Putting on the Heart of Christ

Christ

How the Spiritual Exercises
Invite Us to a Virtuous Life

Gerald M. Fagin, SJ

LOYOLA PRESS.
A JESUIT MINISTRY
Chicago

LOYOLA PRESS.
A JESUIT MINISTRY

3441 N. Ashland Avenue
Chicago, Illinois 60657
(800) 621-1008
www.loyolapress.com

Cover design by Beth Herman Adler
Interior design by Kathryn Seckman Kirsch and Joan Bledig

Library of Congress Cataloging-in-Publication Data
Fagin, Gerald M.
  Putting on the heart of Christ : how the Spiritual exercises invite us to a virtuous
life / Gerald M. Fagin.
      p. cm.
  Includes bibliographical references (p.   ).
  ISBN-13: 978-0-8294-2905-3
  ISBN-10: 0-8294-2905-0
  1. Virtues. 2. Christian life--Catholic authors. 3. Ignatius, of Loyola, Saint,
1491–1556. Exercitia spiritualia. I. Title.
  BV4630.F34 2010
  241'.042--dc22

Printed in the United States of America
09 10 11 12 13 14 Bang 10 9 8 7 6 5 4 3 2 1

*In loving memory of my parents
and my brother and sister
my first school of virtue*

CONTENTS

Acknowledgments

Gratitude was at the heart of Ignatius's response to God and to the giftedness of all of life.

Publication of a book is a special time for gratitude to the many people who have encouraged and supported the author and shared their wisdom to improve the book.

I first wish to thank the Woodstock Jesuit community in Washington, D.C., where the initial research and writing for this book took place. They offered hospitality after hurricane Katrina, as well as support and insight as the book began to emerge.

I want to offer a special thanks to Joe Tetlow, SJ, for his encouragement from the beginning of this project and for graciously writing the foreword to the book.

Also I give thanks to Jerome Neyrey, SJ, whose detailed suggestions from a biblical perspective improved the book and expanded my perspectives.

I express my gratitude also to Judy Deshotels, Barbara Fleischer, Evelyn Jegen, RC, and Mark Thibodeaux, SJ, who all read the manuscript and shared helpful insights and encouragement.

I am grateful to Noel Toomey, OP who during twenty-five years of shared ministry of training spiritual directors, has taught me a great deal about the graces and dynamics of the Exercises.

I am also grateful to the many spiritual directors over the years who have guided me and helped me notice and understand the movement of God in my heart, in particular, the late Vince O'Flaherty, SJ, who directed my second thirty-day retreat and became both mentor and friend.

My thanks also go to my colleagues and students in the Loyola Institute for Ministry who have challenged me to articulate more clearly my ideas about Ignatian spirituality. They are a constant source of support.

Finally, I wish to thank all those at Loyola Press who have brought the book to completion, in particular Joe Durepos who guided this project in its early stages and, especially, Jim Manney, whose skillful editing has made me sound "less like a professor" and made the book more accessible to all who read it.

FOREWORD

You picked up this book. That suggests an interest in the Spiritual Exercises of St. Ignatius Loyola. You must know that they are being given and made by more people in more places and in more ways than at any time in history. And you will have come across the astonishing number of books about ways to give them, ways to make them, purposes for making them, and a lot of studies of their "dynamic." You can reasonably ask, What else can possibly be said?

This book answers that by saying something that is new in several ways. Its explanation of the Spiritual Exercises does not dwell on their structure or on what experts call the "dynamic" experienced in making them. Instead, it looks into each exercise to find how it shapes the person praying and then asks how that affects your life from now on. This life is not a life of piety within the church. Rather, the life it depicts is a life freed of the secularism of our age to live in imitation of Jesus Christ. This book is not about praying in a cocoon, about what happens when you go to a retreat house in the hills, or join a group praying together though long months. This book is about living out the Exercises in this wonderful, exuberant secular nation of ours.

Our nation's tendency right now is not only to separate church and state, but also to question any valid role for religion in everyday life and the marketplace. The deeply vexed question facing every serious disciple of Jesus Christ is how—even whether—to live faithful to him in a culture of corrosive secularity. "The second rate superior minds of a cultivated age," John Stuart Mill argued, "stand always in exaggerated opposition to its spirit." If conservative and liberal Christians neither oppose it excessively nor live excessively absorbed by the secular spirit of this cultivated age, are there alternatives? This book faces that squarely. It suggests how you can—indeed, that you must—live as an active citizen who is a consciously committed disciple of Jesus Christ.

The book makes the case for this in three ways. First, it explores how the Exercises inculcate *virtues,* the permanent dispositions of your heart which you enact daily. The Holy Spirit guides you into these dispositions. The same Holy Spirit is shaping you who shaped the little girl in Nazareth to the point at which she was free and willing to say *yes* to becoming the mother of the Messiah. And the same Holy Spirit shapes you who shaped the boy Jesus of Nazareth as he "grew in wisdom, age, and grace." How did the Spirit do that to the holy Mother and Son, and how does the Spirit do that in you? Can we have any insight into, and joyfully join in cocreating, the person the Spirit has hoped us to be?

The book answers in the positive and in detail. While you pray the Exercises, the author points out, the Spirit is shaping in you habits of the heart such as compunction, generosity, joy, and love. When you *enact those habits of the heart* in your everyday life after you have finished the Exercises, you are becoming what the Spirit hopes you will become—that is, you are "doing God's will." Enacting the virtues the Spirit pours into you as you pray the Exercises, you become the person the Almighty Creator has been hoping in eternity you will become in time. This book goes beyond talk about techniques and methods; it explores how you lead a real life in Christ.

Second, the book implicitly urges leaving behind a current weakness in giving and making the Exercises. These spiritual activities in the interior of each individual too easily occasion withdrawal from real life. This book, rather than argue about that, simply shows the alternative. It addresses the virtues while keeping in touch with the conditions of belief and holiness actually prevalent in the culture's new millennium. The author knows people: for decades, he has been listening to, teaching, and guiding young and mature men and women. But he does not make the too common mistake of writing just from "experience," though his own began with a thirty-day retreat in 1956. No: the author knows about culture, is aware of analyses of modernity such as Alasdair MacIntyre's *After Virtue*. This study probed how influential thinkers like Nietzsche and Kant occasioned what John Allen has called "the hollowness of materialist visions of happiness"—hollow because they have no purpose beyond themselves (*The Making of Benedict XVI*). Fagin also knows the leading thinkers about virtue ethics, James Keenan, SJ, and Richard Gula, SS. He knows and cites serious commentaries on Exercises—by Michael Ivens, SJ, for instance, and John English, SJ.

But Fagin is doing something none of these have done until now. In his realization of the experience of Spiritual Exercises, Fagin has found the way to draw out the habits of the heart that each of the disparate exercises invites you to embrace. Some of the Exercises' virtues seem plain: praying on God's forgiveness obviously inculcates the virtue of forgiveness, and the Call of the King inculcates the virtue of generosity. Some are less obvious: the Ignatian consideration on the Principle and Foundation inculcates the virtue of gratitude as well as the virtue of reverence, and those on Two Standards and the Three Classes inculcate the virtue of prudence. So his analysis of each of the major passages in the Exercises opens not only the "will of God" as an objective truth and not only the spiritual effects that you beg God to give you. Fagin reaches beyond that into the burgeoning human heart to see you develop the virtues of each exercise and the mounting coherence of all the virtues necessary to live purposefully in Christ. What happens in the Exercises shapes to a great extent what happens after them, and not in nebulous ways.

This dynamic has to happen in a corrosively secular culture. So be perfectly clear what you will get in this book: an analysis both of what happens during the Exercises and also of what happens in living out the graces offered and inculcated by the Exercises after they are over. Other commentators are content to send you out on your own at the end of the Exercises, convinced that you have put order into your passions and prayer and you'll figure out what God's will is. Fagin clearly thinks the Exercises can do better than that. He takes on the urgent question that oppresses not a few retreatants: Now what? How do you go day after day living to "praise, reverence, and serve God"? What does it mean in the concrete to "imitate Christ"?

So the urgent question is not about the Exercises, merely. It is about the stark challenge facing Christians to escape the secular spirit of the age. Put the question this way: In this generous, exuberant American culture, how does the life of the disciple of Jesus Christ differ from the life of a really good person who has little or no belief? Do you give bread to the hungry? So do many wonderful men and women, simply because of their humanity. But experts say that if you have accepted the deepening and maturing of the Exercises, you are doing this as Jesus Christ did and does it. This book tells how. Your generosity to the poor rises as an *enactment of a habit of your heart which is the same as the habit of heart that Jesus enacted*—a habit you learned in imitation of Christ when contemplating the life of Jesus of Nazareth. This is a fresh and different appreciation of the Exercises.

There is a third way—a little more technical—in which this book differs from the many current studies of Exercises. The author discusses "the dynamic" of the Spiritual Exercises, as many books do—that is, the interaction of the matter for prayer, God's action, praying and desiring, and spiritual guidance that flow through the thirty days. But Fagin discusses this dynamic in fresh terms. He is aware that most commentators assign two big purposes for going through the Exercises: first, reaching a big decision in life; and second, as they are currently practiced, a deepening in prayer and in relationship with God. He finds both of these good and his treatment deals well with both. But his interest differs: This book explores how the Exercises transform the one who makes them, not in some true but mystical way, unobservable until the process of beatification begins later on. Fagin tells how the transformation happens in palpable ways that can and must be consciously recognized. Then just how *do* the Exercises transform you?

The answer here is direct and focused: by giving a new shape to the habits of the heart that determine your big and small daily decisions and finally who you are growing to be. In this book, the dynamic is not merely about the choices faced and made during the Exercises. The dynamic is not mainly about reshaping your religious sensibility or your faith doing justice. In this book, the dynamic of the Exercises is about shaping you as a person to live a holy life, even though you are embedded in a culture in which ordinary people can live without God. If you wonder what that means, consider that *The Economist* can print a calm description of "summer camp for secular kids" offered in several places in the U.S.—so that agnostic and atheistic children can be encouraged in their life choice.

Ordinary people in America and the entire West live today rather by unchallenged axioms and unreflected convictions than by rationally established beliefs and decisions. Philosophers like Charles Taylor point out that you live in a culture of expressive individualism, which finds meaning in these dicta: "I gotta be me. I gotta do my own thing." Pope Benedict XVI urges that the church finds itself again in the situation it was in when Benedict shaped the force that preserved civilization through the dark ages. His conviction is that Christians must form "little societies of spiritual concentration." Fagin has given those who practice Ignatian spirituality a blueprint for achieving that. His book will interest keenly those who give Exercises and those who want to know about them. It will be a fertile help while you are making Exercises.

Even apart from Exercises, the book will prove rich resource for anyone who wonders how to go about offering hope to a world fixed in time and facing death.

Joseph A. Tetlow, SJ
Montserrat Jesuit Retreat House
Lake Dallas, TX

PREFACE

"Love one another as I have loved you" is the most challenging command in the Gospel. We are to love with the same selfless, faithful, forgiving, and compassionate love that flowed from the heart of Jesus, who loved us even when we were sinners. The invitation of our Christian lives is to put on the mind and heart of Jesus. With that mind and heart, we can love God and others the way Jesus has loved us.

The qualities of heart that are embodied in Jesus have classically been called *virtues*. Virtues shape the kind of people we are and they are the source of our actions . We grow in the Christian life by fostering these virtues and allowing them to direct our lives. We put on the heart of Christ by putting on Christ's virtues. This is the deepest meaning of the imitation of Christ. We do not slavishly mimic his actions, but rather live in a way that embodies his loving heart.

This book will explore how the Spiritual Exercises of Ignatius of Loyola help us grow in virtue and embody the heart of Christ. The Spiritual Exercises are a process of prayer, reflection, and discernment that help bring a person to freedom in order to hear God's call and to respond in faith. Commentators point out different purposes for the Exercises. All agree that the Exercises invite one to a deeper experience of God's love as creative, forgiving, calling, and saving. Some go on to say that the purpose of the Exercises is to discern God's will for one's life and make faith-filled decisions. Others focus on the Exercises as a school of prayer: a way of fostering a person's growth in a relationship with God.

This book suggests another purpose of the Spiritual Exercises: to transform an individual into a certain kind of person with certain virtues or dispositions of heart.

To develop this interpretation of the Exercises, this book mines the insights of a contemporary movement in moral theology called *virtue ethics*. Virtue ethics contend that the real question of ethics is not "What should I do?" but rather "Who should I become?" It is concerned with fostering the virtues necessary to live a Christian life of love of God, and service of neighbor. For one called to discipleship, this means putting on the mind and heart of Jesus and loving as Jesus loved.

Ignatius wanted Christians to be committed "to love and serve the Divine Majesty in all things." (Sp. Ex. 234) In the chapters that follow, the Spiritual Exercises outlined by Ignatius will be related to some of the virtues that define this kind of Christian. This does not imply that there is a rigid link between certain exercises and certain virtues. The connections are meant to be suggestive only. My purpose is to provide a way of naming the graces that are at the heart of the movement and dynamic of the Exercises. I also wish to articulate the desires elicited by the Exercises in the language of virtue. "Ask for what you desire" is a maxim of Ignatian spirituality. This book will relate these desires to the virtues so that we live out of these graces and make decisions based on them.

The purpose of this book is not to propose a new way to make or give the Spiritual Exercises. Rather, I hope to propose a new way of understanding the graces of the Exercises and their formative power in a person's life. I want to show how the Exercises are an invitation to become a certain kind of person: a virtuous person who has taken on the qualities of Christ's heart and a person who can "Love one another as I have loved you."

1 The Spiritual Exercises and the Return to Virtue

Recent decades have seen a surge of interest in both Ignatian spirituality and what is called *virtue ethics*. The Spiritual Exercises of Ignatius of Loyola have for centuries been a widely-used basis for spiritual formation and retreats of all kinds. Virtue ethics is a creative and fertile movement in moral theology. Let's examine each more closely.

The Many Dimensions of the Spiritual Exercises

An Experience

The Spiritual Exercises are first and foremost an *experience*. In their full form, they are an experience of thirty days of solitude, praying four or five hours a day, and a way to encounter God. The Spiritual Exercises are a process intended to lead someone to the freedom of hearing God's call and following that call in faith. The

Spiritual Exercises are a journey of transformation and conversion. They help a person get in touch with the desires of their heart that give voice to God's desires within themselves. Generosity is necessary to make these exercises because they will challenge one always to do more, to open one's heart more fully to God.

A Book

The Spiritual Exercises are a book that outlines a series of exercises. These exercises include prayers, meditations, contemplations, and methods of self-examination, as well as guidelines for discerning God's movements in the human heart. They are exercises for discovering God's will and making decisions. At one level, the content of the book is a set of exercises laid out for the one following them, but at a deeper level, the content of the Spiritual Exercises is what God does within each individual person. It is an exercise book to help one get in touch with one's experiences of God, to be sensitive to those experiences, and to see how God is working within oneself. The director who is guiding a person through the Exercises wants to know what God is doing in a person's heart because the movement of God *is* the content of the Spiritual Exercises. That experience cannot be found in a book, but only in the movements of God in the human heart in prayer and reflection.

A Book for the Spiritual Director

The Exercises are a book for the director, not for the one making the Exercises. The person going through the Spiritual Exercises needs a guide who is knowledgeable of the Exercises and of the spiritual life. The Exercises are adapted to each individual person according to how God is working in the heart of that individual. It is not a handbook or a textbook that one can read, rather something a person must experience. The Exercises are an art form, not a science.

The book was first printed in 1548. Ignatius made 500 copies and he kept all of them. He gave copies to people who had already made the Exercises so that they could direct others.

A Journal

The Exercises are a *journal* of Ignatius's own experience of God, a journal about God moving in his heart. Ignatius spent a year at Manresa after his conversion at Loyola. During that time, he experienced God purifying his dream and making clear that his call was to help souls. Ignatius was called to be an apostolic person, to be a person of the church, and to carry on the work of Jesus. The journal he kept during that year became the basis of the Spiritual Exercises. He refined his journal and adapted it over twenty-five years of directing others through the Exercises. This experience showed him what needed to be put in the book to help the director. But basically the book is the journal of his own conversion experience, a journal about God moving in his heart. As Ignatius talked to other people and led them through the Exercises, he discovered that his journey was really a paradigm of everyone's journey, both the way God works with souls and the way people respond to God. He discovered that this was not just God dealing with him, but the way God dealt with everyone, even though in each case it was very personal and very individual. That is why the Exercises are adapted for each individual person. They are a paradigm, a model, and a pattern for God's dealing with people.

Things to Do

The Exercises are not a book to be read or studied, but rather a book to be prayed. They take God's story, especially as it is narrated in the life of Jesus, and relate it to each individual's own story and life experience. To simply read the Exercises would be like reading a book on jogging and then wondering why one is not in better shape. The Exercises are a book of exercises, of things to be done.

What Ignatius Said about the Exercises

To clarify the meaning and purpose of the Exercises, Ignatius began with a series of guidelines or explanations. He first defined a *spiritual exercise* as any means that helps us come into contact with God. Anything that will dispose our hearts and set us free so we can find God's will in our life such as a prayer, a meditation, a reflection, or a self-examination. Ignatius makes the point that just as there are exercises that one does for physical health, there are exercises one does for spiritual health. His book gives these exercises in a very ordered and structured way.

Ignatius wrote about what he hoped people would derive from these experiences. He hopes people will grow in *knowledge*, but not just head knowledge. He was more interested in felt knowledge or interior knowledge—the intimate understanding of a truth. It is the difference between knowing about Jesus and knowing Jesus, between knowing in our heads that God loves us and experiencing that love in our hearts. This kind of knowledge touches the heart and motivates us to act in an entirely new way. Ignatius is looking for an *intimate interior felt knowledge*. "For what fills and satisfies the soul consists, not in knowing much, but in our understanding the realities profoundly and in savoring them interiorly." (Sp. Ex. 2)[1]

Ignatius seeks *magnanimity* in the one making these Exercises:

> The persons who make the Exercises will benefit by entering upon them with great spirit and generosity toward their Creator and Lord, and by offering all their desires and freedom to him so that His Divine Majesty can make use of their persons and of all they possess in whatsoever way is in accord with his most holy will. (Sp. Ex. 5)

One needs openness and generosity, or, as Ignatius expressed it, "*great desires.*" Ignatius wanted people who were not content where they were, who were restless, and who were looking to give something more. When he sought candidates for the Exercises, he looked for people who wanted to do great things, who wanted to do *more.*

A very important point for understanding Ignatius is his insistence that *God is the director of the* Exercises. He believed the Creator and Lord would touch the individual soul. The personal touch of God is the heart of the Exercises and at the heart of Ignatius's spirituality.

> But during these Spiritual Exercises when a person is seeking God's will, it is more appropriate and far better that the Creator and Lord himself should communicate himself to the devout soul . . . the one giving the Exercises ought to . . . allow the Creator

to deal immediately with the creature and the creature with its Creator and Lord. (Sp. Ex. 15)

God does touch the individual soul through thoughts, desires,
imaginings, and all the feelings that go on inside of a person.
The director is there only to facilitate that conversation between
God and the person making the Exercises. The director does
not give advice or teach them, but only facilitates the personal
encounter of that person with God. The Spiritual Exercises are
about the encounter with God and meeting God in a very personal way.

What Others Say about the Exercises

Over the years, two schools of thought about the purpose of
the Exercises have emerged. George Aschenbrenner calls them
"Electionists" and "Perfectionists." The Electionists see the goal
of the Exercises as "making a wise choice of a state of life in which
to serve God best." The Perfectionists see the goal as "a union
with God most intimate and total."[2]

Ignatius envisioned the Spiritual Exercises as a means to
overcome ourselves, to order our lives, so we could reach an
ordered decision. He saw it as a process of coming to a major
life decision. To make such a decision, we must come to a level
of freedom so choices can be made out of ordered affections. Put
another way, the Exercises help us discover our role in the plan of
salvation—God's will for us. We should ask what is God calling
me to do in my life and how do I fit into God's plan of salvation
of the world?

> The name of spiritual exercises is given to any
> means of preparing and disposing our soul to rid
> itself of all its disordered affections and then, after
> their removal, of seeking and finding God's will in
> the ordering of one's life for the salvation of our
> soul. (Sp. Ex. 1)

The Exercises then are about making decisions, but making decisions out of freedom, not out of disordered ideas, not out of pleasure, power, or prestige.

However, many people make the Exercises primarily to enrich their own spiritual lives. They have already made a commitment to a life in priesthood, religious life, marriage, or single life. They have chosen a profession. They are not making new decisions so much as they are trying to live out the gospel more faithfully in their life circumstances. For many, the primary purpose of the Exercises is to develop and deepen their relationship with God, to come closer to God, to become more intimate with God, and to let God work more deeply within their hearts so that they can draw closer to God.

These two purposes of the Exercises—a way to make decisions and a way to grow in the spiritual life—are complementary, not mutually exclusive. Here I am proposing a somewhat different way of looking at the Exercises. I will look at them through the lens of virtue. To grow in virtue is to grow in our relationship with God and with others. To grow in virtue also deepens our freedom to make decisions out of love and generosity. To make this connection between the Exercises and virtues, I will use some of the practical wisdom found in the contemporary return to virtue.[3]

Virtue Ethics: What Kind of Person Do I Want to Be?

In the last thirty years, attention has shifted in philosophical ethics and moral theology to the place of virtues in Christian life. The focus on the morality of particular actions that has characterized post-Enlightenment thinking has been complemented and, in some cases, replaced by a new emphasis on the human person acting. Action-centered ethics has given way to agent-centered ethics, which is more concerned with the kind of person we are and will become than with what we are to do in a specific situation.[4] Some characterize this as an ethics of *being* in contrast to an ethics of *doing*.

Richard Gula says that an ethics of being is concerned with "those personal qualities disposing us to act in certain ways."

> [These are] patterns of actions, or the habits we acquire, the vision we have of life, the values and convictions or beliefs we live by, the intentions we have, the dispositions which ready us to act as well as the affections which move us to do what we believe to be right.[5]

Instead of analyzing the morality of particular actions, such as termination of life support, premarital sex, abortion, or paying just wages, virtue ethics is concerned with fostering virtues such as compassion, justice, generosity, and love. Rather than centering the discussion on the nature and species of sins, the return to virtue centers on the person doing the actions and the person's dispositions and character.[6] The return to virtue recaptures, in many ways, earlier approaches to ethics that had been lost after the Enlightenment.[7]

Three Key Questions

James Keenan refers to the three questions articulated by Alasdair MacIntyre: Who am I? Who ought I to become? How am I to get there?[8]

Who am I? Virtue ethics describes a person in terms of the virtues the person possesses and practices. Am I loving, generous, grateful, and just?

Who ought I to become? This is the crucial question. Virtue ethics focuses on the goal of our lives. What kind of person do I wish to become? What virtues do I wish to foster and develop? As Keenan puts it, "for the honest person the virtues are not what we acquire in life; they are what we pursue."[9] The end not only motivates actions. It also shapes the content of the actions. The challenge is to make the transition from who we are to who we can become.

How am I to get there? The final question concerns the means to reach our goal of becoming a virtuous person. To answer this question, virtue ethics looks at the ordinary events of our day-to-day lives. Here the focus is on the virtue of prudence as the means of guiding us to actions that will help us become the person we desire to be.

What Is Virtue?

Virtues deal with the ordinary events of our lives. They are concerned with the interplay between our habits of heart and our actions. Virtues are dispositions of heart that guide our actions. If we have the virtue of generosity, we will spontaneously share with others. If we have the virtue of honesty, we will be inclined to tell the truth even when it is difficult. We call people kind or patient or compassionate by the way they habitually behave. Their actions reveal who they are.

At the same time, how we act shapes the habits and dispositions we develop. We become a virtuous person by performing virtuous actions. Our being is formed through our doing, just as our being informs our doing. Virtues are not simply dispositions. They are ways of behaving. We engage in repeated actions that form certain habits that in turn lead to further actions. When we have a regular practice of daily prayer, we become a prayerful person apt to find time to pray each day. When we regularly give thanks for gifts received, we become a grateful person apt to recognize the giftedness of all things. Parents teach their children to say "Thank you" in hopes they will become grateful people. All human actions are moral actions. These actions effect the kind of people we become.

Joseph Kotva makes five generalizations about virtues that are helpful for appreciating the role of virtues in our lives.[10]

Virtues are related to the human good. Virtues are "those states of character that enable or contribute to the realization of the human good."

Virtues encompass the whole range of human activity. They engage not only the rational part of the human person, but also the affective and desiring part of the person.

Virtues are especially related to tendencies to react in expected ways. They are dispositions to strive for particular ends and actions. They "include all those states of character or character traits that influence how we act and choose."

Virtues are products of moral education and growth. They remain stable aspects of our character that provide continuity in our actions.

Virtuous actions must be done for their own sake. Virtue may help us achieve some good or goal, but ultimately they must be performed simply because they are virtuous actions.[11]

Why Are Virtues Important for Christians?

Virtues give us a deeper insight into what it means to follow Jesus. Christians are called to be disciples who model our lives on Gospel values and walk in companionship with Jesus. The call of discipleship means following a person, not primarily following a set of rules.

This is the vision Ignatius set forth in the Spiritual Exercises when he calls us to labor alongside Jesus to carry out God's hopes and dreams for the world, and to bring about the reign of God. The grace we pray for is the grace to know, love, and follow Jesus. Discipleship is not simply about doing certain actions and asking "what would Jesus do?", but also about becoming a certain kind of person. We are called to be loving persons in imitation of Christ, to become forgiving, compassionate, loving people with a passion to carry out the Father's will. It is about making the values that shaped Jesus' ministry our own values. It is about putting on the heart of Jesus and loving as he loved. "Let the same mind be in you that was in Christ Jesus." (Philippians 2:5) Jesus did not talk a great deal about specific moral actions and did not give his disciples many explicit moral directives. He was more concerned about the kind of person we are to become. He told stories and parables about what the reign of God is like. Jesus told stories about ordinary, everyday events and occupations—sowers and shepherds and masters and servants. He spoke about banquets and treasures in a field and lost sheep and buried talents.

These stories tell us what kind of people would be at home in the kingdom of God.

Where Is Your Heart?

This emphasis is especially clear at the beginning of the Sermon on the Mount when Jesus proclaims the Beatitudes—those attitudes of heart that characterize the Kingdom of God. We are to be poor in spirit, pure of heart, merciful, and passionate about justice. Jesus does not focus on the actions of murder and adultery and lying and revenge. He is more concerned about the anger and lust and lack of honesty and vengeance in our hearts that lead to these actions.[12]

The scriptural image for this is a new heart. The Prophets in the Hebrew Scriptures call us to take out our hearts of stone and put on a heart of flesh. Jesus takes this further by modeling for us the new heart and the virtuous person. Jesus is normative for Christian living not on the basis of a particular teaching, but on the basis of who he was and is. He embodies for us the kind of person we ought to become and the sort of right actions we ought to perform. We are called to live out in our lives the virtues of Jesus by putting on his perspective, dispositions, affections and intentions.[13]

The Spiritual Exercises and contemporary virtue ethics both offer a vision of a renewed and transformed heart. The focus of this book is to encourage a conversation between them. The graces of the Spiritual Exercises are a call to identify more deeply with the values and virtues of Jesus. The insights of virtue ethics can enrich our response to the invitation of the Exercises to embrace the person of Jesus as leader and friend.

Reflecting on Your Attitudes of Heart

- How would I describe the heart of Christ?
- What dispositions of the heart come to mind when I think of Jesus?
- What attitudes of the heart do I wish to foster in my own life?
- What kind of person is Jesus inviting me to be at this moment in my life?

Scripture Readings on the Heart

Philippians 2: 1–11 Put on the mind and heart of Christ
Matthew 5: 1–12 The Beatitudes
Ephesians 3: 14–21 May Christ dwell in your heart

2 Reverence: Created in Love

Human beings are created to praise, reverence,
and serve God our Lord.

SP. EX. 23

The foundational grace of the Christian life is an experience of the unconditional love of God manifested in Jesus and poured into our hearts through the power of the Holy Spirit. This experience of God's love is central to the Principle and Foundation located at the beginning of the Spiritual Exercises.

Who Is God for You?

To one approaching the Exercises, one must first answer the following questions: Who is God in your experience? Who are *you*? How do you relate to God? And what is the meaning and value of the world in which we live?

To answer these questions, Ignatius offers a consideration he calls "The Principle and Foundation." It answers the basic question about the purpose of our lives and why we are here.

> Human beings are created to praise, reverence, and serve God, our Lord. The purpose of life is to praise, reverence, and serve God and by this means to save our soul.
>
> The other things on the face of the earth are created for human beings, to help them in the pursuit of the end for which they are created.
>
> From this it follows we ought to use these things to the extent that they help us toward our end and free ourselves from them to the extent that they hinder us from the end.
>
> To attain this, it is necessary to make ourselves indifferent to all created things, in regard to everything which is left to our free will and is not forbidden. Consequently, on our own part, we ought not to seek health rather than sickness, wealth rather than poverty, honor rather than dishonor, a long life rather than a short one, and so in all other matters.
>
> Rather we ought to desire and choose only that which is more conducive to the end for which we were created. (Sp. Ex. 23)

Ignatius presents the Principle and Foundation as a "consideration." It is not a meditation or a contemplation, but rather a reflection on some basic truths that are the foundation of the rest of the Exercises. He says that you have to clarify what God's plan is and who you are before God. What is the plan that God is creating within you and what is the purpose of the life that God has given you? One commentator says that the Principle and Foundation "sketches the worldview of Christian faith as the background against which everything else in the Exercises and in life should be viewed."[1]

At first glance, the Principle and Foundation looks like a philosophical statement, which can lead to an abstract intellectual reflection on the purpose of life. However, Tetlow reminds us that "the sentences of the Principle and Foundation are meant to evoke a religious experience."[2] The Principle and Foundation is rooted in Ignatius's own mystical experience and calls for a heartfelt response to God's creative initiative. This religious experience is described as

> [T]he experience of my intensely personal relationship with God my Creator and Lord, not only as the One who loves and cherishes and forgives me, but also and even more as the One who is at every moment making me, my life world and my self.[3]

Ignatius has invited us to have a deeply personal encounter with God that touches the heart.

How Deeply Does God's Love Penetrate?

The first premise of the Principle and Foundation is that we are created by God. We are creatures totally dependent on God, not simply for our beginning, but for every moment of our existence. We are continually being created by God. This fundamental truth shapes the way we understand ourselves and the world around us. We cannot declare our independence from God or pretend we are autonomous. God's act of creation sustains us in existence and gifts us with ongoing life at each moment. We are always in relationship with God as our Creator and source of life.

The consoling truth in this reality is that we are created out of love. We exist because of God's desire for our life and our salvation. We are loved by God in a radical and unconditional way from the moment of our conception. This is the good news proclaimed by the prophet Isaiah: "But now thus says the Lord, he who created you, O Jacob, he who formed you, O Isreal: Do not fear for I have redeemed you; I have called you by name and you are mine. . . . Because you are precious in my sight, and honored, and I love you . . ." (Isaiah 43:1,4). The prophet compares God's love to the faithful love of a mother "Can a woman forget her nursing child, or show no compassion for the child of her womb? Even these may forget, yet I will not forget you. . . . See, I have inscribed you on the palms of my hands" (Isaiah 49:15–16). We recall too the words of the Psalmist extolling this faithful love of God:

> Praise the Lord, all you nations!
>   Extol him, all you peoples!
> For great is his steadfast love
>   toward us,
> and the faithfulness of the
>   Lord endures forever.
> Praise the Lord! (Psalm 117)

The challenge for many people is to accept God's love as unconditional. This acceptance needs to take place in our hearts as well as our heads.[4] God took the initiative in loving us long before we were able to love in return. We do not need to win God's love. We cannot possibly earn it. The love of God for each person is a pure gift that only calls for response. The Principle and Foundation reminds us that God continues to touch our lives and calls us to a deeper sharing in the life of God.

On one level, the Principle and Foundation can be seen as *diagnostic*. It explores whether a person has truly grasped at an interior level the experience of God's creative and sustaining love. Many contemporary directors of the Exercises begin by inviting those making the Exercises to pray on Scriptural texts that speak of God's faithful and tender love for us as individuals. Even those advanced in the spiritual life need to experience anew that foundational experience of God's love before progressing further in the Exercises. Until people can claim that gift of God's love on a personal level, they cannot hear God's words of forgiveness or the call in freedom in the rest of the Exercises. To enter into the meditations on sin in the first week of the Exercises without a genuine experience of God's love can be a destructive experience. A person cannot come to honest self-knowledge without first knowing they are loved.

Put another way, the Principle and Foundation explores a person's operative image of God. Most people approaching the Exercises would say that they have a positive image of God and would describe God as a God of love and forgiveness and fidelity. The question is whether this intellectual belief is the operative belief in a person's life. Do you *really* believe and act out of a loving image of God, or does an image of God as demanding, punishing, and arbitrary lurk at a deeper level? At a deeper, unconscious level, do you believe that God's love must be earned, that God has rather harsh conditions to be fulfilled, that God expects more than you feel capable of giving? Do you hear these words of Isaiah at the most personal level: "[M]y steadfast love shall not depart from you. . . ."? (Isaiah 54:10).

These are the questions Ignatius would have us ask. He invites us to get in touch with God's continuing creative love as a felt experience that is the foundational grace of a person's relationship with God.

What Reverence Means

The Principle and Foundation introduces us to the wonder and graciousness of creation, to the transcendent majesty of God as origin and source of all creation. Reverence is our response to that majesty and mystery.[5] Rudolph Otto speaks of the *mysterium tremendum et fascinans*—the mystery that is daunting and majestic, yet fascinating.[6] Before the majesty of the Ultimate, we experience fear, yet attraction. We are reluctant to draw near, yet we are also captivated by a power and energy far beyond our own. This reaction to the holy is pervasive in human religious experience. Every religion has some sense of reverence before the Ultimate.

We find this same sense of awe, of fear, and of fascination in the Hebrew and Christian scriptures. We see it when Abraham drops to the ground and bows his face to the earth (Genesis 17:1–3), when Moses takes off his shoes before the burning bush and covers his face (Exodus 3:1–6), when the Israelites are warned that they cannot look on the face of God and live (Exodus 33:20). We see reverence when Peter falls to his knees after the great catch of fish (Luke 5:1–8), when the disciples are awestruck when Jesus calms the storm (Mark 4:35–41), and when Peter, James, and John are overwhelmed at the Transfiguration. (Matthew 17:1–8). Yet there's a paradox in this sense of awe and fear. It leads to a sense of closeness to God. Reverence occurs in the context of the personal love of God that ennobles and enriches the human person. Reverence is an invitation to draw near to God and not be afraid.

This sense of closeness is a reflection of God's desire for us. The restlessness in our hearts, the desire for union with the divine, our pull to self-transcendence—all of these are our response to God's invitation to share in God's life. William Barry speaks of the experience of reverence as "desiring 'I know not what.'" Barry speaks of this desire as an experience "of being touched by the creative desire of God who desires us into being and continues us in being."[7] *Desire* is a key idea. It is vital to understanding the heart of Ignatius and the dynamic of the Exercises. Ignatius is eliciting our deepest desire for God that haunts our souls and fills us with longing for the divine. We feel this desire when we feel reverence.

Ignatius Loyola's Experience of Reverence

Reverence was a basic attitude that shaped Ignatius's relationship with God. It pervaded Ignatius's way of living in the world. The idea of reverence occurs often in the Spiritual Exercises, his *Spiritual Diary*, and in his letters. Ignatius used two Spanish words for reverence: *reverencia* and *acatamiento*. *Acatamiento* refers to veneration and awe and reverence, as well as submission. O'Neill describes it as:

> a happy consciousness of divine presence, an awe suffused with warm attractiveness and resulting in love. In this communing presence submission flows from an awareness of the utter gratuity of creation and redemption.[8]

Acatamiento implies a heightened awareness or consciousness of God's presence. At the same time, it is a loving awe that draws one closer to God. Ignatius refers to it as "an awe which is affectionate."[9]

A passage from Ignatius's *Spiritual Diary* testifies to the profound emotional character of this reverence:

> Before, during, and after Mass there was within me a thought which penetrated deep within my soul, with what great *acatamiento* and reverence I should mention the name of God our Lord on my way to Mass, such that, steeping myself in this reverence and awe (*reverencia y acatamiento*) before Mass, in my room, in chapel, and at Mass, with the tears coming, I put them away promptly, so as to attend to the awe (*acatamiento*), and not seeming as my doing, there came that *acatamiento* which always increases my devotion and my tears.[10]

Not surprisingly, Ignatius counseled others to approach God in prayer with reverence. This is a direction from the Spiritual Exercises:

> A step or two away from the place where I will
> make my contemplation or meditation, I will stand
> for the length of an Our Father. I will raise my
> mind and think how God our Lord is looking at
> me, and other such thoughts. Then I will make an
> act of reverence or humility. (Sp. Ex. 75)

Ignatius also recognized that reverence was especially appropriate when a person was dealing directly with God:

> When we are conversing with God our Lord or
> his saints vocally or mentally, greater reverence is
> demanded of us than when we are using the intellect to understand. (Sp. Ex. 3)

This attitude of reverence is not to be restricted to prayer. Ignatius wanted to foster a sense of reverence in all of life. The Contemplation on Divine Love at the end of the Exercises calls for a sense of reverence for the God who dwells in all things. Ignatius's ability to find God in all things is rooted in this pervasive sense of God's active presence. Ignatius was called "a contemplative in action" because his sense of reverence moved him to action. Ignatius promoted the spiritual practice of daily examination of conscience as a way of fostering an attention to the presence of God in our everyday lives—an attention that leads to a deeper sense of reverence.[11]

For Ignatius, reverence was a basic attitude and it permeated his life. Reverence is emphasized at the beginning of the Exercises because it is essential and foundational to all that follows in the Exercises and to Ignatian spirituality.

Learning to Live Reverently

Reverence is a virtue to be cultivated and practiced. It is a disposition of heart that leads us to the good in all things and draws
us closer to God. Reverence brings us closer to other people
and to the world around us. The reverent person notices and
responds to the mystery of life and the sacredness of all things.
Reverence is an attitude of dependence and humility, an appreciation of the splendor and beauty of all reality, and a longing
for something greater. Reverence is a self-effacing virtue, but it
implies as well a reverence for oneself as a person created and
loved and chosen by God. Reverence gives voice to our desire
for God, our desire to find fulfillment beyond ourselves in the
mystery that embraces us.

Some will argue that contemporary life and culture have
lost a sense of reverence. In an individualized and person-
centered world, it is easy to domesticate God, trivialize relationships, and flee from the sacred. Reverence is not a virtue
to be found only in traditional settings, formal titles, formal
rituals, and attitudes. Each culture must discover its own way
to foster reverence. Each of us must find reverence in the world
in which we live.

In the end, we must tap into our own experience of reverence
by reflecting on contemplative moments of awe. Descriptions of
reverence are only helpful if they are measured against one's own
recalled experience of transcending oneself and opening oneself
to something greater. For example, I remember standing on the
top of a mesa ten thousand feet high overlooking what seemed
to be hundreds of miles of fertile land. I had an experience of
amazement, of silence, of vastness, of expansiveness, of gift.

I felt a sense of wonder that God had almost done too much and thus created out of the sheer joy of creating and sharing goodness.

We feel such things often—in the countless number of stars on a clear night, before a work of art, at the birth of a child, at the moment of dying of a loved one. These contemplative experiences draw us closer to God even as we feel small and unworthy. They are sacred moments that expand the landscapes of our hearts. Ignatius knew reverence when he prayed at night under the stars, but he knew it as well in the busyness of each day. He hoped to elicit that experience throughout the Exercises.

Ignatius believed that anyone who prayerfully considers the basic truth that we are created out of love by a transcendent God of holiness will grow in a sense of reverence. We will have a deepened sense of the sacredness of all things if we think of everything as continually being called and sustained in being by God. We will stand in awe not just before sunsets and mountains, flowers and trees, but also, and especially, before every person we meet. Reverence is a disposition of a heart that allows us to live before the beauty and goodness of every creature and the God who made them. In Ignatian terminology, reverence will enable us to find God in all things.

This first exercise of the Spiritual Exercises begins to transform us into a particular kind of person. Already there is an answer emerging to the questions asked by virtue ethics: Who am I? Who ought I to become? How am I to get there? Reverence is a foundational virtue for putting on the heart of Christ.

Reflecting on the Virtue of Reverence

- Recall and reflect on an experience of reverence and awe in your life.
- Where and how do I experience God being present in my life?
- How can I grow in reverence for God, others, self, and life?
- How can I foster a contemplative heart?

Scripture Readings on Reverence

Psalm 104 God the Creator and Provider
Luke 8:22–25 Jesus Calms a Storm
Luke 9:28–36 The Transfiguration

3 Gratitude: All Is Gift

The other things on the face of the earth are
created for human beings . . .

Sp. Ex. 23

About a year after his conversion, Ignatius received a vision of
God and creation that changed the way he looked at everything.
The vision occurred at the river Cardoner in Manresa in eastern
Spain. Years later he described the vision this way:

> He received such a lucidity in understanding that
> during the course of his entire life—now having
> passed his sixty-second year—if he were to gather
> all the helps he received from God and everything
> he knew, and add them together, he does not think
> they would add up to all that he received on that
> one occasion.[1]

At that moment Ignatius saw the world coming down from
God and returning to God in two great acts: creation and the

Incarnation. He had an overwhelming sense of everything coming to us from the hands of a loving God who desires to share goodness and life. His heart was moved to profound gratitude.

Gratitude does not come easily

Maintaining a sense of gratitude is difficult For us. We easily take things for granted and we cease to see things as gifts. The air we breathe, the water we drink, our health and intelligence, those who love and support us—we can so easily expect these essential things to always be present and available. Only when we lose basic necessities, our health, or our loved ones do we recognize that they were not our creation, but God's gifts to us.

To take something for granted is to cease to acknowledge it as a gift given by someone. We lose touch with the giver. The gift is no longer a gift, but a possession. We claim it as our own and wrap our hands around it and say, "This is mine."

Some years ago, I was moving and it was time to throw away much of what I had accumulated over the years. I had received many gifts such as candles, stoles, books, and religious objects. They were usually connected to an occasion such as a retreat or time spent with a group. When I received them, they were cherished reminders of significant people and moments of grace. However, as I began to sort through them, I began to divide them into two piles. The first pile contained objects that called to mind the people involved and the occasion remembered. The second pile contained objects that seemed to have no connection with anyone in particular. To my embarrassment, I could no longer remember the person or the people who had given them to me. I suddenly realized that the first pile contained gifts; the second, only possessions. The objects in the second pile no longer had a connection with the giver. As you may have guessed, I kept the first pile and discarded the second.

Routine is another obstacle to gratitude. We lose sight of the giftedness of creation because it is always with us. G. K. Chesterton once commented on our expectation that the sun will rise every day. We take it for granted. It is not experienced as a gift, but as a simple fact. He suggested that it would be better to imagine God beginning each day with a decision to give a sunrise to the people he loves. We could see each day as a gift from the hands of a loving God. It reminds us that God is gifting us and loving us each day.

Gratitude is the spontaneous response to the experience of the giftedness of reality. It acknowledges the gift and the giver. Gratitude opens the human heart in love and generosity. Grateful people do not claim things as their own, but cherish everything as given and received. Yet gratitude is elusive. We are grateful for a while, and then we forget. It is a virtue that needs attention.

Gratitude at the Center of the Spiritual Exercises

Though there are only a few explicit references to gratitude in the Spiritual Exercises, gratefulness is at the heart of the dynamic and movement of the Exercises and the experience of the one making the Exercises. The Principle and Foundation at the beginning of the Spiritual Exercises reminds us that we are created out of love. God created us and continues to create us each moment of our existence. God's unconditional love is the source and continuing foundation of our lives. This truth evokes in us both the obligation and the desire to praise, reverence, and serve God.

The Principle and Foundation also announces that the world and everything in it is the product of God's love. Everything that exists is a gift from the hands of a loving God. As the Psalmist proclaims it:

> O Lord, how manifold are your
>   works!
> In wisdom you have made
>   them all;
> the earth is full of your
>   creatures. (Psalm 104, v. 24)

In the words of Ignatius, "The other things on the face of the earth are created for human beings. . . ." For him, a Christian is one who sees everything as a gift from God. Everything points our minds and hearts to the Giver of all good gifts.

Gifts are gifts only when they keep us in touch with a giver. The moment we lose touch with the giftedness of any aspect of our lives, we lose touch with the Giver of all gifts. For Ignatius, everything in the world was a continuing gift from the gracious God who never ceases to give to us. The Principle and Foundation urges us to be aware of the giftedness of our lives.

To see everything as gift is also to see everything as a promise. A gift ceases to be a gift when it only points to the past. A gift is a present reality and a promise of future giving. This is certainly true when we think of God's gifts. The gifts of life and creation that surround us are promises from a faithful God. This awareness leads to trust in God, an assurance that his love is never exhausted or limited.

In the First Week of the Exercises, as a person prays on sinfulness and God's mercy, once again Ignatius encourages the person to pray for gratitude: "conclude with a colloquy, extolling the mercy of God our Lord, pouring out my thoughts to God and giving thanks to God that up to this moment God has granted me life." (Sp. Ex. 61) At the end of a meditation on hell, there is also a prayer for gratitude: "I shall also thank God for this, that up to this very moment God has shown himself so loving and merciful to me." (Sp. Ex. 71) Gratitude for creation, for God's love and for all God's gifts expands into gratitude for God's mercy, for the unmerited and undeserved gift of forgiveness that heals and restores us.

Knowledge of the many gifts and blessings leads one to gratitude which then leads to love and a desire to serve God. This grace and desire capture the core of Ignatian spirituality and sum up all the graces of the Exercises. Strengthened by this grace, one is able to say the final suscipe prayer of total surrender and generosity:

> Take, Lord, and receive all my liberty, my memory,
> my understanding, and my entire will, all that
> I have and possess. You have given all to me. To
> you, O Lord, I return it. All is yours, dispose of it
> wholly according to your will. Give me only your
> love and your grace, for this is sufficient for me.
> (Sp. Ex. 234)

The graced awareness that all has been given by God moves one to gratitude and the freedom to clutch at nothing, but to return everything, even our very selves, to God with the deep conviction that God will continue to grace and gift us.

A basic truth of our lives is that we are surrounded and sustained by God's lavish gift giving. Gratitude is our humble response to God's initiative in loving us and gifting us. The presence of gratitude in response to reflection on the Principle and Foundation is another sign that a person is ready to move on in the Exercises. It signals an openness to God's offer of mercy and God's call to serve.

The theme of gratitude also appears in the contemplation on the Annunciation. Mary's response to God's offer for her to become the mother of God models our response to God's invitations to us: "This will be to consider . . . how our Lady humbles herself and offers thanks to the Divine Majesty." (Sp. Ex. 108) The Christian response to all of the events in the life, death, and resurrection of Jesus is to give thanks to God for the gift of God's love in Jesus.

The final grace prayed for at the end of the Exercises dramatizes the role of gratitude in the mind of Ignatius. In the Contemplation on the Love of God, Ignatius invites the person to reflect on all God's gifts, how God dwells and labors in these gifts, and how all these gifts lead one back to the Giver of all gifts. Ignatius invites the one making the Exercises to share in his vision at the river Cardoner. The grace prayed for in this final contemplation is: "To ask for an intimate knowledge of the many blessings received, that filled with gratitude for all, I may in all things love and serve the Divine Majesty. (Sp. Ex. 233) The final grace prayed for in the Contemplation on the Love of God refers to being "filled with gratitude," but Ganss captures better the movement of the grace of gratitude throughout the

Exercises when he translates the phrase as "stirred to profound gratitude."[2]

A dynamic of gratitude animates the Exercises. The Exercises allow a person to have an experience of gratitude for God's love and generous giving. Moreover, a person may also have an experience of gratitude because he or she was called to labor alongside Jesus, sharing in the paschal mystery of death and Resurrection.

Ignatius Was Saturated in Gratitude

Ignatius considered ingratitude the greatest of all sins and, in fact, the source of all sins. He wrote to Simon Rodriquez, one of his first companions:

> It seems to me in the light of the Divine Goodness, although others may think differently, that ingratitude is the most abominable of sins and that it should be detested in the sight of our Creator and Lord by all of his creatures who are capable of enjoying his divine and everlasting glory. For it is a forgetting of the graces, benefits, and blessings received. As such it is the cause, beginning, and origin of all sins and misfortunes. On the contrary, the grateful acknowledgement of blessings and gifts received is loved and esteemed not only on earth but in heaven.[3]

On one level, this seems a strong statement on the centrality of gratitude, but it is not surprising in light of Ignatius's experience at the river Cardoner and his mystical sense of the giftedness of all of creation. Harvey Egan in writing of Ignatius's mysticism says that:

> Ignatius experienced mystically that gratitude and thanksgiving flowed from his authentic mystical life. To experience the mystery of the triune God in Christ rendered him gracefilled, grateful. He responded appropriately with thanksgiving. . . ."[4]

Hugo Rahner refers to "a characteristic which distinguished the noble heart of Ignatius from the very beginning of his conversion: a truly compassionate gratitude."[5]

To fully appreciate the importance of gratitude in Ignatius's experience and worldview, we look at his other writings. References to gratitude abound in Ignatius's *Spiritual Diary*, his letters and in the *Constitutions of the Society of Jesus*. The *Diary*, in particular, gives us an entry into the heart of Ignatius in his most intimate moments with God. Even his reason for keeping this journal of graces and mystical experiences reveals Ignatius's focus on gratitude. As one biographer put it, "Ignatius jotted down his experiences in the order in which they came, merely to keep alive his memory of them and his gratitude."[6] The Diary contains about a dozen explicit references to gratitude, such as, "After Mass, both in the chapel and later kneeling in my room, I wanted to thank God for such great graces."[7] In fact, most of Ignatius's mystical graces occurred during his prayer in the morning during or after Mass, connecting his sense of gratitude with the central role of Eucharist in his mystical life.

In the *Constitutions of the Society of Jesus*, Ignatius focuses his gratitude on benefactors who supported him and the ministries of the Jesuits. He exhorts Jesuits to pray for the benefactors and to offer them service. This same sentiment of gratitude is evident throughout Ignatius's many letters to benefactors, friends, and Jesuits. For instance, he wrote to his longtime benefactress and friend Isabel Roser, "Our Lord insists that we look to the giver, and love the giver more than the gift, and thus keep the giver before our eyes and in the most intimate thoughts of our heart."[8] All this supports Hugo Rahner's comment about Ignatius that "when the time for gratitude came, there was no restraining him."[9] Gratitude is a touchstone grace that reveals the heart of Ignatius.

Gratitude as a Virtue

Gratitude is the disposition of heart that first *notices* the giftedness of reality. It is attentive to God's presence as the giver of gifts. It is the movement within the human heart that goes beyond the gift to the giver. Gratitude notices the giftedness of the world around us, the giftedness of others, and finally the giftedness of ourselves.

A student of mine rushed out of her house one day, late and distracted, and dropped a book on the ground. As she bent over to pick it up, her eye fell on an iris plant in her garden. Just at that moment, the bulb began to open and reveal the flower. She experienced it as a gift given only for her by a gracious God. Gratitude filled her heart in the midst of a busy day and lifted her heart to God as the source of creation and beauty. She did not look away, but paused to savor the experience and to become more grateful.

Gratitude is a disposition of heart that *remembers* that God is the giver of all good gifts. Gratitude brings us back to the moments of grace so we can savor and appreciate them as gifts. A person grows in gratitude by recalling the gifts God has given and by acknowledging again that God is the source of the gift. This is another reason why Ignatius insisted on the twice-daily practice of examen of conscience, the first step of which is to give thanks for the gifts of the day. It is an opportunity to recognize the gifts that a person has failed to notice or attend to during the day. It is also an opportunity, among other things, to take time to remember and give thanks for the ways God has gifted us with God's presence and care.

Gratitude is a *choice*. Not everything experienced in life is experienced as gift. Moments of loss and tragedy and failure can turn a person's heart to grief, resentment, and anger. The focus shifts from what has been given to what has been lost. At times like this, gratitude becomes a choice to notice and to remember all that has been received and to accept what has happened in hope. The virtue of gratitude disposes us to see the gift dimension of *all* reality, even in the moments of dying. Genuine gratitude is not a naïve or simplistic view of reality that fails to recognize the suffering and challenges of life. Rather it views reality in the larger context of the radical giftedness of all of life and sees reason to rejoice even in difficult circumstances.

Gratitude is the source of *happiness*. Grateful people are happy people because they see the world as gift. Keenan points out that satisfaction is at the root of gratitude.[10] There is little room for gratitude as long as we are looking beyond what we already have in search of something more. When we are satisfied with what we have, we can be content and find a place for thanksgiving.[11]

Gratitude and the Good Life

Gratitude's connection to happiness and satisfaction is confirmed by recent studies on the psychology of gratitude. The psychologist Charles Shelton is especially insightful about the importance of gratitude as a resource for living the "good life."[12] He is concerned with gratitude not simply as a momentary and isolated response to a gift, but gratitude as a constant disposition or a way of life.

Shelton says, "Gratitude offers the hope of kindness and the giving away of goodness to others, while cementing relationships through the perceived good-will of the benefactor and the sharing of gifts in return."[13]

Shelton lists the positive qualities of gratitude. It enriches love because it enables a person to break out of the role of victim and work toward healing. It counteracts the human tendency to focus on the negative rather than on the positive. It limits stress and selfish desires by acting against "feeling-states of self-preoccupation and possible envy." Our own experience shows that feelings of gratitude are incompatible with pettiness and negativism and self-centeredness. When our hearts are filled with thanksgiving, we move beyond minor irritations and deprivations and focus on the larger sense of love and affirmation.

Gratitude expands our hearts and opens them to the richness and giftedness of life. It fosters self-esteem, positive relationships of trust, and leads to joy that encourages sharing of one's gifts.

Gratitude Turns Us Outward

Gratitude impels us to share the gifts received. Gratitude does not turn us inward with a sense of passive contentment but points us outward in service. The experience of being gifted fosters a desire to gift others. We consume what we possess. We cherish and share what we hold as gift. Gratitude moves us beyond mere consumption and arrogant dominion to stewardship, the commitment to enhance and pass on the gifts received.[14]

The Spiritual Exercises foster a commitment to service, and this commitment is the fruit of gratitude. Service can flow out of compulsion or a desire for reward or a desire to be esteemed, but genuine loving service is rooted in an experience of God's love that moves one to service.[15] The experience of gratitude is the driving force behind Ignatius's constant call to action and service. Genuine service flows from a grateful heart anxious to share the gifts received.

The Exercises foster virtues close to the heart of Ignatius. The Principle and Foundation calls a person to reverence and to gratitude. The gratitude elicited in reflecting on creation will expand even further through the experience of forgiveness and call, culminating in the Contemplation of Divine Love. The experience of the Exercises shapes our hearts and transforms us into people in tune with the grateful heart of Christ.

> At that same hour Jesus rejoiced in the Holy Spirit and said, "I thank you, Father, Lord of heaven and earth, because you have hidden these things from the wise and the intelligent and have revealed them to infants; yes, Father, for such was your gracious will" (Luke 10:21).

Reflecting on Gratitude

- List the gifts of your life, both past and present.
- Name the important givers in your life.
- Are there people or things in my life that I have taken for granted?
- Are there people I need to thank?
- How do I share the gifts I have received?

Scripture Readings on Gratitude

Psalms 30, 100, 107
Matthew 11:25–27 Jesus Thanks His Father
Luke 17:11–19 Jesus Cleanses Ten Lepers
Matthew 25:14–30 The Parable of the Talents

4 Freedom: Called to Freedom

. . . it is necessary to make ourselves indifferent to all created things.

Sp. Ex. 23

Freedom is another foundational virtue for living the Christian life. We need freedom in order to transcend the self and respond to the invitation to share in God's life with love. Freedom is also foundational to the Spiritual Exercises. Ignatius makes it clear that the purpose of the Spiritual Exercises is to bring us to the freedom necessary for us to hear God's call and respond with generosity.

What Ignatius Meant by "Indifference"

Ignatius put great emphasis on distinguishing between the goal of life and the means to attain it. The goal or end of life is to praise, reverence, and serve God, and to come to eternal life. All of God's gifts are means to achieve this goal; we should use them accordingly. "From this it follows that I should use these things to the extent that they help me toward my end, and rid myself of them to the extent that they hinder me." (Sp. Ex. 23)

Our temptation is to confuse means and ends to this goal of life. We choose a means first; then try to find a way to use it to reach the end. For example, we decide we want to be married, and we then try to figure out how to praise, reverence, and serve God in the married state. Ignatius would rather have us focus on the goal—to serve God—and then discern the state of life that is *the* best way to achieve this goal. In the words of Ignatius, "I ought to desire and elect only the thing which is more conducive to the end for which I was created." (Sp. Ex. 23)

Making such a choice demands freedom. Ignatius's term for this is *indifference*. For most people, indifference implies a disinterest. "I am indifferent" is another way of saying, "I don't care." However, Ignatius means something quite different by using the word indifference. In fact, it's the opposite. For Ignatius, indifference means that a person is so passionately committed to God and to embracing God's plan that everything else is secondary to that one goal and one purpose. Indifference is the detachment one needs to be able to choose God's plan. In the words of Michael Ivens, indifference is a place in the heart where "the movements of the Spirit can be sensed and things seen in relation to the signs of God's will." He goes on to say that "indifference must be understood in relation to the deeper desires, given by the Spirit, to do whatever conduces more to the praise, reverence, and service of God, and more specifically to follow Christ and to live by the values of the gospel."[1]

Dean Brackley describes indifference even more dramatically. He states, "it means being so passionately and single-mindedly committed, so completely in love, that we are willing to sacrifice anything, including our lives, for the ultimate goal. It means magnanimous generosity, abandonment into God's hands, *availability* (italics his)."[2] This captures some of Ignatius's own passion for God and God's will. One of the graces we pray for in the Principle and Foundation is a passionate desire to choose only God and the freedom to let go of whatever stands in the way of responding to God's love.

What destroys our indifference and compromises our freedom are gifts of God that we become attached to in a disordered way. Of course many of our attachments are properly ordered— friends, loved ones, creative and productive work. But some attachments are disordered. We cling to them. They make it impossible to discern God's call and to respond in generosity. They set boundaries on God's desires for us.

For example, think of a person unable and unwilling to hear an invitation from God for a new ministry because the person cannot imagine leaving a certain city or institution. This may be a person so attached to his or her own agenda that he or she is unable to embrace God's agenda. There are things held so tightly in our hand that we are incapable of opening our hand to receive something new. Here we are not even necessarily talking about sinful attachments, but attachments to things that otherwise may be good and holy.

The Gospel story of the rich young man vividly illustrates a lack of indifference (Matthew 19:16–30). The young man approached Jesus seeking eternal life. He was a good man and faithfully kept the commandments. Then Jesus invited him to another level and said, "If you wish to be perfect, go, sell your possessions and give the money to the poor, and you will have treasure in heaven; then come, follow me." The young man went away sad because he had great possessions. His attachments put a limit on God.

It is interesting that the young man first asked, "Teacher, what good deed must I do to have eternal life." He wanted to know what action he should perform. When he asked for more, Jesus challenged him to put on a new heart that was free enough to let go of whatever he had so he could follow Jesus. The young man had many attachments, many possessions that bound his heart and kept him from hearing the call of Jesus to a fuller and richer life.

This story dramatizes the call of every Christian to come to the freedom to follow Jesus. It asks us to consider the possessions or gifts we clutch at that capture our hearts, the possessions we allow to define us and give us worth.

What Does it Mean to Be Free?

Our God is a God of freedom. The defining moment in God's relationship with the Israelites was the Exodus. God led the Israelites out of slavery into freedom and ultimately into the Promised Land. God molded them into a people. They were freed again when God intervened in their history and brought them back from exile in Babylon.

As God did with the Israelites, Jesus came to set people free. In his inaugural address in the synagogue as he begins his ministry, Jesus makes the mission of the prophet Isaiah his own.

When he came to Nazareth, where he had been brought up, he went to the synagogue on the sabbath day, as was his custom. He stood up to read, and the scroll of the prophet Isaiah was given to him. He unrolled the scroll and found the place where it was written:

> "The Spirit of the Lord is upon
>   me,
> because he had anointed me
> to bring good news to the
>   poor.
> He has sent me to proclaim
>   release to the captives
> and recovery of sight to the blind,
>   to let the oppressed go free,
> to proclaim the year of the
>   Lord's favor."

And he rolled up the scroll, gave it back to the attendant, and sat down. The eyes of all in the synagogue were fixed on him.

Then he began to say to them, "Today this scripture has been fulfilled in your hearing."

Jesus announces that he has come to free people from whatever enslaved them. He will free the prisoners from confinement, the blind from darkness, and the oppressed from their slavery. He came especially to free people from interior captivity of the heart.

The first miracle Jesus performs in Mark's gospel is an exorcism (Mark 1:23–27). It symbolizes Jesus' conflict with the power of evil and darkness that enslaves people. Jesus' act of healing set people free from their diseases. His teaching set them free from ignorance. He tried to set people free from the burden of the Law that in many ways enslaved them. Above all, Jesus came to cast out the fear that bound up their hearts. How often Jesus spoke the words, "Do not be afraid?" Jesus' ministry invited people to the freedom of the children of God. Jesus came to reveal who God is and to dispel false images of God. He came to remind us that God is a God of freedom who invites us to live in such freedom and love.

For example, Paul experienced the freedom of the risen Christ. He announced our freedom from sin, death, and the law, the forces that enslaved people. We experience this freedom through the power of the Spirit. "Now the Lord is the Spirit, and where the Spirit of the Lord is, there is freedom" (2 Corinthians 3:17).

Why Freedom?

God calls us to freedom so we can respond to his graces and invitations in our lives. Freedom is rooted in an experience of God's unconditional love. This is the love we pray for in the Principle and Foundation. God's love for us calls forth our love for God. This is the heart of our freedom and our willingness to let go of everything to attain our goal of deeper union with God.

The psychologist Carl Rogers casts light on this experience of freedom.[3] Rogers postulates that a basic need of all people is "positive regard." This is the experience of receiving acceptance, respect, sympathy, warmth, and love from significant people in our lives. Positive regard leads to "positive *self*-regard."

Most often we receive positive regard from specific things we do—what Rogers calls "conditions of worth." Conditions of worth can be placed on us, often subtly and unconsciously, by parents, teachers, friends, and even spiritual directors. They become obligations to perform in order to experience positive regard or positive self-regard. They can be as trivial as "If you eat your spinach, you are a good child" to more significant conditions like, "If you become a doctor or a priest, you will be worthy of love." These conditions of worth get internalized and we learn to evaluate our worth in light of them.

However, it is possible to give or receive "*unconditional* positive regard"—approval that does not depend on anything we do. The most obvious example is the love of a parent for a child. This is also the way God loves us.

The questions remain, How do we experience God's love? Is it conditional or unconditional? Is God's love a free gift or is it a love that must be earned by fulfilling certain obligations? These are questions that must be answered at a heart level of feeling and attitude.

If we truly experience God's love as freely given, then that love drives out fear. Paul tells us that "But God proves his love for us in that while we still were sinners Christ died for us." (Romans 5:8) It is "unconditional positive regard." Conditional love causes fear. We are afraid that we have not done what's necessary to merit God's love. Fear is dispelled when we experience love as gift. "There is no fear in love, but perfect love casts out fear; for fear has to do with punishment, and whoever fears has not reached perfection and love. We love because he first loved us" (1 John 4:18–19).

This experience of love as pure gift leads us to freedom. This freedom is the gift of the Holy Spirit that is poured into our hearts. "[A]nd hope does not disappoint us, because God's love has been poured into our hearts through the Holy Spirit that has been given to us." (Romans 5:5) When we are afraid we act not out of freedom, but out of compulsion. Compulsion is slavery to something imposed from outside—a duty, an obligation, or a condition placed on being loved. In contrast, when we know we are loved, we are able to act out of our deepest desires, not out of compulsion. We act in free response to a love received, not as a frantic effort to win reward or escape punishment. This gift of love sets us free to love in return.

A wise spiritual director once asked me two "why" questions, and said that the second "why" was more important. The first question was, "Why do you want to join a religious community?" The answer was "To give my life to God." The second question was "Why do you want to give your life to God?" Is it out of fear? Out of compulsion to do what seems to be the best possible thing to do with your life? Or is it out of love for someone who has loved you first?

Another example: "Why do you want to get a PhD?" "I want to be as educated as possible." Why do you want to be as educated as possible?" Is a PhD a condition of your worth? Do you need it because you will then be accepted and worthwhile and looked up to? Or is it because you have a love of teaching and research and you wish to minister to others through teaching? In other words, do these and other decisions flow from freedom and love or from fear and compulsion. Fear leads to compulsion and slavery. Love leads to true desires which lead to freedom.

The Power of a Free Choice

Freedom makes true commitment possible. The freedom to say yes or no out of love enables us to give ourselves wholeheartedly. If we do not have a personal experience of God's love, we may well act out of fear. We may be motivated out of some "should" that compels us to say "yes" in order to be worthy and accepted. An experience of God's love leads to the power to give our life in love. Such freedom flows from a personal relationship with a loving God. We can give our lives fully and freely only to someone who calls us in love.

This freedom is essential for one making the Exercises because it enables one to hear God's call and to respond in love. It also enables one to face one's sinfulness and believe in God's mercy. Throughout the Exercises, God's love is repeatedly revealed to us. Ignatius has us meditate on God's love as creating, forgiving, calling, caring, loving unto death, and calling to risen life. All of these experiences confirm the grace of knowing God's love that leads us to freedom.

Commitment is the highest exercise of the gift of freedom. Freedom comes to fullness in fidelity, when we give ourselves totally to another in love. Freedom is not the capacity for indefinite revision, but the capacity to create something final and lasting. We will talk in a later chapter about fidelity, but for now we can recognize it as a response to love offered and received. We remain faithful to those who have loved us and whom we love in return.

Where Freedom Comes From

We have seen two sources of freedom. The first is our experience of God's unconditional love. Knowing God's love frees us to act out of love and our deepest desires, not out of fear or a sense of inadequacy.

The second source is our trust in a God who is a faithful giver. We trust God because we know that God is a faithful giver. God will continue to give us what we need. Recall the parable in Luke 12:16–21: there is no need to fill our barns for the future. Jesus reminded us of the lilies of the field and the birds of the air that God cares for. We need not be anxious because God will care for us as well.

But at the deepest level, freedom flows from our passion for God alone. We are moved by God's love to center our hearts only on God. This is the heart of Ignatian indifference that sets our hearts free for love and service. In the end, this is putting on the heart of Christ, a heart that trusts in God, a heart so filled with love that it desires to let go and share, and a heart free to seek God's kingdom above all else.

The Foundation of Our Spiritual Lives

In this and the two previous chapters, we have been reflecting on the Principle and Foundation. In this opening consideration of the Exercises, Ignatius invites us to begin our spiritual journey by reflecting on who we are and who God is and on our relationship with God and the world around us. Ignatius lays the foundation of our spiritual lives and reminds us of the most basic truths of our existence. I have suggested that this consideration elicits and fosters three virtues that are essential to our life in God and foundational for all that will follow in the Spiritual Exercises.

First, our awareness that we are created by God out of love moves us to a profound sense of reverence, an awareness of God's presence in all of creation and a sense of affectionate awe before the majesty of God and sacredness of all of creation that, at the same time, draws us closer to God.

Second, our sense of all of creation as a gift from the hands of a loving God calls forth an overwhelming experience of gratitude, of blessings freely given and received. This gratitude moves us to cherish and share the gifts, as well as uniting us ever more deeply to the Giver of all gifts.

Finally, the experience of being loved and gifted centers our hearts on the goal and purpose of our lives and frees us to let go of whatever stands in the way of our hearing and responding to God's invitations. It dispels fear and frees us to act out of love. It focuses our hearts only on God as the source and goal of our deepest desires.

Reverence, gratitude, and freedom are dispositions of heart that enable us to live out our Christian lives. To be aware of God's presence, to be grateful for God's gifts, to be free to hear God's call are absolutely essential to becoming true disciples of Christ. They shape our hearts into the heart of Christ and open us to God's mercy and call. They are the virtues that empower us to "love and serve the Divine Majesty in all things." (Sp. Ex. 233)

Reflecting on Freedom

- When have I not experienced freedom in my life?
- In what ways do I act out of fear rather than love?
- How do I experience Jesus setting me free in my life?
- How can I grow in trust in God as the faithful giver?

Scripture Passages about Freedom

Matthew 19:16–30 The Rich Young Man

Luke: 4:16–21 Jesus Comes To Set Us Free

I John 4:18–19 Love Casts Out Fear.

2 Corinthians 3:17 "where the Spirit of the Lord is, there is
    freedom."

5 Compunction: Human Sinfulness

I will call to memory all the sins of my life.

SP. EX. 56

God loves us unconditionally. God invites us to love freely in return with grateful and undivided hearts that are centered on God alone. But we don't reflect on this truth for very long before realizing that our response to God's love is inadequate. We have not always loved God in return. In some ways, we have been ungrateful, irreverent, and unfree. We have taken God's gifts and made them possessions that we have misused and refused to share. We have not been attentive to God's presence in our lives. We have allowed our hearts to be captured by things other than God so we have not been free to respond in love. We have sinned.

What is Sin?

Ignatius sees sin as ingratitude and irreverence. Earlier I quoted his startling statement that ingratitude is the greatest sin and the root and source of all sin. When we cease to see everything as gift that connects us to the Giver, we take things for granted and claim them as our own. We no longer acknowledge that we have received everything from the hands of a loving God. We consume rather than cherish and misuse rather than share.

For Ignatius, sin is a disorder that poisons our relationships with God, each other, and the world around us. We no longer make choices that are conducive to the end and purpose of our lives. Sin is the disordered attachments that get in the way of our service and love of God and our neighbors. It is an unfreedom that enslaves our hearts and prevents us from praising, reverencing, and serving God. In the words of Michael Ivens, sin for Ignatius is "the refusal to 'use' one's freedom to give reverence and obedience to one's Creator and Lord, in short the refusal to use the gift of freedom to allow God to be God."[1]

Grappling with Sin in the Spiritual Exercises

Ignatius divides the Spiritual Exercises into four weeks." These are not seven-day weeks, but rather stages of growth in our relationship with God. In the Exercises, we experience our sinfulness, God's mercy, conversion, a sense of vocation, and a deeper union with God.

An encounter with one's personal sinfulness and ingratitude happens in the First Week of the Spiritual Exercises. Ignatius first situates our own faulty response to God in the broader context of the history of sin that parallels the history of salvation. He has us consider the fall of the angels and the story of Adam and Eve. Then Ignatius asks us to imagine someone who cuts himself or herself off from God by an act of rebellion and disobedience. We see ourselves as sinners who have been saved by God. We are part of both the history of sin and salvation. Our sin is not an isolated act in human history, but part of a larger failure to respond in love to God's initiatives.

Ignatius then invites us to reflect on our own personal history of sin. This is not intended as a detailed examination of conscience of one's whole life. Rather, Ignatius wants us to claim our own sinfulness and need for conversion. We pray to know our own sin and take responsibility for it, especially in contrast to the grandeur of God. John English says that the purpose of this prayer is to "come to a deep affective realization of our sin and to perceive how unresponsive we have been in the face of so much goodness and so much love."[2] This is not an exercise in self-rejection, but an exercise in genuine self-knowledge before God. It brings home to us our need for salvation and for the gift of God's forgiveness and healing.

Sin is understood in contrast to the holiness of God. In the presence of God, we feel sinful, such as Peter did in the boat. He said , "Go away from me, Lord, for I am a sinful man" (Luke 5:8). Peter felt a sense of awe and unworthiness in response to the miraculous catch of fish in this reading. This was more a statement about God's holiness and majesty than about Peter's state of soul. Peter recognized his inadequate response to Jesus, but even more he acknowledged Jesus' power and holiness.

Ignatius suggests that we repeat these exercises in order to move our understanding of our sin from our heads to our hearts. He wants us to arrive at that deep interior knowledge of the source of our sin. Finally, Ignatius challenges us to imagine and reflect on the ultimate consequences of sin by considering the possibility of eternal loss in hell. Hell dramatizes our capacity to reject God's mercy and love. Hell shows where unbridled selfishness will ultimately lead us—to self-destruction and alienation, far from the face of God.

Sin is Breaking Relationships, Not Laws

Contemporary images of sin resonate well with Ignatius's approach to sin. In response to an act-centered and law-centered approach to sin, contemporary moralists view sin more as a failure to respond to God's offer of love. Sin is imagined as alienation from God, from others, and from the world. Sin is ingratitude and infidelity to God. It is rooted in possessiveness and a sense of self-sufficiency that leads to an inability and unwillingness to respond to the call to discipleship. Sin breaks the covenant relationship with God that was based on mutual love and commitment.

Sin is understood today more as breaking a relationship than breaking a law. The story of sin in the book of Genesis highlights this idea. Adam and Eve violated God's prohibition about eating the fruit of the tree, but at a deeper level, they broke their relationship with God by refusing to accept their dependence on God. They wanted to be autonomous. Moreover, they broke their relationship with each other by trying to blame the other. Finally, their sin ruptured their relationship with the world around them. This is symbolized by their expulsion from the garden and by the pain that will accompany work and childbirth.

Contemporary discussion of sin also stresses what we fail to do as well as what we do—sins of omission as well as commission. In the story of the Good Samaritan, the focus is not on the thief who attacked the traveler, but on the priest and Levite who fail to help him. In the final judgment scene in Matthew's Gospel, people are judged for failing to feed the hungry and clothe the naked. They are not censured for breaking rules or performing evil deeds. We certainly commit sinful acts, but we too often overlook our failures to reconcile with others, to reach out to those in need, to hope in difficult times.

Richard Gula sees sin as a breech of our covenantal relationship with God. He describes sin as a failure "to respect the *worth* of ourselves and others as constituted by God's love; to live in *solidarity* with creation and with one another as covenantal partners; and to develop the virtue of *fidelity* as the proper characteristic of every covenantal relationship."[3] In this view, sin is failure to honor and foster our relationships with God, others, and the world around us. Sin is essentially a failure in virtue.

Jim Keenan describes sin as "a failure to bother to love." He says that this is the scriptural view of sin:

> It captures the sin of Matthew's goats, Lazarus's rich man, the wounded man's priest and Levite, the publican's Pharisee and so on. Each of the Bible stories that refers us to sin, refers us to what one could have done and did not do.[4]

We domesticate our sinfulness by compiling lists of familiar things we do wrong when in fact our greatest failures are failures to be compassionate or concerned. We simply do not take the time or make the effort that love demands.

When we imagine sin in terms of relationship we can see how it is more than a personal failure. Sin inevitably leads to the destruction of community. For example, in the Hebrew Scriptures, this is best illustrated in the story of the Tower of Babel. It is the culmination of the history of sin narrated in the early chapters of Genesis. The attempt to build a tower reaching to God causes the breakdown of communication, symbolized by the diversity of languages. Sin disperses the community. The Pauline image of the Body of Christ captures the communal dimension of sin. Our sins cause pain and suffering to the Body united in Christ. Even the most private sin weakens and impoverishes the Christian community. Sin undermines the covenant that binds us together in love.

Recent attention to social sin and sinful social structures emphasizes its connection to the community even more strongly. In a complex and interdependent world, the greatest sins are not the individual actions we perform out of weakness and malice. Our actions and failures to act create the greater evils of societal structures that lead to injustice and neglect. Social sin "describes the consequences of individual choices which form structures wherein people suffer various forms of oppression," Gula writes.[5] We bear some responsibility for what we do and fail to do in creating and supporting the structures of our society.

Dean Brackley, in his contemporary reading of Ignatius, describes the reality of evil in the social context of poverty and hunger: "When we look through the wide lens, the systemic despoilment of the poor is the most obvious, the most massive and death-dealing sin."[6] He makes clear that we must claim our part in the sin of the world. This moves our experience of sin from the personal level to the level of society. It expands our hearts and, in turn, expands our area of responsibility.

Ignatius's worldview did not include an awareness of social sin. He did not identify the unjust structures of society as embodiments of sin nor did he think of sin in communal or relational terms. Ignatius's understanding of sin would have been more individual and act-oriented. His own battles with scrupulosity taught him that obsessing with particular actions did not lead to peace or bring him closer to God. Ignatius is more concerned with the graces and desires of our hearts than with our individual sins. More important for him is the call to gratitude and freedom that focuses our hearts on God and God's goodness. The more contemporary approach to sin can, however, further expand and enrich Ignatius's sixteenth-century understanding of sin. Reflection on social sin is an essential adaptation of the Exercises in today's context.

The Grace of Sorrow for Our Sin

We have been paying close attention to the particular graces that accompany each movement of the Spiritual Exercises. These graces reveal what Ignatius hoped for us as the Exercises unfolded. They name the deepest desires of our hearts.[7] These desires shape our prayer and direct the movements of our hearts. Throughout our reflections on the Exercises, we will highlight the graces prayed for in each week as a way of capturing the heart of the flow of the Exercises.

In the First Week of the Exercises, Ignatius asks us to pray for "shame and confusion about myself" (Sp. Ex. 48) and for "growing and intense sorrow and tears for my sins." (Sp. Ex. 55) These are the graces we experience in response to a renewed awareness of human sinfulness, especially our own. We are moved to a profound sense of shame and sorrow as we contrast our ingratitude and self-centeredness with the love and grandeur of God.

The other graces prayed for in this First Week are named in the *Triple Colloquy*, a conversation with Mary, Jesus, and the Father. Ignatius proposes that we ask for three graces:

> First, that I may feel an interior knowledge of my
> sins and also an abhorrence of them;
>
> Second, that I may perceive the disorder in my
> actions, in order to detest them, amend myself, and
> put myself in order;
>
> Third, that I may have a knowledge of the
> world, in order to detest it and rid myself of all that
> is worldly and vain. (Sp. Ex. 63)

Here Ignatius wants to take us beyond any morbid dwelling on individual sins to a profound sense of the disorder of sin and the forces of evil in the world. These are not sins that we uncover in our own examination of conscience, but rather the deeper sin that only God can reveal to us. We can only recognize sin as we stand before the gracious love of God freely given. Sin is not simply our comfortable failures and misdeeds that can often mask our deeper sin. Sin is the radical ingratitude and lack of response to God's offer of life that is at the root of all sin.

The Virtue of Compunction

Our contention is that virtues flow from the graces of the Exercises. What dispositions of heart arise when we reflect on our sin before God? In my view, the virtue that flows from shame and sorrow is what has been traditionally known as *compunction.*

Contemporary spiritual authors have written relatively little about compunction, but it is a rich notion in the early Church theologians, the monastic tradition, and the medieval theologians. John Chrysostom, John Cassian, Gregory the Great, and Anselm all wrote about compunction. Michael Driscoll says that compunction signifies "pain of the spirit, a suffering due to the actual existence of sin and human concupiscence, and as a result of our desire for God. The theological connotation is closely parallel to the biblical idea of metanoia, rendered in English as 'penitence.'"[8]

In his Rule, St. Benedict speaks of a compunction of tears and a compunction of heart. In speaking of reverence in prayer, he says: "How much more important, then, to lay our petitions before the Lord God of all things with the utmost humility and sincere devotion. We must know that God regards our purity of heart and tears of compunction, not our many words."[9] He exhorts the monks to observe the season of Lent "by refusing to indulge evil habits and by devoting ourselves to prayer with tears, to reading, compunction of heart, and self-denial."[10]

Compunction is often associated with tears—tears of penitence that turn into tears of joy. Joan Chittester aptly describes these tears: "To the ancients, 'tears of compunction' were the sign of a soul that knew its limits, faced its sins, accepted its needs, and lived in hope."[11] The virtue of compunction seems an appropriate Ignatian virtue because it is so often related to tears, a grace Ignatius asks us to pray for in the First Week.[12]

Compunction pierces the human heart. (The Latin root of the word "compunction" means "to puncture with.") Our heart is pierced with sorrow, but more profoundly by the love of God that purifies our hearts and opens them to God. Benedicta Ward speaks of a twofold meaning of compunction: "This is the first kind of compunction, a piercing of sorrow and dread, which leads, through a realization of its resolution in the love of God, to that other compunction of longing desire for God."[13] Our deepest sorrow arises from knowing we were loved into creation and have not responded to that love. It gives rise to an even deeper desire for God.

In the eleventh century, St. Anselm captures the grace Ignatius would pray for in the First Week some five centuries later:

> Ask urgently that I may have the love that pierces the heart; tears that are humble; desire for the homeland of heaven; impatience with this earthly exile; searing repentance; and a dread of torments in eternity.[14]

One wonders if Ignatius ever read these words while at the University of Paris. Certainly he would have been at home praying them.

Compunction is that deep sense of sorrow and shame that Ignatius invites us to pray for. It is an awareness of sin that leads to repentance and contrition. Compunction does not focus on our failure, but on the one offended. We think of the words from the Act of Contrition: ". . . but most of all, because I have offended you, who are all good and deserving of all my love." Compunction is the sadness that emerges when we realize that we have betrayed or hurt someone we love. It is the heaviness that fills our hearts when we realize that we have distanced ourselves from the very one we most desire, the one who alone can satisfy our restless hearts. Compunction does not turn us inward but outward toward the other.

We need to rediscover compunction. It is often overlooked in our contemporary moral reflection. We have reacted to a past overemphasis on sin by emphasizing the pervasiveness of God's love and forgiveness. We have moved from legalism to a morality of love, from self-rejection to self-esteem, from "only a few are saved" to "all are saved," from the pervasiveness of sin to the near absence of sin. Overall, this has been a theologically sound redis-covery of the Scriptural revelation of God's unconditional love. But it risks overshooting the mark. The danger is that it masks our genuine sinfulness and keeps us from claiming responsibility for our actions.[15]

The Ignatian Exercises remind us not to pass over the first grace of the First Week—an awareness of our sinfulness and our need for salvation. We're often tempted to skip the reality of our sinfulness. We hear people say, "I don't do sin. It is too nega-tive. In the past, it has led me to self-rejection and a devaluing of myself. It is unhealthy to dwell on my sinfulness." However, the power of the Exercises is to help us claim our own sinful-ness as we experience God's unconditional love. This allows us to appreciate the absolute gratuitousness of God's continuing love in forgiving us. We cannot fully appreciate God's mercy without acknowledging our sinfulness. We cannot know the joy of salva-tion without admitting that we need to be saved. Compunction is an essential virtue for everyone who wants to stand honestly before God and know the depths of God's forgiving love.

Compunction flows from a genuine self-knowledge and an acceptance of oneself as a sinner. It is the longing of a penitent heart for healing and reconciliation. It is that longing that opens our hearts to the forgiving love of God that surrounds us and sets us free.

Reflecting on Compunction

- Where are the places of ingratitude and unfreedom in my life?
- What are the ways I fail to respond to the faithful offer of God's love in my life?
- What moves me to sorrow and compunction and leads my heart to a deeper desire for God?
- What are the ways I could be more loving and concerned for others?
- What are the ways I could be more attentive and responsive to the needs of the poor and vulnerable?

Scripture Passages about Compunction

Psalm 51 Prayer for Cleansing and Pardon
Luke 5:1–11 Jesus Calls the First Disciples
Romans 7:14–25 The Inner Conflict
1 Corinthians 13:1–7 The Gift of Love
2 Corinthians 4:7–12 Treasure in Clay Jars

6 Forgiveness: The Mercy of God

I will conclude with a colloquy of mercy.

Sp. Ex. 61

Acknowledging our sin isn't all we do in the First Week of the Exercises. We are also invited to celebrate God's mercy. We are sinners, but we are loved sinners. God's love is ever faithful even when we choose darkness. The God of the First Week is a God of mercy. The person making the Exercises is likely to be a spiritually mature person seeking spiritual growth. For a person of this kind, conversion will mean a deep change of heart that can only arise out of a new personal discovery of God's mercy. Ignatius invites a person to that more radical sense of sinfulness that can only be experienced in the light of God's love. Writes Ivens: "The essential grace of the First Week is that of a conversion arising out of the literally heart-breaking experience of being loved and forgiven."[1] The full experience of the First Week arises when we know our sin and yet know that we are still loved.

Ignatius's Conversations About Mercy

Ignatius expects that our experience of God's mercy will arise in the course of three of the colloquies that occur during the First Week. Colloquies are real conversations with God. In the words of Ignatius, they are to be made "in the way one friend speaks to another, or a servant to one in authority—now begging a favor, now accusing oneself of some misdeed, now telling one's concerns and asking counsel about them." (Sp. Ex. 54) Ignatius expects colloquies to arise spontaneously as we pray, but he suggests content for several of them as we reflect on sin and its consequences. They give voice to the desires of our hearts and reveal to us what God hopes and desires for us.

The first colloquy occurs at the end of the first exercise of the First Week. Ignatius invites us to a conversation with Jesus at the foot of the cross. He says, "Imagine Christ our Lord suspended on the cross before you, and converse with him in a colloquy: How is it that he, although he is the Creator, has come to make himself a human being? How is it that he has passed from eternal life to death here in time, and to die in this way for my sins?" (Sp. Ex. 53)

The reference to Jesus as Creator takes us back to the Principle and Foundation and God's creative love for us. We notice too that this very personal conversation with Jesus emphasizes that Jesus does not simply die for sins, but for *our* sins. This is where we experience the mercy of God poured out in Jesus. Only when we stand before the cross of Christ do we truly know the depth of our sin. Only when we know the depth of our sin do we know the depth of God's mercy. Jesus' death dramatizes the horror of sin and its consequences, but it also reveals God's unrelenting love for us even in our sinfulness. We pray for the grace of sorrow and shame, but in this conversation with Jesus, we celebrate the forgiving love of God. Fleming highlights the importance of this colloquy in defining our relationship with God:

> We are led through our prayer with the crucified Jesus to a wholly new depth of relationship with God. For this is a God who loves us so much that he suffers our shame and confusion, that he sorrows and sheds tears with us, and that he forgives and saves us, and continues to share divine life with us.[2]

The God who created us in love is also a saving God who offers us love and forgiveness in Jesus.

Ignatius then suggests simply that we gaze on Jesus on the cross and "speak out whatever comes to mind." He does not tell us what to say. Jesus only asks us to speak and listen with our hearts to what he desires to say to us. This colloquy sets the backdrop of the First Week. All of our reflection on sin is done in the context of the cross of Jesus and his saving love for us. It is here that we know ourselves as loved sinners.

To further stimulate this conversation with Jesus, Ignatius formulates three challenging questions to ask ourselves: "What have I done for Christ? What am I doing for Christ? What ought I to do for Christ?" How have I acted and how will I act in response to the love of Christ? Ignatius always asks the action question. It is not enough to experience God's love. That love prompts us to *do* something in return. The question "What ought I to do?" will lead us to a sense of God's call in the Second Week of the Exercises.

The theme of mercy recurs in the colloquy at the end of the second exercise: "I will conclude with a colloquy of mercy—speaking and giving thanks to God our Lord for giving me life until now, and proposing, with his grace, amendment for the future." (Sp. Ex. 61) Here gratitude is prompted by the mercy of God. Finally, the experience of mercy also shapes the colloquy at the end of the final meditation on hell: "I will also thank Christ because he has shown me, all through my life up to the present moment, so much pity and mercy." (Sp. Ex. 71)

These conversations about mercy throughout the First Week remind us that our reflection on sin is incomplete without an experience of God's mercy. George Aschenbrenner sums up well the final result of our prayer on sin and God's mercy. He says, "You know now that you are not as good as you have worked hard for years to make yourself seem, but you are much more loved than you could ever have imagined."[3]

The more we know our sin, the more we are overwhelmed by the love of God.

Stories of Mercy from the New Testament

Contemporary directors of the Exercises often suggest scripture passages to help people experience the graces of the First Week. The story of the Prodigal Son is a powerful narrative of God's mercy (Luke 15:11–32). The father rushes out to meet the returning son without recriminations or harsh words, only words of acceptance and reconciliation. The story ends with a celebration as do the two previous parables in Luke's Gospel—the shepherd who finds a lost sheep and the woman who finds a lost coin. Jesus tells this story to assure us of God's mercy. God is more anxious and willing to forgive than we are to be forgiven.

Jesus' actions spoke eloquently of God's mercy toward sinners. He does not condemn the woman caught in adultery but forgives her and challenges others to forgive her. When the accusers disperse, Jesus gently encourages her. "Jesus straightened up and said to her, 'Woman, where are they? Has no one condemned you?' She said, 'No one, sir.' And Jesus said, 'Neither do I condemn you. Go your way, and from now on do not sin again" (John 8:10–11).

Jesus' dealt mercifully with Zacchaeus, the tax collector. Jesus calls him down out of the tree and invites himself to Zacchaeus's house. In response to Zacchaeus' generous signs of repentance, Jesus exclaims: "Today salvation has come to this house, because he too is a son of Abraham. For the Son of Man came to seek out and to save the lost" (Luke 19:9–10).

On the cross Jesus is portrayed as reaching out with the words, "Father, forgive them; for they know not what they are doing" (Luke 23:34). Jesus' forgiveness of those who crucified him gave voice to God's offer of forgiveness to all of us.

One final story captures both the mercy and human sensitivity of Jesus. Peter had denied Jesus three times during the Passion. On the lake shore after the Resurrection, Jesus gives voice to his desire for reconciliation rooted in love. He does not ask for an apology or an admission of guilt from Peter. But he invites Peter to profess his love three times to allow him to ritualize his sorrow and his love for Jesus. "Lord, you know everything; you know that I love you" (John 21:17). Each time Jesus affirms his trust in Peter by asking him to carry on Jesus' ministry of feeding the people. Jesus says, "Feed my sheep" (John 21:17).

The risen Jesus carries on this ministry of forgiveness today. This is the forgiveness that Ignatius wants us to experience in the First Week of the Exercises.

We Forgive Because We Have Been Forgiven

The experience of forgiveness in the First Week opens our hearts to share this gift of forgiveness with others. It empowers us to love as Jesus loved on the cross. The grace of forgiveness is a grace to be shared. Paul said as much to the Corinthians:

"All this is from God, who through Christ reconciled us to himself and gave us the ministry of reconciliation; that is, God was in Christ reconciling the world to himself, not counting their trespasses against them, and entrusting to us the message of reconciliation" (2 Corinthians 18–19).

This is the virtue of *forgiveness*, which we are to show in our dealings with others.

Jim Keenan speaks of this as the virtue of a reconciling spirit. He describes how this virtue pervades the Sermon on the Mount. We are called to be peacemakers, to seek reconciliation on the way to court and before we approach the Eucharist. We are exhorted to turn the other cheek and love our enemies. In the Our Father, we rashly ask God to forgive us as we forgive others. A spirit of reconciliation and the commitment to forgive others is at the heart of the Christian message. It is a virtue that is central to living the Christian life.

It is also one of the most challenging demands of the Gospel. It is hard to tell someone you are sorry. This means admitting that we have failed. But it is even more difficult to say "I forgive you."

These words demand that we let go of any sense of superiority and accept the radical equality and dignity of the other person. Saying "I forgive you" forces us to surrender our claim to harsh feelings. Peter asked Jesus how often he needed to forgive those who offend him. "As many as seven times?" (Matthew 18:21). Peter was looking for a limit on forgiveness. Jesus answers by saying that forgiveness is limitless: "Not seven times, but, I tell you, seventy-seven times" (Matthew 18:21–22). Forgiveness is a virtue, not a duty with certain boundaries. It is a disposition of heart that opens us to forgive others without limits.

Jesus continues his response to Peter by telling the parable of the ungrateful servant. The servant is forgiven a huge debt by his master, but he refuses to forgive a much smaller debt owed to him by a fellow servant. The master is amazed that the servant can see no connection between his forgiveness and the need to forgive another. "You wicked slave! I forgave you all that debt because you pleaded with me. Should not you have had mercy on your fellow slave, as I had mercy on you?" (Matthew 18:32–33). We should forgive others as God has forgiven us. Forgiveness is a grace to be shared. Our readiness to forgive others is a sign that God's forgiveness has truly transformed our hearts.

The story of the Prodigal Son illustrates the point that God's forgiveness has truly transformed our hearts. The prodigal's older brother cannot forgive him and join in the party to celebrate his return. The older brother feels taken for granted and unappreciated and perhaps a little envious of his brother's wild times. The older brother sees no need to be forgiven himself.

Throughout the Gospel, religious leaders convinced of their own righteousness hardened their hearts against sinners. The self-righteous are not disposed to forgive. It is difficult to forgive another when we focus on our own faithfulness. One wonders if those gathered around the woman accused of adultery had ever claimed their own need for forgiveness. In fact, they may well have walked away for fear that Jesus would forgive her and challenge their own unforgiving hearts.

Louis Evely highlights this connection between forgiveness and our own salvation by recalling a scene from a play:

> In one of his plays, Jean Anouilh describes the last judgment as he sees it. The good are densely clustered at the gate of heaven, eager to march in, sure of their reserved seats, keyed up and bursting with impatience. All at once, a rumor starts spreading: "It seems God is going to forgive those others, too!" For a minute, everyone's dumbfounded. They look at one another in disbelief, gasping and sputtering, "After all the trouble we went through!" "If only I'd known this...." "I just can't get over it!" Exasperated, they work themselves into a fury and start cursing God; and at that very instant they're damned. That was the final judgment, you see. They judged themselves, excommunicated themselves.[4]

The damned cannot enter heaven because of their unforgiving hearts. They cannot see that eternal life is a gift given, not a reward earned.

The opposite of the unforgiving older brother is Joseph in the book of Genesis. Joseph was grievously wronged by his brothers, who sold him into slavery because they were envious of him. Later, the tables are turned. Joseph has power over his brothers. They are afraid that he will punish them. But Joseph lets go of his anger and restores the relationship: "But Joseph said to them, "Do not be afraid! Am I in the place of God? Even though you intended to do harm to me, God intended it for good, in order to preserve a numerous people as he is doing today. So have no fear; I myself will provide for you and your little ones." In this way he reassured them, speaking kindly to them" (Genesis 50:19–21).

The virtue of forgiveness proclaims forcefully that there is no place for vengeance in the heart of a disciple. Disciples are to absorb the violence of the world rather than escalate it through retaliation. As Gula puts it, "Revenge believes that the only way to address evil is to imitate it."[5] Revenge does not bring justice, but only more evil and hatred. Revenge traps us in anger and resentment and enslaves us in our past. We are reminded of the old saying, "Resentment is like taking poison and waiting for the other guy to die."[6] If we are not forgiving, we become what we hate. Nothing darkens and constricts our hearts more than unforgiveness and vengeance. Unforgiveness is a way of controlling others and closing our hearts to them, though in the end, unforgiveness controls us and enslaves us. We know of people whose whole lives are defined by their resentments and grudges. They recount slights or unkind actions toward them that happened twenty-five years ago as if they happened yesterday. They view all of life through the lens of past hurts. Much of the energy in their lives is absorbed in replaying injustices they feel they have suffered. There is little room for joy or new experiences of love.

Growing in the Virtue of Forgiveness

By contrast, nothing expands our hearts more than forgiveness. Forgiveness unburdens our hearts and sets us free to live in the present and look to the future. Gula reminds us that "The Greek word we translate as 'forgive' (*aphiemi*) means 'to let go.'"[7] Forgiveness demands that we let go of our resentments and hostility.

Forgiveness is not an unhealthy repression of hurts received. It does not mean denial or forgetting injustices we have experienced. As Gula describes it, "We don't pretend that nothing happened or deny it was wrong; instead, through forgiveness we resolve not to let what happened in the past keep us frozen from moving into the future. . . . Forgiveness makes us free to move beyond hurt and anger and toward reconciliation."[8] We remember the past not to harbor and foster harsh feelings, but rather to learn from it and accept it in freedom.

Forgiving often takes time and it is a goal we work toward. The healing of deep personal wounds takes patience and the grace of God. We cannot root out feelings with an act of the will. We need time to integrate the pain into the larger picture of our lives and situate it in the history of love that sustains us. We can only forgive if we know we are loved and forgiven by God and others.

People close to us—parents, friends, teachers, spouses, colleagues—may have hurt us, either intentionally or unintentionally, in ways that have caused us great pain. Forgiveness is a challenge. We may be called to forgive strangers who have hurt us or those we love. A forgiving heart enables us to discern between justice and vengeance. A forgiving heart helps us know when to stand up for our rights and dignity and when to "turn the other cheek."

The hardest person to forgive is often oneself. Forgiving ourselves means acknowledging that we have not lived up to our own ideals and expectations. We have to take responsibility for our actions. We cannot blame others for our failures nor for the pain these failures have caused us and others. The challenging command of Jesus to "love one another as I have loved you" becomes even more daunting when we rephrase it as "love *yourself* as I have loved you." Genuine self-love includes the ability to forgive ourselves and move on with our lives. The alternative is to live mired in regrets and self-incriminations.

Forgiving others seems an inevitable fruit of a deep experience of being forgiven. The transforming forgiveness of God opens our hearts to be forgiving ourselves. We offended God. In return God sent God's Son to die for us. God returned love for hatred. If we are to love as God loves, we too must return love for hatred. We must offer forgiveness rather than vengeance.

These are the graces of the First Week. The virtue of compunction leads us to the virtue of forgiveness. An experience of God's mercy fosters and leads to a forgiving heart. Once we know we are loved sinners, we can be forgiving sinners. We can forgive both ourselves and others. As the Principle and Foundation led us to *thanks-giving*, the First Week leads us to *for-giving*. These virtues are essential aspects of a heart conformed to the heart of Christ.

Reflecting on Forgiveness

- Recall moments when you have experienced forgiveness from God and others in your life.
- Who are the people I need to forgive?
- Are there resentments or grudges I need to let go of in my life?
- Am I open to receive forgiveness?
- What does it mean for me to love as Jesus loved?

Scripture Passages about Forgiveness

Luke 5:1–11 Jesus Calls the First Disciples

Luke 15 The Parable of the Lost Sheep, the Parable of the Lost Coin, and the Parable of the Prodigal and His Brother

John 8:1–11 The Woman Caught in Adultery

2 Corinthians 5:16–21 Living by Faith

7 Generosity: The Call of the King

*Whoever wishes to come with me must labor
with me.*

Sp. Ex. 95

We experience a sense of being loved and forgiven in the Principle and Foundation and in the First Week of the Exercises. Gratitude for this love and forgiveness expands our hearts. It leads to a desire to share the good news that God loves us and forgives us. Gratitude opens us to service. At the same time, freedom enables us to hear the call to discipleship and to respond in openness. Gratitude empowers us to let go of whatever may hinder our response to God. Freedom from attachment becomes freedom for service.

In the Gospels, two stories of Peter highlight the dynamic connection between forgiveness and service. In the first story, Peter catches nothing after fishing all night. Jesus tells Peter to cast the net on the other side. The skeptical Peter complies and

suddenly catches a boatload of fish. Peter is overwhelmed with a
a deep sense of unworthiness. He says, "Go away from me, Lord,
for I am a sinful man" (Luke 5:8). But Jesus says, "Do not be
afraid; from now on you will be catching people" (Luke 5:10). At
the moment of Peter's profound sense of his unworthiness, Jesus
commissions him to go forth and share the good news.

The second story unfolds on the shore in Galilee after the
Resurrection. Peter expresses his sorrow three times for denial of
Jesus by professing his love for Jesus. Each time Jesus responds by
sending Peter forth to feed the sheep. In both stories, the experience of forgiveness and reconciliation empowers Peter to carry
on the ministry of Jesus.

Like Peter, the same can be said about us. The experience of
being loved and forgiven expands our hearts so that we want to
share God's love with other people. This is the spiritual dynamic
that moves us into the Second Week of the Exercises. The
Second, Third, and Fourth Weeks of the Exercises are part of
a process leading us to a decision about what it means to follow
Jesus. Ignatius invites us to hear the call of Christ and to discern
how to respond to that call.

The Transforming Vision of Ignatius

Ignatius offers a "consideration" as a transition between sin and
forgiveness in the First Week and discipleship in the Second
Week. To understand this consideration, we have to understand
a pivotal event in the life of Ignatius. Some fifteen years after his
conversion, he stopped at a little wayside chapel outside Rome
called La Storta. There he had a vision. He saw Jesus carrying
his cross. Ignatius heard the Father say to Jesus, "Take this man

(Ignatius) to labor with you." And Jesus turned to Ignatius and said, "Come labor with us."

This profound experience confirmed for Ignatius what God was calling him to do. He was placed at the side of the Son under the standard of Christ, which was a standard of poverty and humility and self-abdication. He was to serve Jesus carrying the cross. This experience confirmed a dream that had been planted in the heart of Ignatius at Loyola and then purified at Manresa.

The vision at La Storta shaped Ignatius's call to discipleship in service and fostered a very deep and personal relationship with Jesus. This vision is the background for Ignatius's "consideration" between the First and Second weeks of the Spiritual Exercises. Ignatius calls this consideration the *Call of the King*. It is not quite a meditation, not quite a contemplation. It is just something to think about, something to consider. It invites us to experience our own La Storta experience wherever we are.

The Call of the King

The Call of the King portrays Jesus as a leader who invites us to labor alongside him in suffering and glory, and to share in the work of redemption. Ignatius tells a parable about an earthly king. The earthly king comes before the people and says, "I want to go out and create a better world and bring about peace and justice. I want you all to follow me. It is going to be hard, but in the end we will triumph." Ignatius has us think about the generosity of the temporal king: "I will consider what good subjects ought to respond to a king so generous and kind (Sp. Ex. 94). He asks us to reflect on our response to a leader who says "I can assure you, if you work with me, we can eradicate hunger in the world."

If we believe this, our response is likely to be, "Yes, yes I'll do it. I know it's going to be hard, but I'm willing."

Ignatius tells us this person actually exists. His name is Jesus, and he is inviting us to bring about the reign of God. Ignatius wants us to get in touch with spontaneous generosity and readiness to serve. He wants to capture in this consideration the passion within all of us. As Michael Ivens puts it, the parable of the king is intended to make the person aware "of the resources of energy, love, ambition, and idealism which Christ wishes to enlist in the service of the Kingdom."[1]

The remaining Exercises make sense in this context of openness, generosity, and the desire to serve.

This also answers the question, "What ought I do for Christ?" You'll recall this was asked at the foot of the cross in the First Week of the Exercises. It is the call of the rich young man in the Gospel: Sell everything and come follow me if you want to be perfect. Some people call this the second Principle and Foundation, but now the Principle and Foundation is much more clearly focused on Jesus and on following Jesus.

In the Call of the King, the grace we pray for is not to be deaf to the Lord's call. We should be ready to accomplish the Lord's most holy will. We pray to be open, to be ready, and to be generous. We ask God to give us a generous heart so that we may follow him and be part of the plan. We should all want to be part of this plan and bring about the great work God is involved in.

Moreover, the Call of the King mobilizes our energy. It invites us to get in touch with our dream of making a better world and to see how Jesus fulfills it. Jesus is a leader, a living king who is actively at work in the world around us. He is seeking to bring about the reign of God and is asking us to labor alongside him.

The Call of the King is one of commitment to the person of Jesus and to the mission of Jesus. William Barry says that retreatants making the Exercises at this point desire that "Jesus reveal himself, his values, his dreams, his loves, and his hates so that the retreatant will actually love him as a true friend and leader and become more like him. Retreatants, at this stage, are asking whether they can and may make Jesus and the mission of Jesus the center around which they will organize their lives."[2]

Ignatius envisioned his own relationship with Jesus in the context of the feudal world of earlier centuries. Ignatius thought of himself as a vassal and Jesus as the Lord. It was a personal relationship of love and friendship, of entering into and sharing the experience of the other person. It was mutual service and fidelity. It was that kind of personal bond that Ignatius had with Jesus and that he invites us to have as well. Jesus for him was his provider, his protector, his leader, and his friend; and he invites us to relate to Jesus as provider, protector, leader, and friend.[3]

Our God Is a Generous God

Generosity is a spontaneous movement of the heart to give of oneself and share one's resources. "What shall I give to the Lord for all the Lord has given to me?" (Psalm 116:2). Christian generosity is first a response to the generosity of God toward us.

The Principle and Foundation focuses on God's generosity in creating the world and everything in it. We have nothing that we have not received from God. All of this flows from God's boundless generosity. The very nature of God is to give in unmeasured love. The history of salvation is a history of God's generosity toward God's people. God protects and sustains people. God's offer is repeated covenants filled with promises of faithful love.

For Christians, God's generosity comes to fullness in the gift of his Son. "For God so loved the world that he gave his only Son, so that everyone who believes in him may not perish but may have eternal life" (John 3:16). Jesus is the incarnation of God's generosity, and a total outpouring of self in love. Jesus' own life embodies that divine generosity. The ministry of Jesus models a generous life of service to those in need. He teaches, heals, feeds, and forgives the people. In the end, he gives himself completely by embracing his passion and death. For example, we read in Paul's letter to the Philippians:

> Let the same mind be in you that was in Christ Jesus
> who, though he was in the form of God,
>   did not regard equality with God
>   as something to be exploited,
> but emptied himself,
>   taking the form of a slave,
>   being born in human likeness.
> And being found in human form,
>   he humbled himself
>   and became obedient to the
>   point of death—
> even death on a cross. (Philippians 2: 5–8)

Moreover, Paul emphasizes God's generosity again in his second letter to the Corinthians: "For you know the generous act of our Lord Jesus Christ, that though he was rich, yet for our sakes he became poor, so that by his poverty you might become rich" (2 Corinthians 8:9). God's generosity is revealed in Jesus coming among us and giving his life for us. Furthermore, Jesus also reveals the generosity of God by inviting us to friendship and a share in the very life of God. God's generosity pervades the Scripture and challenges us to be generous toward others. Our generosity flows out of and mirrors our experience of God's generosity toward us.

Magis: Ignatius's Call to Generosity

Ignatius believed that a spirit of generosity is necessary for anyone making the Spiritual Exercises.

> The persons who make the Exercises will benefit by entering upon them with great spirit and generosity toward their Creator and Lord, and by offering all their desires and freedom to him so that His Divine Majesty can make use of their persons and of all they possess in whatsoever way is in accord with his most holy will. (Sp. Ex. 5)

The Call of the King brings generosity to the forefront. To hear and respond to the invitation of Jesus, we need a generous heart and a desire to do more in the world. To go forward in the Exercises, we need a desire to serve without reservation. Generosity is especially urgent because those who follow Jesus face great challenges. In the Call of the King Jesus says, "Therefore whoever wishes to come with me must labor with me, so that following me in the pain he or she may follow me also in the glory." (Sp. Ex. 95)

The Call of the King is a diagnostic exercise that tests a person's degree of generosity. One cannot be a disciple unless one is willing to offer oneself freely for others. Only those with generous hearts can follow Jesus to the cross and suffer and die with Jesus for love of others. Only those with generous hearts can respond to the call of Jesus to "love one another as I have loved you."

Ignatius's word for this quality of generosity is *magis* (more). The driving force of his spirituality is a desire to always do more, to ask himself, "What more can I do?" With Ignatius, there is never a sense that we can be satisfied with what we have already done. We have never done enough. He searches for the way of greater service and love. How can we be *more* generous, *more* loving, *more* compassionate, *more* zealous, and *more* involved in the work of the Kingdom?

Ignatius's *magis* is not the drive of the perfectionist to do what is best or most demanding. It is the drive to reach higher and seek the greater good. As Michael Ivens points out, the *magis* is not the product of compulsive behavior that relies only on one's own efforts.

> This insistence on the 'more' must nevertheless be dissociated from a self-driven ethic ("must try harder") with which the Ignatian *magis* is sometimes associated. We are concerned with the 'more' of Christ's invitations and of the expanding possibilities of his grace, not the 'more' of compulsion.[4]

The Ignatian commitment to the "Greater Glory of God" captures this passion to respond ever more generously to the call of God to labor alongside Jesus in the work of the Kingdom.

Ignatius says as much as he concludes the Call of the King. He says:

> Those who desire to show *greater* devotion and to distinguish themselves in total service to their eternal King and universal Lord . . . will make offerings of *greater* worth and moment, and say: "Eternal Lord of all things, I make my offering, with your favor and help. I make it in the presence of your infinite Goodness, and of your glorious Mother, and of all the holy men and women in your heavenly court. I wish and desire, and it is my deliberate decision, providing only that it is for your *greater* service and praise, to imitate you in bearing all injuries and affronts, and any poverty, actual as well as spiritual, if your most Holy Majesty desires to choose and receive me into such a life and state." (Sp. Ex. 97–98) (Italics are added by the author)

Ignatius asks the retreatant to listen to this prayer and not to say it. In the words of David Fleming, "we listen to the prayer response of those who want to be more devoted and to signalize themselves in their service to their Lord."[5] We can say the prayer ourselves only when we receive the grace of generosity.

We pray for this grace in the Prayer for Generosity, a prayer attributed to Ignatius because it gives expression to the desire of his heart in response to the call of the King.

> Eternal Word, only begotten Son of God,
> Teach me true generosity.

Teach me to serve you as you deserve.
To give without counting the cost,
To fight heedless of wounds,
To labor without seeking rest,
To sacrifice myself without thought of any reward
Save the knowledge that I have done your will.
        Amen.

Growing in the Virtue of Generosity

The virtue of generosity is a disposition of the heart to give spontaneously of oneself, to reach out to others in love and concern, and to seek the good of others. A generous heart does not measure its response and goes beyond what is expected or required or owed. A generous heart asks for nothing in return.

Generosity prompts us to act selflessly and to share our resources of time, talent, and treasure. We call someone generous when we are surprised, humbled, and touched by their actions, and when there is no rational explanation for their gracious gestures of love and sharing. Generosity moves us to service of others. The heart of a disciple is shaped by generosity. It is not surprising that Paul lists generosity among the fruits of the Spirit. Paul writes, "By contrast, the fruit of the Spirit is love, joy, peace, patience, kindness, generosity, faithfulness, gentleness, and self-control" (Galatians 5:22–23). Generosity is a grace to be prayed for and desired by anyone who hears the call of the Lord.

Ignatius tries to elicit this generous attitude of heart because he believed that God had planted it in every heart. We are made in the image and likeness of God who is generous. Our spontaneous generosity may have been muted by our sin and selfishness, but it can be enlivened by an experience of the unconditional love of God that knows no bounds.

The call to generosity will be deepened as the retreatant contemplates the generosity of Jesus narrated in the Gospel stories of his life, death, and resurrection. The Call of the King is a first step in putting on the generous heart of Christ and forming us into a person who will carry on the selfless ministry of Jesus.

Reflecting on Generosity

- What are the ways I experience the generosity of God?
- What specific scenes in the Gospels speak to me about Jesus' generosity?
- What inhibits my generosity in reaching out to others and sharing my resources with them?
- How can I respond *more* generously to God's love and Jesus' call to discipleship?

Scripture Passages about Generosity

Psalm 116:2 Thanksgiving for the Recovery from Illness
Isaiah 1—13 "Here I am, Lord, send me."
Mark 10:17–31 The Rich Man
2 Corinthians 8:9 Encouragement to be Generous

8 Faith: The Incarnation

The three Divine Persons decide in their eternity that
the Second Person should become a human being.

Sp. Ex. 102

The Call of the King invites us to respond in generosity to follow the call of Jesus in love and service. But to follow Jesus we must know Jesus. Jesus is the focus of the Second Week of the Exercises. We follow Jesus from his birth and baptism to his public ministry. We encounter the risen Christ through the events of his life. We contemplate the Gospel scenes of Jesus' life and allow them to transform us and open our hearts to the person of Jesus. Throughout this Second Week, we pray to know Christ more intimately, so we will love him more deeply and follow him more closely.

Contemplating the Incarnation

Hugo Rahner describes Ignatian spirituality as "from above." Ignatius sees the world as coming down from God as a gift and then returning to God. Our purpose in life is to discover how we can help bring the world back to God. This "from above" quality of Ignatius's vision is captured in a contemplation on the Incarnation, the first contemplation of the Second Week. Ignatius asks us to envision three scenes: the Trinity looking down from heaven, the world in need of redemption, and the scene of the Annunciation.

> Here it is how the three Divine Persons gazed on the whole surface or circuit of the world, full of people; and how, seeing that they were all going down into hell, they decide in their eternity that the Second Person should become a human being, in order to save the human race. And thus, when the fullness of time had come, they sent the angel St. Gabriel to Our Lady. (Sp. Ex. 102)

We view the world through God's eyes and see the plan of salvation unfold. We recognize the world's need and our own need of redemption and reflect on God's compassionate response. As we search our hearts for a response to this wonderful outpouring of God, Ignatius takes us to the scene of the Annunciation. Mary's response of yes to God's invitation to become the mother of God models our response to Jesus' invitation to be part of God's plan. God calls each of us and, like Mary, we are called to answer yes.

While contemplating the Incarnation, Ignatius tells us to see what is happening, listen to what is being said, watch what people are doing, and then reflect on this and draw some profit from it. The contemplation on the Incarnation ends with a conversation with the Trinity, the incarnate Word, and Mary, begging "favors according to what I perceive in my heart, that I may better follow and imitate Our Lord, who in this way has recently become a human being." (Sp. Ex. 109)

This contemplation dramatizes Ignatius's vision of the divine plan of salvation. This is the horizon against which all the events of Jesus' life will be seen. The life, ministry, death, and Resurrection of Jesus are the unfolding of that plan. Michael Ivens comments, "The constant return to the Incarnation serves to keep the whole Second Week experience within the context of the vision proposed in the opening contemplation, the vision of a needy world in relation to the Trinity."[1]

Contemplating the Birth of Jesus

Ignatius now asks us to contemplate the Nativity of Jesus. We imagine ourselves on the journey to Bethlehem and at the birth of Jesus. We picture the scene, and then once again we are to see the persons involved. We listen to what they are saying, consider what they are doing, and reflect on all that is going on. We are to enter into the scene just as if we were there, contemplating the Holy Family and "serving them in their needs." As all of this happens, Ignatius says, "in order that the Lord may be born in greatest poverty; and that after so many hardships of hunger, thirst, heat, cold, injuries, and insults, he may die on the cross! And all this for me!" (Sp. Ex. 116) Ignatius wants us to appropriate the values of Jesus in contrast to the values of the world and to personalize the events in Jesus' life. We are being invited to put on the heart of Christ and to allow the events of his life to transform us.

In the child Jesus, God becomes suddenly approachable. God shares our human limitations, embraces our human condition, and becomes one of us. All of this is done for us. We recall the words of Ignatius earlier in the Exercises when he invites us to pray at the foot of the cross. Ignatius asks, "How is it that he, although he is the Creator, has come to make himself a human being? How is it that he has passed from eternal life to death in time, and to die in his way for my sins?" (Sp. Ex. 53).

The contemplation on the Nativity is not a reflection on a doctrine. It is a personal encounter with Jesus who has become human for us. It is a vivid dramatization of Jesus' humility and poverty. During the next two days of the Exercises, Ignatius directs us to pray on the hidden life of Jesus—his presentation in the Temple, the flight into Egypt, the obedience of Jesus to his parents, and the finding of Jesus in the temple. We grow in the knowledge and love of Jesus so we will be moved to follow him as his disciples.

Praying with the Imagination

The contemplations on the Incarnation and the Nativity are models for the way we are to pray with all the Gospel scenes throughout the rest of the Exercises. We are to use our imaginations. Ignatius thought that God speaks to us through our imaginations. This imaginative prayer engages us as a whole person and leads to a deep interior, affective knowledge of Jesus as teacher, healer, leader, and model. As we enter into Christ's experience, he enters into our own. We become the people in the Gospel as we imagine him healing the sick, casting out demons, and feeding and forgiving people. Jesus heals us, feeds us, forgives us, sets us free, and calls us to follow. George Aschenbrenner affirms that "the Holy Spirit effects an engagement of your whole person with the mystery in an encounter with the risen Jesus. . . . The mystery is happening right now, and you, as more than an objective spectator, are participating firsthand."[2] In other words, this contemplation is not simply a nostalgic recollection of past events. The events are present to the believer *here and now.*

Such imaginative involvement in the life events of Jesus does more than dramatize his actions so we can imitate them. As we enter into the Gospel scenes, we uncover the heart of Jesus, the motives and desires that shaped and inspired his actions. Ivens explains:

> In contemplating a Gospel narrative, a believer truly in search of God and his will encounters the living Christ, who through this narrative reaches out to such persons, drawing them into union with himself, and sharing with them his own vision and desires.[3]

Aschenbrenner speaks of contemplation as helping us "to learn Jesus, to enter the tabernacle of his heart, to encounter him in an intimate and zealous faith."[4] The method of imaginative prayer that characterizes the last three weeks of the Exercises is a creative way to put on the heart of Jesus. The fruit of this prayer is not only a graced discernment of what God is calling us to do. This prayer also shapes our hearts into the compassionate and loving heart of Christ.

Faith: An Attitude and an Act

Contemplating the mystery of the Incarnation and the historical scene of the Nativity touches the human heart in myriad ways. It calls forth a rich variety of responses. As we stand before the reality of God made flesh out of love for us, we are moved to wonder and reverence, to have gratitude and hope, humility and joy, and, above all, to have love. Almost every virtue is evoked by this foundational truth of our faith.

Here I will focus on the virtue of faith. Faith is both an attitude of heart and an act of surrender and assent. Mary is presented most clearly as the model of that faith response. She says yes in faith and trust to God's invitation to share in the plan of salvation. Ignatius wishes to elicit that same disposition of faith from us. The disciple relies on God and puts faith in the Lord Jesus.

Faith is our response to God's self-revelation. It is a response to God calling us and inviting us to new life and salvation. Faith is the response of our whole person. We believe *in* God before we believe *that* certain doctrines are true. As Avery Dulles explains, "In believing we assent primarily to God who reveals and only secondarily to this or that particular truth that we believe on the authority of God."[5] If we focus on revelation as only a set of propositions to be believed, then faith is primarily an assent of the mind to those truths. If we understand revelation in the broader sense of God's self-communication to us, our faith becomes a personal commitment, a giving of oneself to God. Furthermore, Dulles states, "Faith, without ceasing to be an assent of the mind, involves a trusting commitment of the whole person to God who reveals, together with fidelity and obedience to the saving message."[6] This description of faith certainly expresses more adequately the faith of Mary at the Annunciation and the faith that Ignatius invites us to in contemplating the events of Christ's life.

What the Scriptures Say about Faith

In the Hebrew Scriptures, faith is a personal relationship of trust in God. The trust is rooted in God's fidelity to God's promises, a fidelity that has been experienced in the personal and communal lives of the people. The God of the covenant, who led them out of slavery in Egypt, sustained them in the desert, and guided and protected the people is absolutely reliable. Faith is an act of confidence in God's steadfast love and kindness. John O'Donnell summarizes it in this way:

> When one looks at the Old Testament understanding of faith, one sees that faith has to do with that which is reliable, that which gives security, that which can be trusted. Faith presupposes a correspondence between that which is promised and that which is realized.[7]

The root words for faith in the Hebrew Scriptures are *aman* and *batah*. Mary Ann Fatula describes the meaning of these words:

> The Hebrew word *aman* ("to be firm, solid"—and thus "true") speaks a personal relationship with the God on whose strength and absolute sureness we

> can literally stake our lives. . . . To have faith is to
> abandon ourselves without reserve into the arms of
> this God whose faithfulness to us is more sure than
> our own existence.[8]

Fatula adds that *batah* conveys "the dynamic force of our actively trusting God, confidently expecting every good from the God who cannot fail us."[9]

To have faith in God means to trust and rely on God and to be obedient to God's word.

In the Old Testament Abraham and Sarah stand as the paradigms of faith in God. They believed in God even when it seemed that the promises of God could not be fulfilled. The Book of Genesis says Abraham ". . . believed the Lord; and the Lord reckoned it to him as righteousness" (Genesis 15:6). Abraham surrendered to God in obedience when asked to sacrifice his son. He trusted that God would be faithful to God's word.

In the New Testament, faith is described as belief in Jesus and in the preaching of the good news. Faith is accepting Christ and surrendering and committing oneself to him. Paul speaks of the "obedience of faith" (Romans 1:5), the commitment of our lives to Jesus. The letter to the Hebrews offers the often-quoted definition of faith: "Now faith is the assurance of things hoped for, the conviction of things not seen" (Hebrews 11:1). Faith is connected with trust and with knowledge. There is a clear emphasis on faith as trust in God and God's promises, but it also leads to knowledge of God and God's revelation. Faith invites us to affirm and profess basic truths about God and Jesus and salvation.

What Tradition Says About Faith

As the theological tradition developed, the understanding of faith focused more and more on the intellectual assent to certain truths of the faith. This later intellectual approach to the virtue of faith is articulated by Thomas Aquinas in the Middle Ages and by the Council of Trent in the sixteenth century. Aquinas states:

> To believe is an act of mind assenting to divine truth by virtue of the command of the will as this is moved by God through grace; in this way the act stands under the control of the free will and is directed toward God. (S. Th. I–II, q. 2, art. 9)

Vatican I speaks of faith as "a supernatural virtue whereby, inspired and assisted by the grace of God, we believe that what God has revealed is true . . ." DS 3008).[10] Both expressions focus on faith as an intellectual assent to the truths of the faith.

Vatican II offers a more nuanced view of faith in its document on revelation. It sees revelation as God's self-communication. Vatican II approaches faith in more existential and personalist categories that speak of a free human response and commitment:

> The "obedience of faith" (Rom. 16:26) must be given to God who reveals, an obedience by which one entrusts one's whole self freely to God, offering "the full submission of intellect and will to God who reveals (Vatican I DS 3008), and freely assenting to the revelation given by him. (DV 5)

Thus Vatican II sees faith as something that engages the whole person. It calls forth trust and commitment, as well as assent to revelation. Faith includes assent to doctrines and revealed truths. But more than that, faith is a bold act of trust and a graced surrender to God and a commitment to God's invitation to new life. It is our "yes" to God's self-revelation in Christ.

Faith, in the end, is grounded in an experience of God's love. We believe in God, we trust God, and we rely on God because we have a felt knowledge of God's faithful love for us. We trust God and God's promises because we have experienced God's unconditional love for us. The graces of the Principle and Foundation, as well as the graces of the Second Week of the Exercises, are the source of our faith in a God whose love for us is manifested in God's taking on human flesh in Jesus. The virtue of faith is fostered by the virtues of reverence, gratitude, freedom, compunction, and forgiveness.

Growing in the Virtue of Faith

Mary at her Annunciation models faith for us. She shows us that faith is more than assent, but is also trust, commitment, obedience, and submission. Mary trusted in God's promises, was obedient to God's word of invitation in her life, surrendered to the mystery before her, and committed herself to be part of God's plan of salvation in Jesus.

At the same time, we can easily romanticize the Gospel scene—Mary is at prayer, an angel appears, and she says a faith-filled yes. The Scripture also tells us that she was deeply troubled and wondered what the angel's greeting meant. Certainly the angel's explanation only left her with more questions and concerns. She did not say yes because she fully understood or had all her questions answered. She said yes in faith and trust. We do Mary a disservice to think she had some infused knowledge that dispelled all her doubts. She was a young woman of extraordinary faith. The "yes" at the Annunciation was not the first "yes" in her life nor would it be the last.

The really significant yeses in our lives also demand a great deal of trust and openness. We cannot know all the implications of them. We respond to the gift of God's call in our lives. We say yes in hope and trust. Like Mary, we say "yes" to something being born in us that must grow and mature and take a shape we cannot predict. We are called to that depth of faith as we contemplate the story of the Annunciation and all the stories of the life of Jesus in the rest of the Exercises. We are called to trust, obedience, surrender, and commitment in our own lives. We will hear an invitation to share in the work of Jesus and respond and live in faith.

Living in faith demands surrender to the stories of God and Jesus recorded in the Scriptures. Christian faith especially demands that we let the stories of Jesus shape our minds and hearts. Paul Wadell says that to live in faith means that we "appropriate these stories, striving to embody their viewpoints, values, and vision as our own. To assent to the truths of faith portrayed in the Scripture is to allow them to become the interpretative framework for our world."[11]

Wadell feels we need these narratives "to mold and shape us, especially in the attitudes and virtues of Jesus."[12] Ignatian imaginative prayer on the Gospel stories is a powerful way to grow in faith by putting on the heart of Christ. As Jesus trusted, obeyed, surrendered, and committed his life to the Father, we are to respond in the same way. All the contemplations on the Gospels throughout the Exercises foster growth in the virtue of faith that empowers us to trust God and commit ourselves to service.

Reflecting on Faith

- What are the moments in my life when I have been asked to surrender to God and the mystery of God's plan?
- Recall the significant yeses in my life when I responded to God's call to commitment?
- When have I been called upon to trust in God and God's faithfulness?
- What are the challenges to my faith, the sources of doubt and uncertainty?

Scripture Readings on Faith

Luke 1:26–38 Annunciation
Mark 5:24–34 "Your faith has made you well."
Mark 9:14–24 "I believe; help my unbelief."
John 11:17–27 Martha's act of faith

9 Prudence: Discernment/
The Two Standards/
Three Classes of Persons

Consider how Christ calls and desires all persons
to come under his standard.

Sp. Ex. 36

The Spiritual Exercises offer a means of discerning God's will and coming to a life decision. This life decision, what Ignatius calls the Election, is at the heart of the Exercises. On the fourth day of the Second Week of the Exercises, after the reflecting on the Call of the King and contemplating the events of Christ's birth and hidden life, Ignatius introduces the person to "the consideration of the states of life."

While continuing our contemplations of Christ's life, we begin simultaneously to explore and inquire:

> In what state or way of life does the Divine Majesty
> want us to serve him? (Sp. Ex. 135)

Ignatius invites us to make an Exercise that he calls the Two Standards. This is a foundation, background, and horizon against which the decision is to be made. These two standards dramatize the conflicting values and tactics of Christ and the forces of darkness. They bring to consciousness the struggle between good and evil in the world around us and in our own hearts, and between the forces that lead us toward God and the forces that lead us away from God.

The Two Standards: Where Is My Place in the Struggle?

Ignatius has us imagine two great armies: the army of Christ and the army of Satan. Satan is seated on a throne of fire and smoke, an image of the fear that takes away our freedom and enslaves us. Satan entices us to possessions, to great honor, and ultimately to pride. In striking contrast, Christ is sitting in a lowly place: humble, gentle, and attractive. Christ invites us to poverty, rejection, and humility, which lead to freedom.

We pray for the grace to understand these contrasting values and tactics so we can live out of freedom and not be seduced by the false values of the world around us. Our desire is to embrace the values of Christ and turn away from the values of Satan. If our heart is in harmony with the heart of Christ, we will be able to discover his call for us and respond in generosity.

For Ignatius, this cosmic struggle between good and evil is played out both in our hearts and in the larger world. The struggle is waged between light and darkness, between egoism and altruism, and between death and life. Ignatius contrasts riches, honor, and pride with poverty, rejection, and humility.

These simple descriptions point to two contrasting sets of values. Jesus stands for the values of the Gospel, the Beatitudes, the Sermon on the Mount. He calls us to simplicity, poverty of spirit, selflessness, sharing, compassion, cooperation, concern for others, community, inclusion, and solidarity with the poor. In contrast, Satan calls us to consumerism, competition, narcissism, individualism, exclusion, and suspicion of others. The self-centered values of Satan conflict with the Gospel values of Jesus. Jesus is the person for others, the person of compassion who went about helping the poor and the broken. Jesus' values are those of the Good Samaritan who stops on the road and reaches out in compassion to the person in the ditch. They are the values in the final judgment scene in Matthew when people are asked, "And when was it that we saw you a stranger and welcomed you, or naked and gave you clothing? And when was it that we saw you sick or in prison and visited you?" (Matthew 25:38–39). In following Jesus we are invited to live out of these values, to put on the mind and heart of Jesus and to make decisions rooted in those values. We respond generously in the Call of the King to follow Jesus and labor alongside him and carry on the mission of Jesus. Now we have to discover what it means to follow Jesus in our own life circumstances. This decision must flow from a heart in tune with the heart of Christ.

Dean Brackley calls the Two Standards the contrast between the Babylon Project and the Jerusalem Project—the upward mobility of the world and the downward mobility of Jesus. He moves the discussion out of a purely individual realm to the broader social context.[1] The Babylon Project of Satan includes covetousness, status symbols, the social ladder, arrogant pride, competition, domination, fear and mistrust, and, in the end, cover-up. The Jerusalem Project of Jesus includes faith, indifference to honors, sharing, humility as solidarity, communities of equals, and cooperation. The two projects are played out in societal structures of race, gender, and class. Upward mobility embodies a lack of respect for the dignity of others and disregard for the poor and outcasts. Downward mobility promotes equality, an option for the poor, and a profound sense of solidarity with all people—all essential components of a just society. This larger social context of today's struggle between good and evil is an indispensable horizon for any genuine apostolic discernment or life decision.[2] We live out our discipleship in both the personal and the social realm.

The Two Standards meditation also describes the tactics of the forces of good and evil. Satan instills in us a desire for possessions, an obsession with the things of the world, a concern for recognition and honor. He seeks a heart enslaved by pride and self-sufficiency. Christ leads us from a poverty of spirit. He fosters a disregard for human honor, a humble heart aware of God's gifts and free to let go of those gifts and to share them with others.

Three Classes of Persons: How Free Am I?

To make a good decision we need to be free. Ignatius now offers a reflection that explores our freedom to hear and respond to the call of God in our lives. He calls it the Three Classes of Persons.

Three persons each acquire a large sum of money. Each is attached to the sum. They recognize their attachment and desire to be rid of it so that they can serve God freely. Each of the three reacts differently to the situation.

The first person talks about getting rid of the attachment but does nothing about it. This person procrastinates until death.

The second person does everything but the one thing that needs to be done. This person negotiates with God, trying to entice God to come around to his or her way of thinking. The person "desires to get rid of the attachment, but in such a way that she or he will keep the acquired money; and that thus God will come to where this person desires." (Sp. Ex. 154) As Ivens puts it, "the second class effectively confines the will of God to the boundaries of their own unfreedom (as opposed to expanding the boundaries of freedom in order to discern the will of God)."[3]

The third person is free. This person "desires to get rid of the attachment, but in such a way that there remains no inclination either to keep the acquired money or to dispose of it. (Sp. Ex. 155) This person's only desire is to praise and serve God. This is the person who is willing to sell everything to buy the treasure in the field. This person is free to act out of his or her deepest desires.

This is the grace we are to pray for. The Three Classes meditation is not simply an interesting case study. It is a prayerful exercise that acknowledges that only God can empower our wills to act out of freedom. The grace prayed for is the grace of indifference or freedom to let go of any attachments that would hinder us from embracing God's will. Ignatius describes the purpose of the Exercises as "to overcome oneself and to order one's life without reaching a decision through some disordered affection." (Sp. Ex. 21) As a person moves into the time of election in the retreat, Ignatius returns to this fundamental grace of freedom that is an essential prerequisite for making a decision rooted in an attachment to God alone.

Discernment: What Is God's Will for Me?

Ignatius builds on the Two Standards meditation with his Rules for Discernment. These lay out in more detail the subtle movements of these good and evil spirits within us. "Discernment of spirits is the grace Ignatius has you pray for as you ponder these two conflicting mentalities."[4]

Discernment is the art and the gift of discovering God's will for us in the concrete circumstances of our lives. David Lonsdale describes discernment as:

> [T]he art of appreciating the gifts that God has given us and discovering how we might best respond to that love in our daily life. It is a process of finding one's own way of discipleship in a particular set of circumstances, a means of responding to the call of Christian love and truth in a situation where there are often conflicting interests and values and choices to be made.[5]

Discernment is always done in the context of Christian love and seeking truth. It helps us choose that course of action which most authentically answers the deepest desires and longings of our hearts and the movement of the Spirit of God within us.

Discernment presupposes that life is a mystery to be embraced and lived out, not a problem to be solved. It also presupposes that life is a process of growing in a relationship with God, with the world and the people around us, and ultimately with ourselves. The foundation of Ignatius's approach to discernment is the belief that God touches the individual soul, that God is at work in the heart of each individual person.

Some distinguish between discernment of spirits and the discernment of God's will. Discernment of spirits is a process of sifting through the movements of our hearts in order to determine which movements lead us toward God and which movements move us away from God. The discernment of God's will includes this discernment, but also involves considering the Word of God, the teaching of the Church, our gifts, and the responsibilities and commitments of our lives. We need to listen to the voice of the Spirit at work in our hearts, but we also need to be attentive to the Spirit speaking to us through the community and through the realities of our lives.

Ignatius's Rules for Discernment are guidelines to help us be aware of and understand the movements in our hearts so we can be led by the good movements and not be led astray by the evil movements. Ignatius describes them as:

> Rules to aid us toward perceiving and then understanding, at least to some extent, the various motions which are caused in the soul: the good motions that they may be received, and the bad that they may be rejected. (Sp. Ex. 313)

The first challenge is to notice, to be attentive. The problem is not that God is silent. The problem is our attentiveness. Usually we are not paying attention to the interior movements of our hearts. We do not notice the shifting moods of sadness and joy, of anxiety and peace. We do not recognize these affections as the work of the Spirit of God within us and as the voices of darkness that lead us away from the truth. Ignatius offers guidelines that make us more attentive to these movements.

Noticing is not enough. We also need to understand these interior movements. Ignatius calls them consolation and desolation. Consolation is the sense of peace and joy, the attraction to the things of God. It fills our hearts with an experience of God's love. We grow in faith and hope and love. Desolation is an experience of sadness and anxiety and separation from God. God seems absent and we feel a lack of faith and hope and love. Ignatius counsels us on what to do in times of desolation and consolation. He alerts us to the tactics of the evil spirit and to the deception of false consolation. Ignatius presumed that anyone who is seriously searching for God's plan will experience these movements of consolation and desolation. He also knew from his own experience that people need help in sifting through these movements. To discover and name these movements of God demands wisdom and sensitivity and openness to God and the direction of others.

How to Make a Decision

Ignatius suggests certain methods and procedures for making a significant life choice. First, all decisions must be made in the light of the end for which we were created. We first focus on the goal of our lives, which is to praise, reverence, and serve God, and only then decide on the means to the goal. We first decide to be disciples of Jesus and then choose how to live out that disciple-ship in our lives. (Sp. Ex. 169)

There are times when the direction God is calling us is abso-lutely clear. At other times, we are moved strongly by the spirits instilling feelings of consolation and desolation. At still other times, we are more tranquil and at peace. In these times of tran-quility Ignatius tells us to use our reason to weigh the advantages and disadvantages of the options before us. He also suggests that we use our imagination. We should ask the questions: What advice would we give others in the same situation? What would we think about this decision if we were looking back on it from the end of our lives? Ignatius thought that some process of dis-cernment would be at the heart of our significant life decisions. It would be unreflective at times, but at other times it would be conscious and measured. His guidelines for discernment enable us and our spiritual guides to be more reflective in following the movements that lead us to wise choices. We seek to act in love and avoid the deceptions that lead us to choices made out of fear and unfreedom. Ignatius challenged us to engage our whole person in making a decision—our intellect, our will, our imagination, as well as our feelings and affections.

The process of discernment and decision-making is not com-plete until we ask God for confirmation. We bring the decision to God and ask God to affirm it and strengthen us to live it out. We ask: Can I walk with the decision in faith and be at peace with it? The confirmation will come from the peace and harmony we feel with the decision before God. The confirmation will also come from the events and circumstances that support the deci-sion and make living it out possible.[6]

The Virtue of Prudence

We have been exploring how the Spiritual Exercises transform us into a certain kind of person. Here we can see that Ignatius's focus on discernment and faith-filled decision-making forms us in the virtue of prudence.

The virtue of prudence is often referred to as *practical wisdom*. Prudence is right judgment about what one should do. As George Evans puts it, "Prudence, the 'know how' virtue of the practical intellect, seeks the best way to do the right thing in specific circumstances."[7] It is the intellectual virtue that enables us to find the right means for a good end. Prudent people make wise choices to promote their personal good and the common good.

Prudence has taken on the connotations of caution and reluctance to act. In fact, prudence implies action that is thoughtful and effective in achieving a goal. Paul Philibert adds that "Prudence connects the everyday with the ultimate. . . . (It) knows how to make everything one does serve the overall purpose of life, namely, moving more deeply into God."[8] Jim Keenan, in his analysis of the virtue of prudence in Thomas Aquinas, emphasizes the role of this virtue in choosing the proper means:

> (Prudence) recognizes the ends to which a person is naturally inclined, it establishes the agenda by which one can pursue those ends, it directs the agent's own performance of the pursued activity, and finally, it measures the rightness of the actions taken. Prudence, in short, guides the agent to living a self-directed life that seeks integration.[9]

This connection to the ultimate end and purpose of life resonates with Ignatius's emphasis on choosing the best means to achieve our final end. Prudence presupposes the freedom fostered in the Exercises and gives priority to the end over the means. Prudence would also make decisions formed by the values of Christ presented in the meditation on the Two Standards. The prudent person will not be led astray by the deceits of the spirit of darkness.

The prudent person is also open to the gifts of the Holy Spirit. The traditional seven gifts of the Holy Spirit are wisdom, knowledge, understanding, counsel, fortitude, piety, and fear of the Lord. These gifts are supernatural dispositions of the soul that make the soul receptive and docile to the inspirations of the Holy Spirit. They facilitate the operation of the virtues by moving us beyond our rational faculties and opening us to the movement and inspiration of grace in our hearts.

Prudence, Wisdom, and the Art of Discernment

The gift of wisdom is closely related to the virtue of prudence and the art of discernment. Wisdom empowers us to taste and savor the things of God. It is a knowledge born of love that allows us to know what leads us toward God and what leads us away from God. It makes us sensitive to the movements of God in our hearts and in our world. It implies a familiarity with God and the ways of God that is the fruit of prayer. Wisdom is the gift of the Spirit that attunes our heart to the heart of God and puts us in harmony with God and God's desires. In this way, it brings to fullness the virtue of prudence.[10]

Prudence and discernment are closely related. A discerning person is a prudent person. The gift of wisdom takes the natural virtue of prudence to a level of faith where it becomes openness to the work of the Spirit. Discernment further places the search for right decision and action in the context of discovering God's will. The question moves beyond what is good and right to the hopes and desires of God for us in the particular circumstances of our lives. Discernment seeks for the good and right thing in the context of discipleship and our call to labor with Jesus. Richard Gula highlights this connection between prudence and discernment of spirits:

> Prudence, in the teaching of St. Thomas, is the virtue which enables a person to discover the best way to do the right action (ST II–II, q. 51). Prudence listens to experience, one's own and others, it seeks counsel, it looks into the future to anticipate difficulties and to size up consequences. It sifts through all these to come to a decision which fits the particular configuration of circumstances at hand. It chooses the best way to do the right thing for now. . . . (Thomas's) interpretation of prudence goes beyond the application of the objective criteria of moral norms and aligns the virtue of prudence more closely with discernment's attending to the internal stirrings of the heart.[11]

Prudence, then, listens to the movements of our hearts, seeks advice, foresees the consequences, and finally makes a practical choice. When infused with grace and perfected by the gift of wisdom, the virtue of prudence is at the heart of discernment.

As a person grows in the gift of wisdom and grows in the art of discernment, the person grows in prudence. All of this is the work of the Spirit that is fostered through meditation and contemplative prayer. One of the fruits of the Exercises is a growth in prudence, wisdom, and discernment. In the Exercises one prays for the gift of discernment. One might pray as well for wisdom and prudence. The Gospel parable of the wise and foolish virgins reminds us that following Jesus demands wisdom and prudence, as well as love and simplicity.

Reflecting on Prudence

- How can I be more attentive to the voice of God in my life?
- What are the values that shape my judgments and decisions?
- In my life, what are the obstacles to freedom that keep me from responding to God's call in love?
- How can I grow in wisdom and a discerning heart?

Scripture Readings on Prudence

Deuteronomy 4: 5–8 A wise and discerning people
Deuteronomy 30:11–20 The word is very near to me
Galatians 5:16–25 The fruits of the Spirit
Romans 11:33–36 The wisdom and knowledge of God

10 Hospitality: The Public Life of Jesus

Frequently to call to mind the life and mysteries of Christ our Lord.

Sp. Ex. 130

The Second Week of the Spiritual Exercises fosters a renewed desire to follow Jesus. We walk with Jesus to discern how we are to labor with him. We come to know and love Jesus as companion and friend. The imaginative form of prayer that Ignatius recommends in this Second Week invites us to enter into the events of Jesus' life and assimilate more deeply his qualities of the heart. Bill Spohn remarks that, "[t]he story that runs through the Old and New Testaments sets the pattern for Christian identity, for the 'sorts of persons' Christians are called to become."[1] Reliving and entering into the stories of Jesus' life changes our attitudes and dispositions of heart.

Ignatius proposes events from Christ's public life for contemplation during eight days of the Second Week of the Exercises:

Day Five: Christ's departure from Nazareth and
    his baptism by John
Day Six: Christ's temptations in the desert
Day Seven: How Andrew and others followed
    Christ
Day Eight: The Sermon on the Mount
Day Nine: Christ walks on the water
Day Ten: How Christ preached in the temple
Day Eleven: The raising of Lazarus
Day Twelve: Palm Sunday

These events seem to be appropriate background for one making a decision. They focus on Jesus' own vocation at his baptism, his temptations, the call of the disciples, the values of the kingdom, and ministry. In the supplementary material at the end of the Exercises, Ignatius adds eight more passages for contemplation: the miracle at Cana, Christ casting the sellers out of the temple, Christ calming the storm, the apostles sent to preach, the conversion of Mary Magdalene, the feeding of the five thousand, the transfiguration, and the supper at Bethany where Mary Magdalene anoints the head of Jesus.

During the retreat the director will choose texts for meditation that suit the particular needs of the retreatant and respond to the movement of God in the heart of the retreatant. At times, retreatants need to experience the healing touch of Jesus or be fed or consoled or challenged by Jesus. The director is not limited to the passages suggested by Ignatius.

Different passages reveal different qualities of Jesus' life and elicit different virtues in the one making the Exercises. Here I will focus on one event in Jesus' life, one suggested by Ignatius in his supplementary material. This is an example of how the Exercises can foster a particular virtue in someone contemplating the life of Christ and lead the person to a deeper knowledge and love of Jesus.

Feeding the Five Thousand

The most frequently told story in the New Testament is Jesus' feeding of the five thousand. It appears in all four Gospels and more than once in two of them. The story recalls God's gracious act of feeding the Israelites in the desert and points to Jesus' loving ongoing act of feeding us in the Eucharist. It reminds us of our deeper hunger for God. The story calls forth an image of a faithful and lavish God who cares for the people God has chosen.

The miracle of the loaves calls to mind many virtues. The story invites us to faith; it shows God's desire to give us all that we need. It invites us to trust that Jesus will feed us, just as the multitude trusted that Jesus would feed them in the desert. The story invites compassion; we are challenged to be people who reach out to those in need. I want to focus on the virtue of hospitality. This is a central virtue for a follower of Christ.

Meeting a God of Hospitality

God is the ultimate host. God created a world as a place to welcome all living creatures. In the Old Testament this act of hospitality is symbolized in the Garden of Eden. It was a place where Adam and Eve could be at home and free to grow into whom God called them to be. Later in the history of God's people, God called them out of slavery, fed them in the desert, and finally welcomed them into the Promised Land. The psalmist gives voice to the Israelites' experience of God's hospitality:

> The Lord is my shepherd, I shall
>   not want.
> He makes me lie down in
>   green pastures;
> he leads me beside still waters;
>   he restores my soul.
> He leads me on right paths
>   for his name's sake.
> Even though I walk through the darkest valley,
>   I fear no evil;
> for you are with me;
>   your rod and your staff—they comfort me.
> You prepare a table for me
>   in the presence of my enemies;
> You anoint my head with oil; my cup overflows.
> Surely goodness and mercy
>   shall follow me
> all the days of my life;
> And I shall dwell in the house
>   of the Lord
> my whole life long. (Psalm 23)

The psalm is an eloquent profession of faith in God's graciousness in making a place for people, especially in times of trouble.

Hospitality is praised in the stories of Abraham welcoming the three strangers and caring for their needs (Genesis 18:1–15) and of the widow of Zarephath who shared what little she had with the prophet Elijah (1 Kings 17:9–24). In both cases, the hospitality was rewarded. In the first story, the travelers announce that Abraham's wife Sarah will give birth to a son; in the second story, Elijah raises the widow's son from the dead and gives her a gift of oil and meal. As God was hospitable to the Israelites, so they were called to be hospitable and welcome the stranger. For us, hospitality means welcoming strangers into our homes and offering them protection and food.

Jesus witnessed to the hospitality of God. Jesus depended on the hospitality of others for he had "nowhere to lay his head" (Luke 9:58). Though he had no home, Jesus made a place for everyone. He accepted them and made a place for them at the table. Jesus welcomed the sinner and the unclean. He welcomed prostitutes, tax collectors, and all those whom society rejected. Jesus included the excluded.

Moreover, Jesus fed the people when the disciples wanted to send them away. He embraced the children whom the disciples tried to turn away.

To image God for us, Jesus told a story of a father welcoming home a prodigal son. At the Last Supper, Jesus was the model host who not only prepared the meal, but even washed the feet of the disciples as a gesture of acceptance and love. On the cross, he welcomed the good thief who asked to be remembered. "This day you will be with me in Paradise." On the lakeshore after the resurrection, Jesus again became the host as he cooked breakfast for the disciples and invited them to be at home. He rewarded the hospitality of the disciples on the road to Emmaus by revealing himself to them in the breaking of the bread. We continue to experience the hospitality of Jesus each time we gather for Eucharist and Jesus welcomes us to the meal of the Kingdom.

Lucien Richard says hospitality is a central part of Jesus' proclamation of the Kingdom. The Kingdom brings about social transformation that integrates the poor and the marginal into society.

> The Christian vision expressed in the Kingdom of God is one of hope founded in compassion for the whole of humanity, especially for those who are at the margins of society. Jesus' announcement of the Kingdom of God is expressed in terms of welcome and warning. All are welcome, but especially the poor, the stranger, the marginal. . . . The story of the Kingdom generates invitation, welcome, and challenge.[2]

The Kingdom of God is the place of hospitality for all, especially the stranger and the outcast. Paul proclaims that the Kingdom is where, "You are no longer strangers and aliens, but you are citizens with the saints and also members of the household of God (Ephesians 2:19).

The final act of Jesus' hospitality is powerfully portrayed in the judgment scene in Matthew's Gospel. Jesus is the ultimate host in making a place for us in the eternal kingdom: "Then the king will say to those at his right hand, 'Come, you that are blessed by my Father, inherit the kingdom prepared for you from the foundation of the world'" (Matthew 25:34). The criterion for entrance into the kingdom is our own hospitality toward others, especially those in need. Jesus said, "For I was hungry and you gave me food, I was thirsty and you gave me something to drink, I was a stranger and you welcomed me, I was naked and you gave me clothing, I was sick and you took care of me, I was in prison and you visited me" (Matthew 25:35–36). He makes clear that the hospitality that we show toward each other is hospitality shown toward Jesus himself. "Amen, I say to you, whatever you did for one of these least brothers of mine, you did for me" (v. 40).

Hospitality is at the heart of Christian ministry. It becomes our way of responding in love to God's hospitality toward us.

The Virtue of Hospitality: An Attitude of Heart

Hospitality is much more than a simple welcome or an offer of food or drink. Hospitality is an attitude of heart that opens us to others and receives them on their own terms. Henri Nouwen speaks of hospitality as a move from hostility to friendship:

> Hospitality, therefore, means primarily the creation of a free space where the stranger can enter and become a friend instead of an enemy. Hospitality is not to change people, but to offer them space where change can take place. . . Hospitality is not a subtle invitation to adopt the lifestyle of the host, but the gift of a chance for the guest to find his own.[3]

The challenge is to offer friendship without binding the guest and freedom without leaving them alone. "The real host is the one who offers that space where we do not have to be afraid and where we can listen to our own inner voices and find our own personal way of being human."[4] It means providing space where new life can be found and everyone's gifts can flourish. To do so, we have to be at home ourselves and be willing to lay down our fears of change. We have to be willing to be vulnerable and open to new ways of doing things. We have to let go of our narcissism and exaggerated individualism.

Hospitality means *openness* to what guests and strangers bring to us. We receive a revelation from the guest which can change us and enrich our lives and open us to new possibilities and ways of thinking and living.

Hospitality implies *attentiveness* to the other and to the needs of others, even anticipating their needs. As Gula explains, "The key to hospitality is 'paying attention.' . . . When we pay attention, we divest ourselves of self-preoccupation. To be hospitable we have to get out of ourselves and become interested in the other."[5]

Often our lack of hospitality is simply the failure to notice and acknowledge others and their needs—the needs of the larger world and the needs of those closest to us. Jesus models that attentiveness. He noticed the sick, the excluded, the hungry, those that others passed by. God continues to be attentive. As we contemplate the ministry of Jesus, we are called to heighten our awareness of others so that we can carry on the ministry of Jesus.

Hospitality demands *commitment* on both sides. It is not a superficial gesture. As Richard describes it:

> Hospitality has to do with the bringing about of a commitment between guests and hosts. The relations that sustain such a commitment are expressed in mutuality and welcoming. Hospitality involves an authentic partnership that resembles covenantal relationship.[6]

Jesus saw hospitality and inclusiveness as a constant disposition of heart toward those in need, an offering of self that engaged the whole person in relation to others.

Finally, genuine hospitality is not a duty but a *pleasure*. As Keenan points out, "Many of us can be dutiful hosts. But we know the difference between hosting as a duty and hosting as a pleasure. Only the latter benefits both host and guest."[7] God is the joyful host who takes pleasure in making a home for us. Hospitality should be a pleasure for us as well. We can be polite or courteous or civil without being hospitable. Hospitality implies enjoying and appreciating the guests and their gifts.

The joy of hospitality is highlighted in the story of Martha and Mary. Both women are hospitable toward Jesus by welcoming him into their home. Martha is hospitable in serving Jesus and preparing the meal. Mary is hospitable by listening to Jesus and spending time with him. The story reminds us that we are challenged to be hospitable in both ways: we listen to others and are present to them, but we also serve them in their needs. Jesus chides Martha not because she fails to be hospitable, but because her anxiety and fretting cause her to lose any joy and pleasure in her service. Hospitality of both word and service should expand our hearts and enrich our lives as well as the lives of others.

Living a Life of Hospitality

The hospitality of God manifested in Jesus encourages us to open our hearts in hospitality. We first think of hospitality with regard to others. The heart of Jesus included everyone. As we put on the heart of Jesus, we too are moved to create a space for everyone, to exclude no one from our circle of concern and love. Hospitality offers a home for all, regardless of race, religion, age, sexual orientation, political persuasion, or economic status. To do this, we must often die to self, to an exaggerated sense of privacy and to an unbending attachment to our plans and agendas. In particular, our hospitality must extend to the stranger in our midst, to those in need, and to those abandoned. Hospitality is a posture of openness and welcome that finds a place for all God's people.

We often identify hospitality with care for the stranger. We may neglect hospitality as a virtue to be practiced toward those closest to us—our family and friends and coworkers. Yet it is important to create a space where those dear to us can find a home. Henri Nouwen speaks of the need for hospitality between parents and children, teachers and students, healers and patients. Though we may not think of parents as offering hospitality toward their children, Nouwen observes that, "What parents can offer is a home, a place that is receptive but also has the safe boundaries within which their children can develop."[8] As good hosts, parents must be able both to receive their children as gifts and offer them care, but also be willing to let them go when it is time to leave.

The teacher-student relationship can also be seen as creating a space for growth:

> Teaching, therefore, asks first of all the creation
> of a space where students and teachers can enter
> into a fearless communication with each other and
> allow their respective life experiences to be their

primary and most valuable source of growth and maturation.[9]

Such a vision of teaching goes beyond the model of simple communication of information and opens new possibilities for both teachers and students.[10]

Finally, there is the relationship between the healer and patient. Nouwen sees all of us as potential healers who provide a place for one's story to be heard:

> Healing is the humble but also very demanding task of creating and offering a friendly empty space where strangers can reflect on their pain and suffering without fear, and find the confidence that makes them look for new ways right in the center of their confusion.[11]

Many everyday encounters can become moments of healing and reconciliation if we offer family and friends a place to be heard and accepted and loved without conditions. Hospitality is an attitude of heart that can frame our lives and move us to be attentive and present to all those we encounter.

We experience the hospitality of God each day of our lives. God makes a place for us in the Christian community, especially at the Eucharist. God's hospitality is offered through the hospitality of others and we become the hospitality of God for others.

Our first response to God's hospitality should be to extend hospitality to God. We want to create a space for God to be at home with us. We want to open our hearts to allow God to reveal Self to us, not on our terms, but on God's terms. This is the Advent grace we pray for—to wait, watch, and welcome God into our lives. At the Last Supper Jesus made it clear that God desires to make his home with us. He says, "Those who love me will keep my word, and my Father will love them, and we will come to them and make our home with them" (John 14:23).

Prayer is a stance or posture of hospitality toward God, a stance of faith, trust, and love that invites God into our hearts. Prayer is openness, availability, and presence. God has spoken first, so we come to pray as listeners to God's Word, not as initiators of the conversation. Prayer is that attentiveness to God that notices the abiding presence of God within us. We do not have to look for God. God has already found us. Prayer is a dialogue with God, initiated by God, where we enter into conversation with God. Prayer is the space where we welcome God

The Second Week of the Exercises leads us to an encounter with Jesus and a more intimate knowledge of his heart. We enter imaginatively into many stories of the public life of Jesus. In each story, Jesus, in distinctive ways, reveals the attitudes of heart that prompt his acts of love and service. These virtues of Jesus can be elicited and fostered in our hearts as we contemplate Jesus. The story of the feeding of the multitude reveals Jesus' heart as a welcoming heart that made space for all. As we pray through the public life of Jesus we are invited to put on that same welcoming heart and act out in our lives the hospitality of God.

Reflecting on Hospitality

- What are the ways I can expand the landscape of my heart?
- What are the ways I have experienced the hospitality and the fidelity of God in my life?
- What are the ways I am hospitable toward God? How am I hospitable toward those around me?
- Whom do I exclude from the circle of my concern?

Scripture Readings on Hospitality

John 6:1–15 Feeding the Five Thousand
Luke 10:38–42 Jesus Visits Martha and Mary
Luke 23:39–43 Jesus Welcomes the Good Thief
John 21:1–23 Jesus Appears to the Disciples

11 Humility: The Three
Ways of Being Humble

I desire and choose poverty with Christ poor.

Sp. Ex. 167

Ignatius engaged the whole person in making life choices. In the Call of the King consideration, Ignatius appealed to the *imagination* to elicit profound generosity for following Christ the leader. In the Two Standards, he encourages us to pray for an *understanding* of the tactics of the forces of good and evil. In the meditation on the Three Classes of Persons, he instructs us to ask for God's grace to strengthen our *wills* to choose out of our freedom so we can embrace God's particular call for us.

On the fifth day of the Second Week, Ignatius offers another exercise that touches our *hearts* and challenges us to reach beyond simple indifference to a personal love of identity with Christ in a special way. This is an exercise in humility. It challenges us to examine our disposition of heart as we approach a decision.

The Three Ways of Being Humble

The ways of humility are concerned with our relationship with Christ and with our attitude of love toward Christ. George Ganss clarifies that in the Three Ways of Being Humble, "Ignatius is dealing successively with *three ways or manners of being lovingly humble*."[1] Ganss further explains that loving humility emerges as the climax of the spiritual or mystical journey that Ignatius records in his *Spiritual Diary*. In the context of this consideration, Ivens comments that "Humility is in fact nothing other than the love of God, but to call this love 'humility' is to pinpoint especially the quality of other-directedness in love, love as handing oneself over in trust, letting God be Lord of one's being."[2] Ignatius, then, is describing three ways of loving from simple obedience to active indifference to the love of imitation and identification.

The first kind of love is expressed in an attitude of obedience to the law of God. Such obedience is necessary for salvation, but it is not adequate for making a free decision in love. It allows us to choose good over evil, but not to choose between goods. The second kind of love is an attitude of indifference or freedom that was described in the Principle and Foundation. This is the freedom to let go of everything that stands in the way of my love and service of God. Such indifference is necessary for genuine discernment and a free choice to follow God's call. It speaks of a heart ready to follow God's desires and hopes for us. Ignatius expects someone at this stage of the retreat to be at this level of love.

The third kind of love calls us to a higher love of imitation and service. It is the desire to be with Christ and to share in his suffering.

In order to imitate Christ our Lord better and to be more like him here and now, I desire and choose poverty with Christ poor rather than wealth; contempt with Christ laden with it rather than honors. Even further, I desire to be regarded as a useless fool for Christ, who before me was regarded as such, rather than as a wise or prudent person in the world. (Sp. Ex. 167)

This third degree of love is a grace to be prayed for. We should beg "to be chosen for this third, a greater and better way of being humble, if the service and praise of the Divine Majesty would be equal or greater." (Sp. Ex. 168) This third level of love and humility is not necessary for a good election. It is the attitude of heart of someone deeply in love with Christ and desirous of being identified with him. This is the love of solidarity with the beloved.

Michael Ivens sums up the three ways of loving: "The three kinds of humility can be characterized as 'love of the creature', 'love of the servant', 'love of the friend'." [3] This certainly resonates with the call of Christ to us as disciples to move from obedience to the law to the posture of a servant to the intimacy of friendship. Jesus says, "I do not call you servants any longer . . . but I have called you friends" (John 15:15). As disciples we are invited to the third way of love of identification with Christ as our leader and friend.

The Virtue of Humility

Humility is a virtue rooted in the truth of who we are and the giftedness of our lives. It recognizes that all is gift from the creative and salvific love of God. True humility does not deny or dismiss our gifts, but accepts them as given freely by a loving God. Humility acknowledges our dependence on God, but celebrates that God is lavish and generous and faithful to God's promises. At the same time, humility accepts our limitations and our sinfulness and our need for God's forgiving love. It is aware of the ways we claim God's gifts as our own and misuse and hoard them instead of sharing them with others.

Humility is a virtue fostered all throughout the Exercises from the Principle and Foundation to the final contemplation on the love of God. The Principle and Foundation reminds us that everything is a gift from the hands of a loving God, the God who created us out of love and preserves us in love. It reminds us of our total dependence on God for all we possess. The first week of the Exercises leads us to knowledge of our ingratitude and unfreedom. It humbles us in the sense of confronting us with our absolute need for God. It assures us that we are loved sinners, unworthy of the love shared with us through God's mercy. The Call of the King calls us to follow Jesus and share in the work of Jesus, but it deepens our awareness that God's call is unmerited and that in the end we are unworthy servants. The Standard of Christ leads us to humility that flows from a deep sense of poverty and the freedom to let go of everything in response to the call of Christ. As we have just seen, the Three Ways of Humility describe to us the levels of love that draw us finally to a love that desires humiliation and rejection with Christ. The Third and Fourth weeks of the Exercises dramatize the gift of salvation offered to us through the dying and rising of Jesus. Finally, as we will see in Chapter 16, the Contemplation on the Love of God reinforces the giftedness of everything in our lives and moves us to gratitude and the desire to love and serve God in all things. One who makes the Exercises is called throughout to put on the heart of Christ who humbled himself.

Humility in the Scripture

In the Hebrew Scriptures, the humility of the Israelite people is based on their sense of total dependence on God. They can claim nothing as their own and rely only on God. God created them and chose them and led them out of slavery. They stand before God who is all powerful and holy and in reverence and awe acknowledge their lowliness and total reliance on God. "Humility is the attitude of the *anawim*, the poor of Yahweh, who have no resources of their own but submit themselves wholly to the will of God, who always hears the cry of the poor."[4] They are chosen by God, but not for their own merits, but out of the gracious love of God. "It was not because you were more numerous than any other people that the Lord set his heart on you and chose you— for you were the fewest of all peoples. It was because the Lord loved you and kept the oath that he swore to your ancestors, that the Lord has brought you out with a mighty hand, and redeemed you from the house of slavery, from the hand of Pharoh king of Egypt" (Deuteronomy 7:7–8).

The Israelites trust in God and God's fidelity, not in their own accomplishments. The prophet Jeremiah exhorts the people to "Hear and give ear; do not be haughty . . ." (Jeremiah 13:15). The Psalmist assures the people that "[g]ood and upright is the Lord; therefore he instructs sinners in the way. He leads the humble in what is right, and teaches the humble his way (Psalm 25:8–9). Finally, the prophet Micah sums up what God asks of the Israelites, "He has told you, O mortal, what is good; and what does the Lord require of you but to do justice, and to love kindess, and to walk humbly with your God?" (Micah 6:8).

This same humility is manifested in the New Testament, first in the faith of Mary as she accepts the call of God to be the mother of God. At the Annunciation, she acknowledges her unworthiness before God while surrendering to God's will. Then in the stirring Canticle placed on her lips at the scene of the Visitation, she gives voice to the depth of humility before the greatness of God:

> My soul magnifies the Lord,
> > and my spirit rejoices in God
> > > my Savior,
> for he has looked with favor on
> > the lowliness of his
> > > servant.
> Surely, from now on all
> > generations will call me
> > > blessed;
> for the Mighty One has done
> > great things for me,
> and holy is his name.
> His mercy is for those who fear
> > him
> from generation to generation.
> He has shown great strength with his arm;
> > he has scattered the proud in
> > > the thoughts of their
> > > > hearts.

He has brought down the
>   powerful from their
>   thrones,
and lifted up the lowly;
he has filled the hungry with
>   good things,
and sent the rich away empty.
He has helped his servant Israel,
in remembrance of his mercy,
according to the promise he
>   made to our ancestors,
to Abraham and to his
decendents forever.
(Luke 1: 46–55)

Mary models the meaning of humility: the absolute dependence on God and God's fidelity. She proclaims how God reaches out to the humble, lifts them up, and continues to bless them. Her humility opened her heart to the fullness of God's grace in Jesus.

Jesus' own coming among us is portrayed as a profound act of humility and self-emptying love:

who, though he was in the form
of God,
did not regard equality with God
as something to be exploited.
but emptied himself,
taking the form of a slave,
being born in human likeness.
And being found in human form,

> he humbled himself
> and became obedient to the point of death—
> even death on a cross. (Philippians 2:6–8)

Jesus did not clutch at what was rightly his, but let go of his divine status of immortality and freedom from death to embrace the human condition and become one with us. He was even willing to accept the humiliation of the cross out of love for humankind.

Jesus lived in this humility throughout his life. His lived humility gave special meaning to his invitation to his disciples to "Take my yoke upon you, and learn from me; for I am gentle and humble of heart, and you will find rest for your souls" (Matthew 11:29). Jesus criticized the religious leaders for their desire for honors and titles and recognition. He told his disciples, "The greatest among you will be your servant. All who exalt themselves will be humbled, and all who humbles themselves will be exalted" (Matthew 23:11–12). He addressed the parable of the Pharisee and the tax collector to "some who trusted in themselves that they were righteous and regarded others with contempt" (Luke 18:9). He contrasted the proud Pharisee who thanked God for setting him above others with the tax collector who "standing far off, would not even look up to heaven, but was beating his breast and saying, 'God, be merciful to me, a sinner'" (Luke 18:13). Jesus says that the tax collector went home justified and says: "for all who exalt themselves will be humbled, but all who humble themselves will be exalted" (Luke 18:14).

Humility is at the heart of discipleship. Children in Jesus' society were lowly, without rights, yet he says, "Let the little children come to me; do not stop them, for it is to such as these that the kingdom of God belongs. Truly I tell you, whoever does not

receive the kingdom of God as a little child will never enter it"
(Mark 10:14–15). Humility is also dramatized in Luke's Gospel
in the story of the centurion who seeks the cure of his servant. The
soldier says to Jesus through his servants, "Lord, do not trouble
yourself, for I am not worthy to have you come under my roof;
therefore I did not presume to come to you. But only speak the
word and let my servant be healed" (Luke 7:6–7). Jesus' response
is simply, "I tell you, not even in Israel have I found such faith."

All throughout the Gospel, the message is clear: humility
is the basic attitude of heart necessary to be a disciple of Jesus.
Without humility, one is not open to God's invitation to the
kingdom and to discipleship.

Jesus Washes the Feet of the Disciples

The most powerful gesture of humility recorded in the Gospels
appears in John's Gospel at the Last Supper on the night before
Jesus died. Before giving the Eucharist to his disciples, he did
something that dramatized the nature of his relationship with
them. He washed their feet.

This moving gesture of Jesus is clearly an act of humility that
challenges the disciples to a humble stance of service to others.
But, as Sandra Schneiders points out, something much more profound is being acted out in Jesus' simple gesture.[5] Accepting Jesus'
offer of humble service means accepting a new view of human
relationships and ultimately of salvation. Jesus' action sets a new
standard for Christian service and Christian community, a new
standard of humility and love.[6]

Footwashing is an act of serving. In John's Gospel, Jesus
defines his salvific work by means of this gesture. Jesus' ultimate

act of service and love will be laying down his life for us. "No greater love than this has one than to lay down one's life for one's friends." Here the act of footwashing is a prophetic action that symbolizes the ultimate act of self-giving: his passion and death.

Schneiders highlights the deeper meaning of the footwashing by describing three different models of service. "In the first model service denotes what one person (the server) must do for another (the served) because of some right or power that the latter is understood to possess."[7] In this model, service is understood within the structures of domination and inequality. This is the service of a slave to a master.

In the second model of service, one person does something freely for another because of the other person's needs. Though at first glance this model seems loving and disinterested, it still implies an inequality and even dominance because one person is acting out of a certain superiority to the other. One person possesses something the other needs and cannot provide for themselves. For instance, a rich person may generously give resources to a poor person.

The third model of service is friendship, the only human relationship based on equality. "Service rendered between friends is never exacted and creates no debts, demands no return but evokes reciprocity."[8] Service between friends is pure self-gift. The third model of service clarifies Jesus' salvific work. Jesus' ultimate self-gift of offering his life for our salvation was not "the master's redemption of unworthy slaves but an act of friendship."[9] Jesus gave his life for his friends. True humility leads to the love of friendship.

Jesus' footwashing was more than an act of humility to be imitated by others. Jesus was acting out the Gospel call to abolish all inequality and domination and to establish a new social order rooted in friendship and love that expresses itself in mutual service.

> By washing his disciples' feet, Jesus overcame by love the inequality that existed by nature between himself and those whom he had chosen as friends. He established an intimacy with them that superseded his superiority and signaled their access to everything that he had received from his Father (see John 15:15), even to the glory that he had been given as Son (see 17:22).[10]

The community of disciples is characterized by the love of friendship that Jesus acts out in washing the disciples' feet. Service in this community will not be an expression of domination or superiority but rather an act of humility and an expression of mutual friendship among equals. This becomes clear when Jesus challenges the disciples to do for one another what he has done for them—wash one another's feet.

This interpretation of the footwashing gives content to Jesus' words in chapter 14 of John, "Love one another as I have loved you." If Jesus loves us as friends, as equals without any claimed superiority or posture of domination, we are to love one another in the same way. We are to be friends of one another and express that friendship in mutual loving service. In fact, we are to lay down our lives for our friends. True friendship always leads to service because the friend is always interested in the good of the other. Jesus modeled that total self-gift in his death and resurrection and he invites us to love one another with the same total and selfless love.

Jesus' washing of the disciples' feet recalls Ivens' description of the three ways of humility as three ways of loving—the love of the creature, the love of the servant, and the love of the friend. Jesus' gesture of love and humility at the Last Supper clearly calls us as disciples beyond the love of the servant to the love of friendship. Jesus' gesture, in the context of his passion and death, images for us the third way of love that desires in friendship to share in the humiliations and rejection of the Beloved.

Living a Life of Humility

Putting on the heart of Christ means first and foremost putting on a humble heart. Humility disposes us to see life as a gift and to let go of any sense of self-sufficiency. As Jesus accepted the truth of who he was before Abba, we too celebrate that we are loved and gifted creatures called to friendship with God. Humility reminds us of our brokenness and need for forgiveness. It opens us to the faithful and forgiving love of God that frees our hearts to love and serve.

Humility makes love possible. It promotes genuine self-love and self-esteem that is the foundation of love of others. At the same time, humility enables us to let go of self-interest and reach out to others as Jesus did. The first letter of Peter exhorts us to humility and love of one another:

> Finally, all of you, have unity of spirit, sympathy,
> love for one another, a tender heart, and a humble
> mind Do not repay evil for evil or abuse for abuse;
> but, on the contrary, repay with a blessing. It is for

this that you were called—that you might inherit
a blessing. (1 Peter 3:8–9)

Paul's famous lyric description of love offers a rich vision of a
humble heart. He writes:

> Love is patient, love is kind; love is not envious or
> boastful or arrogant or rude. It does not insist on its
> own way; it is not irritable or resentful; it does not
> rejoice in wrongdoing, but rejoices in the truth. It
> bears all things, believes all things, hopes all things,
> endures all things. (1 Corinthians 13:4–7)

These passages connect humility to love; they remind us
that the two virtues support and enrich each other. Without
humility, we cannot live in love because we will always focus on
ourselves and our accomplishments and not on the good of the
other. Humility opens us to the mutuality and reciprocity of
friendship.

This brings us back to Ignatius's meditation on the Three
Ways of Humility. The three ways of humility are three ways
of loving. All throughout the Second Week, as we make a life
choice, Ignatius invites us to reflect on the kind of love that motivates us. We make good decisions when we act out of a sense of
our giftedness and the desire to share those gifts with others.
We make good decisions when we respond out of humility and
selflessness to the needs of others. We make good decisions when
we put on the humble heart of Jesus and love others as he has
loved us.

We grasp the full meaning of the third way of love when we enter into the Third Week of the Exercises, where we walk with Jesus in his passion and death and pray for the grace "to sorrow with Christ in sorrow." (Sp. Ex. 203) We embrace in a new way the desire to be with Christ in his suffering and we appreciate on a personal level the invitation to the third level or way of humility.

The first contemplation at the beginning of the Third Week is on the Last Supper. It serves as a transition into the passion story. In the second point for reflection in that contemplation, Ignatius asks us to consider the gesture we have reflected on in this chapter, Jesus washing the disciples' feet:

> He washed his disciples' feet, even those of Judas. He began with St. Peter; and Peter, thinking of the Lord's majesty and his own lowliness, was reluctant to consent. "Lord," he asked, "are you going to wash my feet?" But Peter failed to understand that the Lord was giving an example of humility, and therefore the Lord said: "I have given you an example, so that as I have done, so you also should do." (Sp. Ex. 289)

This gesture dramatizes Jesus' invitation to all of us as disciples to live in loving humility and friendship. As we move in the next two chapters into the events of Jesus' suffering and death, the grace of humility prayed for in the Three Ways of Humility will continue to challenge us to make the humble heart of Jesus our own.

Reflecting on Humility

- How can I better acknowledge my total dependence on God and my need for God's forgiving love?
- What are the ways I need to empty myself and let go of my own self-interest so I can be of greater service to others?
- How does Jesus' gesture of washing the disciples' feet dramatize his invitation to me to live in loving humility and humble service?
- What are the ways I am called to wash the feet of others as a humble friend?

Scripture Readings on Humility

Luke 7:1–10 Jesus Heals a Centurion's Servant
John 13:1–20 Jesus Washes the Disciples' Feet
Philippians 2:5–11 Imitating Christ's Humility
Luke 1:46–56 Mary's Song of Praise
1 Corinthians 13:4–7 The Gift of Love

12 Fidelity: The Agony in the Garden

He began to pray and his sweat became like drops of blood.

LUKE 22:44

The invitation to follow Jesus in discipleship is an invitation to share in his life and ministry and to carry on that ministry. But discipleship also implies entering into Jesus' experience of dying and rising. "If you wish to follow me, you must take up your cross and follow me" (Mark 8:34). Ignatius's confirming vision at La Storta was an experience of being invited by Jesus to labor with him carrying his cross. Ignatius knew that his call to service would entail suffering and rejection. He was fully aware that to journey with Jesus was to journey with him on the way of the cross.

The Third Week: Entering Christ's Passion

In the Third Week of the Exercises, Ignatius invites the one making the Exercises to be with Christ in his Passion. The focus of the Second Week was to know Jesus more intimately, to love him more fully, and to follow him more generously. Now in the Third Week, the grace prayed for is to move out of oneself, to be united with Christ, and to share in his suffering. Ivens speaks of a "shift from more *external* graces of knowledge, love and committed discipleship, to graces of a more immediately participatory sort—suffering *with* Christ. . . ."[1] It is a grace of union. It will lead to a deeper love of Jesus and a more faithful and realistic commitment to service.

Ignatius begins with a model contemplation for approaching the passion of Jesus. He entitles it, "How Christ our Lord went from Bethany to Jerusalem for the Last Supper." It includes three preludes, six points, and a colloquy. After introducing the scene and focusing our imaginations on the road from Bethany to Jerusalem, he asks us to pray for "sorrow, regret, and confusion, because the Lord is going to his Passion for my sins." (Sp. Ex. 193) In the second contemplation, Ignatius describes the grace more fully as "sorrow with Christ in sorrow; a broken spirit with Christ so broken; tears; and interior suffering because of the great suffering which Christ endured for me." (Sp. Ex. 203) We pray for the grace to enter into Jesus' sorrow and suffering in a personal and intimate way. Jesus' suffering is connected to our sins and to his personal love for us. He goes to his Passion "for my sins" and his suffering is suffering he "endured for me." We cannot be innocent spectators in the contemplations of Jesus' passion. We are saved by his suffering and death embraced in love for us.

The final three points of the contemplation relate directly to the passion.

The Fourth Point. Consider what Christ our Lord
suffers in his human nature, or desires to suffer,
according to the passage being contemplated.
Then one should begin here with much effort
to bring oneself to grief, sorrow, and tears, and
in this same manner to work through the points
which follow.

The Fifth Point. Consider how his divinity hides
itself; that is, how he could destroy his enemies
but does not, and how he allows his most holy
humanity to suffer so cruelly.

The Sixth Point. Consider how he suffers all this for
my sins, and so on; and also ask: What ought I
to do and suffer for him? (Sp. Ex. 195–197)

The fourth and sixth points reinforce the grace prayed for—sorrow and tears that are intensified by awareness that Jesus "suffers
all this for my sins." Our response is to echo the question asked
at the foot of the cross in the first meditation of the First Week:
"What ought I to do and suffer for him?" Sorrow and grief lead
to action, action that responds in love to the one who "loved us
and gave himself up for us" (Ephesians 5:2). In a note after the
second contemplation, Ignatius encourages the one making the
Exercises to reinforce throughout the day the grace prayed for
by fostering "an attitude of sorrow, suffering, and heartbreak, by
calling often to memory the labors, fatigue, and sufferings which
Christ our Lord suffered. . . . " (Sp. Ex. 206).

The fifth point highlights that Jesus truly enters into the suffering of his Passion as a human being. He does not hide behind
his divinity or deflect the pain. He becomes weak so that we may

be strong. Jesus surrenders to the human situation and embraces our human condition.

Ignatius offers no suggestions for what to speak about in the colloquy at the end of the contemplation, but elsewhere he says that in colloquies we "ought to converse and beg according to the subject matter" and that "I ought to ask for what I more earnestly desire in regard to some particular matters." (Sp. Ex. 199) Certainly in the context of the contemplations on the passion, each person is moved to speak to Jesus from their own deep sorrow and gratitude for all that Jesus has suffered for them. Perhaps the wordless prayer that best expresses what is in our hearts are the tears that Ignatius invites us to ask of God.

Confirming a Decision

For Ignatius, an absolutely essential element in discernment is the grace of confirmation. Any decision made in discernment must be brought to God for confirmation. Is this truly what God is calling me to do? Does this decision resonate with my deepest desires and embody God's hopes and dreams for me? The decision has been made in the Second Week. In the Third Week Ignatius invites the person to bring that decision to Jesus who is suffering and dying. Can I bring my decision to the cross of Christ and feel peace and a sense of integrity? Does the decision made manifest a willingness to suffer with Christ? To love without counting the cost? The cross of Christ can reveal our selfishness. As we stand before Christ's love poured out in his suffering and death, we are challenged to examine the depth of our own love and the generosity of our hearts. We ask the question posed in the sixth point: What ought I to do and suffer for him? We ask, What more can I do for Christ?

The Third Week also seeks confirmation in a second sense: the strength we need to carry out decisions. There is always the temptation to doubt our ability to carry out decisions. Have we made an unrealistic decision in the midst of the fervor of a retreat? Have we committed to something beyond our ability? Have we made a rash or imprudent decision? Have we set ourselves up for failure?

In the Third Week, we seek the grace to rely on God's strength and not our own. We ask for the grace to be faithful to the commitment we have made. This confirmation might even come in an experience of dryness and desolation in the Third Week that in the end strengthens the commitment and moves it beyond the level of feeling. Confirmation is the strength we need to remain faithful to the commitment we have made.

The Virtue of Fidelity

The second contemplation of the Third Week takes us from the Last Supper to the garden of Gethsemane. The agony in the garden dramatizes Jesus' own struggle to remain faithful to the Father's will. Jesus acknowledges his own reluctance to carry out God's plan of salvation, yet he trusts that God will sustain and strengthen him by love. "And going a little farther, he threw himself on the ground and prayed, 'My Father, if it is possible, let this cup pass from me, yet not what I want but what you want'" (Matthew 26:39). This scene mirrors the temptations of Jesus in the desert when he was tested by the evil spirit and encouraged to be another kind of Messiah than the one God called him to be.

Would he be a miracle worker who would captivate the people and build his own kingdom, or would he rely only on God's word and seek only God's kingdom? Jesus chose fidelity to God's call, even if it meant his own suffering and eventual death.

Jesus' struggle in the garden is a powerful contrast to the original garden of Eden, where Adam and Eve chose the lures of power and self-reliance. As Jesus surrendered to God's will in the desert and in the garden, he set the human race free from the pride and self-destruction of the original choice. It is fitting that Ignatius places us in the garden with Jesus after inviting us to contemplate the Last Supper. In the garden we will find the strength to remain faithful to the commitment we have made in the Second Week of the Exercises.

Contemplation on the Passion fosters many virtues, but I wish to focus on the virtue of fidelity. Fidelity is at the core of Jesus' heart. To put on the heart of Jesus is to put on a faithful heart.[2]

The root of our fidelity is God's own fidelity. The Hebrews experienced God as faithful to God's promises, even when they were not faithful. God was *hesed*, the one who kept promises, the God of faithful love.

> Praise the Lord, all you nations!
>   Extol him, all you peoples!
> For great is his steadfast love
>   toward us,
> and the faithfulness of the
>   Lord endures forever.
> Praise the Lord!
> (Psalm 117; see also Psalm 40:11; Psalm 89:8, 24;
>   Psalm 98:3)

God made covenants with the people. With the covenants came promises that God would be their God and that they would be God's people. Faithfulness was at the heart of the covenants and faithfulness is what God asked. "For I desire steadfast love and not sacrifice, the knowledge of God rather than burnt offerings" (Hosea 6:6). When the people were in slavery and later in exile, God promised to save them and lead them to a Promised Land, to lead them out of exile, to make of them a great nation. God kept the promises he made to Abraham and Moses and David and to all the generations after them. God asked the prophet Hosea to model God's faithfulness to the people by marrying an unfaithful woman and remaining faithful to her. The history of Israel is the history of God's fidelity to the people and God's constant care for them.

Jesus is the definitive revelation of God's fidelity. Jesus is God's "yes" that once and for all assures us that God is faithful. "For in him every one of God's promises is a 'Yes'" (2 Corinthians 1:20). Jesus fulfilled the prophecies that spoke of a Spirit-filled one who would come to save the people. Jesus himself remained faithful to who the Father called him to be. Jesus remained faithful to his mission from God. In the end, Jesus was faithful to the Kingdom of God that he came to proclaim and to make a reality. He would reach out to the poor and bring healing and reconciliation to all people. He announced a kingdom of justice and peace with a special commitment to those excluded and oppressed in society.

Jesus also made promises to send a Holy Spirit who would guide the disciples into truth and keep them faithful. He gave them the promised gift of the Holy Spirit on Easter night, when he appeared to the disciples in the upper room. The Holy Spirit is the ongoing manifestation of God's fidelity, an assurance that

God is with us and continues to gift us with love. The story of God's fidelity in sending the Spirit is narrated in the Pentecost event in the Acts of the Apostles. The Holy Spirit descends on the disciples and empowers them to preach the Gospel and to carry on the ministry of Jesus. God's fidelity continues to be revealed in the ongoing presence of the Spirit in the life of the Christian community.

Christians are called to be faithful as God is faithful. We are to be faithful to the promises of our baptism and faithful to the commitments we have made to others in our lives. Like Jesus' fidelity in the Garden, our fidelity is about the strength and courage to carry out commitments made in generosity. This is especially true in difficult times when we are tempted to retreat from our commitments. The virtue of fidelity empowers us to remain constant, even when we have to pay a great price to do so.

Fidelity and trust are interrelated virtues. We trust God because God is faithful. We are moved to be faithful because we trust God. Others trust us because we are faithful. To be faithful is to be trustworthy. The faithful person is the one who can be trusted. God has entrusted us with many gifts and we are challenged to be trustworthy with those gifts. Our fidelity is embodied in our wise and generous use of the gifts of God. We are faithful when we cherish what has been given to us. To squander our gifts is to be unfaithful to God and to ourselves.

Gula develops further the image of the two gardens as a lesson in fidelity and trust. "Both can be seen as stories of what we do with our freedom to live as trustworthy partners in covenant."[3] Adam and Eve distrusted God and eventually stopped trusting each other. They were unfaithful to who God invited them to be. By contrast, Jesus in the Garden trusts in God and remains faithful to his mission. Jesus believes that God's faithful love will be with him. Trustworthiness is at the core of fidelity.

Fidelity is not about rigidity and mindless conformity. Fidelity must always be creative and open to new invitations. It demands we be responsive to new circumstances and new situations. At times fidelity means letting go of a decision or way of doing things that no longer makes sense and embracing something new and never before imagined. The spirit of fidelity may well guide us into new and surprising ways of being faithful. God often calls us to change. To refuse to change or adapt may be the greatest infidelity. Fidelity always calls us to be responsive to new ways of finding God by living in love.

Fidelity in Relationships

We are faithful to people, not to things. We can speak of being faithful to a cause or a project, but the richest meaning of fidelity is fidelity to God or to those we love. As Keenan puts it, by fidelity "a person develops and nurtures the affective bonds of any relationship—whether with spouse, friend, family or community member, colleague, or fellow citizen."[4] Fidelity in this sense centers on those we we are committed to in our lives. Fidelity is the virtue that defines our primary responsibilities and demands our commitment to those to whom we owe special care.

We also grow in fidelity in our everyday lives as noted by the example below:

> Fidelity is practiced by the staff member who is always punctual, by the usher who reliably assumes his usual task, by the hospice worker who sits with

a dying person, by the parent who shows up for Little League, by the AA member who sets up for the meeting.[5]

As we practice simple acts of fidelity, we grow in the habit of faithfulness and draw closer to the heart of Christ. We are faithful to our relationship with God when we take time for prayer and try to be attentive to the movement of God in our hearts. We are faithful to others when we are attentive to their needs and reach out with care and compassion. Adult sons and daughters are called to be faithful to elderly parents in need of daily support and care. Parents are called to be faithful to a handicapped child with special needs. Fidelity is lived out in simple acts of kindness and generosity and in the ordinary obligations of the day.

Jesus and Friendship

The virtue of fidelity is fully manifested in friendship, the bond of love that unites people in shared openness and mutual care and concern for each other. Fidelity is manifested in especially difficult times of trial and suffering, but it is also embodied in the simple acts of taking the time to listen to the other, sharing joys and quiet moments, and celebrating successes and grieving losses. The virtue of fidelity moves our hearts out of ourselves and focuses them on those we love.

Jesus' fidelity was manifested in his relationships with the people he encountered in the Gospel stories. Jesus befriended people. He called them together, taught them, healed them, forgave them, and ate with them. We think of his wonderful friendships with the apostles, Martha and Mary, with Lazarus, and with so many others. The Gospel is filled with stories of Jesus reaching out to those in need and offering the hand of friendship. We think of Zaccheus whom Jesus invited to come down out of the tree so he could come to his home. Jesus befriended tax collectors and prostitutes and all those excluded as unclean by the religious establishment. He laid down his life for his friends, surrendering to the forces of evil, so he could set his friends free. Jesus was faithful to the end. His fidelity was rooted in the friendship he offered to all those he met.

Jesus experienced Abba's love as friendship. Jesus invites us to share that Abba experience by calling us to be friends. "As the Father has loved me, so I have loved you" (John 15:9). In a startling invitation on the night before he died, Jesus called us to be not servants, but his friends (John 15:15). As a true friend he revealed all that he knew of God and desired to make his home with us. Jesus wanted us to be where he was. Even when his disciples betrayed him, he remained faithful. Jesus loved us as friends and that is how he invited us to love one another. "Love one another as I have loved you." We are to love as Jesus loved, to be a friend as Jesus is a friend to us. Human friendship is the sacrament of God's faithful love for us. When we love one another in fidelity, we reveal God's love to one another.

Fidelity at the Center

Contemplation on the Passion of Christ calls to mind many virtues of Christ's heart and elicits those virtues in our hearts. We may think of courage and fortitude and patience, but certainly at the center of Christ's suffering and death is the virtue of fidelity. Jesus is the revelation of God's fidelity to God's promises.

Jesus' trust in God enabled him to be faithful even when faced with his own suffering and death. We find in Jesus' faithfulness to God the model and source of our own faithfulness. The fidelity revealed in Jesus strengthens us to remain faithful to the commitments of our lives, but we are also called to live out that fidelity each day in simple acts of love and concern. Our deepest fidelity is acted out in our faithfulness and trust in our relationships, especially in friendship. As friends of God, we are called to love one another in friendship. We are called to put on the faithful and loving heart of Jesus.

Reflecting on Fidelity

- Where am I called to fidelity in my life?
- Where are the places I have not been faithful?
- How have I experienced God's fidelity?
- Who are the people in my life who deserve my fidelity?
- Who are the people in my life who deserve my friendship?

Scripture Readings on Fidelity

Psalm 117 Universal Call to Worship
2 Corinthians 1:20 Jesus is the "yes" of God
Luke 22:39–46 Jesus Prays at the Mount of Olives
John 14:1–29 Promises of Jesus at the Last Supper

13 Compassion: The Passion and Death of Jesus

Ask for sorrow and confusion, because the Lord is going to his Passion for my sins.

SP. EX. 193

Ignatius wants the reality of Jesus' death to sink into the heart of the one making the Exercises. He invites us to accompany Jesus through the events of his Passion and death and to pray for the grace of sorrow, grief, and tears. At the end of the Third Week he asks us to spend the day contemplating the whole Passion of Christ. We're to reflect "throughout that whole day and as frequently as possible how the most holy body of Christ our Lord was separated from his soul and remained apart from it, and where and how it was buried. Consider, too, Our Lady's loneliness along with her deep grief and fatigue; then, on the other hand, the fatigue of the disciples." (Sp. Ex. 208) Finally, Ignatius adds that "when the whole Passion has been completed, he or she can take another day to review it as a whole. . . ." (Sp. Ex. 209) He encourages us to spend time at the tomb with Jesus dead and to identify with the sadness and desolation of Mary and the disciples. Christ has died for our sins, and Ignatius does not want us to escape the horror and the wonder of Jesus' death out of love for us.

The truth is that we cannot know Jesus until we stand at his cross and his tomb. Only there can we understand Jesus' mission and understand who we are called to be. Without the cross and tomb, we cannot confront the mystery of our lives and of suffering and death. Only at the foot of the cross can we truly know the depth of our sin and the depth of Jesus' love for us. The cross speaks of the depth and power of God's love. "For God so loved the world that he gave his only Son, so that everyone who believes in him may not perish but have eternal life" (John 3:16). As Paul says, "while we were still sinners, Christ died for us." (Romans 5:8) or even more poignantly, "He loved me and He gave himself for me" (Galatians 2:20).

Ignatius points out that the cross brings us face to face with the humanity of Jesus, with the realization that he entered fully into the human condition, including pain and suffering. Jesus made himself vulnerable and subject to suffering and death. We cannot avoid the stark reality that Jesus embraced our humanity with all its sorrows and pains and that he understands our human condition. That is why Ignatius challenges us to enter deeply into the experience of Jesus' death.

The Call of the Cross

The call to discipleship is a call to take up our cross and follow Jesus. But what does it mean to take up our cross? What does the cross call us to?

First, the cross calls us to enter into the death and Resurrection of Jesus—the Paschal Mystery of Christ's dying and rising. We first experience this in our baptism. As Paul says, "Do you not know that all of us who have been baptized into Christ Jesus were baptized into his death? Therefore we have been buried with him by baptism into death, so that, so that, just as Christ was raised from the dead by the glory of the Father, so too we might walk in the newness of life" (Romans 6:3–4). As Christians, we are called to die each day so that others may live. "So death is at work in us, but life in you" (2 Corinthians 4:12). In the words of Dietrich Bonhoeffer, "When Christ calls a person, he bids the person come and die."[1] Or as Bonhoeffer puts it more starkly in another place, "There are only two ways possible of encountering Jesus: we must die or we must put Jesus to death."[2]

Contemplation on the passion of Jesus challenges us to insert ourselves into the salvific plan of Jesus. We are called to be personally integrated into the Paschal Mystery and to accept a more conscious participation in the building up of God's Kingdom. To enter into the dying of Jesus, we must give up attachments that divide our hearts. We must let go of egoism and individualism, of prejudices and biases, and of insensitivity to the suffering of the world around us. We only begin to understand the cross of Christ when we participate in it in our everyday lives.

The cross also calls us to find the suffering Christ in our suffering sisters and brothers. Christ continues to suffer in his Body. We encounter Christ each day in the poor and exploited of the world. The final judgment scene in Matthew's Gospel dramatizes this powerful connection between Jesus and the needy of the world.

> Then the righteous will answer him, "Lord, when was it that we saw you hungry and gave you food, or thirsty and gave you something to drink? And when was it that we saw you a stranger and welcomed you, or naked and gave you clothing? And when was it that we saw you sick or in prison and visited you?" And the king will answer them, "Truly I tell you, just as you did it to one of the least of those who are members of my family, you did it to me." (Matthew 25:37–40)

The cross of Christ is a constant reminder of our call as disciples to be suffering servants through committed Christian service. As Jesus "came to serve and not be served" (Mark 10:45), so all Christians are challenged to live lives of service. This mandate to serve others is rooted in our Christian baptism, in our own share in the dying and rising of Jesus. To be faithful to our baptism demands that we reach out to those in need and work to shape a society of peace and justice.

In the end, we recognize that we were not saved simply by the suffering of Jesus, but by the love of Jesus that was willing to give his life to set us free. The cross calls us to live in love, a love that often leads to suffering and always expresses itself in loving action. The desire to be of service to others flows from a compassionate heart that notices and responds to those in need.

The Virtue of Compassion

The God of the Hebrew Scriptures was a compassionate God. In the words of the Psalmist:

The Lord is gracious and merciful,
slow to anger and abounding
in steadfast love.
The Lord is good to all,
and his compassion is over all
that he has made. (Psalm 145:8–9)

The words of the prophet Isaiah also give assurance of God's unending compassion:

For the mountains may depart
and the hills be removed,
But my steadfast love shall
not depart from you,
and my covenant of peace
shall not be removed,
says the Lord, who has
compassion on you. (Isaiah 54:10)

God's heart was moved by the suffering of the people. God reached out to the people enslaved in Egypt and in exile in Babylon. God was compassionate toward the people wandering in the desert. God was concerned for the poor and God inspired the prophets to challenge the people to care for the widows and the orphans.

Throughout his life Jesus embodied this compassion of God. He showed compassion for outcasts and sinners, for the marginalized, the hungry, the sick, and the grieving. Often we read in the Synoptic Gospels that Jesus was moved with compassion. Examples include:

"When he saw the crowds, he had compassion for them, because they were harassed and helpless, like sheep without a shepherd." (Matthew 9:36)

When he went ashore, he saw a great crowd; and he had compassion for them and cured their sick. (Matthew 14:14)

Then Jesus called his disciples to him and said, 'I have compassion for the crowd, because they have been with me now for three days and have nothing to eat; and I do not want to send them away hungry, for they might faint on the way. (Matthew 15:32)

Moved with compassion, Jesus touched their eyes. Immediately they regained their sight and followed him. (Matthew 20:34)

Jesus' compassion extended to the crowds without food in the desert, the lepers who were excluded from society, the blind and the deaf who felt isolated, and the possessed who experienced in a special way the power of darkness in their lives.

A moving example of Jesus' compassion is narrated in the story of the widow of Nain whose only son had died (Luke 7:11–17). Jesus comes upon the funeral procession. He is moved at the sight of the grieving mother. "When the Lord saw her, he had compassion for her and said to her, 'Do not weep'" (Luke 7:13). Jesus stops the procession and tells the young man to get up. When the man sat up and began to speak, Jesus gave him to his mother. He showed the same compassion at the tomb of Lazarus. His grief is joined with the grief of Martha and Mary as he weeps for his friend. Jesus calls Lazarus forth to life and tells the people to set him free.

The ministry of Jesus was a ministry of compassion. He acted out the compassion of God that he encouraged others to accept. The heart of Jesus was clearly a heart of compassion that reached out to all those in need.

Stories of compassion

Jesus also told stories of compassion to dramatize the compassion of God. He revealed the compassionate heart of God by comparing God to a shepherd in search of a lost sheep. In the same chapter of Luke's Gospel, Jesus tells the story of a lost son who returns to his father. We are told that "while he was still far off, his father saw him and was filled with compassion; he ran and put his arms around him and kissed him" (Luke 15:20).The compassionate father is a powerful image of the compassionate heart of God.

The story of the Good Samaritan is the story that best captures the compassion of God and our own call to compassion. Jesus tells the story in response to a lawyer who asks him, "Who is my neighbor?" Jesus does not respond directly to the question, but rather describes what it means to be a neighbor. The neighbor is the one who shows compassion. As James Keenan points out, preachers and theologians have long interpreted the story as the story of our redemption. The man in the ditch is Adam wounded by sin.

> The priest and the Levite, representing the tradition and the law, are unable to do anything for Adam. Along comes the Samaritan (Christ) who tends to Adam's wounds, takes him to the inn (the church), gives a down payment (his life) for Adam's healing (our salvation), and promises to return for him (to pay in full the cost of redemption) and take him to where he dwells (the Kingdom).[3]

The story speaks of the compassion of God for God's people, but it also challenges us as disciples to do as Jesus has done.

The story teaches us three elements about compassion. First, compassion demands that we first notice those in need. We can desensitize ourselves so that even the suffering right before our eyes does not make an impression on us. We can do this on a global scale when we cease to notice the suffering of the homeless, hungry, and exploited of the world. We can fail to notice those people we encounter each day—friends, coworkers, and loved ones who need our attention and care. The Good Samaritan noticed the man in the ditch. He included him in his circle of concern. Compassion means noticing the needs of others.

The second element of compassion is a feeling of care and concern for the person in need. The priest and the Levite saw the man in the ditch, but their hearts were not moved to pity or compassion because they feared becoming unclean. For them ritual purity was a greater value than compassion. Only the

Samaritan was moved with compassion. Michael Downey sees compassion as

> [The] capacity to be attracted and moved by the fragility, weakness, and suffering of another. It is the ability to be vulnerable enough to undergo risk and loss for the good of another. Compassion involves a movement to be of assistance to the other, but it ineluctably entails a movement of participation in the experience of the other in order to be present and available in solidarity and communion.[4]

Compassion is a movement of the heart toward the other who is in need. It enters into the suffering of the other and identifies at some level with their pain. The extent of our compassion depends on the extent of our circle of concern. Who do we care for? Are there certain people or groups of people that are excluded from our care? Are there certain people we consider unworthy of attention? The compassionate heart of Jesus knew no bounds. It stepped across social and religious boundaries to include everyone whether they be Jew or Gentile, slave or free, clean or unclean, sinner or righteous by the Law. As disciples of Jesus, our compassion must also be inclusive of all, with a special concern for the poor.

Compassion, however, cannot stop at the level of feeling. Genuine compassion moves us to appropriate action. It demands that we become involved in reaching out to the person in need. As Michael Ivens puts it, "Compassionate feelings, whatever their intensity, fall short of the true grace of compassion unless they contain the sense of involvement, of responsibility, on our side."[5] The Samaritan was not simply moved to compassion. He went to the man, bandaged his wounds, and took him to an inn and took care of him. He even arranged for the man's continued care by promising to return and pay for any future expenses. Compassion must include acts of mercy that effectively respond to the pain of the other.

The final judgment scene of Matthew's Gospel reminds us of the central role of compassion in the Kingdom of God. People are judged by their compassion, not by observance of the law or pious religious practices.

> Then the King will say to those at his right hand, "Come, you that are blessed by my Father, inherit the kingdom prepared for you from the foundation of the world; for I was hungry and you gave me food, I was thirsty and you gave me something to drink, I was a stranger and you welcomed me, I was naked and you gave me clothing, I was sick and you took care of me, I was in prison and you visited me." (Matthew 25:34–36).

The blessed are rewarded because they noticed people in need, were moved to compassion, and acted to relieve suffering. To care for those in need is to care for Jesus. To neglect those in need is to neglect Jesus. The blessed are rewarded for what they did. Those who are lost are condemned for what they failed to do. Our greatest sins are often sins of omission, including our failures to act out of compassion. In the end, we are judged by the depth of compassion in our hearts. Have we put on the compassionate heart of Jesus?

Works of Mercy

Another way to approach the virtue of compassion is to reflect on mercy as the way God deals with us and the way we are to deal with one another. James Keenan proposes that mercy is the distinctive element of Catholic morality. He sees it as the condition for salvation, the heart of the theological tradition, and Christianity's self-definition.[6] He defines mercy as "the willingness to enter the chaos of others to answer them in their need."[7] Keenan highlights the story of the Good Samaritan as the foundational story that defines love of neighbor as the practice of mercy. The primal act of mercy is God's act of creation that brought order out of chaos. The defining act of Christianity was God's entry into the chaos of human existence in the Incarnation. We may think of mercy in terms of forgiveness, but ultimately it is about caring for those in need.

Keenan explores the rich tradition of the corporal and spiritual works of mercy as practices that embody the practice of mercy. To feed the hungry, give drink to the thirsty, clothe the naked, shelter the homeless, care for the sick, visit the imprisoned, and bury the dead are actions that exemplify Christian service. Christian service is also exemplified through the spiritual works of mercy of admonishing sinners, instructing the ignorant, counseling the doubtful, comforting the sorrowful, bearing wrongs patiently, forgiving injuries, and praying for the living and the dead. When Jesus exhorts his followers to "[b]e merciful, just as your heavenly Father is merciful" (Luke 6:36), he is inviting us to reach out to those in need and care for them. To speak of mercy is to speak of compassion, the compassion of God lived out in the compassion of Jesus.

Compassion for Jesus

In the Third Week of the Exercises we are invited to suffer with Jesus in his Passion and death. This compassionate sharing in the suffering of Jesus is ultimately the source of our own compassionate ministry. We are not simply to imitate Jesus' compassion for others but to root our compassion in Jesus. We are moved to compassionate action for our suffering brothers and sisters because we see Jesus in them. "And the King will answer them, 'Truly I tell you, just as you did it to one of the least of these who are members of my family, you did it to me'" (Matthew 25:40). As David Fleming articulates it, "Compassion is first of all experienced when we stay with Jesus throughout the events of his passion."[8] He adds "Compassion in all our relationships with others and in all our ministries of whatever kind is grounded in our having experienced this intimacy with Jesus, especially in his passion and death."[9]

The Third Week calls us to a deep personal union with Jesus. It is only this personal union with Jesus that will sustain our ministry of compassion. Dean Brackley highlights this connection between our compassion for Jesus and our compassion for our suffering brothers and sisters. "Contemplating the suffering and death of Christ intensifies our union with him. It should also draw us to know and love the crucified people of today."[10] Our love for the suffering Jesus shapes our own hearts into the compassionate heart of Jesus. This confirms our commitment to live our lives in service to those in need. The root of our compassion is our compassion for Jesus and for our suffering brothers and sisters who are Christ's body today.

Reflecting on Compassion

- How do I experience the compassion and care of others toward me?
- Who is in most need around me?
- How do I reach out to those in my life and in the world in need?
- How am I called to act for justice in solidarity with others?

Scripture Readings about Compassion

Psalm 103 Thanksgiving for God's Goodness
Matthew 9:35–38 The Harvest is Great, the Laborers Few
Luke 10:25–37 The Parable of the Good Samaritan
Matthew 25: 31–46 The Judgement of the Nations

14 Joy: The Resurrection

The grace to be glad and to rejoice intensely because of the great glory and joy of Christ our Lord.

Sp. Ex. 221

Modern Scriptural scholarship and theological reflection have emphasized the unity of the whole Paschal Mystery. The dying and rising of Jesus are one continuous event that is the source of our salvation. We are baptized into the dying and rising of Jesus, not simply into the death of Jesus. For many centuries, Christian spirituality focused on the invitation to share in the suffering of Jesus. The Resurrection was divorced from the work of salvation and seen only as a proof of Christ's divinity and as a reward at the end of time for those who loved God and lived faithful lives. It reinforced a view of the world as a place of suffering and trial far removed from the joys of the next life. This approach was quite distinct from the lived experience and theology of St. Paul.

The Third and Fourth weeks of the Spiritual Exercises are an experience of the unity of the Paschal Mystery. The Third Week invites us into a personal encounter with Christ suffering and dying. The Fourth Week invites us to pray with the risen Christ. For both weeks the focus is being present with Christ and sharing in his experience. The unity of the two weeks is found in Christ's lived experience of dying and rising. The grace in both weeks is a union with Christ in both sorrow and joy. To know, love, and follow Christ, we must encounter not only the Christ of the Passion, but also the risen Christ. The risen Christ is the Christ we meet each day in prayer, worship, and community.

A Contemplation on the Resurrection

The first contemplation of the Fourth Week serves as a guide for all the Resurrection contemplations in the Exercises. After recalling Jesus' death, his descent into hell, and his appearance to his Blessed Mother, Ignatius calls on our imaginations to picture both the Holy Sepulcher and the room where Jesus appeared to Mary. It is here where we are to ask for the grace that defines the fourth week of the Exercises: "the grace to be glad and to rejoice intensely because of the great glory and joy of Christ our Lord." (Sp. Ex. 221)

Like the grace of the Third Week, this grace calls us out of ourselves to the other. As we joined in the sorrow of Jesus, now we ask to join in his joy. The focus is not on our joy at the thought of our salvation. We focus on the joy of Jesus, who has moved beyond suffering and death to his risen life of glory with the Father. We rejoice because Jesus rejoices, though as Ivens points out, "Christ's joy is not only for himself but for us."[1] As we know from our experience, it is not always easy to join in someone else's joy, especially if we are in pain. It is a challenge to put aside our heavy heart to rejoice with another person, even someone we love. To enter into the joy of Jesus and to be with him in his joy helps to keep the focus on Jesus and his experience. At the same time, we know that Jesus' Resurrection and joy are a pledge of our own resurrection and eternal glory. Knowing this, we have every reason to also rejoice.

Ignatius lays out five points and a colloquy for the model contemplation. The fourth and fifth points are especially important:

> The Fourth Point. Consider how the divinity, which seemed hidden during the Passion, now appears and manifests itself so miraculously in this holy Resurrection, through its true and most holy effects. (Sp. Ex. 223)
>
> The Fifth Point. Consider the office of consoler which Christ our Lord carries out, and compare it with the way friends console one another. (Sp. Ex. 224)

The Fourth Point contrasts the way Jesus revealed himself in the previous week and in this week. In the Third Week, Jesus' human weakness and vulnerability took center stage and his divine power and strength seemed overshadowed. Now, in the Resurrection, Jesus' divinity shines forth in his glory and loving presence with the disciples.

The Fifth Point highlights the heart of the ministry of the risen Jesus. The risen Jesus comes to console. Most of the Resurrection appearances have a pattern of movement from sadness and fear to joy and peace. From Mary Magdalene being present at the tomb of Jesus, to the disciples on the road to Emmaus, and the disciples huddled in the upper room—in each case people have lost heart and are unsure of their future. They are afraid and deeply saddened by what has happened and are unclear where to turn. Yet in each case, Jesus appears and dispels the sadness, filling them with hope and giving comfort. Jesus gives them the promised gift of the Holy Spirit. The gift of the Holy Spirit lifts their hearts and assures them of God's fidelity to God's promises. Ignatius invites us to notice Jesus doing this in all the Resurrection appearances that we will consider during the Fourth Week. This is how the risen Jesus relates to us as well. It opens our hearts to Jesus' consoling ministry toward us.

Finally, Ignatius asks us to compare Jesus' work of consolation "with the way friends console one another." Through the contemplations of the life, death, and Resurrection of Jesus, we enter more deeply into an intimate relationship of friendship with Jesus. "I no longer call you servants. I call you friends." The Resurrection appearances are deeply personal encounters with a friend.

The Resurrection Brings Joy

Three significant truths rooted in the Resurrection open a window to the grace and virtues of the Fourth Week. In particular, they highlight some of the reasons for our joy.

First, the Resurrection is a proclamation that Jesus is alive and present with us. In the Resurrection appearances, the disciples experienced Jesus in their midst. The same Jesus who had walked with them now again touched their lives, and spoke and ate with them. But Jesus was radically changed. Clearly, Jesus had not simply come back to life like Lazarus did. Jesus now lived the glorious life beyond death, but he was again with them. The Resurrection proclaims that Jesus is with us as well. Luke's story of the Ascension is not a declaration of Jesus' absence. Luke is announcing that Jesus is now present in every space and time. We encounter Jesus in the Scripture, in the sacraments, and in our brothers and sisters. As we recall the stories of the Resurrection appearances, Christ is once again with us, forgiving, feeding, and consoling.

Second, death has been conquered. Death opens the way to eternal life. Jesus gives witness to God's faithfulness even in death. We need not be afraid of death since it is not the end, but the beginning of eternal life. Jesus' Resurrection gives meaning to suffering and death as a way to salvation.

Third, Jesus' Resurrection affirms the value of the human person and the world in which we live. Jesus was raised as a whole person—body and soul. Jesus did not take on human flesh and then discard it. Jesus retained his whole humanity. Along with the doctrines of the Incarnation and the Eucharist, the Resurrection assures us that God has identified with matter. God has embraced the human condition. A profound unity forever exists between God and the world, between spirit and matter. As Christians, we do not believe simply in the immortality of the soul. We believe in the immortality of the human person. Jesus' Resurrection and ours speak of continuity between this life and the next. Jesus' Resurrection also acknowledges the value of creation.

> For the creation waits with eager longing for the
> revealing of the children of God; for the creation
> was subjected to futility, not of its own will but by

the will of the one who subjected it, in hope that
creation itself will be set free from its bondage to
decay and will obtain the freedom of the glory of the
children of God. We know that the whole creation
has been groaning in labor pains until now; and not
only the creation, but we ourselves, who have the
first fruits of the Spirit, groan inwardly while we
wait for adoption, the redemption of our bodies.
(Romans 8:19–23)

As the Principle and Foundation says, this world is a gift of an
all-loving God. Our faith in the Resurrection assures us that
everything of beauty and love and creativity lasts forever. The
Resurrection is the foundation of a holistic view of the human
person and an incarnational and sacramental view of life.

Jesus is with us, death has been destroyed, and human life
and activity have lasting value—these are all reasons to rejoice.

The Joy of God

How often do we think of God rejoicing? How often do we think
of God taking delight in God's creation and in the people God
has created? Yet the prophet Isaiah tells the people of Israel:

> For Zion's sake I will not keep silent,
>   and for Jerusalem's sake I will not rest,
> until her vindication shines out like the dawn,
>   and her salvation like a burning torch.
> The nations shall see your vindication,
>   and all the kings your glory;

and you shall be called by a new name
>   that the mouth of the LORD will give.
You shall be a crown of beauty in the hand of the
>   LORD,
>   and a royal diadem in the hand of your God.
You shall no more be termed Forsaken,
>   and your land shall no more be termed
>   Desolate;
but you shall be called My Delight Is in Her,
>   and your land Married;
for the LORD delights in you,
>   and your land shall be married.
For as a young man marries a young woman,
>   so shall your builder marry you,
and as the bridegroom rejoices over the bride,
>   so shall your God rejoice over you.

>>   (Isaiah 62:1–5)

God does not simply love the people. God delights in the people and rejoices over them.

Jesus tells stories of God rejoicing over the repentance of sinners. In the fifteenth chapter of the Gospel of Luke, Jesus recounts three parables, all ending in God's rejoicing. When the shepherd finds the lost sheep, he places the sheep on his shoulders, rejoicing. Then he calls all his friends together and says to them, "Rejoice with me, for I have found my sheep that was lost" (Luke 15:6). The story ends with Jesus announcing that "Just so, I tell you, there will be more joy in heaven over one sinner who repents than over ninety-nine righteous persons who need no repentance" (Luke 15:7). The second story is about a woman who finds her lost coin and again invites her friends to rejoice with her. "'Rejoice with me, for I have found the coin that I had lost.' Just so, I tell you, there is joy before the angels of God over one sinner who repents" (Luke 7:9–10). Finally, in the story of the Prodigal Son, the father rejoices at the son's return and throws a banquet to celebrate his homecoming. ". . . let us eat and celebrate; for this son of mine was dead and is alive again; he was lost, and is found! And they began to celebrate" (Luke 7:23–24). When the older brother objects to the celebration, the father's response is, "But we had to celebrate and rejoice, because this brother of yours was dead and has come to life; he was lost and has been found" (Luke 7:32). Jesus images God as a shepherd, a woman, and a father—all of whom rejoice over finding what was lost. Our God is a God of joy who takes delight in God's people.

Jesus rejoices. When the seventy sent out by Jesus returned, they "returned with joy, saying, 'Lord, in your name even the demons submit to us!'" (Luke 10:17). Jesus, however, exhorts them, "Nevertheless, do not rejoice at this, that the spirits submit to you; but rejoice that your names are written in heaven" (Luke 10:20). In Luke's gospel, it is at this moment that Jesus prays to his Father:

> At that same hour, Jesus rejoiced in the Holy Spirit and said, "I thank you, Father, Lord of heaven and earth, that you have hidden these things from the wise and intelligent and revealed them to infants; yes, Father, for such was your gracious will. All things have been handed over to me by my Father; and no one knows who the Son is except the Father, or who the Father is except the Son and any one to whom the Son chooses to reveal him. (Luke 10:21–22)

Jesus rejoices because God has revealed the mysteries of the Kingdom to the humble and simple of the world. Too often Jesus has been portrayed as overly serious and solemn. The suffering Christ has taken center stage and too little time is given to reflecting on Jesus' joy in life, in his disciples and friends, in the beauty of creation, and above all, in the love of his Father.

In the Fourth Week, Ignatius invites us to be with Jesus in his joy. We imagine the joy of Jesus at his Resurrection. His Father has raised him up. There will no more suffering or tears. His trust in the Father has been rewarded and Jesus can rejoice in the love of his Father. The words at his baptism, "This is my beloved Son in whom I am well pleased," have taken on a new meaning. The mission of his life is accomplished. He has proclaimed the Reign of God and now in his Resurrection that Reign has been established. Certainly he now rejoices in the Holy Spirit with a renewed sense of hope and peace. Jesus' heart is filled with joy.

The desire of Jesus is that we will share in his joy. At the Last Supper, Jesus uses the rich image of the vine and the branches to describe our intimate union with him. He invites us to abide in his love:

> As the Father has loved me, so have I loved you;
> abide in my love. If you keep my commandments,
> you will abide in my love, just as I have kept my
> Father's commandments and abide in his love. I
> have said these things to you so that my joy may
> be in you, and that your joy may be complete.
> (John 15:9–11)

Jesus returns to that theme of joy later in his discourse:

> So you have pain now; but I will see you again,
> and your hearts will rejoice, and no one will take
> your joy from you. On that day you will ask
> nothing of me. Very truly, I tell you, if you ask
> anything of the Father in my name, he will give it
> to you. Until now you have asked nothing in my
> name; ask, and you will receive, so that your joy
> may be complete. (John 16:22–24)

Finally, in his great priestly prayer for unity at the end of the discourse, Jesus says to his Father, "But now I am coming to you, and I speak these things in the world so that they may have my joy made complete in themselves" (John 17:13). Jesus prays that we may share in his joy, a joy rooted in God's love and the power of the Resurrection.

In the letter to the Colossians, the Pauline writer says, "I am now rejoicing in my sufferings for your sake, and in my flesh I am completing what is lacking in Christ's afflictions for the sake of his body, that is, the church . . ." (Colossians 1:24). It is a profound affirmation of our vocation to share in the redemptive work of Jesus. It gives meaning to our suffering and unites us in the Body of Christ by plunging us more deeply into the Passion of Jesus. But have we ever considered that perhaps we are also invited to fill up what is lacking in the joys of Christ? We share in the work of redemption by entering into the whole Paschal Mystery, not simply the dying of Jesus. There are many joys that Jesus never had the opportunity to experience because he lived in a particular time and in a particular place. Jesus continues to suffer in his Body, but does he also continue to rejoice in that same Body? When we marvel at a beautiful sunset, enjoy a meal with a friend, witness the birth of a child, fall in love, or are captivated by a Beethoven symphony, are we not filling up the joys of Jesus? Not only do our sufferings and afflictions unite us with the sufferings of Jesus and so lead us to salvation and expand the Reign of God, but also our joys and celebrations unite us with the joys of Jesus and so lead us to a fuller experience of eternal life and thus enrich the Kingdom.

Is it any wonder that the Psalmist exclaims: "This is the day that the Lord has made; let us rejoice and be glad in it" (Psalm 118:24). Should we be surprised that the Psalmist exhorts us to "Make a joyful noise to the Lord, all the earth; break forth into joyous song and sing praises" (Psalm 98:4)? The letter to the Philippians gives a similar injunction: "Rejoice in the Lord, always; again I will say, Rejoice" (Philippians 4:4). Mary gives voice to her own joy in her Magnificat when she prays: "My soul magnifies the Lord, and my spirit rejoices in God my Savior. . ." (Luke 1:46–47). We rejoice because we know in faith that we are loved and saved and cherished by God. Christian joy is rooted in God's love and fidelity toward us and the assurance that one day we will hear the words, "enter into the joy of your master" (Matthew 25:21, 23).

The Virtue of Joy

Joy is a gift of the Holy Spirit that expands our hearts and opens us to the presence of God in our lives. Joy is rooted in our faith in God and God's promises fulfilled in Jesus. We rejoice because we have encountered the risen Christ and because God has poured the Holy Spirit into our hearts. Joy is a virtue that disposes us to see reality with the eyes of faith and to trust that God can bring good out of evil, life out of death. Joy disposes us to see the goodness of the world and not be overwhelmed by the pain and suffering that so often seems to have the upper hand. Joy reveals the presence of God and assures us that God is with us. Joy is a fruit of the grateful heart, the reverent heart, the free heart. In fact, joy flows from all the other virtues and enhances them.

At the same time, genuine joy comes out of suffering. Christian joy does not detour around the challenges and struggles of life. It is a fruit of the Paschal Mystery of dying and rising. Joy emerges out of a dying to self and an embracing of suffering. It is tested in the fire of suffering and loss. It is life that has arisen out of dying. In fact, Christian joy often exists in the midst of suffering. It is the grace to believe and hope even when there seems little reason for faith and hope. The poor and others who seem to have little reason to rejoice are often joyful. They are sustained by a profound sense of God's love and care for them. They know that God is with them. Joy sees the face of God in the world.

Joy is expansive. Like the disciples who saw the risen Jesus, we find it hard to keep joy to ourselves. In his book *Enough Room for Joy*, William Clarke, SJ, tells a story about a trip to the beach with a group of mentally challenged adults living in one of the L'Arche communities founded by Jean Vanier. One mentally challenged adult was playing in the sand. A staff member asked him to draw a tree. He eagerly sketched the outline of a tree in the sand. The staff member asked him to draw a house. He sketched a house with a chimney with smoke. Then, the staff member playfully asked him to draw a picture of joy. With a somewhat puzzled look, the man looked far down the beach, first to the right and then to the left, and said "I cannot draw joy. There is not enough room." The joy of God is like that. It is limitless. The heart of Jesus sets no boundaries on love and life.

The Fourth Week of the Exercises elicits the grace and fosters the virtue of joy. This grace and virtue mirrors the joy of the heart of Christ and surrounds our hearts with the joy only God can give. To put on the heart of Christ is to put on a joyful heart that is filled with the infinite love of God that raised up Jesus and will raise us as well.

Reflecting on Joy

- What brings joy to my heart?
- What reasons do I have for rejoicing?
- What stands in the way of my joy?
- How can I share more fully in other people's joy?
- How can I fill up the joys of Jesus?

Scripture Readings about Joy

Isaiah 62:1–5 God Rejoices
Luke 15 God rejoices when the lost are found
John 15:9–11 Jesus the True Vine
Philippians 4:4 "Rejoice in the Lord always"
Luke 1:46–55 Mary's Song of Praise

15 Hope:The Disciples on the Road to Emmaus

Consider the office of consoler which Christ our Lord carries out.

Sp. Ex. 224

Some of the most poignant words found in the Scripture are voiced by the two disciples on the road from Jerusalem to Emmaus on the first Easter morning: "We had hoped . . ." (Luke 24:21). They express the sadness and discouragement of Jesus' disciples after his death. They had hoped he was the Messiah and the Reign of God had arrived. They had hoped that all God's promises would be fulfilled. But the death of Jesus seemed to have destroyed hope.

That morning there were rumors that the tomb was empty and that Jesus had appeared to some of the disciples. Was there reason to hope again? The two disciples were confused and perhaps a bit cynical when Jesus appeared to them on the road and rekindled their hope. What the two disciples experienced that afternoon was repeated in the lives of many of Jesus' followers in the days after the Resurrection.

Ignatius lists fourteen Resurrection appearances of Jesus as material for contemplation during the fourth week of the Exercises. Here we will focus on one of these—the story of the disciples on the road to Emmaus—and we will reflect on the virtue of hope as a disposition of heart fostered by all the stories of Jesus' appearances.

Ignatius's focus in the Fourth Week is on joy and rejoicing with Jesus. He does not mention hope or invite us to pray for it. Yet hope will be elicited and strengthened if one prays on Jesus' resurrection and the disciples' experience of the risen Lord. Our hope is rooted in our faith in God's fidelity in raising Jesus from the dead and God's promise to us in Jesus that we too will be raised to eternal life.

Hope is central in the Gospel story of Jesus' appearance to the disciples on the road to Emmaus. Their hope had been shaken by the events surrounding Jesus' Passion and death. They are walking away from Jerusalem, the place where the disciples were gathered on that Easter day. They had lost the source, object, and motive of their hope. "We had hoped." But they meet a stranger who listens to them. As he opens the Scripture to them, they ask him to stay with them. Only as they break bread and share fellowship do they finally recognize Jesus. Now their hearts were burning within them. Once again they had reason to hope in the preaching and promises of Jesus.

In this Resurrection story, Jesus appears to ordinary disciples—Cleopas and another unnamed man or woman disciple. They are pilgrims going the wrong way. The story assures us that Jesus is present to every pilgrim searching for answers, whether filled with faith or struggling with doubt. The story affirms that Jesus will stay with us if we ask. Christians have retold this story throughout the centuries because they believe that Jesus continues to meet us in the Scripture, in the Eucharist, and in those we meet along the way. This encounter with the risen Christ is the foundation of our faith and our hope. The pattern of all resurrection appearances is a passage from sadness, discouragement, and dejection to joy, renewed faith, and a sense of hope.

The Emmaus story also shows that renewed hope is a stimulus to mission. The disciples on the road to Emmaus rushed back to Jerusalem to tell the community their joyful experience of the risen Lord, but they also recognized that their rekindled hope was a gift not only for themselves, but for all the disciples. They experienced a new confidence that God would be faithful to all God's promises and that they were to be part of building the promised reign of God. Hope was a gift given to the whole community, a gift that would sustain them in the turbulent early years of expansion and persecution.

Hope in the Scripture

The Hebrew Scriptures tell the story of God's intervention in human history—creation, call, forgiveness, and redemption of a people chosen by God. They narrate God's repeated offers of a covenant with the people, covenants often broken by the people but always renewed by a faithful and persistent God. God leads the people, saves them, and sets them free. God is near to the people and protects them and sends them leaders and prophets to guide and challenge them.

But the Hebrew Scriptures are also a history of God's promises. God is always calling the people into a new future full of hope. The God of the Israelites is a God faithful to promises for present care and future reward. How often had the Israelites said the words later voiced by the disciples on the road, "We had hoped"? Yet God continued to send them prophets to stir up their hope in times of defeat and exile.

> For surely I know the plans I have for you, says the
> Lord, plans for your welfare and not for harm, to
> give you a future with hope. Then when you call
> upon me and come and pray to me, I will hear you.
> When you search for me, you will find me; if you
> seek me with all your heart, I will let you find me,
> says the Lord, and I will restore your fortunes and
> gather you from all the nations and all the places
> where I have driven you, says the Lord, and I will
> bring you back to the place from which I sent you
> into exile. (Jeremiah 29:11–14)

Jeremiah assures the people that God has not abandoned them. If they turn to the Lord, the Lord will lead them back to the land God promised them. The stirring words of the Prophet called the people again to hope, a hope founded on God's recurring intervention in their lives. The Prophet goes on to say:

> Thus says the Lord: Keep your voice from
> weeping, and your eyes from tears; for there is a
> reward for your work, says the Lord: they shall

come back from the land of the enemy; there
is hope for your future, says the Lord: your
children shall come back to their own country.
(Jeremiah 31:16–17)

No wonder the Psalmist cries out: "By awesome deeds you
answer us with deliverance, O God of our salvation; you are
the hope of all the ends of the earth and of the farthest seas"
(Psalm 65:5).

The Israelites relied on the Lord because God had always
been faithful even when they were unfaithful. Their hope rested
in Yahweh because God had chosen them and made them a great
people and given them the land God had promised. In their time
of exile, the people hoped and trusted the Lord would again save
them. Their hope was rooted in all that God had done for them
throughout their history as a people.

> Confident reliance on God, eager longing for His
> fidelity to be manifested, patient bearing of pres-
> ent trials in view of God's promises of vindication,
> and taking refuge with God as one's rock or for-
> tress to escape one's foes are all attitudes of Old
> Testament hope.[1]

In the end, their hope was fulfilled in a new covenant written in
their hearts.

In the New Testament, hope is rooted in Jesus and his
Resurrection as the manifestation of God's fidelity to God's
promises. Jesus is God's revealing promise to us and the source of

our hope. Jesus is the proof of God's faithfulness. As God raised up Jesus, we are assured that God will raise us up also. Jesus is the anticipation of our resurrection. As we share in his suffering, we will also share in his glory. "Through him you have come to trust in God who raised him from the dead and gave him glory, so that your faith and hope are set on God" (1 Peter 1:21; see also 1:3 in the same letter).

The first verses of the Letter to the Ephesians dramatically reveal God's plan of salvation in Christ (Ephesians 1:3–14). They detail how God chose us in Christ, destined us for adoption, redeemed us through the blood of Christ, and revealed the mystery of God's will. The verses end with reference to our hope in Christ:

> In Christ we have also obtained an inheritance,
> having been destined according to the purpose
> of him who accomplishes all things according to
> his counsel and will, so that we, who were the
> first to set our hope on Christ, might live for the
> praise of his glory. In him you also, when you
> had heard the word of truth, the gospel of your
> salvation, and had believed in him, were marked
> with the seal of the promised Holy Spirit; this is
> the pledge of our inheritance toward redemption
> as God's own people, to the praise of his glory.
> (Ephesians 1:11–14)

Our hope for the future is strengthened by our present experience of God's Spirit poured into our hearts. We are already heirs of the promises of God, yet we still live in hope of their fulfillment.

The Virtue of Hope

Hope is about expectation and trust and confidence. We hope for things we do not yet have. "For in hope we were saved. Now hope that is seen is not hope. For who hopes for what is seen? But if we hope for what we do not see, we wait for it with patience" (Romans 8:24–25). Hope is a virtue of longing and restlessness and desiring for what is not yet a reality, but what we trust will become a reality in the future. Hope is a basic human stance that presumes an ultimate meaning to life and the world in which we live. We can foster hope, but ultimately it is a gift rooted in our reliance on God's fidelity. To become a person of hope is to surrender to God's grace in our lives and allow God to strengthen our faith. The source of our hope is God's faithfulness to promises, a faithfulness expressed most dramatically in Jesus and the gift of the Spirit. Our hope grows out of our experience of God's unconditional love for us. We hope in a God who loves us, who says through the prophet Isaiah, ". . . But my steadfast love shall not depart from you . . ." (Isaiah 54:10).

We most often think of hope in terms of future reward. We hope for Resurrection and eternal life. We hope for the coming of God's reign in its fullness. Our faith offers us the sure hope of immortality. As God raised Jesus from the dead, we too will one day be raised. This hope of eternal life consoles us and strengthens us as we face our mortality and as we try to deal with the death of loved ones. We are people of hope because we believe that God will raise us up and offer us a share in God's life.

At the same time, we hope for God's care for us in the present. Our hope is not restricted to God's promise of life after death or the ultimate fulfillment of God's reign in the next life. Our hope is not centered solely on the life to come. Our hope is that God will be with us and support us in our everyday lives.

> He said to his disciples, "Therefore I tell you, do not worry about your life, what you will eat, or about your body, what you will wear. For life is more than food, and the body more than clothing. Consider the ravens: they neither sow nor reap, they have neither storehouse nor barn, and yet God feeds them. Of how much more value are you than the birds! . . . Consider the lilies, how they grow: they neither toil nor spin; yet I tell you, even Solomon in all his glory was not clothed like one of these. But if God so clothes the grass of the field, which is alive today and tomorrow is thrown into the oven, how much more will he clothe you—you of little faith! (Luke 12:22–28)

Our hope assures us that God will do more than reward us in the next life. God will be a constant source of strength in our daily struggles and challenges. Richard Gula remarks: "Hope enables us to find meaning in whatever happens because hope rests on the faith conviction that all is sustained by the graciousness of God."[2] God has promised to be with us as we strive to live out our commitments in fidelity. We hope in God's faithful presence and support, especially in times of difficulty.

Another manifestation of hope is our belief that God can continue to work in and through us and do great things within us. We are always tempted to passively accept our present level of growth and sanctity. We lose hope that God can do more within us and through us. We no longer look for new possibilities in life or ministry. We limit God to promises already fulfilled and fail to embrace new promises that stretch our imaginations and dreams. Hope opens our hearts to God's hopes and dreams for us and our world. Hope is not content with the "already." Hope always envisions and believes in the "not yet."

Hope invites us to patience and endurance. We are called to wait on the Lord. We accept that God's time is not our time. Hope is most needed in times of darkness and difficulty. As Jim Keenan puts it, "Hope is the willingness to not give up on one's faith, precisely when, in a manner of speaking, one draws no consolation from it."[3] Hope sustains us in times of trial.

> Hope is the Spirit entering into our tired, exhausted, fearful selves, offering us a way to continue the dialogue, to continue standing face to face with the living God. Whatever enables us to continue to believe in the face of death, doubt, uncertainty, or fear, is hope.[4]

Thus a Christian hopes in the midst of suffering and death. Until we have felt the pain, the meaninglessness, the seeming loss of what we love, our hope will remain naïve optimism or wishful thinking. Real hope comes when we find a reason to keep going in suffering and death. The traditional symbol of hope is an anchor because hope keeps us secure in times of storm so we are not blown about and thrown off course. "We have this hope, a sure and steadfast anchor of the soul . . ." (Hebrews 6:19).

The virtue of hope also disposes our hearts to be committed, courageous, and generous. Hope is more than passive acceptance. It motivates us to act now. A person of hope recognizes that God invites us to help build the reign of God. Michael Scanlon describes well the tension yet ultimate connection between hope for eternity and hope for the realization of God's reign in the present world. Do we hope for eternal life or do we hope for a more just and peaceful world?

> The new line of division among Christians is revealed in the answer to the question, "What can we hope for?" For "traditional" Christians the answer remains: eternal life after death for the purified soul. For "progressive" Christians the answer is partially in agreement: yes, ultimately eternal life, but penultimately a more just, more peaceful world order."[5]

The exclusive focus on the fulfillment of God's promises in the next life can undermine our commitment to transform the world in which we live. Hope is directed not only to the next life, but also to present history.

An awareness of the central role of hope in creating a better world characterizes much of Christian theology in the last fifty years. As Monika Hellwig notes: "Many forces combined in the mid-20th century to bring the virtue of hope into prominence in

Christian theology and spirituality, and to give it a this-worldly, active and communitarian turn."[6] In other words, there has been a shift from setting our hearts on the next life to committing ourselves to a better world, from passive acceptance to active involvement in building the reign of God, and from personal happiness in heaven to the transformation of relationships and the structures of society. The virtue of hope moves us to more than personal efforts to gain eternal life. Our mission is to share in the labor of bringing God's promises to fulfillment. Hope too gives us perseverance, the strength to continue to struggle for justice and a better world. Hope sustains us as we face the arduous work of renewing society's structures. Without hope, we would lose resolve and despair of ever changing the world in which we live. Because we hope in God's promises, we trust that our efforts will bring forth change. But hope also invites us to humility. It highlights the simple truth that the ultimate success of the reign of God depends finally on God's power, not our own. Hope reminds us that "Unless the Lord builds the house, we labor in vain who build it."

This new emphasis on the role of hope in creating a better world was articulated in the twentieth century by theologians of hope like Jurgen Moltmann, Johann-Baptist Metz, and Wolfhart Pannenberg. They returned to the biblical categories of promise and hope and sought to understand history in terms of the future. History was understood as a linear progression that offers the possibility of the radically new and original. God is imaged not as "above us," but as "ahead of us" as a God of promise pulling us into the future and missioning us to create a new future. This call to mission was echoed by Third World liberation theologians who connected hope to a commitment to deal with suffering, poverty, and exploitation in the world. In the words of Hellwig:

These theologians address themselves to the discernment and analysis of the authentic intermediate objects of hope—those transformations in relationships, values, expectations, and structures of society that are steps in the direction of the full realization of the reign of God among us.[7]

Hope, then, becomes a dynamic force that moves a Christian to action for justice. Hope should not detach the Christian from the world or foster escape from the world. Hope is a disposition to action that engages the Christian in the world. At the same time, this this-worldly, active, communitarian, and social understanding of hope does not deny the longing of the human heart for personal happiness and the fullness of God's reign in the life to come. Hellwig sums it up well:

The challenge for Christian spirituality and pastoral strategy in our times is to rediscover in depth the personal and communitarian dimensions of the theological virtue of hope, and especially to keep discerning in changing circumstances the interdependence of the personal and social dimensions of hope for the true quest and welcoming of the reign of God coming among us.[8]

In the end, the tension between this world and the next finds resolution in the continuity between the reign of God now and the reign of God to come in fullness. As we actively hope for a world of peace and justice, we contribute to the eternal reign of God that is the final object of our hope.

Living in Hope

Paul prayed for the Christians of Rome: "May the God of hope fill you with all joy and peace in believing, so that you may abound in hope by the power of the Holy Spirit" (Romans 15:3). The Resurrection of Jesus is the source of our joy, our peace, and our hope. Paul clearly connects these gifts in our Christian lives. Though Ignatius asks a person to pray for joy rather than hope during the Fourth Week, hope will certainly be elicited from the heart of anyone who enters imaginatively and prayerfully into the stories of the Resurrection appearances. Like the disciples on the road, like the disciples in the upper room and the women at the tomb, encountering the risen Christ rekindles our trust in God. We have the deep assurance that God will keep promises just as God fulfilled all God's promises in the Resurrection of Jesus.

As we come to the end of the four weeks of the Exercises, we recognize that the virtue of hope actually finds its roots in all the graces prayed for throughout the Exercises from the Principle and Foundation to the Resurrection of Jesus. Our hope is grounded in the felt knowledge of the love of God that creates for us, forgives us and calls us to follow Jesus. Hope flows out of our response to God's love calling us to life, saving us, and inviting us to eternal life now and in the future. The dynamic of the Exercises and the movement of the graces lead a person to a faith-filled confidence in God's faithful love.

The hope fostered throughout the Exercises also sends us forth to share the good news and continue the ministry and mission of Jesus. Only in hope can we discern and embrace the Call of the King and the mission given to us in Jesus. Only in hope can we discover the courage and boldness to be disciples laboring at the side of Jesus. The Exercises mold us into people of hope who rely on the promises of God. We know in faith and hope that what God has started, God will bring to completion.

Reflecting on Hope

- What are God's hopes and dreams for me and for our world?
- What new possibilities and areas of growth do I hope for myself and others?
- How does my hope in God sustain me in times of trial and difficulty?
- What is my role in helping fulfill God's promises for a more just and peaceful world?

Scripture Readings on Hope

Jeremiah 29:11–14 A Future Full of Hope
Luke 12:22–34 Do Not Worry
Ephesians 1:11–18 Spiritual Blessings in Christ
Romans 8:18–25 Future Glory

16 Love: The Contemplation on the Love of God

Love ought to manifest itself more by deeds than by words.

Sp. Ex. 230

In the Contemplation on the Love of God, the final exercise of the Spiritual Exercises, Ignatius invites us to reflect on the love of God—the central grace and reality throughout the Exercises. The person making the Exercises has experienced the love of God as creating, forgiving, calling, saving, and inviting to eternal life. This final exercise is a summary of all that has gone before and an expression of the heart of Ignatian spirituality.

The Contemplation on the Love of God is a call to an intimate knowledge and love and service of God. The exercise tries to bring us to a place where we can love and serve the Divine Majesty in all things. The grace we pray for is an interior knowledge, deep in our heart, of all the great good that we have received. This knowledge elicits profound gratitude. When we really grasp the gifts of God in our lives, we are moved to gratitude. Stirred by this gratitude, we are able to love and serve God in all things.

Ignatius leads us through a series of steps. First, he offers two prenotes. The first prenote is that love is expressed in deeds not just in words. It is not enough just to say nice things to God. The call is to be lived out in action. If anything captures Ignatius, it is that sense of always asking, "What do I have to *do?*" Ignatius's mysticism of service impelled him to find God's will and labor for God's glory and the good of others.

The second prenote is that love consists of a mutual giving and sharing of what one possesses. Love is mutuality. As God has given all this to us, we are to give it all to God and share it with God and share it with those around us. It is in mutual sharing that the unity of the lover and the beloved is realized.

Ignatius then offers four points for our consideration. First, he invites us to call to mind the blessings and favors we have received—the gifts of our family, friends, education, and ministry. We reflect on how much God has done for us, how much God has given us, and how much God desires to give God's very self to us.

Next Ignatius invites us to consider how God dwells in what God gives us. God does not simply give us all these gifts and then leave us on our own. God actually dwells in creation. Above all God is dwelling in us and in our hearts. We are the temple of God. The temple is a wonderful image throughout the Scripture of the place where God resides. The central role of the Temple is obvious in the Hebrew Scriptures. In the New Testament Jesus says that he is the temple where God resides. In the early church, the community was acknowledged as the temple of God. You find God in the community. Paul finally says that every Christian is the temple of God because God dwells in our hearts. "Do you not know that you are God's temple and that God's Spirit dwells in you?" (1 Corinthians 3:16).

Ignatius's third point is that God doesn't just dwell in us in a passive way. God works and labors in creation for us, bringing the world back to God, moving people's hearts, and trying to move the world toward the reign of God. God is active and engaged in the world.

Finally, in the fourth point, Ignatius says: Consider all the gifts and blessings as coming down from above, so that I will be led back to the source of all good. If we consider everything coming down from God, from above, our hearts will go back to the giver. If it is all a gift, the gift will lead us back to the giver. And that is where our hearts should finally reside, in the giver.

All of this is not speculation for Ignatius. The purpose of this contemplation is not just speculation, it is surrender. It is to give our hearts back to God and is a call to service.

Finding God in All Things

The Principle and Foundation was about the transcendence of God: God above us sending gifts down. This final contemplation focuses on the immanence of God: God in our midst, in our presence, and God in creation. God's active presence calls us to service and gratitude. If there are two words you remember from Ignatius, they are service and gratitude. Gratitude leads us to service.

Ignatius invites us to pray for that deep interior knowledge of the giftedness of creation that moves us to love in return and to render service. It is a movement from thanksgiving to thankfully giving ourselves in service. If Jesus labors for us and Jesus labors with us, we are invited to share with him in his labor and bring the reign of God to completion.

This contemplation then captures the heart of Ignatian spirituality because it is telling us to find God in all things. Where is God? God is in the midst of everything. God is dwelling and laboring here. God is in everything about us, including our own hearts. That is where we find God. What is Ignatian spirituality about? It is about finding God in all things. That is what this contemplation is trying to let sink deep into our hearts.

Another phrase often used about Ignatius was first used by Jerome Nadal, one of the early Jesuits who knew Ignatius extremely well. In fact, Ignatius said Nadal knew him better than he knew himself. Somebody asked Nadal, "How do you sum up Ignatius?" Nadal answered, "He is a contemplative man even in the midst of action." That phrase is rooted in the contemplation on the love of God. The contemplative in action is not someone who prays a lot and then goes out to do something. Rather, one is praying in the very midst of doing things. You are a contemplative in the midst of the very things you are doing. In action you are finding God, relating to God, you are in touch with God.

The Contemplation on the Love of God is also a transition out of the retreat into our everyday lives. Where's God? We are going to find God out there. The temptation is to stay in the retreat, to build three tents and stay on top of the mountain, as the disciples wanted to do at Jesus' Transfiguration. The retreat has been wonderful, but now, go do something. It is Jesus' voice at the Ascension saying, "Why are you standing here idly looking up to heaven?" In this contemplation, Ignatius gives us the mission and the energy to go forth to find God in our everyday lives and to be of service to one another.

Perhaps Ignatius's most famous prayer is the suscipe. He invites us to say this prayer in the Contemplation on the Love of God.

> Take, Lord, and receive all my liberty, my memory, my understanding, and my entire will. You have given all to me. Now I return it. Everything is yours. Do with it what you will. Give me only your love and your grace and that is enough for me.

It is a prayer of surrender: "You have given everything to me. I give it back. Just give me your love and your grace and that is enough for me." It is the total freedom of surrendering everything so one can follow Jesus and live out the call of the Gospel.

This prayer of total surrender completes the cycle of creation and redemption. All things come from God and all things go back to God. God has gifted the world in creation and in the incarnation. We return that gift—both as an act of personal surrender and as a way to labor with Christ to bring all things back to God. We want to bring everything back to the Giver of all Gifts.

God's Love for Us

Ignatius's Contemplation on the Love of God focuses our attention on God's love for us and our response in love. It elicits the virtue of love that is the foundation of our Christian lives. The first letter of John reveals the heart of the Christian message: God is love and we as Christians are to love one another.

> Dear friends, let us love one another, for love comes from God. Everyone who loves has been

> born of God and knows God. Whoever does not
> love does not know God because God is love. This
> is how God showed God's love among us. God
> sent God's one and only Son into the world that
> we might live through him. This is love: not that
> we loved God, but that God loved us and sent
> his Son as an atoning sacrifice for our sins. Dear
> friends, since God so loved us, we also ought to
> love one another. . . . God is love. Whoever lives in
> love lives in God, and God in them. . . . We love
> because God first loved us. (1 John 7—11, 16, 19)

Christian love is a response to God's love for us. Since God loved first, Christians are motivated not by fear of punishment or a compulsion to earn God's love, but by gratitude for love already offered. As we have seen throughout the Exercises, we experience God's love as creating, redeeming, sanctifying and gifting us with eternal life. In fact, God's inner Trinitarian life is a life of communication, sharing, and the love of friendship, and that love pours itself out in the Holy Spirit. We are invited to live that life of God, to live in friendship and love.

This love of God is revealed dramatically in the Hebrew Scriptures where God is portrayed as a faithful lover of Israel.

> Praise the Lord, all you nations! Extol the Lord,
> all you peoples! For great is his steadfast love
> toward us, and the faithfulness of the Lord
> endures forever. Praise the Lord! (Psalm 117)

God's faithful and forgiving love is acted out in the series of covenants God makes with the Israelites. God is always faithful, even when the people are not. God's love is the root of the people's election. Out of love, God chooses them as God's people and gives them the land and protects them from their enemies. The prophets use the image of marriage to portray the relationship between God and the people. The prophet Isaiah uses maternal imagery to highlight God's love for the people: "Can a woman forget her nursing child, or show no compassion for the child of her womb? Even these may forget, yet I will not forget you. See, I have inscribed you on the palms of my hands . . ." (Isaiah 49:15–16). Even more simply, the prophet speaks in Yahweh's name, "Because you are precious in my sight, and honored and I love you . . ." (Isaiah 43:4). Certainly, the image of God in the Hebrew Scriptures is far from simple and unambiguous. There is a clear revelation of a steadfast love of God for the people that belies the stereotype of an Old Testament God of vengeance versus a New Testament God of love.

In the New Testament, God's faithful and persistent love is manifested in Jesus. "For God so loved the world that he gave his only Son, so that everyone who believes in him may not perish but may have eternal life" (John 3:16). Throughout his life Jesus revealed God's forgiving and life-giving love for the people. He healed and forgave people and told stories of God's mercy and faithfulness. In the end, Jesus manifested God's love by loving us even unto death. As Paul poignantly states it, Jesus "loved me and gave himself for me" (Galatians 2:20). Paul also reminds us that Jesus loved us even when we were sinners (Romans 5:8). It is not surprising that Paul exclaims:

> For I am convinced that neither death, nor life,
> nor angels, nor rulers, nor things present, nor
> things to come, nor powers, nor height, nor depth,

> nor anything else in all creation, will be able to
> separate us from the love of God in Christ Jesus
> our Lord. (Romans 8:38–39)

In John's Gospel, Jesus speaks of his own love for his disciples and all those disciples who will follow after. At the Last Supper Jesus assures them that "[a]s the Father has loved me, so I love you; abide in my love" (John 15:9). Jesus goes on to offer friendship: "I do not call you servants any longer, because the servant does not know what the master is doing; but I have called you friends, because I have made known to you everything that I have heard from my Father. You did not choose me but I chose you" (John 15:15–16).

The love that Jesus offers is a love of friendship that invites the disciples to intimacy and mutuality. At the end of his discourse at the Last Supper, Jesus prays to his Father, asking that the disciples may share in the divine love that is the inner life of God: "I made your name known to them, and I will make it known, so that the love with which you have loved me may be in them, and I in them" (John 17:26). In Romans, Paul says that this divine love is given to us through God's Spirit, "God's love has been poured into our hearts through the Holy Spirit that has been given to us" (Romans 5:5). The love of God is the presence of the Holy Spirit who is the love between the Father and the Son.

Our Response to God's Love

Christian love is our response to this love of God manifested in Jesus and poured into our hearts by the Holy Spirit. As Pope Benedict states it: "Since God has first loved us (cf. 1 John 4:10), love is now no longer a mere 'command'; it is the response to the gift of love with which God draws near to us."[1] When asked by the Pharisees "Which commandment in the law is the greatest,?" Jesus responded:

> You shall love the Lord your God with all
> your heart, and with all your soul, and with
> all your mind. This is the greatest and first
> commandment. And a second is like it: You shall
> love your neighbor as yourself. On these two
> commandments hang all the law and the prophets.
> (Matthew 22:37–40)

Jesus lays out a twofold commandment for those who have experienced God's love. They are to love God and love their neighbor. In fact these two commands are really one command that expresses our response to God's love. Jesus first quotes the exhortation from the book of Deuteronomy to love God totally with our whole being. He then makes a surprising connection with the command from the book of Leviticus to love our neighbor as ourselves. In John's Gospel, Jesus calls this a new command: "I give you a new commandment, that you love one another. Just as I have loved you, you should love one another. By this everyone will know that you are my disciples, if you have love for one another" (John 13:34-35). What should distinguish disciples of Jesus is their love for one another.

What is most challenging about that love is that disciples are to love one another in the way that Jesus has loved them. "This is my commandment, that you love one another as I have loved you" (John 15:12). We are to imitate Jesus' self-sacrificing love that loved us even unto death. We must be willing to give our lives for one another.

In the Sermon on the Mount, Jesus spells out the implications of Christian love. If Jesus has loved us even when we were sinners, we in turn are to love even those who sin against us:

> You have heard that it was said, "You shall love your neighbor and hate your enemy." But I say to you, Love your enemies and pray for those who persecute you, so that you may be children of your Father in heaven; for he makes his sun to rise on the evil and the good, and sends rain on the righteous and on the unrighteous. For if you love those who love you, what reward do you have? Do not even the tax collectors do the same? And if you greet only your brothers and sisters, what more are you doing than others? Do not even the Gentiles do the same? Be perfect, therefore, as your heavenly Father is perfect.
> (Matthew 5:43–48)

Christian love calls us to love even our enemies. We are to forgive others in the same way that God has forgiven us. Paul speaks of us as agents of reconciliation:

> So if anyone is in Christ, there is a new creation: everything old has passed away; see, everything has become new! All this is from God who reconciled us to himself through Christ, and has

> given us the ministry of reconciliation; that is, in
> Christ God was reconciling the world to himself,
> not counting their trespasses against them, and
> entrusting the message of reconciliation to us.
> (2 Corinthians 5:17–19)

Forgiveness is a gift given to us by God to share with others. Christian love challenges us to let go of resentments and open our hearts to those who may have offended us.

Christian love is inclusive. Jesus loved sinners and all those that society excluded from its circle of concern: the unclean, the tax collectors, the lepers. Jesus' love knew no boundaries. In fact, Jesus' love stepped across boundaries that separated people. He embraced everyone as neighbor. In particular, Jesus' love reached out to those in need. He had special concern for the poor, the exploited, the neglected in society, and those who had no voice or rights. This concern is dramatized in the story of the Good Samaritan and in the final judgment scene in Matthew's Gospel when the only criteria for distinguishing between those blessed and those cursed are how they responded to those in need.

> Then the king will say to those at his right hand,
> 'Come, you that are blessed by my Father, inherit
> the kingdom prepared for you from the foundation
> of the world; for I was hungry and you gave me
> food, I was thirsty and you gave me something to
> drink, I was a stranger and you welcomed me, I
> was naked and you gave me clothing, I was sick

and you took care of me, I was in prison and you
visited me. (Matthew 25:34–36)

When the righteous ask the king when they did all these things,
the king responds: "Truly I tell you, just as you did it to one of the
least of those who are members of my family, you did it to me"
(Matthew 25:40). Jesus identifies with the least of society and
urges us to give them special concern. Christian love has a preferential love for the poor. Christian love prompts us to compassion
and justice and service.

Christian love also calls us to self love. We are to love others
as we love ourselves. This implies a generous love of self rooted
in God's love for us. The Gospel calls us to a valuing of ourselves
as lovable, as created and loved by God. We are called to love
ourselves even in our brokenness and need for God. We are challenged as well to forgive ourselves as God forgives us. We cannot
genuinely love and forgive others if we do not love and forgive
ourselves. Self-love allows us to see ourselves through God's eyes
and to claim our dignity as images of God loved into existence.

Love as a Virtue

Love is the driving force of our lives. It is the fundamental disposition of heart that motivates us to go beyond ourselves in care
and concern for others. Love is the desire of our hearts for self-
transcendence. It is the passion that moves us to be one with God
and others. Love is a feeling, but, more importantly, it is a choice
of the will to turn toward others. True love is altruistic, compassionate, faithful, and self-sacrificing. It disposes us to act always
for the good of others, to give of ourselves.

Ignatius rightly stresses that love is shown in deeds, not just in words, yet, as James Keenan expresses it, "Charity is concerned more with the interior life than with the external act, more concerned with the heart than with the deed."[2] Love is an interior attitude of heart that leads to gracious action. It is a desire that finds fulfillment in acts of faithful service. Love is the source of community that binds us together and unites us with God and others in Christ's Body. As a theological virtue, it empowers us to love with the love of God that is poured into our hearts.

Love is the source of all the virtues. Thus, it is fitting that it is the final virtue we reflect upon. Love gives birth to gratitude, reverence, generosity, faith, prudence, fidelity, joy, and hope, and to all the virtues touched on in this book.

In the Contemplation on the Love of God, Ignatius invites us to end the Spiritual Exercises where we begin, with God's love. The Exercises begin with the experience of God's love in creation. They culminate in a profound experience of God's love as pervading and giving meaning to all of life. This is why the final grace prayed for in the Spiritual Exercises is to love and serve God in all things. Perhaps the words of the letter to the Ephesians best express the desire of Ignatius's heart for those who come to the end of the Exercises:

> I pray that, according to the riches of his glory,
> he may grant that you may be strengthened in
> your inner being with power through his Spirit,
> and that Christ may dwell in your hearts through
> faith, as you are being rooted and grounded
> in love. I pray that you may have the power to
> comprehend, with all the saints, what is the

breadth and length and height and depth, and to
know the love of Christ that surpasses knowledge,
so that you may be filled with all the fullness of
God. (Ephesians 3:16–19)

Reflecting on Love

- What are the ways I experience God's steadfast love in my life?
- How do I give expression to my love for God?
- What are the ways I am called to love and care for my neighbor?
- Are there those whom I fail to include in my love?

Scripture Readings about Love

1 John 4:7–21 Love is from God

Romans 5:1–11 God's love has been poured into our hearts

Romans 8:31–39 Nothing can separate us from the love of God

Ephesians 3:14–20 Rooted and grounded in love

John 13:34–35 Love one another as I have loved you

Conclusion: Go and Do Likewise

Ignatius Loyola spent the last fifteen years of his life serving as the Superior General of the newly approved Society of Jesus. He had no doubt envisioned being a missionary sent by the pope to respond to the needs of the church throughout the world. Instead God called him through his Jesuit brothers to lead the Society of Jesus in its early years of growth and development. One of the tasks before him in those years was to write Constitutions for the new religious order.

The Constitutions could have been written as a rather dry and uninspiring set of statutes and rules to be applied rigidly, but, as George Ganss points out, Ignatius "skillfully wove into the legislative prescriptions the spiritual motivation for carrying them into practice. As a result, his book is a classic of spirituality as well as of religious legislation."[1] The Constitutions is not simply a juridical document that lays out procedures and guidelines, but also a spiritual document that includes motivation for living life in the Society of Jesus. The same vision and values that give shape to the Spiritual Exercises are at the heart of the Constitutions. Ignatius always had in mind the end for which we are created and what is more conducive to that end. Thus Ganss further describes the Constitutions as a manual for discernment.

> His Constitutions is not merely a set of precepts but also, perhaps more importantly, a manual of discernment toward helping superiors or members to discover the better choices in the opinions they meet: Which option is likely to result, in the long run, to lead to greater glory of the Divine Majesty?[2]

Ignatius refers to growth in virtues throughout the Constitutions, but I wish to focus on his description in Part IX of "the kind of person the superior general should be."[3] The superior general as described by Ignatius can be seen as an ideal person formed in Ignatian spirituality and shaped by the Spiritual Exercises. In fact, Ignatius organizes the Constitutions around the process of formation of Jesuits, beginning with the admission of candidates, then their spiritual and intellectual formation, and ultimately their final incorporation into the Society and how their ministries are to be chosen.[4] The description of the general comes at the end of that process as a model of the fully formed Jesuit, a Jesuit living out of the graces of the Exercises.

It is interesting to note that virtue plays a central role in the life of the superior general. After naming intimacy or familiarity with God in prayer and action as the first quality desired in the general, Ignatius adds that:

> The second quality is that he should be a person whose example in the practice of all virtues is a help to the other members of the Society. Charity

should be especially resplendent in him, toward all his fellowmen and above all toward the members of the Society; and genuine humility too should shine forth, that these characteristics may make him highly lovable to God our Lord and to men. (Cons. #725)

As his description of the general unfolds, Ignatius also mentions kindness, magnanimity, fortitude of soul, and prudence. He adds that these qualities "include the general's perfection in relation to God: further, what perfects his heart, understanding, and execution. . . ." (Cons. #724) Ignatius, then, acknowledges these qualities as dispositions of the heart. The final paragraph of his description begins with: "Finally, he ought to be one of those who are most outstanding in every virtue. . . ." (Cons. #735) Clearly, Ignatius believed that a person formed in the Society of Jesus over many years by the graces and movements of the Exercises would be a person of outstanding virtue, a person whose heart was in tune with the heart of Christ.

Ganss also points out that this portrait of the ideal superior "has long been regarded as a self-portrait made subconsciously by Ignatius himself."[5] More importantly, Ganss notes that Ignatius "has also left an ideal which all members of his order can well seek to approach."[6] I would add that, with certain modifications, what Ignatius is really describing are the ideal qualities and virtues of any person who has made the Exercises. Anyone who has prayed through the Exercises and prayed for the graces of the Exercises will be formed in the dispositions of heart named by Ignatius in describing the superior general; in fact, the person will be schooled "in the practice of all virtues."

Part X of the Constitutions, the final part, sums up all the preceding sections of the Constitutions and gives an overview of the Society and its spirit. Ignatius is concerned with "how the whole body of the Society can be preserved and developed in its well being." He begins by acknowledging that the Society was instituted and is preserved and developed through the grace of God (Cons. #812). Human means are essential, but in the end those means which unite the person with God are more important than any human means.

> The means which unite the human instrument with God and so dispose it that it may be wielded dexterously by his divine hand are more effective than those which equip it in relation to men. Such means are, for example, goodness and virtue, and especially charity, and a pure intention of the divine service, and familiarity with God our Lord in spiritual exercises of devotion, and sincere zeal for souls for the sake of glory to him who created and redeemed them and not for any other benefit. Thus it appears that care should be taken in general that all the members of the Society may devote themselves to the solid and perfect virtues and to spiritual pursuits, and attach greater importance to them than to learning and other natural and human gifts. For they are the interior gifts which make those exterior means effective toward the end which is sought. (Cons. #813)

Ignatius makes a clear distinction between the natural gifts that God gives as Creator and the supernatural gifts God gives as the

Author of grace. We may no longer be comfortable with this sharp distinction between the natural and the supernatural, but it does highlight the balance and interconnectedness of God's gifts. It is important to notice again that in this final part of the Constitutions, Ignatius gives a prominent place to virtue as a means to growth in the spiritual life and in apostolic effectiveness.

This brief reflection on the Constitutions of the Society of Jesus highlights how Ignatius saw the importance of virtues in the life of someone dedicated to live out the graces and insights of the Spiritual Exercises. Ignatius's description of the qualities of the ideal superior general and of those fully formed in Ignatian spirituality within the Society of Jesus is a portrait of any person whose heart has been transformed by the experience of God's unconditional love, forgiveness, call, and invitation into the Paschal Mystery that is central to the Spiritual Exercises. The graces planted and fostered in the Exercises grow into the virtues that give shape to the heart of a disciple. Late in his life, as Ignatius drafted the Constitutions, his own heart had been molded into the virtues he expected to see in anyone who had made the Exercises. He envisioned growth in the spiritual life as a growth in these virtues. The language of the Exercises was a language of grace and desire, but certainly one fruit and embodiment of those graces and desires was a virtuous heart open to God's call to draw closer to the heart of Christ.

Virtues and the Exercises and the Heart of Christ

The goal of this book has been to foster a conversation between the Spiritual Exercises and the life of the virtues. The purpose of the book is not to propose a new way to give or make the

Exercises, nor to offer a new interpretation of the Exercises. The goal has been to explore the Exercises through the lens of the return to virtue that characterizes much of contemporary philosophical ethics and moral theology. The desire has been to use the virtues as a way to understand more deeply and appreciate more fully the graces of the Exercises. Ignatius was not only concerned in the Exercises with one-time graces, but more deeply with attitudes of heart that shape all our decisions and actions and sustain us in a life of service.

The virtues discussed here are examples of dispositions of heart that are fostered by the Exercises. The list is not complete, but only a way to begin the conversation and encourage further reflection on the connection between the virtues and the Exercises. Ignatius did not envision people making the Exercises more than once. It was to be a once-in-a-lifetime experience that committed a person to a life of service as a disciple of Jesus. Rather quickly, however, people began to make them, often in modified forms, more frequently, even annually. The Sixth General Congregation of the Society of Jesus in 1608 decreed that every Jesuit should make an eight-day retreat based on the Exercises every year.[7] Certainly, the repetition of the Exercises makes sense if we view them as a school of prayer or as a means to deepen, renew, and assimilate more personally the graces of the Exercises at different stages of our lives.

Recognizing the Exercises as a way to foster Christian virtues also motivates a person to make the Exercises more frequently. We need to continually promote and develop those foundational virtues that flow out of the experience of the Exercises. Also at different moments in our lives, particular virtues become more important. At times we may need to be more grateful or generous or faithful or compassionate. At other times, our life circumstances may call us to be more reverent or courageous or hopeful or loving.[8] The Exercises call us to embrace more deeply the dispositions of heart that are necessary to love and serve God and others. The virtues flow out of the desired graces we pray for, but they are also the source of actions that strengthen and plant those graces more solidly in our hearts. The Exercises in all their rich adaptations can become an effective means to enrich our spiritual lives through growth in virtue.

Virtues are dispositions of heart, but they also guide our decisions and determine how we act. Thus we grow in virtue by performing virtuous acts. We become more compassionate by acts of compassion, more humble by acts of humility, more generous by acts of generosity. There are certainly opportunities while making the Exercises in solitude to perform acts of virtue, but the Exercises first elicit dispositions of heart that shape the kind of person we are. During a Nineteenth Annotation retreat (a retreat in the midst of daily life over six or eight months), there are certainly many occasions to practice virtues first fostered in the Exercises. The frequent, even annual, retreat based on the Exercises allows us to practice acts of virtue in our everyday lives and then return to the Exercises to strength the attitudes of heart that are most needed for Christian living.

Throughout the Exercises, Ignatius asks us to pray for what we desire. These desires have been planted in our hearts by a God who loves us and desires our happiness. Our desires, our longing for God, are simply a reflection of God's desires and longing for us. The Exercises are a process that helps us discover what God desires us to do with our lives, what choices will lead us closer to God and a deeper share in God's life. In light of the questions posed by virtue ethics, however, we can also ask: What kind of person does God desire us to become? The virtues discussed in this book are at least an initial description of who God desires us to become, the kind of person God desires us to be. Of course, we have the model of that person in Jesus. The heart of Jesus reveals to us what God desires us to become. God desires that we put on the heart of Jesus. The Spiritual Exercises offer a powerful way to identify with the heart of Jesus and make it our own.

In the parable of the Good Samaritan, Jesus tells a story of compassion and loving action. The Samaritan models a disciple who reaches out to the one in need. What Jesus says at the end of that parable captures Jesus' desire for us. As Spohn explains:

> The basic command that Jesus gives at the end of the Good Samaritan story invites Christians to think analogically: "Go and do likewise" (Luke 10:37). The mandate is not "Go and do exactly the same" as the Samaritan. It is decidedly not "Go and do whatever you want." The term "likewise" implies that Christians should be faithful to the story of Jesus yet creative in applying it to their context.[9]

Jesus does not exhort us to a slavish imitation of certain actions. In fact, Jesus does not lay out exactly what to do. At the same time, he does not simply recommend that we do whatever we want. We are to act *like* the Good Samaritan. We are to be attentive to those in need. We are to be moved by compassion at their plight, and that compassion should drive us to act creatively and responsibly to offer support and assistance. Jesus does not tell us exactly what to do when we see a homeless person or meet a beggar on the street. He does tell us the attitudes of heart that should motivate and inform our response. We are to respond with the heart of Christ. Our response will be dictated by the circumstances and our resources, but most of all by the dispositions of heart that shape all our actions.

A virtuous and discerning heart rooted in the heart of Christ will guide us in the way of discipleship. Richard Gula expresses it well:

> Discipleship is not concerned with reproducing point for point the external aspects of the master's life and work. It is concerned, rather, with making the master's wisdom, dispositions, and spirit shape our own character so that we will prefer spontaneously the way of life that harmonizes with the master's.[10]

Jesus invites us to see things in a new way, to be disposed to act in a new way, and to do things for new reasons.[11] Ultimately, Jesus calls us to become who Jesus is. We are invited to become a new person with a new heart. We see others as Jesus does when we see others as neighbors and sisters and brothers, when we look at the world through the eyes of the poor, and when we see the world as a place where God's reign is breaking in. We are disposed to act as Jesus does when we act out of freedom and fidelity and love, when we are moved by compassion and generosity, when we are sustained by hope and trust in God and others. We act for the reasons Jesus did when we seek only the good and freedom of others and reconciliation with them, when we do all for the glory of God, when we seek first the Kingdom of God and let go of all else. We become who Jesus is when we have opened our hearts completely to God's love and our lives become a faith-filled response of love and service. Then, and only then, can we say with Paul, "I live now, not I, but Christ lives in me." The Spiritual Exercises of Ignatius offer us a graced way to put on the heart of Christ and become who Christ is and who Christ longs for us to become.

For Reflection

- What kind of person is God calling me to become?
- Which virtues are most important for me at this time in my life?
- How can I more fully put on the heart of Christ and "go and do likewise"?
- As I finish this reflection, what do I ask of God? What are the desires of my heart?

Scripture Readings

Ezekiel 36:26–29 The Renewal of Israel

Jeremiah 29:11–14 A future full of hope

1 Corinthians 3:10–23 I belong to Christ

Philippians 3:7–16 That I may gain Christ and be found
    in him

REFERENCES

References for Chapter 1: The Return to Virtue

1. George Ganss, *The Spiritual Exercises of Saint Ignatius: A Translation and Commentary*. (St. Louis: Institute of Jesuit Sources, 1992) #2. Further references to the Exercises will be given in the text.

2. George Aschenbrenner, *Stretched for Greater Glory*. (Chicago: Loyola Press, 2004) 10.

3. For scholarly and popular commentary on the Spiritual Exercises, see Michael Ivens, *Understanding the Spiritual Exercises*. (Herefordshire, England: Gracewing, 1998); David Fleming, *Like the Lightning*. (Saint Louis: Institute of Jesuit Sources, 2004); George Aschenbrenner, *Stretched for Greater Glory*; John English, *Spiritual Freedom*, 2nd Edition, (Chicago: Loyola Press, 1995).

4. See James Keenan, "Virtue Ethics: Making a Case As It Comes of Age" *Thought*, Vol. 67, No. 265 (June 1992) and Joseph Kotva, *The Christian Case for Virtue Ethics*. (Washington, D.C.: Georgetown University Press, 1996).

5. Richard Gula, *Reason Informed by Faith*. (New York: Paulist Press, 1989) 7.

6. See Kotva, 12.

7. Reflecting on the virtues is not a new idea. Much of the discussion of virtue ethics is rooted in a Neo-Aristotelian ethic and in the writings of Thomas Aquinas, the great Medieval Dominican theologian, about the role of virtues in our moral and spiritual lives.

8. James Keenan, "Virtue Ethics." *Christian Ethics: An Introduction*. ed. Bernard Hoose (London: Cassell, 1998) 84. See Alasdair MacIntyre, *After Virtue* (Notre Dame, Indiana: University of Notre Dame Press, 1981).

9. Keenan, 85.

10. Kotva, 23–25.

11. For more on virtue ethics, see the works by Keenan, Kotva, and McIntyre already cited. Also Daniel Harrington and James Keenan, *Jesus and Virtue Ethics* (Chicago: Lanham, 2002) and William Spohn, "The Return of Virtue Ethics," *Theological Studies*, Vol. 53, March, 1992, 60–75.

12. For a more in-depth presentation of this, see Kotva, Ch. 5. Keenan summarizes Kotva on this topic in Harrington and Keenan, *Jesus and Virtue Ethics*, 67–71.

13. For a fuller development of these ideas, see Gula, *Reason Informed by Faith*, 185–198. In particular, Gula speaks about the perspectives, dispositions, affections, and intentions of one committed to Jesus and then paints a challenging portrait of discipleship.

References for Chapter 2: Reverence

1. George Ganss, *Ignatius of Loyola.* (New York: Paulist, 1991) 393, n. 18.
2. Joseph Tetlow, "The Fundamentum: Creation in the Principle and Foundation," *Studies in the Spirituality of Jesuits*, Vol. 21, No. 4 (September 1989) 49.
3. Tetlow, 2.
4. For a wonderful reflection on God's love for us, see Tony Campbell, *God First Loved Us.* (New York: Paulist Press, 2001).
5. Throughout this section, I will depend heavily on the work of Charles O'Neill on reverence in Ignatius, "Acatamiento: Ignatian Reverence in History and in Contemporary Culture," *Studies in the Spirituality of Jesuits*, Vol. 8, No. 1, (January 1976).
6. Rudolf Otto, *The Idea of the Holy.* trans. John Harvey (New York: Oxford, 1958).
7. William Barry, *Finding God in All Things.* (Notre Dame: Ave Maria Press, 1991) 34–43. Barry offers a number of helpful examples from literature to dramatize this experience.
8. O'Neill, 3.
9. O'Neill, 5.
10. O'Neill, 4.
11. George Aschenbrenner, "Consciousness Examen," *Review for Religious* 21 (January 1972), 14–21. He presents a contemporary understanding of the Ignatian examen of conscience.

References for Chapter 3: Gratitude

1. *A Pilgrim's Journey: The Autobiography of St. Ignatius Loyola.* trans. Joseph Tylenda, SJ (San Francisco: Ignatius Press, 2001) #30.
2. Ganss, *Ignatius of Loyola.* (New York: Paulist, 1991) 176.
3. *Letters of St. Ignatius of Loyola.* trans. William J. Young, SJ (Chicago: Loyola University Press, 1959) 55. This quotation is cited in my article on Ignatian gratitude, "Stirred to Profound Gratitude," *Review for Religious*, March-April 1995, 237–252. The ideas in this section of the chapter are taken from that article. The article gives further references to the works of Ignatius on gratitude.

4. Harvey Egan, SJ, *Ignatius Loyola the Mystic*. (Wilmington: Michael Glazer, 1987) 114.

5. Hugo Rahner, *St. Ignatius Loyola: Letters to Women*. trans. Kathleen Pond and S. A. H. Weerman (New York: Herder and Herder, 1960) 169.

6. Ganss, 232.

7. Citation from Antonio De Nicolas, *Powers of Imagining*. (Albany: State University of New York Press, 1986) 196. *Spiritual Diary* #41.

8. Ignatius, *Letters*, 10.

9. H. Rahner, *St. Ignatius Loyola: Letters to Women*, 170.

10. Keenan, *Virtues for Ordinary Christians*. (Kansas City: Sheed and Ward, 1996) 121–123.

11. See Keenan, *Virtues for Ordinary Christians*, 122.

12. See Charles Shelton, "Gratitude, Moral Emotions and the Moral Life." A monograph adapted from a lecture presented April 15, 2002, at Indiana University, Bloomington, Indiana. Copyright by the Indiana University Foundation. He develops these ideas more fully in "Gratitude: Considerations from a Moral Perspective," *The Psychology of Gratitude*, eds. Robert A. Emmons and Michael E. McCullough (Oxford University Press, 2004). See also, Shelton, "Graced Gratitude," *The Way*, Vol. 42, No. 3 (July 2003). It is beyond the scope of this brief chapter to present Shelton's insightful ideas on rooting gratitude in a moral standard and a notion of the good.

13. Shelton, "Gratitude, Moral Emotions and the Moral Life, 15

14. It is beyond the scope of our reflection here, but it is important to consider the contemporary critique of anthropocentrism in dealing with the issue of stewardship. Ignatius's words that "The other things on the face of the earth are created for human beings . . ." need to be reenvisioned in the light of the larger universe story. For a reflection on the Exercises and ecology, see Neil Vaney, SM, *Christ in a Grain of Sand* (Notre Dame, Indiana: Ave Maria Press, 2004).

15. See Wilkie Au, "Ignatian Service, Gratitude and Love in Action," *Studies in the Spirituality of Jesuits*. Vol. 40, No. 2 (Summer 2008) 4.

References for Chapter 4: Freedom

1. Michael Ivens, *Understanding the Spiritual Exercises*. (Herefordshire, England: Gracewing, 1998) 32.

2. Dean Brackley, *The Call to Discernment in Troubled Times*. (New York: Crossroad, 2004) 12.

3. Cf. Carl Rogers, *On Becoming a Person*. (Boston: Houghton Mifflin Co., 1961) or T. L. Holdstock and C. R. Rogers, "Person-Centered Therapy,"

in R. Corsini, ed., *Current Personality Theories*. (Itasca, Ill.: F. E. Peacock Publishers Inc., 1977) 132. Secondary source: Robert Lundin, *Theories and Systems of Psychology*, 4th Ed. (Lexington, Mass.: D.C. Heath and Company, 1991) 351-356.

References for Chapter 5: Compunction

1. Michael Ivens, *Understanding the* Spiritual Exercises. (Herefordshire, England: Gracewing, 1998) 51.
2. John English, *Spiritual Freedom*, 2nd Edition. (Chicago: Loyola Press, 1995) 77.
3. Richard Gula, *Reason Informed by Faith*. (New York: Paulist, 1989) 92. (His italics).
4. James Keenan, *Moral Wisdom*. (Lanham: Sheed and Ward, 2004) 57.
5. Gula, *Reason Informed by Faith*, 116.
6. Dean Brackley, *The Call to Discernment in Troubled Times*. (New York: Crossroad, 2004) 27.
7. E. Edward Kinerk, "Eliciting Great Desires: Their Place in the Spirituality of the Society of Jesus," *Studies in the Spirituality of Jesuits*, Vol. 16, No. 5, (November 1984).
8. Michael Driscoll, "Compunction" in *New Dictionary of Catholic Spirituality*, ed. Michael Downey (Collegeville, Minn.: Liturgical Press, 1995) 193.
9. Timothy Fry, ed., *The Rule of Saint Benedict*. (New York: Random House, 1998) Ch 20, 29.
10. Fry, Ch. 49, 49.
11. Joan Chittister, *The Rule of Benedict*. (New York: Crossroad, 1992) 90.
12. Ignatius's own frequent experience of tears is documented in his *Spiritual Diary*.
13. Benedicta Ward, trans., *The Prayers and Meditations of St. Anselm*. (Harmondsworth: Penguin Books, 1973) 54.
14. Ward 202. Benedicta Ward highlights this passage in *The Prayers and Meditations of St. Anselm* as an example of the centrality of compunction in his prayer. She says, "This passage is set in a prayer of tears and longing and is indeed the two-edged sword of compunction, piercing with terror and tenderness, fear and delight." 55.
15. Jim Keenan highlights the truth that we may well be bigger sinners than we admit. It is easy to "domesticate" and "trivialize" our sin. See *Moral Wisdom*, 47–65.

References for Chapter 6: Forgiveness

1. Ivens, 44.
2. David Fleming. *Like the Lightning.* (Saint Louis: Institute of Jesuit Sources, 2004) 94. Fleming emphasizes that this encounter with Christ on the cross challenges us to ask ourselves how we understand and image salvation.
3. George Aschenbrenner, *Stretched for Greater Glory.* (Chicago: Loyola Press, 2004) 62.
4. Louis Evely, *That Man Is You.* (Westminster, Maryland: Newman Press, 1964) 92–93.
5. Gula, *The Good Life.* (New York: Paulist Press, 1999) 108.
6. Quoted in John Sheehan, "Love Your Enemies," *America*, November 17, 2003, 10.
7. Gula *The Good Life*, 110.
8. Gula, *The Good Life*, 111.

References for Chapter 7: Generosity

1. Michael Ivens, *Understanding the Spiritual Exercises.* (Herefordshire, England: Gracewing, 1998) 78.
2. William Barry, *Finding God in All Things.* (Notre Dame, Indiana: Ave Maria, 1991) 74.
3. For a fuller discussion of this, see Robert Schmidt, "The Christ-Experience and Relationship in the Spiritual Exercises," *Studies in the Spirituality of Jesuits*, Vol. 6, No. 5, October 1974.
4. Michael Ivens, 75n.
5. David Fleming, *Like the Lightning.* (St. Louis: The Institute of Jesuit Sources, 2004) 109–110.

References for Chapter 8: Faith

1. Michael Ivens, *Understanding the Spiritual Exercises.* (Herefordshire, England: Gracewing, 1998) 89.
2. George Aschenbrenner, *Stretched for Greater Glory*, (Chicago: Loyola Press, 2004) 81.
3. Michael Ivens, *Understanding the Spiritual Exercises.* (Herefordshire, England: Gracewing, 1998) 90.
4. George Aschenbrenner, *Stretched for Greater Glory*, (Chicago: Loyola Press, 2004) 79–80.
5. Avery Dulles, "Faith," *Systematic Theology*, Vol. 1, Francis Fiorenza and John Galvin, eds., (Minneapolis: Fortress, 1991) 107.

6. Ibid., 116.

7. John O'Donnell, "Faith" *The New Dictionary of Theology*, Joseph Komanchak, Mary Collins, and Dermot Lane, eds. (Wilmington: Michael Glazier, 1989) 376.

8. Mary Ann Fatula, "Faith" *The New Dictionary of Catholic Spirituality*, Michael Downey, ed., (Collegeville: Liturgical Press, 1993) 379.

9. Ibid.

10. Translation from *The Christian Faith in the Documents of the Catholic Church*, edited by J. Neuner and J. Dupuis, New York: Alba House, 1982, p. 42.

11. Paul Wadell, "Faith," *The Collegeville Pastoral Dictionary of Biblical Theology.* ed. Carroll Stuhlmuller (Collegeville: Liturgical Press, 1996) 304.

12. Ibid.

References for Chapter 9: Prudence

1. Dean Brackley, *The Call To Discernment in Troubled Times*. (New York: Crossroad, 2004) 78–104.

2. Brackley also draws a contrast between the standards in terms of false humility and "ressentiment" (resentment) versus magnanimity. False humility denies the gifts of God and the work of God within us. It fosters fear and discouragement and self-hatred and a sense of inadequacy that stifles the work of the Spirit. "Ressentiment" leads to a desire for revenge that denigrates the strengths and values and privileges of others. What Christ calls us to is magnanimity that claims an appropriate sense of self-esteem and giftedness and leads to generous action. Brackley emphasizes that the standard of Christ is not about self-rejection or devaluing of self. (109–124)

3. Michael Ivens, *Understanding the Spiritual Exercises*. (Herefordshire, England: Gracewing, 1998) 117.

4. Aschenbrenner, 90.

5. David Lonsdale, *Eyes to See, Ears to Hear*. (Maryknoll, New York: Orbis, 2000) 64. For additional information on Ignatian discernment, see Jules Toner, *A Commentary on St. Ignatius's Rules for Discernment of Spirits*. (St Louis: Institute of Jesuit Sources, 1982); Timothy Gallagher, *The Discernment of Spirits*. (New York: Crossroad, 2005); Timothy Gallagher, *Spiritual Consolation*. (New York: Crossroad. 2007); Wilkie Au and Noreen Cannon Au, *The Discerning Heart*. (New York: Paulist Press, 2006).

6. Ignatius describes the times and methods of making a decision in the *Spiritual Exercises*, Nos. 175–188. For a discussion of these methods, see Ivens, 128–145.

7. George Evans, "Cardinal Virtues," *The New Dictionary of Catholic Spirituality*. (Collegeville: Liturgical Press, 1993) 114.

8. Paul Philibert, "Virtue," *The New Dictionary of Catholic Spirituality*, 1005.

9. James Keenan, "The Virtue of Prudence (IIa IIae, qq.47–56)," in Stephen Pope, ed., *The Ethics of Aquinas*. (Washington, D.C.: Georgetown University Press, 2002) 259–271. Keenan presents a much more complete discussion of the virtue of prudence than can be presented here. See also Jean Porter, *The Recovery of Virtue*. (Louisville, Kentucky: Westminster/John Knox Press, 1990) 155–171 and Josef Pieper, *The Four Cardinal Virtues*. (Notre Dame, Indiana: University of Notre Dame Press, 1966) 3–40.

10. There is an obvious connection between the gift of wisdom and prudence because wisdom perfects the speculative reason in making judgments about truth. Thomas Aquinas, however, suggests that the gift of wisdom relates to the theological virtue of love and that the gift of counsel more properly perfects the virtue of prudence because it is connected to our practical reason. I have chosen, however, to highlight the connection between wisdom and prudence in light of the rich biblical tradition about wisdom.

11. Richard Gula, *Reason Informed by Faith*. (New York: Paulist, 1989) 316

References for Chapter 10: Hospitality

1. William Spohn, *Go and Do Likewise*,(New York: Continuum, 1999) 13.

2. Lucien Richard, *Living in the Hospitality of God*. (New York: Paulist Press, 2000) 41.

3. Henri Nouwen, *Reaching Out*. (New York: Doubleday, 1975) 51.

4. Nouwen, 73.

5. Richard Gula, *Reason Informed by Faith*. (New York: Paulist Press, 1989) 180.

6. Lucien Richard 35. Richard goes on to reflect on hospitality in terms of impoverishment, dispossession, powerlessness, compassion, and service, 44–73.

7. James Keenan, *Virtues for Ordinary Christians*. (Kansas City: Sheed and Ward, 1996) 111.

8. Nouwen, 57.

9. Nouwen, 60.

10. For a brief reflection on spiritual direction as a ministry of hospitality, see Gerald Fagin, SJ, "The Spirituality of the Spiritual Director," *Presence; The Journal of Spiritual Directors International*, Vol. 8, no. 3 (October 2002) 15–16.

11. Nouwen, 68.

References for Chapter 11: Humility

1. George Ganss, *The* Spiritual Exercises *of Saint Ignatius.* (St. Louis: The Institute of Jesuit Sources, 1992) 175, n. 86. (Italics his).

2. Michael Ivens, *Understanding the* Spiritual Exercises. (Herefordshire, England: Gracewing, 1998) 123.

3. Ivens, 123–124.

4. William Shannon, "Humility," *The New Dictionary of Catholic Spirituality.* (Collegeville: Liturgical Press, 1993) 517.

5. Sandra Schneiders, *Written That You May Believe* (New York: Crossroad, 1999). In this section on the washing of the feet, I am using material from my earlier discussion of this action in Barbara Fleischer and Gerald Fagin, "The Sacramentality of Friendship and Its Implications for Ministry," in *A Sacramental Life: A Festschrift Honoring Bernard Cooke* (Marquette University Press, 2003) 231–252.

6. Jerome Neyrey distinguishes between foot washing as transformation and foot washing as ceremony. As a transformational ritual, it initiates Peter and the other disciples into a new, elite status. "Jesus requires Peter to undergo a status transformation ritual to become 'wholly clean' in order to merit a new, elite inheritance or status with Jesus. . . . Peter's foot washing ritual has to do with his transformation into the role of an elite, public witness to Jesus with accompanying risk of death. . . ." Jerome Neyrey, *The Gospel of John.* (Cambridge University Press, 2007) 228.

7. Schneiders, 170.

8. Ibid, 172.

9. Ibid, 172.

10. Ibid, 173.

References for Chapter 12: Fidelity

1. Michael Ivens, *Understanding the* Spiritual Exercises. (Herefordshire, England: Gracewing, 1998) 146.

2. Clearly, Jesus exemplified many other virtues in his agony in the garden. For example, Jerome Neyrey makes a convincing case that in Luke's Gospel Jesus in the garden is portrayed as practicing the virtue of courage. See *The Passion According to Luke.* (New York: Paulist Press, 1985) 54. This is yet another example of how any given meditation in the *Spiritual Exercises* can foster many different virtues.

3. Gula. *The Good Life.* (New York: Paulist Press, 1999) 72.

4. Keenan, *Virtues for Ordinary Christians.* (Kansas City: Sheed and Ward, 1996) 59.

5. Keenan, 63.

References for Chapter 13: Compassion

1. Dietrich Bonhoeffer, *The Cost of Discipleship*. (New York: Macmillan, 1963) 99.
2. Dietrich Bonhoeffer, *Christ the Center*. (New York: Harper and Row, 1978) 35.
3. James Keenan, *The Works of Mercy*. (Lanham: Sheed and Ward, 2005) 2–3.
4. Michael Downey,"Compassion," *The New Dictionary of Catholic Spirituality* (Collegeville: Liturgical Press, 1993) 192.
5. Michael Ivens, *Understanding the* Exercises. (Herefordshire, England: Gracewing,1998) 151.
6. James Keenan, *The Works of Mercy*. (Lanham: Sheed and Ward, 2005) 1–5
7. Keenan, xiii.
8. David Fleming, *Like the Lightning*. (Saint Louis: The Institute of Jesuit Sources, 2004) 119.
9. Fleming, 120.
10. Dean Brackley, *The Call to Discernment in Troubled Times*. (New York: Crossroad, 2004) 173.

References for Chapter 14: Joy

1. Michael Ivens, *Understanding the* Spiritual Exercises. (Herefordshire, England: Gracewing, 1998) 162, n. 3.

References for Chapter 15: Hope

1. J.E. Fallon, "Hope," *New Catholic Encyclopedia* Vol. VII (New York: McGraw-Hill, 1967) 141.
2. Richard Gula, *The Good Life*. (New York: Paulist Press, 1999) 101.
3. James Keenan, *Virtues for Ordinary Christians*. (Kansas City: Sheed and Ward, 1996) 43.
4. Ibid. 45–46.
5. Michael Scanlon, "Hope," *The New Dictionary of Theology*, Joseph Komonchak, Mary Collins, and Dermot Lane, eds. (Wilmington: Michael Glazer, 1989) 497.
6. Monika Hellwig, "Hope," *The New Dictionary of Catholic Spirituality*, Michael Downey, ed. (Collegeville: Liturgical Press, 1993) 511.
7. Hellwig, 513.
8. Hellwig 514.

References for Chapter 16: Love

1. Pope Benedict XVI, "Deus Caritas Est: Encyclical," *Origins* Vol. 35, No. 33, February 2, 2006, 542.
2. James Keenan, *Virtues for Ordinary Christians.* (Kansas City: Sheed and Ward, 1996) 49.

References for the Conclusion

1. George Ganss, *Ignatius of Loyola.* (New York: Paulist Press, 1991) 277.
2. Ibid, 278.
3. *Cons* # 723–35. The authoritative English translation of the Constitutions is: Saint Ignatius of Loyola, *The Constitutions of the Society of Jesus*, translated, with an introduction and a commentary by George Gnass, SJ (St. Louis: The Institute of Jesuit Sources, 1970). Further references to the Constitutions will be given in the text, using the standard paragraph numbers. The book referred to above by Ganss, *Ignatius of Loyola,* gives helpful representative selections from the Constitutions, focusing on paragraphs of a more spiritual nature.
4. In an insightful essay on the *Constitutions of the Society of Jesus,* Janos Lukacs highlights the developmental pattern and design of the Constitutions. He argues that the Constitutions cannot be understood apart from an experience of making the Exercises and that the Constitutions promote a dynamic psycho-spiritual movement toward God similar to the progression toward God found in the Exercises. "The Incarnational Dynamic of the Constitutions," *Studies in the Spirituality of Jesuits*, Vol. 36, No. 4, Winter, 2004.
5. Ganss, *The Constitutions of the Society of Jesus,* 309, n. 1.
6. Ibid.
7. In fact, counting a thirty-day experience of the Exercises in both the novitiate and tertianship and an annual eight-day retreat, a Jesuit who lives fifty years in the Society spends more than fourteen months of his life in retreat, praying for the graces of the Exercises.
8. Cf. Gerald M. Fagin, "The Spiritual Exercises and a Spirituality for the Later Years," *The Way*, Vol. 43, No. 1, January 2004, 67–79.
9. William Spohn, *Go and Do Likewise.* (New York: Continuum, 1999) 4.
10. Richard Gula, *The Good Life.* (New York: Paulist, 1999) 79.
11. See Spohn for an extensive treatment of the perception, dispositions and identity of the disciple, 73–187.

The Color of Justice

Race, Ethnicity, and Crime in America

FIFTH EDITION

SAMUEL WALKER
University of Nebraska at Omaha

CASSIA SPOHN
Arizona State University

MIRIAM DELONE
Fayetteville State University

WADSWORTH
CENGAGE Learning

Australia • Brazil • Japan • Korea • Mexico • Singapore • Spain • United Kingdom • United States

The Color of Justice: Race, Ethnicity, and Crime in America, Fifth Edition

Samuel Walker, Cassia Spohn, Miriam DeLone

Senior Publisher: Linda Schreiber-Ganster

Acquisition Editor: Carolyn Henderson Meier

Editorial Assistant: Virginette Acacio

Media Editor: Andy Yap

Marketing Manager: Marcia Locke

Marketing Coordinator: Sean Foy

Senior Marketing Communication Manager: Heather Baxley

Manufacturing Director: Marcia Locke

Content Project Management: PreMediaGlobal

Art Director: Maria Epes

Print Buyer: Karen Hunt

Rights Acquisitions Specialist Text & Images: Dean Dauphinais

Cover Designer: Riezebos Holzbaur/Tae Hatayama

Cover Photo Credit: Steve Allen

Compositor: PreMediaGlobal

© 2012, 2009, 2007 Wadsworth, Cengage Learning

For product information and technology assistance, contact us at **Cengage Learning Customer & Sales Support, 1-800-354-9706**

For permission to use material from this text or product, submit all requests online at **www.cengage.com/permissions**. Further permissions questions can be emailed to **permissionrequest@cengage.com**.

Library of Congress Control Number: 2011927746

Student Edition:

ISBN-13: 978-1-111-34692-8

ISBN-10: 1-111-34692-5

Wadsworth
20 Davis Drive
Belmont, CA 94002-3098
USA

Cengage Learning is a leading provider of customized learning solutions with office locations around the globe, including Singapore, the United Kingdom, Australia, Mexico, Brazil and Japan. Locate your local office at **www.cengage.com/global**.

Cengage Learning products are represented in Canada by Nelson Education, Ltd.

For your course and learning solutions, visit **www.cengage.com**.

Purchase any of our products at your local college store or at our preferred online store **www.cengagebrain.com**.

Printed in the United States of America
2 3 4 5 6 7 15 14 13 12

Brief Contents

Contents

Preface

Since the fourth edition of **The Color of Justice** was published, issues of race and ethnicity with respect to crime have remained major issues in American political life. Immigration, in particular, has become an even greater controversy than before. Unlike most books on criminal justice, this edition of **The Color of Justice** provides a wealth of information on the fastest-growing minority segment of the American population, the Hispanic and Latino community. The question of racial profiling—for example, police making traffic stops solely on the basis of drivers' race—continues to be a national controversy. Questions of profiling are not confined to traffic stops; they have been raised with regard to national security and immigration enforcement as well. The debate over the death penalty has also entered a new phase in the last few years, with new and disturbing evidence of miscarriages of justice such as innocent people being sentenced to death. Many of the convicted offenders recently exonerated through DNA evidence have been African Americans. Finally, the economic crisis that struck the nation in 2007–2008 has forced state and local criminal justice agencies to make significant reductions in personnel and services. This has made it difficult to maintain basic levels of service—police patrol, probation and parole services, and so on—and these cutbacks often affect people of color most heavily. In short, controversies involving race and ethnicity still pervade the criminal justice system, and new issues are continually arising.

ORGANIZATION

This book is divided into eleven chapters. The organization is designed to guide students through a logical exploration of the subject, beginning with a discussion of the broader social context for race and ethnicity in American society and then moving to the different components of the criminal justice system: police, courts, corrections, the death penalty, and juvenile justice.

NEW TO THIS EDITION

In the fifth edition, we have significantly updated research and included the most current statistics available, particularly regarding Hispanic groups. We have also included material on some of the most important recent developments in the field—racial profiling in the context of homeland security, for instance, as well as hate crime legislation, the disproportionate attention given to crime victims according to race, minority youth victimization rates, the intersection of race and domestic violence, the impact of the financial crisis on the criminal justice system, and much more:

- Chapter 1, "Race, Ethnicity, and Crime," has been revised to reflect changes in the state of racial and ethnic relations in the United States and how those changes relate to the criminal justice system.

- Chapter 2, "Victims and Offenders," includes a reexamination of media depictions of crime victims, especially the race of victims, and also includes expanded discussions of environmental racism, immigration and crime, and additional theoretical perspectives on the causes of criminal violence and hate crime.

- Chapter 3, "Race, Ethnicity, Social Structure, and Crime," features data on the social and economic status of African Americans, Hispanics, and white Americans that has been completely updated, with particular attention paid to the impact of the economic recession and the growing inequalities in America.

- Chapter 4, "Justice on the Street," contains greatly expanded coverage of racial profiling, incorporating new data from studies of traffic enforcement and new perspectives on the nature of the problem and how it can be controlled. Special attention is given to some of the promising innovations regarding police accountability designed to curb police misconduct, and also problem-oriented policing, which show promise of controlling crime, particularly in neighborhoods of color.

- Chapter 5, "The Courts," includes new material reflecting recent research on the relationship between race/ethnicity, pretrial detention and sentencing, as well as a discussion of the treatment of illegal immigrants in federal courts and expanded coverage of the ways in which race and ethnicity influence prosecutorial charging and plea bargaining decisions. It also includes a discussion of the Duke Lacrosse case and the case of the Jenna Six.

- In Chapter 6, "Justice on the Bench," there is expanded coverage of race and ethnicity in the jury selection process, with a focus on the 2010 report by the Equal Justice Initiative that documented disparities in eight southern states. There also is a new section on racial profiling in the courtroom, which examines the use of cultural stereotypes of the Hmong people.

- In Chapter 7, "Race and Sentencing," there are new sections on sentencing illegal immigrants and Asian Americans in federal courts, as well as new material on Devah Pager's work on the "mark of a criminal record" and a discussion of unconscious racial bias among judges. Chapter 7 also includes new research exploring the direct and indirect effects of race and ethnicity on sentencing in state and federal courts.

- Chapter 8, "The Color of Death," features a new section on gendered racism in the use of the death penalty, updated material on Supreme Court decisions that affect the use of capital punishment, and a discussion of the racial justice acts that have been recently enacted. Also in Chapter 8 is a new section focusing on race and the probability of execution.

- Chapter 9, "Corrections in America," has updated information on federal and state incarceration, jail populations, and tribal jails. The chapter also provides updated information for international incarceration rates and prison gangs and presents new research that addresses the role of race in parole board decision making and in post-release hostility.

- Chapter 10, "Minority Youth and Crime," includes a more extensive discussion of explanations for the higher violent victimization rate among racial and ethnic minority youth and new material on racial and ethnic disparities in arrests of juveniles; it also features a new section that discusses the victimization of African American girls.

List of Reviewers:

Gail Beaudoin, University of Massachusetts at Lowell

Brenda Berretta, Middle Tennessee State University

Michele P. Bratina, Indiana University of Pennsylvania

T. D. Coleman, Rochester, South University

Ken Ezell, Fort Valley State University

Angelina Forde, University of Tennessee

Jay Gilliam, University of Illinois Springfield

Lora Lempert, University of Michigan-Dearborn

Faith Lutze, Washington State University

James P. Mayes, North Carolina A&T State University

Kathleen Rettig, Creighton University

Mike Seredycz, University of Wisconsin-Parkside

Susan F. Sharp, University of Oklahoma

Karen Sternheimer, University of Southern California

Quanda Stevenson, The University of Alabama

Rob Tillyer, University of Texas at San Antonio

SUPPLEMENTS

Cengage Learning provides a number of supplements to help instructors use *The Color of Justice: Race, Ethnicity, and Crime in America* in their courses and to aid students in preparing for exams. Supplements are available to qualified adopters. Please consult your local sales representative for details.

For the Instructor

INSTRUCTOR'S RESOURCE MANUAL WITH TEST BANK An improved and completely updated *Instructor's Resource Manual with Test Bank* has been developed by Shannon Portillo at George Mason University. The manual includes learning objectives, detailed chapter outlines, key terms, chapter summaries, discussion questions, student activities and assignments, and Internet resources. Each chapter's test bank contains questions in multiple-choice, true–false, fill-in-the-blank, and essay formats, with a full answer key. The test bank is coded to the chapter objectives that appear in the main text and includes the page numbers in the main text where the answers can be found. Finally, each question in the test bank has been carefully reviewed by experienced criminal justice instructors for quality, accuracy, and content coverage. Our "Instructor Approved" seal, which appears on the front cover, is our assurance that you are working with an assessment and grading resource of the highest caliber.

POWERPOINTS Created by David Makin at Washington State University, these handy Microsoft PowerPoint slides, which outline the chapters of the main text in a classroom-ready presentation, will help you in making your lectures engaging and in reaching your visually oriented students. The presentations are available for download on the password-protected website and can also be obtained by emailing your local Cengage Learning representative.

THE WADSWORTH CRIMINAL JUSTICE VIDEO LIBRARY So many exciting new videos—so many great ways to enrich your lectures and spark discussion of the material in this text. Your Cengage Learning representative will be happy to provide details on our video policy by adoption size. The library includes these selections and many others.

- *ABC® Videos.* ABC videos feature short, high-interest clips from current news events as well as historic raw footage going back 40 years. Perfect for discussion starters or to enrich your lectures and spark interest in the material in the text, these brief videos provide students with a new lens through which to view the past and present, one that will greatly enhance their knowledge and understanding of significant events and open up new dimensions in learning. Clips are drawn from such programs as *World News Tonight, Good Morning America, This Week, PrimeTime Live, 20/20,* and *Nightline,* as well as numerous ABC News specials and material from the Associated Press Television News and British Movietone News collections.

- *Cengage Learning's "Introduction to Criminal Justice Video Series"* features videos supplied by the BBC Motion Gallery. These short, high-interest clips from CBS and BBC news programs—everything from nightly news broadcasts and specials to CBS News Special Reports, CBS Sunday Morning, 60 Minutes, and more—are perfect classroom discussion starters. Designed to enrich your lectures and spark interest in the material in the text, these brief videos provide students with a new lens through which to view the past and present, one that will greatly enhance their knowledge and understanding of significant events and open up new dimensions in learning. Clips are drawn from BBC Motion Gallery.

- *Films for the Humanities.* Choose from nearly 200 videos on a variety of topics such as elder abuse, supermax prisons, suicide and the police officer, the making of an FBI agent, and domestic violence.

CRIMINAL JUSTICE MEDIA LIBRARY

Cengage Learning's Criminal Justice Media Library includes nearly 300 media assets on the topics you cover in your courses. Available to stream from any Web-enabled computer, the Criminal Justice Media Library's assets include such valuable resources as Career Profile Videos featuring interviews with criminal justice professionals from a range of roles and locations, simulations that allow students to step into various roles and practice their decision-making skills, video clips on current topics from ABC® and other sources, animations that illustrate key concepts, interactive learning modules that help students check their knowledge of important topics, and Reality Check exercises that compare expectations and preconceived notions against the real-life thoughts and experiences of criminal justice professionals. The Criminal Justice Media Library can be uploaded and used within many popular Learning Management Systems. You can also customize it with your own course material. You can also purchase an institutional site license. Please contact your Cengage Learning representative for ordering and pricing information.

For the Student

Careers in Criminal Justice Website
Available bundled with this text at no additional charge. Featuring plenty of self-exploration and profiling activities, the interactive Careers in Criminal Justice Website helps students investigate and focus on the criminal justice career choices that are right for them. Includes interest assessment, video testimonials from career professionals, resumé and interview tips, and links for reference.

CL eBook

CL eBook allows students to access Cengage Learning textbooks in an easy-to-use online format. Highlight, take notes, bookmark, search your text, and, in some titles, link directly into multimedia: CL eBook combines the best aspects of paper books and ebooks in one package.

1

Race, Ethnicity, and Crime
American's Continuing Crisis

GOALS OF THE CHAPTER

After you have read this chapter:

1. You will understand the basic goals of the book as a whole.
2. You will have an understanding of how race and ethnicity are central to understanding crime and criminal justice in America.
3. You will be able to discuss recent trends in criminal justice, the current crime situation in America, emerging problems in the criminal justice system, and how all of these factors affect race, ethnicity, and justice.
4. You will be familiar with the difference between race and ethnicity. You will also understand whether or not these are really scientific categories, and how they are used by the U.S. Census Bureau and by criminal justice agencies.
5. You will understand the quality of commonly used criminal justice data (for example, arrests) and whether they provide an accurate picture of what actually happens in the justice system.
6. You will be able to discuss the difference between disparities and discrimination with regard to race and ethnicity.

Race, Ethnicity, and Justice in America

More than 100 years ago, the great African American scholar W. E. B. Du Bois declared, "The problem of the twentieth century is the problem of the color line."[1] Racism and racial discrimination, he argued, were the central problems facing modern society.

Who is "Juanita"?

With respect to race and ethnicity, Who or what am I? Am I white? Black? Latino? How would I know? Is it just what I say I am? Or is it what someone else calls me? Or what label the government places on me? These questions are fundamental to an intelligent discussion of race, ethnicity, and justice in America. We cannot begin to discuss whether or not there are inequalities or whether discrimination exists unless we have accurate data on how people of different races or ethnicities are treated in the justice system.

Many people mistakenly think the answers to these questions are easy. They are not. Consider, for example, the case of "Juanita," as discussed in the report *Donde esta la justicia?* Her father is Puerto Rican and her mother is African American. How would she be classified if she were arrested? In Arizona she would define her own race or ethnicity. In California she would be counted as African American. In Michigan she would be classified as Hispanic and then be assigned to a racial group. In Ohio she would be recorded as biracial.

In short, we have a serious problem. This chapter is designed to help navigate our way through this very complex but very basic issue.

SOURCE: Adapted from Building Blocks for Youth, *Donde esta la justicia?* (East Lansing: Michigan State University, 2002).

Much the same can be said about crime and justice in American society today. Nearly every problem related to criminal justice issues involves matters of race and ethnicity, including arrests, sentencing, corrections, involvement in crime, and public trust and confidence in the criminal justice system. Some examples include:

- In 2009 the incarceration rate for African American males in state and federal prisons was 6.7 times the rate for whites (4,749 versus 708, respectively, per 100,000). The incarceration rate for Hispanic American males was 2.6 times greater than for whites (1,822 per 100,000). There were also disparities in the incarceration of white and African American females, but not as great as for males.[2]

- A 2010 Arizona law directing local police to check the immigration status of anyone they suspected to be undocumented created a national controversy and several lawsuits challenging the law. Critics charged that it would inevitably lead to ethnic profiling against Hispanic and Latino people.

- Rates of rape and sexual assault against Native American women are higher than for either white or African American women. Effective criminal justice responses to crimes against Native Americans, moreover, are complicated by jurisdictional problems arising from the unique legal status of Native American tribes as sovereign nations.[3]

- Racial profiling—the allegation that police officers stop African American drivers or pedestrians because of the color of their skin and not because of actual violations of laws—continues to be a national controversy. The issue was highlighted in 2009 when Cambridge, Massachusetts, police arrested Harvard Professor Henry Louis Gates for disturbing the peace at his home.[4]

- In 2007, 19 percent of American Muslims said they faced discrimination, and 15 percent said they felt Americans viewed Muslims as terrorists.[5]

- Sex trafficking—holding people in bondage for purposes of commercial sex—is an international problem that involves perhaps over 2 million people a year worldwide.[6] In the United States, the principal victims of sex trafficking are immigrants from Asia, Africa, or Eastern Europe; that is, people of all different races and ethnicities who are exploited because of their desperation to come to the United States.

- The Innocence Project has found that among prisoners exonerated by DNA evidence, 70 percent are people of color: 61 percent African American; 30 percent non-Hispanic white; and 1 percent Asian.[7]

Since the mid-1960s, crime has been a central issue in American politics. For many white Americans, the crime issue is an expression of racial fears: fear of victimization by African American offenders and fear of racial integration of neighborhoods. For its 2001 annual report on *The State of Black America*, The National Urban League surveyed 800 African Americans. One question asked, "In general, do you think the criminal justice system in the United States is biased in favor of blacks, is it biased against blacks, or does it generally give blacks fair treatment?" Seventy-four percent of the respondents thought that it is biased against African Americans, whereas only 15 percent thought that the system is fair.[8]

In short, on both sides of the color line, there are suspicion and fear: a sense of injustice on the part of racial minorities and fear of black crime on the part of whites. American society is deeply polarized over the issues of crime, justice, and race. This polarization of attitudes toward crime is especially strong with respect to the death penalty. In 2009, 52 percent of African Americans opposed the death penalty for persons convicted of murder, compared with 27 percent of whites. (In previous polls, Latino Americans fell somewhere in between whites and African Americans).[9]

Fear of crime is higher among people of color for some crimes than it is for whites. In 2009 more African Americans expressed fear of "getting mugged" (an armed robbery) than whites (37 versus 28 percent). This is a legitimate concern, because African Americans are in fact victims of robbery at a higher rate than whites.[10] At the same time, for many whites, crime is a code word for fears of social change, and fears of racial change in particular. A study of community crime control efforts in Chicago, for example, found that neighborhood organizations usually were formed in response to perceived changes in the racial composition of their neighborhoods.[11]

IS DISCRIMINATION JUST A MYTH?

Some critics, however, argue that the criminal justice system is not racist, and that allegations of systematic discrimination are based on myth. One of the most forceful advocates of this position is Heather MacDonald, a fellow at the

Manhattan Institute. She argues that the primary cause of the high rate of incarceration of African Americans is involvement in criminal behavior, not discrimination by the criminal justice system.[12]

MacDonald's argument frames the issues we will examine in this book. What are the facts regarding criminal behavior and the performance of the criminal justice system? Is there systematic discrimination, or not? If discrimination exists but is not systematic, how do we characterize it? What accounts for racial and ethnic disparities in arrest rates and imprisonment rates?

In her article, "Is the Criminal-Justice System Racist?" MacDonald makes the following arguments:

- The homicide rate among African Americans is seven times higher than among white non-Hispanic Americans (and since murder is a crime most likely to result in a prison sentence, that explains part of the imprisonment disparity).

- African Americans represent 56 percent of all robbery arrests (in 2008 it was 52 percent according to the Uniform Crime Reports from the FBI) and about 40 percent of all arrests for violent crime arrests (again, these are crimes most likely to result in a prison sentence).

- Victimization studies have found a parity between the reported race of robbers and offenders committing aggravated assault and the race of arrestees for these crimes (suggesting no discrimination in arrests).

- A 1994 Justice Department study of felony cases found that African Americans arrested for a felony had a lower chance of being prosecuted and a lesser chance of being convicted at trial than whites.[13]

- Statements by some of the leading criminologists (for example, Michael Tonry) that differences in criminal offending by race and ethnicity and not discrimination account for the large racial disparities in prison population.

MacDonald's points are based on solid criminological data, and for that reason must be taken seriously. But are they the last word on the subject? After all, statistics can be interpreted in many different ways. This is not saying that MacDonald has misused them in a dishonest way. One of the main issues we will deal with in this book is that "facts" do not speak for themselves. On all of the most important issues, there are often conflicting data and legitimate differences of opinion among experts about how data should be interpreted.

There are some important issues that MacDonald does not cite that present a very different picture. They include:

- With respect to drugs, arrests of African Americans and Latinos far exceed reported drug usage compared with whites.[14]

- The fact that African Americans arrested for felonies are less likely to be prosecuted and less likely to be convicted at trial may be explained by the fact that they may be arrested on weaker evidence. Some research suggests that the apparent "leniency" in later stages of the system represents decisions that correct for inappropriate arrest decisions.[15]

- The higher rates of offending among African Americans and Latinos can be explained by inequalities in the American social system that are criminogenic: disparities in education, employment, health care, and so on. (We discuss this in detail in Chapter 3.)

- People of color are victimized by violent and property crimes at a higher rate than white Americans. This is partly because they live in neighborhoods where robbers and burglars live, and thus are convenient targets, and also because of the failure of local criminal justice systems to develop effective responses to the problems of drugs, gangs, domestic violence, and other crimes.

The last point raises an issue that is central to this book. As our subtitle indicates, our purpose here is to examine race, ethnicity, *and* crime. We want to take a big picture view, looking at all the factors related to crime. It is a mistake to examine only what happens within the criminal justice system. Chapter 3 is devoted to these very important external social and economic factors.

THE SCOPE OF THIS BOOK

This book offers a comprehensive, critical, and balanced examination of the issues of crime and justice with respect to race and ethnicity. We believe that none of the existing books on the subject is completely adequate.[16]

First, other books do not offer a *comprehensive treatment* of all the issues on crime and the administration of criminal justice. There are many excellent articles and books on particular topics, such as the death penalty or police use of deadly force, but none cover the full range of topics in a complete and critical fashion. As a result, there are often no discussions of whether relatively more discrimination exists at one point in the justice system than at others. For example, is there more discrimination by the police in making arrest decisions than, say, by prosecutors in charging? Harvard University's Christopher Stone points out that our knowledge about most criminal justice issues is "uneven."[17] There are many important questions about which we just do not have good information.

Second, the treatment of race *and* ethnicity in criminal justice textbooks is very weak. They do not identify race and ethnicity as a major issue or clarify the difference between race and ethnicity, and they fail to incorporate important literature on police misconduct, felony sentencing, the employment of racial minorities, and other important topics.[18]

Third, few books or articles discuss all racial and ethnic groups. Most focus entirely on African Americans. Coramae Richey Mann points out that "the available studies focus primarily on African Americans and neglect other racial minorities."[19] Although research on Hispanic Americans has been growing in recent years, there are still major gaps in our knowledge. There is still little good research on Native Americans or Asian Americans. *The Color of Justice* includes material on all groups, along with material on Americans of Middle

Eastern origin, who, in the wake of the terrorist attacks on September 11, 2001, allege that they have been the victims of racial profiling and other forms of discrimination.

An important contribution of this book is to highlight the significant *differences between the experiences of various racial and ethnic groups* with respect to crime and justice. African Americans and Latinos, for example, have different experiences with the police and different attitudes toward their local police departments. The experience of Native Americans is completely different from those two groups.

In this regard, *The Color of Justice* takes a *contextual approach* and emphasizes the unique historical, political, and economic circumstances of each group. Alfredo Mirandé, author of *Gringo Justice*, argues that historically "a double standard of justice" has existed, one for Anglo Americans and one for Chicanos.[20] Marianne O. Nielsen, meanwhile, argues that the subject of Native Americans and criminal justice "cannot be understood without recognizing that it is just one of many interrelated issues that face native peoples today," including "political power, land, economic development, [and] individual despair."[21]

Additionally, this book takes into account the many other contexts that affect crime and justice: regional differences (the southeast versus the rest of the country), urban versus rural; differences in local political cultures that affect the quality of the police, how courts operate, and the use of the death penalty.

Because there has been little comparative research, it is often difficult to make useful comparisons of the experiences of different groups. We do not know, for example, whether Hispanic Americans are treated worse, better, or about the same as African Americans. We have chosen to title this book *The Color of Justice* because it covers *all* people of color.

Fourth, this book keeps up with the *important recent changes* in criminal justice. Just since the last edition, a number of important changes have occurred. These include:

- Congress in 2010 reduced the 100-to-1 disparity in federal sentences for crack versus powder cocaine. Since the federal sentencing guidelines were adopted in 1987, many analysts have argued that the 100-to-1 disparity has had a terribly disparate impact on African Americans.[22]

- New York State in 2009 revised the 1973 Rockefeller Drug Laws, which imposed very severe sentences and had a disparate impact on racial and ethnic minorities.[23]

- The immigration and crime debate has suddenly emerged as a major political issue in America (see the detailed discussion later in this chapter).

- The Mexican drug cartels have surfaced as a major problem, creating a problem of narco-terrorism that has serious effects on the United States as well as Mexico.[24]

- In 2009 the number of prisoners in state prisons declined for the first time in 38 years. A report by the Pew Center on the States found that part of the reason is that several states have adopted policies to reduce the use of imprisonment. Although the motive has been to control costs, the impact on racial and ethnic minority communities is significant.[25]

- In July 2010 Congress passed the Tribal Law and Order Act, which made a number of major changes in the criminal justice systems on Native American reservations. Previous law limited tribal courts to sentencing offenders to no more than one year in prison. The new law raised the limit to three years, letting judges give appropriate sentences to people who have committed serious violent offenses.

Fifth, this book offers *a critical perspective* on the available evidence, something that few other books on the subject do. Data on arrests and sentencing, for example, are extremely complex. Interpreting traffic stop data to determine if there is racial profiling is a major issue among criminologists. There is an important distinction between disparities and discrimination (see the discussion later in this chapter). Other books often gloss over these complexities.

We have already applied a critical analysis to Heather MacDonald's argument that racism in the criminal justice system is a myth. We provide a critical analysis of the other side of the argument as well, examining closely the evidence her critics cite. We do the same with the data offered by both sides in the debate over immigration and crime.

In the end, we disagree with Heather MacDonald's argument that racism in the criminal justice system is a "myth."[26] Our analysis of the data finds that she ignores several important points and selectively interprets some data without presenting alternative explanations. Our view is that abundant evidence on racial and ethnic disparities in the administration of justice can only be explained in terms of biased attitudes and practices.

We also reject Christopher Stone's conclusion, in his report to the President's Initiative on Race, that there is "strong reason for optimism" regarding race, ethnicity, and criminal justice.[27] The authors of this book are not quite so optimistic. There are indeed some areas of progress in the direction of greater equality and fairness in the criminal justice system. The employment of African Americans and Latinos in the justice system has made some real progress. At the same time, however, persistent patterns of racial and ethnic disparities remain. Discrimination appears to be deeply rooted in the application of the death penalty, for example.

Finally, as Darnell F. Hawkins points out, American sociologists and criminologists have done a very poor job of studying the relationship of race, ethnicity, and crime. In particular, there is an absence of solid theoretical work that would provide a comprehensive explanation for this extremely important phenomenon. The main reason for this, Hawkins argues, is that "public discourse about both crime and race in the United States has always been an ideological and political mine field."[28] On the one side, racist theories of biological determinism attribute high rates of crime among racial and ethnic minorities to genetic inferiority. On the other side, the mainstream of American criminology has downplayed racial differences in criminal behavior and emphasized the inadequacy of official crime data. The extreme sensitivity of the subject has tended to discourage rather than stimulate the development of theoretical studies of race, ethnicity, and crime.

OBJECTIVES OF THE BOOK

The Color of Justice has several objectives. First, it presents the best and most recent research on the relevant topics: the patterns of criminal behavior and victimization, police practices, court processing and sentencing, the death penalty, and prisons and other correctional programs.

Second, it offers a critical interpretation of the existing data and addresses the key questions: Is there systematic discrimination in the criminal justice system? Can patterns of discrimination be explained better in terms of contextual discrimination? What does that term mean? If this pattern exists, where do we find it? How serious is it? What are the causes? Have any reforms succeeded in reducing it?

Third, *The Color of Justice* offers a multiracial and multiethnic view of crime and justice issues. The United States is comprised of many different races, ethnic groups, and cultural lifestyles. Unfortunately, most of the research has ignored the rich diversity of contemporary society. There is a great deal of research on African Americans and criminal justice but relatively little on Hispanics, Native Americans, and Asian Americans. In addition, much of the criminal justice research confuses race and ethnicity. This book clarifies the distinction between the two, examining the impact of crime and justice.

Finally, *The Color of Justice* does not attempt to offer a comprehensive theory of the relationship of race, ethnicity, and crime. Although Hawkins makes a persuasive case for the need for such a theory, this book has a more limited objective. It seeks to lay the groundwork for a comprehensive theory by emphasizing the general patterns in the administration of justice with respect to race and ethnicity. We feel that the available evidence permits us to draw some conclusions about that subject. The development of a comprehensive theory will have to be the subject of a future book.

THE COLORS OF AMERICA:
RACIAL AND ETHNIC CATEGORIES

The United States is increasingly a multiracial, multiethnic society. Findings from the 2010 census had not yet been released as this is written (you can probably check them now), but the 2008 estimates are reliable. The American population in 2008 was, by race, 65.4 percent non-Hispanic white, 12.1 percent Black or African American, 1 percent Native American, and 0.3 percent Asian/Pacific Islander. With regard to race, 12.5 percent reported Hispanic ethnicity.[29] These figures represent significant changes from 30 years ago, and demographers are predicting steady changes in the immediate future. As Figure 1.1 indicates, Hispanics are the fastest-growing racial or ethnic group in the United States, increasing from 6.4 percent of the population in 1980 to an estimated 17.8 percent by the year 2020. As we will discuss later in a section called "The Geography of Justice," the racial and ethnic population is unevenly distributed, with important effects on crime and justice.

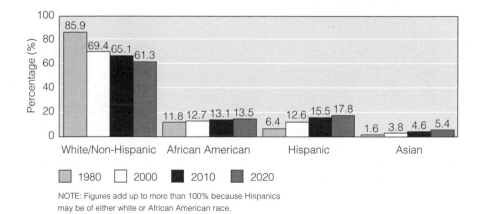

NOTE: Figures add up to more than 100% because Hispanics may be of either white or African American race.

FIGURE 1.1 U.S. Population, 1980–2020 (projected)

SOURCE: U.S. Bureau of the Census. *Interim Projections by Age, Sex, Race, and Hispanic Origin* (Washington, DC: Bureau of the Census, March 2004).

Racial and Ethnic Categories

Race and ethnicity are extremely complex and controversial subjects. The categories the Census Bureau and other government agencies use, and that most people use in everyday conversation, are problematic and do not accurately reflect the reality of American life.

Much of the data we will use in this book is from the U.S. census. It is very important to understand that *the census is based on self-reported identity*. Are you black or white? It depends on what you say you are. Are you Hispanic or not? It depends on your own self-identity. A Pew Center report, "*Who's Hispanic*," explains this issue through a series of questions and answers. For example: "Q. My mom is from Chile and my dad is from Iowa. I was born in Des Moines. Am I Hispanic? A. You are if you say so."[30]

Race Traditionally, race has referred to the "major biological divisions of mankind," which are distinguished by color of skin, color and texture of hair, bodily proportions, and other physical features.[31] The traditional approach identifies three major racial groups: Caucasian, Negroid, and Mongoloid.

Anthropologists and sociologists do not accept the strict biological definition of race. Because of intermarriage and evolution over time, it is virtually impossible to identify exclusive racial categories. Scientists have not been able to determine meaningful differences among people who are referred to as white, black, and Asian. J. Milton Yinger maintains that "we cannot accept the widespread belief that there are a few clearly distinct and nearly immutable races. Change and intermixture are continuous."[32]

Experts regard the concept of race as "primarily a social construct."[33] That is to say, groups define themselves and have labels applied to them by other groups. Usually, the politically and culturally dominant group in any society defines the labels that are applied to other groups. At times, however, subordinate groups assert themselves by developing their own labels. Racial designations have changed over the centuries as a result of changes in both political power and racial attitudes. Yinger argues that the critical categories for social analysis are the "socially visible 'racial' lines, based on beliefs about race and on administrative and political classifications, rather than genetic differences."[34]

A good example of the politics of racial categories is the history of the classification and labeling of African American people in the United States. Historically, the attitudes of whites—and official policy—embodied the racist "drop of blood" theory: anyone with the slightest African ancestry was defined as "black," even when a majority of that person's ancestors were white or Caucasian.[35] Following this approach, many datasets in the past used the categories of "white" and "nonwhite." The federal government today prohibits the use of the "nonwhite" label.[36]

The problem with traditional racial categories is obvious when we look at American society. Many people have mixed ancestry. What, for example, is the "race" of the child whose father is African American and mother is of Irish American heritage? Or the child whose mother is Japanese American and whose father is of European background? Or the child whose mother is Native American and whose father is Hispanic? Many "white" Americans have some ancestors who were African American or Native American. Few African Americans have ancestries that are purely African.

Issues related to classifying multiracial and multiethnic people are not abstract ideas; they have very real, and often cruel, human meaning. An article in the *New Yorker* magazine highlighted the case of Susan Graham of Roswell, Georgia, who complained, "When I received my 1990 census form, I realized that there was no race category for my children." She is white, and her husband is African American. She called the Census Bureau and was finally told that children should take the race of their mother. No rational reason was given about why the race of her husband, the children's father, should be arbitrarily ignored. Then, when she enrolled the children in kindergarten, the school classified them as "black." Thus, she pointed out, "My child has been white on the United States census, black at school, and multiracial at home—all at the same time."[37]

The bureaucratic problems related to classification of people have important human implications. Classification systems label people and inevitably tend to imply that some groups are inferior to others. The Association of MultiEthnic Americans and related groups are particularly concerned about the impact of classifications and labels on children.[38]

The problem of classifying multiethnic and multiracial people has important implications for criminal justice data. What if the National Crime Victimization Survey (NCVS) calls the Graham household? Would their household be classified as "white" or "black"? What if one of their children were the victim of a robbery? Would the victimization survey record that as a "white" or "black" victimization?

Members of the major racial and ethnic groups are divided among themselves about which term they prefer. The National Urban League surveyed 800

Focus on an Issue
The Bell Curve Controversy: Race and IQ

A national storm of controversy erupted in the fall of 1994 over a book titled *The Bell Curve* by Richard J. Herrnstein and Charles Murray.[39] The authors argue that success in life is determined largely by IQ: the smarter people succeed, whereas those with lower intelligence, as measured by standard IQ tests, fail and end up at the bottom of the social scale. The authors contend that those at the low end of the IQ scale do poorly in school and are more likely to be unemployed, receive welfare, and commit crime.

The Bell Curve is now over 15 years old, but we need to examine it because the issue of race and IQ continues to arise, and many stereotypes are an ingrained part of popular folklore. Let us sort our way through the myths and misunderstandings and get at the truth.

The most provocative and controversial parts of Herrnstein and Murray's thesis are the points that intelligence is inherited and that there are significant differences in intelligence between races. The authors cite data indicating that Asian Americans consistently score higher on IQ tests than white European Americans, who, in turn, score higher than African Americans. Herrnstein and Murray are very clear about the policy implications of their argument: because intelligence is mainly inherited, social programs designed to improve the performance of poor children, such as Head Start, are doomed to failure and should be abandoned.

The Bell Curve was attacked by psychologists, anthropologists, and sociologists, among others.[40] Critics disputed the authors' assumptions that there is some entity called "intelligence" that is inherited and that IQ tests are a valid measure of intellectual capacity.

Critics also disputed the authors' handling of the evidence regarding intelligence tests, the impact of environmental factors as opposed to inherited factors, and the effect of programs such as Head Start. There is evidence, for example, that Head Start does improve IQ test scores in addition to children's later success in life.

One point is relevant to the discussion in this chapter. Herrnstein and Murray argue that there are basic, inherited differences in intelligence between races. We reject that argument on the grounds that the vast majority of anthropologists and sociologists do not accept the idea of separate races as distinct biological entities. If there are no scientifically valid racial differences, the basic argument of *The Bell Curve* falls apart.

In response to the long controversy, the American Anthropological Association (AAA) in 1994 issued an official "Statement on 'Race' and Intelligence." (Note in this statement and the one cited in Box 1.1 that the AAA places the word race in quotation marks as a way of indicating that the concept does not have any scientific validity.) The AAA makes the following statement:

> The American Anthropological Association (AAA) is deeply concerned by recent public discussions which imply that intelligence is biologically determined by race. Repeatedly challenged by scientists, nevertheless these ideas continue to be advanced. Such discussions distract public and scholarly attention from and diminish support for the collective challenge to ensure equal opportunities for all people, regardless of ethnicity or phenotypic variation.

Earlier AAA resolutions against racism (1961, 1969, 1971, 1972) have spoken to this concern. The AAA further resolves:

> WHEREAS all human beings are members of one species, Homo sapiens, and

(Continued)

WHEREAS, differentiating species into biologically defined "races" has proven meaningless and unscientific as a way of explaining variation (whether in intelligence or other traits),

THEREFORE, the American Anthropological Association urges the academy, our political leaders and our

communities to affirm, without distraction by mistaken claims of racially determined intelligence, the common stake in assuring equal opportunity, in respecting diversity and in securing a harmonious quality of life for all people.

The full AAA statement is available on the organization's website (http://www.aaanet.org).

B o x 1.1   American Anthropological Association, Statement on "Race," 1998 (excerpt)

In the United States both scholars and the general public have been conditioned to viewing human races as natural and separate divisions within the human species based on visible physical differences. With the vast expansion of scientific knowledge in this century, however, it has become clear that human populations are not unambiguous, clearly demarcated, biologically distinct groups. Evidence from the analysis of genetics (for example, DNA) indicates that most physical variation, about 94%, lies within so called racial groups. Conventional geographic "racial" groupings differ from one another only in about 6% of their genes. This means that there is greater variation within "racial" groups than between them. In neighboring populations there is much overlapping of genes and their phenotypic (physical) expressions.

Throughout history whenever different groups have come into contact, they have interbred. The continued sharing of genetic materials has maintained all of humankind as a single species.

SOURCE: The full statement, along with other materials, can be found on the website of the American Anthropological Association (http://www.aaanet.org).

African American adults, asking them which term they preferred. About half (51 percent) preferred black and 43 percent preferred *African American*.[41] Reports by the Pew Hispanic Center find complex patterns of self-identification among Hispanics. When asked what is the first term they use to identify themselves, slightly more than half use their country of origin (i.e., Mexico, Nicaragua). About one third (34 percent) prefer "Hispanic" and 13 percent prefer Latino.

As these examples suggest, the complex multicultural reality of American society means that the categories used by government agencies such as the Census Bureau are, as one person put it, "illogical."[42]

The U.S. Census Bureau classifies people on the basis of self-identification—that is, your racial or ethnic identity is what you say it is. Many people have protested the requirement of having to choose one or another racial category. The Association of MultiEthnic Americans (AMEA) was established to fight for the right of people with mixed heritage to acknowledge their full identity. AMEA proclaimed "victory" in October 1997 when the Office of Management and Budget (OMB) adopted new federal guidelines allowing people to identify themselves in terms of more than just one race.[43] Most of the data in this book use the racial categories established by the OMB, which are required for use by all federal agencies, including the Census Bureau.

The OMB also revised the names used for many of the racial groups. The new categories are (1) American Indian or Alaska Native; (2) Asian; (3) Black or African American; (4) Hispanic or Latino; (5) Native Hawaiian or Other Pacific Islander; and (6) white. Previously, OMB used only the term *black*; the new category is *Black or African American*. Persons may also identify themselves as Haitian or Negro. Previously, only the term *Hispanic* was used. The new guidelines use *Hispanic or Latino*. The OMB considered, but rejected, a proposal to use *Native American* and retained the old term *American Indian*.

The OMB defines a black or African American person as anyone "having origins in any of the black racial groups of Africa." It defines a white person as anyone "having origins in any of the original peoples of Europe, the Middle East, or North Africa." Accordingly, a person who is from Morocco or Iran is classified as "white," and someone from Nigeria or Tanzania is classified as "black." The category of American Indians includes Alaska Natives and "original peoples of North and South America (including Central America)." Asian includes people from the Far East, Southeast Asia, or the Indian subcontinent. Pacific Islanders are no longer in the same category with Asians and are now included with Native Hawaiians in a separate category.[44]

The OMB concedes that the racial and ethnic categories it created "are not anthropologically or scientifically based." Instead, they represent "a socialpolitical construct." Most important, OMB warns that the categories "should not be interpreted as being primarily biolological or genetic in reference."[45]

Ethnicity   Ethnicity is not the same thing as race. *Ethnicity* refers to differences between groups of people based on cultural customs, such as language, religion, foodways, family patterns, and other characteristics. Among white Americans, for example, there are distinct ethnic groups based primarily on country of origin: Irish Americans, Italian Americans, Polish Americans, and so on. Yinger uses a three-part definition of ethnicity: (1) The group is perceived by others to be different with respect to such factors as language, religion, race, ancestral homeland, and other cultural elements; (2) the group perceives itself to be different with respect to these factors; and (3) members of the group "participate in shared activities built around their (real or mythical) common origin and culture."[46]

The Hispanic or Latino category is extremely complex. First, Hispanic is an ethnic designation, and individuals may belong to any racial category. Thus, some Hispanics identify themselves as white, others consider themselves African American, and some identify as Native Americans. In the past, criminal justice agencies, following the federal guidelines, have classified Hispanics as white but have not also collected data on ethnic identity. As a result, most criminal justice data sets do not provide good longitudinal data on Hispanics.

Second, the Hispanic American population is extremely diverse in several respects. Hispanics are divided among native born Americans and immigrants. Some immigrants are naturalized citizens, others are in the United States as permanent residents or on visas, and some are undocumented immigrants. Hispanics also differ with regard to their country of origin, which includes Mexico, Puerto Rico, Cuba, Central America, South America, and others. All people born in Puerto Rico are automatically U.S. citizens. Although widely used, these categories are not consistent or logical. Mexico and Cuba are countries, whereas Central America and South America are regions consisting of several nations. Mexican Americans are the largest single group within the Hispanic community, making up 58.4 percent of the total in the 2000 census. Puerto Ricans are the second largest (9.6 percent), and Cubans are third (3.2 percent).[47]

(In another curious variation, some demographic studies classify as Hispanic or Latino people whose origins involve 20 Spanish-speaking countries. This excludes Portugal and Brazil, where Portuguese rather than Spanish is spoken. The U.S. census, however, is not affected by this because it relies on self-reported identity; if you are of Brazilian heritage and you say you are Hispanic, you are Hispanic.)[48]

Arab Americans   Arab Americans represent a special case because the community is extremely diverse and does not fit into any of the categories used by the U.S. census. The census records most Arab Americans as "Caucasian," but that label does not adequately describe the diverse community. With respect to the physical indicators that are popularly used to define "race," such as skin color or hair texture, Arab Americans are as diverse as are "white" and "black" Americans. The term Arab Americans is, in fact, a social construct that includes people of many different national origins, religions, and ethnicities.[49]

Many people assume that Arab Americans are religiously all Muslim, but this is not true. Arab Americans are Muslim, Christian, Druze, and other religions. Even Christian Arabs are divided among Protestant, Catholic, and Greek Orthodox. In terms of national origins, Arab Americans trace their heritage to Lebanon, Syria, Iraq, Kuwait, Morocco, Algeria, and many other countries. (Many people assume that Turkish people are Arabs. In fact, Turkish is a national identity, referring to people who are citizens of Turkey, and they consist of several different ethnic identities.) Because of this, most Arabs are classified as white or Caucasian by the U.S. census. Finally, with regard to ethnicity, Arab Americans may be Kurds, Berbers, Armenian, Bedu, or members of other groups.

We do not know exactly how many Muslims there are in the United States because the census does not collect data on religious affiliation. (There are private surveys and estimates, however.) Estimates of the total number range from 1.3 million (the American Religious Identification Survey) to 7 million (the Council on American-Islamic Relations). About 25 percent of all Muslims in the United States are converts, most of whom are African Americans. Malcolm X is probably the most famous person to have fallen in this category. Religious services are sometimes given in several languages: Urdu, Arabic, or English.

"Minority Groups" as a Label   The term *minorities* is widely used as a label for people of color. The United Nations defines minority groups as "those nondominant groups in a population which possess and wish to preserve stable ethnic, religious or linguistic traditions or characteristics markedly different from those of the rest of the population." The noted sociologist Louis Wirth adds the element of discrimination to this definition: minorities are those who "are singled out from the others in the society in which they live for differential and unequal treatment, and who therefore regard themselves as objects of collective discrimination."[50]

Use of the term *minority* is increasingly criticized. Among other things, it has a pejorative connotation, suggesting "less than" something else, which in this context means less than some other groups. The new OMB guidelines for the Census Bureau and other federal agencies specifically "do *not* identify or designate certain population groups as 'minority groups.'"[51] Many people today prefer to use the term *people of color.*

Some American cities are now majority African American or Latino. The Miami-Dade County metropolitan area in 2009, for example, was 62.5 percent Hispanic, 20 percent African American, and 18 percent white non-Hispanic. Los Angeles in 2009 was almost 50 percent Hispanic. As a result, in a number of cities more than half of the police officers are African Americans or Latino, non-Hispanic white being a minority. In these situations, which group is the "majority" and which is the "minority"? From a national perspective, you get one answer. A local perspective gives you a different one.

Diversity within Racial and Ethnic Groups   Another important complicating factor is the diversity that exists within racial and ethnic groups. As our previous discussion indicates, both the Latino and the Arab American communities include people of very different national origins. The African American community, meanwhile, consists of people whose families have been in the United States for hundreds of years and recent immigrants from Africa. Some recent immigrants from Africa, for example, do not wish to be labeled African Americans because they consider themselves strictly African.

The Hispanic community is extremely diverse. It includes native born Americans and immigrants. Among the native born, some families have been in the United States for many generations, whereas others are first-generation Americans. Immigrants include both legal and unauthorized or undocumented persons. Some immigrants speak English fluently, others speak only their native language, and many are bilingual.

The Native American community is divided among 562 tribal governments recognized by the Bureau of Indian Affairs (which does not necessarily include all tribes), some of which have very different languages, cultural traditions, and tribal political institutions. The Cherokee tribe is the largest, with 302,569 members according to the 2000 census. The second largest is the Navajo tribe, with 276,775 members. One third (34 percent) of Native Americans live on reservations or designated areas.[52] Each racial and ethnic group, meanwhile, is divided by social class, with both wealthy and poor members. Social class has a major impact on peoples' experiences with the criminal justice system.

The census category of Asian, Native Hawaiian, and Pacific Islanders includes many diverse groups. For example, Asian Americans include many people of Chinese or Japanese origin whose families have been in the United States for generations, and also many very recent immigrants. The economic status of these different groups is often very different. Many Native Hawaiians, meanwhile, are also well established economically, socially, and politically. Bureau of Justice Statistics (BJS) data on crime victimization, however, collapse these very different people into a single category. The National Council on Crime and Delinquency, however, argues that it is important, where possible, to disaggregate the Asian American population into its different components because some may have greater involvement with the justice system than the group as a whole.[53]

Diversity has many impacts. A Vera Institute of Justice study of police relations with immigrant communities in New York City concluded that "immigrant groups are not monolithic, [but] are made up of ethnically, culturally, socio-economically, and often linguistically diverse subgroups...." This has important implications for criminal justice agencies. The Vera Institute report advised that police departments must "reach out to a variety of community representatives," even within one racial or ethnic group.[54]

One reason criminal justice agencies need to reach out to immigrant groups is that recent arrivals to the United States do not necessarily understand our legal system. A number of scholars have noted that they do not share the "legal consciousness" that long-time American residents have.[55] This legal consciousness includes a sense of "inherent rights" and entitlements regarding the legal system. In practice, this includes a sense of your right to call the police if you have a problem, a right to be treated respectfully by the police and other officials, and a right to file a complaint if you are not treated properly.

The Politics of Racial and Ethnic Labels

There has always been great controversy over what term should be used to designate different racial and ethnic groups. The term *African American*, for example, is relatively new and became widely used only in the 1980s. It has begun to replace *black* as the preferred designation, which replaced *Negro* in the 1960s. *Negro*, in turn, replaced *colored* about 25 years earlier. The leading African American civil rights organization is the National Association for the Advancement of Colored People (NAACP), founded in 1909. Ironically, *colored* replaced *African* much earlier. In some respects, then, we have come full circle in the past 150 years. As John Hope Franklin, the distinguished African American historian and former chair of President Clinton's Initiative on Race, points out in his classic history of African Americans, *From Slavery to Freedom*, the subjects of his book have been referred to by "three distinct names ... even during the lifetime of this book."[56]

What label do African Americans prefer? A 2007 Gallup Poll found that 24 percent prefer African American, 13 percent prefer black, and 61 percent say it does not matter.[57]

The controversy over the proper label is *political* in the sense that it often involves a power struggle between different racial and ethnic groups. It is not just a matter of which label but who chooses that label. Wolf argues that "the function of racial categories within industrial capitalism is exclusionary."[58] The power to control one's own label represents an important element of police power and autonomy. Having to accept a label placed on you by another group is an indication of powerlessness.

The term *black* emerged as the preferred designation in the late 1960s as part of an assertion of pride in blackness and quest for power by African Americans themselves. The African American community was making a political statement to the majority white community: "This is how we choose to describe ourselves." In a similar fashion, the term *African American* emerged in the 1980s through a process of self-designation on the part of the African American community. In this book, we use the term *African American*. It emerged as the preferred term by spokespeople for the African American community and was adopted by the OMB for the 2000 census and continued for 2010 (and can be used along with *black*, *Negro*, and *Haitian*). It is also consistent with terms commonly used for other groups. We routinely refer to Irish Americans, Polish Americans, and Chinese Americans, for instance, using the country of origin as the primary descriptor.

It makes sense, therefore, to designate people whose place of origin is Africa as African Americans. The term *black* refers to a color, which is an imprecise descriptor for a group of people whose members range in skin color from a very light yellow to a very dark black.

A similar controversy exists over the proper term for Hispanic Americans (see Box 1.2). Not everyone, including some leaders of the community itself, prefers this term. Some prefer *Latino*, and others use *Chicano*. As we previously noted, a majority of Hispanics refer to themselves by their country of origin, but about one third use the term *Hispanic* and the remainder prefer *Latino*.[59] A 2005

B o x   1.2   Donde está la justicia?

The term *Hispanic* has been used to refer to people of Spanish descent. The term refers, in part, to people with ties to nations where Spanish is the official language. The U.S. government and legal system historically have insisted on categorizing all Spanish-speaking people as Hispanic and treating them as a monolithic group, regardless of cultural differences.

The term *Latino*, however, generally refers to people with ties to the nations of Latin America and the Caribbean, including some nations where Spanish is not spoken such as Brazil. It also encompasses people born in the United States whose families immigrated to this country from Latin America in the recent past and those whose ancestors immigrated generations ago. Like the term Hispanic, the categorization Latino is a general one that does not recognize the diversity of ethnic subgroups (for example, Puerto Rican, Dominican, Guatemalan, Peruvian, and Mexican).

SOURCE: Adapted from Francisco A. Villarruel and Nancy E. Walker, *Donde está la justicia? A Call to Action on Behalf of Latino and Latina Youth in the U.S. Justice System* (East Lansing, MI: Institute for Youth, Children, and Families, 2002).

Pew Hispanic Center survey found that 36 percent prefer the term Hispanic, 21 percent prefer Latino, and the others have no preference.[60] Many Anglo Americans incorrectly refer to Hispanics as Mexican Americans, ignoring the many people who have a different country of origin. The OMB accepted the term *Latino*, and both the 2000 and 2010 censuses uses the category of Hispanic or Latino. In this book we use the term *Hispanic*. It is more comprehensive than other terms and includes all of the different countries of origin.

We use the term *Native Americans* to designate those people who have historically been referred to as American Indians. The term *Indians*, after all, originated through a misunderstanding, as the first European explorers of the Americas mistakenly thought they had landed in Asia.

The term *Anglo* is widely used as a term for white Americans, but it is not an accurate descriptor. Only a minority of white Americans trace their ancestry back to the British Isles, to which the term Anglo refers. The often-used pejorative term WASP (white, Anglo-Saxon, Protestant) is also inaccurate because many white Americans are Catholic, Jewish, or members of some other religious group, and are not Anglo-Saxon.

In short, the term *white* is as inaccurate as *black*. People who are commonly referred to as white have a wide range of skin colors, from very pale white to a dark olive or brown. The term *Caucasian* may actually be more accurate.

The Quality of Criminal Justice Data on Race and Ethnicity

Serious analysis of the racial and ethnic dimensions of crime and justice requires good data. Unfortunately, the data reported by criminal justice agencies are not always reliable. The first problem is that on many important subjects there are no data at all on race or ethnicity. The majority of the published research to date involves African Americans. Although there are important gaps and much remains to be done, we do have a reasonably good sense of how African Americans fare at the hands of the police, prosecutors, judges, and correctional officials. Hispanic Americans, however, have until very recently been neglected. Even less research is available on Native Americans and Asian Americans. Consequently, we will not be able to discuss many important subjects in detail in this book (for example, the patterns of police arrest of Hispanics compared with those of whites and African Americans).

A second problem involves the quality of the data. Criminal justice agencies do not always use the same racial and ethnic categories. The problem is particularly acute with respect to Hispanic Americans. Many criminal justice agencies collect data only on race and use the census categories of white and black, counting Hispanics as whites. This approach, however, masks potentially significant differences between Hispanics and non-Hispanic whites. This has important implications for analyzing the nature and extent of disparities in the criminal justice system. If we assume that Hispanics are arrested at a higher rate than non-Hispanic whites (a report finds that Hispanic drivers are arrested by the police at a much higher rate than whites),[61] the available data not only eliminate Hispanics as a separate group but also raise the overall non-Hispanic arrest rate.

Some data systems use the categories of "white" and "nonwhite." This approach incorrectly treats all people of color as members of the same race. As noted earlier, the OMB prohibits government agencies from using the term *nonwhite*.

Classifying Hispanics and non-Hispanic whites as "white" has a major impact on official data and the picture that is presented of the criminal justice system. Holman analyzed how using a "white/black" classification system results in an overcount of non-Hispanic whites in prison and an undercount of Hispanics. In 2009, 57.2 percent of all federal prisoners were "white." But 32 percent were Hispanic, meaning that only about 25 percent were non-Hispanic whites (39 percent were African American), so if you only used the "white" category you would give a misleading picture of federal prisoners. In New Mexico, the misrepresentation was even worse. Official data indicated that 83 percent of prisoners were white, when in fact only 28.9 percent were non-Hispanic white and 54.1 percent were Hispanic.[62]

The National Council on Crime and Delinquency argues that classifying Hispanics as white has the effect of "inflating White rates [for example, for arrest] and deflating African American rates in comparison."[63] For example, the data on adults on death row in 2008 indicate that 56 percent were "white" and 42 percent African American. But since the "white" category includes Hispanics, it simultaneously ignores them altogether as a distinct group while overstating the presence of non-Hispanic whites on death row.[64]

In short, be on guard whenever you see data on "white" and "black" or "nonwhite" people in the justice system. These data do not accurately reflect the reality of crime and justice in America.

The Uniform Crime Reports (UCR) data from the Federal Bureau of Investigation (FBI) are useless with respect to many important issues related to race, ethnicity, and crime. First, the data used to create the Crime Index, "crimes known to police," do not include data on race and therefore do not tell us anything about victimization by race. Second, the FBI data on arrests use the categories of white, black, American Indian or Alaska Native, and Asian or Pacific Islander. There is still no separate category for Hispanics. Fortunately, the NCVS does collect data on Hispanics and non-Hispanics, and it is a rich source of data on this issue. The BJS National Prisoner Statistics program also reports data on white, black, and Hispanic prisoners.

With respect to Native Americans, Gary LaFree points out that they "fall under the jurisdiction of a complex combination of native and nonnative legal entities" that render the arrest data "problematic."[65] Zoann K. Snyder-Joy characterizes the Native American justice system as "a jurisdictional maze" in which jurisdiction over various criminal acts is divided among federal, state, and tribal governments.[66] It is not clear, for example, that all tribal police agencies report arrest data to the FBI's UCR system. Thus, Native American arrests are probably significantly undercounted.

An additional problem is that the FBI has changed the categories for Asian Americans over the years, making longitudinal analysis impossible.

The appendices in the *Sourcebook of Criminal Justice Statistics* reveal a serious lack of consistency in the use of the Hispanic designation among criminal justice agencies.[67] In the National Corrections Reporting Program, for example, Colorado, Illinois, Minnesota, New York, Oklahoma, and Texas record Hispanic prison inmates as "unknown" race. Ohio records Native Americans and Asian Americans as "unknown" race. California, Michigan, and Oklahoma classify only Mexican Americans as Hispanic, apparently classifying people from Puerto Rico, Cuba, and South America, for example, as non-Hispanic.

In addition, the criminal justice officials responsible for classifying persons may be poorly trained and may rely on their own stereotypes about race and ethnicity. The race of a person arrested is determined by what the arresting officer puts on the original arrest report. In the Justice Department's Juvenile Court Statistics, race is "determined by the youth or by court personnel." We are not entirely sure that all of these personnel designate people accurately.

In short, the official data reported by criminal justice agencies are very problematic, which creates tremendous difficulties when we try to assess the fate of different groups at the hands of the criminal justice system. The disparities that we know to exist today could be greater or smaller, depending on how people have been classified. We will need to be sensitive to these data problems as we discuss the various aspects of the criminal justice system in the chapters ahead.

The Crime and Immigration Controversy

Immigration emerged as a major national controversy in 2010 when Arizona passed a new law requiring state and local police to inquire into immigration status. The controversy touches several separate issues relating to crime, immigration, and unauthorized immigration: Do immigrants contribute to high rates of crime? Do unauthorized immigrants in particular contribute to high crime rates? Who should be responsible for immigration enforcement? Only federal authorities, or local police as well? Will this law lead to racial profiling?

It is important to examine these issues in detail in Chapter 1 because they relate directly to issues we will cover throughout the book, for example the social and economic status of groups and the impact on criminal behavior, how public attitudes about different groups affect criminal justice policy, the long history of police–community relations problems, and the impact of specific crime-fighting policies on policing and the criminal justice system.

The Arizona Law   Arizona Bill 1070 directs state and local law enforcement officers to enforce federal immigration laws. Immigration is clearly a federal responsibility. Whether state and local officers also have the authority to enforce them is an issue still to be resolved in the courts. (The legal question involves "preemption," whether federal law completely preempts state law on any issue.) The most controversial portions of the Arizona law are: (1) that officers are directed to make a reasonable attempt" to determine someone's immigration status "where reasonable suspicion exists that the person is an alien who is unlawfully present in the United States"; and (2) that the police must determine the immigration status of any person arrested "before the person is released."

Sorting Out the Issues on Immigration, Unauthorized Immigration, and Crime

The Number of Immigrants   As we will do with other controversial issues in this book, we begin with some basic facts about immigration, undocumented or unauthorized immigrants, and immigrants and crime. In 2008 there were 40,000,000 foreign-born people in the United States. This included 28,000,000 legal immigrants (half of whom were naturalized citizens) and an estimated 12,000,000 unauthorized immigrants. Of the unauthorized immigrants, 7,000,000 million (or 60 percent) were from Mexico, and another 1,300,000 million from Central America. There were also 1,300,000 unauthorized immigrants from Asia, 525,000 from Europe or Canada, and 190,000 from the Middle East.[68]

Public Attitudes about Immigration   Public opinion polls consistently indicate that Americans are very concerned about illegal immigration. A CBS News poll in May 2010 found that 56 percent of Americans thought illegal immigration was a "very serious" problem and 28 percent thought it was "somewhat serious," for a total of 84 percent. Other polls have found similar results. Americans do not, however, think illegal immigrants are responsible for an increase in crime. A May 2010 Fox News poll found that only 6 percent regarded crime as their "biggest concern" regarding illegal immigration. Far more important were "overburdening the government" (44 percent) and "taking jobs from citizens" (19 percent).[69]

Immigration and Crime   Although public opinion polls indicate that Americans do not associate unauthorized immigrants with crime, many politicians have made it an issue. What are the facts on this subject? The evidence suggests that immigrants, both legal and unauthorized, are not responsible for higher levels of crime.

Graham C. Ousey and Charis E. Kubrin examined violent crime trends in cities with populations greater than 100,000 (n = ___) between 1980 and 2000. They found that immigration negatively affected crime; cities that experienced increases in immigration also experienced decreases in crime. It should be

---

B o x 1.3   A Note on "Generations"

There is a lot of confusion over the proper terms for different "generations" of Americans. Someone who immigrates to the United States is a "first generation" American. His or her children are "second generation." A separate issue involves citizenship. A "second generation" person would be a "first generation citizen," unless of course his or her parents became naturalized, in which case the parents would be "first generation citizens." There is no such thing as a "second generation immigrant"; only one generation can immigrate.[70]

noted that the time period included a time of rising violent crime rates (1980s) and sharply falling crime rates (1993–2000). Tim Wadsworth also found that between 1999 and 2000, cities that experienced the largest increases in immigration (of all types) had the largest decreases in homicide and robbery in the same time period. His study involved FBI UCR data for 459 cities with populations greater than 50,000 people. The period studied included the years of the great "crime drop," when serious crime experienced a tremendous decline. And although victims generally report only 40 percent of crimes (47 percent of personal crimes and 37 percent of property crimes in 2007), criminologists argue that all but a few homicides are discovered by the police.[71]

How do we explain the negative impact of immigration on crime? Ousey and Kubrin offer an interesting interpretation. Immigrant families have lower rates of divorce and single parent households. Criminologists have long established that both of those factors are associated with higher rates of delinquency and crime. The 2009 Pew Hispanic Center on young Hispanics, *Between Two Worlds*, found that immigrant Hispanics were less likely to be involved in a gang, or know someone who is, than American-born Hispanics. Young Hispanics are more likely to be incarcerated than young non-Hispanic whites, but only half as likely to be incarcerated than young African Americans.[72]

Impact of the Arizona Law on Policing I: Profiling?   The major criticism of the Arizona law is that it will lead to racial profiling. If officers are required to check on the immigration status of people they stop (for whatever reason), what basis will they use to form a "reasonable suspicion" that the person may be an unauthorized immigrant? Critics argue that it will inevitably be skin color and/or English language capacity. There are many people in this country legally who "look" Hispanic and who either do not speak English or have a Spanish accent. At the same time, it is very unlikely that officers will develop "reasonable suspicion" about Anglo non-Hispanic people. The result, critics charge, will be racial—or in this case ethnic—profiling.

Another controversial feature of the law is that when a person is detained because of suspicion about immigration status, the police cannot release that person until his or her immigration status has been determined. This process could take hours or longer. The result is that many legal residents of the United States will be deprived of their liberty for no reason other than suspicion about their immigration status.

In the Media
Updates on the Immigration Enforcement Controversy

How has the media handled the ongoing controversy over immigration and crime? Do recent news stories cite criminological research on immigrants and crime? How have the courts ruled on the Arizona law?

If there is any evidence of actual racial profiling related to immigrants, do news stories reflect that? Who do they quote in their stories? Do they quote leading criminologists?

Impact of the Law on Policing II: Police-Community Relations   Many police chiefs and law enforcement organizations oppose the Arizona law because it will adversely affect police–community relations and undermine community policing. Tensions between the police and communities of color have been a long-standing problem in policing.

In 2008 the Police Chiefs Executive Research Forum (PERF), a professional association of chiefs and top managers, issued a policy statement opposing immigration by local law enforcement.[73] Several chiefs pointed out that immigrants, both legal and unauthorized, are victims of crime. They are more likely to be paid in cash, which makes them easy prey for robbers, and because they fear being questioned about their immigration status, they are very reluctant to call the police and report the crime. Also, many immigrants are victims of domestic violence but do not call the police because they are afraid that they or other family or friends will be subject to immigration enforcement. Many immigrants are witnesses of crime but are reluctant to come forward to help the police. For all these reasons, the Police Foundation in 2009 concluded that local agencies "should employ community-policing and problem-solving tactics to improve relations with immigrant communities and resolve tension caused by expanding immigration."[74]

Police chiefs are also concerned that giving officers responsibility for immigration enforcement will strain their resources and make it difficult to perform their basic responsibilities. This problem has become worse in the economic recession of 2008–2010, when police departments have been unable to hire to replace retiring officers, and in some cases have been forced to lay off officers. Local jails, moreover, often do not have the space to hold large numbers of unauthorized immigrants. (Remember, there are 12 million unauthorized immigrants across the country.) Local courts are also overburdened with cases, and they are facing cutbacks because of the recession. In Iowa, state courts were closed one day a week as a cost-saving measure. In short, many police chiefs fear that immigration enforcement could harm their traditional law enforcement mission. In 2009 the Police Foundation, after an extensive review, concluded that the various costs of participating in federal immigration enforcement "outweigh the benefits."[75]

Enforcement under the 287(g) Program   In fact, some local law enforcement agencies already engage in immigration enforcement. Under Section 287(g) of the 1996 immigration reform act, local police and sheriffs can establish written agreements with the federal Immigration Control and Enforcement (ICE) agency. The agreement specifies that local officers are trained in immigration enforcement and then authorized to cooperate with federal officials under their direction. Local offices are then authorized to question people about their immigration status, arrest suspects without a warrant for suspected immigration violations, and five other actions. A 2008 PERF report found that only 4 percent of local agencies had signed such an agreement, however.

One underlying issue is that violating federal immigration law is a civil and not a criminal offense. That is, you can be deported for violating the law but you cannot be sentenced to prison. Some states have a rule that local police cannot enter into 287(g) agreements because officers in the state do not have authority to enforce federal civil laws.

The Children of Unauthorized Immigrants   Under the U.S. Constitution, a person born in this country is automatically a U.S. citizen. Some opponents of illegal immigration charge that at least some immigrants come to the United States specifically to deliver a baby, and thereby have a child who is a U.S. citizen. As a result, they want to revise the Fourteenth Amendment to the Constitution to disallow citizenship to the children of illegal immigrants. That would require going through the entire process for amending the Constitution. Opponents of this idea reply that it would stop the historic U.S. policy of welcoming people to this country.

What are the facts surrounding this intense controversy? The U.S. Census estimates in 2008 that of the 4,300,000 babies born in the United States, 340,000 were born to undocumented immigrants (or approximately 8 percent of all babies).[76] This statistic alone illustrates only part of the story, however. First, not all of these babies are born to Hispanic parents. As already noted, 60 percent of illegal immigrants are from Mexico, with another 18 percent from Central and South America, but the remaining 22 percent are from other regions. Second, there is no persuasive evidence (e.g., social science research, in-depth investigative journalism) that any immigrants come to the United States specifically to deliver a baby. The allegation that they do is simply speculation. Third, there is no data on how long undocumented immigrants on average have been in the United States when their first child is born. The fact that many have been in the United States for some time refutes the allegation that they came to the United States specifically to have a child.

THE GEOGRAPHY OF RACIAL
AND ETHNIC JUSTICE

Because of two factors, the "geography of justice" in the United States varies across the country. First, the primary responsibility for criminal justice lies with city, county, and state governments. The federal government actually plays a very small role in the total picture of criminal justice. Second, the major racial and ethnic groups are not evenly distributed across the country. The population of California in 2008 was estimated to be 36 percent Hispanic, compared with 4 percent for Iowa. Mississippi was 37 percent African American, compared with 4.5 percent for Minnesota. Atlanta was 57 percent African American compared with 8 percent for Seattle. As a result, issues of race and ethnicity are far more salient in some areas compared with others.

Although the United States as a whole is becoming more diverse, most of this diversity is concentrated in a few regions and metropolitan areas. One study concluded that "most communities lack true racial and ethnic diversity."[77] In 1996 only 745 of the 3,142 counties or county equivalents had a white population that was below the national average. Only 21 metropolitan areas qualified as true "melting pots" (with the percentage of the white population below the national average and at least two minority groups with a greater percentage than the national average).

The distribution of the Hispanic population is even more complex. More than half (51 percent) live in just two states, Texas and California. About 83 percent of these people are Mexican Americans. Puerto Rican Americans, the second largest Hispanic group in the United States, are concentrated on the East Coast, with almost 41 percent living in New York and New Jersey. In New York City, Puerto Ricans are the largest Hispanic national origins group (789,172 people in 2000, out of a total of 8,000,000 Hispanics), and Dominicans are second, with 406,806 people. People from Mexico are a small part of the New York City population, being only 186,872 people. About 67 percent of all Cuban Americans live in Florida. Native Americans are also heavily concentrated. Just less than half (45 percent) live in four states: Oklahoma, Arizona, New Mexico, and California.[78]

The uneven distribution of the major racial and ethnic groups is extremely important for criminal justice. Crime is primarily the responsibility of state and local governments. Thus, racial and ethnic issues are especially salient in those cities where racial minorities are heavily concentrated. For example, the context of policing is very different in Detroit, which is 82 percent African American, than in Minneapolis, where African Americans are only 18 percent of the population. Similarly, Hispanic issues are far more significant in San Antonio, which is 59 percent Hispanic, than in many other cities where few Hispanics live.[79]

These disparities illustrate the point we made earlier that in some areas the traditional "minority" has become the majority. This has important implications for criminal justice. Population concentration translates into political power and the ability to control agencies. Mayors, for example, appoint police chiefs. If a county is a majority African American or Hispanic, those groups are able to control the election of the sheriff. African Americans have served as mayors of most of the major cities: New York; Los Angeles; Chicago; Philadelphia; Detroit; Atlanta; Washington, DC; and others. David Dinkins was elected the first African American mayor of New York City in 1990. There have also been African American police chiefs or commissioners in each of these cities.

The concentration of African Americans in the Southeast has at least two important effects. This concentration gives this group a certain degree of political power that translates into elected African American sheriffs and mayors. These officials, in turn, may appoint African American police chiefs. For instance, by 2002 Mississippi had 950 elected African American officials, more than any other state, including several elected sheriffs. In 2008 Texas led the nation with 2,245 elected Hispanic officials.[80]

DISPARITY VERSUS DISCRIMINATION

Perhaps the most important question with respect to race and ethnicity is whether there is discrimination in the criminal justice system. Many people argue that it is pervasive, whereas others believe that intentional discrimination does not exist. Mann presents "a minority perspective" on the administration of justice, emphasizing discrimination against people of color.[81] MacDonald, as we discussed earlier, argues that the idea of systematic racism in the criminal justice system is a "myth."[82]

Debates over racial and ethnic discrimination in the criminal justice system are often muddled and unproductive because of confusion over the meaning of "discrimination." It is, therefore, important to make two important distinctions. First, there is a significant difference between disparity and discrimination. Second, discrimination can take different forms and involve different degrees of seriousness. Box 1.4 offers a schematic diagram of the various forms of discrimination, ranging from total, systematic discrimination to pure justice.

Disparity refers to a difference but one that does not necessarily involve discrimination. Look around your classroom. If you are in a conventional college program, almost all of the students will be relatively young (between the ages of 18 and 25). This represents a disparity in age compared with the general population. There are no children, few middle-aged people, and probably no elderly students. (This will be less true at educational institutions that cater to adults pursuing continuing professional development. They will necessarily have an older student body.) This is not a result of discrimination, however. These older groups are not enrolled in the class mainly because the typical life course

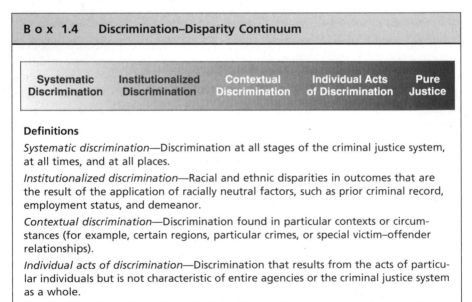

B o x 1.4   Discrimination–Disparity Continuum

Systematic Discrimination	Institutionalized Discrimination	Contextual Discrimination	Individual Acts of Discrimination	Pure Justice

Definitions

Systematic discrimination—Discrimination at all stages of the criminal justice system, at all times, and at all places.

Institutionalized discrimination—Racial and ethnic disparities in outcomes that are the result of the application of racially neutral factors, such as prior criminal record, employment status, and demeanor.

Contextual discrimination—Discrimination found in particular contexts or circumstances (for example, certain regions, particular crimes, or special victim–offender relationships).

Individual acts of discrimination—Discrimination that results from the acts of particular individuals but is not characteristic of entire agencies or the criminal justice system as a whole.

Pure justice—No racial or ethnic discrimination at all.

is to attend college immediately after high school. The age disparity, therefore, is the result of factors other than discrimination.

The example of education illustrates the point that a disparity is a difference that can be explained by legitimate factors. In criminal justice, the crucial distinction is between legal and extralegal factors. *Legal factors* include the seriousness of the offense, aggravating or mitigating circumstances, or an offender's prior criminal record. These are considered legitimate bases for decisions by most criminal justice officials because they relate to an individual's criminal behavior. *Extralegal factors* include race, ethnicity, gender, social class, and lifestyle. They are not legitimate bases for decisions by criminal justice officials because they involve group membership and are unrelated to a person's criminal behavior. It would be illegitimate, for example, for a judge to sentence all male burglars to prison but place all female burglars on probation, despite the fact that women had committed the same kind of burglary and had prior records similar to those of many of the men. Similarly, it would be illegitimate for a judge to sentence all unemployed persons to prison but grant probation to all employed persons. It is illegitimate for a police officer to disregard a sexual assault allegation by a woman who is poor, dressed shabbily, and appears to have been drinking.

Discrimination, however, is a difference based on *differential treatment* of groups without reference to an individual's behavior or qualifications. A few examples of employment discrimination will illustrate the point. Until the 1960s, most Southern police departments did not hire African American officers. The few that did, moreover, did not allow them to arrest whites. Many Northern police departments, meanwhile, did not assign African American officers to white neighborhoods.[83] These practices represented differential treatment based on race—in short, discrimination. Also during that time period, airlines hired only young women as flight attendants. This approach represented a difference in treatment based on gender rather than individual qualifications. The flight attendants were also automatically terminated if they married. Because no male employees were fired for being married, this practice represented a form of sexual discrimination.

African Americans were excluded from serving on juries because they were illegally disenfranchised as voters and, therefore, were not on jury lists. This practice represented racial discrimination in jury selection. Let us imagine a rural county in the northwestern United States, however, where there are no African American residents. The absence of African Americans from juries would represent a racial disparity but not discrimination. Consider another hypothetical case. Imagine that a police department arrested only African Americans for suspected felonies and never arrested a white person. That situation would represent racial discrimination in arrest.

The questions we deal with in the real world, of course, are not quite so simple. There are, in fact, racial disparities in jury selection and arrest: according to the Equal Justice Initiative, African Americans are less likely to serve on juries,[84] and more African Americans are arrested than whites for crimes of violence. The question is whether these disparities reflect discrimination. The evidence on these two difficult issues is discussed in Chapter 4 (arrests) and Chapter 6 (jury selection).

It is also important to remember that the word *discrimination* has at least two different meanings. One has a positive connotation. It is a compliment to say that someone has "discriminating taste" in music, food, or clothes. The person discriminates against bad food and bad music. The other meaning of *discrimination* has a negative connotation. When we say that someone "discriminates against African Americans or Hispanics," we mean that he or she makes invidious distinctions based on negative judgments about an entire group of people—that is, the person discriminates against all African Americans without reference to a particular person's qualities (for example, ability, education, or experience). Acts that involve racial or ethnic discrimination in employment, housing, or the administration of justice are illegal.

The Law of Discrimination

Discrimination occurs whenever people are treated differently. An act of discrimination is illegal when it is prohibited by law. Several different parts of the American legal system make discrimination illegal. The Fourteenth Amendment to the Constitution declares that "nor shall any state ... deny to any person within its jurisdiction the equal protection of the law." This provision applies to the states and not the federal government. If a state barred African Americans or women from serving on juries (as some states once did) it would be a violation of the Fourteenth Amendment.

A number of federal laws also forbid discrimination. The most important is Title VII of the 1964 Civil Rights Act, which holds that "It shall be an unlawful employment practice for an employer to fail or refuse to hire or to discharge any individual, or otherwise to discriminate against any individual with respect to his compensation, terms, conditions, or, privileges of employment, because of such individual's race, color, religion, sex, or national origin ...." This law covers employment discrimination by private employers and government agencies, which would include police, court, and correctional agencies. Other federal laws prohibit other forms of discrimination, such as in housing (the 1968 Fair Housing Act), age, disability (The 1990 Americans With Disabilities Act [or ADA]), and others.

State constitutions and laws also prohibit discrimination. The constitution of each of the 50 states has a provision similar to the Fourteenth Amendment guaranteeing equal protection of the laws. All states also have laws prohibiting discrimination in employment, housing, and other areas. Finally, cities have municipal ordinances that also make discrimination illegal.

Although the Fourteenth Amendment and federal, state, and local laws prohibit discrimination, in court a plaintiff has to prove that his or her experience involved discrimination. An African American who is stopped while driving and given a traffic ticket has to prove that the stop and the ticket were based on race. A Hispanic defendant sentenced to prison has to prove that the sentence was based on national origin. A Native American who is not hired as a parole officer has to prove that it was based on race. Proving discrimination in court is often very difficult. In most cases, other factors entered into the decision, and the decision was not clearly based on race or ethnicity. In Chapter 4 we will discuss the difficulty of proving racial profiling based on official data on traffic enforcement.

The Discrimination–Disparity Continuum

To help clarify the debate over this issue, let us review Box 1.4. *Systematic discrimination* means that discrimination occurs at all stages of the criminal justice system, in all places, and at all times. That is to say, there is discrimination in arrest, prosecution, and sentencing (stages); in all parts of the country (places); and without any significant variation over time.

Institutionalized discrimination involves disparities in outcomes (for example, more African Americans than whites are sentenced to prison) that result from established (institutionalized) policies. Such policies do not directly involve race. As D. E. Georges-Abeyie explains, "The key issue is result, not intent. Institutionalized racism is often the legacy of overt racism, of de facto practices that often get codified, and thus sanctioned by de jure mechanisms."[85]

Some criminal courts, for example, have bail policies granting pretrial release to defendants who are currently employed. This policy is based on the reasonable assumption that an employed person has a greater stake in the community and is less likely to flee than an unemployed person. The policy discriminates against the unemployed, and, because racial minorities are disproportionately represented among the unemployed, they are more likely to be denied bail. Thus, the bail policy has a race effect: a racial disparity in the outcomes that is the result of a criterion other than race. The racial disparity exists not because any judge is racially prejudiced, but because judges apply the rules consistently.

Employment discrimination law recognizes the phenomenon of institutionalized discrimination with reference to "disparate impact." A particular hiring policy may be illegal if it has an especially heavy impact on a certain group and is not demonstrably job related. In policing, for example, police departments formerly did not hire people who were shorter than 5'6". This standard had a disparate impact on women, Hispanics, and Asian Americans and is now no longer used.

Contextual discrimination involves discrimination in certain situations or contexts. There are a number of examples in the criminal justice system. Racial profiling involves discrimination in the context of traffic enforcement. The same pattern may not appear with regard to robbery and burglary arrests, however. Some unprofessional court systems may have patterns of extreme racial or ethnic disparities that are not found in more professionalized court systems where court officials are better trained and guided by formal policies. One important example is discrimination based on victim–offender relationship. As we will see in Chapter 8, the odds that the death penalty will be given are greatest when an African American murders a white person, whereas there is almost no chance of a death sentence when a white person murders an African American. This factor has been found in the context of other felony sentencing as well. It also appears that drug enforcement has a much heavier impact on African Americans and Hispanics than routine police work does.

Organizational factors represent another contextual variable. Some police departments encourage aggressive patrol activities (for example, frequent stops and frisks). The Kerner Commission found that "aggressive preventive patrol" aggravated tensions between the police and racial minority communities.[86] In Cincinnati, lawsuits against the police department resulted in a Consent Decree that directed the department to implement problem-oriented policing and as a result end its practice of heavy-handed crime fighting that had provoked racial riots and martial law in 2001.[87]

Thus, departments with different patrol policies may have less conflict with minority communities. Some police departments have very bad records in terms of use of physical force, but others have taken steps to curb misconduct.

Individual acts of discrimination involve those carried out by particular justice officials. For instance one police officer is biased in making arrests, whereas others in the department are not; one judge sentences minorities very harshly, whereas other judges in the same court do not. These are discriminatory acts, but they do not represent general patterns of how the criminal justice system operates.

Finally, at the far end of the spectrum in Box 1.4 is the condition we label *pure justice*. This means that there is no discrimination at any time or place in the criminal justice system.

As we discussed earlier, MacDonald argues that the idea that the criminal justice system is racist is a "myth."[88] Using our discrimination–disparity continuum, she probably falls somewhere in the area of contextual discrimination and individual discrimination (although she does not go into this in detail). The earlier book by William Wilbanks is clearly in these categories, because he conceded that individual acts of discrimination exist. Mann, however, argues that there is systematic discrimination: "The law and the legal system [have] perpetuated and [continue] to maintain an ingrained system of injustice for people of color."[89]

Throughout the chapters that follow, we will grapple with the question of whether disparities represent discrimination. For example, there are racial and ethnic disparities in arrests by the police. In Chapter 4, we examine the evidence on whether these data indicate a clear pattern of discrimination—and if so, what kind of discrimination (contextual, individual, or systematic). Chapter 4 also examines the difficulties in interpreting traffic stop data to determine whether there is a pattern of illegal racial profiling. There is also evidence of disparities in plea bargaining and sentencing. Chapters 5, 6, and 7 wrestle with the problem of interpreting the data to determine whether there are patterns of discrimination. Chapter 8 examines the data on the death penalty and the race of persons executed.

A THEORETICAL PERSPECTIVE ON RACE, ETHNICITY, AND CRIME

There are many different theories of crime and criminal justice. We believe that the available evidence on race, ethnicity, and crime is best explained by a theoretical perspective known as *conflict theory*.

The basic premise of conflict theory is that the law is used to maintain the power of the dominant group in society and to control the behavior of individuals who threaten that power.[90] A classic illustration of conflict theory involves the law of vagrancy. Vagrancy involves merely being out in public with little or no money and no clear "purpose" for being there. Vagrancy is something engaged in only by the poor. To make vagrancy a criminal act and to enforce vagrancy laws are means by which the powerful attempt to control the poor.

Conflict theory explains racial disparities in the administration of justice as products of broader patterns of social, economic, and political inequality in U.S. society. These inequalities are the result of prejudicial attitudes on the part of the white majority and discrimination against minorities in employment, education, housing, and other aspects of society. Chapter 3 explores these inequalities in detail. Conflict theory explains the overrepresentation of racial and ethnic minorities in arrest, prosecution, imprisonment, and capital punishment as both the product of these inequalities and an expression of prejudice against minorities.

Conflict theory has often been oversimplified by both advocates and opponents. Criminal justice research has found certain "anomalies" in which racial minorities are not always treated more harshly than whites. For example, there are certain situations in which African American suspects are less likely to be arrested than white suspects. Hawkins argues that these anomalies can be explained through a revised and more sophisticated conflict theory that takes into account relevant contingencies.[91]

One contingency is crime type. Hawkins claims that African Americans may be treated more leniently for some crimes because officials believe that these crimes are "more normal or appropriate for some racial and social class groups than for others."[92] In the South during the segregation era, for example, African Americans often were not arrested for certain crimes, particularly crimes against other African Americans. The dominant white power structure viewed this behavior as "appropriate" for African Americans. The fact that minority offenders were being treated leniently in these situations is consistent with conflict theory because the outcomes represent a racist view of racial minorities as essentially "childlike" people who cannot control their behavior.

A second contingency identified by Hawkins involves the race or ethnicity of the offender relative to the race of the victim. Much research has found that the criminal justice system responds more harshly when the offender is a person of color and the victim is white, particularly in rape and potential death penalty murder cases. According to conflict theory, such crimes are viewed as challenges to the pattern of racial dominance in society. The same crime is not perceived as a threat when it is intraracial (for example, white offender/white victim, African American offender/African American victim). A relatively lenient response to crimes by minorities against minorities or crimes in which a racial or ethnic minority is the victim is explained by conflict theory in terms of a devaluing of the lives of minority victims.

There may also be important contingencies based on population variables. It may be that crimes by racial minorities are treated more harshly when minorities represent a relatively large percentage of the population and therefore are perceived as a social and political threat. A substantial body of research has explored the "minority threat" thesis, which holds that racial or ethnic disparities will be greater where the white majority feels threatened by a large or growing racial or ethnic minority population in that jurisdiction.[93] At the same time, some research on imprisonment has found that the disparity between white and African American incarceration rates is greatest in states with small minority populations.[94] In this context, minorities have little political power.

Alternative Theories

Conflict theory is a sociological explanation of criminal behavior and the administration of justice in that it holds that social factors explain which kinds of behavior are defined as criminal; which people commit crime; and how crimes are investigated, prosecuted, and punished. Sociological explanations of crime are alternatives to biological, psychological, and economic explanations. These other factors may contribute in some way to explaining crime but, according to the sociological perspective, do not provide an adequate general theory of crime.[95] Conflict theory also differs from other sociological theories of crime. Consensus theory holds that all groups in society share the same values and that criminal behavior can be explained by individual acts of deviance. Conflict theory does not see consensus in society regarding the goals or operation of the criminal justice system. Conflict theory also differs from Marxist theory, although there are some areas of agreement. Conflict theory and Marxist theory both emphasize differences in power between groups. Marxist theory, however, holds that there is a rigid class structure with a ruling class. Conflict theory, meanwhile, maintains a pluralistic view of society in which there are different centers of power—business and labor, farmers and consumers, government officials and the news media, religious organizations, public interest groups, and so forth—although they are not necessarily equal. The pluralistic view also allows for changes in the relative power of different groups.

CONCLUSION

The question of race and ethnicity is a central issue in American criminal justice—perhaps the central issue. The starting point for this book is the overrepresentation of racial and ethnic minorities in the criminal justice system. This chapter sets the framework for a critical analysis of this fact about contemporary American society. We have learned that the subject is extremely complex. First, the categories of race and ethnicity are extremely problematic. Much of the data we use are not as refined as we would like. Second, we have learned that there is much controversy over the issue of discrimination. An important distinction exists between disparity and discrimination. Also, there are different kinds of discrimination. Finally, we have indicated the theoretical perspective about crime and criminal justice that guides the chapters that follow.

DISCUSSION QUESTIONS

1. Is there systematic discrimination in the criminal justice system or not? You have read brief statements on two sides of the issue. Which ones did you find most interesting? What do you most want to learn more about in the chapters ahead?

2. What are the differences between *race* and *ethnicity*? Give some examples that illustrate the differences.

3. When social scientists say that the concept of race is a "social construct," what exactly do they mean?

4. What are the most recent developments in the debate over immigration and crime? Search the Web and see if there is any new important evidence. What has happened with the lawsuits over the 2010 Arizona immigration enforcement law? Has the case reached the U.S. Supreme Court?

5. Do you think the U.S. census should have a category of "multicultural" for race and ethnicity? Explain why or why not. Would it make a difference in the accuracy of the census? Would it make a difference to you?

6. Explain the difference between *discrimination* and *disparity*. Give one example from some other area of life.

NOTES

1. W. E. B. Du Bois, *The Souls of Black Folk* (New York: W. W. Norton, 1999), p. 17.

2. Bureau of Justice Statistics, *Prison Inmates at Midyear 2009—Statistical Tables* (Washington, DC: Department of Justice, 2010), Table 18. NCJ 230113.

3. Ronet Bachman, Heather Zaykowski, Rachel Kallmyer, Margarita Poteyeva, Christina Lanier, *Violence Against American Indian and Alaska Native Women and the Criminal Justice Response: What is Known* (Washington, DC: Department of Justice, 2008). NCJ 223691. Available at http://www.ncjrs.org.

4. David Harris, *Profiles in Injustice: Why Racial Profiling Doesn't Work* (New York: New Press, 2002); ACLU, *Driving While Black* (New York: ACLU, 1999).

5. Pew Research Center, *Muslim Americans: Middle Class and Mostly Mainstream* (Washington, DC: Pew Research Center, 2007). Available at http://pewresearch .org/.

6. Siddharth Kara, *Sex Trafficking: Inside the Business of Modern Slavery* (New York: Columbia University Press, 2009).

7. Current data are available at the website: http://www.innocenceproject.org.

8. National Urban League, *State of Black America, 2001* (New York: National Urban League, 2001).

9. Bureau of Justice Statistics, *Sourcebook of Criminal Justice Statistics*, 2010, online edition, Table 2.52.2009. Available at http://www.albany.edu/sourcebook.

10. Bureau of Justice Statistics, *Sourcebook of Criminal Justice Statistics*, 2010, online edition, Table 2.39.2009.

11. Dennis Rosenbaum, D. A. Lewis, and J. Grant, "Neighborhood-Based Crime Prevention: Assessing the Efficacy of Community Organizing in Chicago," in *Community Crime Prevention: Does It Work?* Dennis Rosenbaum, ed. (Newbury Park, CA: Sage, 1986), pp. 109-139.

12. Heather MacDonald, "Is the Criminal-Justice System Racist?", *City Journal* 18 (Spring 2008). Available at http://www.city-journal.org/printable.php?id=2563.

13. Bureau of Justice Statistics, *Felony Defendants in Large Urban Counties*, 1994 (Washington, DC: Department of Justice, 1998). NCJ 164616.

14. Substance Abuse and Mental Health Services Administration [SAMSA], *Results from the 2008 National Survey on Drug Use and Health: National Findings* (Washington, DC: Department of Health and Human Services, 2009). Available at http://www.oas.samhsa.gov/nsduh/2k8nsduh/2k8Results.pdf.

15. Joan Petersilia, *Racial Disparities in the Criminal Justice System* (Santa Monica: Rand Corporation, 1983).

16. See, for example, Shaun L. Gabbidon and Helen Taylor Greene, *Race and Crime* (Thousand Oaks: Sage Publications, 2005); David Cole, *No Equal Justice: Race and Class in the American Criminal Justice System* (New York: The New Press, 1999); Katheryn K. Russell, *The Color of Crime* (New York: New York University Press, 1998); Gregg Barak, Jeanne M. Flavin, and Paul S. Leighton, *Class, Race, Gender, and Crime* (Los Angeles: Roxbury, 2001); Michael Tonry, *Malign Neglect* (New York: Oxford University Press, 1996); Coramae Richey Mann, *Unequal Justice* (Bloomington: Indiana University Press, 1988); Ronald Barri Flowers, *Minorities and Criminality* (Westport, CT: Greenwood, 1988); William Wilbanks, *The Myth of a Racist Criminal Justice System* (Monterey, CA: Brooks/Cole, 1987); Joan Petersilia, *Racial Disparities in the Criminal Justice System* (Santa Monica, CA: Rand, 1983).

17. Christopher Stone, "Race, Crime, and the Administration of Justice: A Summary of the Available Facts" (paper presented to the Advisory Board of the President's Initiative on Race, May 19, 1998); National Institute of Justice, *NIJ Journal* 239 (April 1999): 26-32.

18. Samuel Walker and Molly Brown, "A Pale Reflection of Reality: The Neglect of Racial and Ethnic Minorities in Introductory Criminal Justice Textbooks," *Journal of Criminal Justice Education* 6 (Spring 1995), pp. 61-83.

19. Mann, *Unequal Justice,* p. viii.

20. Alfredo Mirandé, *Gringo Justice* (Notre Dame, IN: University of Notre Dame Press, 1987), p. ix.

21. Marianne O. Nielsen, "Contextualization for Native American Crime and Criminal Justice Involvement," in *Native Americans, Crime, and Justice*, Marianne O. Nielsen and Robert A. Silverman, eds. (Boulder, CO: Westview, 1996), p. 10.

22. The Sentencing Project, *Federal Crack Cocaine Sentencing* (Washington, DC: The Sentencing Project, n.d.).

23. The reform of the Rockefeller Drug Law and reforms in other states are described in Nicole D. Porter, *The State of Sentencing 2009: Developments in Policy and Practice* (Washington, DC: The Sentencing Project, 2010). Available at http://www.sentencingproject.org.

24. Howard Campbell, *Drug War Zone: Frontline Dispatches from the Streets of El Paso and Juarez* (Austin: University of Texas Press, 2009).

25. Pew Center on the States, *Prison Count 2010*, Rev. April 2010 (Washington, DC: Pew Center on the States, 2010). See also Bureau of Justice Statistics, *Prisoners and Yearend 2009—Advance Counts* (Washington, DC: Department of Justice, 2010). NCJ 230189.

26. MacDonald, "Is the Criminal-Justice System Racist?" MacDonald's argument is far stronger and more data-based than the earlier William Wilbanks, *The Myth of a Racist Criminal Justice System* (Monterey, CA: Brooks/Cole, 1987).

27. Stone, "Race, Crime, and the Administration of Justice," p. 1.

28. Darnell F. Hawkins, "Ethnicity, Race, and Crime: A Review of Selected Studies," in *Ethnicity, Race, and Crime*, D. F. Hawkins, ed. (Albany: State University of New York, 1995), p. 40.

29. U. S. Bureau of the Census, *American Community Survey*. Available at http://www.census.gov/acs/www.

30. Jeffrey Passel and Paul Taylor, *Who's Hispanic?* (Washington, DC: Pew Research Center, 2009).

31. The concept of race is both problematic and controversial. For a starting point, see Ashley Montagu, *Statement on Race*, 3rd ed. (New York: Oxford University Press, 1972), which includes the text of and commentary on four United Nations statements on race.

32. J. Milton Yinger, *Ethnicity: Source of Strength? Source of Conflict?* (Albany: State University of New York Press, 1994), p. 19.

33. Paul R. Spickard, "The Illogic of American Racial Categories," in *Racially Mixed People in America*, Marla P. Root, ed. (Newbury Park, CA: Sage, 1992), p. 18.

34. Yinger, *Ethnicity*, p. 19.

35. Christine B. Hickman, "The Devil and the One Drop Rule: Racial Categories, African Americans, and the U.S. Census," *Michigan Law Review* 95 (March 1997), pp. 1161-1265.

36. U.S. Office of Management and Budget, Directive 15, *Race and Ethnic Standards for Federal Statistics and Administrative Reporting*, OMB Circular No. A-46(1974), rev. 1977 (Washington, DC: U.S. Government Printing Office, 1977).

37. Lawrence Wright, "One Drop of Blood," *The New Yorker* (July 25, 1994), p. 47.

38. See the Association of MultiEthnic Americans website at http://www.ameasite.org.

39. Steven Fraser, ed., *The Bell Curve Wars: Race, Intelligence, and the Future of America* (New York: Basic Books, 1995).

40. National Urban League, *State of Black America*, 2001.

41. Richard J. Herrnstein and Charles Murray, *The Bell Curve: Intelligence and Class Structure in American Life* (New York: The Free Press, 1994).

42. Pew Hispanic Center, *2002 National Survey of Latinos* (Los Angeles: Pew Hispanic Center, 2002). See also Pew Hispanic Center, *Hispanic Trends: A People in Motion*

(Los Angeles: Pew Hispanic Center, 2005). Available at http://www.pewhispanic .org.

43. Pew Hispanic Center, *2002 National Survey of Latinos* (Los Angeles: Pew Hispanic Center, 2002). See also Pew Hispanic Center, *Hispanic Trends: A People in Motion* (Los Angeles: Pew Hispanic Center, 2005). Available at http://www .pewhispanic.org.

44. Office of Management and Budget, "Revisions to the Standards for the Classification of Federal Data on Race and Ethnicity," (October 30, 1997). Available at http://www.whitehouse.gov/omb/fedreg/ombdir15.html.

45. Ibid.

46. James Paul Allen and Eugene James Turner, *We the People: An Atlas of America's Ethnic Diversity* (New York: Macmillan, 1988). Yinger, *Ethnicity*, pp. 3-4.

47. U.S. Bureau of the Census, *U.S. Hispanic Latino Population, Census 2000* (Washington, DC: Census Bureau, 2004). Available at http://www.census.gov. See also reports by the Pew Hispanic Center at http://www.pewhispanic.org.

48. Passel and Taylor, *Who's Hispanic?*

49. Nadine Naber, "Ambiguous Insiders: An Investigation of Arab American Invisibility," *Ethnic and Racial Studies* 23 (January 2000), pp. 37-61. Helen Hatab Samhan, "Who Are Arab Americans?" Grolier Multimedia Encyclopedia, available on the website of the Arab American Institute: http://www.aaiusa.org/pages/publications/.

50. United Nations quoted in Yinger, *Ethnicity*, p. 21. Louis Wirth, "The Problem of Minority Groups," in *The Science of Man in the World Crisis*, Ralph Linton, ed. (New York: Columbia University Press, 1945), p. 123.

51. Office of Management and Budget, "Revisions to the Standards."

52. U.S. Census, *We The People: American Indians and Alaska Natives* (Washington, DC: Bureau of the Census, 2006).

53. Bureau of Justice Statistics, *Asian, Native Hawaiian, and Pacific Islander Victims of Crime* (Washington, DC: Department of Justice, 2009). NCJ 22503. National Council on Crime and Delinquency, *Created Equal: Racial and Ethnic Disparities in the US Criminal Justice System* (Oakland, CA: NCCD, March 2009), p. 2.

54. Anita Khashu, Robin Busch, Zainab Latif, and Francesca Levy, *Building Strong Police-Immigrant Community Relations: Lessons from a New York City Project* (New York: Vera Institute, 2005). Available at http://www.vera.org.

55. Cecilia Menjivar and Cynthia L. Beharano, "Latino Immigrants' Perceptions of Crime and Police Authorities: A Case Study from the Phoenix Metropolitan Area," *Ethnic and Racial Studies,* 27 (January 2004), pp. 120-148.

56. John Hope Franklin and Alfred A. Moss Jr., *From Slavery to Freedom: A History of African Americans*, 7th ed. (New York: Knopf, 1994), p. xix.

57. Frank Newport, "Black or African American?" *Gallup News Service*, September 28, 2007.

58. Eric R. Wolf, *Europe and the People without History* (Berkeley: University of California Press, 1982), pp. 380-381.

59. Pew Hispanic Center, *2002 National Survey of Latinos*, and Pew Hispanic Center, *Hispanic Trends: A People in Motion* (2005). Available at http://www.pewhispanic .org.

60. Pew Hispanic Center, *Hispanics: A People in Motion* (2005), p. 19.

61. Bureau of Justice Statistics, *Contacts Between the Police and the Public: Findings from the 2002 National Survey* (Washington, DC: U.S. Department of Justice, 2005). NCJ 207845.

62. Barry Holman, *Masking the Divide: How Officially Reported Prison Statistics Distort the Racial and Ethnic Realities of Prison Growth* (Alexandria: National Center on Institutions and Alternatives, 2001). Bureau of Justice Statistics, *Sourcebook of Criminal Justice Statistics*, 2010 online edition, Table 60022.2009.

63. National Council on Crime and Delinquency, *Created Equal*, p. 1.

64. Bureau of Justice Statistics, *Capital Punishment*, 2008 (Washington, DC: Department of Justice, 2010).

65. Gary LaFree, "Race and Crime Trends in the United States, 1946–1990," in *Ethnicity, Race, and Crime*, pp. 173-174.

66. Zoann K. Snyder-Joy, "Self-Determination and American Indian Justice: Tribal versus Federal Jurisdiction on Indian Lands," in *Ethnicity, Race, and Crime*, p. 310.

67. Bureau of Justice Statistics, *Sourcebook of Criminal Justice Statistics, 2010, Online edition* (Washington, DC: U.S. Government Printing Office, 2005), app. 4.

68. Jeffrey S. Passel and D'Vera Coh, *A Portrait of Unauthorized Immigrants in the United States* (Los Angeles: Pew Hispanic Center, 2009).

69. PollingReport.com, August 18, 2010, "Summary of recent public opinion polls regarding immigration." Available at http://www.pollingreport.com/immigration.htm.

70. See the discussion of these and related issues in Pew Hispanic Center, *Between Two Worlds: How Young Latinos Come of Age in America* (Los Angeles: Pew Hispanic Center, 2009), p. ii.

71. Graham C. Ousey and Charis E. Kubrin, "Exploring the Connection Between Immigration and Violent Crime Rates in U.S. Cities, 1980–2000," *Social Problems* 56 (2009): 447-473. Tim Wadsworth, "Is Immigration Responsible for the Crime Drop? An Assessment of the Influence of Immigration on Changes in Violent Crime Between 1990 and 2000," *Social Science Quarterly* 91 (June 2010): 531-553. Bureau of Justice Statistics, *Sourcebook of Criminal Justice Statistics*, 2010 online edition, Table 3.33 2007.

72. Pew Hispanic Center, *Between Two Worlds: How Young Latinos Come of Age in America* (Los Angeles: Pew Hispanic Center, 2009).

73. Police Executive Research Forum, *Police Chiefs and Sheriffs Speak Out on Local Immigration Enforcement* (Washington, DC: PERF, April 2008).

74. Police Foundation, *The Role of Local Police: Striking a Balance Between Immigration Enforcement and Civil Liberties* (Washington, DC: Police Foundation, 2009), pp. 4-5.

75. Police Foundation, *The Role of Local Police*, p. 4.

76. Pew Hispanic Center, *Unauthorized Immigrants and Their U.S.-Born Children* (Los Angeles: Pew Hispanic Center, August 11, 2010).

77. William H. Frey, "The Diversity Myth," *American Demographics* 20 (June 1998), p. 41.

78. Pew Hispanic Center, *Hispanics of Puerto Rican Origin in the United States*, 2007 (Los Angeles: Pew Hispanic Center, 2009). Bureau of the Census, *Statistical Abstract of the United States*, 2011, Table 19.

79. U.S. Census Bureau, *Statistical Abstract of the United States*, 2011, Table 23.

80. U.S. Census Bureau, *Statistical Abstract of the United States*, 2011, Tables 413, 414.

81. Mann, *Unequal Justice,* pp. vii–xiv.

82. MacDonald, *"Is the Criminal Justice System Racist?"*

83. W. Marvin Dulaney, *Black Police in America* (Bloomington: Indiana University Press, 1996).

84. Equal Justice Initiative, *Illegal Racial Discrimination in Jury Selection: A Continuing Legacy* (Montgomery, AL: Equal Justice Initiative, 2010).

85. D. E. Georges-Abeyie, "Criminal Justice Processing of Non-White Minorities," in *Racism, Empiricism, and Criminal Justice,* B. D. MacLean and D. Milovanovic, eds. (Vancouver: Collective, 1990), p. 28.

86. National Advisory Commission on Civil Disorders [Kerner Commission], *Report* (New York: Bantam Books, 1968), p. 304.

87. Samuel Walker and Morgan Macdonald, "An Alternative Remedy," *George Mason University Civil Rights Law Journal* (2009).

88. MacDonald, "Is the Criminal Justice System Racist?" Wilbanks, *The Myth of a Racist Criminal Justice System,* p. 5.

89. Mann, *Unequal Justice,* p. 160.

90. Richard Quinney, *The Social Reality of Crime* (Boston: Little, Brown, 1970).

91. Darnell Hawkins, "Beyond Anomalies: Rethinking the Conflict Perspective on Race and Criminal Punishment," *Social Forces* 65 (March 1987), pp. 719-745.

92. Ibid.

93. Malcolm D. Holmes, "Minority Threat and Police Brutality: Determinants of Civil Rights Criminal Complaints in U.S. Municipalities," *Criminology* 38 (May 2000), p. 343.

94. Alfred Blumstein, "Prison Populations: A System out of Control," in *Crime and Justice: A Review of Research,* Michael Tonry and Norval Morris, eds., Vol. 10 (Chicago: University of Chicago Press, 1988), p. 253.

95. Ronald L. Akers and Christine S. Sellers, *Criminological Theories,* 5th ed. (New York: Oxford University Press, 2008).

2

✳

Victims and Offenders
Myths and Realities about Crime

Popular Images of Victims and Offenders: A Racial Hoax

Bethany Storro's face revealed scars from an incident in September 2010. This twentysomething, white female reported to police that she was at a coffee shop when a stranger spoke to her and threw acid in her face. What type of person would do this? Her report to the police offered a description of the unnamed offender: black female. An indictment of modern race relations: it was a racial hoax. Newspaper reports referred to Storro as "obviously deeply troubled," but "she was sane enough to make a calculated decision to maximize sympathy and deflect suspicion. She blamed it on a black person."[1] The "mad black woman imagery" reflects a disturbing imagery present in modern society about the linkages between race and crime.

The news media exert a powerful impact on how Americans think about crime and justice. Unfortunately, the image the media create is often wildly distorted. Even worse, many of those distorted images have serious racial implications, perpetuating racial stereotypes about criminals and their victims. This chapter attempts to cut through those distorted images and present an evidence-based picture of victims and offenders in America.

GOALS OF THE CHAPTER

In this chapter we describe the social context of crime in the United States. The chapter starts with a discussion of the types of crimes and criminals that catch the attention of the American public and then presents the picture of the typical victim and typical offender from government victimization and arrest reports.

After you have read this chapter:

1. You will understand the basic patterns of who commits major crimes and who the principal victims are. You will have a solid grasp of the racial- and ethnic-group patterns related to both victims and offenders.

2. You will be able to sort your way through basic data on crimes and victims and be able to spot occasions when the news media present a distorted picture of crime in America.

3. You will understand the concept of "racial hoaxes" and the role they play in distorting public understanding of crime.

4. You will understand the category of "hate crimes," with special reference to race and ethnicity, and how they are different in important respects from what are called "street crimes" (for example, robbery and burglary).

5. You will have a good understanding of the racial and ethnic aspects of gangs in American, both in communities and in prisons.

6. You will understand the different theoretical explanations for the racial and ethnic gap in offending and victimization.

MEDIA AND CRIME

Racial Hoaxes

Racial hoaxes have a particularly powerful impact on public images of victims and offenders. Katheryn K. Russell asserts that a racial hoax occurs "when someone fabricates a crime and blames it on another person because of his race OR when an actual crime has been committed and the perpetrator falsely blames someone because of his race."[2] Hoaxes receive a lot of publicity because they are typically sensational and violent crimes that grab media attention. People remember them because of their sensational character. One infamous racial hoax was the case of Susan Smith's assertion that an African American man stole her car and kidnapped her children.[3] Smith was a white women. It was later revealed that she drove her car, with her children trapped in their car seats, into a nearby lake. Russell argues that such hoaxes have social and psychological consequences for individuals and the community and significant legal costs.[4] In this 1994 case in South Carolina, state and federal officials spent nine days looking for the alleged offender before she confessed to driving the car into the lake and killing her children. Smith's attempt to blame someone else for the crime was successful (even if temporarily) because it tapped in to widely held societal fears about the typical criminal.

Russell documents known racial hoaxes in the United States from 1987 to 1996. Although she found that racial hoaxes "are perpetrated by people of all races, classes, geographic regions and ages,"[5] the majority of racial hoax cases were perpetrated by a white person charging an African American person (70 percent of the cases), with a smaller number of African Americans charging whites in racial hoaxes.[6] (In this discussion the "perpetrator" is the person who makes a false claim of a crime, not a person who actually commits the alleged crime.) Hoax perpetrators have been charged with filing false police reports, but this occurs in less than half of the documented cases.[7]

In her book, *The Color of Crime*, Russell makes a compelling argument for a strong legal response to the perpetration of racial hoaxes. She argues that legislation should be passed, similar to hate-crime legislation, that allows for a sentence enhancement to such charges as filing a false police report in the case of racial hoaxes. Such a law would be similar to one proposed in New Jersey in 1995; it would punish citizens who falsely incriminate another as the perpetrator of a crime or submit a fictitious report based on race, color, or ethnicity (as well as religion and sexual orientation).[8] In addition to a sentence enhancement (fine, fee, additional supervision/incarceration), the person convicted would have to reimburse the law enforcement agencies whose search actions resulted from the racial hoax.

Race and Gender of Crime Victims

Some crime stories capture the attention of the public more than others, arguably because of the nature of the offense, the type of victim, and the type of offender. Recently, media outlets have been charged with favoring the presentation of some crime stories over others. The media consistently portray violent crime as more common than property crime when in fact violent crimes are only about ten percent of all reported crimes.[9] Additionally, the media often suggest crime is increasing at astronomical rates when in fact the great American crime drop (see Chapter 1) brought crime rates to historic lows.

Some critics also charge that the media show bias in the coverage of missing persons, arguing that print and television coverage of stories focuses on missing white women and tends to ignore missing women of color. *Essence* magazine contends, for example, that "when black women disappear, the media silence is deafening."[10] Specifically, some media critics charge that attention the media give to such cases such as Laci Peterson, Natalee Holloway, and Chandra Levy far outweighs the emphasis placed on such cases as Evelyn Hernandez, LaToyia Figueroa, and Ardena Carter.

Perhaps the typical American recognizes the details of one of the following pairs of missing person victims but not the other.

The first pair of victims is connected by time and location/geography:

> In 2004 Laci Peterson, a missing white female who was eight months pregnant, was found dead in the San Francisco Bay Area. Most Americans know not just the details of her disappearance from her home, the search for her whereabouts, and the subsequent recovery of her body but also that her husband, Scott Peterson, was charged and convicted of this offense.

> Few Americans are aware that a few months before Laci Peterson's body was discovered, the decapitated body of a young, pregnant Hispanic woman,

Evelyn Hernandez, was found. Details of her missing person / murder case were not extensively covered by the national media.

The second pair of victims is connected by time, but not geography:

In May 2005 Natalee Holloway, a white American teenager, was reported missing in Aruba. Her story made headlines almost from the moment that she was reported missing. Print and news media covered the incident extensively for weeks following her disappearance.

In July 2005, 24-year-old LaToyia Figueroa, who was pregnant, was reported missing. Her body was later recovered, and her boyfriend was charged with murder. However, her story was initially ignored by the national media, some suggest because she was not white.

The third pair of victims is connected by time and occupation:

In 2003 Chandra Levy, a white female intern in Washington, DC, disappeared on a morning jog. Considerable attention was paid to her search and recovery in nationwide news stories.[11]

In 2003 Ardena Carter, a young African American graduate student in Georgia, went missing on her way to the library. Her disappearance and the subsequent recovery of her body garnered no more than regional news coverage.[12]

Critics of the media coverage of these types of missing person cases argue that the public is being misled about who is really missing.[13] Department of Justice data, for example, indicate that in California, nearly twice as many Hispanic women (7,453) are missing than white women (4,032).[14] The National Center for Missing Adults reports that of the more than 47,000 people missing in 2005, 29,553 were white or Hispanic, 13,859 were African American, 1,199 were Asian American, and 685 were Native American.[15] Of these missing persons, 53 percent were men.

This pattern of more media emphasis on white, female missing persons is not necessarily intentional; nonetheless it does signal a devaluation of the lives of nonwhite victims of crime. Professor Todd Boyd notes that the media's decision to focus on white women and not women of color may be "an unconscious decision about who matters and who doesn't."[16] He asserts, "In general, there is an assumption that crime is such a part of black and Latino culture that these things happen all the time. In many people's minds it's regarded as being commonplace and not a big deal."

A BROADER PICTURE OF THE CRIME VICTIM

Our perceptions of crime are shaped to a large extent by the highly publicized crimes featured on the nightly news and sensationalized in newspapers. We read about young African American or Hispanic males who sexually assault, rob, and

Focus on an Issue
Central Park Jogger

In 1989 a group of minority male teenagers were convicted of attacking and raping a woman who was jogging in New York's Central Park. The Central Park Jogger Case has long been used to illustrate the media emphasis on certain types of crimes (violent crime), with certain types of crime victims (white females), and with certain types of offenders (a "gang" of young, minority males). Does this incident reflect a "typical" criminal event? Many people believe that it does: a white victim falling prey to the violence of minority gang activity. But the evidence suggests that it is *not* the typical criminal event. First, more than 80 percent of crimes reported to the police are property crimes.[17] Second, a disproportionate number of crime victims are minorities. Third, interracial (between-race) crimes are the exception, not the rule. Finally, not all group activity is gang activity, not all gang actions are criminal, and not all gang members are racial or ethnic minorities.

Additionally, an article in the *New York Times* several weeks after the well-publicized event described here helps put this victimization in perspective. A total of 29 rapes were reported in the city that week (April 16–22, 1989), with 17 African American female victims, 7 Hispanics, 3 whites, and 2 Asians.[18] Thus, the typical rape victim was in fact a *minority* female. Although the 29 reports from the New York Police Department did not indicate the race of the offender, other sources, including the national victimization data discussed later in this chapter, demonstrate that rape is predominantly an intrarracial (within-race) crime.[19]

Subsequent to the investigation of this event, five young males of color were eventually convicted and incarcerated for perpetrating this attack, each serving up to 8 years in prison. In 2002, with the assistance of DNA analysis, it was revealed that the five convicted youths were not the actual offenders.[20] The actual offender has now been identified and has confessed to the offense.[21] Note that these details became known only after the young offenders had served their sentences. Thus, this infamous case is an example of wrongful prosecution based on faulty police work, including very questionable interrogation techniques, that had a devastating impact on young men of color.

---

murder whites, and we assume that these crimes are typical. We assume that the typical crime is a violent crime, that the typical victim is white, and that the typical offender is African American or Hispanic. As Charles Silberman observes, this topic is difficult to address:

> In the end, there is no escaping the question of race and crime. To say this is to risk, almost guarantee, giving offense; it is impossible to talk honestly about the role of race in American life without offending and angering both whites and blacks—and Hispanic browns and Native American reds as well. The truth is terrible, on all sides; and we are all too accustomed to the soothing euphemisms and inflammatory rhetoric with which the subject is cloaked.[22]

In short, compelling evidence suggests that the most widely held picture of crime, criminal, and crime victim in America is at best incomplete and at worst inaccurate, particularly as it concerns race and ethnicity of crime victims. Victimization data, in fact, reveal that people of color are more likely than whites in most circumstances to be victimized by crime.

In the sections that follow, we use victimization data to paint a broad picture of the crime victim, allowing for a view of which racial and ethnic groups are disproportionately the victims of crime. We begin by discussing the National Crime Victimization Survey, the source of most data on criminal victimization in the United States. We then compare the household victimization rates of African Americans and whites, as well as Hispanics and non-Hispanics. Personal victimization rates (property and violent offense) are then compared for African Americans, whites, "other" race,★ and "two or more" races, as well as for Hispanics and non-Hispanics. We conclude this section with a discussion of homicide victimization events.

The National Crime Victimization Survey

The most systematic source of victimization information is the National Crime Victimization Survey (NCVS). The survey, which began in 1973, is conducted by the Bureau of Census for the Bureau of Justice Statistics (BJS). Survey data are used to produce annual estimates of the number and rate of personal and household victimizations for the nation as a whole and for urban, suburban, and rural comparisons.[23]

Interviews are conducted at six-month intervals to ask whether household members have been the victims of selected major crimes during the last six months. Information is collected about/from persons aged 12 and older who are members of the household selected for the sample. The sample is chosen on the basis of the most recent census data to be representative of the nation as a whole. The NCVS data presented here are estimates based on the interviews of 41,500 households and 73,600 individuals aged 12 years and older. The response rates for the 2007 survey were very high: 90.3 percent of eligible households and 86.2 percent of eligible individuals responded.[24]

Members of selected households are contacted either in person or by phone every six months for three years. Household questionnaires are completed to describe the demographic characteristics of the household (income, number of members, and so on). The race and ethnicity of the adult completing the household questionnaire is recorded from self-report information as the race and ethnicity of the household. Starting in 2003, respondents can self-report more than one race. Incident questionnaires are completed for both household offenses and personal victimizations. The designated head of the household is questioned about the incidence of household burglary, household larceny, and motor-vehicle theft. Personal victimization incident questionnaires are administered to household members aged 12 and older, probing them to relay any victimization incidents of rape, robbery,

---

★This term is used to report Asian, Native Hawaiian, Pacific Islander, Native American, and Alaskan Native

assault, and personal larceny. Those who report victimizations to interviewers are asked a series of follow-up questions about the nature of the crime and the response to the crime. Those who report personal victimizations are also asked to describe the offender and their relationship (if any) with the offender. Some sample personal victimization questions are as follows:

> During the last six months:
>
> Did anyone beat you up, attack you, or hit you with something such as a rock or a bottle?
>
> Did anyone take something directly from you by using force, such as by a stickup, mugging, or threat?
>
> Was anything stolen from you while you were away from home—for instance, at work, in a theater or restaurant, or while traveling?

In many ways, the NCVS produces a more complete picture of crime and the characteristics of those who are victimized by crime than official police records. Most important, it includes victimizations not reported to the police. As the NCVS has consistently reported for over 30 years, only slightly more than one-third of all crimes are reported. In addition, the survey includes questions designed to elicit detailed information concerning the victim, the characteristics of the offender(s), and the context of the victimization. This information is used to calculate age-, sex-, and race-specific estimates of victimization. In addition, estimates of interracial and intraracial crime can be calculated. Furthermore, supplements to the survey are done periodically to address victimization issues such as identity theft and school crime and safety.

In addition, for an individual year, the information on race includes white, African American, "other" (a combined category for Asian, Pacific Islander, Native Alaskan, and Native American respondents), and two or more races for those household heads self-designating as biracial or multiracial. Ethnicity is limited to Hispanic and non-Hispanic only. It is important to remember that Hispanics may be of any race (see Chapter 1). NCVS designations are determined by census categories, so the Hispanic category includes all individuals of Spanish origin (Mexican American, Chicano, Mexican, Puerto Rican, Cuban, Central, or South American) regardless of racial identity. (The NCVS is a vast improvement over the FBI UCR system, which still uses the categories of "white" and "black" with no reference to ethnicity.)

The NCVS is an invaluable source of data, but it does have certain limitations. For example, it does not cover commercial crime (such as convenience store robberies or bank robberies), white collar crime, kidnapping, or homicide; the estimates produced are for the nation as a whole, central city compared to suburban areas. It does not, therefore, give us data on particular cities or states. Homeless people are not interviewed; and responses are susceptible to memory loss, telescoping (reporting a crime that occurred more than a year ago, which is outside the scope of the survey), exaggeration (for example, I lost $1,000 in property when in fact it was only $20), misunderstandings about crime categories (for example, robbery versus burglary), and interviewer bias.

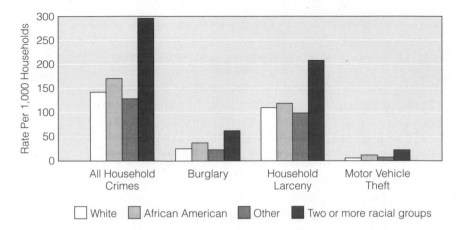

FIGURE 2.1   Household Victimization Rates, by Race of Head of Household, 2007

SOURCE: Bureau of Justice Statistics, *Criminal Victimization in the United States*: 2007 Statistical Tables. Available at: bjs.ojp.gov/content/pub/html/cvus/property_crimes_head_of_household703.cfm.

Household Victimization

The NCVS makes a basic distinction between household crimes and personal crimes. As noted, the NCVS questions the designated head of household about crimes against the household—burglary, household larceny, and motor vehicle theft. It is clear that household victimization rates vary by race and ethnicity (see Figure 2.1).[25] The lowest victimization rate for all household crime combined is the "other" group consisting of Asians, Pacific Islanders, Alaska Natives, and Native Americans, followed closely by white households. Looking at crime by individual category, this general pattern holds for "other" and white households, with the exception of the household burglary victimization rate, which is higher for white households. While African American households have higher rates (overall and individually) than both of these racial groups, their overall rate and rate per individual crime are surpassed by the "two or more" racial group.

The 2007 estimates of household victimization rates by ethnicity indicate that overall victimization rates are higher for Hispanic households than the victimization rates for non-Hispanic households.[26] Figure 2.2 shows higher rates for Hispanics for all household crimes combined (207 per 1,000 households compared to 158 per 1,000 households) and for each household crime individually. The largest disparity in victimization rates is for motor vehicle theft, where Hispanic households are estimated to have a rate more than two times that of non-Hispanic households.

The Effect of Urbanization

The racial differences in household (property) victimization rates and personal violent victimization rates discussed thus far are differences for the United States as a whole. A number of criminologists have asserted that victimization patterns can be

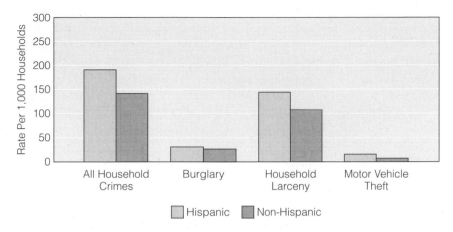

FIGURE 2.2   Household Victimization Rates, by Ethnicity of Head of Household, 2007

SOURCE: Bureau of Justice Statistics, *Criminal Victimization in the United States*: 2007 Statistical Tables. Available at: bjs.ojp.gov/content/pub/html/cvus/property_crimes_head_of_household703.cfm.

expected to vary by such structural characteristics as "urbanization." This section explores victimization rates by degree of urbanization: urban, suburban, and rural. In the most recent data available from the NCVS (Table 2.1), household victimization rates are highest for African American and white households in urban areas and for the combined "other" racial group (Native American / Alaska Native, and Asian / Pacific Islander) in the rural areas.[27] African American household victimization rates are higher than white and "other" household rates for the urban and suburban areas but are lowest comparatively in the rural areas. Hispanic household victimization rates are highest in rural areas and remain higher than non–Hispanic households in both suburban and rural areas as well.

Regarding violent victimization rates by urbanization, generally victimization rates are highest in rural areas and decline in suburban areas, with the lowest

TABLE 2.1   **Racial and Ethnicity Property Crime Victimization Rate by Urban, Suburban, and Rural Setting, 1993–1998**

	Crime Rate Per 1,000 Households		
	Urban	Suburban	Rural
Race			
African American	348.6	295.5	200.0
White	341.7	252.4	210.6
Other	295.4	253.9	342.8
Ethnicity			
Hispanic	386.4	337.8	271.6
Non-Hispanic	335.2	249.9	209.6

SOURCE: Detis T. Duhart, *Urban, Suburban, and Rural Victimization, 1993–1998* (Washington, DC: Bureau of Justice Statistics, 2000). Available at http://www.ojp.usdoj.gov/bjs/.

rates in rural areas. However, some important exceptions to this pattern exist. African Americans in urban areas have the highest victimization rates for rape (4.6 per 1,000), robbery (14.5 per 1,000), and aggravated assault (17.0 per 1,000). Whites have the highest simple assault rate in urban areas (36.5 per 1,000), but the highest overall simple assault rate is for the "other" race category in rural areas (46.8 per 1,000). What is the explanation for such patterns? The social threat hypothesis is most often used in urban settings, but perhaps the introduction of racially diverse populations into racially homogenous rural settings can be seen as a similar source of threat.

Personal Victimization

In addition to questioning the head of the household about crimes against the household, the NCVS interviewers ask all household members aged 12 or older whether they themselves have been the victim of rape (worded as sexual assault), robbery, assault, or personal theft within the past six months. This information is then used to estimate victimization rates for the nation as a whole and for the various subgroups in the population.

Consistent with the pattern of racial disparity found in household victimizations, these estimates reveal that African Americans are more likely than either whites or members of other racial or ethnic groups to be the victims of violent crimes, however, the highest victimization rate is reported for persons self-identified as "two or more races." As shown in Table 2.2, the overall violent victimization rate for African Americans is 24.3 per 1,000 persons in the population aged 12 or older, 19.9 per 1,000 for whites, 11.4 per 1,000 for other races

T A B L E 2.2   Personal Victimization Rates by Type of Crime and by Race and Ethnicity of Victims, 2007

| | Victimization Rates[a] | | | | | |
| | Race | | | | Ethnicity | |
	White	African American	Other	Multi-Race	Hispanic	Non-Hispanic
Crimes of Violence (all)	19.9	24.3	11.4	73.8	18.6	21.0
Rape	1.0	0.05	1.2	5.5	0.3	1.1
Robbery	1.9	4.9	1.8	10.8	3.9	2.2
Assault	17.0	18.8	8.3	57.5	14.5	17.8
Aggravated	3.2	4.4	2.7	13.3	3.0	3.5
Simple	13.9	14.4	5.7	44.2	11.4	14.3
Crimes of Theft	0.6	1.9	1.1	0.06	1.0	0.07
All Offenses	20.5	26.2	12.5	73.8	19.6	21.1

[a]Victimization rates per 1,000 persons aged 12 and older.
SOURCE: Sourcebook of criminal justice statistics online. Available at http://www.albany.edu/sourcebook/pdf/t342007.pdf.

(combined group of Native American / Alaska Native and Asian / Pacific Islanders), and 73.8 per 1,000 for the multi-race respondents.

The racial differences across crime-specific types of violence reveal interesting observations. In particular, African Americans and biracial/multiracial respondents are more than twice as likely as whites and other race respondents to be the victims of rape and to be the victims of robbery, with a similar pattern for aggravated assault. The victimization rate for simple assault is more similar for whites and African Americans, with the biracial/multiracial respondents having a rate three to four times higher than all other racial groups.

Table 2.2 also displays personal victimization rates by ethnicity. Overall, in 2007 non–Hispanics had slightly higher victimization rates than Hispanics (21.0 per 1,000 population versus 18.6 per 1,000 population). This comparison does not hold for all years of the NCVS reports—for example, in 2000 Hispanic respondents reported higher victimization rates (30.8 per 1,000 persons aged 12 or older compared with 28.8 per 1,000).[28] Victimization rates for 2007 also vary by type of crime. Hispanics have the highest victimization rates for robbery, whereas non–Hispanics have higher victimization rates for rape, assault, and simple assault. Rates for aggravated assault are essentially identical across ethnic groups.

A recent analysis of the violent offense of carjacking (done by pooling several years of NCVS data), reveals that African Americans were three times as likely to be victims of carjacking than whites.[29] Box 2.1 also shows additional NCVS information on the violent victimization of college students by race and ethnicity compared to similar age respondents who are not college students.

B o x 2.1   College Students and Violent Victimization

The Bureau of Justice Statistics has pooled several years of National Crime Victimization Survey (NCVS) data (1995–2002) to offer a picture of violent victimization of college students. About 7.9 million people per year from ages 18 to 24 years were enrolled in college during this time. The consistent pattern of age, race, and victimization from the NCVS data set is that young minorities have routinely higher violent victimization rates than whites. However, white college students have higher rates of violent victimization than African American students and students of "other" races (65 per 1,000 students compared to 52 and 37 per 1,000 students, respectively). Nonstudent victimization rates (ages 18–24) are substantially higher, with African American and whites having the highest rates (83 and 65 per 1,000 population compared to the numbers outlined previously). African American students have the highest victimization rates for robbery and aggravated assault, but white students have higher rates of victimization for simple assault and rape victimization.

A unique aspect of this data set is that Hispanics are coded to be of any race, so their victimization rates can be compared to whites and African Americans, rather than simply non-Hispanics. A review of these data indicates that Hispanics have an overall violent victimization rate that is higher than the rate for African Americans but lower than the rate for whites. The exception to this pattern is the Hispanic victimization rate for rape—it is higher than any other racial/ethnic group in the study.

SOURCE: Katrina Baum and Patsy Klaus, "Violent Victimization of College Students, 1995–2000," *Bureau of Justice Statistics Report* (Washington, DC: Government Printing Office, January 2005).

Finally, the personal theft rates (pocket picking, purse snatchings) are highest for African Americans and the multiracial category compared with whites and "other races," with the multiracial group reporting a rate two times higher than African Americans. In contrast to the predominant violent offense pattern for ethnicity above, Hispanics have a higher rate of personal theft victimizations than non-Hispanics.

In July 2004, the NCVS questionnaire included questions to offer ongoing estimates of identity theft. The household heads were asked about identity theft experiences by members of the household, with nearly 8 million households indicating one member of the household reporting at least one event of identity theft.★ White and "other" race households had identity theft levels near the national average from the survey of 6.6 percent. African American households reported somewhat lower instances of identity theft at 5.8 percent of households. While white and biracial/multiracial households reported a substantially higher 11.4 percent victimization level. The ethnicity of the head of household also indicated variance on the level of identity theft, with nearly 8 percent of non-Hispanic households experiencing identity theft and approximately 5 percent of Hispanic households.[30]

The Effects of Urbanization

An analysis of victimization trends by the BJS using NCVS data from 1993 to 1998 indicates that urbanization is a key aspect of understanding violent victimization. The BJS report also indicated that urban residents, who accounted for 29 percent of the U.S. population, reported 38 percent of all violent and property crime victimizations. Suburban residents comprise 50 percent of the population and experience 47 percent of the victimizations. Rural residents are least likely to experience criminal victimization; they comprise 20 percent of the population and experience 20 percent of all criminal victimizations.[31]

Interesting convergence and divergence patterns by urbanization and race/ethnicity are discussed in this section. Victimization rates for all groups are highest in urban areas and lowest in rural areas. As we know from discussions earlier in this chapter it is important to disaggregate victimization rates by type of crime, as well as urbanization. This characteristic pattern is present in the combined violent and property victimization rates for African Americans and whites, as well as for Hispanics and non-Hispanics. Victimization rates for African Americans and whites are very similar in suburban and rural areas, with whites having a higher rate (34 per 1,000 population) than African Americans (31 per 1,000 population) in rural areas. In urban areas, the rate for African Americans (68 per 1,000 population) is higher than the rate for whites (59 per 1,000 population). In contrast, the violent victimization rate for "other races" (for example, Native Americans and Asian Americans) is substantially higher in rural areas than in urban areas.

★Identity theft for the purposes of the NCVS are: unauthorized credit card use, another existing account, and misuse of personal information.

The most recent victimization data indicate that although the overall property victimization rate is highest for African Americans and highest in urban areas, there are some interesting differences when we look more closely.[32] Personal theft victimization rates are always higher for whites, particularly in urban areas. The household burglary and motor vehicle theft rates for African Americans and whites nearly converge in rural areas.

Focus on an Issue
Violent Victimization and Women of Color

Research on the characteristics of victims of violent crime generally focuses on the race of the victim, the ethnicity of the victim, or the sex of the victim. There are relatively few studies that examine the interrelationships among race, ethnicity, sex, and violent victimization or that attempt to determine if the risk factors for violent victimization are different for white women and women of color.

Two studies of nonlethal violent victimization addressed these issues. Janet L. Lauritsen and Norman A. White used data from the National Crime Victimization Survey (NCVS) to identify the risk of violence for African American, white, and Hispanic females. Because they were interested in the potential relationship between neighborhood characteristics and risk for violence, they classified violent incidents according to whether they occurred within respondents' neighborhoods (that is, within one mile of their homes). They also differentiated between incidents involving strangers and those involving nonstrangers.[33]

Lauritsen and White found that the overall risk of nonlethal violence was lowest for white females and highest for African American females, with Hispanic females in the middle. They also found that (1) women, regardless of race/ethnicity, faced a lower risk of violence in their own neighborhoods; (2) African

American women faced a substantially higher risk of violence at the hands of nonstrangers than either white or Hispanic women; and (3) both African American and Hispanic women faced higher risks of violence at the hands of strangers than did white women. These racial/ethnic differences, which persisted when the authors controlled for other characteristics of the respondent that might be associated with risk of victimization, diminished or disappeared when they included a measure of neighborhood disadvantage in their models. When neighborhood disadvantage was taken into consideration, they found that Hispanic females, but not African American females, had a higher risk of nonstranger violence than white females and that neither Hispanic females nor black females faced a higher risk of stranger violence than white females. Further analysis revealed that African American, white, and Hispanic women who lived in disadvantaged neighborhoods had higher risks for stranger and nonstranger violence than African American, white, and Hispanic women who lived in more advantaged communities. According to the authors, this means that "the reduction of violence is unlikely to require group-specific solutions, but will require attention to both community and individual factors that foster safety and harm reduction"[34]

(Continued)

Laura Dugan and Robert Apel took a somewhat different approach to studying violent victimization of women of color. They combined eight years of NCVS data, which generated enough cases to explore risk factors for white, African American, Hispanic, Asian / Pacific Islander, and Native American females. In predicting violent victimization, the authors controlled for the respondent's age; home environment (type of residence, marital status, number of children younger than age 12, and whether the respondent went out every night); and such things as the respondent's income, education, and job situation. They found that Native American women faced the greatest risk of violent victimization, followed by black women, Hispanic women, white women, and Asian / Pacific Islander women. The rate for Native American women, in fact, was almost twice the rate for black women.[35]

The authors of this study discovered that the factors that predicted violent victimization were not the same for each group of women. Although being married was a protective factor for all women and going out every night and moving often were risk factors across the board, the other factors had more variable effects. Living in an urban area, for example, increased the risk of violent victimization only for African American and Native American women, and living in public housing was a risk factor only for Hispanic women.

Living alone with at least one child, having a job, and working while in college all had particularly strong effects on victimization of Asian / Pacific Islander woman.

The authors also found interesting racial/ethnic differences in the characteristics of the violent victimization incidents that women experienced. White women were the least likely to be victimized by someone using a weapon but were the most likely to be victimized by a spouse. African American women, however, were the group most likely to be victimized by a boyfriend or at home; they also were the most likely to be victimized with using a weapon and to be seriously injured. Asian / Pacific Islander women were the most likely to be victims of impersonal crimes (for example, robbery), to be victimized by strangers, and to be victimized by more than one offender. African American women were the most likely to call the police to report the victimization; Asian women were the least likely to do so. Hispanic females were the least likely to be victimized in the home, and Native American females were the most likely to be victimized by someone who was using drugs or alcohol at the time of the incident.

The results of these two studies suggest that explanations for the violent victimization of women are complicated and that it is "naive to assume that all women are uniformly put at risk or protected regardless of their cultural background"[36]

Lifetime Likelihood of Victimization

Although annual victimization rates are important indicators of the likelihood of victimization, they "do not convey the full impact of crime as it affects people."[37] To gauge the impact of crime, we must consider not just the odds of being victimized within the next few weeks or months but the possibility of being robbed, raped, assaulted, or burglarized at some time in our lives. Although the odds of being victimized during any 12-month period are low, the odds of ever being victimized may be high. Whereas only 16 out of

10,000 women are rape victims annually, for example, the lifetime likelihood of being raped is much greater: nearly 1 out of every 12 females (and 1 out of every 9 black females) will be the victim of a rape at some time during her life.[38]

Box 2.2   Native Americans and Violent Crime

Information on the victimization rates of Native Americans is difficult to compile. This group represents less than 1 percent (0.5 percent) of the sample population of non-Hispanic respondents in the National Crime Victimization Survey (NCVS). Given that the incidence of victimization in the general population is rare, documenting a rare event in a small population is challenging. The Bureau of Justice Statistics has pooled a number of years (1992–2001) to reveal a picture of Native American (nonfatal) violent victimization: 101 violent victimizations occurred per 1,000 population of Native Americans aged 12 and older. The average violent victimization rate for Native Americans was 2.5 times the rate for whites (41 per 1,000), twice the rate for African Americans (51 per 1,000), and 4.5 times that rate for Asians (22 per 1,000).[39]

When the victimization rates are disaggregated by crime type, Native Americans have higher victimization rates in almost all categories. Their robbery and assault victimization rates are twice that of whites and African Americans. However, the rape victimization rate for Native Americans is higher than for whites but lower than for African Americans. Additionally, in contrast to the general intraracial victimization patterns of white and African American crime, Native Americans report that 6 of 10 violent offenses were committed by someone they perceived to be white.[40]

Ronette Bachman and colleagues' recent report on "Violence Against American Indian and Alaska Native Women" reveals that sexual assault victimizations are more likely to be reported by "a friend, family member, or another official" then the victim herself. Additionally, victims reported being aware of a subsequent arrest in only 6 percent of sexual assault cases. This review of victimization data also revealed that "lifetime prevalence rates for physical assaults are also higher for American Indian and Alaska Native women compared to other women … [they] are more likely to be assaulted by known offenders compared to strangers."[41]

What is the impact of having such little information on victimization events of Native Americans? What should be the prevention response to such victimization? What should be the crime control response to such victimization? Bachman et al. argue that:

> The unique position of American Indian and Alaska Native tribes as both sovereign and dependent creates problematic jurisdictional barriers that sometimes prohibit an effective criminal justice response to American Indian and Alaska Native victims of violence. Several federal laws have limited tribal government's power to prosecute offenders including the Major Crimes Act (1885), which mandated that virtually all violent crimes committed on tribal lands were to be prosecuted by the federal government. Although tribes have the power to concurrently prosecute cases of violence, the Indian Civil Rights Act (1968) mandates that tribal courts are not permitted to punish offenders with more than $5,000 in fines, one year in jail or both. Importantly, tribal sovereignty in punishing offenders does not apply to non-American Indian and Alaska Natives (*Oliphant v. Suquamish Indian Tribe*, 435 U.S. [1978]).[42]

B o x   2.3   Asian Americans, Native Hawaiians, Pacific Islanders, and Violent Crime

---

Asian Americans, Native Hawaiians, and Pacific Islanders make up less than 4 percent of the population, but they account for 3 percent of property crime victimization in the United States and only 2 percent of nonfatal violent crimes. To estimate their victimization rates, the BJS pooled several years of NCVS (2002–2006) data. These rates indicate that Asian Americans, Native Hawaiians, and Pacific Islanders have a substantially lower victimization rate than non-Asian Americans.

Average Annual Violent Victimization Rate by Race/Hispanic Origin and Type of Crime, 2002–2006

	Rate per 1,000 persons aged 12 or older
Asian/NH/PI	10.6
White	22.6
African American	29.1
Hispanic	24.1
Native AM / AL Native	56.4

Rates for individual violent victimizations indicate that only for robbery are Asian/NH/PI victimization rates essentially the same as the next lowest group (whites).[43]

Additional unique patterns emerge from these NCVS analyses with pooled years of data. For example, compared to the non-Asian racial groups, Asian/NH/PI have a higher percentage of stranger assaults for both males (59 percent compared to 77 percent) and females (34 percent compared to 51 percent). Similarly, the persistent pattern of intraracial crime events does not hold true for Asian American victimizations. When Asian American respondents were asked to report the perceived race of the offender, less than 30 percent of offenders were identified as Asian Americans, whereas 35 percent were identified as white and 26 percent as African American.[44]

Recall that the NCVS data presented earlier on violent victimization combined Asian / Native Hawaiian / Pacific Islander with Native American / Alaska Native into a group called "other." What questions emerge when looking at victimization data from this viewpoint of pooled data, which allows for the disaggregation of Asian, Native Hawaiian, Pacific Islander from Native American / Alaskan Native? Given the relatively low victimization rates of one group compared to the high victimization rates of the contrasting constituent group, what victimization patters remain hidden from view? What mistakes are policy makers vulnerable to if looking at the aggregate information compared to the disaggregate information?

The BJS used annual victimization rates for a 10-year period to calculate lifetime victimization rates. These rates, which are presented in Table 2.3, indicate that about five out of six people will be victims of a violent crime at least once during their lives and that nearly everyone will be the victim of a personal theft at least once. There is no difference in the African American and white rates for personal theft, and only a slight difference in the rates for violent crimes.

T A B L E 2.3   Lifetime Likelihood of Victimization

	Percentage Who will be Victimized[a]	
	African Americans	Whites
Violent crimes	87	82
Robbery	51	27
Assault	73	74
Rape (females only)	11	8
Personal theft	99	99

[a]Percentage of persons who will experience one or more victimizations starting at 12 years of age.
SOURCE: Bureau of Justice Statistics, U.S. Department of Justice, *Lifetime Likelihood of Victimization* (Washington, DC: U.S. Government Printing Office, 1987).

For the individual crimes of violence, the lifetime likelihood of being assaulted is nearly identical for African Americans and whites; about three of every four people, regardless of race, will be assaulted at some time during their lives. There are, however, large racial differences for robbery, with African Americans almost twice as likely as whites to be robbed. The lifetime likelihood of rape is also somewhat higher for African American females than for white females. Thus, for the two most serious (nonmurder) violent crimes, the likelihood of victimization is much higher for African Americans than for whites.

Homicide Victimization

The largest and most striking racial differences in victimization are for the crime of homicide. In fact, all of the data on homicide point to the same conclusion: African Americans, and particularly African American males, face a much greater risk of death by homicide than do whites.

Although the NCVS does not produce estimates of homicide victimization rates, there are a number of other sources of data. A partial picture is available from the Supplemental Homicide Reports, 2008 (SHR), submitted by law enforcement agencies to the U.S. Federal Bureau of Investigation (FBI) as part of the Uniform Crime Reports (UCR) Program.[45] This information is collected when available for single victim–single offender homicides. These data reveal that a disproportionate number of homicide victims are African American. In 2008 African Americans constituted no more than 15 percent of the population but comprised more than 47.7 percent of all homicide victims. Whites are underrepresented in homicide figures, compared to the population, but they did make up the largest number of victims, with whites comprising 48.3 percent of homicide victims. Asian / Pacific Islander and Native America / Alaska Natives make up the smallest group of homicide victims at less at 1.5 percent and 1 percent respectively.[46]

Focus on an Issue
Victim Assistance: Should Race Matter?

Although most observers agree that the American criminal justice system should treat suspects and offenders in a colorblind fashion, how should we treat victims? Gregg Barak, Jeanne M. Flavin, and Paul S. Leighton[47] argue that victim assistance should take the race, ethnicity, gender, and even class of the victim into consideration. They state, "Victim counseling needs to be sensitive to cultural values through which the victimization experience is interpreted. Rehabilitation and intervention programs likewise need to build on cultural values for maximum effectiveness."[48] For example, a victim of domestic violence may need different services depending on their social realities: a Hispanic woman with children, no employment history, and a limited working knowledge of English will require different services than a white woman with children, a professional employment history, and a command of English.

In Bachman and colleagues' exploration of domestic violence among Native American women, they assert that "some American Indian and Alaska Native communities are developing culturally sensitive interventions for violence against American Indian and Alaska Native women both within and outside of the criminal justice system. These family or community forums emphasize restorative and reparative approaches to justice. One example of this is the Navajo Peacemaking system. Other culturally sensitive victim support services are being created across the country, in both urban settings as well as on rural tribal lands."[49]

Should the criminal justice system be entirely color blind, even in response to victims? Or does justice actually require the system to be color conscious in some situations? Do you support the victim advocate's position that victim services should be racially, ethnically, and culturally sensitive in their victimization responses?

The SHR data reveal that homicide is a more significant risk factor for African Americans than for whites. Whereas homicide rates have decreased among all groups since the early 1990s, the homicide rate in 2002 indicated that African Americans were six times more likely to be murdered than whites (20.8 per 100,000 population compared to 3.3 per 100,000 population).[50] Even more striking, the rate for African American males was nearly 8 times the rate for white males and 24 times the rate for white females. The rate for African American females exceeded the rate for white females, approaching that of white males.

The BJS analysis of homicide trends from 1976 to 2002 reveals that homicide circumstances of homicides often vary by race.[51] For example, although whites and African Americans are equally likely to be victims of gun homicides, whites constitute more than half of the victims in arson and poison cases. Additionally, African Americans are the majority of victims in homicides involving drugs, and whites are the majority victim in sex-related homicides and gang-related homicides.

Summary: A More Comprehensive Picture of the Crime Victim

The victimization data presented in the preceding sections offer a more comprehensive picture of the crime victim than is found in common perceptions and media presentations. These data reveal that African Americans, Asian / Pacific Islanders, Native Americans, and Hispanics are often more likely than whites and non-Hispanics to be victims of household and personal crimes. These racial and ethnic differences are particularly striking for violent crimes, especially robbery. African Americans—especially African American males— also face a much greater risk of death by homicide than whites. It thus seems fair to conclude that in the United States, the groups at greatest risk of becoming crime victims are those that belong to racial and ethnic minority groups.

Focus on an Issue
Environmental Racism Claims Brought under Title VI of the Civil Rights Act

As Michael Fischer notes, since "the early 1980s, environmental justice advocates have been publicizing and protesting the fact that environmental hazards at the workplace, in the home, and in the community are disproportionately visited upon poor people and people of color." Environmental racism builds on the foundation of the civil rights movement and the term was coined by African American civil rights activist Benjamin Chavis. This term is used most commonly to refer to the enactment or enforcement of any policy, practice, or regulation that negatively affects the environment of marginal low-income and/or racially homogeneous communities at a disproportionate level; thus, the battle against environmental racism includes claims by Native Americans, African Americans, and Hispanic Americans. Fischer notes that environmental racism may occur if "the actions of those federally-funded state agencies create a racially discriminatory distribution of pollution, then a violation of Title VI has occurred and a civil rights lawsuit is warranted."[52]

Bullard contends that "people of color in all regions of the country bear a disproportionate share of the nation's environmental problems," including air pollution, soil pollution, dumps, and so on. In 2010, as director of a center dedicated to grassroots efforts to fight for environmental justice, he observed that a 2007 study

> found race to be the most potent predictor of where commercial hazardous waste facilities are located. Environmental injustice in people of color communities is as much or more prevalent today than 20 years ago. People of color make up the majority (56%) of the residents living in neighborhoods within two miles of the nation's commercial hazardous waste facilities and more than two-thirds (69%) of the residents in neighborhoods with clustered facilities.[53]

Are there instances of environmental racism in your community or region? Go to the Environmental Justice Resource Center at Clark University (http://www.ejrc.cau.edu/) for more details on specific contaminated sites.

PICTURE OF THE TYPICAL OFFENDER

For many people the term "crime" evokes an image of a young African American male who is armed with a handgun and who commits a robbery, a rape, or a murder. In the minds of many Americans, "crime" is synonymous with "black crime." It is easy to see why the average American believes that the typical offender is African American. The crimes that receive the most attention—from the media, from politicians, and from criminal justice policy makers—are "street crimes" such as murder, robbery, and rape. These are precisely the crimes for which African Americans are arrested at a disproportionately high rate. In 2008, for example, 50.1 percent of those arrested for murder, 546.7 percent of those arrested for robbery, and 32.2 percent of those arrested for rape were African American.[54]

Arrest rates for serious violent crimes, of course, do not tell the whole story. Although violent crimes may be the crimes we fear most, they are not the crimes that occur most frequently. Moreover, arrest rates do not necessarily present an accurate picture of offending. Many crimes are not reported to the police, and many of those reported do not result in an arrest.

In this section we use a number of criminal justice data sources to paint a picture of the typical criminal offender. We summarize the offender data presented in official police records, victimization reports, and self-report surveys. Because each of these data sources varies both in terms of the offender information captured and the "point of contact" of the suspect with the criminal justice system, the picture of the typical offender that each produces also differs somewhat. We note these discrepancies and summarize the results of research designed to reconcile them.

Official Arrest Statistics

Annual data on arrests are produced by the UCR system, which has been administered by the FBI since 1930. Today the program compiles reports from more than 17,000 law enforcement agencies across the country, representing 95 percent of the total U.S. population (more than 288 million Americans). The annual report, *Crime in the United States*, offers detailed information from local, state, and federal law enforcement agencies on crime counts and rates as well as arrest information.

Problems with UCR Data

The information on offenders gleaned from the Uniform Crime Reports is incomplete and potentially misleading because it includes only offenders whose crimes result in arrest. The UCR data exclude offenders whose crimes are not reported to the police and offenders whose crimes do not lead to arrest. A second limitation is that the UCR reports include arrest statistics for four racial groups (white, African

American, Native American, and Asian), but they do not present any information by ethnicity (Hispanic versus non-Hispanic). See "Focus on an Issue: A Proposal to Eliminate Race from the Uniform Crime Report" for further discussion of the controversy surrounding the reporting of race in UCR figures.

A substantial proportion of crimes are not reported to the police. In fact, the NCVS reveals that fewer than half of all violent victimizations and only one-third of all property victimizations are reported to the police. Factors that influence the decision to report a crime include the seriousness of the crime and the relationship between the victim and the offender; violent crimes are more likely than property crimes to be reported, as are crimes committed by friends or relatives rather than strangers.[55]

Victimization surveys reveal that victims often fail to report crimes to the police because of a belief that nothing could be done, the event was not important enough, the police would not want to be bothered, or it was a private matter. Failure to report also might be based on the victim's fear of self-incrimination or embarrassment resulting from criminal justice proceedings that result in publicity or cross-examination.[56]

Focus on an Issue
A Proposal to Eliminate Race from the Uniform Crime Report

In October 1993 a group of mayors, led by Minneapolis Mayor Donald Fraser, sent a letter to the U.S. Attorney General's office asking that the design of the Uniform Crime Report (UCR) be changed to eliminate race from the reporting of arrest data. The mayors were concerned about the misuse of racial data from crime statistics. They charged that the current reporting policies "perpetuate racism in American society" and contribute to the general perception "that there is a causal relationship between race and criminality." Critics of the proposal argued that race data are essential to battling street crime because they reveal who the perpetrators are.

Although the federal policy of reporting race in arrest statistics has not changed, Fraser was instrumental in pushing a similar request through the Minnesota Bureau of Investigation. The final result in Minnesota was the following disclaimer in state crime publications:

"Racial and ethnic data must be treated with caution ... [E]xisting research on crime has generally shown that racial or ethnic identity is not predictive of criminal behavior within data which has been controlled for social and economic factors." This statement warns that descriptive data are not sufficient for causal analysis and should not be used as the sole indication of the role of race and criminality for the formation of public policy.

Using inductive reasoning, the over-representation of minority race groups in arrest data can be suggestive of at least two causal inferences: (1) certain racial groups characterized by differential offending rates, or (2) arrest data reflective of differential arrest patterns targeted at minorities. What steps must a researcher take to move beyond descriptions of racial disparity in arrest data to an exploration of causal explanations for racial patterns evident in arrest data?

The NCVS indicates that the likelihood of reporting a crime to the police also varies by race. African Americans are slightly more likely than whites to report crimes of theft and violence to the police, whereas Hispanics are substantially less likely than non-Hispanics to report victimizations to the police. Michael J. Hindelang found that victims of rape and robbery were more likely to report the victimization to the police if there was an African American offender.[57]

Even if the victim does decide to report the crime to the police, there is no guarantee that the report will result in an arrest. The police may decide that the report is "unfounded"—in this case, an official report is not filed and the incident is not counted as an "offense known to the police." Furthermore, even if the police do file an official report, they may be unwilling or unable to make an arrest. In 2003 only about 20 percent of all index crimes were cleared by the police; the clearance rate for serious crimes ranged from 13.1 percent for burglary to 62.4 percent for murder.[58]

Police officer and offender interactions also may influence the inclination to make an arrest, and cultural traditions may influence police–citizen interactions. For instance, Asian communities often handle delinquent acts informally, when other communities would report them to the police.[59] Hispanic cultural traditions may increase the likelihood of arrest if the Hispanic's tradition of showing respect for an officer by avoiding direct eye contact is interpreted as insincerity.[60] African Americans who appear "hostile" or "aggressive" also may face a greater likelihood of arrest.[61]

The fact that many reported crimes do not lead to an arrest, coupled with the fact that police decision making is highly discretionary, suggests that we should exercise caution in drawing conclusions about the characteristics of those who commit crime based on the characteristics of those who are arrested. To the extent that police decision making reflects stereotypes about crime or racially prejudiced attitudes, the picture of the typical offender that emerges from official arrest statistics may be racially distorted. If police target enforcement efforts in minority communities or concentrate on crimes committed by racial minorities, then obviously racial minorities will be overrepresented in arrest statistics.

A final limitation of UCR offender information centers on the information not included in these arrest reports. The UCR arrest information fails to offer a full picture of the white offender entering the criminal justice system. Specifically, additional sources of criminal justice data present the white offender as typical in the case of many economic, political, and organized crime offenses. Russell, in detailing the results of her "search for white crime" in media and academic sources, supports the view that the occupational (white-collar) crimes for which whites are consistently overrepresented may not elicit the same level of fear as the street crimes highlighted in the UCR but nonetheless have a high monetary and moral cost.[62] (See Box 2.4 for information on the "operationalization," or measurement, of race in crime data.)

Arrest Data

The arrest data presented in Table 2.5 reveal that the public perception of the "typical criminal offender" as an African American is generally inaccurate.

Examination of the arrest statistics for all offenses, for instance, reveals that the typical offender is white; more than two-thirds (69.2 percent) of those arrested in 2008 were white, less than one-third (28.3 percent) were African American, and less than 3 percent were Native American or Asian. Similarly, more than half of those arrested for violent crimes and roughly two-thirds of those arrested for property crimes were white. In fact, the only crimes for which the typical offender was African American were murder, robbery, and gambling.[63]

Examining the percentage of all arrests involving members of each racial group must be done in the context of the distribution of each group in the population. In 2008 whites comprised approximately 83 percent of the U.S. population, African Americans comprised 13 percent, Native Americans comprised less than 1 percent, and Asians comprised 3 percent. A more appropriate comparison, then, is the percentage in each racial group arrested *in relation* to that group's representation in the general population, rather than simply stating the "typical offender" by the largest proportion of offenders by racial group.

Thus although whites are the people most often arrested in crime categories reported in the UCR, it appears that African Americans are arrested at a disproportionately high rate for *nearly* all offenses. The total combined rate for all

---

B o x 2.4   The Operationalization of Race in Criminal Justice Data

The concept of race is measured—operationalized—in a number of ways, depending on the discipline and depending on the research question. Most biologists and anthropologists recognize the difficulties with using traditional race categories (white, black, red, yellow) as an effective means of classifying populations, and most social scientists rely on administrative definitions for recordkeeping, empirical analysis, and theory testing. Given these conditions, however, the term "race" still carries the connotation of an objective measurement with a biological/genetic basis.

As Knepper[64] notes, the recording of race in the UCR can be traced to a practice that has no formal theoretical or policy relevance. From available accounts, this information was recorded because it was "available" and may be a side effect of efforts to legitimize fingerprint identification. Currently, the UCR manual gives detailed information on the definitions for index offenses and Part 2 offenses and provides specific instructions about the founding of crimes and the counting rules for multiple offenses. What is lacking, however, are specific instructions on the recording of race information. Administrative/census definitions provided by local law enforcement agencies on agency arrest forms are calculated and reported, but no criteria for the source of the information are given. Thus, some records will reflect self-reporting by the offender, whereas others will reflect observations of police personnel. Some police arrest reports have "black," "white," "Native American," and "Asian," whereas many use the category of "other." Still others use "Hispanic" in the race category, rather than a separate ethnicity. Given that the FBI does not currently request or report ethnicity in the UCR, much information is lost.

The FBI's National Incident-Based Reporting System does log additional information based on race and ethnicity for victims and offenders, but the information available in that data set for 2004 reflects on only 20 percent of the U.S. population in 26 states.[65]

T A B L E 2.4   Percent Distribution of Arrests by Race, 2008

	White (%)	African American (%)	Native American (%)	Asian American (%)
Total	69.2	28.3	1.3	1.1
Part 1 Crimes				
Murder and nonnegligent manslaughter	47.9	50.1	1.0	1.1
Forcible rape	65.2	32.2	1.2	1.4
Robbery	41.7	56.7	0.7	0.9
Aggravated assault	63.3	34.2	1.4	1.2
Burglary	66.8	31.4	0.9	0.9
Larceny-theft	68.1	29.3	1.3	1.4
Motor-vehicle theft	59.7	38.1	1.1	1.2
Arson	75.8	21.7	1.2	1.2
Violent Crime	58.3	39.4	1.2	1.1
Property Crime	67.4	30.1	1.2	1.3
Part 2 Crimes [Selected]				
Other assaults	65.2	32.2	1.4	1.2
Vandalism	75.3	22.0	1.5	1.2
Weapons: carrying, possessing, etc.	56.7	41.7	0.7	0.9
Prostitution and commercialized vice	55.7	40.9	0.8	2.6
Sex offenses (except forcible rape and prostitution)	73.5	24.0	1.1	1.4
Drug abuse violations	63.8	34.8	0.6	0.7
Gambling	22.6	75.0	0.3	2.1
Driving under the influence (DUI)	87.3	10.0	1.3	1.3
Drunkenness	82.5	15.0	1.9	0.6
Disorderly conduct	63.4	34.1	1.6	0.8
Vagrancy	59.8	37.8	1.9	0.5

SOURCE: *Crime in the United States, 2008* (Washington, DC: U.S. Department of Justice, 2009). Available at http://www.fbi.gov/ucr/cius2008/data/table_43.html.

offenses (see Table 2.4) indicates that the arrest rate for African Americans is two times higher than would be predicted by their representation in the population. The disproportion is even larger for the most serious Part 1 / index offenses reported in the UCR; the arrest rate is two and a half times higher for African Americans than predicted by their representation in the population.

Among the individual offenses, however, the degree of African American overrepresentation varies. The largest disparities are found for robbery and murder. The arrest rate for African Americans is nearly four times what we would expect for murder and robbery, given their representation in the population. These differences also are pronounced for rape, motor vehicle theft, gambling, vagrancy, stolen property offenses, and weapons offenses.

Table 2.4 also presents arrest statistics for whites, Native Americans, and Asians. Whites are overrepresented for some UCR offenses. Specifically, whites are overrepresented for driving under the influence (DUIs) and liquor law violations compared to their representation in the general population. Whites are found in numbers consistent with their representation in the population for drunkenness arrests.

The overall pattern for Native American arrest figures is a slight overrepresentation compared to their representation in the population (1.3 percent of those arrested versus 0.8 percent in the population); however, the pattern across crimes is more erratic. For Part 1 / index crimes, Native Americans are slightly more likely to be arrested for violent crime (particularly forcible rape and aggravated assault) and for property crimes (particularly larceny-theft) than their representation in the population suggests. Native Americans are overrepresented in several Part 2 offenses, including other assaults, vandalism, offenses against family and children, liquor law violations, drunkenness, disorderly conduct, and vagrancy. The proportion of Native American offenders arrested for a number of offenses—robbery, fraud, embezzlement, receiving stolen property, prostitution / commercialized vice, and gambling—is lower than what is expected given their proportion in the population. Additionally, the arrest figures for a number of other offenses— murder, robbery, aggravated assault, burglary, and drug abuse violations—are consistent with their proportion in the general population.

Caution is required when interpreting Native American arrest figures because arrests made by tribal police and federal agencies are not recorded in UCR data. Using information from the Bureau of Indian Affairs, K. Peak and J. Spencer[66] found that although UCR statistics revealed lower-than-expected homicide arrest rates for Native Americans, homicide rates were nine times higher than expected across the 207 reservations reporting.

For overall figures and each index offense, Asian Americans are underrepresented in UCR arrest data (1.2 percent of arrests in 2008 compared to 3 percent of the population). The notable exception to the pattern of underrepresentation is the Part 2 offense of gambling. Although 2008 data reveal 2.1 percent of arrests for gambling are of Asians, UCR arrest figures have been as high as 6.7 percent. The arrest rate for this offense can reach twice what is expected given the representation of Asians in the population. Notably, Asian Americans are underrepresented in arrest figures for arson, fraud, drug abuse violations, disorderly conduct, and vagrancy.

In 2008 James A. Fox and Mark L. Swatt released a report based on FBI supplemental homicide reports that in the five-year period of their study (2002–2007) overall (not race spefific) homicide reports revealed little fluctuation. However, homicides involving young black male perpetrators rose by 43 percent and young black male victims rose by 31 percent. This increase was not present in the white male homicide and victim populations, regardless of age. Fox and Swatt also note a

Focus on an Issue
Immigration and Crime: Fear versus Fact

Many reserachers and social critics are concerned that the infromation we "know" about crime is distorted. The negative images of immigrants being criminals and immigration rates causing crime rates to rise is commonly presented by both news figures and politicians. These messages are numerous and constant, especially in light of immigrations numbers doubling in the past decade. However, U.S. crime rates have not increaesed during this time. Crime rates have fallen in most cases, remained stable in others, and even declined dramatically in other areas. On a community level, two recent studies come to the same conclusion about the crime benefit of immigrant populations. First, a California study revealed that "California cities with large populations of recently arrived immigrants showed no significant relationship between immigrant inflows and property crimes, and a negative relationship with violent crimes."[67]

Second, Stowell and colleagues' research asserts that the multivariate findings from their multijusrisdictional data set

"indicate that violent crime rates tended to decrease as metropolitan areas experienced gains in their concentration of immigrants. The inverse relationsip is especially robust for the offense of robbery. Overall, our results support the hypothesis that the broad reductions in violent crime during recent years are potentially attributable to increases in immigration."[68]

Regarding public perceptions about immigrants being more crime prone, the Public Policy Institute of California cites a national poll taken in 2006 that "asked adults nationwide whether they thought immigrants were more or less likely than native residents to be involved in criminal activity. Most respondents (68 percent) replied 'not much difference,' while 19 percent repled 'more likely' and 12 percent 'less likely.'"[69] The most accurate answer for street crimes appears to be "less likely," as self-report data and incarceration data present a similar picture of crime by immigrants as less likely than native born and socialized populations.[70]

race-specific trend in the use of guns during homicides, with a nearly 50 percent increase in the use of guns by young (ages 14–24), black male perpetrators. They further note there are few geographic differences in this trend, so it is not just a big city, East or West Coast problem. In short "a majority of states and a majority of cities have experienced increases in homicides committeed by young black offenders compared with smaller increases or even decreases among their white counterparts."[71]

Fox and Swatt also express concern about the consistent rise in gun use in homicide victimizations since 1976. The trend present for gun use by white homicide offenders peaked in the early 1990s, while gun use among black offenders, particularly under the age of 25, has continued to increase. In 2007 nearly 85 percent of black homicide offenders under the age of 25 used guns.[72]

According to the report by Fox and Swatt that presents homicide rates by age and race, the highest homicide offending rates are found among young, black males between 18 and 24, roughly nine times higher than the offending rate for white males of the same age group. Similarly, the victimzation rates are highest for young, black males ages 18 to 24, with a rate nearly eight times higher than that for white males of the same age group.

Supplemental homicide reports from 2008 reveal that the peak age for homicide offending for males is between 17 and 24; it drops significantly after the age of 30. Women are identified as commiting less than 10 percent of homicides, and their offending patterns mirror those of males with the peak offending years between 17 and 24 and a significant decline after age 30. While blacks are identified as homicide offenders in more than 50 percent of cases where the offender race is known, the peak age of offending varies little by race of offender. The main difference by age and race is that black offenders start offending at high levels at an earlier age than white offenders (13 to 16 years of age), but white offenders continue to offend at a significant rate until a later age range (into their 40s).

Perceptions of Offenders by Victims

Clearly African Americans are arrested at a disproportionately high rate. The problem, of course, is that we do not know the degree to which arrest statistics accurately reflect offending. As noted previously, not all crimes are reported to the police and not all of those that are reported lead to an arrest.

One way to check the accuracy of arrest statistics is to examine data on offenders produced by the NCVS. Respondents who report a "face-to-face" encounter with an offender are asked to indicate the race of the offender. If the percentage of victims who report being robbed by an African American matches the percentage of African Americans who are arrested for robbery, we can have greater confidence in the validity of the arrest statistics. We can be more confident that differences in the likelihood of arrest reflect differences in offending.

If, however, the percentage of victims who report being robbed by an African American is substantially smaller than the percentage of African Americans who are arrested for robbery, we can conclude that at least some of the disproportion in the arrest rate reflects what Hindelang refers to as "selection bias" in the criminal justice system. As Hindelang notes, "If there are substantial biases in the UCR data for *any* reason, we would expect, to the extent that victimization survey reports are unbiased, to find large discrepancies between UCR arrest data and victimization survey reports on racial characteristics of offenders."[73]

Problems with NCVS Offender Data

There are obvious problems in relying on victims' "perceptions" of the race of the offender. Respondents who report a victimization are asked if the offender was white, African American, or some other race. These perceptions are of questionable validity because victimizations often occur quickly and involve the element of shock. In addition, victim memory is subject to decay over time and to "retroactive reconstruction" to fit the popular conception of a criminal offender.

If a victim believes that the "typical criminal" is African American, this may influence his or her perception of the race of the offender.

Relying on victims' perceptions of offenders' race creates another potential problem. If these perceptions are based on skin color, they may be unreliable indicators of the race of an offender. There are many very light-skinned African Americans and dark-skinned "white" people. Hispanics are of a wide range of skin colors. A person may self-identify in a way not reflected by his or her skin color. Thus, individuals may appear in different racial groupings in victimization reports than they do on a police arrest report. A light-skinned offender who identifies himself as Hispanic and whose race is thus recorded as "other" in arrest data might show up in victimization data as "white." If this occurs with any frequency, it obviously will affect the picture of the offender that emerges from victimization data.

Perceptions of Offenders

With these caveats in mind, we present the NCVS data on the perceived race of the offender for single-offender violent victimizations. As Table 2.5 shows, although the typical offender for all of the crimes is white (or is perceived to be white), African Americans are overrepresented as offenders for all of the offenses listed. The most notable disproportion revealed by Table 2.5 is for robbery, with 37 percent of the offenders in single-offender robberies identified as African American. Also, African Americans are overrepresented as offenders for rape/sexual assault, aggravated assault, and simple assault. Note that the "not known" category ranges from 17.0 percent of respondents for rape / sexual assault to 7.3 percent of respondents for simple assault cases.

We argued earlier that one way to check the accuracy of arrest statistics is to *compare* the race of offenders arrested for various crimes with victims' perceptions of the race of the offender. These comparisons are found in Table 2.6. There is a

T A B L E 2.5   Perceived Race of Offender for Single-Offender Crimes of Violence

Type of Crime	Perceived Race of the Offender			
	White	African American	Other	Race not known
All Crimes of Violence	59.0%	22.4%	10.8%	7.9%
Rape/Sexual Assault	48.8	18.1	16.2	17.0
Robbery	39.7	37.0	15.2	8.9
Assault	61.1	21.4	10.1	7.4
Aggravated	56.2	24.1	12.0	7.6
Simple	62.8	20.5	9.5	7.3

SOURCE: Bureau of Justice Statistics, *Criminal Victimization in the United States—Statistical Tables, 2006* (Washington, DC: U.S. Department of Justice, 2008). Available at http://bjs.ojp.usdoj.gov/content/pub/pdf/cvus0602.pdf.

T A B L E 2.6   **A Comparison of UCR and NCVS Data on Offender Race, 2006**

	Whites		African Americans		Other	
	Arrested	Perceived	Arrested	Perceived	Arrested	Perceived
Rape	65.3	58.8	32.5	21.8	2.2	19.5
Robbery	42.2	43.2	56.3	40.3	1.6	8.8
Aggravated Assault	63.2	60.1	34.5	26.0	2.3	12.9
Simple Assault	65.2	67.8	32.2	22.1	2.6	10.2

SOURCE: Federal Bureau of Investigation, *Crime in the United States, 2006*. Available at http://www.fbi.gov/ucr/cius2006/data/table_43.html; Bureau of Justice Statistics, *Criminal Victimization in the United States—Statistical Tables, 2006*. Available at http://bjs.ojp.usdoj.gov/content/pub/pdf/cvus0602.pdf.

relatively close match in the figures for white offenders for robbery and aggravated assault between victim perception data and arrest data. These comparisons also suggest that whites may be overrepresented in arrest data for rape and underrepresented in arrest data for simple assault. For African Americans, however, the pattern is more consistent—that is, African Americans are represented in arrest figures in much higher proportions than the perception of offenders from victim interviews for all offenses examined, with more than one-third higher representation in arrest figures than in victim-perception percentages. These comparisons indicate that the racial disproportion found in arrest rates for these four offenses cannot be used to resolve the dilemma of differential arrest rates by race versus a higher rate of offending among African Americans. It may be reasonably argued that such evidence actually suggests the presence of both differentially high offending rates by African Americans for serious violent offenses *and* the presence of differentially high arrest rates for African Americans, particularly for rape offenses.

The comparison of "other" race offers a consistent pattern of underrepresentation of "other" race in arrest figures compared to the victim-perception figures. This observation could mean that Asian / Pacific Islander and Native American / Alaska Native are committing crimes at a higher rate than they are arrested for. However, these figures also suggest that NCVS respondents may be classifying offenders they perceive as Hispanic/Latino/Mexican in appearance to be of "other" race. Citizens commonly assume that Hispanic is a racial category, not an ethnic category. It may be argued, then, that dark-skinned offenders who do not appear African American may be classified as "other" because Hispanic is not an option for the race-identification question. Additionally, NCVS respondents are not asked to identify the perceived ethnicity of the offender.

Hindelang used early victimization data to determine which of these explanations (differential offending versus differential enforcement) was more likely. His initial comparison of 1974 arrest statistics with victimization data for rape, robbery, aggravated assault, and simple assault revealed some evidence of "differential selection for criminal justice processing"[74] for two of the offenses examined. For rape and aggravated assault, the percentage of African American offenders in the victimization data was smaller (9 percentage points for rape, 11 percentage points for aggravated assault) than the proportion found in UCR arrest statistics.

However, once Hindelang controlled for victimizations that were reported to the police, the discrepancies disappeared and the proportions of offenders identified as African American and white were strikingly similar. Hindelang concluded that "it is difficult to argue (from these data) that blacks are no more likely than whites to be involved in the common law crimes of robbery, forcible rape, assault."[75]

Hindelang's analysis of victimizations reported to the police also revealed a pattern of differential reporting by victims. Specifically, Hindelang found that for rape and robbery, those victimized by African Americans were more likely than those victimized by whites to report the crime to the police. Hindelang suggested that this is a form of selection bias—victim-based selection bias.

Hindelang concluded his comparison of UCR arrest rates and victimization survey data by separating the elements of criminal justice—system selection bias, victim-based selection bias, and differential offending rates. He argued that both forms of selection bias were present but that each was outweighed by the overwhelming evidence of differential involvement of African Americans in offending.

Using NIBRS arrest data (17 states), Stewart J. D'Alessio and Lisa Stolzenberg try to disentangle differential offending from differential enforcement by deriving research questions from the social threat hypothesis. They use racial composition of a jurisdiction to approximate the social threat of racial minority populations to determine if law enforcement arrest practices vary by the racial composition of reporting jurisdictions, and thus differentiate differential arrest practices from differential offending practices. They report that the odds of arrest were actually higher for whites than blacks in three of the four crime types examined. They conclude that their findings suggest that "the disproportionately high arrest rate for black citizens is most likely attributable to differential involvement in reported crime rather than to racially biased law enforcement practices."[76]

Self-Report Surveys

Self-report surveys are another way to paint a picture of the criminal offender. These surveys question respondents about their participation in criminal or delinquent behavior. Emerging in the 1950s, the self-report format remains a popular source of data for those searching for descriptions and causes of criminal behavior. One of the advantages of asking people about their behavior is that it gives a less-distorted picture of the offender than an official record because it is free of the alleged biases of the criminal justice system. However, it is not at all clear that self-report survey results provide a more *accurate* description of the criminal offender.[77]

Problems with Self-Report Surveys

One of the major weaknesses of the self-report format is that there is no single design used. Moreover, different surveys focus on different aspects of criminal behavior. Not all self-report surveys ask the same questions or use the same or similar populations, and very few follow the same group over time. Usually, the sample population is youth from school settings or institutionalized groups.

In addition to the problems of inconsistent format and noncomparable samples, self-report surveys suffer from a variety of other limitations. The accuracy of self-report data is influenced by the respondents' honesty and memory and by interviewer bias.

One of the most confounding limitations in criminal justice data sets is present with self-report surveys: the comparisons are overwhelmingly between African Americans and whites. Little can be said about Native Americans, Asian Americans, or Hispanic Americans. Some studies suffer from the additional limitation of homogenous samples, with insufficient racial representation. These limitations make it difficult to draw conclusions about how many members of a racial group commit delinquent activity (prevalence) and how frequently racial minorities commit crime (incidence).

Although self-report surveys generally are assumed to be reliable and valid, this assumption has been shown to be less tenable for certain subgroups of offenders.[78] Specifically, it has been shown that there is differential validity for white and African American respondents. Validity is the idea that, as a researcher, you are measuring what you think you are measuring. Reverse record checks (matching self-report answers with police records) have shown that there is greater concurrence between respondent answers and official police arrest records for white respondents than for African American respondents.[79] This indicates that African American respondents tend to underreport some offending behavior.

Delbert Elliot and colleagues caution against a simplistic interpretation of these findings.[80] They find that African American respondents are more likely to underreport index-type offenses than less-serious offenses. Therefore, they suggest that this finding may indicate the differential validity of official police records rather than differential validity of the self-report measures by race. An example of differential validity of police records would occur if police reported the clearly serious offenses for whites and African Americans but reported the less serious offenses for African Americans only. In short, most self-report researchers conclude that racial comparisons must be made with caution.

Characteristics of Offenders

Usually juvenile self-report surveys record demographic data and ask questions about the frequency of certain delinquent activities in the last year. The delinquent activities included range in seriousness range from less-serious actions like skipping class and drinking liquor to more-serious behaviors such as stealing something worth more than fifty dollars, stealing a car, or assaulting someone.[81]

Early self-report studies, those conducted before 1980, found little difference in delinquency rates across race (African American and white only). Later, more refined self-report designs have produced results that challenge the initial assumption of similar patterns of delinquency.[82] Some research findings indicate that African American males are more likely than white males to report serious criminal behavior (prevalence). Moreover, a larger portion of African Americans than whites report a high frequency of serious delinquency (incidence).[83]

Theoretical Explanations for the Racial Gap in Offending

Theoretically driven empirical research into the connections among race, ethnicity, and crime helps answer the question of whether minorities have differential offending rates compared to whites. Perhaps the most recent and comprehensive analysis of the race and prevalence and race and incidence issues was done by Huizinga and Elliot[84] with six waves of the National Youth Survey (NYS) data. This self-report survey is a longitudinal study that began in 1976 and uses a national panel design. This study offers the only national assessment of individual offending rates based on self-report studies for a six-year period. See Box 2.5, "Monitoring the Future," for additional information on self-report delinquent behavior.

Community Influence on the Racial Gap in Offending Rates

Criminological theory at the beginning of the twentieth century focused on immigrant communities with reportedly high delinquency rates to develop such

---

B o x 2.5   Monitoring the Future

The only student-based self-report survey done on a yearly basis with a nationwide sample is Monitoring the Future.[85] Responses to their delinquency questions reveal few differences in self-report delinquent behavior by white compared to African American youth. White youth were slightly more likely to report being in a serious fight within the last year, using a weapon to get something from a person, taking something from a store, and taking a car that did not belong to someone in their family. African American youth were slightly more likely to report taking something from a store without paying for it, taking something not belonging to them worth less than $50, and going into some house or building without permission.

David Huizinga and Elliot explored whether African American youth have a higher prevalence of offending than whites and whether a higher incidence of offending by African Americans can explain differential arrest rates. Their analysis revealed few consistent racial differences across the years studied, either in the proportion of African American and white youth engaging in delinquent behavior or the frequency with which African American and white offenders commit delinquent acts. Contrary to Hindelang, they suggest that the differential selection bias hypothesis cannot be readily dismissed because the differential presence of youth in the criminal justice system cannot be explained entirely by differential offending rates.[86]

Focus on an Issue
Code of the Street: Predicts Violent Delinquency

In Elijah Anderson's work, he sets forth a "Code of the Street" perspective to explain the causes of violent delinquency among African Americans. This work suggests a learning environment conducive to the commission of violence as individuals develop "social identities" consistent with the predominant street culture.[87] Recent work by Eric Stewart and Ronald Simons offers a multivariate analysis of the "code of the street" perspective by testing two key hypotheses, finding support for each. Using a data set of 700 African American youth in response to a survey designed to "identify neighborhood and family processes that contribute to African American children's development in families living in a wide variety of community settings,"[88] these researchers found the following:

> First, based on the assumption of the existence of a neighborhood-based street culture of violence, Stewart and Simons hypothesize that "neighborhood street culture would be related significantly to violent delinquency above and beyond individual level street code values."[89] Their findings indicate that neighborhood street culture does in fact predict violent delinquency beyond the individual respondent's personal commitment to street code values.

Second, based on the ideas presented by Anderson that suggest "the neighborhood street culture moderates the effect of individual-level street code values of violence" thus leading to the assumption that "neighborhood street culture tends to amplify the violence-provoking effect of personnel commitment to the street code" Stewart and Simons proposed a second hypothesis in which they expect: "the effect of street code values to be associated strongly with violent delinquency in settings where strong evidence is found of a neighborhood street culture." Their findings indicate that support for the position that "neighborhood street culture moderates individual-level street code values on violence in neighborhoods where street culture is widespread."[90]

Theoretical explanations based on the importance of neighborhood effects as a locus for and moderator of causes of offending by race have received substantial support from the works of Anderson, Stewart and Simons, Stowell and colleagues (discussed earlier in the chapter), and Sampson and colleagues (discussed earlier in the chapter).

---

theories as Social Disorganization theory and Culture Conflict theory. More recent research by Sampson and colleagues indicates that minority immigrant populations in Chicago neighborhoods have lower rates of self-reported delinquency than white and African American populations. In their recent cohort study Sampson and colleagues find that first generation immigrants from Puerto Rico and Mexico have lower self reported delinquency rates than second- and third-generation immigrants.

Furthermore, Sampson and colleagues find that self-report data collected in a cohort study of juvenile and young adults from Chicago neighborhoods indicate that there is a gap in offending between African American, Mexican, Puerto Rican, and white youth. In an attempt to explain these descriptive findings, they control for neighborhood level effects, individual constitutional characteristics (IQ and impulsivity), and so on. Once controlling for the economic indicators, the gap in offending by race and ethnicity effectively disappears.[91]

Drug Offenders

A prevalent image in the news and entertainment media is the image of the drug user as a person of color. In particular, trend arrest data for nonalcoholic drug abuse violations reflect an overrepresentation of African Americans and often an overrepresentation of Native Americans for alcohol-related offenses. A more comprehensive picture of drug users emerges from self-report data that asks respondents to indicate their use of and prevalence of use behavior for particular drugs. In a recent report on the use of licit and illicit drugs among people of color, Monitoring the Future (MTF) provides patterns for Whites, African Americans, and Hispanics, while patterns of drug use for Native Americans and Asian youth come from the National Institutes of Health (NIH).

The most recent Monitoring the Future report on licit and illicit drug use by race offers several details about drug use by race:[92]

- African American twelfth-grade youth report the lowest use of all licit and illicit drugs reviewed, with whites having the highest reported use rates for such drugs as marijuana, powder cocaine, inhalants, LSD, Ecstasy, OxyContin, and Ritalin.

- Hispanic twelfth graders report the highest use rates for crystal meth and heroin (with and without a needle).

- Crack use rates are highest among twelfth-grade Hispanics, followed whites, with the lowest use rates by African Americans.

The National Institutes of Health report on Drug Use Among Racial and Ethnic Minorities adds the following elements to the picture of drug use in the United States:[93]

- About 6 percent of the U.S. population aged 12 and older are current illegal drug users, with Native American / Alaska Native populations having just over 12 percent current illicit drug users.

- About 3 percent of Asian / Pacific Islanders are current illegal drug users, but specific ethnicities have different rates (there are more than 60 separate racial/ethnic groups and subgroups identified by the U.S. Census), with Chinese Americans at 1 percent, Asian Indian Americans at 2 percent, Vietnamese Americans at over 4 percent, Japanese Americans at 5 percent, and Koreans closer to 7 percent.

Additionally, the HIH report indicates that Native American youth begin using a variety of drugs (not limited to alcohol) at an earlier age than white youth. Inhalant use is twice as high among Native American youth than it is among other racial groups.

In short, there is no clear picture of the typical drug user/abuser. Additional race differences are evident in results from a school-based survey by the Centers for Disease Control and Prevention, which indicate that self-reported lifetime crack use is highest among Hispanic students, followed by lower percentages for whites and even lower percentages for African Americans. However, the National Household Survey on Drug Abuse data reveal the disturbing observation that a far greater number of African American and Hispanic youth (approximately one-third) reported seeing people sell drugs in the neighborhood occasionally or more often than whites did (less than 10 percent).

Summary: A Picture of the Typical Criminal Offender

The image of the typical offender that emerges from the data examined here conflicts somewhat with the image in the minds of most Americans. If by the phrase "typical offender" we mean the offender who shows up most frequently in arrest statistics, then for all crimes except murder and robbery the typical offender is white, not African American.

As we have shown, focusing on the *number* of persons arrested is somewhat misleading. It is clear from the data discussed thus far that African Americans are arrested at a disproportionately high *rate*. This conclusion applies to property crime and violent crime. Moreover, victimization data suggest that African Americans may have higher offending rates for serious violent crime, but examinations of victim perception of offender with official arrest data reveal that some of the overrepresentation of African American offenders may be selection bias on the part of criminal justice officials, but this dilemma remains unsettled.

If part of the view of the typical criminal offender is that the typical drug offender is a minority, we have shown that self-report data from youth populations in the United States reveal that people of color do not have consistently higher drug-use rates than whites. This picture varies slightly by type of drug, with Hispanic youth showing higher rates of use with some drugs and Native American youth with other drugs, but there is little evidence of differential patterns of higher use rates by African Americans than other racial groups.

CRIME AS AN INTRARACIAL EVENT

In the minds of many Americans, the term "crime" conjures up an image of an act of violence against a white victim by an African American offender.[94] In the preceding sections we demonstrated the inaccuracy of these perceptions of victims and offenders; we illustrated that the typical victim is a racial minority and that the typical offender, for all but a few crimes, is white. We now turn to a discussion of crime as an *intraracial* event.

National Crime Victimization Survey

Few criminal justice data sources, including the NCVS, offer comprehensive information on the racial makeup of the victim–offender dyad. Recall that the NCVS asks victims about their perceptions of the offender's race in crimes of violence and data presented distinguish among only African Americans, whites, and "others" (victims' perceptions of the offender as Hispanic are not available).

With these limitations in mind, NCVS data on the race of the victim and the perceived race of the offender in single-offender violent victimizations can be examined.[95] These data indicate that almost all violent crimes by white offenders were committed against white victims (73 percent). This pattern also characterized the individual crimes of robbery, sexual assault, aggravated assault, and simple assault. The typical white offender, in other words, commits a crime against another white person.

This intraracial pattern of violent crime is also reported by African American victims. In short, crimes of robbery, sexual assault, aggravated assault, and simple assault of African Americans are predominantly intraracial. The only NCVS crime type that does not follow this pattern is a white robbery victim with injury. These victims are nearly as likely to be victimized by perceived offenders who are white or African American.

Uniform Crime Report Homicide Reports

A final source of data on the victim–offender pair is the Supplemental Homicide Report. Contrary to popular belief, a 29-year review of UCR SHRs reveals that homicide is essentially an intraracial event.[96] Specifically, in 2008,

- 80 percent of African American murder victims were slain by other African Americans;

- 91 percent of whites were victimized by whites;

- 63 percent of Asian / Hawaiian / Pacific Islanders were victimized by Asian / Hawaiian / Pacific Islanders; and

- 57 percent of Native American / American Indians were victimized by Native American / American Indians.

The small percentage of interracial homicides are more likely to occur with young victims and young offenders and are slightly more likely to be black-on-white offenses than white-on-black offenses. This analysis also reveals that when crimes are interracial they are more likely to be stranger homicides (3 in 10 are interracial) than homicides by victim or acquaintance (1 in 10 are interracial).[97]

Summary

The general pattern revealed is one in which white offenders consistently victimize whites, whereas African American offenders, and particularly African American males, more frequently victimize both African Americans and whites. As noted, the politicizing of black criminality continues, and the emergence of and subsequent focus on racial hoaxes persists.[98] See "Focus on an Issue" sections for a discussion of the politicizing of black criminality and the persistence of racial hoaxes.

Focus on an Issue
Politicizing Black-on-Black Crime

"Much attention has been devoted to 'black-on-black' crime ... It is not unusual to see in the written press or to hear in the electronic media stories depicting the evils of living in the black community. [This] has occurred with such frequency that some individuals now associate black people with criminality. Simply put, it has become fashionable to discern between crime and black-on-black crime. Rarely does one read or hear about white crime or 'white-on-white' crime. This is troubling when one considers that most crimes, including serious violent crimes, are committed by and against whites as well as blacks."[99]

Some researchers have challenged the assertion that crime is predominantly intraracial.[100] These critics point to the fact that a white person has a greater likelihood of being victimized by an African American offender than an African American has of being victimized by a white offender. Although this is true, it does not logically challenge the assertion that crime is predominantly an intraracial event. Remember that the NCVS reveals that the typical offender is white, not African American.

The exception to the predominant intraracial pattern of crime occurred with the examination of Native American and Asian victimization patterns. Native Americans report most victimizations occurring by whites, and Asians report victimizations occurring almost equally by whites, African Americans, and other racial groups (with no group committing the majority of offenses).

CRIME AS AN INTERRACIAL (HATE) EVENT

Not all interracial criminal events are considered hate crimes. The term "hate crime" (or bias crime) is most often defined as a common law offense that contains an element of prejudice based on the race, ethnicity, national origin, religion, sexual orientation, or disability status of the victim (some statutes add gender). Generally, hate-crime legislation is enacted in the form of enhancement penalties for common law offenses (ranging from assault to vandalism) that have an element of prejudice. Justifications for the creation of such legislation include the symbolic message that certain actions are exceptionally damaging to an individual when they are "provoked" by the status of race and ethnicity and that such actions are damaging to the general community and should be condemned.

The FBI has been mandated by Congress to collect and disseminate information on hate crime in the United States.[101] In 2008 the FBI Hate Crime Data Collection Program received reports from nearly 13,690 law enforcement agencies, representing nearly 85 percent of the U.S. population. The FBI offers this caution in its annual report: "The reports from these agencies are insufficient to allow a valid national or regional measure of the volume and types of crimes motivated by hate; they offer perspectives on the general nature of hate crime occurrence."

The FBI received reports of 7,783 bias-motivated criminal incidents in 2008, consisting of 9,168 offenses. Most offenses reported (60 percent) involved crimes

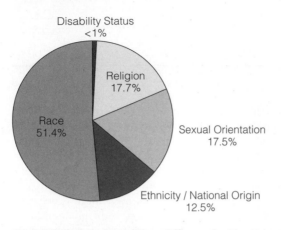

FIGURE 2.3   Hate-Crime Offenses, by Bias Type, 2007

SOURCE: *FBI Hate Crime Report*, 2008.
NOTE: Disability status (antiphysical and antimental) constitutes 0.4 percent of offenses in 2003 and is not included in this figure.

against a person, with 39.0 percent of the offenses designated as property offenses. A small number of offenses (less than 1 percent) were designated as crimes against society.[102] The most common offense was destruction/vandalism of property (32.4 percent), followed by the crimes of intimidation (29.5 percent), simple assault (12.8 percent), and aggravated assault (11.1 percent).[103] More than half of the reported hate-crime offenses involved race bias (51.3 percent), with another 17.5 percent reflecting bias based on religion, and 13.7 percent reflecting a bias based on ethnicity/national origin (Figure 2.3). The victims of race bias crimes were reflective of all race categories, including a multiracial group category. More than 70 percent of bias incidents classified by race of the victim occurred against African Americans. The incidents of race-based hate crimes occurred against Native Americans and Asian Americans at almost the same percentages as their representation in the general population (1.2 percent and 3.4 percent). White victims of hate crime incidents are not overrepresented in relation to their presence in the population, but at 17.3 percent of reported victims they are the second largest group of race-based hate crime victims. The ethnicity / national origin information is available for Hispanic and other ethnicity / national origin. Hispanics are the most common hate-crime ethnicity /national origin–based victims, at 60 percent of reported incidents.[104]

Offender information is also available in the FBI Hate Crime Reporting Program reports. This information is provided by victims reporting their perceptions, rather than being based on arrest or charging information. In 51.6 percent of the hate-crime offenses reported, the offender was known and the perception of race was reported by the victim. In these cases suspected offenders were most often identified as white (61 percent), but suspected offenders represented all four race categories and were occasionally identified as multiracial.[105] In short, all race groups have individuals who have been victimized by bias crimes and all race groups have individuals who are suspected offenders of bias crimes.

Information on the trends of victimization and offending in bias-crime events is limited, but patterns for both whites and African Americans have emerged. Whites are most often victimized by African Americans, and African Americans are most often victimized by whites.[106] In 2008 Native Americans were most likely to identify whites as the typical offender in bias-crime incidents. Additionally, although Native Americans are rarely identified as offenders, they were as likely to have white victims as African American victims. Asian Americans most often identify their offenders as white, whereas the offender identified as Asian American is found to victimize African Americans more than the other racial groups.[107]

In 2005 the Bureau of Justice Statistics released a Special Report comparing the picture of hate crime incidents and offenders that appears in victim self-report survey information (the NCVS) with the picture found in police-based data (UCR).[108] The NCVS requires corroborating evidence of hate-based motivation before it records an event as a hate crime. Specifically, the offender must use derogatory language, display a hate symbol, or have a confirmed hate crime report by local law enforcement. Pooling several years of NCVS data (2000–2003) results in an average of 191,000 hate incidents, of which 92,000 were reported to police (44 percent). These data reveal approximately 3 percent of all violent crimes reported in the NCVS were perceived by the victim as hate crimes. Nearly one-third of the offenses were violent crimes such as rape and serious assault, and nearly 25 percent of the offenses were household vandalism that was perceived to be motivated by hate. The most common motivation identified by victims was based on race (55 percent), association with someone of a different race (such as a multiracial couple; 31 percent), or ethnicity (29 percent).

Key information describing the offender and the incident is also available from the NCVS data. Offenders are predominately male and most likely to be white and a stranger to the victim. The event is most likely to be a violent crime and occur in a public place. When comparing hate offenders to non-hate offenders, NCVS data reveals that perceived gang membership and use of weapons does not vary from hate to non-hate-related events. However, a larger percentage of females are identified as offenders in hate events than non-hate events. Similarly, the perceived racial makeup of offenders is different with hate and non-hate related events. Forty-four percent of offenders are white in hate events; 62 percent of offenders are identified as white in non-hate events. Conversely, a larger percentage of hate offenders are perceived as African American than non-hate offenders (39 percent compared to 24 percent).[109]

When the racial composition of victims and offenders is examined, interesting differences appear. First, white victims report that nearly half of their offenders were white offenders and nearly half of the offenders were African American. However, African American victims perceive their offenders to be white in more than 85 percent of offenses, with African American offenders identified in only 15 percent of cases.[110]

The official UCR recording of hate crime incidence from this time period (2000–2003) gives an annual average of 8,227 incidents.[111] What accounts for the disparity? First, the motivation of association is not recognized by the UCR classification system (identified above as the second most common motivation in the NCVS). Second is the lack of victimization reporting to the police. The NCVS respondents reveal the hate incidents they report to the police are confirmed by police investigation in fewer than 10 percent of incidents. This study also reveals that victims are less likely to report hate-related events to the police than similar non-hate-related events. Additionally, the NCVS data may reflect an overreporting by respondents, perhaps due to telescoping events forward in time.

James Jacobs argued that hate-crime statutes create a law unlikely to deter and its implementation will widen social division. He also argued that hate-crime legislation represents an ill-advised insertion of the civil rights paradigm into the criminal law. Specifically, he reasons that civil rights legislation is an attempt to extend "positive rights and opportunities to minorities and women ... directed at the conduct of government officials and private persons who govern, regulate, or sell goods and services. By contrast, hate crime law deals with conduct that is already criminal and with wrongdoers who are already criminals." He concluded that the "possibility that criminals can be threatened into not discriminating in their choice of crime victims is slight."[112]

In a recent study examining the potential for community disorganization to explain the occurrence of hate crime, Christopher Lyons hypothesized that socially disorganized communities will have higher rates of hate crime. In his multivariate analysis of communities in Chicago he characterized social disorganization with such measures as youths who skipped school, the presence of graffiti, and fighting in front of a respondent's house. He also controlled for unemployment, poverty, percentage of families on public assistance, and percentage of families with single mothers. Additionally, he controlled for racial composition and percentage change in minority racial composition over the last decade. The dependent variables for this study were the occurrence of anti-black and anti-white hate crimes. His findings indicate that "anti-black hate crimes are most numerous in relatively organized communities with *higher* levels of informal social control, and *especially* in internally organized white communities undergoing the threat of racial invasion" and are most common in "economically affluent communities." Anti-white hate crimes, however, have a different set of causes, since these crimes are identified as "somewhat more likely in disadvantaged communities, especially with higher levels of residential mobility."[113]

Lyons concludes that "the correlates of anti-black crimes are distinguishable from those of crime in general," while anti-white crime, "like other forms of crime ... appear[s] to be the product of social disorganization brought about by population turnover."[114] The logical extension of this research is that different prevention strategies may be needed for different types of hate crime incidents. Moreover, this research again highlights the importance of criminological theory based on neighborhood context to explain the causes of crime and victimization (this is addressed more in Chapter 3).

Focus on an Issue
Disability and Crime Victims

The FBI Hate Crimes statistics report bias incidents occurring against people with disabilities. Although these events are rare—85 incidents in 2008, and approximately 1 percent of all reported hate crime incidents—this status of victimization is still relevant to a discussion of minorities and criminal justice. These data distinguish between those with physical disabilities (33 percent) and those with mental disabilities (67 percent). Of the known reported incidents, 60 percent occurred in the residence/home, higher than the percentage for this location for any other bias crime offense.[115]

A recent report from the Bureaus of Justice Statistics based on the National Crime Victimization Survey indicated that roughly 10 percent of bias crimes are directed at respondents with disabilities. The gender of disability victimizations did not differ significantly; however, a larger percentage of disbility bias offenses were committed against whites identifying a disability than against African Americans identifying a disability. The vicimization of Hispanics was significantly lower than for non-Hispanics. Age differences emerged in

these data that indicate a higer percentage of disiblity-based bias crimes occurred against people aged 21 and over, compared with respondents aged 20 or younger.[116]

Victims identifying their offenders indicated that their offenders were more likely to be a combination of male/female offenders than one or the other, significanlty more likely to be white than African American, and more likely to be 20 or younger than 21 or older. This report indicates significantly more victimizations during this time period than the FBI Hate Crime statistics that police agencies report.

Although no indication is offered in the NCVS data about the relationship between the victim and the offender, Karla Westjohn's review of crime victimizations of the blind in Illinois indicated that the vast majority of victimizers of the disabled are people known to the victim. Westjohn also challenges stereotypes that disabled people can also be offenders, because some of the offenders known to the victim were also disabled. She also asserts the need for law enforcement and the courts to be more responsive to disabled victims as able witnesses.[117]

ETHNIC YOUTH GANGS

In the minds of most Americans, the words *gang*, *race*, and *crime* are inextricably linked. Recall the incident described at the beginning of this chapter, in "Focus on an Issue: Central Park Jogger" (p. 13), in which a woman was raped and believed to be attacked by a group of minority teenagers in Central Park. The media labeled these youths a "gang." This designation, however, was challenged by those who argued that the teenagers allegedly involved in the incident were not organized, had no gang identity, and behaved more like a mob than a gang.[118] This insistence on the perceived "group" nature of the offense led investigators to arrest and the court to convict the "gang" suspects, ignoring the evidence of the single "real" offender identified later by DNA testing.

A comprehensive review of recent research on ethnic youth gangs is beyond the scope of this chapter. Instead we discuss some of the prevailing myths about gangs and gang membership and summarize research on ethnic gang activities. Although there is no universally accepted definition of a gang, the term is generally used to refer to a group of young people who recognize some sort of organized membership and leadership and who, in addition, are involved in criminal activity.[119]

Gang Myths and Realities

We have shown that popular perceptions of crime, crime victims, and criminal offenders often are inaccurate. Many of the prevailing beliefs about gangs are similarly mistaken. In the sections that follow we discuss some of the myths surrounding gangs and gang activity. We show that although there is an element of truth in each of these myths, there also are a number of inaccuracies.

Myth 1: Gangs are a uniquely twentieth and twenty-first century phenomenon. L. Sante documents that some historians believe there is evidence to suggest that gangs began in the Unites States just after the Revolutionary War, around 1783. Still others document the emergence of street gangs in growing American cities several decades later, in the early 1800s.[120]

A recent report on the "History of Gangs in the United States" also documents unique regional factors that have contributed to the emergence of gangs around the country.[121] For example, Northeast and Midwest gangs are largely rooted in the immigration patterns from white ethnic groups leaving Europe for America. These groups were settling in large industrial cities in very segregated housing situations and experienced prejudices that made achieving the American Dream difficult (see subculture theory in Chapter 3). In the West, the clash of American expansion and preexisting Mexican cultures lead to the emergence of street gangs. Subsequent immigration patterns to the West Coast from Mexico, immigrants looking for farm work, contributed to the growth of street gangs. Migration patterns by African Americans moving from the South to these three regions (the Northeast, the Midwest, and the West) added an additional dimension of gang formation that is still prevalent today. In the decades to come additional groups of Hispanics (Puerto Ricans, Panamanians, Cubans, and so on) and Asian immigrants (Filipinos, Chinese, Vietnamese, and so on) would continue to fuel the gang cultures in these regions. Native American gangs would emerge at a later point, both on and off tribal lands.[122]

Myth 2: All gang members are African American and belong either to the Bloods or the Crips. The Bloods and the Crips *are* predominantly African American and are very widely known. These two gangs are heavily involved in illegal drug activities and are characterized by a confederation of local gangs that stretch across the country.[123] They are not, however, exclusively African American. S. Mydans[124] provided examples of well-to-do white youth joining California Crips and Bloods.

Although members of the racial minority groups we focus on in this book are overrepresented in gangs, they do not comprise the entire gang problem. (It is somewhat misleading to categorize gangs as Hispanic or Asian. The terms "Hispanic" and "Asian" are very broad and mask the variety within each group. In reality, gangs are ethnically specific by nationality; there are Puerto Rican, Cuban, Mexican American, Vietnamese, Cambodian, Korean, Chinese, and Japanese gangs.)

The earliest gangs in the Northeast region of the United States were predominantly white, reflecting the major waves of European immigration, first from northern and Western European countries and later from middle and Eastern European countries. These immigration trends, along with the rapid growth of industrial center cities, left a situation of poverty and unemployment that created fertile ground for the formation of gangs. Sante notes the earliest gangs were commonly Irish, with the Chinese establishing tongs as early as 1860. Italian and Jewish gangs emerged after the Civil War.[125]

Currently, white ethnic gangs are not as prevalent. Covey and colleagues[126] argue that "the relative absence of white ethnic gangs in official studies may be a product of a number of factors including the difficulty of identifying them[127] and biases in reporting and public perception."[128] Many of the white ethnic groups that do exist are characterized by white supremacist activities or Satanism.

Myth 3: Gangs are only found in large cities. It is important to understand that the gang phenomenon is not a homogeneous one. Although many gangs *are* located in urban areas, gangs are increasingly found in suburban and rural communities and on Indian reservations.[129] The National Youth Gang Survey in 2007, collected by the National Youth Gang Center from law enforcement agencies, estimated that gangs were present in 86 percent of large cities and 35 percent of smaller cities. Additionally, this survey revealed that suburban and rural counties each reported the presence of gangs (50 percent and 15 percent).[130] The National Youth Gang Center also tracks the size of urban, suburban, and rural gangs over time. Since 2002 the general estimate of the number of self-identified gang problem jurisdictions went up 25 percent. However this increase was largely fueled by the 33 percent rise in suburban gangs compared to the 12 percent rise in large city gangs.

Myth 4: All gangs are involved in selling drugs and drug trafficking. Many, but not all, gangs are involved in illegal drug activities. Many of the original gangs on the East Coast were made of laborers and were more concerned about territory than criminal activity for profit. Moreover, at least some of the modern gangs existed before they began selling drugs. It is possible that gangs have been exploited because of their structure and organization to sell drugs and that this lucrative activity serves as a reason for recruitment and expansion.

Drug use is common in most gangs, but the emphasis placed on drug sales varies by the character and social organization of the gang.[131] Many researchers challenge the idea that selling drugs is usually an organized gang activity involving all gang members.[132] In their study of Denver youth, Finn-Aage Esbensen and David Huizinga distinguished between a gang involved in drug activity and individual gang members selling drugs. They found that 80 percent of youth respondents said that their gangs were involved in drug sales, but only 28 percent admitted to selling drugs themselves.[133] In short, although gang members were found to be more active in drug-related crimes (use and sales) than non-gang youth, not all gang members sold drugs.

In a recent National Youth Gang Survey, law enforcement agencies reported that 51 percent of all gangs in rural counties were believed to be organized specifically for the purpose of drug trafficking, whereas 41 percent of those in large cities were identified as organized for drug trafficking. Drug trafficking by gangs is perceived as being less common in suburban areas (39 percent of all gangs) and small cities (26 percent of all gangs).[134]

Related to the myth that all gang members sell drugs is the notion that drugs and violence are inextricably linked. In fact there is a complex relationship between drugs and violence in gangs. Jeffrey Fagan found that regardless of the level of drug dealing within a gang, violent behaviors still occurred, with the majority of incidents unrelated to drug sales. He concluded that "for gang members, violence is not an inevitable consequence of involvement in drug use and dealing."[135] David G. Curry and Scott H. Decker also noted the prevalence of violence in gang activity, pointing out that much of this violence is intraracial.[136]

Moreover, an assessment of gang activity across the country documents the emerging trend toward the use of technology in the commission of crime. These new criminal endeavors are identified as identity theft, pirating of videos and movies, and email fraud schemes.[137]

Myth 5: Gangs are the result of poverty and a growing underclass. It is overly simplistic to attribute the existence of gangs solely to poverty. The National Youth Gang Survey indicated that although the majority of gang members are identified as underclass, 35 percent were identified as working class, 12 percent as middle class, and 3 percent as upper middle class.[138] Gangs exist for a variety of reasons: the growth of the underclass, the disintegration of the African American and Hispanic family, poverty, difficulty assimilating into American culture, marginality, political and religious reasons, and general rebellion against adult and conventional society.[139] However, Curry and Decker argued that gang formation and gang delinquency are more likely to be explained at a community level rather than at an individual level.[140]

Myth 6: All gang members are males. Although it is true that males are overrepresented in gang membership, there are female gang members and female gangs. The early sociological literature on gangs only discussed males; females who accompanied male gang members were often described in terms of an "auxiliary"—present, but not a formal part of the criminal activity.

More recent studies have found both fully active female gang members and a few solely female gangs. Researchers estimate that females represent between 10 percent and 25 percent of all gang members. The 2007 National Gang Survey indicates that nearly one in seven jurisdictions reports that more than half of their gangs have female members, with smaller cities reporting the largest percentage of female gang members compared to larger cities, suburban counties, and rural counties.[141] Anne Campbell identified several all-female gangs in New York City. "The Sandman Ladies," for example, were Puerto Rican females with a biker image. "The Sex Girls" were African American and Hispanic females involved in drug dealing. Currently, female gang members are known to assist with the "movement of drugs and weapons for male gang members and [the gathering of] intelligence from rival gangs."[142]

The presence of female gang members differs by ethnicity as well. Females are found in Hispanic, African American, and white ethnic gangs, but they appear to be conspicuously absent in both journalistic and scholarly accounts of Asian American gangs.[143]

Myth 7: Youth gangs involve only young people and have few ties to organized crime. For a number of years gang researchers have documented generational patterns of gang membership in a number of Hispanic and African American gangs. More than 25 percent of all law enforcement agencies in one survey indicated that gangs in their jurisdiction were associated with organized crime. Law enforcement agencies report that street gangs are associated with Mexican drug organizations, Asian organized crime groups, Russian organized crime, and outlaw motorcycle gangs.[144]

Varieties of Ethnic Gangs

We already noted that, contrary to popular wisdom, all gang members are not African Americans. There are also Hispanic, Native American, Asian, and white gangs. The National Youth Gang Survey indicated that 49 percent of gang members are identified as Hispanic, 35 percent as African American, 9 percent as white, and 9 percent as other.

Covey and colleagues stated, "[Ethnicity] is not the only way to understand gangs, but gangs are organized along ethnic lines, and it would be a mistake to ignore ethnicity as a variable that may affect the nature of juvenile gangs."[145] Most ethnic gangs reflect a mixture of their members' culture of origin and the American "host" culture; indeed, many gangs form as the result of a clash between the two cultures.

African American

The most widely known African American gangs are the Bloods and the Crips. Each gang has unique "colors" and sign language to reinforce gang identity. It is believed that these gangs are really "national confederations of local gangs" in American cities.[146] They are characteristically very territorial and often are linked to drug distribution.

Other African American gangs exist across the United States. Researchers have identified many big-city African American gangs that are oriented toward property crime rather than drug sales. In addition; African American gangs have formed around the tenets of Islam, with corresponding political agendas.[147]

Native American

The circumstances among which Native American youth are becoming part of the gang culture in the United States include the emerging presence of gangs in the semi-sovereign tribal lands throughout the country and the formation of gangs located in urban and rural nonreservation areas. Specifically, the Navajo nations have documented the presence of youth gangs consisting of tribal members. They have reported the presence of more than 50 gangs with nearly 1,000 members on the tribal lands.[148] Some Native American gangs identify themselves with the native culture of their unique areas (such as the Native Outlawz and Native Mob), whereas other gang names indicate alliances with more nationally recognized groups like the Bloods and Gangster Disciples (with names like the Indian Bloods and Native Gangster Disciples). Actual evidence of structural alliances with these other urban gangs seems to be in doubt. Some gang researchers speculate that such affiliation is "utilized for the purposes of notoriety and intimidation." Most gang crimes on tribal lands seem to be property-based, but there is increasing concern about violence and drug distribution (especially methamphetamine and marijuana).[149]

Asian American

As previously stated, there are a variety of Asian ethnic gangs. Most Asian gang researchers attribute the formation of these gangs, at least in part, to feelings of alienation due to difficulty assimilating into American culture.[150] Similarities between Asian gangs include an emphasis on economic activity and a pattern of intraracial victimization. The tendency to victimize others in the Asian community may contribute to lower reporting rates of gang victimization to local law enforcement. Asian gangs are found in coastal cities in western states, such as California and Oregon, but also in East Coast cities in New York, Massachusetts, and Connecticut.[151]

The origins of Chinese American gangs can be traced to the early 1890s and the secret "Tong" societies. Chinese American gang activity has increased with the relaxation of immigration laws in the mid-1960s. The research on Chinese gangs reveals that these entities have a commitment to violence, both for its own sake (gang warfare) and also as a means for generating income (through robbery, burglary, extortion, and protection). Gang researchers report that it is not unusual for Asian organized crime groups to work with street gangs in such activities as "drug trafficking, credit card fraud, illegal gambling and money laundering." K. Chin noted that generally the structure of Chinese American gangs is very hierarchical; he also explains that gang members may participate in legitimate business, establish drug distribution and sale networks, and form national and international networks.[152] Vietnamese American gang activity is not as structured as that of Chinese American gangs. The increase in gang activity for this ethnic group can also be tied to an influx in immigration. Overall, Vietnamese American gang activity is less violent, usually economically oriented, and most likely to target other Vietnamese Americans.[153]

Hispanic

Hispanic gangs have identifiable core concerns: brotherhood/sisterhood, machismo, and loyalty to the barrio (neighborhood). Many Hispanic gangs have adult and juvenile members, and gang members may be involved in the use and sale of drugs. The importance of machismo may explain the emphasis of many Hispanic gangs on violence, even intragang violence.[154]

Hispanic gangs make up the largest ethnic population of gang membership in the country. Hispanic gangs have the most gang members in large cities, small cities, and suburban counties. This trend reverses for rural counties where Hispanic gangs comprise 32 percent of gang members, while African American gang members comprise 44 percent of the indentified gang members. Prominent Hispanic gangs vary by region. In the western part of the country, Sur 13 and The Latin Kings are most evident. The former is strongly associated with the prison gang Mexican Mafia (discussed in Chapter 9). Law enforcement agencies have identified Hispanic gangs in Northern California in alliance with outlaw motorcycle gangs to transport drugs (primarily methamphetamine). International connections emerge with such gangs as the MS-13 (Mara Salvatrucha), which has El Salvadoran roots. Other gangs are reported to have connections to crime groups in Honduras, Guatemala, and other Central American countries.[155]

The National Alliance of Gang Investigators reports that some Central American gang members, from El Salvador and Honduras, have gained Temporary Protective Status (granted by the Bureau of Immigration and Custom's Enforcement) in the United States as a result of the gang prosecution efforts in their own countries. The Department of Homeland Security requires migrants to be deported if they have been convicted of a felony or two or more misdemeanors, but some gang members are able to remain for a period of time if they are looking for work.[156]

White

The white ethnic gangs—composed of Irish, Polish, and Italian youth—identified by researchers earlier in this century are less evident in today's cities. Contemporary white ethnic gangs are most often associated with rebellion against adult society; with suburban settings; and with a focus on white supremacist, domestic terrorist, or Satanist ideals. Larger cities report that about 8 percent of gangs are comprised of white members, while smaller cities and suburban and rural counties identify between 14 percent and 17 percent of gang members as white.[157]

"Skinheads" may be the most well-known example of a white ethnic gang. Covey and colleagues describe them in this way: "Skinhead gangs usually consist of European American youths who are non-Hispanic, non-Jewish, Protestant, working class, low income, clean shaven and militantly racist and white supremacist."[158] Skinheads have been located in cities in every region of the country and have been linked to adult domestic terrorist organizations such as the White Aryan Resistance (WAR) and other Neo-Nazi movements. Skinheads are unique in the sense that they use violence not to protect turf, protect a drug market, or commit robberies, but rather "for the explicit purpose of promoting political change by instilling fear in innocent people."[159]

Youth gangs with connections to domestic terrorist groups comprise less than 10 percent of known gang activity. These groups include the Ku Klux Klan, Aryan Resistance, National Socialist Movement, and various militia groups. Little evidence exists of youth gang connections with international terrorist groups because most evidence suggests recruitment is more common in adult prisons (see Chapter 9).[160]

"Stoner" gangs, another form of white ethnic gangs, are characterized by an emphasis on Satanic rituals. This doctrine is supplemented by territoriality and the heavy use of drugs.[161]

In recognizing the racial nature of gangs it is important to clarify the role of racism in the formation of gangs. Most gangs are racially and ethnically homogenous. Some researchers argue that this situation is merely reflective of the racial and ethnic composition of neighborhoods and primary friendships—that is, "where schools and neighborhoods are racially and ethnically mixed, gangs tend to be racially and ethnically mixed."[162]

Although violent conflicts do occur between and within ethnic gangs, violence is seldom the reason for gang formation. Racism as a societal phenomenon that creates oppressive conditions can contribute to gang formation. However, individual racism explains very little in terms of the formation of gangs or the decision to join gangs. Skinhead membership is a notable exception, being almost exclusively a function of individual racism.[163]

CONCLUSION

We began this chapter with a discussion of the presentation of crime stories in the media in comparison to their actual occurrence. We argued that incidents like missing person reports and racial hoaxes shape perceptions of crime in the United States. In the minds of many Americans, the typical crime is an act of violence involving a white victim and a minority offender. We have used a variety of data sources to illustrate the inaccuracy of these perceptions and offer a more comprehensive view of victimization and offending.

We have shown that people of color are overrepresented as victims of both household and personal crime and have demonstrated that this pattern is particularly striking for crimes of violence. We have demonstrated that the typical offender for all crimes except robbery and gambling is white; however, African Americans are arrested at a disproportionately high rate. We also have shown that most crimes involve an offender and victim of the same race, which means that crime is predominantly an intraracial event.

The information provided in this chapter may raise as many questions as it answers. Although we have attempted to paint an accurate picture of crime and victimization in the United States, we are hampered by limitations inherent in existing data sources. Some victimization events are not defined as crimes by the victims, many of those that are defined as crimes are not reported to the police, and many of those reported to the police do not lead to an arrest. There is no data set that provides information on all crimes that occur.

We have attempted to address this problem by using several different sources of data. We believe that we can have greater confidence in the conclusions we reach if two or more distinct types of data point in the same direction. The fact that both NCVS data and data from the SHRs consistently reveal that racial and ethnic minorities are more likely than whites to fall victim to crime, for example, lends credence to the need for a more comprehensive picture of victims and offenders. Similarly, the fact that a variety of data sources suggest that crime is predominantly an intraracial event enhances our confidence in this conclusion as well.

We have less confidence in our conclusions concerning the racial makeup of the offender population. Although it is obvious that African Americans are arrested at a disproportionately high rate, particularly for murder and robbery, it is not clear that this reflects differential offending rather than selective enforcement of the law. Arrest statistics and victimization data both indicate that African Americans have higher rates of offending than whites, but some self-report studies suggest that there are few, if any, racial differences in offending. We suggest that this discrepancy limits our ability to draw definitive conclusions about the meaning of the disproportionately high arrest rates for African Americans.

One final caveat seems appropriate. The conclusions we reach about victims and offenders are based primarily on descriptive data; they are based primarily on percentages, rates, and trends over time. These data are appropriate for describing a disproportionate representation of people of color as the victims of crime and as the criminal offender, but these data are not sufficient for drawing conclusions concerning causality. The data we have examined in this chapter can tell us that the African American arrest rate is higher than the white arrest rate for a particular crime, but they cannot tell us why this is so. We address issues of causation in subsequent chapters.

DISCUSSION QUESTIONS

1. What do you think? Should states have racial hoax sentence enhancement statutes? What should the content of such legislation be?

2. Does the media systematically discriminate against crime victims, favoring white victims? Or is the discrimination contextual (see Chapter 1)? How does the media cover racial hoaxes? Does this coverage perpetuate the view of young African American males as the typical criminal offenders?

3. What are some of the possible explanations for the overrepresentation of minorities as crime victims? Are minority communities particularly vulnerable to crime? Why?

4. The descriptive information in UCR arrest data depicts an overrepresentation of African American offenders for most violent and property crimes. What are the possible explanations for such disparity? Is this picture of the offender the result of differential offending rates or differential enforcement practices? What must a researcher include in a study of "why people commit crime" to advance beyond a description of disparity to test for a causal explanation?

5. Should hate be a crime? What arguments can be made to support the use of sentencing enhancement penalties for hate crimes? What arguments can be made to oppose such statutes? Are hate-crime laws likely to deter offenders and reduce crime?

6. What are the social and psychological costs of racial hoaxes? Should perpetuating a racial hoax be a crime? What should the penalty for such an offense be?

7. If most youth gangs are racially and ethnically homogenous, should law enforcement use race- and ethnic-specific strategies to fight gang formation and to control gang crime? Or should law enforcement strategies be racially and ethnically neutral? What dilemmas are created for police departments that pursue each of these strategies? Is the likely result institutional or contextual discrimination?

NOTES

1. Nikole Hannah-Jones, "The Sordid History of Racial Hoaxes," posted on *The Root,* September 21, 2010, 11:49 A.M. http://www.theroot.com/views/sordid-history-racial-hoaxes.

2. Katheryn K. Russell, *The Color of Crime* (New York: New York University Press, 1998), p. 70.

3. Ibid.

4. Ibid.

5. Ibid., p. 76.

6. Ibid.

7. Ibid., p. 75.

8. Ibid., p. 88.

9. *Crime in the United States,* 2008 (Washington, DC: U.S. Department of Justice, 2009).

10. National Center for Missing Adults, quoted in Anne-Marie O'Connor, "Media Coverage of Missing Women Draws Ire," *Lincoln Journal Star*, Monday, August 8, 2005, p. 8A.

11. Erin Bruno, quoted in Fahizah Alim, "Missing White Women Get Lion's Share of Media Coverage," *Sacramento Bee*, June 28, 2005.

12. Ibid.

13. Ibid.

14. Ibid.

15. Erin Bruno, quoted in Anne-Marie O'Connor, "Media Coverage of Missing Women Draws Ire," *Lincoln Journal Star*, Monday, August 8, 2005, p. 8A.

16. Professor Todd Boyd, quoted in Anne-Marie O'Connor, "Media Coverage of Missing Women Draws Ire," *Lincoln Journal Star*, Monday, August 8, 2005, p. 8A.

17. According to Uniform Crime Report index crime totals for 2000, roughly 90 percent of crimes were property crimes. It is believed that rapes are severely underreported, but similar arguments can be made for property crimes, especially fraud. Even if the rape numbers are low, the numbers of violent criminal events do not overshadow property crime.

18. *New York Times* (May 29, 1989), p. 25.

19. Robert M. O'Brien, "The Interracial Nature of Violent Crimes: A Reexamination," *American Journal of Sociology* 92 (1987), pp. 817–835.

20. Joe Mahony, "Five Cleared in Central Park Jogger Assault," *Daily News* (New York), January 7, 2005.

21. Ibid.

22. Charles Silberman, *Criminal Violence, Criminal Justice* (New York: Random House, 1978), pp. 177–118.

23. The original National Crime Survey (NCS) was renamed the National Crime Victimization Survey (NCVS) to clearly emphasize the focus of measuring victimizations. The Bureau of Justice Statistics was formerly the National Criminal Justice and Information Service of the Law Enforcement Assistance Administration.

24. Bureau of Justice Statistics, *Criminal Victimizations in the United States: 2007 Trends* (Washington, DC: Government Printing Office, 2009).

25. Bureau of Justice Statistics, *Criminal Victimizations in the United States: 2007 Statistical Tables Index (Table 16).* Available at http://bjs.ojp.usdoj.gov/content/pub/html/cvus/property_crimes_head_of_household703.cfm.

26. Bureau of Justice Statistics, *Criminal Victimizations in the United States: 2007 Statistical Tables Index (Table 17).* Available at http://bjs.ojp.usdoj.gov/content/pub/html/cvus/ethnicity341.cfm.

27. Detis T. Duhart, *Urban, Suburban, and Rural Victimization, 1993–1998* (Washington, DC: U.S. Department of Justice, 2000). Available at http://www.ojp.usdoj/bjs/.

28. Callie M. Rennison, *Criminal Victimization, 2000* (Washington, DC: U.S. Department of Justice, 2001).

29. *Criminal Victimization, 2004.* Available at www.ojp.usdoj.gov/bjs/cvict_v.htm.

30. Lynn Langton and Katrina Baum, Identity Theft Reported by Households, 2007— Statistical Tables (June 2010; NCJ 230742).

31. Duhart, *Urban, Suburban, and Rural Victimization, 1993–1998.*

32. *Criminal Victimization in the U.S., 2002.* Available at http://www.ojp.usdoj.gov/bjs.

33. Janet L. Lauritsen and Norman A. White, "Putting Violence in Its Place: The Influence of Race, Ethnicity, Gender, and Place on the Risk for Violence," *Crime and Public Policy* 1 (2001), pp. 37–59.

34. Ibid., p. 51.

35. Laura Dugan and Robert Apel, "An Exploratory Study of the Violent Victimization of Women: Race/Ethnicity and Situational Context," *Criminology* 41 (2003), pp. 959–977.

36. Ibid., p. 972.

37. Bureau of Justice Statistics, *Lifetime Likelihood of Victimization* (Washington, DC: U.S. Department of Justice, 1987), p. 1.

38. Ibid., p. 3.

39. Callie Rennison, *Violent Victimization and Race, 1993–1998*. Available at http://www.ojp.usdoj.gov/bjs/pub/pdf/vvr98.pdf. See also, Lawrence A. Greenfeld and Steven K. Smith, *American Indians and Crime* (Washington, DC: Bureau of Justice Statistics, 1999).

40. Ibid.

41. Ronette Bachman, Heather Zaykowski, Rachel Kallmyer, Margarita Poteyeva, and Christina Lanier, *Violence Against American Indian and Alaska Native Women and the Criminal Justice Response: What is Known* (National Institute of Justice Publication, 2008), p. 7.

42. Ibid., pp. 7–8.

43. Erika Harrell, *Asian, Native Hawaiian, and Pacific Islander Victims of Crime*. Available at http://www.ojp.usdoj.gov/bjs/abstract/anhpivc.htm.

44. Renisson, *Violent Victimization and Race*.

45. Easy access to the *FBI Supplemental Homicide Reports, 1980–2008*, is available at http://www.ojjdp.gov/ojstatbb/ezashr/asp/vic_selection.asp.

46. *Homicide Trends in the US, 1976–2002*. Available at http://www.ojp.usdoj.bjs/homicide/race.htm.

47. Gregg Barak, Jeanne M. Flavin, and Paul S. Leighton, *Class, Race, Gender, and Crime: Social Realities of Justice in America* (Los Angeles: Roxbury, 2001).

48. Ibid., p. 102.

49. Bachman, Zaykowski, Kallmyer, Poteyeva , and Lanier, *Violence Against American Indian and Alaska Native Women and the Criminal Justice Response*, p. 10.

50. *Homicide Trends in the US, 1976–2002*.

51. Ibid.

52. Michael Fischer, "Environmental Racism Claims Brought under Title VI of the Civil Rights Act," Environmental Law 25 (1995), p. 285; Commission for Racial Justice, United Church of Christ, *Toxic Wastes and Race In The United States: A National Report On The Racial and Socioeconomic Characteristics of Communities With Hazardous Waste Sites* (New York: Public Data Access, Inc., 1987).

53. Robert Bullard, Dumping in Dixie: Race, Class, and Environmental Quality (1990). Accessed at http://www.ejrc.cau.edu; Robert Bullard, "Message from the Director," accessed at http://www.ejrc.cau.edu, November 29, 2010.

54. U.S. Department of Justice, *Crime in the United States, 2008*. Available at http://www.fbi.gov/ucr/ucr.htm.

55. Rennison, *Criminal Victimization, 2000*.

56. D. L. Decker, D. Shichor, and R. M. O'Brien, *Urban Structure and Victimization* (Lexington, MA: D.C. Heath, 1982), p. 27.

57. Michael J. Hindelang, "Race and Involvement in Common Law Personal Crimes," *American Sociological Review* 43 (1978), pp. 93–109.

58. U.S. Department of Justice, *Crime in the United States, 2003*.

59. John Huey-Long Song, "Attitudes of Chinese Immigrants and Vietnamese Refugees toward Law Enforcement in the United States," *Justice Quarterly* 9 (1992), pp. 703–719.

60. Margorie Zatz, "Pleas, Priors, and Prison: Racial/Ethnic Differences in Sentencing," *Social Science Research* 14 (1985), pp. 169–193.

61. Donald Black, "The Social Organization of Arrest," in *The Manners and Customs of the Police*, Donald Black, ed. (New York: Academic Press, 1980), pp. 85–108.

62. Russell, *The Color of Crime*.

63. Crime in the United States, 2008 (Washington, DC: U.S. Department of Justice, 2009). Available at http://www.fbi.gov/ucr/cius2008/data/table_43.html.

64. Paul Knepper, "Race, Racism and Crime Statistics," *Southern Law Review* 24 (1996), pp. 71–112.

65. Available at http://www.fbi.gov/about-us/cjis/ucr/frequently-asked-questions/nibrs_faqs.

66. K. Peak and J. Spencer, "Crime in Indian Country: Another Trail of Tears," *Journal of Criminal Justice* 15 (1987), pp. 485–494.

67. Kristin Butcher and Morrison Piehl, *San Diego Union-Tribune*, March 2008.

68. Eric Stowell, Steven Messner, Kelly McGreever, and Lawrence Raffalovich, "Immigration and the Recent Violent Crime Drop in the United States: A Pooled, Cross-sectional Time-Series Analysis of Metropolitan Areas," *Criminology* 47 (2009): 889–928.

69. Public Policy Institute of California, *Immigration and Crime, June 2008*. Available at http://www.ppic.org.

70. Sampson et al., 2005; Butcher and Piehl, 2005.

71. James A. Fox and Marc L. Swatt, "Recent Surge in Homicides Involving Young Black Males and Guns: Time to Reinvest in Prevention and Crime Control." Available at http://www.jfox.neu.edu/Documents/Fox%20Swatt%20Homicide%20Report%20Dec%2029%202008.pdf.

72. Ibid., Table 10.

73. Hindelang, "Race and Involvement in Common Law Personal Crimes," p. 93.

74. Ibid., p. 99.

75. Ibid., pp. 100–101.

76. Stewart J. D'Alessio and Lisa Stolzenberg, "Race and the Probability of Arrest," *Social Forces* 80 (2003), pp. 1,381–1,397.

77. Gwynn Nettler, *Explaining Crime*, 3rd ed. (New York: McGraw-Hill, 1984).

78. Patrick G. Jackson, "Sources of Data," in *Measurement Issues in Criminology*, Kimberly Kempf, ed. (New York: Springer-Verlag, 1990).

79. Michael Hindelang, Travis Hirschi, and Joseph G. Weis, *Measuring Delinquency* (Beverly Hills, CA: Sage, 1981); Delbert Elliot, David Huizinga, Brian Knowles, and Rachel Canter, *The Prevalence and Incidence of Delinquent Behavior: 1976–1980: National Estimates of Delinquent Behavior by Sex, Race, Social Class, and Other Selected Variables* (Boulder, CO: Behavioral Research Institute, 1983); Robert M. O'Brien, *Crime and Victimization Data* (Beverly Hills, CA: Sage, 1985).

80. Elliot et al., *The Prevalence and Incidence of Delinquent Behavior*.

81. National Youth Survey questionnaire in O'Brien, *Crime and Victimization Data*.

82. O'Brien, *Crime and Victimization Data*.

83. Delbert S. Elliot and S. S. Ageton, "Reconciling Race and Class Differences in Self-Reported and Official Measures of Delinquency," *American Sociological Review* 45 (1980), pp. 95–110; Hindelang et al., *Measuring Delinquency*.

84. Ibid.

85. Principal Investigators of the Monitoring the Future Project are Lloyd D. Johnston, Jerald G. Bachman, and Patrick M. O'Malley. Data available in the *Sourcebook of Criminal Justice Statistics, 2000.* Available at http://www.albany.edu/sourcebook/.

86. David Huizinga and Delbert S. Elliot, "Juvenile Offenders: Prevalence, Offender Incidence, and Arrest Rates by Race," *Crime and Delinquency* 33 (1987), pp. 206–223.

87. Elijah Anderson, "The Code of The Streets," *Atlantic Monthly* 273 (1994), pp. 81–94; Elijah Anderson, *Code of the Street: Decency, Violence, and the Moral Life of the Inner City* (New York: W.W. Norton, 1999).

88. Eric Steward and Ronald Simons, "Race, Code of the Street, and Violent Delinquency: A Multilevel Investigation of Neighborhood Street Culture and Individual Norms of Violence," *Criminology* 48 (2010), pp. 569–605.

89. Ibid., p. 756.

90. Ibid., pp. 578, 570.

91. Robert Sampson, Jeffrey Morenoff, and Stephen Raudenbush, "Social Anatomy of Racial and Ethnic Disparities in Violence," *American Journal of Public Health* 95 no. 2 (2005), pp. 224–232.

92. Lloyd D. Johnston, Patrick M. O'Malley, Jerald G. Bachman, and John E. Schulenberg, *Demographic Subgroup Trends for Various Licit and Illicit Drugs, 1975–2009* (The University of Michigan Institute for Social Research, Ann Arbor, MI, 2010).

93. National Institute of Health, *Drug Use Among Racial/Ethnic Minorities*, Report No. 95–3888. (Washington, DC: U.S. Government Printing Office, 1995); see also revised report, 2003.

94. Lori Dorfman and Vincent Scharaldi, "Off Balance: Youth, Race, and Crime in the News," Berkeley Media Studies Group, 2001. Available at http://www.buildingblocksforyouth.org/media.html.

95. NCVS, 2003.

96. C. Puzzanchera and W. Kang, "Easy Access to the FBI's Supplementary Homicide Reports: 1980–2008" (2010). Available at http://www.ojjdp.gov/ojstatbb/ezashr/.

97. Ibid.

98. Bing and Russell, "*Politicizing Black-on-Black Crime*"; Russell, *The Color of Crime.*

99. Bing, "*Politicizing Black-on-Black Crime*"; Russell, *The Color of Crime.*

100. William Wilbanks, "Is Violent Crime Intraracial?" *Crime and Delinquency* 31 (1985), pp. 117–128.

101. Hate Crimes Act of 1990; Violent Crime and Law Enforcement Act of 1994; Church Arson Prevention Act, 1996.

102. Federal Bureau of Investigation, *Hate Crime Statistics, 2008.* Available at http://www.fbi.gov/ucr/hatecm.htm.

103. Ibid., p. 6.

104. Federal Bureau of Investigation, *Hate Crime Statistics, 2008.* Available at http://www.fbi.gov/ucr/hatecm.htm. Table 1.

105. Ibid., p. 1.

106. Ibid., Table 5.

107. Ibid., p. 14.

108. Caroline Wolf Harlow, *Hate Crime Reported by Victims and Police* (Washington, DC: BJS, 2005).

109. Ibid.

110. Ibid.

111. *Hate Crime Statistics, 2000–2003*. Available at http://www.fbi.gov/ucr.

112. James Jacobs, "Should Hate be a Crime?" *Public Interest* (1993), pp. 3–14.

113. Christopher Lyons, "Community (Dis)Organization and Racially Motivated Crime," *American Journal of Sociology* 113 (2007), p. 848.

114. Ibid., p. 847.

115. *Hate Crime Statistics, 2008*. Available at www.fbi.gov/ucr/hatecm.htm. Tables 1, 10.

116. Federal Bureau of Investigation, *Hate Crime Statistics, 2008*. Available at: http://www.fbi.gov/ucr/hatecm.htm.

117. Karla Westjohn, "Beyond Stereotypes and Good Intentions: An Examination of Blindness and Criminal Victimization," Master's Thesis. (Western Illinois University, 2008).

118. A. K. Cohen, "Foreword and Overview," in *Gangs in America*, C. Ronald Huff, ed. (Newbury Park, CA: Sage, 1990).

119. Herbert C. Covey, Scott Menard, and Robert J. Franzese, *Juvenile Gangs* (Springfield, IL: Charles C. Thomas, 1992).

120. Luc Sante, *Low Life: Lures and Snares of Old New York* (New York: Vintage Books, 1991).

121. James C. Howell and John P. Moore, "History of Street Gangs in the United States," Washington, DC: Bureau of Justice Assistance, *National Gang Center Bulletin* 4 (2010).

122. M. K. Conway, *Gangs on Indian Reservations* (Washington, DC: U.S. Department of Justice, Federal Bureau of Investigation, 1998).

123. Covey, et al., *Juvenile Gangs*.

124. Seth Mydans, "Not Just the Inner City: Well To Do Join Gangs," *New York Times* National (April 10, 1991), A–7.

125. Luc Sante, *Low Life: Lures and Snares of Old New York* (New York: Vintage Books, 1991).

126. Covey et al., *Juvenile Gangs*, p. 64.

127. C. J. Friedman, F. Mann, and H. Aldeman, "Juvenile Street Gangs: the Victimization of Youth," *Adolescence* 11 (1976), pp. 527–533.

128. William J. Chambliss, "The Saints and The Roughnecks,'" *Society* 11 (1973), pp. 341–355.

129. National Alliance of Gang Investigators Association, *2005 National Gang Threat Assessment*. Available at http://ojp.usdoj.gov/BJA/what/2005_threat_assesment.pdf.

130. Office of Juvenile Justice and Delinquency Prevention, 2009. *Highlights of the 2007 National Youth Gang Surveys*. Available at www.ncjrs.gov/pdffiles1/ojjdp/225185.pdf.

131. C. Ronald Huff ("Youth Gangs and Public Policy," *Crime and Delinquency* 35 [1989], pp. 528–537) identifies three gang types: hedonistic, instrumental, or predatory; Jeffrey Fagan ("The Social Organization of Drug Use and Drug Dealing

Among Urban Gangs," *Criminology* [1989], pp. 633–666) identified four gang types: social gangs, party gangs, serious delinquents, and organized gangs.

132. Malcomb W. Klein, Cheryl Maxson, and Lea C. Cunningham, "'Crack,' Street Gangs, and Violence," *Criminology* 29 (1991), pp. 623–650; Scott H. Decker and Barrick Van Winkle, "Slinging Dope: The Role of Gangs, and Gang Members in Drug Sales," *Justice Quarterly* 11 (1994), pp. 583–604.

133. Finn-Aage Esbensen and David Huizinga, "Gangs, Drugs, and Delinquency," *Criminology* 31 (1993), pp. 565–590.

134. Highlights of the 1999 National Youth Gang Survey, Office of Juvenile Justice and Delinquency Prevention, 2000. Available at http://www.iir.com/nygc/.

135. Fagan, "The Social Organization of Drug Use and Drug Dealing Among Urban Gangs."

136. David G. Curry and Scott H. Decker, *Confronting Gangs: Crime and Community* (Los Angeles: Roxbury, 1998).

137. National Alliance of Gang Investigators Association, 2005 Threat Assessment, pp. 3–5.

138. Highlights of the 1999 National Youth Gang Survey, Office of Juvenile Justice and Delinquency Prevention, 2000. Available at http://www.iir.com/nygc/.

139. J. M. Hagedorn, *People and Folks* (Chicago: Lake View Press: 1989); D. Ronald Huff, *Gangs in America*; W. K. Brown, "Graffiti, Identity, and the Delinquent Gang," *International Journal of Offender Therapy and Comparative Criminology* 22 (1978), pp. 39–45; J. W. C. Johnstone, "Youth Gangs and Black Suburbs," *Pacific Sociological Review* 24 (1981), pp. 355–375; Thrasher, *The Gang*; J. D. Moore and Vigil R. Garcia, "Residence and Territoriality in Chicano Gangs," *Social Problems* 31 (1983), pp. 182–194; Ko-Lin Chin, Jeffrey Fagan, and Robert J. Kelly, "Patterns of Chinese Gang Extortion," *Justice Quarterly* 9 (1992), pp. 625–646; Calvin Toy, "A Short History of Asian Gangs in San Francisco," *Justice Quarterly* 9 (1992), pp. 645–665; M. G. Harris, *Cholas: Latino Girls in Gangs* (New York: AMS Press, 1988); J. D. Vigil, *Barrio Gangs* (Austin, TX: University of Texas Press, 1988); Anne Campbell, *Girls in the Gang: A Report from New York City* (Oxford: Basil Blackwell, 1984); E. G. Dolan and S. Finney, *Youth Gangs*; James F. Short, Jr., and Fred L. Strodbeck, *Group Process and Gang Delinquency* (Chicago: University of Chicago Press, 1965).

140. Curry and Decker, *Confronting Gangs*.

141. Mydans, "Not Just the Inner City"; Esbensen and Huizinga, "Gangs, Drugs and Delinquency"; Jeffrey Fagan, "Social Process of Delinquency and Drug Use Among Urban Gangs," in *Gangs in America*, C. Ronald Huff, ed. (Newbury Park, CA: Sage, 1990); Anne Campbell, *The Girls in the Gang*, 2nd ed. (Cambridge, MA: Basil Blackwell, 1991).

142. National Alliance of Gang Investigators Association.

143. Covey et al., *Juvenile Gangs*.

144. Ibid.

145. Covey et al., *Juvenile Gangs*, p. 49.

146. Ibid., p. 52.

147. John P. Sullivan, Third Generation Street Gangs, *Crime and Justice International Magazine* (April 24, 2011), available at: http://cjmagazine.com.

148. *Omaha World Herald*, September 18, 1997.

149. National Alliance of Gang Investigators Association, *2005 Threat Assessment,* pp. 11–12.

150. James D. Vigil and S. C. Yun, "Vietnamese Youth Gangs in Southern California," in *Gangs in America*; Chin et al., "Patterns in Chinese Gang Extortion"; Toy, "A Short History."

151. Covey et al., *Juvenile Gangs,* p. 67; NAGIA, *2005 Threat Assessment,* p. 18.

152. K. Chin, "Chinese gangs and extortion," in *Gangs in America,* C. Ronald Huff, ed. (Newbury Park, CA: Sage, 1990).

153. Vigil and Yun, "Vietnamese Youth Gangs in Southern California."

154. Covey et al., *Juvenile Gangs.*

155. NAGIA, *2005 Threat Assessment,* pp. 7–8.

156. Ibid., p. 9.

157. National Youth Gang Survey (2007).

158. Covey et al., *Juvenile Gangs,* p. 65.

159. Mark S. Hamm, *American Skinheads* (Westport, CT: Praeger; 1994), p. 62.

160. NAGIA, *2005 Threat Assessment,* p. 5.

161. I. A. Spergel, "Youth Gangs: Continuity and Change," in *Crime and Delinquency: An Annual Review of Research*, vol. 12, Michael Tonry and Norval Morris, eds. (Chicago: University of Chicago Press; 1990).

162. Covey et al., *Juvenile Gangs,* p. 48

163. Hamm, *American Skinheads.*

3

✳

Race, Ethnicity, Social Structure, and Crime

GOALS OF THE CHAPTER

The goals of this chapter are to examine the broader structure of American society with respect to race and ethnicity and to analyze the relationship between social structure and crime. As we learned in Chapter 2, people of color are disproportionately involved in the criminal justice system, as crime victims, offenders, persons arrested, and persons in prison. In very general terms, there are two possible explanations for this overrepresentation. The first is discrimination in the criminal justice system. We explore the data related to this issue in Chapters 4 through 10. The second explanation involves structural inequalities in American society. This chapter examines the relationships among race and ethnicity, the social structure, and crime.

We should first define what we mean by social structure. Social structure is "a general term for any collective social circumstance that is unalterable and given for the individual."[1] The analysis of social structure reveals *patterned relationships between groups of people* that form the basic contours of society. The patterned relationships are related to employment, income, residence, education, religion, gender, and race and ethnicity. In combination, these factors explain a person's circumstances in life, relationships with other groups, attitudes and behavior on most issues, and prospects for the future.

This chapter explores the very complex relationship among social and economic inequality, race and ethnicity, and participation in crime.

After you have read this chapter:

1. You will be able to knowledgeably discuss social and economic inequality, race and ethnicity, and crime.
2. You will better understand the nature and extent of inequality in American society with respect to racial and ethnic minorities.

3. You will be able to explain whether the social and economic gap between whites and people of color is narrowing or growing.

4. You will understand how inherited wealth perpetuates inequality in terms of opportunities for employment and education.

5. You will understand what we know about the relationship between social and economic inequality and crime, and how the leading theories of crime help explain that relationship.

6. You will be knowledgeable about the impact of reform efforts designed to reduce inequality, including the civil rights movement and different anti-poverty efforts.

A SNAPSHOT OF SOCIAL INEQUALITY AND CRIMINAL JUSTICE

Raymond Towler walked out of prison in May 2010, after serving 28.5 years for crimes he did not commit. He had been erroneously accused and convicted of rape, felonious assault, and kidnapping. The Innocence Project secured his exoneration and release through DNA evidence. The main evidence against him was the eyewitness testimony of the 11- and 12-year-old victims. The jury ignored the testimony of friends who corroborated his statement that he was home at the time of the crime. No physical evidence tied him to the crime. In 2010 DNA testing of one of the victim's underwear excluded him as the perpetrator. Towler is African American; the two victims are white.

Sixty percent of the over 260 convicted people exonerated by the Innocence Project through the use of DNA evidence have been African Americans. Another 8 percent have been Hispanic. They served an average of 13 years in prison for crimes they did not commit. Eighty-four percent were convicted of sexual assault, and 76 percent were convicted at least in part on the basis of incorrect eyewitness identification. Over half of those misidentifications, moreover, were cross-racial, with a white accuser and an African American suspect. Not only are eyewitness identifications always problematic, but research has also found cross-racial identifications are filled with problems, because of both stereotyping and lack of familiarity with different races. In short, being African American makes you more likely to be falsely convicted of a serious crime and sentenced to many years in prison.[2]

INEQUALITY AND CRIME

Long-Term Trends and the Recession

Inequality is directly related to crime. Social and economic inequality explains a great deal about who commits crime, who are the victims of crime, who is arrested and prosecuted, and who goes to prison. Does inequality cause crime?

No. All poor people do not commit crime, and poverty does not make someone become a criminal. But it does involve circumstances that do contribute to criminal behavior.

The United States has had long-standing patterns of social and economic inequality by race and ethnicity. African Americans, Hispanics, and Native Americans are much worse off by every measure than are non-Hispanic whites and Asian Americans. In this chapter we will explain how those factors directly affect crime and criminal justice and account for much of the much-publicized disparities in the prison population.

Two Societies?

In 1968 the Kerner Commission warned that "our Nation is moving toward two societies, one black, one white—separate and unequal."[3] Twenty-four years later, political scientist Andrew Hacker published a book on American race relations titled *Two Nations: Black and White, Separate, Hostile, Unequal.*[4] Hacker's subtitle indicates that the Kerner Commission's dire warning has come true: instead of moving toward greater equality and opportunity, since the 1960s we have moved backward.

The situation, moreover, has worsened in just the last few years because of the recession that struck in 2008. Unemployment is up, job opportunities are down, and the mortgage crisis that has forced many people out of their homes has hit African Americans and Hispanics particularly hard. The unemployment rate for African American teens in September 2010 was almost 50 percent, creating what some call a "national crisis."[5]

ECONOMIC INEQUALITY

The extraordinary 50 percent unemployment rate was partly a result of the recession, but it was also a severe manifestation of historic economic inequalities based on color in America that have a direct impact on crime and criminal justice.[6]

There are three important patterns of economic inequality in America: (1) a large gap between rich and poor, without regard to race or ethnicity; (2) a large economic gap between white Americans and racial minorities; and (3) the growth of the very poor—a group some analysts call an underclass—in the past 30 years. (We discuss the concept of an underclass later on pp. 11–13).

The standard measures of economic inequality are income, wealth, unemployment, and poverty status. In studying social and economic inequality, there is increased social science interest in the concept of well-being. It includes not just the traditional measures of employment, income, educational attainment, health and access to insurance but also the quality of a person's family life, the social and physical environment, and personal safety.[7] The latter two indicators are particularly important for people of color, since they are more likely to live

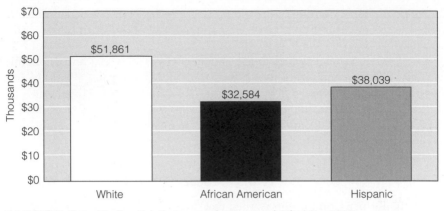

FIGURE 3.1 Median Family Income, by Race and Ethnicity, 2009

in high crime neighborhoods, and as a result to live in fear of crime and be victimized. The recession has aggravated these factors.

Income

Median family income is a standard measure of economic status. U.S. Census Bureau data reveal wide gaps between racial and ethnic groups. In 2009 the median household income in the United States for African American families was only 63 percent that of white Americans ($51,861 for whites versus $32,584 for African Americans and $38,039 for Hispanic families; see Figure 3.1).[8] Historical trends put these figures in perspective. African Americans made significant progress relative to whites in the 1950s and 1960s, but since then, according to the National Research Council, "the economic status of blacks relative to whites has, on average, stagnated or deteriorated."[9]

The median household income figures mask significant differences within racial and ethnic groups. One of the most significant developments over the past 40 years has been the growth of an African American middle class.[10] A similar class difference exists within the Hispanic community. These cleavages are the result of two factors. First, the civil rights movement opened the door to employment for African Americans and Hispanics in careers from which they previously had been excluded: white-collar, service, and professional-level jobs. Second, the end of blatant housing discrimination has allowed middle class African Americans and Hispanics to move out of segregated neighborhoods. This process, however, has resulted in a concentration of poverty in the older neighborhoods, with a concentration of factors that reinforce disorder and crime.

Among both African Americans and Hispanics, then, there is a greater gap between the middle class and the poorest than at any other time in our history. Later, we will see how changes in housing patterns among people of color have resulted in a greater concentration of disadvantage in certain areas. This has a direct impact on crime in poor neighborhoods.

Wealth

Annual income is only part of the story of poverty and inequality. An even greater gap involves wealth. *Income* measures how much you earn in any year. *Wealth* includes all the assets you own: your home (or homes, for some people); your cars and boats; other property (the rent you earn from a property is counted as income, but its basic value is wealth); your savings, including stocks and bonds; and so forth. The family that owns a house, for example, has far more wealth than the family that rents.

In 2004 (the most recent data available) white Americans had 13 times the net wealth of African American families and 9 times that of Hispanic families: $113,822 versus $8,650 for African Americans and $13,375 for Hispanic households (Figure 3.2).[11] These huge gaps have major implications, both direct and indirect, for crime and criminal justice.

The reasons for the huge gap in net worth are easy to understand. Middle-class people are able to save each month; the poor struggle to get by with what they have. Savings are used to buy a house, stocks. Savings can also be used to send children to college, which gives them a head start in life over their less-fortunate peers. Students who graduate with no student loan debts, because their parents could pay for college, have an additional advantage. The family's net wealth increases as the value of their home increases. Middle-class people, moreover, typically buy houses in neighborhoods where property values are rising. Lower-middle-class families, regardless of race, are often able to buy homes

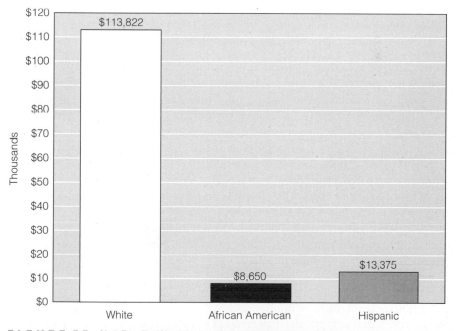

FIGURE 3.2 Net Family Wealth, by Race and Ethnicity, 2004

only in neighborhoods where property values are stagnant. As a result, their wealth does not increase very much. Poor people, of course, cannot buy a house at all, and as a result continually fall behind in terms of wealth.

The recession has altered this traditional analysis. Housing values have plummeted, and for many people that is their principal source of wealth. When they lost their jobs (or even one member of a two-earner family), they could not make their house payments and experienced foreclosure. The recession has hit the middle class very hard, and these people's economic status and future have fallen as it has for people of color.

Wealth plays an important role in perpetuating inequality. Traditionally, it cushioned a family against temporary hard times, such as loss of a job. The lower-middle-class person who is laid off, even temporarily, may lose his or her home; as a result, the family slides down the economic scale. Wealth is also transferred to the next generation. We have already discussed how it buys education and the resulting advantage for children.

It is also clear that the gap between whites and African Americans remains wide, despite the tremendous changes over the decades as a result of the civil rights movement. In a comprehensive survey of American race relations, the National Research Council concluded, "The status of black Americans today can be characterized as a glass that is half full." It found "persisting disparities between black and white Americans." Although many individuals have made significant progress and enjoy considerable wealth and status, a significant fraction of African Americans still cannot move into mainstream America. Later in this chapter we will examine the impact of the civil rights movement and other social changes on the problem of persistent inequality.

The "Family Thing": Inheritance

Contributing to wealth is a factor some people call the "family thing": inheritance. When people die, they leave their children their estate in the form of cash, stock, or property. But that is really true only for some people and not most Americans. In a powerful analysis of the gap between whites and African Americans, Thomas Shapiro argues that "inheritance is a frightful conveyor and transmitter of inequality." In a series of family interviews, he found that 25 percent of white families enjoyed an inheritance from parents or other family members, compared with only 5 percent of African American families. And that is only part of the story. One study found that among those inheriting anything, whites averaged $144,652, whereas African American families averaged only $41,985.[12] The Federal Reserve, meanwhile, estimates that the average white American family inherits $20,000 from their parents, whereas the average African American family inherits $2,000.

Inheritances give people receiving them a number of advantages. It can help tide over a young person who is still trying to find a job and career. It helps to buy a house, particularly a more expensive house in a better neighborhood. Shapiro argues that almost half of all whites (46 percent) made the down payment on their houses with help from family or other sources in addition to their own

TABLE   3.1

Part A: Percentage of Wealth Owned by Richest 1 Percent of Americans, 1972–2007

	1972	2007
Richest 1 Percent	29.1	34.6
Remaining 99 Percent	70.9	65.4

Part B: Distribution of Wealth, 2007

Richest 1 Percent	34.6
Next 19 Percent	50.5
Remaining 80 Percent	15.0

savings. Only 12 percent of African Americans enjoyed that extra help. A house in a middle-class neighborhood is more likely to increase in value than one in an economically marginal neighborhood—thereby increasing a family's wealth over time. Education data, moreover, consistently show that student performance in middle-class neighborhood schools is consistently better than in poor neighborhoods. Thus, being able to buy into a better neighborhood means "buying" your children a better education.

The Growing Gap between the Very Rich and Most Americans

The gap between the very richest Americans and most Americans in terms of both annual income and total wealth has actually been growing over the last few decades. As Table 3.1, Part A indicates, in 1972 the richest 1 percent of Americans owned 29.1 percent of all the wealth, compared with 70.9 percent by the remaining 99 percent of the population. Thirty-five years later, in 2007, the richest had increased their share to 34.6 percent, and the remaining 99 percent's share had declined to 65.4 percent. Even more revealing, in 2007 the top 1 percent owned 34.6 percent of the wealth, the next 19 percent owned 50.5 percent, and the "bottom" 80 percent (that is, most Americans) owned only 15 percent (Table 3.1, Part B).[13]

Unemployment

A large racial and ethnic gap in unemployment has existed for decades. In September 2010 the official unemployment rate for whites was 8.7 percent, compared with 12.4 for Hispanics and 16.1 for African Americans. Even before the recession, the gap existed. In 1990, a good economic year, the white unemployment rate was 4.8 percent, but it was 8.2 for Hispanics and 11.4 for African Americans.[14] The African American unemployment rate has been consistently about twice the white rate. Thus, even in good times the unemployment rate gap has persisted.

The official data on unemployment are incomplete, however. First, there are serious problems with the official unemployment rate. The official unemployment rate counts only those people who are *actively seeking employment.* (In a similar way, the official crime rate only counts crimes that are reported to police.) It does not count three important groups: (1) discouraged workers who have given up and are not looking for work; (2) part-time employees who want full-time jobs but cannot find them; and (3) workers in the "underground economy," who are paid in cash to avoid paying taxes and Social Security withholding. During a recession, when job opportunities are scarce, it is even more likely that people will not bother to look for work. Many economists believe that people of color are disproportionately represented among those not counted by the official unemployment rate.[15]

Equally important, the official unemployment rate is much higher for teenagers than for adults. The September 2010 unemployment rate for all teenagers (ages 16–19) was 26 percent (compared with 9.8 for adult men over the age of 20). Particularly alarming, the African American teen unemployment rate in September 2010 was almost 50 percent (49 percent according to the Bureau of Labor Statistics).[16]

The unemployment rate data reveal important differences within the Hispanic community related to national origins. The unemployment rate for Hispanics of Mexican and Puerto Rican origin is consistently higher than for those of Cuban origin.[17] The situation with regard to Native Americans is probably the bleakest of any group. Reliable data are difficult to find, but estimates put the adult unemployment rate on some reservations at over 40 percent. There are important differences among tribes and reservations. The Pine Ridge reservation in South Dakota is particularly poor, whereas the Arizona tribal reservations are much better off financially.[18]

The recession has had one important effect on Hispanic employment. As job opportunities fell, immigration declined. The Pew Hispanic Center found that between March 2007 and March 2009, the number of unauthorized immigrants entering the United States was only one third what it had been in 2000–2005.[19]

Later in this chapter we discuss the major theories of crime as they relate to race and ethnicity. For virtually every theory, the teenage unemployment rate is particularly relevant in terms of the likelihood of participation in crime. The peak years of criminal activity for Index crimes occur when people are between the ages of 14 and 24. Arrests peak at age 18 for violent crimes and at age 16 for property crimes. The persistently higher rates of unemployment for African American and Hispanic teenagers help explain their higher rates of criminal activity compared with those of whites.

Poverty Status

Yet another measure of economic status is the percentage of families in poverty. The federal government first developed an official definition of poverty in 1964 that was designed to reflect the minimum amount of income needed for an adequate standard of living. In 2009 the official poverty line was $22,050 for a family of four. That year, 14.3 percent of all Americans were below the poverty line, up from 12.5 percent in 2004. A strong racial and ethnic gap exists here as with other indicators. In 2009, 9.4 percent of non-Hispanic whites were in poverty, compared with 25.8 percent of African Americans and 25.3 percent of Hispanics. Even worse, economists have estimated that the official government poverty line is actually only half of what people really need to live adequately. Thus, a family of four really needs an income of $44,100 a year.[20]

The most disturbing aspect of the poverty figures is the percentage of children living below the poverty line. According to the National Center for Children in Poverty, in October 2009 about 20.7 percent of all children in the United States—15 million total—lived in families under the official poverty line. (Be careful with the data. Some reports refer to "low-income" families, which is a different category than "poverty." In 2010 the low-income ceiling for a family of four in Cleveland was $51,800. [The ceiling varies according to the cost of living in different areas.] About 42 percent of all children were in "low-income" families in 2009). The impact of poverty is especially strong on racial and ethnic minority groups. In the same year an estimated 25.8 percent of African American and 25.3 percent of Hispanic children lived in poverty level families.[21]

Because childhood low-income status is associated with so many other social problems—inadequate nutrition, single-parent households, low educational achievement, high risk of crime victimization, and high rate of involvement in crime—the data suggest a grim future for a very large percentage of racial and ethnic minority children.

Insurance Coverage

Another important measure of well-being is insurance coverage. An estimated 50 million Americans had no health insurance in 2009 (up from 46 million in just one year). That included 12 percent of non-Hispanic whites, 21 percent of African Americans, and 32.4 percent of Hispanics.[22]

Lack of health insurance makes a big difference in a person's life. If you cannot take care of routine health problems, you are likely to develop major health problems that affect your economic status. If you are chronically sick, you have trouble holding a steady job. Prenatal health care is extremely important for the health of the fetus, with major impacts later in life. In 2007, 62 percent of personal bankruptcies in the United States were due to medical bills not covered by insurance (up from 46 percent in 2001).[23] Bankruptcy causes many families to fall from middle- or even upper-middle-class status to lower-class or even poverty status.

Social Capital and Cultural Capital

An important aspect of economic status and the possibility of upward mobility is social and cultural capital. We typically think of "capital" in terms of money alone, but it takes other forms as well. Theorist Pierre Bourdieu identified three different types of capital. Economic capital, obviously, refers to financial resources. Social capital refers to a person's network of friends, relationships, and other contacts. Cultural capital includes education, knowledge, or skills that give a person an advantage.[24]

Social capital is defined by the World Bank as "the institutions, relationships, and norms that shape the quality or quantity of a society's social interactions."[25] The sources of social capital include families, communities, and organizations. With respect to employment, one important form of social capital is having family, friends, or neighbors who are able to offer jobs (for example, in a small family business) or personal referral to someone who is able to offer a job.

There are two categories of social capital: private and collective. Private social capital involves resources that an individual has; for example, the uncle who gives you a job in his small business. Collective social capital is resources that an entire group enjoys. This is particularly important at the neighborhood level. One neighborhood, for example, may have many strong religious institutions, which in turn promote social cohesion and sponsor activities that benefit the entire area. We will explore the importance of this later in our discussion of social disorganization theory (pp. 19–21).[26]

Social and cultural capital have huge implications for individuals, their status in life, their prospects for the future, and also their likelihood of becoming criminals. Having a family member who owns a business and can offer you a job is a form of social capital. Having a job and a chance to move up in the business means you are much more likely to establish a law-abiding lifestyle. Knowing how to repair cars or air conditioning units is a skill—a form of cultural capital— that is also likely to lead to employment. People often learn these skills from their relatives and so a stable family often contributes directly to the development of cultural capital. A parent who is a business owner, a lawyer, or a doctor; who can serve as a role model and inspiration; and who can transmit the lore of how to succeed in those occupations is another form of social and cultural capital. These examples illustrate how inequality is perpetuated as social and cultural capital are transmitted from one generation to the next.[27]

Families are a particularly important form of social and cultural capital. Sociologists and psychologists agree that the family is the primary unit for transmitting values to children. These values include, for example, self-respect, self-reliance, hard work, and respect for other people. If a family is dysfunctional, these values are not effectively transmitted to the children. The condition of poverty is generally associated with single-parent families, which are less able to transmit positive values.

Criminologist Elliot Currie illustrated the point by citing a comparative study of juvenile delinquents who graduated from the Lyman School in Massachusetts and the Wiltwyck School in New York in the 1950s. The predominantly white Lyman graduates often had personal connections who helped them find good employment. One graduate explained: "I fooled around a lot when I was a kid.... But then I got an uncle on the [police] force. When I was twenty he got me my first job as a traffic man."[28] The predominantly African American and Hispanic graduates of Wiltwyck did not have similar kinds of personal resources. As a result, they recidivated into criminal activity at a much higher rate. In short, the conditions of extreme poverty diminish the human and social capital that young people possess and, as a consequence, contribute to higher rates of criminal activity.

The noted sociologist Alejandro Portes points out, however, that social capital can also have a downside. Networks of groups in a neighborhood may promote criminal activity. A drug gang, for example, offers income, protection from other criminals, and a sense of belonging.[29]

The World Bank argues that government institutions, "the public sector," are an important part of the network of social capital. Assume that a neighborhood has stable families and a strong sense of community. Responsive government institutions can help translate their aspirations and efforts into effective services: good schools, attractive parks for recreation, a public transportation system that allows people to find and hold jobs, and so on. Obviously, the police and the criminal justice system are also important elements of this process. If the police effectively control crime and disorder, community members will feel better about their neighborhood and feel empowered to work for its improvement. The community policing movement of the past 20 years has been built on the idea that policing can be made more effective through partnerships with community organizations.

If neighborhood residents do not trust the police, however, they are less likely to cooperate with them in solving crime and other problems. Residents will also feel worse about their neighborhood. For this reason, the quality of police–community relations is extremely important. Chapter 4 discusses in detail the state of police–community relations and the effectiveness of programs to improve them.

The Debate over the Underclass

Those observers who take the most pessimistic view about poverty in America often use the term *underclass* to describe the very poor who are concentrated in the inner cities. The question of the existence of an underclass is more than a matter of semantics. It makes a great deal of difference whether the term is merely another euphemism for poor people (that is, "the poor," "the deprived," "the impoverished," "the disadvantaged," "the at-risk," and so on), which implies that the economic status of people at the bottom has not changed in any fundamental way, or whether it describes the emergence of a new kind of poverty in America.[30]

The crucial point about the underclass involves the impact of the conditions surrounding the very poor. Most important, they involve a concentration of factors that are heavily associated with criminal activity: dysfunctional families, a lack of nearby job opportunities, a concentration of bad peer influences and an absence of positive role models, and bad schools. For these reasons, the underclass tends to perpetuate itself.

Evidence suggests that the nature of urban poverty has changed in significant ways. First, the industrial sector of the economy has eroded, eliminating the entry-level jobs that were historically available to the poor. Second, conditions in the underclass generate circumstances and behavior that perpetuate poverty.

Gary Orfield and Carole Ashkinaze's study of economic conditions in Atlanta during the 1980s found growing inequality amid overall growth and prosperity. The authors found that although most people in the Atlanta metropolitan area fared better economically, "the dream of equal opportunity is fading fast for many young blacks in metropolitan Atlanta." For the African American poor in the inner city, "many of the basic elements of the American dream—a good job, a decent income, a house, college education for the kids—are less accessible ... than was the case in the 1970s."[31] Most of the economic growth occurred in the largely white suburbs, whereas opportunities declined in the predominantly African American inner city. At the same time, most of the expanding opportunities occurred in the service sector of the economy: either in white-collar professional-level jobs or in minimum-wage service jobs (for example, fast food). The poor cannot realistically compete for the professional-level jobs, and many of the service-sector jobs do not pay enough to support a family. A minimum-wage job paying $7.25 per hour (the federally mandated level in 2010) yields an annual income of $14,500 ($7.25 × 40 hours / week × 50 weeks). This is only 66 percent of the official poverty line of $22,050 for a family of four (2009 official figure).

Patterns of residential segregation contribute to the development of the urban underclass. Job growth over the past 30 years has been strongest in suburban areas outside the central cities. Inner-city residents, regardless of color, find it extremely difficult both to learn about job opportunities and to travel to and from work. Public transportation systems are either weak or nonexistent in most cities, particularly with respect to traveling to suburban areas. A private car is almost a necessity for traveling to work. Yet one of the basic facts of poverty is the lack of sufficient money to buy a reliable car. Concentration of the very poor and their isolation from the rest of society erode the social networks that are extremely important for finding employment. And, finally, as we have already mentioned, the recession has hit poor and low-income people particularly hard, aggravating the trends over the previous 30 years.

Studies of the job-seeking process have found that whites are more likely to be referred to jobs by friends or family who have some information about a job or connection with an employer. Racial and ethnic minorities are less likely to have these kinds of contacts, which are an important element of social capital. The problem is especially acute for members of the underclass, who are likely to have very few personal contacts that lead to good jobs.[32]

The pessimistic analysis of the changes in Atlanta in *The Closing Door* is still compatible with the more optimistic aspects of Stephan and Abigail Thernstroms' analysis. Atlanta has a large and growing African American professional and middle class. These individuals and families live in the suburbs, as do their white counterparts. Their very real progress, however, coexists in the Atlanta metropolitan area with the lack of progress by very poor African Americans trapped in the inner city. Robert D. Crutchfield explains the economic situation in the inner city in terms of a *dual labor market*. What economists call the *primary* market consists of good, well-paying jobs with fringe benefits (especially health care coverage) and good prospects for the future. The *secondary* market consists of low-paying jobs with limited fringe benefits and uncertain prospects for the future. He argues that the secondary market "has an effect on individual propensity to engage in crime." Individuals are less "bonded" to their work (and, by extension, to society as a whole) and to the idea that hard work will lead to a brighter future. Additionally, the inner city involves concentrations of people in the secondary market, who then "spend time with each other, socialize with one another, and at times even victimize each other."[33]

The pattern of economic change that affected Atlanta, a growing city, had even more negative effects on declining industrial cities such as New York and Chicago. Economic expansion there was concentrated in the suburban areas, and the inner cities declined significantly. Such older industrial cities did not experience the same rate of growth in the suburbs, and the decline in industrial jobs was even more severe. The relationship of the underclass to crime becomes clearer when we look at it from the standpoint of neighborhood community social structure.

COMMUNITY SOCIAL STRUCTURE

The social structure of communities has an important impact on crime. *Community* in this respect refers to both large metropolitan communities and local neighborhoods. The social structure of a community involves the spacial distribution of the population, the composition of local neighborhoods, and patterns of interaction between and within neighborhoods.

Residential Segregation

American metropolitan communities are characterized by strong patterns of residential segregation. As already indicated, this has an impact on patterns of criminal activity. Segregation itself is nothing new. Historically, American cities have always been segregated by race, ethnicity, and income. New arrivals to the city—either immigrants from other countries or migrants from rural areas—settled in the central city, with older immigrant groups and the middle class moving to neighborhoods farther out or to suburban communities. Racial and ethnic segregation in housing has been the result of several factors: the historic practice of de jure segregation, covert discrimination, and group choice. In the South and some Northern communities, local ordinances prohibited African Americans from living in white neighborhoods.

Particularly in the North, many property owners adopted restrictive covenants that prohibited the sale of property to African Americans or Jews. Real estate agents maintained segregation by steering minority buyers away from white neighborhoods. Banks and savings and loan companies refused to offer mortgages in poor and minority neighborhoods—a practice known as "redlining." Finally, segregation has been maintained by personal choice. People often prefer to live among members of their own group. Thus, European immigrants tended to form distinct ethnic neighborhoods, many of which still exist (for example, Little Italy).

Despite federal and state laws outlawing housing discrimination, residential segregation persists today. Social scientists have devised an index of residential segregation that measures the proportion of neighborhoods in any city that are racially homogeneous. The data indicate that in the 1980s, from 70 to 90 percent of the people in the major cities lived in racially homogeneous neighborhoods.

The residential segregation indices for both Detroit and Chicago in 1980 were 88, meaning that 88 percent of all people lived in either all-white or all–African American neighborhoods. In practical terms, this means that for a white person living in Detroit, an estimated 93 percent of the "potential" contacts with other people would involve other whites. For African Americans, 80 percent of the "potential" contacts would involve other African Americans. In New York City and Los Angeles, the residential segregation indices were 78 and 79, respectively.[34]

Interestingly, residential segregation is less severe for Hispanics (Dissimilarity Index = 50) than it is for African Americans (Dissimilarity Index = 65). The DI is a statistical technique for measuring the extent to which neighborhoods or census tracts consist primarily (or even entirely) of one group as opposed to being diverse in their population.[35]

Residential Segregation and Crime

Residential segregation has a direct impact on crime. Research has found that it has a significant effect on homicides. Most of the research on this subject has involved African Americans, but Ben Feldmeyer found that segregation has the same effect with Hispanics.[36] Most important, it concentrates high-rate offenders in one area, which has two significant consequences. First, the law-abiding residents of those areas suffer high rates of robbery, burglary, and other predatory crimes. In 2007 the household burglary rate was almost three and a half times higher for the poorest households (less than $7,500 annual income) than the highest income group ($75,000 a year or more). The robbery and auto theft rates were also higher. The obvious questions are: Why do burglars prey on the households that have the least? Why not go where there is more to steal? The answer to both is that burglars themselves are generally poor, and they attack the most available homes, those in the immediate neighborhood.[37, 38]

Second, the concentration of high-rate offenders in an area affects criminal activity. Peer group influence matters. Teenagers in high crime areas have disproportionate contact with people already involved in criminal activity: drugs, gangs, illegal weapons possession, and so on. They have much less contact with law-abiding peers. As Crutchfield points out, unemployed or marginally employed people in the secondary labor market "spend more time with each other," and as a result, they are more likely to influence each other in the direction of a greater propensity to commit crime.[39]

Even in stable families, the sheer weight of this peer influence overwhelms positive parental influence. In the worst of situations, teenagers are coerced into joining crime-involved gangs. Thus, many individuals are socialized into crime when this would not be the case if they lived in a more diverse neighborhood with less crime. In one of the great ironies of recent history, some of the great gains of the civil rights movement have hurt the poorest racial minority communities. Since the 1960s, the civil rights movement has opened up employment opportunities in business and the professions, creating a greatly expanded African American middle class. At the same time, the end of blatant residential segregation has created housing opportunities for families in the new African American middle class. Following the example of their white counterparts, these families move out of low-income, inner-city neighborhoods and into the suburbs.

The result is that the old neighborhoods abandoned by the African American middle class are stripped of important stabilizing elements—what William Julius Wilson refers to as a "social buffer."[40] The neighborhood loses its middle-class role models, who help socialize other children into middle-class values, and an important part of its natural leadership, the people who are active in neighborhood associations and local school issues. Wesley G. Skogan reports that educated, middle-class, home-owning residents are more likely to be involved in neighborhood organizations than are less educated, poorer, renting residents.[41] And, as we have already noted, the middle class is composed of the people who can provide the social networks that lead to good jobs.

All of these factors contribute directly to neighborhood deterioration and indirectly to crime. As more of the people with better incomes move out, the overall economic level of the neighborhood declines. Houses often go from owner-occupied to rental property. As the area loses purchasing power, neighborhood stores lose business and close. James Q. Wilson and George Kelling, two of the early theorists of community policing, argue that the physical deterioration of a neighborhood (abandoned buildings and cars, unrepaired houses, and so forth) is a sign that people do not care and, consequently, is an "invitation" to criminal behavior.[42] As the composition of the neighborhood changes, meanwhile, an increasing number of crime-involved people move in, changing the context of peer pressure in the neighborhood.

Skogan describes the impact of fear of crime on neighborhood deterioration as a six-stage process. It begins with withdrawal. People choose to have less contact with other neighborhood residents; the ultimate form of withdrawal is to move away. This leads to a reduction in informal control over behavior by residents: people no longer monitor and report on the behavior of, say, their neighbors' children. Then, organizational life declines: fewer residents are active in community groups. These factors lead to an increase in delinquency and disorder. As the neighborhood becomes poorer, commercial decline sets in. Local shops close and buildings are abandoned. The final stage of the process is collapse. At this point, according to Skogan, "there is virtually no 'community' remaining."[43] Community policing, it should be noted, is designed to stop this process of deterioration. First, many community policing efforts address small signs of disorder that cause people to withdraw. Second, police-initiated partnerships and block meetings are designed to strengthen networks among residents and help to give them a feeling of empowerment or collective efficacy in dealing with neighborhood problems.[44]

The Impact of Crime and Drugs

Crime has a devastating impact on neighborhoods—an impact that is intensified in very poor neighborhoods. First, it results in direct economic loss and physical harm to the crime victims. Second, the resulting high fear of crime damages the quality of life for everyone in the area. Third, persistent high rates of crime cause employed and law-abiding people to move out of the neighborhood, thereby intensifying the concentration of the unemployed and high-rate offenders. Fourth, crime damages local businesses, in the form of both direct losses and inability to obtain insurance. Eventually, many of these businesses move or close, with the result that the immediate neighborhood loses jobs. Those that stay frequently charge higher prices to make up for their losses.

The drug problem hit poor neighborhoods with devastating effect, particularly with the advent of crack cocaine in the mid-1980s. Drug trafficking fostered the growth of gangs and led to an increase in gang-related violence, including drive-by shootings that sometimes kill innocent people. Moreover, crack cocaine appears to be more damaging to family life than other drugs are. Mothers addicted to crack seem more likely to lose their sense of parental responsibility. The phenomenon of pregnant women becoming addicted to crack has resulted in a serious problem of crack-addicted babies.[45]

In some drug-ridden neighborhoods, the drug trade is the central feature of neighborhood life. Entire blocks have become "drug bazaars" with open drug sales. The drug trade is often a highly organized and complex activity, with people watching for the police, negotiating the sale, obtaining the drugs, and holding the main supply. The buyers are frequently outsiders, and the drug market represents what economists call *economic specialization*, with one part of society providing services to the rest of society.[46] Police departments have experimented with drug enforcement crackdowns (short-term periods of intensive arrest activity), but there is no evidence that this strategy has any long-term effect on reducing the drug trade.[47]

When drug and gang activity begins to dominate a neighborhood, it becomes virtually impossible for law-abiding residents to shield themselves and their children from illegal activity. The peer pressure on juveniles to join gangs becomes extremely intense. Often, kids join gangs for their own protection.

Because of drive-by shootings and other gang-related violence, the streets are even less safe than before. This is the stage that Skogan describes as neighborhood "collapse."[48]

Well-Being

The quality of life people enjoy involves more than the material aspects of income and wealth. Social scientists now conceptualize this factor in terms of well-being. Income and wealth do count. Being employed rather than unemployed matters tremendously. Getting an inheritance (or knowing that you will) makes a big difference. Having health insurance coverage not only means you are more likely to be treated and treated quickly for an illness but it also eliminates the anxiety that comes from not being insured and not knowing how you will pay any medical bills. Social and cultural capital are also important. Being part of a stable family increases your happiness and makes possible other enjoyable activities. Being part of an extended family that provides love, understanding, and possible help in times of crisis makes a big difference.

Your well-being is also affected by the quality of life in your neighborhood. Poor neighborhoods are typically filled with dilapidated or abandoned buildings. It is hard to take pride in this kind of area. An important part of vibrant and healthy neighborhoods is social bonds among residents and participation in organizations such as religious institutions and civic groups. Knowing other people and knowing that they care about you and the neighborhood provides a great deal of satisfaction. As we will see later (pp. 20–21), criminological research has found that neighborhoods with these kinds of bonds are likely to have lower rates of crime than similar neighborhoods that do not have these bonds. Being able to work together to fight disorder and crime is referred to as "collective efficacy."[49] Finally, well-being is directly affected by the level of crime in two ways. First, you are more likely to be the victim of crime. The NCVS, as we have already mentioned, consistently finds that poor people experience higher levels of crime than middle- and upper-middle-class people. Higher levels of victimization, meanwhile, lead to higher levels of fear of crime. Feeling safe and free to walk the streets of your area is an important component of well-being.

THEORETICAL PERSPECTIVES ON INEQUALITY AND CRIME

The second important issue addressed in this chapter is the relationship between inequality and crime. We have established that significant economic inequality prevails between the white majority and racial and ethnic minorities. To what extent does this inequality contribute to the racial and ethnic disparities in crime and criminal justice? To help answer this question, we turn to the major theories of criminal behavior. In different ways, each one posits a relationship between inequality and crime that helps explain the disparities within crime and criminal justice.

Social Strain Theory

Robert Merton's social strain theory holds that each society has a dominant set of values and goals along with acceptable means of achieving them. Not everyone is able to realize these goals, however. The gap between approved goals and the means people have to achieve them (for example, I want to be rich and famous, but I am a high school dropout with no job skills) creates what Merton terms *social strain*.[50]

As Steven F. Messner and Richard Rosenfeld argue in *Crime and the American Dream*, the dominant goals and values in American society emphasize success through individual achievement.[51] Success is primarily measured in terms of material goods, social status, and recognition for personal expression (for example, through art or athletics). The indicators of material success include a person's job, income, place of residence, clothing, cars, and other consumer goods.

The accepted means of achieving these goals are also highly individualistic, emphasizing hard work, self-control, persistence, and education. The American work ethic holds that anyone can succeed if only he or she will work hard enough and keep trying long enough. Failure is regarded as a personal, not a social, failure. Yet, as we have seen, many people in the United States do not enjoy success in these terms: unemployment rates remain high, and millions of people are living in poverty. Minorities are the victims of racial and ethnic discrimination.

Merton's theory of social strain holds that people respond to the gap between society's values and their own circumstances in several different ways: rebellion, retreatism, and innovation. Some of these involve criminal activity.

Rebellion involves a rejection of society's goals and the established means of achieving them, along with an attempt to create a new society based on different values and goals. This stage includes revolutionary political activity, which in some instances might be politically related criminal activity such as terrorism. Rebellion can also take the form of artistic expression. Many famous artists rebelled against established norms, created new art forms, and eventually became very famous. Think of the novelist James Joyce or folk/rock pioneer Bob Dylan.

Retreatism entails a rejection of both the goals and the accepted means of achieving them. A person may retreat, for example, into drug abuse, alcoholism, vagrancy, or a countercultural lifestyle. Retreatism helps explain the high rates of drug and alcohol abuse in America. Many forms of drug abuse involve criminal behavior: the buying and selling of drugs, robbery or burglary as a means of obtaining money to purchase drugs, or involvement in a drug trafficking network that includes violent crime directed against rival drug dealers.

There is considerable debate among criminologists over the relationship between drugs and crime.[52] There is no clear evidence that drug abuse is a direct cause of crime. Studies of crime and drugs have found mixed patterns: some individuals began their criminal activity before they started using drugs, whereas for others, drug use preceded involvement in crime. Moreover, some individuals "specialize" and either use (and/or sell) drugs but engage in no other criminal activity, or they commit crimes but do not use illegal drugs.[53]

Innovation involves an acceptance of society's goals but a rejection of the accepted means of attaining them—that is, some forms of innovation can be negative rather than positive. Crime is one mode of innovation. The person who embezzles money seeks material success but chooses an illegitimate (criminal) means of achieving it. Some Wall Street investors pushed the limits of the law in developing new ways to make money. In some cases, they did break the law and were eventually caught and prosecuted. Gang formation and drug trafficking are manifestations of entrepreneurship and neighborhood networking. Unfortunately, they lead to lawbreaking and often have destructive side effects (for example, gang-related shootings) rather than law obedience. These are examples of what Alejandro Portes and Patricia Landolt refer to as the "downside" of social capital.[54] The person who steals to obtain money or things is seeking the external evidence of material success through illegal means.

Applying the Theory

Social strain theory helps explain the high rates of delinquency and criminal behavior among racial and ethnic minorities in the United States. Criminal activity will be higher among those groups that are denied the opportunity to fulfill the American dream of individual achievement. The theory also explains far higher rates of retreatist (for example, drug abuse) and innovative (for example, criminal activity) responses. The high levels of economic inequality experienced by minorities, together with continuing discrimination based on race and ethnicity, mean that minorities are far less likely to be able to achieve approved social goals through conventional means.

Differential Association Theory

Edwin Sutherland's theory of differential association holds that criminal behavior is learned behavior. The more contact a person has with people who are already involved in crime, the more likely that person is to engage in criminal activity.[55]

Applying the Theory

Given the structure of American communities, differential association theory has direct relevance to the disproportionate involvement of racial and ethnic minorities in the criminal justice system. Because of residential segregation based on income and race, a person who is poor, a racial or ethnic minority, or both is more likely to have personal contact with people who are already involved in crime. The concentration of people involved in crime in underclass neighborhoods produces enormous peer pressure to become involved in crime. In neighborhoods where gangs are prevalent, young people often experience tremendous pressure to join a gang simply as a means of personal protection. In schools where drug use is prevalent, juveniles will have more contact with drug users and are more likely to be socialized into drug use themselves. As noted earlier, Crutchfield argues that the secondary labor market brings together high concentrations of people with a weak attachment to their work and the future, who then socialize with one another and influence one another's propensity to commit crime.[56]

Parents have a basic understanding of differential association theory: they warn their children to avoid the "bad" kids in the neighborhood and encourage them to associate with the "good" kids. This also explains choices people make in where they live. They choose what they see as "good" neighborhoods, where there are "good" schools and where their children will not meet "bad" kids.

Social Disorganization Theory

Followers of the Chicago school of urban sociology developed the social disorganization theory of crime.[57] Focusing on poor inner-city neighborhoods, this theory holds that the conditions of poverty undermine the institutions that socialize people into conventional, law-abiding ways of life. As a result, the values and behavior leading to delinquency and crime are passed on from one generation to another.

The Chicago sociologists found, for example, that recent immigrants tended to have lower rates of criminality than the first American-born generation. Immigrants were able to preserve old-world family structures that promoted stability and conventional behavior. These older values broke down in the new urban environment, however, which led to higher rates of criminality among the next generation. The Chicago sociologists noted the spatial organization of the larger metropolitan areas, with higher rates of criminal behavior in the poorer inner-city neighborhoods and lower rates in areas farther out.

The conditions of poverty contribute to social disorganization and criminality in several ways. Poverty and unemployment undermine the family, the primary unit of socialization, which leads to high rates of single-parent families. Lack of parental supervision and positive role models contributes to crime and delinquency. The concentration of the poor in certain neighborhoods means that individuals are subject to strong peer group influence tending toward nonconforming behavior. Poverty is also associated with inadequate prenatal care and malnutrition, which contribute to developmental and health problems that, in turn, lead to poor performance in schools.

The principal proponent of social disorganization theory today is Robert J. Sampson, whose research has focused on Chicago neighborhoods. Out of his research has emerged the related theory of collective efficacy.[58] If the people in a neighborhood have resources they can rely on as a group, they can resist and possibly even overcome the impact of social disorganization. Measures include friendship networks, control of teenagers' activity on the streets, and participation in neighborhood organizations. These resources include bonds among neighborhood residents based on mutual trust; strong neighborhood institutions such as churches, synagogues, or mosques; and neighborhood leaders such as small business owners or religious leaders. One of the basic principles of community policing and problem-oriented policing is that neighborhood-focused police efforts can help communities develop the resources (including trust in the police) that represent collective efficacy.[59]

Applying the Theory

Social disorganization theory helps explain the high rates of crime and delinquency among racial and ethnic minorities. As our discussion of inequality suggests, minorities experience high rates of poverty and are geographically concentrated in areas with high rates of social disorganization. Sampson's research on Chicago found that neighborhoods with higher levels of collective efficacy had lower levels of violent crime, after controlling for other variables.

In Baltimore, Maryland, Ralph Taylor, Stephen Gottfredson, and Sidney Brower interviewed residents of 687 households, asking whether they belonged to neighborhood organizations and whether they felt responsible for conditions in their neighborhood. People who answered affirmatively to both questions were more likely to live on neighborhood blocks with lower levels of violent crime than people on blocks who did not belong to organizations and did not feel responsible for their area.[60]

Social disorganization theory is consistent with other theories of crime. It is consistent with social strain theory, in that persons who are subject to conditions of social disorganization are far less likely to be able to achieve the dominant goals of society through conventional means and, therefore, are more likely to turn to crime. It is consistent with differential association theory, in that neighborhoods with high levels of social disorganization will subject individuals, particularly young men, to strong influences tending toward delinquency and crime.

Social disorganization theory and the related theory of collective efficacy underpin a number of criminal justice innovations, particularly community policing and problem-oriented policing. As Sampson puts it, the more promising approach to controlling crime is in "changing places, not people."[61] Traditional rehabilitation programs seek to change people; community policing and related approaches seek to change the quality of life in neighborhoods. Community policing and problem-oriented policing, for example, seek to reduce social disorder and to make neighborhoods appear safer and actually be safer. Reducing the fear of crime helps to keep people from moving out of the area and also to be more involved in neighborhood activities. "Hot spots" policing, meanwhile, is directed toward specific areas where crime is concentrated. Crime prevention through environmental design seeks to eliminate features that invite crime (for example, hidden walkways or building entrances).[62]

Culture Conflict Theory

Culture conflict theory holds that crime will be more likely to flourish in heterogeneous societies where there is a lack of consensus over society's values.[63] Human behavior is shaped by norms that are instilled through socialization and embodied in the criminal law. In any society, the majority not only defines social norms but also controls the making and the administration of the criminal law. In some instances, certain groups do not accept the dominant social values. They may reject them on religious or cultural grounds or feel alienated from the majority because of discrimination or economic inequality. Conflict over social norms and the role of the criminal law leads to certain types of lawbreaking.

One example of religiously based culture conflict involves peyote, a cactus that has mild hallucinogenic effects when smoked and that some Native American religions use as part of their traditional religious exercises.[64] Today, many observers see national politics revolving around a "culture war" involving such issues as abortion, homosexuality, and religion in the public schools.[65] Some groups believe that abortion is murder and should be criminalized; others argue that it is a medical procedure that should be governed by the individual's private choice.

Applying the Theory

Culture conflict theory helps explain some of the differential rates of involvement in crime in society, which is extremely heterogeneous, characterized by many different races, ethnic groups, religions, and cultural lifestyles. The theory encompasses the history of racial conflict—from the time of slavery, through the Civil War, to the modern civil rights movement—as one of the major themes in U.S. history. There is also a long history of ethnic and religious conflict. Americans of white, Protestant, and English background, for instance, exhibited strong prejudice against immigrants from Ireland and southern and eastern Europe, particularly Catholics and Jews.[66]

An excellent example of cultural conflict in American history is the long struggle over the consumption of alcohol that culminated in national Prohibition (1920–1933). The fight over alcohol was a bitter issue for nearly 100 years before Prohibition. To a great extent, the struggle was rooted in ethnic and religious differences. Protestant Americans tended to take a very moralistic attitude toward alcohol, viewing abstinence as a sign of self-control and a means of rising to middle-class status. For many Catholic immigrant groups, particularly Irish and German, alcohol consumption was an accepted part of their cultural lifestyle. The long crusade to control alcohol use represented an attempt by middle-class Protestants to impose their lifestyle on working-class Catholics.[67]

Conflict Theory

Conflict theory holds that the administration of criminal justice reflects the unequal distribution of power in society.[68] The more powerful groups use the criminal justice system to maintain their dominant position and to repress groups or social movements that threaten their position.[69] As Hawkins argues, conflict theory was developed primarily with reference to social class, with relatively little attention to race and ethnicity.[70]

The most obvious example of conflict theory in action was the segregation era in the South (1890s–1960s), when white supremacists instituted de jure segregation in public schools and other public accommodations.[71] The criminal justice system was used to maintain the subordinate status of African Americans. Because African Americans were disenfranchised as voters, they had no control or influence over the justice system. As a result, crimes by whites against African Americans went unpunished, and crimes by African Americans against whites were treated very harshly—including alleged or even completely fabricated offenses.[72] Meanwhile, outside of the South, discrimination also limited the influence of minorities over the justice system. The civil rights movement has eliminated de jure segregation and other blatant forms of discrimination. Nonetheless, pervasive discrimination in society and the criminal justice system continues.

Applying the Theory

Conflict theory explains the overrepresentation of racial and ethnic minorities in the criminal justice system in several ways. The criminal law singles out certain behavior engaged in primarily by the poor. Vagrancy laws are the classic example of the use of the criminal law to control the poor and other perceived "threats" to the social order. The criminal law has also been used against political movements challenging the established order: from sedition laws against unpopular ideas to disorderly conduct arrests of demonstrators.

Finally, "street crimes" that are predominantly committed by the poor and disproportionately by racial and ethnic minorities are the target of more vigorous enforcement efforts than are those crimes committed by the rich. The term *crime* refers more to robbery and burglary than to white-collar crime. In these ways, conflict theory explains the overrepresentation of racial and ethnic minorities among people arrested, convicted, and imprisoned.

Routine Activity Theory

Routine activity theory shifts the focus of attention from offenders to criminal incidents. Marcus Felson explains that the theory examines "how these incidents originate in the routine activities of everyday life."[73] Particularly important, the theory emphasizes the extent to which the daily routine creates informal social control that helps prevent crime or undermines those informal controls and leads to higher involvement in crime. (Informal social control includes, for example, the watchfulness of family, friends, and neighbors. Formal social control is exercised by the police and the rest of the criminal justice system.) Felson offers the example of parental supervision of teenagers. He cites data indicating that between 1940 and the 1970s, American juveniles spent an increasing amount of time away from the home with no direct parental supervision.[74]

These changes are rooted in the changing nature of work and family life in contemporary society (as opposed to some kind of moral failing). These circumstances increase the probability that young people will engage in crime. To cite an earlier example, in the 1920s many people were alarmed that the advent of the automobile created the opportunity for young men and women to be alone together without direct parental supervision, with a resulting increase in premarital sexual behavior.

Applying the Theory

Routine activity theory is particularly useful in explaining crime when it is integrated with other theories. If parental supervision represents an important informal social control, then family breakdown and single-parent households will involve less supervision and increase the probability of more involvement in crime. High rates of teenage unemployment will mean that more young people will have free time on their hands, and if unemployment is high in the neighborhood, they will have more association with other unemployed young people, including some who are already involved in crime.

The Limits of Current Theories

All of the theories discussed here attempt to explain the relationships among race, ethnicity, and crime in terms of social conditions. Hawkins argues that this approach represents the liberal political orientation that has dominated American sociology and criminology through most of this century. He also believes that there are important limitations to this orientation. The liberal emphasis on social conditions arose out of a reaction to racist theories of biological determinism, which sought to explain high rates of crime among recent European immigrants and African Americans in terms of genetic inferiority. Herrnstein and Murray's controversial book, *The Bell Curve*, represents a recent version of this approach. The liberal emphasis on social conditions, however, tends to become a form of social determinism, as criminologists focus on the social pathologies of both minority communities and lower-class communities. Although consciously avoiding biologically based stereotypes, much of the research on social conditions has the unintended effect of perpetuating a different set of stereotypes about racial and ethnic minorities.[75]

Hawkins suggests that if we seek a comprehensive explanation of the relationships among race, ethnicity, and crime, the most promising approach will be to combine the best insights from liberal criminology regarding social conditions and conflict perspectives regarding both the administration of justice and intergroup relations.[76]

INEQUALITY AND SOCIAL REFORM

The most disturbing aspect of social inequality in America has been its persistence over 30 years despite a national effort to reduce or eliminate it. Paul E. Peterson refers to this as the "poverty paradox": not just the persistence of poverty in the richest country in the world but its persistence in the face of a major attack on it.[77] The civil rights movement fought to eliminate racial discrimination, and several different government policies sought to create economic opportunity and eliminate poverty. In the 1960s, liberals adopted the War on Poverty and other Great Society programs; in the 1980s, conservative economic programs of reducing both taxes and government spending sought to stimulate economic growth and create job opportunities.

Not only has inequality persisted, but as Hacker, Orfield, and Ashkinaze all argue, the gap between rich and poor and between whites and minorities has also gotten worse in many respects.[78] What happened? Did all the social and economic policies of the past generation completely fail?

There are four major explanations for the persistence of inequality, poverty, and the growth of the underclass.[79] Many liberals argue that it is the result of an inadequate welfare system. Social welfare programs in the United States are not nearly as comprehensive as those in other industrialized countries, lacking guaranteed health care, paid family leave, and comprehensive unemployment insurance. Other liberals argue that it is the result of the transformation of the national (and international) economy that has eliminated economic opportunities in the inner city and reduced earnings of many blue-collar jobs. Many conservatives argue that the persistence of poverty is the result of a "culture of poverty" that encourages attitudes and behavior patterns that keep people from rising out of poverty. Closely related to this view is the conservative argument that many government social and economic programs provide disincentives to work. These conservatives believe, for example, that the welfare system encourages people not to work and that the minimum wage causes employers to eliminate rather than create jobs.

The prominent African American social critic Cornell West argues that the traditional liberal–conservative debate on the relative importance of social structure versus individual character is unproductive. He points out that "structures and behavior are inseparable, that institutions and values go hand in hand."[80] In short, the problem of the persistence of inequality is extremely complex. The next section examines some of the major forces that have reshaped American life in the past generation and their impact on inequality.

The Impact of the Civil Rights Movement

The civil rights movement between 1945 and 1965 was one of the most important events in U.S. history. A revolution in the law ended *de jure* discrimination in public schools (the Supreme Court's landmark 1954 decision in *Brown v. Board of Education*) and public accommodations in the South (the 1964 Civil Rights Act), ended discrimination in voting (the 1965 Voting Rights Act), and established equality as national policy.[81] The movement inspired attacks on other forms of discrimination. Title VII of the 1964 Civil Rights Act banned employment discrimination against women. The 1990 Americans with Disabilities Act outlawed employment discrimination against people with disabilities. In 1967 the Supreme Court declared unconstitutional a Virginia law barring interracial marriage. A number of states and cities have banned discrimination against people on the basis of their sexual orientation.[82]

The civil rights revolution had a profound impact on the operations of every social institution, including the criminal justice system. Public schools in the South were racially integrated. Police departments began hiring African American officers. As a result of greater voter participation, the number of African American elected officials increased dramatically, from 33 nationwide in 1941 to 1,469 in 1965 and 8,830 in 1998. The total number of Hispanic elected officials increased from 3,174 in 1985 to 5,129 in 2007.[83]

With the development of educational and employment opportunities, African American and Hispanic middle classes emerged, and some individuals became wealthy business owners or professionals. Despite this progress, however, many analysts argue that the gaps between white and African American, and white non-Hispanic and Hispanic remain large. The National Academy of Sciences in 1989, for example, found a large gap between middle class African Americans those members of their race still in poverty.[84] Not everyone agrees with this pessimistic assessment, however. In *America in Black and White: One Nation, Indivisible*, Stephan Thernstrom and Abigail Thernstrom argue that African Americans have made remarkable progress since the 1940s, economically, socially, and politically, observing that "The signs of progress are all around us."[85]

Using Gunnar Myrdal's classic study of American race relations, *An American Dilemma* (1944), as their baseline, they find that the percentage of African American families in poverty fell from 87 percent in 1940 to 21.9 percent in 2000. The number of African Americans enrolled in college increased 30-fold in the same period, increasing from 45,000 students in 1940 to 1,400,000 in the late 1990s. Contrary to Hacker's pessimistic assessment that we are "two nations,"(p. 3 of this chapter) they argue that we are today less separate; less unequal; and, in their view, less hostile than was the case in 1940.[86]

Where does the truth lie? Is the United States progressing, stagnating, or regressing in terms of social and economic inequality? The answer is that there is a degree of truth in all three interpretations. It depends on which segment of the population we are talking about. We can make sense of this complex subject by taking the approach we suggested in Chapter 1: disaggregating it into distinct components and contexts.

First, it depends on what baseline you use. The Thernstroms use 1940 as a baseline, and few can question the amount of progress since that time, when segregation still prevailed in the South and there was much discrimination in the rest of the country. When you use the mid-1970s as your baseline, however, a very different picture emerges. African American progress has stagnated (even the Thernstroms concede this point), and in some respects their situation has gotten worse. The real income for all working Americans has also fallen since then.

Second, aggregate data on African Americans disguises the simultaneous development of a new middle class and the deteriorating status of the very poor.[87] A similar trend exists for Hispanics. Asian Americans are also divided into those who are doing well and those who are not. Among Native Americans, some individuals and entire tribes have benefited from the economic opportunities provided by the development of tribal gaming, whereas others remain mired in poverty.

Economists generally blame the economic stagnation since the 1970s on the disappearance of industrial-level jobs, particularly from the inner city, including the transfer of manufacturing plants to other countries. The economic policies of both liberal Democratic and conservative Republican presidents since the 1960s have attempted to stimulate the economy and create jobs. The major liberal Democratic effort was the War on Poverty, begun in 1965 with the Economic Opportunity Act. The federal attack on poverty and inequality also included major programs related to health care, education, Social Security, food stamps, and other forms of government assistance. The major conservative Republican effort in the 1980s involved tax cuts (for example, Reaganomics in the 1980s, the Bush tax cuts of 2002), which seek to stimulate investment that will create jobs.

The impact of these different measures is a matter of great controversy. Conservatives argue that the War on Poverty and other liberal policies of the 1960s not only failed to eliminate poverty but actually made things worse by impeding economic growth and removing the incentives for poor people to seek employment.[88] Liberals, meanwhile, argue that Reaganomics and the Bush tax cuts increased the gap between rich and poor, benefiting the wealthy and eliminating programs for the poor. The data suggest that neither of the policies has reduced the disappearance of manufacturing jobs, or halted the increasing structural in American society.

The complex changes in the economy over the past three decades have directly affected the racial and ethnic dimensions of crime and criminal justice. The persistence of severe inequality and the growth of the underclass have created conditions conducive to high rates of crime. The different theories of crime we discussed earlier—social strain theory, differential association theory, social disorganization theory, culture conflict theory, conflict theory, and routine activity theory—all would predict high rates of crime, given the changes in the economy that have occurred. Because racial and ethnic minorities have been disadvantaged by these economic trends, these theories of crime help explain the persistently high rates of crime among minorities.

CONCLUSION

The American social structure plays a major role in shaping the relationships among race, ethnicity, and crime. American society is characterized by deep inequalities related to race, ethnicity, and economics. There is persistent poverty, and minorities are disproportionately represented among the poor. In addition, economic changes have created a new phenomenon known as the urban underclass.

The major theories of crime explain the relationship between inequality and criminal behavior. In different ways, social strain, differential association, social disorganization, culture conflict, conflict, and routine activity theories all predict higher rates of criminal behavior among the poor and racial and ethnic minorities.

DISCUSSION QUESTIONS

1. Do you agree with the Kerner Commission's conclusion that we are "moving toward two societies, one black [and] one white"? Explain your answer.

2. Explain the difference between income and wealth. How, according to some analysts, does wealth perpetuate inequality?

3. Explain how residential discrimination on the basis of race or ethnicity contributes to crime.

4. What is meant by the concepts of human capital and social capital? How do they affect criminal behavior?

5. What has been the impact of the civil rights movement on crime and criminal justice?

6. Which theory of crime do you think best explains the prevalence of crime in the United States?

7. Explain the concept of collective efficacy. What impact does it have on crime in a neighborhood?

NOTES

1. E. F. Borgatta and M. L. Borgatta, *Encyclopedia of Sociology*, vol. 4 (New York: Macmillan, 1992), p. 1,970.

2. The Innocence Project, *260 Exonerated: Too Many Wrongfully Convicted* (New York: The Innocence Project, 2010). Available at http://www.innocenceproject.org.

3. Kerner Commission, *Report of the National Advisory Commission on Civil Disorders* (New York: Bantam Books, 1968), p. 1.

4. Andrew Hacker, *Two Nations: Black and White, Separate, Hostile, Unequal* (New York: Scribner's, 1992).

5. "The 'Unspoken National Crisis'—Black Teenage Unemployment Nears 50 Percent," *A3P News Team*, October 13, 2010.

6. "The 'Unspoken National Crisis'—Black Teenage Unemployment Nears 50 Percent," *A3P News Team*, October 13, 2010.

7. Urban Institute, *America's Children in Brief: Key National Indicators of Well-Being, 2010* (Washington, DC: Urban Institute, 2010).

8. U.S. Bureau of the Census, *Income, Poverty, and Health Insurance Coverage in the United States: 2009* (Washington, DC: Bureau of the Census, September 2010).

9. Gerald David Jaynes and Robin Williams Jr., eds., *A Common Destiny: Blacks and American Society* (Washington, DC: National Academy Press, 1989), p. 6.

10. Stephan Thernstrom and Abigail Thernstrom, *America in Black and White: One Nation, Indivisible* (New York: Simon & Schuster, 1997).

11. Population Reference Bureau, *Large Wealth Gap Among U.S. Racial and Ethnic Groups* (Washington, DC: PRB, September 2010); Lawrence Mishel, Jared Bernstein, and Heidi Shierholz, *The State of Working America 2008/2009*, Economic Policy Institute Book (Ithaca: Cornell University Press, 2009).

12. Thomas M. Shapiro, *The Hidden Cost of Being African American: How Wealth Perpetuates Inequality* (New York: Oxford University Press, 2004), pp. 67–71, 84.

13. G. William Domhoff, "Wealth, Income, and Power," (September 2005, Updated September 2010) *Who Rules America? http://sociology.ucsc.edu/whorulesamerica/*. The website provides updated data. The book version is G. William Domhoff, *Who Rules America? Challenges to Corporate and Class Dominance*, 6th ed. (New York: McGraw-Hill, 2010).

14. U.S. Bureau of Labor Statistics, *The Unemployment Situation: September 2010* (Washington, DC: Department of Labor, 2010). Available at http://www.dol.gov; U.S. Bureau of Labor Statistics, *Unemployment Rate Demographics September 2010* (Washington, DC: Department of Labor, 2010); Census Bureau, *2010 Statistical Abstract*, Table 576.

15. Bureau of Labor Statistics, *How the Government Measures Unemployment* (2010). Available at http://www.bls.gov/cps_htgm.htm; Hacker, *Two Nations*, p. 105.

16. "The 'Unspoken National Crisis'—Black Teenage Unemployment Nears 50 Percent," *A3P News Team*, October 13, 2010.

17. Bureau of the Census, *Statistical Abstract, 2006*, Table 41.

18. Tom Rodgers, "Native American Poverty: A Challenge Too Often Ignored," *Spotlight on Poverty and Inequality*, http://www.spotlightonpoverty.org/ExclusiveCommentary.aspx?id=0fe5c04e-fdbf-4718-980c-0373ba823da7.

19. Jeffrey Passel and D'Vera Cohn, *U.S. Unauthorized Immigration Flows Are Down Sharply Since Mid-Decade* (Los Angeles: Pew Hispanic Center, September 1, 2010).

20. U.S. Bureau of the Census, *Income, Poverty, and Health Insurance Coverage in the United States: 2009* (Washington, DC: Bureau of the Census, 2010); National Center for Children in Poverty, *Basic Facts About Low-Income Children: Birth to Age 18* (New York: Columbia University, July 2005).

21. U.S. Bureau of the Census, *Income, Poverty, and Health Insurance Coverage in the United States: 2009*. See also Bureau of the Census, *Poverty in the United States: 2002* (Washington, DC: Bureau of the Census, 2003); National Center for Children in Poverty, *Basic Facts About Low-Income Children, 2009* (Washington, DC: NCCP, 2010). Available at http://www.nccp.org.

22. U.S. Bureau of the Census, *Income, Poverty, and Health Insurance Coverage in the United States: 2009* (Washington, DC: Bureau of the Census, 2010), p. 23.

23. "Medical Bills Prompt More Than 60 Percent of U.S. Bankruptcies," *CNN Health*, June 5, 2009.

24. Pierre Bourdieu and Jean-Claude Passeron, *Reproduction in Education, Society and Culture* (Newbury Park, CA: Sage, 1990).

25. *What Is Social Capital?* World Bank Group, PovertyNet. Available at http://www.worldbank.org/poverty.

26. Hartmut Esser, "The Two Meanings of Social Capital," in Dario Castiglione, Jan W. Van Deth, and Guglielmo Wolleb, eds., *Handbook of Social Capital* (New York: Oxford University Press, 2008), pp. 22–49.

27. Toby L. Parcel and Elizabeth G. Menaghan, *Parents' Jobs and Children's Lives* (New York: Aldine deGruyter, 1994), p. 1.

28. Elliot Currie, *Confronting Crime* (New York: Pantheon Books, 1985), p. 243. The original study is by William McCord and Jose Sanchez, "The Treatment of Deviant Children: A Twenty-Five Year Follow-Up Study," *Crime and Delinquency* 29 (March 1983), pp. 239–251.

29. Alejandro Portes and Patricia Landolt, "The Downside of Social Capital," *The American Prospect* 26 (May–June 1996), pp. 18–21, 94; Mark E. Warren, "The Nature and Logic of Bad Social Capital," in Castiglione, et al., eds., *Handbook of Social Capital*, pp. 122–149.

30. William Julius Wilson, *The Truly Disadvantaged* (Chicago: University of Chicago Press, 1987); Christopher Jencks and Paul E. Peterson, eds., *The Urban Underclass* (Washington, DC: Brookings Institution, 1991); William Julius Wilson, ed., *The Ghetto Underclass* (Newbury Park, CA: Sage, 1993).

31. Gary Orfield and Carole Ashkinaze, *The Closing Door: Conservative Policy and Black Opportunity* (Chicago: University of Chicago Press, 1991), p. xiii.

32. Jaynes and Williams, *A Common Destiny*, p. 321.

33. Robert D. Crutchfield, "Ethnicity, Labor Markets, and Crime," in *Ethnicity, Race, and Crime*, D. F. Hawkins, ed. (Albany: State University Press of New York, 1995), p. 196.

34. Jaynes and Williams, *A Common Destiny*, pp. 78–79.

35. Ben Feldmeyer, "The Effects of Racial/Ethnic Segregation on Latino and Black Homicide," *Sociological Quarterly* 51, no. 4 (2010), pp. 600–623.

36. Ruth D. Peterson and Lauren J. Krivo, "Macrostructrual Analyses of Race, Ethnicity, and Violent Crime: Recent Lessons and New Directions for Research," *Annual Review of Sociology* 31 (2005), pp. 331–356; Feldmeyer, "The Effects of Racial/Ethnic Segregation on Latino and Black Homicide."

37. Bureau of Justice Statistics, *Criminal Victimization, 2007* (Washington, DC: Department of Justice, 2008), Table 5. NCJ 224390.

38. Bureau of Justice Statistics, *Criminal Victimization, 2007*, Table 5.

39. Crutchfield, "Ethnicity, Labor Markets, and Crime," p. 196.

40. Wilson, *The Truly Disadvantaged*, pp. 137, 144; see also Bill E. Lawson, "Uplifting the Race: Middle-Class Blacks and the Truly Disadvantaged," in *The Underclass Question*, Bill E. Lawson, ed. (Philadelphia: Temple University Press, 1992), pp. 90–113.

41. Wesley G. Skogan, *Disorder and Decline* (New York: Free Press, 1990), pp. 132–133.

42. James Q. Wilson and George Kelling, "Broken Windows: The Police and Neighborhood Safety," *Atlantic Monthly* 249 (March 1982), pp. 29–38.

43. Wesley Skogan, "Fear of Crime and Neighborhood Change," in *Communities and Crime*, A. Reiss and M. Tonry, eds. (Chicago: University of Chicago Press, 1986), pp. 215–220.

44. Wesley G. Skogan and Susan M. Hartnett, *Community Policing, Chicago Style* (New York: Oxford University Press, 1997).

45. The problem has been exaggerated in much of the news media coverage but is a serious problem nonetheless. See Dale Gieringer, "How Many Crack Babies?" in *Drug Prohibition and the Conscience of Nations*, Arnold Trebach and Kevin B. Zeese, eds. (Washington, DC: Drug Policy Foundation, 1990), pp. 71–75.

46. Peter Reuter, Robert MacCoun, and Patrick Murphy, *Money from Crime: A Study of the Economics of Drug Dealing in Washington, DC.* (Santa Monica, CA: Rand Corporation, 1990).

47. Lawrence W. Sherman, "Police Crackdowns," in *Crime and Justice: An Annual Review of Research*, vol. 12, Michael Tonry and Norval Morris, eds. (Chicago: University of Chicago Press, 1990).

48. Skogan, "Fear of Crime and Neighborhood Change," p. 220.

49. Robert J. Sampson, Stephen W. Raudenbush, and Felton Earls, "Neighborhoods and Violent Crime: A Multilevel Study of Collective Efficacy," *Science* 277 (August 15, 1997), pp. 918–924.

50. Robert K. Merton, *Social Theory and Social Structure* (New York: Free Press, 1957).

51. Steven F. Messner and Richard Rosenfeld, *Crime and the American Dream*, 4th ed. (Belmont, CA: Cengage, 2006).

52. Michael Tonry and James Q. Wilson, eds., *Drugs and Crime, Crime and Justice: A Review of Research*, vol. 13 (Chicago: University of Chicago Press, 1990).

53. David N. Nurco, Timothy W. Kinlock, and Thomas E. Hanlon, "The Drugs–Crime Connection," in *Handbook of Drug Control in the United States*, James A. Inciardi, ed. (New York: Greenwood, 1990), pp. 71–90.

54. Alejandro Portes and Patricia Landolt, "Unsolved Mysteries: The Tocqueville Files II," *The American Prospect* 7, no. 26 (May–June 1996), p. 10.

55. Edwin H. Sutherland, *Principles of Criminology*, 3rd ed. (Philadelphia: Lippincott, 1939).

56. Crutchfield, "Ethnicity, Labor Markets, and Crime," p. 196.

57. W. I. Thomas and Florian Znaniecki, *The Polish Peasant in Europe and America* (Boston: Gorham, 1920); Clifford R. Shaw, Frederick M. Forbaugh, and Henry D. McKay, *Delinquency Areas* (Chicago: University of Chicago Press, 1929).

58. Robert J. Sampson and W. Byron Groves, "Community Structure and Crime: Testing Social-Disorganization Theory," *American Journal of Sociology* 94 (January 1989), pp. 774–802; Sampson, Raudenbush, and Earls, "Neighborhoods and Violent Crime."

59. Michael S. Scott, *Problem-Oriented Policing: Reflections on the First 20 Years* (Washington: Department of Justice, 2000); Jack R. Greene, "Community Policing in America: Changing the Nature, Structure, and Function of the Police," in *Policies, Processes and Decisions of the Criminal Justice System* (Washington, DC: Department of Justice, 2000), pp. 299–370.

60. Ralph Taylor, Stephen Gottfredson, and Sidney Brower, "Block Crime and Fear: Defensible Space, Local Social Ties, and Territorial Functioning," *Journal of Research in Crime and Delinquency* 21 (1984), pp. 303–331.

61. Robert J. Sampson, "Crime and Public Safety: Insights From Community-Level Perspectives on Social Capital," in *Social Capital and Poor Communities*, Saegert, et al., eds. (New York: Russell Sage Foundation, 2001), pp. 89–114.

62. Scott, *Problem-Oriented Policing: Reflections on the First 20 Years*; Greene, "Community Policing: Changing the Nature, Structure, and Function of the Police."

63. Thorsten Sellin, *Culture Conflict and Crime*, Bulletin 41 (New York: Social Science Research Council, 1938).

64. Christopher Vecsey, ed., *Handbook of American Indian Religious Freedom* (New York: Crossroad, 1991).

65. James Davison Hunter, *Culture Wars: The Struggle to Define America* (New York: Basic Books, 1991).

66. Gustavus Myers, *History of Bigotry in the United States* (New York: Random House, 1943).

67. Joseph R. Gusfield, *Symbolic Crusade* (Urbana: University of Illinois Press, 1966).

68. Austin T. Turk, *Criminality and Legal Order* (Chicago: Rand McNally, 1969); Richard Quinney, *The Social Reality of Crime* (Boston: Little, Brown, 1970).

69. Allen E. Liska, ed., *Social Threat and Social Control* (Albany: State University Press of New York, 1992).

70. Darnell F. Hawkins, "Beyond Anomalies: Rethinking the Conflict Perspective on Race and Criminal Punishment," *Social Forces* 65 (March 1987), pp. 719–745;

Darnell F. Hawkins, "Ethnicity: The Forgotten Dimension of American Social Control," in *Inequality, Crime, and Social Control*, George S. Bridges and Martha A. Myers, eds. (Boulder, CO: Westview, 1994), pp. 99–116.

71. C. Vann Woodward, *The Strange Career of Jim Crow*, 3rd ed., rev. (New York: Oxford University Press, 1974).

72. Gunnar Myrdal, *An American Dilemma* (New York: Harper & Brothers, 1944).

73. Marcus Felson, *Crime and Everyday Life* (Thousand Oaks, CA: Pine Forge Press, 1994), p. xi.

74. Ibid., p. 104.

75. Darnell F. Hawkins, "Ethnicity, Race, and Crime: A Review of Selected Studies," in *Ethnicity, Race, and Crime*, pp. 31, 39–41.

76. Ibid.

77. Paul E. Peterson, "The Urban Underclass and the Poverty Paradox," in The Urban Underclass, pp. 3–27.

78. Hacker, *Two Nations: Black and White, Separate, Hostile, Unequal.* Orfield and Ashkinaze, *The Closing Door: Conservative Policy and Black Opportunity.*

79. Paul E. Peterson, "The Urban Underclass and the Poverty Paradox," in *The Urban Underclass,* pp. 3–27.

80. Cornell West, *Race Matters* (Boston: Beacon, 1993), p. 12. Summarized in Peterson, "The Urban Underclass and the Poverty Paradox," in *The Urban Underclass,* pp. 9–16.

81. Richard Kluger, *Simple Justice* (New York: Vintage Books, 1977).

82. *Loving* v. *Virginia*, 388 U.S. 1 (1967). Peter Wallenstein, *Tell the Court I Love My Wife: Race, Marriage, and Law. An American History* (New York: Palgrave, 2002).

83. Data on African American elected officials are regularly compiled by the Joint Center for Political and Economic Studies (http://www.jointcenter.org). Data on Hispanic elected officials are compiled by the National Association of Latino Elected Officials (http://www.naleo.org). These data are also reported in Bureau of the Census, *Statistical Abstract of the United States.*

84. Jaynes and Williams, *A Common Destiny*, p. 4.

85. Thernstrom and Thernstrom, *America in Black and White*, p. 17.

86. Ibid., p. 534.

87. Ibid., Chapter 7, "The Rise of the Black Middle Class," pp. 183–202.

88. Charles Murray, *Losing Ground: American Social Policy, 1950–1980* (New York: Basic Books, 1984).

4

✳

Justice on the Street?
The Police and Racial and Ethnic Minorities

GOALS OF THE CHAPTER

This chapter explores the complex issues in the relationship between the police and racial and ethnic minority communities and helps sort through the sometimes conflicting evidence on race, ethnicity, and criminal justice.[1] The first section outlines a *contextual approach* that helps resolve the apparent contradictions in the available evidence. The second section examines *public opinion* about the police, comparing the attitudes of whites, African Americans, and Hispanics (unfortunately, there is little evidence on other racial and ethnic groups). The third section *reviews the evidence* on police behavior, beginning with the most serious action, use of deadly force, and proceeding through the less-serious police activities. The fourth section deals with citizen complaints against the police, reviewing the evidence on the extent of misconduct and the ways police departments handle citizen complaints. The final section examines *police employment practices*. Particular attention is given to the law of employment discrimination and the historic problem of discrimination against racial and ethnic minorities.

After you have read this chapter:

1. You will be familiar with the most important issues related to police and people of color.
2. You will be able to make sense of the complex data on police arrests, use of force, use of deadly force, and racial profiling.
3. You will be able to discuss the difference between racial disparities and racial discrimination.

4. You will be able to discuss the most important reforms in policing and whether or not they have succeeded in reducing racial disparities.

5. You will be knowledgeable about police–community relations programs and which ones work and do not work in terms of improving relations between the police and communities of color.

6. You will be familiar with the trends in the employment of people of color in policing, and you will be able to discuss what difference it makes in terms of actual police work.

UNEQUAL JUSTICE?

A Famous Incident

It is one of the most famous incidents in all of U.S. police history. On March 3, 1991, Los Angeles police officers stopped an African American man named Rodney King after a high-speed chase and proceeded to savagely beat him. The beating was videotaped by an observer across the street, and when the tape was broadcast around the country on television, a national uproar broke out. The term "Rodney King" became shorthand for all police abuse. When several of the officers involved were acquitted of criminal charges a year later, a major riot broke out in Los Angeles. Officers were subsequently convicted on federal civil rights charges. The beating also led to the Christopher Commission Report (1991), which proposed sweeping reforms in the Los Angeles Police Department. The Rodney King incident summarized a range of issues we will consider in this chapter: police use of force, race discrimination, effective remedies for misconduct, and how controversial incidents often provoke reforms.

Race and ethnic controversies continue to be at the center of problems facing U.S. police forces.

■ In 2010 the federal government indicted nine New Orleans police officers for fatal shootings of African Americans during Hurricane Katrina in 2005. Investigations of the shootings by the New Orleans Police Department had been superficial and had exonerated the officers.[2]

■ Arizona created a national controversy when it passed an immigration enforcement law in 2010 requiring officers to check on the immigration status of people they arrest. Critics charged the law would result in racial and ethnic profiling. The law was temporarily stayed by a federal court.

■ The arrest of Harvard Professor Henry Louis Gates, a distinguished African American scholar, for disturbing the peace in Cambridge, Massachusetts, created a national controversy over racial profiling. Even President Barack Obama got involved in the controversy and held a meeting with Gates and the officer at the White House.

■ A riot erupted in Cincinnati in April 2001 after the fifteenth fatal shooting of an African American man by the Cincinnati police between 1996 and 2001.

The shooting led to a Justice Department "pattern or practice" suit against the police department. The suit, and a parallel one by civil rights groups, resulted in consent decrees requiring major reforms of the Cincinnati police department.

In a 2010 report on *The Changing Environment for Policing, 1985–2008*, David Bayley and Christine Nixon list the issues of "new immigrants, both legal and illegal," and "Racial discrimination" as among the six challenges facing American policing.[3] The issue of racial profiling is only part of a larger pattern of racial disparities in the criminal justice system. A report by the Police Executive Research Forum (PERF) places the issue of racial profiling in a broader context. Racial bias does not occur just in traffic enforcement but can occur in any and all phases of law enforcement—traffic stops, arrests, failure to provide service, and so forth. This chapter examines the full range of police activities to identify possible patterns of bias.[4] Racial and ethnic minorities are arrested, stopped and questioned, and shot and killed by the police out of proportion to their representation in the population. In 2008 African Americans represented 12 percent of the population, but they represented 40 percent of all arrests for violent crimes and 56 percent of all robbery arrests. They are shot and killed by police four times as often as whites, down from a ratio of 8:1 in the early 1970s.[5]

Hispanic communities, meanwhile, are often simultaneously over-policed and underserved by the police. Many Hispanics who are bona fide American citizens are stereotyped as illegal immigrants and subject to inappropriate traffic stops. At the same time, many Hispanics are reluctant to call the police for routine problems, in part because of fear they will be subject to immigration law enforcement.[6] The federal government through 287(g) agreements authorizes local police to enforce federal immigration laws—a power they did not previously have. Some Hispanic people do not call the police because they either do not speak English or have limited English proficiency.

Native American reservations have seriously inadequate law enforcement resources, despite crime rates that are much higher than in the rest of American society. The most recent Justice Department report found serious problems arising from conflicting authority among federal, state, local, and tribal law enforcement agencies; inadequate funding among tribal agencies; poor training; and high turnover rates among tribal officers. Additionally, reservations often involve vast geographic areas (as large as 500,000 acres in some cases), and many crime victims lack telephones.[7] The economic recession that hit the country in 2007-2008 has had important consequences for the police and communities of color and all low-income neighborhoods. State and local governments faced severe budget crises and had to begin making significant cuts in services. This included local police. The most extreme example was the city of Camden, New Jersey, which in January 2011 laid off 46 percent of its police officers. Obviously, cutting a police department in half restricts its ability to provide effective police services: responding to 911 calls, investigating crimes, engaging in innovative problem-oriented or community policing programs.[8]

The impact of the economic recession is particularly acute for communities of color. Typically, they involve the poorest cities (such as Camden or Oakland,

California) and have the fewest resources in terms of tax bases that can sustain adequate public services. A significant reduction in police services, such as patrol and response to 911 calls, meanwhile, may result in higher crime rates. Many victims of crime may stop calling to report the crime. When this happens, of course, the crime does not enter the FBI UCR system, and the result is that the official crime data does not reflect the actual level of crime. So we may not know whether crime has gone up–or if it has by how much. At this point, we don't know the full impact of a major reduction in police services. It seems obvious, however, that poor communities and communities of color will suffer more than economically better off ones.

A CONTEXTUAL APPROACH

This chapter adopts a contextual approach to help understand the complex and at times contradictory evidence related to police and racial and ethnic minorities. This approach disaggregates the general subject of policing into four specific contexts that affect relations between the police and minorities (Table 4.1).

First, different racial and ethnic groups have very different experiences with the police. As noted in Chapter 1, we cannot talk about "minorities," or even "racial and ethnic minorities," as a homogeneous category. African Americans, Hispanics, Native Americans, and Asian Americans all have somewhat different experiences with the police. Hispanics are less likely to be stopped by the police than either African Americans or non-Hispanic whites. African Americans, meanwhile, have the least favorable attitudes toward the police. We will look at these variations throughout this chapter.[9]

A survey of six racial and ethnic groups in New York City found "major differences" in how they respond to being a crime victim. If there were an incident of "family violence," 80 percent of Dominicans and Colombians said they

T A B L E 4.1   Contexts of Policing

Variations by racial and ethnic group

  African American, Hispanic, Native American, Vietnamese, etc.

Variations by police department

  More professional vs. less professional
  High rates of use of deadly force vs. low rates

Variations within each racial and ethnic group

  By social class and by nationality group
  Recent immigrants vs. long-time residents
  Middle class vs. poor

Variations by department units, policing strategy, or crime problem

  Patrol unit vs. gang unit vs. traffic enforcement unit
  War on drugs efforts, immigration enforcement, anti-terrorism programs

would be "very likely" to report it to the police, compared with 66 percent of African Americans and 65 percent of Asian Indians. Similar differences were found for break-ins and drug sales.[10] The major factor explaining differences in dealing with the police was the sense of ethnic group community empowerment. People were more likely to report crimes to the police if they believed their own racial or ethnic community "was likely to work together to solve local problems" and if they believed their community had some political power. A sense of community powerlessness reduced the likelihood of reporting crimes. In short, the experience of a racial or ethnic community itself—its cohesion and political power—plays a major role in its relationship with the police, and these experiences vary considerably from group to group.

Marianne O. Nielsen, meanwhile, argues that the Native American experience with the criminal justice system "cannot be understood without recognizing that it is just one of many interrelated issues that face Native peoples today," including "political power, land, economic development, [and] individual despair."[11]

Second, police departments have very different records with regard to racial and ethnic minority community relations. Some departments do a much better job of controlling officer use of deadly force. A 2001 survey by the *Washington Post* found that the rate of fatal shootings by police is seven or eight times higher in some cities than in others.[12] In Cincinnati there were 15 fatal shootings of African American men between 1996 and 2001. After a riot following the last shooting in 2001, the Justice Department and civil rights groups both sued the city. The resulting two consent decrees required major changes in the police department, and abusive conduct was reduced.[13]

Third, social class makes a difference, with the result that there are important differences within racial and ethnic minority communities. Ronald Weitzer's research in Washington, DC, found significant differences in perceptions of the police by low-income and middle-class African Americans in the city. Low-income and middle-class African Americans believed that race makes a difference in how police treat individuals, whereas middle-class whites had a much more favorable view of police–community relations in their own neighborhoods.[14] African American and Hispanic communities vary by income, with both middle-class and poor elements. All the public opinion surveys indicate that young men have a very different—and far more negative—experience with the police than do adults or young women (discussed later).

Fourth, variations by police units and tactics and policing philosophy have very different impacts on communities. In the North Carolina State Highway Patrol (NCSHP), for example, the Criminal Investigation Team (CIT) made 73 percent of all searches in traffic stops in 1997, compared with 27 percent by the other eight troops in the NCSHP. After the department cut the CIT in half by 2000, the number of stops and searches dropped accordingly.[15] Later in this chapter we will explain how racial profiling in traffic stops occurs in three different contexts: the war on drugs, people being "out of place," or "crackdowns" on crime or gangs. In short, profiling does not necessarily occur in all places and times in one jurisdiction. Aggressive patrol tactics with frequent stops of citizens create resentment among young men. Drug enforcement efforts are disproportionately directed at minority communities. Later, we will discuss some problem-oriented policing projects that focus on a short list of suspected high rate offenders and avoid the negative impact of "sweeps" and "crackdowns" that alienate law-abiding citizens of color.

To sum up, we have to be careful about generalizing about racial or ethnic groups, including whites, and the police. We have to focus on particular kinds of police actions and their effects on particular groups of people in society.

A LONG HISTORY OF CONFLICT

Conflict between the police and racial and ethnic minorities is nothing new. There have been three major eras of riots related to police abuse: 1917–1919, 1943, and 1964–1968. The Cincinnati riots of 2001 were only the latest chapter in a long history of conflict and violence.[16] The pattern of civil disorders in this country is depressingly similar. Noted African American psychologist Kenneth Clark told the Kerner Commission in 1967 that reading the reports of the earlier riots was like watching the same movie "re-shown over and over again, the same analysis, the same recommendations, and the same inaction."[17] That was in 1967. This chapter will cite evidence of reforms in recent years that do appear to have brought about significant reductions in racial disparities.

Alfredo Mirandé, meanwhile, defines the long history of conflict between Hispanics and the police in terms of "gringo justice." Taking a broad historical and political perspective, he sees a fundamental "clash between conflicting and competing cultures, world views, and economic, political and judicial systems."[18] Conflict with the police is a product of the political and economic subordination of Hispanics, their concentration in distinct neighborhoods or barrios, and stereotyping of them as criminals. The so-called Zoot Suit Riot in Los Angeles in 1943 involved attacks on Hispanic men by police and by white Navy personnel on shore leave.[19] In Chapter 1 and later in this chapter we discuss the national controversy surrounding the 2010 Arizona law that requires local police to enforce federal immigration law.

THE POLICE AND A CHANGING AMERICA

The changing demographic face of the United States because of immigration presents a special challenge for the police. Between 1980 and 2008, the Hispanic population increased from 6.4 percent of the U.S. population to 13 percent; they are now the largest people of color community in the country.[20] These changes create potential conflict related to race, ethnicity, cultural values, lifestyles, and political power. Many new U.S. residents do not speak English and are not familiar with U.S. laws and police practices. Historically, the police have often aggravated conflicts with new arrivals and powerless people. The police have

---

B o x   4.1   The Challenges of Policing New Immigrant Communities:

Many people who do not speak English well

Reluctance to report crime

Fear of police

Impact of federal immigration enforcement

Confusion over role of local police in enforcing immigration laws

Misunderstandings arising from cultural differences

Problematic encounters between individuals and police officers

SOURCE: Matthew Lysakowski, Albert Antony Pearsall, III, and Jill Pope, *Policing in New Immigrant Communities* (Washington, DC: Department of Justice, 2009). http://www.cops.usdoj.gov.

---

represented the established power structure, resisted change, and reflected the prejudices of the majority community.

A report by PERF argues that, contrary to past practice, the police can "help prevent open conflict, mitigate intergroup tensions within a community and build meaningful partnerships among the diverse populace of modern cities."[21]

A Community Oriented Policing Services (COPS) Office report on *Policing in New Immigrant Communities* based on studies of five local communities and their police departments (including Lowell, Massachusetts; Nashville, Tennessee; and Prince William County, Virginia) found that "Many immigrants—refugees especially—come from places where police are corrupt and abusive." Lowell, for example, has many Cambodian refugees who fled the murderous Khmer Rouge genocide of the 1970s. With regard to cultural differences, for example, it is a "normal cultural practice" in El Salvador when stopped by the police to get out of the car and approach the officer. This is contrary to standard U.S. police practice and would generally be regarded as a threatening move. The report also found that many Cambodian immigrants keep their wallets in their socks. So when a police officer asks to see a driver's license a person would reach for his or her socks, a move that many officers might mistake as reaching for a handgun or knife.[22]

The COPS report identified several *promising practices* designed to improve relations between the police and new immigrant communities. One is to create a specialized unit for immigrant communities. The Charlotte-Mecklenburg Police Department (North Carolina) took this step several years earlier, creating a special International Unit to help the department respond more effectively to all of the new immigrant groups in the community, which include Hispanic, Hmong, Vietnamese, and Asian Indians.[23] The COPS report also recommended partnering with agencies facing similar challenges regarding new immigrant communities. Other important steps include strong leadership from the chief or sheriff, training officers about cultural differences, recruiting a more diverse police force, and community internships as a part of police cadet training.

One starting point is for the police to develop language capacity that enable them to communicate effectively with members of the community who do not speak English or have only a limited English proficiency (LEP). One private firm (Network Omni Translation [http://www.networkomni.com]) provides translation services in a number of languages under contract with law enforcement agencies and other organizations. The San Francisco Office of Citizen Complaints has information on its website available in over 50 languages, including Spanish, Chinese, and Arabic.[24]

In some instances, however, police departments do not in fact provide the language services they are required to provide, and say that they offer. A 2010 report by the Justice Department found that the New York Police Department (NYPD) "often fails" to meet its language obligations. The most commonly spoken languages other than English in the city are Spanish, Chinese, Russian, and Italian. Not all officers in the field are provided with cell phones that connect with Language Line, which provides translations under contract. As a result, officers often rely on bystanders to translate. This creates special problems in domestic violence cases when officers rely on family members, who cannot be assumed to be neutral in a domestic conflict. The Justice Department was particularly critical of the police for sometimes relying on children to translate, in violation of the department's own policy. The NYPD disputed the report and filed a 17-page rebuttal defending its practices.[25]

As the New York situation illustrates, most major U.S. cities have significant populations speaking several different languages. Even when services are available under contract, it requires considerable management and supervisory effort to ensure that they are in fact available and are used.

PUBLIC ATTITUDES ABOUT THE POLICE

Public attitudes about the police provide a good starting point for understanding relations between the police and people of color. Race and ethnicity are consistently the most important factors in shaping attitudes about the police. Yet, these attitudes are complex and often surprising. The vast majority of all Americans express confidence in the police. Among all Americans in 2009, 88 percent expressed either a "great deal" or "some" confidence, and only 10 percent expressed "very little" confidence (Table 4.2). A significant racial gap existed, however. Whereas only 6 percent of whites had "very little" confidence,

T A B L E 4.2   Confidence in the Police, 2009

	Great deal/ Quite a lot	Some	Very little	None
All	59%	29	10	1
White	63	30	6	1
Black	38	31	27	4

SOURCE: Gallup Poll, 2009, as reported in Bureau of Justice Statistics, Sourcebook of Criminal Justice Statistics, online edition, Table 2.12 2009. http://www.albany.edu.

27 percent of African Americans did. (Unfortunately, this poll did not distinguish between Hispanics and non-Hispanic whites, so that important data is missing).

When the question changes from overall confidence in the police to whether the police engage in excessive force, or whether you or someone you know has been treated unfairly, the racial gap widens. In an earlier survey, 37 percent of African Americans said they had been "unfairly stopped by police," compared with only 4 percent of whites.[26] In another poll, more than half of African Americans (58 percent) felt that the police in their community did not treat all races fairly, compared with only 20 percent of whites and 27 percent of Hispanics.[27]

The public opinion data contradict the popular image of complete hostility between the police and people of color. The vast majority of African Americans and Hispanics are law-abiding people who rarely have contact with the police. Their major complaint is inadequate police protection in their neighborhoods. A Police Foundation survey in Washington, DC, found that 54.8 percent of African American residents feel there are "too few" police officers in their neighborhood; only 25.7 percent of whites felt that way about their neighborhoods.[28]

Quality of life in the neighborhood also has a strong impact on attitudes toward the police. People who live in high crime areas generally rate the police less favorably. Because African American and Hispanic neighborhoods tend to have higher crime rates than white neighborhoods, this affects their attitudes toward the police. Weitzer found that middle-class African Americans in Washington, DC, had a much more favorable view of relations with the police in their neighborhood than did poor African Americans. Their attitudes on this point, in fact, were much closer to those of white, middle-class Washington residents than of poor African Americans.[29]

Surveys over the past 30 years have found that public attitudes toward the police have been remarkably stable. In 1967 the President's Crime Commission reported that only 16 percent of nonwhites rated the police as "poor," and a 1977 survey found that only 19 percent of African Americans rated their police as "poor," compared with 9 percent of whites. A survey of 500 Hispanic residents of Texas found that only 15 percent rated their local police as "poor."[30] The racial and ethnic gap has remained in virtually every study over the past 40 years.

Highly publicized controversial incidents have a short-term effect on public attitudes. In the immediate aftermath of the 1991 Rodney King beating, the percentage of white Los Angeles residents who said they "approve" of the Los Angeles police fell from more than 70 percent to 41 percent. The approval ratings by African Americans and Hispanics in the city, which were low to begin with, also fell. The approval ratings of all groups eventually returned to their previous levels, but white attitudes did so much more quickly than those of minority groups.[31]

Age is the second most important factor in shaping attitudes toward the police. Young people, regardless of race, consistently have a more negative view of the police than do middle-aged and elderly people. This is not surprising. Young men are more likely to be out on the street, have contact with the police, and engage in illegal activity. At the same time, lower-income people have more negative attitudes toward the police than do upper-income people.

The 2009 PEW Hispanic Center National report on young Hispanics, for example, found that 29 percent of all Hispanic young males and 13 percent of females had been questioned by the police in the past year. That is an extraordinarily high percentage.[32]

Hostile relations between the police and young, low-income men are partly a result of conflict over lifestyles. Carl Werthman and Irving Piliavin found that juvenile gang members in the early 1960s regarded their street corner hangouts as "a sort of 'home' or 'private place.'" They sought to maintain control over their space, particularly by keeping out rival gang members. Their standards of behavior for their space were different from what adults, especially middle-class adults, and the police considered appropriate for a public area.[33]

Perceptions of Police Officer Conduct

A growing body of research indicates that citizen attitudes are heavily influenced by how they feel officers treat them in an encounter. This avenue of research represents an important alternative to overall assessments of "the police" and yields valuable insights. It is not *what* the police do, but *how* they do it. This research is based on the concept of procedural justice, which holds that in any situation levels of satisfaction are mainly determined not by the outcome of encounters with the police but by the process, or what happens in encounters.[34] Being stopped by the police and given a traffic ticket is an outcome. The process involves whether the officer is courteous and respectful. This phenomenon has a close analogy in education. A student is naturally upset by a low grade (for example, a D). If the teacher takes the time to explain the basis for the grade (failure to mention important points covered in class, incomplete sentences, and so on), the student is more likely to understand and accept the result. If the teacher, on the other hand, refuses to meet and explain the grade, the student is likely to be even more upset.

Research supports the procedural justice perspective. Wesley G. Skogan found that people who had been stopped by the police had more favorable attitudes if they felt they were *treated fairly*, if the officer(s) *explained the situation* to them, were *polite*, and *paid attention* to what they had to say on their own behalf. Procedural justice research in other areas of life (for example, employment) consistently finds that people are more satisfied if they feel they had a chance to tell their side of the story. Skogan found important racial and ethnic differences in citizen perceptions, however. African Americans and Spanish-speaking Hispanics, for example, were "far less likely to report that police had explained why they had been stopped." Less than half of the African Americans and Hispanics thought the police treated them politely, and both groups thought they were treated unfairly.[35]

These findings have important policy implications, suggesting that it is possible for the police to improve public attitudes and improve relations with racial and ethnic minority communities. Department policies, training, and supervision that increase officer courtesy and listening skills are likely to improve police–community relations.

POLICING RACIAL AND ETHNIC MINORITY COMMUNITIES

As already noted, it is not appropriate to talk about "racial and ethnic minorities" as a homogeneous group. These individuals have different types of experiences with the police.

The African American Community

Historically, the primary focus of police–community relations problems has been the African American community. Thirty years ago, David H. Bayley and Harold Mendelsohn observed, "[T]he police seem to play a role in the life of minority people out of all proportion to the role they play in the lives of the dominant white majority."[36] This is still true today and is the result of differences in income level, reported crime, and calls for police service.

African Americans are more likely than other Americans to be the victims of crime. The National Crime Victimization Survey (NCVS) reports that between 2001 and 2005 their overall violent crime victimization rate was higher than all other racial and ethnic groups except for Native Americans: 28.7 per 1,000 for African Americans, compared with 24.3 for Hispanic and 22.8 for non-Hispanic whites. The robbery rate for African Americans was more than twice the rate for non-Hispanic whites (4.3 per 1,000 compared with 2.0).[37]

African Americans do, however, report crimes to the police at a slightly higher rate than whites do. African American women, for example, reported 60.2 percent of all violent victimizations to the police, compared with 47.1 for white women. They call the police at a higher rate despite their less favorable ratings of them.[38]

Because there is generally more crime in African American neighborhoods police departments assign higher levels of police patrol there than in white neighborhoods. The combination of more crime and more police patrol results in higher levels of contact between police and residents. It also explains both the higher arrest rate and the higher rate of African Americans being shot and killed by the police. Some African American parents are so fearful of the police that they make special efforts to teach their children to be very respectful when confronted by a police officer. They are afraid that their children (and particularly their sons) might be beaten or shot if they display any disrespect.[39]

A survey of Cincinnati residents before the 2001 riot found that nearly half (46.6 percent) of all African Americans said they had been personally "hassled" by the police, compared with only 9.6 percent of all whites. *Hassled* was defined as being "stopped or watched closely by a police officer, even when you had done nothing wrong."[40]

The Hispanic Community

A report to the U.S. Justice Department concluded, "Latinos may have unique experiences with police which shape attitudes toward law enforcement officials."[41] The Hispanic community also experiences higher rates of crime than does the non-Hispanic white community. The robbery rate is about 43 percent higher for Hispanics than for non-Hispanics. Hispanics in 2007 reported property crimes to the police at about the same rate as whites and African Americans; African Americans reported violent crimes at a slightly higher rate than Hispanics or whites.[42]

Hispanics initiate contact with the police less frequently (167 per 1,000 people) than either whites (221 per 1,000) or African Americans (189 per 1,000) and are also less likely to be stopped by the police for a traffic violation. One study found that the police did not stop many Hispanic drivers because officers decided that they probably would not be able to communicate with Spanish-speaking drivers, and, therefore, nothing would result from the stop.[43]

Several factors help explain the patterns of interactions between Hispanics and the police. Hispanics who do not speak English have difficulty communicating with the police and may not call. As the COPS report indicated, some Hispanics fear that calling the police will expose members of their community to investigation regarding immigration status. Carter found that the Hispanic community's sense of family often regards intervention by an "outsider" (such as a police officer) as a threat to the family's integrity and, in the case of an arrest, as an attack on the father's authority.[44] (Other studies of Hispanic families, however, have found considerable variations that suggest that Carter employed inappropriate stereotypes.)

A series of focus groups in a Midwestern city found significant differences between how Hispanic, African American, and white residents would respond to an incident of police misconduct. Members of the predominantly Spanish-speaking group were far more fearful of the police, far less knowledgeable about the U.S. legal system, and less likely to file a complaint than either whites or African Americans. Much of the fear of the police was related to concern about possible immigration problems.[45]

Skogan explored the differences between English-speaking and non–English-speaking Hispanics. Non–English-speaking Hispanics were much less likely to report crimes: only 9 percent of respondents, compared with 35 percent of English-speaking Hispanics and 27 percent of African Americans. They were also less likely to report a neighborhood problem to the police (8 percent, compared with 19 percent of English-speaking Hispanics and 14 percent of African Americans).[46]

The Native American Community

A particularly severe problem exists with regard to violent crime victimization among Native Americans. Between 2001 and 2005, according to the NCVS, the violent crime victimization rate for Native Americans was two and a half times that for non-Hispanic whites (56.8 per 1,000 versus 22.8) and twice the rate for African Americans (28.7). The differences were especially acute for the crime of simple assault.[47]

Native Americans occupy a unique legal status in the United States, which has an important effect on their relations with the police. Native American tribes are recognized as semi-sovereign nations with broad (although not complete) powers of self-government within the boundaries of the United States. There are more than 500 federally recognized Native American tribes and about 330 federally recognized reservations, and approximately 200 have separate law enforcement agencies.[48]

Competing authority among tribal police agencies, county sheriff or city police departments, and federal authorities creates serious problems for effective law enforcement. In any specific case—say, a robbery—jurisdiction depends on *where* the crime was committed, *what* the crime was, and *who* committed it. Tribal police have jurisdiction only over crimes committed on Indian lands by Native Americans. A crime committed by any other person on a reservation is the responsibility of the county sheriff. In addition, tribal authorities have jurisdiction only over less serious crimes. Murder and robbery, for example, are the responsibility of federal authorities. The 2010 Tribal Law and Order Act revised some of the traditional restrictions, and it remains to be seen if it will enhance the effectiveness of law enforcement.[49]

Native American policing is also complex because there are five different types of tribal law enforcement agencies: (1) those operated and funded by the federal Bureau of Indian Affairs (BIA); (2) those federally funded but operated by the tribe under an agreement with the BIA (called PL 96–638 agencies); (3) those operated and funded by the tribes themselves; (4) those operated by tribes under the 1994 Indian Self-Determination Act; and (5) those operated by state and local governments under Public Law 280.[50]

Reports to the National Institute of Justice (NIJ) in 2001 and 2008 found serious problems with policing on Native American lands. In addition to the jurisdictional problems among different agencies, tribal police departments suffer from inadequate budgets and equipment, poor management, high levels of personnel turnover, and considerable political influence. There are also serious practical problems on many reservations. Some reservations involve vast territory (500,000 acres in some cases), and many residents do not have telephones. Thus, it is often difficult for people to report crimes or request police services, and even then it may take a very long time before officers can arrive at the scene.[51] The Bureau of Justice Statistics (BJS) reports that the victimization rate for violent crimes among Native Americans is twice that of other Americans;[52] reservations have problems with youth gangs and domestic violence. Most tribal agencies are very small (10 or fewer sworn officers), and only half have a 911 emergency telephone service. About half (42.6 percent) cross-deputize their officers with the local county sheriff's department, meaning that their officers have law enforcement powers off the reservation. About two-thirds of all sworn officers employed by tribal departments are Native Americans, and about 56 percent are members of the tribe they serve. The 2001 NIJ report concludes that most of these problems are the legacy of federal Native American policy that has historically served the interests of the federal government rather than the goal of tribal autonomy and self-governance.[53]

In response to the problems with Native American criminal justice, Congress in 2010 passed the Tribal Law and Order Act. The law removed some of the sentencing restrictions on tribal courts (allowing more than one-year sentences for serious crimes, for example); allowed greater crime information sharing between tribal, state, and federal agencies; and improved existing federal programs to provide assistance to tribal police, courts, and correctional agencies. The U.S. Department of Justice also maintains the Office of Tribal Justice (http://www.justice.gov/otj/), which offers information, resources, and assistance on crime, drug abuse, gaming, civil rights, and other issues.

Asian, Native Hawaiian, and Pacific Islanders

Asian, Native Hawaiian, and Pacific Islander Americans have the lowest victimization rates of any racial or ethnic group in the United States. Between 2002 and 2006, according to the NCVS, their violent crime victimization rate (10.6 per 1,000) was less than half the rate for non-Asians (24.1). As a consequence, they have much lower rates of contact with the police. Even when they are victimized, they are much less likely to report property crimes to police than whites, African Americans, or Hispanic Americans, although they report violent crimes more often than some groups and less often than others.[54]

The Middle Eastern Community

The terrorist attack on the United States on September 11, 2001, raised fears of discrimination against Arab Americans on the basis of national origin, religion, or immigration status. There are an estimated 4 million Arab Americans in the United States, representing about 2 percent of the U.S. population. The American–Arab Anti Discrimination Committee (ADC; http://www.adc.org) reports increased incidents of discrimination following 9/11, including 80 incidents where Arab Americans were removed from airplanes solely because of their appearance and not any illegal conduct. A 2008 ADC report found that violent hate crimes declined in the years after 9/11; they stabilized at a level just a bit higher than the pre-2001 level. The main source of discrimination remains stereotyping by overzealous and poorly trained officials, and in some cases other passengers, at airports.[55]

Several policing issues concern the Arab American community. The first is racial profiling, whereby the police, particularly federal authorities, identify individuals as suspects solely on the basis of their national origin. In the wake of 9/11, there were a number of incidents involving discrimination against Arab Americans attempting to fly on airlines. The 2008 ADC report found relatively few instances of discrimination by local police and concluded that the most serious problems involved the Joint Terrorism Task Forces (JTTF) coordinated by the federal government.[56]

A second issue involves hate crimes, specifically attacks on Arab Americans because of their national origin or religion. The ADC reported more than 700 violent attacks on Arab Americans in the first nine weeks following the 9/11 terrorist attack.

There are also issues related to the federal war on terrorism. Soon after 9/11, the FBI set out to interview 5,000 Arab American men in the United States, not as criminal suspects but simply as potential sources of information about possible terrorists. Many Arab Americans regarded this as intimidating and a form of racial profiling.

Focus on an Issue

Enforcing Federal Immigration Laws

As we discussed in Chapter 1 (pp. 1–38), there is a huge national controversy over whether local police should enforce immigration laws. Traditionally, local police did not because immigration is covered by federal law. To clarify one point that is widely misuderstood, being in the United States without proper documentation is not a crime, it is a civil law violation. You can be deported, but you cannot be sent to prison. (Although, in practice, thousands of people spend time in detention awaiting resolution of their residency status.) Enforcement of federal immigration laws is the responsibility of the federal Immigration and Customs Enforcement (ICE) agency. ICE has cooperative agreements with many local law enforcement agencies through the 287(g) program that authorizes the local agencies to assist ICE in immigration enforcement.

The major controversy today centers on the 2010 Arizona law authorizing local police in the state to enforce immigration laws. The most important part of the law is the section that *requires* police to check on the immigration status of people with which they have contact. Critics charge that this requirement will lead to racial and ethnic profiling. (As this is written, the Arizona law has been challenged in the courts. Also, other states and local governments are considering similar laws. Check the Web for news about recent developments.)

Many local police officials argue that enforcing immigration laws will interfere with their basic responsibilities. In 2002 the California Police Chiefs Association sent a letter to the U.S. Attorney General opposing local police enforcement of immigration laws. At a 2008 forum of police chiefs, many argued that illegal immigrants may be "even less likely to report being a victim of crime." This is especially true with regard to the victims of domestic violence.[57] Local police argue that it will create conflict with immigrant communities with whom they want to develop good relations and, as a result, interfere with their basic responsibilities for crime and disorder. Many Hispanics already are afraid to call the police because they worry about potential immigration problems for themselves, members of their families, or friends. Local police also argue that they are already overburdened with responsibilities (and that has gotten worse because of the 2008–2010 recession) and cannot take on new duties.

In March 2011 the Police Executive Research Forum issued a report, "Police and Immigration," calling for restraint by local police departments regarding immigration enforcement. The report described the efforts of six police departments in exercising restraint and also making special efforts to develop and maintain good relations with immigrant communities. In Prince William County, Virginia, for example, the police chief persuaded the County Board of Supervisors to scale back an immigration law because the original bill would adversely affect his department's relations with immigrant communities. The Minneapolis Police Department, meanwhile, has made a special effort to maintain good relations with its very large Somali population (the largest concentration of Somali immigrants in the United States). The PERF report made a strong recommendation that "Officers should be prohibited from arresting and detaining people for the sole purpose of investigating their immigration status." Additionally, local police departments "should encourage all victims [of crime] and witnesses to report crimes, regardless of their immigration status."[58]

POLICE USE OF DEADLY FORCE

Fatal shootings by the police continue to stir controversy. On New Year's Day 2009, Oscar Grant, an African American, was shot and killed by a transit police officer on the Bay area BART transportation system in Oakland, California. The shooting was recorded by a cell phone camera. The officer claimed he thought he was firing his TASER and not his firearm. (Note that TASER is a trademarked name. The generic name for these weapons is electronic control device [ECD].) In 2010 a jury convicted the officer of the lesser crime of involuntary manslaughter rather than second degree murder. The verdict sparked protests alleging racism in both the shooting and the verdict. In September 2010 angry crowds protested against the Los Angeles police after an officer shot and killed an immigrant bearing a knife in MacArthur Park.[59]

Historically, police shootings have been the most explosive issue in police–community relations. In the 1970s, the police fatally shot eight African Americans for every one white person. By 1998, as a result of new policies controlling police use of deadly force, the ratio had been reduced to 4:1. James Fyfe, one of the leading experts on the subject, asked whether the police have "two trigger fingers," one for whites and one for African Americans and Hispanics.[60]

One of the most significant police shootings in U.S. history occurred on October 3, 1974, in Memphis, Tennessee. A lawsuit eventually reached the Supreme Court, which issued a landmark decision on police shootings. Two Memphis police officers shot and killed Edward Garner, a 15-year-old African American. Garner was 5'4" tall, weighed 110 pounds, and was shot in the back of the head while fleeing with a stolen purse containing $10. The Memphis officers acted under the old *fleeing felon rule*, which allowed a police officer to shoot to kill, for the purpose of arrest, any fleeing suspected felon. The rule gave police officers very broad discretion, allowing them to shoot, for example, a juvenile suspected of stealing a bicycle worth only $50. Edward Garner's parents sued, and in 1985 the Supreme Court declared the fleeing felon rule unconstitutional in *Tennessee* v. *Garner*. The Court ruled that the fleeing felon rule violated the Fourth Amendment protection against unreasonable searches and seizures, holding that shooting a person was a seizure.[61]

Police officers, of course, did not shoot every suspected fleeing felon. The data, however, suggest that they were much more likely to shoot African Americans than whites. Between 1969 and 1974, for example, police officers in Memphis shot and killed 13 African Americans in the "unarmed and not assaultive" category but only one white person (Table 4.3). In fact, half of all the African Americans shot were in that category.[62] The permissive fleeing felon rule allowed officers to act on the basis of prejudices and stereotypes. White officers were more likely to feel threatened by African American suspects than by white suspects in similar situations. Because the typical shooting incident occurs at night, in circumstances in which the officer has to make a split-second decision, it is often not clear whether the suspect has a weapon.

There is little data on the shootings of Hispanics and none on Native Americans or Asian Americans. Once again, the available data are inadequate with regard to

T A B L E 4.3   Citizens Shot and Killed by Police Officers, Memphis

	1969–1974		1985–1989	
	White	African American	White	African American
Armed & assaultive	5	7	6	7
Unarmed & assaultive	2	6	1	5
Unarmed & not assaultive	1	13	0	0
Totals, by race	8	26	7	12
Total		34		19

SOURCE: Adapted from Jerry R. Sparger and David J. Glacopassi, "Memphis Revisited: A Reexamination of Police Shootings after the Garner Decision," *Justice Quarterly* 9 (June 1992), pp. 211–225.

race and ethnicity. The BJS report on deadly force trends from 1976 to 1998 uses the categories of "white" and "black." Hispanics shot and killed by the police were probably classified as "white." (See our discussion of these data problems in Chapter 1.) The result is that the gap between African Americans and non-Hispanic whites is probably even greater than the report indicates. In an earlier study, William A. Geller and Kevin J. Karales found that between 1974 and 1978, Hispanics were about twice as likely to be shot and killed by the Chicago police as whites, but only half as likely to be shot as African Americans.[63]

There are substantial differences among police departments regarding the number and rate of citizens shot and killed. Controlling for violent crime (an extremely relevant variable on this issue), Washington, DC, police shot and killed almost seven times as many citizens as did Boston police officers between 1990 and 2000 (6.35 per 10,000 violent crimes versus 0.91 per 10,000).[64] These variations highlight the importance of the contextual approach to police–community relations and the importance of differences in departmental policies and the enforcement of those policies and discipline of officers.

Disparity versus Discrimination in Police Shootings

The data on people shot and killed by the police raise the question that pervades all studies of race, ethnicity, and criminal justice: Data often indicate a disparity, but does that also mean that illegal discrimination exists?[65] Does the 4:1 ratio represent discrimination, or does it reflect a disparity that can be explained by factors other than race, such as involvement in crime?

The first step in addressing this question is to examine who is "at risk" for being shot by the police. Women are not at great risk because they have a very low level involvement in violent crimes that involve a weapon. Young men are at risk because of their involvement in such crimes. Young African American men are most heavily involved in such crimes, and this explains part of their overrepresentation among persons shot by the police. This does not settle the matter, however. Historically, far more shootings of African Americans have involved circumstances where police use of deadly force was questionable, given the circumstances of the case.[66]

Long-term Changes in Police Use of Deadly Force

The Supreme Court's *Garner* decision discussed earlier is only one of several factors that have brought about long-term changes in police use of deadly force. Lorie Fridell identifies the other forces for change. A second factor is social science research that documented racial disparities in persons shot and killed and raised public consciousness about this problem. A third factor involves police departments developing formal policies governing when officers can and cannot use deadly force. We discuss this in detail shortly. These policies are part of a general movement to control discretion in criminal justice. A fourth factor affecting police practice is the demand for racial justice as part of the larger civil rights movement. When we discuss racial profiling, we will examine evidence that publicity about discrimination affects police practices. And a fifth factor, with regard to shootings in particular, is that civil liability for unjustified deaths at the hands of the police, and the resulting damage awards, has forced local governments to take steps to avoid such tragedies in the future.[67]

Controlling Police Shootings

One clear point emerges from the long-term data on police shootings: department policies can reduce the number of people shot and killed by the police and in the process narrow the racial disparity. In the 1970s, in response to protests by civil rights groups, police departments began to replace the old fleeing felon rule in favor of the *defense of life* rule, limiting shootings to situations that pose a threat to the life of the officer or some other person. Many departments also prohibit warning shots, shots to wound, and shots at or from moving vehicles. Officers are now required to fill out a report any time they discharge their weapon. These reports are then subject to an automatic review by supervisors.

Fyfe found that the defense of life rule reduced firearms discharges in New York City by almost 30 percent in just a few years. Across the country, the number of people shot and killed by police declined from a peak of 559 in 1975 to 300 in 1987. Follow-up data on Memphis, meanwhile, indicate a significant reduction in racial disparities in shootings. Particularly important, as Table 4.3 indicates, between 1985 and 1989 no people of either race were shot and killed in the fleeing felon category. The overall number of people shot and killed decreased significantly, and the racial disparity was cut in half. The defense of life rule may not have changed police officer attitudes, but it did alter their behavior, curbing the influence of racial prejudice. Similar policies in departments across the country had the same effect.[68]

A Special Problem: Police-on-Police Shootings. One very disturbing aspect of police use of deadly force has been the shooting of fellow, off-duty officers by on-duty officers. The actual number is very low: only 26 between 1981 and 2009, according to a New York State Task Force report. But in the most recent 25-year period, 10 of the 14 officers shot and killed in this way have been people of color. Such shootings are usually highly publicized, and they create under-standable fear among officers of color. It is understandable how such shootings occur. The incidents often occur in high crime areas, particularly in large departments where the on-duty officers may not know all of the other officers. The Task Force made a number of recommendations for dealing with this problem, including better policies for how off-duty officers conduct themselves, scenario-based training for all officers, and programs to reduce unconscious racial bias among officers.[69]

"POLICE BRUTALITY": POLICE USE OF PHYSICAL FORCE

Q: Did you beat people up who you arrested?

A: No. We'd just beat people in general. If they're on the street, hanging around drug locations ...

Q: Why?

A: To show who was in charge.[70]

This exchange between the Mollen Commission and a corrupt New York City police officer in the mid-1990s dramatized the unrestrained character of police brutality in poor, high-crime neighborhoods in New York City. Police brutality has been a historic problem with U.S. police. As far back as 1931 the Wickersham Commission reported that the "third degree," the "inflicting of pain, physical or mental, to extract confessions or statements is extensively practiced."[71] The 1991 Rodney King beating is probably the most notorious recent example of police use of excessive physical force. A 1998 report by Human Rights Watch concluded, "Race continues to play a central role in police brutality in the United States."[72]

The Mollen Commission defined brutality as the "threat of physical harm or the actual infliction of physical injury or pain." Citizen perceptions of force are much broader. In the 2005 Police-Public Contact Survey, 83 percent of people who experienced police use of force felt that it was "excessive," and the responses varied only slightly be race and ethnicity. The New York City Civilian Complaint Review Board classifies 16 specific police officer actions in the "force" category, including physical force, choke hold, firing a gun, pointing a gun, using pepper spray, using a police radio or flashlight as a club, and other actions.[73]

The term *police brutality* is a political slogan with no precise legal meaning. We use the term *excessive force*, defined as any physical force that is more than reasonably necessary to accomplish a lawful police purpose. It is important to distinguish between *force* and *excessive force*. A police officer is legally justified in using force to protect himself or herself from physical attack, or to subdue a suspect who is resisting arrest, or to accomplish a lawful police purpose. Any amount of force more than the minimal amount needed is excessive.

B o x 4.2   Your Own Research on Police Use of Force Policies

Many police departments now place their policy and procedure manuals on the Web. Search for the websites of the Minneapolis, Seattle, Kansas City, and Los Angeles police departments and examine their use-of-force policies. Are there any significant differences? Do they clearly define what constitutes excessive force? Do law enforcement agencies in your community (the major police department, the sheriff's department, small suburban departments) put their policy and procedure manuals on the Web? If so, how do they compare with other departments?

There is much controversy over the prevalence of police use of excessive force.[74] Critics of the police argue that it is a routine, nightly occurrence, whereas others believe that it is a rare event. Research, however, has consistently put the use of force at between 1 and 2 percent of all encounters between police and citizens. The 2005 BJS police–citizen contact survey found police officers used force or threatened to use force (an important factor that is not included in most studies) in 1.6 percent of all encounters with citizens.[75] In the 2002 survey most respondents (75.4 percent) felt that the force was excessive, and whites (71.6 percent) were almost as likely as African Americans (77.7 percent) to report feeling it was excessive. These responses, of course, represent the perception of the citizen. Observational studies of police work have found that in the judgment of the independent observer, about one-third of all uses of force are excessive or unjustified.[76]

The 2005 BJS report found that African Americans were more than three times as likely to experience force (4.4 percent of all encounters) than whites (1.2 percent). Particularly disturbing is the fact that the disparity had increased since 2002. The BJS police–public contact survey does collect data on Hispanics, and it found that they were more likely than whites but less likely than African Americans to experience police use of force (2.3 percent of all encounters, down from 2002).[77]

Some critics of the police have trouble believing the estimate that police use or threaten to use force in only 1.6 percent of all encounters. It is important to remember, however, that most encounters are very routine: a residential burglary call where the officers simply take a report; a problem-free traffic ticket; a call for police assistance. Research has consistently found that certain problem situations are more likely to involve the use of force than others. The police use force four or five times more frequently against people being arrested, people who challenge their authority, and people who are drunk or on drugs. Common sense suggests this is predictable, given the nature of those encounters.

The issue of challenges to police authority raises some questions. Some people believe that the police overreact to even legitimate questions from citizens. They refer to this police practice as "contempt of cop."[78] Albert Reiss found that almost half of the victims of excessive force had either defied the officer's authority (39 percent of all cases) or resisted arrest (9 percent of all cases). Donald Black's data revealed another important pattern, however—African Americans were far more likely to be disrespectful to the police than were whites after controlling for all other variables.[79] It seems obvious that African American males are more likely to be disrespectful because of the long history of police–community relations problems. The impact of this pattern on arrests is discussed later in this chapter.

Reiss concluded that race *per se* is not a determining factor in the use of excessive force: "Class rather than race determines police misconduct."[80] The typical victim of excessive force is a lower-class male, regardless of race. Other observers, however, disagree with this interpretation and see a systematic pattern of police use of force against young minority men.

The race or ethnicity of the officer has little apparent influence on the use of physical force. The majority of excessive force incidents are intraracial—that is, citizens are mistreated by a police officer of the same racial or ethnic group. The data on citizen complaints against police are revealing. In New York City, whites represented 53.4 percent of all officers in 2009 and 49.5 percent of all officers receiving citizen complaints; African Americans represented 16.4 percent of all officers and 17.2 percent of those receiving complaints; Hispanics represented 28.4 percent of all officers and 25.2 percent of those receiving complaints. A similar pattern has existed in San Jose, California.[81] Robert E. Worden found a very complex pattern of use of force, with African American officers somewhat more likely than white officers to use reasonable levels of force but less likely to use improper force.[82]

At the same time, however, police officers of different races have very different perceptions of how the police in general use force and treat people of color and the poor. A Police Foundation survey of officers nationwide found that 57 percent of African American officers agreed or strongly agreed with the statement "Police officers are more likely to use physical force against blacks and other minorities than against whites in similar situations," compared with only 5 percent of white officers. The responses to this statement reflected not what officers said they personally do, but what they perceived officers in general do (which probably means other officers in their own department).[83]

The data on officer involvement in excessive use of force parallel the data on the use of deadly force. In neither case is it a simple matter of white officers shooting or beating people of color. In both cases, officer behavior is heavily determined by the contextual or situational variables: location (high-crime versus low-crime precinct); the perceived criminal involvement of the citizen; the demeanor of the citizen; and, in the case of physical force, the social status of the citizen.

Our contextual approach suggests that the use of physical force has special significance for racial minority communities. Even if the overall rate of use of force is only 1.6 percent of all encounters, incidents are concentrated among lower-class men and criminal suspects, which means they are disproportionately concentrated among racial and ethnic minorities. Reiss pointed out that incidents accumulate over time, creating a perception of systematic harassment.[84] Ronald Weitzer and Stephen A. Tuch asked Washington, DC, residents if they felt police used excessive force in their neighborhood. Among African Americans,

30 percent felt it happened "very often" or "fairly often," compared with only 8 percent of whites and 23 percent of Hispanics.[85]

Finally, police use of force has special political significance for minorities. Because the police are the symbolic representatives of the established order, incidents of excessive force are perceived as part of the broader patterns of inequality and discrimination in society.

The evidence on whether formal policies over police use of non-lethal force actually reduce the inappropriate force incidents is less clear than the evidence regarding the impact of policies on police shootings. Physical force incidents are far more numerous and there is no consensus over what kinds of actions constitute "force," or what is "excessive" force. By comparison, with deadly force, there is no ambiguity over whether a gun was fired or whether someone was shot and killed. In a review of the subject, William Terrill argues that there are many empirical questions regarding non-lethal force that need to be addressed.[86]

DISCRIMINATION IN ARRESTS?

The question of race discrimination in arrests has been a controversy in American policing for a half a century. Civil rights advocates charge that discrimination does exist. Police officials reject that accusation. Any proven discrimination would be a violation of the Fourteenth Amendment guarantee of equal protection of the law. Official FBI data on arrests clearly indicate a racial disparity in arrests. As we have already noted, African Americans are disproportionately represented among people arrested. As we discussed in Chapter 1, Heather MacDonald rejects the discrimination interpretation by arguing that African Americans are involved in more serious crimes.[87] The long-term accumulation of arrests is very significant. Robert Tillman found that of all people arrested in California, 66 percent of all African American men were likely to be arrested before the age of 30 years, compared with only

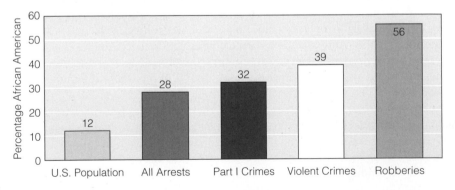

FIGURE 4.1 Arrests of African Americans, 2009

SOURCE: Federal Bureau of Investigation, *Uniform Crime Reports, 2009* (Washington, DC: Federal Bureau of Investigation, 2010), Statistical Tables, Table 43.

34 percent of white men.[88] Since the FBI does not report data on ethnicity, there are no national data on arrest rates for Hispanics. This represents a major gap in our knowledge about policing. Native Americans, meanwhile, represent 0.8 percent of the U.S. population but 1.1 percent of all persons arrested.[89]

The arrest data clearly indicate a racial disparity, but does that disparity represent illegal discrimination? There has been considerable research on the subject over the years. In the first quantitative study, Donald Black found that arrest decisions were shaped by situational factors (strength of the evidence; seriousness of the crime; the victim's preference; the relationship between the victim and offender; and the suspect's demeanor, particularly if he or she was disrespectful toward the officer). The race of the suspect was not a major determinant of arrest decisions. Using data from the same study, Albert Reiss concluded that social class rather than race was the major factor in who gets arrested.[90] Subsequent studies, however, found that race was a factor in arrests. Douglas A. Smith, Christy Visher, and Laura A. Davidson concluded that "race does matter" and that African American suspects were more likely to be arrested than whites.[91]

Tammy Rinehart Kochel, David B. Wilson, and Stephen D. Mastrofski recently reviewed all of the studies of race and arrests and concluded that "race matters." Many studies were methodologically weak, and researchers based their review on 27 methodologically sound studies. They found a "strong consistency" regarding race in those studies. On average, the probability of a white person being arrested was 0.20, whereas the probability for nonwhites was 0.26. In other words, the chances of arrest are about 30 percent higher for African Americans after controlling for other relevant variables. The race effect, in fact, is higher than that found in studies of sentencing.[92]

The Question of the Suspect's Demeanor. One particularly complex issue involves the impact of the suspect's demeanor. Black found that African Americans were arrested more often than whites, mainly because they were more often disrespectful to police officers. Thus, they were arrested for their demeanor and not their race.[93] The issue is more complex than the data seem to indicate, however. Young African American men are more likely to have more negative attitudes toward the police (see discussion earlier in this chapter) because of the long history of bad police–community relations. A vicious cycle results. Expressing their hostility toward police officers results in higher arrest rates, which only heightens their feelings of alienation and hostility.

David A. Klinger, however, questioned Black's interpretation of the impact of demeanor. He argued that the study did not specify when the hostile demeanor occurred. If it occurred after the actual arrest was made—and it is understandable that a person might express anger at that point—it did not cause the arrest.[94]

Impact of the War on Drugs

The war on drugs is one of the major contributors to racial disparities in arrest. FBI data indicate that African Americans were 34 percent of all people arrested for drug offenses in 2009. Yet, Monitoring the Future and other studies have found that African Americans, who represent only 12 percent of the population, are only somewhat more likely to report using drugs. The difference between these figures is the result of police actions. It is important to remember that drug enforcement is different from enforcement of ordinary street crimes such as robbery or burglary. For those offenses, the police are reactive, responding to 911 calls from victims. Drug use and sale, however, are victimless crimes. No victim calls the police. Enforcement is proactive, meaning that the police choose to engage in enforcement, and they must make decisions about where to concentrate their efforts. The data on arrests strongly suggest that these decisions involve disproportionately targeting neighborhoods where most of the residents are people of color.[95]

Impact of an Arrest Record

Being arrested, regardless of the outcome of the case, has enormous consequences for the person arrested. An arrest record can affect chances of employment or housing. If one group is disproportionately arrested, their employment opportunities will be adversely affected to the same degree. If the arrest results in a conviction, it can affect a person's sentence in a subsequent offense, where prior criminal history is taken into account. In addition, Justice Department surveys of state criminal history information systems have consistently found that many do not include information on the final disposition of cases. As a result, someone whose case was dismissed, or who was acquitted, will still have an official arrest record with the implication of a conviction.[96] Joan Petersilia, in her book on offenders returning to the community from prison, argues that legal restrictions on employment of people with criminal histories is one of many formal obstacles to their reintegrating into the community and establishing law-abiding lives.[97]

Reducing Disparities in Police Use of Force and Arrests: Recent Research

Can the use of force and arrests be reduced? Several recent developments provide reasons for cautious optimism on this issue.

★★ The Los Angeles Police Department (LAPD) has had a long history of bad police-community relations, involving complaints about unjustified shootings and excessive use of force. The department's history is marked by a major riot in 1965; the Rodney King beating in 1991 and the 1992 riot that followed the acquittal of officers involved; and the 1998–2000 Rampart Scandal. As a result of Rampart, the U.S. Justice Department sued the LAPD for a pattern of civil rights violations and obtained a Consent Decree in 2001. The Consent Decree required the LAPD to make a number of reforms related to use of force and accountability. The department was required to improve procedures for investigating use of force incidents, implement an early intervention system (EIS) for tracking officer performance (known as TEAMS II in the LAPD), and improve its citizen complaint process. Did these reforms make any difference? Did they change officer behavior and improve community relations?[98]

A Harvard University evaluation found evidence of genuine improvements. Between 2004 and 2008 use of the most serious forms of force by LAPD officers declined by 30 percent. Use of force incidents involving African American and Hispanic people, moreover, declined more than they did against whites. Moreover, use of force declined even though arrests rose 6 percent in the period. This suggests that officers were working somewhat harder but exercising force more carefully. The overall rate of force per 10,000 arrests declined from 8.1 to 6.2 percent. This is a significant achievement in a police department long troubled by a reputation for heavy-handed policing.[99]

★★ Cincinnati, meanwhile, experienced a major riot in 2001 after the fatal shooting of the fifteenth African American man in five years by the police department. As a result, both local civil rights groups and the Justice Department sued the city and obtained two separate consent decrees. The Justice Department consent decree required a set of management reforms similar to those in Los Angeles designed to increase accountability. The civil rights suit (actually there were several separate suits that were consolidated) required the police department to adopt problem-oriented policing and eliminate the heavy-handed policing tactics that generated friction with the community.[100]

★★ One of the most promising directions for reducing the discriminatory aspect of police use of force and "get tough" crime-fighting strategies involves focused problem-oriented policing (POP) programs. In general, POP is closely related to community policing and involves focusing on specific crime and disorder problems and neighborhoods.

The relevant POP programs are derived from the highly praised Boston Gun Project, which as one of its components targeted a specific list of known gang leaders and subjected them to a variety of close surveillance and intervention strategies by police, probation and parole officers, and social service agencies.[101]

The Cincinnati Initiative to Reduce Violence (CIRV) conducted "call-in" meetings, where known high-rate offenders were given a deterrent message by the police (for example, that they individually would be subject to intensive police efforts if there was another murder) and then offered a range of social services (employment, education, drug counseling) if they wanted to end their criminal activity. Representatives of social service agencies attend the call-in meetings. In Lowell, Massachusetts, police officers, correctional officers, and social service workers would "flood" a neighborhood after a shooting and communicate the same messages as in the Cincinnati CIRV program: tough enforcement for specific suspects, along with offers of various treatment programs. In both Cincinnati and Lowell, evaluations found evidence of successful crime reduction.[102]

The evaluation of the Lowell program in particular characterized it as "focused deterrence." Traditional deterrence-oriented programs (for example, a tough new drunk driving law; harsher sentences for gun crimes) have not generally been successful because they are addressed to a broad audience, with the result that the deterrence message is usually lost. Focused deterrence may be more effective because it is directed in person to a very small group of people. From our perspective, by focusing on known suspects, this approach avoids the problems of traditional police "crackdowns" or "sweeps" that typically result in stops, frisks, and arrests of large numbers of people, who are almost always young African American or Hispanic males. Not only are these traditional approaches ineffective in terms of crime fighting, they aggravate police–community relations by sweeping up many law-abiding people of color. In Cincinnati, moreover, there was evidence that African American residents of one particularly high crime neighborhood greatly appreciated the fact that the police were targeting gang members who were preying on them.[103]

POP versus Traditional Crime-Fighting Strategies. The success of focused, problem-oriented policing programs highlights the negative impact of many traditional crime-fighting strategies on police–community relations. The strategies include "sweeps," "crackdowns," and "zero-tolerance" programs. Sweeps and crackdowns involve short-term intensive police–enforcement efforts where the police make many arrests of suspected drug dealers and/or gang members. The problem with this approach is that they sweep up many law-abiding people, or even some people who have committed crimes but where there is insufficient evidence for a prosecution. The result is that most of the cases are dismissed, leaving no meaningful impact on crime and strong feelings of being harassed by the police.

In the late 1980s, several departments adopted zero-tolerance or "quality of life" policing, most famously in New York City. This strategy involves concentrating on relatively minor crimes, such as public urination or loitering. It is based on the "broken windows" theory that enforcing minor crimes and disorders sends a message that major crimes will not be tolerated. Some people arrested for a minor crime turn out to be in possession of an illegal gun or are wanted on outstanding warrants.[104] Crime did decline substantially in New York City in the 1990s, but there was much controversy over the causes and also the effects of quality of life policing. Crime declined nationally during this period and so was not unique to New York City. Critics, meanwhile, argued that aggressive policing was perceived as harassment, particularly by young men of color. In fact, New York City experienced severe police–community relations problems in the 1990s as a result of several controversial shootings and the savage beating of Abner Louima in 1997.[105]

More research is needed on this highly important subject, but it appears that well-planned POP programs that focus on a short list of known offenders may be capable of achieving both effective crime reduction *and* improved police-community relations.

TRAFFIC STOPS: RACIAL PROFILING

Robert Wilkins, an African American attorney, was stopped by the Maryland state police on Interstate 95 and subjected to a prolonged detention and illegal search. To support Wilkins's case, his lawyers sponsored observational research on traffic and enforcement patterns on I-95. The research found that African Americans did not speed on I-95 at a higher rate than that of white drivers but constituted 73 percent of all drivers stopped for possible violations. Even worse, they represented 81 percent of all drivers whose cars were searched after being stopped.[106]

Focus on an Issue
The Chicago Gang Ordinance

Gangs are a serious problem in many cities. Gangs have controlled drug trafficking, been responsible for gun violence, and intimidated law-abiding citizens, creating a climate of fear in neighborhoods. In an effort to control gangs, Chicago enacted a Gang Congregation Ordinance in 1992. The story of the law is an excellent example of a "crackdown" approach to crime fighting: a policy designed to get tough with crime that in practice resulted in massive arrests of people of color (see the discussion, pp. 25–26).

The Chicago gang ordinance made it a crime for a known "gang member" to "loiter" on the street with one or more people with "no apparent purpose." In enforcing the law, Chicago police officers had to "reasonably believe" the person was a gang member, order the person to disperse, and make an arrest if the person did not disperse. Violations could be punished by a fine of $500 and/or 6 months in jail and/or 120 days of community service.

In three years, the Chicago police issued 80,000 dispersal orders and arrested 42,000 people. Enforcement of the law fell heavily on the African American and Hispanic communities in Chicago. The police department enforced it only in areas where it believed gangs were a problem, but it did not inform the public about which areas they were. The basic question became, "Did the law give the police too much discretion in enforcing the law?"

The Supreme Court ruled the Chicago Gang Ordinance unconstitutional in the case of *Chicago* v. *Morales* (1999). The Court found the law unconstitutionally vague. The definition of loitering was vague and did not distinguish between standing on the street for a good purpose (waiting for a friend) or a bad purpose (planning a crime). There was no *mens rea* requirement—that is, the police did not have to show that a person had criminal intent. Almost comically, the law did not apply to people who were moving and excluded specific acts that are the most intimidating kinds of conduct (for example, approaching someone in a possibly threatening manner). Finally, the law violated the First Amendment right of freedom of association, which includes the right to freely travel in public places.

The law also raised the issue of lists of gang members compiled by police departments. The Chicago law authorized officers to enforce the law against people it "reasonably believed" to be gang members. But how does an officer know that? Is there an official list, or is the officer making a subjective judgment on the spot? If the department does have a list, how was it compiled? Who provided the information? Was the information verified? If a young man dropped out of a gang he belonged to was he still listed as a "gang member"? How do you ever get off the list? In many cities there have been controversies over the arbitrary and discriminatory uses of police department gang lists.

FURTHER READING

Chicago v. *Morales*, 527 U.S. 41 (1999).

Malcolm Klein, *The American Street Gang* (New York: Oxford, 1995).

Charles M. Katz, "The Establishment of a Police Gang Unit: An Examination of Organizational and Environmental Factors," *Criminology* 39 (2001), pp. 37–75.

The racial profiling controversy involves several related issues: Does racial profiling in fact exist? How can we measure police activity to determine whether it exists? What is the best method of controlling officer behavior in traffic enforcement and eliminating any racial or ethnic bias?[107]

The Wilkins case played a major role in focusing national attention on racial profiling. *Racial profiling* is defined as the use of race as an indicator in a profile of criminal suspects, with the result that drivers are stopped either entirely or in part because of their race or ethnicity and not because of any illegal activity. Civil rights leaders coined the term "driving while black" to describe this practice. A 2004 Gallup Poll found that 53 percent of all Americans believe that racial profiling is "widespread." It is surprising that 50 percent of white Americans believe it, compared with 67 percent of African Americans and 63 percent of Hispanics. The issue is not confined to traffic enforcement either. All racial and ethnic groups also believe that racial profiling is widespread in shopping malls and stores.[108]

The Use of Race in Law Enforcement

The profiling controversy focuses our attention on the crucial question of when a citizen's race or ethnicity can and cannot legitimately be used in law enforcement. This includes traffic enforcement, pedestrian stops, frisks, and arrests. Most important, stopping someone *solely* because of race or ethnicity is clearly an illegal form of discrimination. In practice, however, traffic stops and arrests usually involve a complex mix of factors—gender, location, height, weight, clothing, behavior, and so on—and it is often difficult to determine if race was the real reason. This leads to a difficult question: "Can the police use race as one of several factors in making a traffic stop" (for example, along with make of the vehicle, the location of the stop, and so on)? If race is one element in a *general profile* (for example, young African American male driving a BMW), a traffic stop or arrest is probably illegal. A stop or arrest is legal, however, in a situation where race or ethnicity is one of several descriptors of a *particular suspect* (for example, male, young, tall, wearing baseball jacket and cap, and white).[109]

Profiling Contexts

Racial profiling occurs in at least three different contexts. One is the *war on drugs*, where officers are targeting African Americans or Hispanics in the belief that they are very likely to be engaged in drug trafficking. This approach represents a profile of criminal suspects based on racial and ethnic stereotypes. The ACLU argues that the Drug Enforcement Administration (DEA) has encouraged racial profiling by state and local departments through its "Operation Pipeline." DEA training materials, they claim, stereotype African Americans and Hispanics as drug traffickers. A 2010 report by the Rights Working Group adds that profiling occurs in counterterrorism measures and immigration enforcement (see our discussion in Chapter 1, pp. 20–24, and in this Chapter, pp. 7–8).[110]

A second context involves stopping citizens who appear to be *out of place*, such as an African American in a predominantly white neighborhood or a white in a predominantly African American neighborhood. In this context, racial stereotypes lead to the assumption that a person does not "belong" in an area because of his or her race and therefore must be engaged in some criminal activity. It ignores the fact that an African American in a predominantly white neighborhood may in fact live there, or may have white friends who live there, or may be there for business or professional purposes (for example, an insurance salesperson calling on a customer). Similarly, the white person in a predominantly African American neighborhood might have some legitimate personal or business-related reason for being there (for example, real estate sales). In a study of traffic stops in a predominantly white community bordering a largely African American city, Albert J. Meehan and Michael J. Ponder confirmed this interpretation. They found that the "proactive surveillance" of African American drivers "significantly increases as African Americans travel farther from 'black' communities and into white communities."[111]

A third context involves a *crackdown on crime*. In this case, the police department has decided to get tough on street crime through an aggressive stop, question, and frisk policy. It is likely to focus on a high-crime neighborhood, which, in turn, is likely to be an African American or Hispanic community. As a result, virtually all of the people stopped will be racial or ethnic minorities.[112]

The Data on Traffic Stops

The BJS national survey of police–citizen contacts provides the best data on police traffic stop practices (Table 4.4). Several important patterns emerge from this study. First, traffic stops are the most common form of encounter between police officers and citizens, accounting for 56.3 percent of all contacts in 2005.[113] Second, the 2005 police–public contact survey reported smaller racial disparities than the previous 2002 survey. Later, we will discuss whether this indicates some progress in dealing with racial profiling.

Third, the greatest racial disparities exist with respect to what happens *after* the initial stop. In the 2002 survey whites and African Americans were issued tickets almost equally, whereas Hispanic drivers were more likely to be ticketed. Both African Americans (5.8 percent) and Hispanics (5.2 percent) were more than twice as likely as whites (2 percent) to be arrested in a traffic stop. Finally, African Americans (2.7 percent) and Hispanics (2.4 percent) were three times as likely to have force used against them as whites (0.8 percent). Similar findings

T A B L E 4.4   Experiences with Traffic Stops, 2002 and 2005

Percentage of each group experiencing

	Stopped		Searched		Force Used	
	2002	2005	2002	2005	2002	2005
White	8.8	8.9	3.5	3.6	1.1	1.2
African American	9.2	8.1	10.2	9.5	3.5	4.4
Hispanic	8.6	8.9	11.4	8.8	2.5	2.3

SOURCE: Bureau of Justice Statistics, *Contacts Between Police and the Public, 2005* (Washington, DC: Department of Justice, 2007), Tables 1, 8, 9.

regarding what happens after the initial stop have been reported in almost all other studies of traffic enforcement.[114]

Interpreting Traffic Stop Data

As is the case with the deadly force and physical force data, the traffic stop data raise difficult questions related to interpretation. There is a question of whether racial and ethnic disparities in traffic stops represent a pattern of discrimination. The basic problems that criminologists have been wrestling with are: What *benchmark* or *baseline* should be used to interpret the traffic stop data? How would we know whether a certain percentage of stops of African Americans is too high? When does a disparity become a pattern of discrimination? Lorie Fridell's comprehensive discussion of this issue, *By the Numbers*, makes it very clear that there are no simple answers and that great care must be taken when interpreting a set of traffic stop data.[115]

Most traffic stop data collection efforts have used the resident population data as a benchmark. The report by the San Jose Police Department, for example, found that Hispanics represented 43 percent of all drivers stopped but only 31 percent of the San Jose population. These data clearly indicate a disparity in the percentage of Hispanics stopped by the police. But do they represent a pattern of illegal discrimination? Other studies have found similar disparities.[116]

Resident population data are not good benchmarks or baselines for traffic stop data, however. They do not represent who is at *risk of being stopped* for a possible traffic violation. An at-risk estimate would take into account the percentage of a racial or ethnic group who are licensed drivers and who actually drive and, most important, the percentage of actual traffic law violators who are members of various racial and ethnic groups.[117] The 2002 police–public contact survey, for example, found significant racial and ethnic differences in driving patterns. Among whites, 93.3 percent drive "a few times a year or more," compared with only 78.9 percent of African Americans and 77.7 percent of Hispanics.[118] In short, whites are far more at risk for a traffic stop. The Monitoring the Future survey found similar racial differences. In 2009, 34.1 percent of African American high school students responded that they drove "not at all," compared with only 13.6 percent of whites.[119]

In the racial profiling lawsuits in Maryland and New Jersey, the plaintiffs conducted direct observation of traffic on the interstate highways in question. Observers on the highways estimated the percentage of drivers in each racial and ethnic category, the percentage in each group who were violating the law, and then the racial breakdown of drivers actually stopped. In both Maryland and New Jersey, African Americans were not observed violating the law at a higher rate than white drivers were. These data provided convincing evidence that African American drivers were being stopped not because of their driving behavior or the condition of their cars but for some other reason—their race.[120]

The research strategy used in the lawsuits in Maryland and New Jersey was facilitated by the fact that it occurred on interstate highways, which are confined spaces with limited access, and where the police focus on one task, traffic enforcement. This research strategy, however, is very difficult to apply in normal city traffic situations. Cities are large geographic areas where citizens are moving about in many different ways and where the police are performing many different tasks: enforcing the law, maintaining order, and serving the community. In this constantly changing environment, it is difficult to estimate the number of traffic violators.[121]

Direct observation is the best method for studying traffic enforcement, but it is also very expensive, requiring a number of trained observers surveying traffic over an extended period of time. Consequently, it has been used only on special occasions, either through a research grant or as part of a lawsuit.

An alternative approach is to use *peer officer comparisons*, or *internal benchmarking*. Walker argues that this approach adapts the basic principles behind police EIS. EIS are data-based management tools that collect and analyze police officer performance data (citizen complaints, officer use of force reports, and so on) to identify officers who have a relatively high number of indicators of problematic behavior compared with their peers.[122] The proper peer comparisons involve officers working similar assignments (for example, a high crime area on the same shift). This approach permits identifying officers who stop more African American or Hispanic drivers than their peers. Because both the racial and ethnic composition and the crime rate of the area is the same, any disparities in traffic stops or arrests suggest that bias might be a factor. EIS result in a formal intervention for officers identified by the system. This can involve counseling, training over issues related to traffic stops or cultural diversity, or reassignment.

The PERF Policy on Traffic Enforcement

The most comprehensive recommended policy for handling traffic stops is in a PERF report, *Racially Biased Policing: A Principled Response*.[123] (See Box 4.3.) It clearly states that race cannot be the sole or even the primary factor in determining whether to stop a citizen. Officers may, however, take race or ethnicity into account when it is information related to a "specific suspect or suspects" that links the suspect or suspects to a particular crime. This information, moreover, must come from a "trustworthy" source. In practice, the police can use race when they have a report of a robbery committed by a young male, white/African American/Hispanic, wearing a baseball cap and a red coat, and driving a white, late-model SUV. They cannot, however, stop all white/African American/Hispanic males simply because police have reports of robberies committed by a male in one of those racial or ethnic categories.

The PERF policy also recommends specific steps that police officers should take to help reduce the perception of bias. Officers should "be courteous and professional" in a traffic stop, "state the reason for the stop as soon as practical," "answer any questions the citizen may have," "provide name and badge number when requested," and "apologize and/or explain if he or she determines that the reasonable suspicion was unfounded."[124] Procedural justice research (p. 42) has found that how the police act has a major impact on citizen attitudes toward police.[125]

Eliminating Bias in Traffic Enforcement

Several strategies have been developed to combat racial and ethnic bias in traffic stops. The traditional strategy of law enforcement organizations involves a

---

B o x 4.3   Excerpts from the Police Executive Research Forum (PERF) Recommended Policy on Traffic Stops

A. Policing Impartially

1. Investigative detentions, traffic stops, arrests, searches, and property seizures by officers will be based on a standard of reasonable suspicion or probable cause in accordance with the Fourth Amendment of the U.S. Constitution. Officers must be able to articulate specific facts and circumstances that support reasonable suspicion or probable cause for investigative detentions, traffic stops, arrests, nonconsensual searches, and property seizures.

   Except as provided below, officers shall not consider race/ethnicity in establishing either reasonable suspicion or probable cause. Similarly, except as provided below, officers shall not consider race/ethnicity in deciding to initiate even those nonconsensual encounters that do not amount to legal detentions or to request consent to search.

   Officers may take into account the reported race or ethnicity of a specific suspect or suspects based on trustworthy, locally relevant information that links a person or persons of a specific race/ethnicity to a particular unlawful incident(s). Race/ethnicity can never be used as the sole basis for probable cause or reasonable suspicion.

2. Except as provided above, race/ethnicity shall not be motivating factors in making law enforcement decisions.

SOURCE: Police Executive Research Forum, *Racially Biased Policing: A Principled Response* (Washington, DC: Author, 2001), pp. 51–53.

---

combination of *exhortation and training.* Many police chief executives have issued statements that race discrimination is prohibited. Such statements are an important function of leadership. Departments have also offered specific training on the proper use of race in traffic stops. Many critics, however, argue that these steps, while important, do not necessarily control officer actions on the street.

The second strategy, favored by civil rights groups, has been to demand that law enforcement agencies *collect data on all traffic stops.* Several states have passed laws requiring data collection, and a large number of departments have begun data collection voluntarily. A federal data collection law has been pending in Congress for several years.[126]

A third strategy involves law enforcement agencies adopting *policies and procedures* governing how officers conduct traffic stops. The consent decree in the Justice Department suit against the New Jersey State Police, for example, requires officers to notify their dispatcher when they are about to make a stop and to report the vehicle license number and the reason for the stop. Officers must also complete detailed reports on each stop, and supervisors are required to review each report carefully.[127] Many other departments have adopted similar policies. These requirements are designed to ensure that officers are accountable for each stop by documenting it. Many departments have also installed video cameras in patrol cars, which will document the stops and any inappropriate behavior by the officer. They can also challenge false claims of officer misconduct.

A final strategy involves litigation, suing police departments for race discrimination. The Wilkins case we discussed earlier involved a lawsuit, and it accomplished several important things. First, it resulted in the Maryland State Police being required to develop new policies and procedures to control traffic stops. Second, more than any other single event, it brought national attention to the problem of "driving while black" and led to the other reforms we have discussed.[128]

The Impact of Formal Policies: The Case of the Customs Bureau

The U.S. Customs Bureau represents a case study in how formal policies can effectively control racial bias. A 2000 report on the Customs Bureau found significant disparities in searches of passengers entering the United States. African American women were more likely to be searched than either white women or African American males, even though they were less likely to be found possessing contraband. Customs agents had almost unlimited discretion to choose who to search, and the guidelines for identifying suspicious people were extremely vague.[129]

In response, the Customs Bureau developed a shorter and more specific list of indicators that could justify a search and a requirement that agents obtain supervisors' approval for particular kinds of searches. The result was a much lower number of searches and a higher "hit rate" (the percentage of searches that found contraband). These changes reduced the number of unnecessary searches where no contraband was found, most of which involved people of color. In short, the Customs Bureau was "working smarter": instead of indiscriminate searches that are unproductive and offend many innocent people, searches were better targeted toward possible suspects.[130]

Another Success Story? The Impact of the
Media on Police Conduct

Does publicity affect police behavior, and can media coverage help to reduce racial disparities? Donald Tomaskovic-Devey found that the combination of news media coverage and the introduction of state legislation requiring traffic stop data collection reduced racial disparities in stops, searches, and "hit rates" (the percentage of searches that successfully find contraband material) in the North Carolina State Highway Patrol (NCSHP). The racial profiling problem was concentrated in the Criminal Investigation Team (CIT) in the NCSHP, which in 1997 conducted 70 percent of all searches by the NCSHP. The number of officers in CIT was cut almost in half (from 25 to 13) by 2000, and the number of searches by the unit also fell by half. Both of these changes were probably a response to the controversy surrounding racial profiling. The percentage of African American drivers stopped declined from 56.3 to 42.4 percent, and the ratio of black to white drivers searched was nearly halved. Finally, the "hit rate" among black drivers rose by 50 percent (from 24 to 36 percent).[131]

As with the Customs Bureau experience, these data suggest that the NCSHP was working "smarter" and more effectively. It targeted fewer drivers and was more successful in choosing who to search. While the exact cause of these changes is not absolutely definite, and further research is needed, the data support the interpretation that publicity about racial profiling had a significant impact on NCSHP officers. They knew they were in the spotlight and changed their behavior to avoid negative publicity. Racial profiling expert David Harris concludes that "Media Attention Matters." The changes in NCSHP traffic enforcement may also have been in response to a data collection bill in the state legislature. This leads Harris to add that "Legislative Attention Matters." He ends by arguing that there is no single solution to the complex problem of race and policing and recommends a "pragmatic, multidimensional approach involving many different strategies, including publicity, legislation (including even proposed legislation), litigation, data collection, formal administrative policies, training and supervision." Together, these changes can add up to important changes in policing.[132]

The argument for a multidimensional approach is supported by other evidence. The rate of traffic fatalities on American highways (measured in terms of fatalities per 100,000 miles driven) has fallen steadily since the 1920s. Policy analysts argue that this has not been the result of a single approach—especially "get tough" drunk driving "crackdowns"—but of many changes: improved roads and signage, safer vehicles, seat belts, air bags, and driver education. All of these small changes have added up to a major change.[133]

National-level Progress on Racial Disparities?

The most recent national data on traffic stops suggests there may be some progress in reducing racial disparities in traffic enforcement. The 2005 BJS report on *Contacts Between Police and the Public* found that the percentage of African American drivers stopped by police had declined from 9.2 percent of all African Americans in 2002 to 8.1 percent. The percentage of whites, meanwhile, rose slightly, and they were actually more likely to be stopped than African Americans.[134] Additionally, the percentage of African American drivers searched by the police declined from 10.2 percent in 2002 to 9.5 in 2005. This was still much higher than the 3.6 percent of white drivers who were searched, however.

Why would traffic stops of African Americans show a national decline? It is possible that all of the national efforts on racial profiling have had some positive effect. These efforts include publicity about the problem, protests by civil rights leaders, new police department policies on the use of race in policing, and better training for officers. The exact answers are not clear at this point, and more research is needed. It will also be important to see if the downward trend occurs in future police–citizen contact surveys.

Continued Progress? The Impact of the Recession

As we indicated at the beginning of this chapter the economic recession has had a significant impact on state and local governments. Many police departments have been forced to lay off officers or simply not hire new ones to replace those who retire. These reductions threaten the capacity of police departments to engage in innovative programs to address problems of crime and relations with communities of color. There are simply fewer officers, and departments struggle to provide basic patrol services and respond to 911 calls. Equally serious, the budget crisis diverts time and energy away from thinking about innovative programs. The evidence we have reviewed in this chapter indicates that many police departments have made genuine progress in dealing with crime and police misconduct. It is not clear that this progress will continue because of the economic recession.

STREET STOPS AND FRISKS

Closely related to traffic stops is the police practice of stopping pedestrians on the street and questioning or frisking them, or both. This practice has long been a source of police–community tensions and is often referred to as a field interrogation (FI). The police have traditionally used FIs as a crime-fighting policy designed to "emphasize to potential offenders that the police are aware of" them and to "reassure the general public that the patrol officers are actively engaged in protecting law-abiding citizens." Some police departments use an "aggressive preventive patrol" strategy to encourage FIs. More than 40 years ago, the Kerner Commission found that such a strategy aggravated tensions with African American communities.[135]

Stops and frisks have recently been particularly controversial in New York City, where the police department maintains an aggressive street enforcement program and has been sued as a result. A 2010 report found that African Americans and Hispanics in the city were nine times more likely to be stopped by the police as were whites (street stops, not traffic stops), but they were arrested at the same rate (about 6 percent for both groups). To put it in other terms, the "hit rate" for whites was relatively high: stops yielded a much higher rate of arrest. Stops of people of color, in contrast, yielded a much lower arrest rate. Civil rights activists charged that the high rate of stops without arrests represented discriminatory harassment.[136]

Several aspects of the NYPD stop-and-frisk policy deserve comment. First, it is huge and growing. In 2009, 575,000 people were stopped by the police, up from less than 200,000 in 2003. It is designed as a crime-fighting tactic. In 2009, however, only about 12 percent of all stops resulted in an arrest or summons, and only 762 guns were seized. The hit rate on guns, moreover, was higher for whites than for African Americans (guns found in 1.7 percent of all stops versus 1.1 for African Americans). Supporters of the policy argue that it has reduced crime, but the great crime decline began in the early 1990s (in New York City and nationally), at least 10 years before the aggressive policy began. Conservative commentator Heather MacDonald argues that police stops data are based on areas with high crime rates and racial and ethnic data on who are involved in serious crimes. It is legitimate to ask, however, whether the negative cost in police–community relations is worth the apparently limited crime fighting value.[137]

Special Issue: Stereotyping and Routine Police Work

An underlying problem regarding traffic stops and stops and frisks is the tendency of police officers to act on stereotypes of categories of people. Jerome Skolnick argued many years ago that stereotyping is inherent in police work. Officers are trained to be suspicious and look for criminal activity. As a result, they develop "a perceptual shorthand to identify certain kinds of people" as suspects, relying on visual "cues": dress, demeanor, context, gender, and age. Thus, a young, low-income man in a wealthy neighborhood presents several cues that trigger an officer's suspicion in a way that a middle-aged woman or even a young woman in the same context does not.[138] Race is often a "cue." A young, racial minority man in a white neighborhood is likely to trigger an officer's suspicion because he "looks out of place"—although he could be an honors student who attends church regularly and has never committed a crime. By the same token, if an officer encounters two middle-class white men in an African American neighborhood that sees a high level of drug trafficking, the officer will likely suspect that they are there to buy drugs. Because African American men are disproportionately arrested for robbery, police officers can fall into the habit of stereotyping all young, racial minority men as offenders. With traffic stops, certain types of vehicles also serve as "cues": officers believe that certain kinds of people drive certain kinds of cars, with the result that vehicles are a proxy for race and class. In their study of how police officers form suspicions about citizens, Roger G. Dunham and Geoffrey P. Alpert questioned the stereotyping argument, however. They found that "behavior" was the most important factor, followed by specific information about a suspect, the time and place of the event, and the suspect's appearance.[139]

Harvard law professor Randall Kennedy asks the question, "Is it proper to use a person's race as a proxy for an increased likelihood of criminal conduct?"[140] Can the police stop an African American man simply because the suspect in a crime is African American or because of statistical evidence that young, African American men are disproportionately involved in crime, drug, or gang activity? He points out that the courts have frequently upheld this practice as long as race is one of several factors involved in a stop or an arrest and the stop is not done for purposes of harassment.

Kennedy then makes a strong argument that race should never be used as the basis for a police action "except in the most extraordinary of circumstances." First, if the practice is strictly forbidden, it will reduce the opportunity for the police to engage in harassment under the cloak of "reasonable" law enforcement measures. Second, the current practice of using race "nourishes powerful feelings of racial grievance against law enforcement authorities." Third, the resulting hostility to the police creates barriers to police–citizen cooperation in those communities "most in need of police protection." Fourth, permitting the practice contributes to racial segregation because African Americans will be reluctant to venture into white neighborhoods for fear of being stopped by the police.[141]

VERBAL ABUSE

Verbal abuse by police officers is one of the more common criticisms civilians have about the police. Some words, such as racial, ethnic, or gender epithets, are clearly wrong. Other words are often perceived as rude or discourteous. An officer may speak in a sharp tone of voice or refuse to answer a civilian's question, and that is often perceived as offensive. Calling somebody a name such as "asshole" or "scumbag" may not appear racially or ethnically motivated, but these words may be perceived as such in an encounter on the street between a white officer and a minority suspect.

For police officers, derogatory language is often used as a control technique. Mervin F. White, Terry C. Cox, and Jack Basehart argue that profanity directed at citizens serves several functions: to get their attention; keep them at a distance; and label, degrade, dominate, and control them.[142] It is also often a moral judgment. As middle-class professionals, police officers often look down on people who do not live by their standards, including criminals, chronic alcoholics, and the homeless.

Verbal abuse is especially hard to control. The typical incident occurs on the street, often without any witnesses except other police officers or friends of the civilian, and it leaves no tangible evidence (unlike a physical attack). Consequently, most complaints about verbal abuse become "swearing contests" in which the civilian says one thing and the officer says just the opposite. Few people bother to file formal complaints about this kind of behavior, however. In the second quarter 2010, only 5 of the 581 complaints investigated by the San Francisco Office of Citizen Complaints involved racial or sexual slurs; another 20 involved discourtesy. Other civilian complaint agencies have reported similarly low rates of complaints in these categories.[143]

POLICE OFFICER ATTITUDES AND BEHAVIOR

Are police officers prejudiced? What is the relationship between police officer attitudes and the behavior of police on the street? The evidence on these questions is extremely complex. As Douglas A. Smith, Nanette Graham, and Bonney Adams explain, "Attitudes are one thing and behavior is another."[144]

Bayley and Mendelsohn compared the attitudes of Denver police officers with those of the general public and found that police officers were "only slightly more [prejudiced] than the community as a whole." Eight percent of the officers indicated that they disliked Spanish-surnamed people, compared with 6 percent of the general public. When asked about specific social situations (for example, "Would you mind eating together at the same table?" or "Would you mind having someone in your family marry a member of a minority group?"), the officers were less prejudiced against Spanish-surnamed people than the general public was but were more prejudiced against African Americans.[145]

Bayley and Mendelsohn's findings are consistent with other research indicating that police officers are not significantly different from the general population in terms of psychological makeup and attitudes, including attitudes about race and ethnicity. Police departments, in other words, do not recruit a distinct group of prejudiced or psychologically unfit individuals. Bayley and Mendelsohn found that on all personality scales, Denver police officers were "absolutely average people."[146]

The attitudes of officers are often contradictory, however. Smith and colleagues found that the overwhelming majority of police officers (79.4 percent) agreed or strongly agreed with the statement "Most people in this community respect police officers."[147] At the same time, however, most (44.2 percent) believed that the chances of being abused by a community member were very high. The characteristics of an officer's assignment affect perception of the community. Officers assigned to racial or ethnic minority communities, high-crime areas, and poor neighborhoods thought they received less respect from the public than did officers working in other areas.

Reiss found that officer attitudes did not reflect behavior. About 75 percent of the officers in his study were observed making racially derogatory remarks, yet they did not engage in systematic discrimination in arrest or use of physical force.[148] One factor limiting the impact of attitudes is the bureaucratic nature of police work. An arrest is reviewed first by a supervisor and then by other criminal justice officials (prosecutor, defense attorney, and judge). News media coverage is also possible. The potentially unfavorable judgments of these people control an officer's behavior.

Much of the research on police officer attitudes was conducted in the 1960s or early 1970s. Since then, police employment practices have changed substantially. Far more African American, Hispanic, female, and college-educated officers are employed today. The earlier research based on a disproportionately white, male police force may no longer be valid.[149] In fact, the Police Foundation study of police abuse of authority found striking differences in the attitudes of white and African American officers. African American officers, by a huge margin, are more likely to believe that police officers use excessive force and use excessive force more often against racial and ethnic minorities and the poor.[150]

Police departments generally offer sensitivity or cultural diversity training for their officers. These programs usually cover the history of race relations, traditional racial and ethnic stereotypes, and explanations of different racial and ethnic cultural patterns. Questions have been raised about the effectiveness of these programs, however. Some critics fear that they may be counterproductive and only reinforce negative attitudes. Classroom training, moreover, does not adequately reproduce the reality of street encounters between officers and civilians. Policies that directly address behavior—such as the PERF policy on traffic enforcement—are more likely to produce positive changes.[151] Geoffrey P. Alpert, William C. Smith, and Daniel Watters argue that, "Mere classroom lectures ... are insufficient" and emphasis needs to be placed on actual on-the-street behavior.[152]

POLICE CORRUPTION AND PEOPLE OF COLOR

Police corruption has a special impact on minority communities. Most police corruption involves vice activities—drugs, gambling, prostitution, after-hours night clubs—that historically have been segregated in low-income and racial minority neighborhoods.

In the 1990s, the New York City Mollen Commission exposed a pattern of corruption and violence in the poorest African American and Hispanic neighborhoods. Officers took bribes for protecting the drug trade, beat up drug dealers, broke into apartments, and stole drugs and money.[153] Historically, police corruption has been concentrated in poor and racial minority neighborhoods because that is where illegal vice crimes have been concentrated. This pattern reflects a more general pattern of unequal law enforcement. The poor and minorities have not had the political power to demand the kind of law enforcement available to many white people and other members of the middle class. The result has been that vice and the resulting corruption are concentrated in poor and minority neighborhoods. The nonenforcement of the law is as much a form of discrimination as overenforcement.

Police corruption harms racial and ethnic minorities in several ways. First, allowing vice activities to flourish in low-income and minority communities represents an unequal and discriminatory pattern of law enforcement. Second, the existence of open drug dealing or prostitution degrades the quality of neighborhood life. Third, vice activities encourage secondary crime—the patrons of prostitutes are robbed; after hours clubs are the scenes of robbery and assault; and competing drug gangs have shoot-outs with rival gangs. Fourth, community awareness of police corruption damages the reputation of the police. In 2008, 16 percent of African Americans thought the ethical standards of the police were "low" or "very low," compared with only 8 percent of whites.[154] In Washington, DC, a study by the Police Foundation found that 19.4 percent of Hispanic residents and 14 percent of African Americans, compared with only 7.2 percent of whites, feel that police officers in the city are "dishonest."[155]

POLICE–COMMUNITY RELATIONS PROGRAMS

Police departments have tried different strategies for improving police–community relations. Some have proved to be more effective than others.

Special PCR Units

In response to the riots of the 1960s, most big-city police departments established special police–community relations (PCR) programs to resolve racial and ethnic tensions. Most involved a separate PCR unit within the department. PCR unit officers spent most of their time speaking in schools or to community groups.[156] Some PCR units also staffed neighborhood storefront offices to make the department more accessible to community residents who either were intimidated by police headquarters or found it difficult to travel downtown. Another popular program was the "ride-along," which allowed citizens to ride in a patrol car and view policing from an officer's perspective.

The PCR programs of the 1960s were not effective. A Justice Department report concluded that they "tended to be marginal to the operations of the police department," with little direct impact on patrol and other key operations.[157] Public education and ride-along programs mainly reached people who already had favorable attitudes toward the police. In the 1970s, most departments reduced or abolished their PCR programs.

Community Policing and Problem-Oriented Policing

Community policing represents an entirely new approach to policing, and some programs have had positive effects on police–community relations. The ambitious Chicago Alternative Police Services (CAPS) program includes a series of regular meetings between patrol beat officers and community residents.[158] The major difference is that under community policing, these meetings are designed to develop two-way communication, with civilians providing input into police policies. The old PCR programs mainly involved one-way communication from the police to the community—in short, a standard public relations effort where the organization attempts to sell itself to the public.

In a national survey of public attitudes about the police, Weitzer and Tuch found that people who believe that community policing is practiced in their neighborhood are less likely to believe that the police frequently use excessive force. The study did not verify whether the police were actually practicing community policing in particular neighborhoods or whether it had a real effect on police conduct. Nonetheless, the belief that it exists has a positive effect on attitudes.[159] Skogan and Hartnett found that community policing had a positive effect on citizens' attitudes toward the police in Chicago. Both African Americans and whites who lived in community policing districts were less likely to believe that police use of excessive force was a problem; similarly they were less likely to believe that the police stopped too many people.[160]

Community policing works only if residents are aware of and involved in the program. Skogan found that in Chicago Hispanics who spoke Spanish were significantly less aware of the CAPS (Chicago Alternative Policing Strategy) than were other groups. They were also the group least likely to have attended a neighborhood beat meeting to discuss neighborhood problems with community policing officers. African Americans, by contrast, were the most likely to have attended a beat meeting. Hispanics now represent more than 26 percent of the Chicago population, and an estimated 60 percent of them indicate that they prefer to speak Spanish. Spanish-speaking Hispanics were least likely to have learned about CAPS from another person (as opposed to television or a printed brochure). In short, special efforts are needed to involve this component of Chicago residents in the community policing program.[161]

As we discussed earlier (pp. 25–26), carefully focused POP programs that target a short list of known offenders avoid the problems associated with "sweeps" and "crackdowns," which involve stopping, frisking, and arresting many people who are not engaged in serious criminal activity. This only creates deep resentment and aggravates police–community relations.

Responding to Community Concerns

Responding to specific community concerns is one way that police departments have tried to develop better relations with communities of color. In one of the best examples, the San Diego Police Department voluntarily decided to collect traffic stop data to determine if there was a pattern of racial profiling. San Diego was the first police department in the country to conduct voluntary data collection. San Jose, California, quickly did the same, and many other departments followed their example.

In his introduction to the first traffic stop data report, San Jose police chief William Lansdowne explained that his department "prides itself upon being responsive to the needs and concerns of everyone who lives, works, learns, plays, and travels within San Jose."[162] Undertaking data collection—a difficult, time-consuming effort that is not popular with all the officers—indicates that the chief was willing to give real meaning to those words.

The Boston Gun Project, meanwhile, was widely credited with both reducing crime and improving relations with minority communities in the 1990s. Gun violence was a major community concern in the African American community. The Ten Point Coalition involved a partnership between the police department and the religious community.[163] The Coalition maintained several activities: "Adopt-a-Gang" programs, where churches provide drop-in centers for young people; neighborhood crime-watch programs; partnerships with community health centers to provide counseling for families with problems; and rape crisis centers for battered women.[164]

A major concern among racial and ethnic minority communities is that police departments do not care about them and are unwilling to acknowledge mistakes that affect their communities. In 2005 the Los Angeles Sheriff's Department took a dramatic step in the direction of expressing concern about a controversial incident. Sheriff's deputies fired 120 shots at an African American man in a vehicle who they believed was an armed suspect. He was wounded and arrested but found to be not the suspect. In a remarkable gesture, the deputies involved publicly apologized to the community for the impact of the incident on the community. There is no record of officers in any department ever apologizing for their actions in this manner. At the same time, the sheriff personally expressed his concern, speedily revised the department's shooting policy, and disciplined the officers. All of these steps represented an effort to repair the damage done by an excessive use of force by officers.[165]

Reducing Officer Misconduct

The National Academy of Sciences report concluded that one way to improve police–community relations is to improve officer conduct and to reduce incidents of misconduct.[166] As mentioned earlier, civilians are sensitive to how officers treat them. In Skogan's study of Chicago, civilian attitudes were heavily influenced by whether they felt they were treated fairly, whether the officer explained the situation to them, whether the officer was polite, and whether the officer listened to what they had to say about the situation.[167] Concern about how officers treat people arises from the field of procedural justice. Research by Tom Tyler and other experts in this field has found that people's attitudes are affected by how they are treated and not necessarily by the outcome of the interaction.[168]

We have already discussed how formal policies on use of deadly force have had some success in reducing police shootings of citizens (pp. 16–19). Policies have also been adopted to reduce the use of excessive physical force. The PERF policy on traffic stops, for example, recommends that officers explain the reason for the stop and apologize if there is no violation of the law or the stop was based on a mistaken identity.[169]

Experts argue that the police need to train their officers to be able to deal with different cultures in America's increasingly diverse society. *Cultural competence* is defined as being aware of the dynamics of interactions between people of different cultures and developing both agency policies and skills among agency personnel to address these dynamics. Issues related to cultural competence arise not just in criminal justice but also in health care, education, and other social services. Georgetown University sponsors a National Center for Cultural Competence devoted to research and training on this issue.[170]

The NYPD, meanwhile, prepared a Fact Sheet on Arab communities. It includes a section on "What Codes of Conduct Should I Know When Entering an Arab's Home?" It explains that in "many Arab Muslim households [people] remove their shoes at the door because carpeting is used for prayers."[171] The Charlotte-Mecklenburg, North Carolina Police Department created a special International Unit to respond to all of the new cultural groups in the community. The county had experienced high rates of immigration of Hispanics, Hmong, Vietnamese, and Indians. The unit produced a manual for all officers in the department that, for example, explained traditional medical practices of coining and cupping that leave marks on the body and are often misinterpreted as physical abuse.[172]

CITIZEN COMPLAINTS AGAINST THE POLICE

One of the greatest sources of tension between the police and minorities is the perceived failure of police departments to respond adequately to citizen complaints about police misconduct. The development of external citizen oversight agencies, which now exist in virtually all big cities, is a response to this problem.[173]

African Americans file a disproportionate number of all complaints against the police. In New York City, for example, African Americans made 57 percent of all complaints filed with the Civilian Complaint Review Board in 2009, even though they represent only 23 percent of the city's population.[174] The Hispanic complaint rate (25 percent of all complaints), on the other hand, was nearly comparable to the city's population (27 percent). Similar patterns have been found in other citizen complaint agencies.

T A B L E 4.5   **Race and Ethnicity of Officers Receiving Complaints, Compared to Composition of the Department, New York City, 2009**

	Percentage of Officers Receiving Complaints	Percentage of Officers in the Department
White	49.5	53.4
African American	17.2	16.4
Hispanic	28.4	25.6
Asian	4.6	4.5

SOURCE: New York City Civilian Complaint Review Board, *Status Report, January–December 2009* (New York: Civilian Complaint Review Board, 2010), Statistical Appendices, Table 9.

Several factors may affect the tendency of Hispanics not to file complaints. Language barriers are a problem for all people who do not speak English or have limited English capacity (LEP). An increasing number of police departments and complaint agencies now provide information about the complaint process in Spanish and Asian languages appropriate to the local community. The San Francisco Office of Citizen Complaints has a link on its website providing information in dozens of languages. Many recent immigrants do not understand the nature of the citizen complaint process and assume that they need an attorney. A study based on interviews with Hispanic immigrants found that many immigrants do not have the "legal consciousness" of long-time resident Americans and do not understand that they have a right to file a complaint against a government official.[175] Also, many recent immigrants from Mexico or other Latin American countries are extremely fearful of the police because complaining about an officer in those countries can result in serious retaliation, even death.

Racial and ethnic minorities accuse police departments of failing to adequately investigate complaints and not disciplining officers who are guilty of misconduct. Internal affairs complaint procedures have often been denounced as "cover-ups."[176] A survey in Washington, DC, found that 75.3 percent of African Americans believe that police department investigations of alleged officer misconduct are biased. Meanwhile, 65.6 percent of Hispanic residents and 81.8 percent of Asians also feel the process is biased. It is surprising that more than half of whites (56.1 percent) also think that complaint investigations are biased.[177] Lack of faith in complaint procedures is one reason why most people who feel they are victims of police abuse do not even file a formal complaint. One study found that only 30 percent of those people who felt they had a reason to complain about a police officer took any kind of action, and only some of them contacted the police department. Most people called someone else (a friend or some other government official).[178]

Historically, some departments have actively discouraged citizen complaints. The Kerner Commission found evidence of this in the 1960s. In the 1990s the Christopher Commission found that officers at Los Angeles police stations discouraged people from filing complaints and sometimes even threatened them with arrest. Additionally, officers frequently did not complete Form 1.81, which records an official complaint. In response to criticisms about how it handled complaints, the Los Angeles Police Department established a special toll-free number as a complaint hotline. A study by the American Civil Liberties Union in Los Angeles, however, found that only 13 percent of the people calling local police stations were given the toll-free number. Other callers (71.9 percent) were told that there was no such number or that the officer could not give it out or they were put on hold indefinitely.[179]

Police department internal affairs (IA) or professional standards units traditionally have handled civilian complaints. The police subculture is very strong, however, and IA officers tend to protect their colleagues and the department against external criticism. William A. Westley found that the police subculture emphasizes "silence, secrecy, and solidarity." Under the informal "code of silence," officers often are willing to lie to cover up misconduct by fellow officers.[180] The Christopher Commission concluded that in Los Angeles, "the greatest single barrier to the effective investigation and adjudication of complaints is the officers' unwritten 'code of silence.'" The code "consists of one simple rule: an officer does not provide adverse information against a fellow officer."[181] The Mollen Commission investigating police corruption in New York City found the "pervasiveness" of the code of silence "alarming." The commission asked one officer, "Were you ever afraid that one of your fellow officers might turn you in?" He answered, "Never," because "cops don't tell on cops."[182]

As a result, most citizen complaints become "swearing contests": the civilian alleges one thing, and the officer denies it. Police departments sustain an average of only 10.4 percent of all complaints.[183]

One alternative to traditional complaint investigation is to mediate complaints. Mediation is a voluntary process in which the complainant and the officer meet face-to-face (usually for about an hour) with a professional mediator supervising the session. The point of mediation is not to establish guilt but to foster a dialogue that leads to better understanding on both sides of the issue. The end result is often simply an agreement that each side has listened to and understands the other person's point of view. Vivian Berger, an experienced mediator in New York City, argues that mediation is particularly appropriate for complaints when the officer and the complainant are of different races or ethnic groups. She explains that many complaints are not formally about race (for example, the allegation is discourtesy) but that "they are really about race"—that is, the complaint is the result of misunderstandings that are rooted in racial or cultural differences. Mediation provides a structured process in which both sides have to listen to each other. In many cases, this can help bridge the racial divide.[184]

CITIZEN OVERSIGHT OF THE POLICE

To ensure better handling of complaints against the police, civil rights groups have demanded external or civilian oversight of complaints. Civilian oversight is based on the idea that people who are not police officers will be more independent and objective in investigating complaints. Despite strong opposition from police unions, civilian review has spread rapidly in recent years. There are now more than 100 oversight agencies in the United States, covering almost all of the big cities and many smaller cities.[185]

Some civilian oversight agencies have original jurisdiction for investigating complaints themselves (for example, the San Francisco Office of Citizen Complaints). Others provide some civilian input into investigations conducted by IA officers (for example, the Kansas City Office of Citizen Complaints). Some procedures systematically audit the performance of the IA unit (for example, the Denver Independent Police Monitor).[186]

There is some evidence that civilian review enhances public confidence in the complaint process. In 1991, for example, San Francisco had five times as many complaints per officer as Los Angeles. It is unlikely that people in San Francisco simply complain more than people in Los Angeles. It is more likely that an external civilian review procedure enhances civilians' belief that their complaints will receive a fair hearing.[187]

To better serve civilians who want to file a complaint, an increasing number of departments and civilian oversight agencies have taken a number of steps: (1) accepting complaints at locations other than police headquarters; (2) accepting complaints over the phone or by email; (3) accepting anonymous complaints; (4) providing a toll-free telephone number for complaints; (5) providing detailed information about the complaint process on their websites; and (6) providing information and complaint forms in all of the languages appropriate for the community.

POLICE EMPLOYMENT PRACTICES

"Not Your Father's Police Department"

As America changes, police departments also need to change their officer workforce in order to represent the communities they serve. Lack of diversity and outright discrimination in employment have been historic problems for the American police. Things have changed in recent decades, however. Law Professor David Sklansky sums up the changes in an article entitled, "Not Your Father's Police Department."[188]

The relevant questions today are: How much progress has been made? Is this sufficient progress? How do we measure that progress? What standard do we apply to determine whether a law enforcement agency employs a sufficient number of African American, Hispanic, Asian, or women police officers?

Discrimination in the employment of officers of color has a long history. During the segregation era (1890s–1960s), southern cities did not hire any African American officers. Even in northern cities, African American officers were seriously underrepresented. The Kerner Commission found that in 1967 African Americans were 23 percent of the population in Oakland, California, but only 2.3 percent of the police officers.[189]

The former Boston police commissioner Paul Evans recognized the need for a diverse workforce in terms of practical law enforcement. He stated, "I know that having African American and Hispanic and Vietnamese officers, people of different backgrounds and cultures who can conduct comfortable interviews with crime victims and can infiltrate crime rings that aren't white—I know the need for that is just common sense."[190]

Employment discrimination occurs in three different areas of policing: initial hiring, assignment to shifts and specialized units, and promotion to higher rank. Initial hiring is the most visible and easiest to control. Assignment to specialized units is much less visible to the public, but it has significant impact on an officer's potential for promotion.

Trends in African American and Hispanic Employment

Since the 1960s, some progress has been made in the employment of racial and ethnic minority police officers (Figure 4.2). In 1960 an estimated 3.6 percent of all sworn officers in the United States were African Americans. By 2003 the figure had increased to 11.7 percent. Hispanics represented about 9.1 percent of all sworn officers that year. (Little data exist on Hispanic officers for earlier years.) Unfortunately, BJS has not compiled data for more recent years.[191]

National data on police employment are misleading because, as noted in Chapter 1, the racial and ethnic groups are not evenly distributed across the country. It is necessary to look at particular police departments to see whether they represent the communities they serve. The Commission on Accreditation for Law Enforcement Agencies (CALEA) accreditation standards for law enforcement agencies require that "the agency has minority group and female employees in the sworn law enforcement ranks in approximate proportion to the makeup of the available work force in the law enforcement agency's service community."[192]

The Equal Employment Opportunity (EEO) Index provides a good measure of whether a department represents the community it serves. The EEO Index compares the percentage of minority group officers with the percentage of that

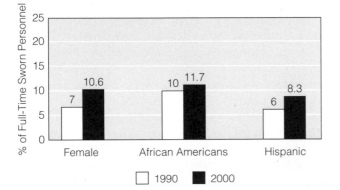

FIGURE 4.2 African American, Hispanic, and Female Officers, 1990–2000

SOURCES: Bureau of Justice Statistics, *Law Enforcement Management and Administrative Statistics*, 1990, (Washington, DC: Department of Justice, 1992); *Bureau of Justice Statistics, Law Enforcement Management and Administrative Statistics*, 2000, (Washington, DC: Department of Justice, 2003).

group in the local population. If, for example, a community is 40 percent African American and 30 percent of the officers are African American, the EEO Index is 0.75.[193] The EEO Index permits a meaningful analysis of individual departments. In 2009 New York City Police Department had an EEO Index of 0.68 for African Americans; the city population was 23 percent African American compared with 16 percent for NYPD officers. This was a significant improvement from the 48.8 EEO index in 2004. The EEO Index for Hispanic officers was 0.84 (28 percent Hispanic population and 23 percent Hispanic officers). This was an improvement from an EEO Index of 66.6 in 2004.[194]

The Boston Police Department provides an example of how an employer can take active steps to increase racial and ethnic minority employment. Former Police Commissioner Paul Evans found that the local civil service rules made exceptions for job candidates with special skills. Because Boston has a significant Haitian population, Evans was able to use these rules to hire officers who could speak Haitian Creole and thus could communicate better with Haitian residents. Evans then extended this practice to include job applicants who could speak Spanish, Vietnamese, or Chinese.[195]

Los Angeles offers another interesting perspective on minority employment. In 1992 the police department had a perfect EEO Index (1.00) for African Americans (14 percent of both the population and the sworn officers). Yet the Rodney King incident revealed that the department had a serious race relations problem. The Christopher Commission found a racist climate within the department, with officers making racist comments over the department's computerized message system.[196] In short, merely employing racial minority officers does not automatically eliminate police–community relations problems. The quality of policing is largely determined by the organizational culture of the department, which is the combined product of leadership by the chief, formal policies on critical issues such as the use of force, and rank-and-file officer peer culture.

In some police departments, non–Hispanic white officers are now the minority. In Texas, the San Antonio Police Department today is about 46 percent Hispanic, 48 percent white, and 6 percent African American. The city population is 61 percent Hispanic, 28 percent non–Hispanic white, and 6 percent African American.[197]

Employing more officers who can speak Spanish facilitates relations with the Hispanic community. Hispanic officers will likely lead to that result, although white non–Hispanic officers who speak Spanish will accomplish the same result. A study of police and Hispanic civilian interactions in a Midwestern city found that although language barriers did not create any major crises (even violent incidents arising from an inability to communicate), they did create delays in the delivery of services and some frustration on the part of officers. When handling a situation in which the civilians did not speak English, officers either found a family member or bystander who could translate or simply "muddled through" with "street Spanish."[198]

Relatively few Native Americans and Asian Americans are employed as sworn police officers in departments other than tribal law enforcement agencies (where Native Americans are about 56 percent of all officers). The Justice Department's report *Law Enforcement Management and Administrative Statistics* provides the most systematic set of data. A few police departments do have a significant number of Asian American officers. They represented 13 percent of the officers in San Francisco in 2000, for example. Native Americans, however, are substantially underrepresented, even in states with the largest Native American populations. They are only 1 percent of the sworn officers in Albuquerque, New Mexico, for example.[199]

The Law of Employment Discrimination

Employment discrimination based on race or ethnicity is illegal. The Fourteenth Amendment to the U.S. Constitution provides that "No state shall … deny to any person … the equal protection of the laws." Title VII of the 1964 Civil Rights Act prohibits employment discrimination based on race, color, national origin, religion, or sex. The 1972 Equal Employment Opportunity Act extended the coverage of Title VII to state and local governments. In addition, state civil rights laws prohibit employment discrimination on the basis of race or ethnicity. According to Section 703, "It shall be an unlawful employment practice for an employer … to fail or refuse to hire or to discharge any individual, or otherwise to discriminate against any individual with respect to his compensation, terms, conditions, or privileges of employment, because of such individual's race, color, religion, sex, or national origin."[200]

The Affirmative Action Controversy

The most controversial aspect of employment discrimination is the policy of affirmative action. The Office of Federal Contract Compliance defines affirmative action as "results-oriented actions [taken] to ensure equal employment opportunity [which may include] goals to correct under-utilization … [and] backpay, retroactive seniority, makeup goals and timetables." Affirmative action originated in 1966 when President Lyndon Johnson issued Executive Order 11246 directing all federal contractors to have affirmative action programs. Some affirmative action programs are voluntary, whereas others are court ordered; some have general goals, whereas others have specific quotas.

An affirmative action program consists of several steps. The first is a census of employees to determine the number and percentage of racial minorities and women in different job categories. The data are then used to identify underutilization. *Underutilization* exists where the percentage of employees in a particular job category is less than the percentage of potentially qualified members of that group in the labor force. If underutilization exists, the employer is required to develop a plan to eliminate it. Recruitment programs usually include active outreach to potential minority applicants, mainly through meetings with community groups and leaders. The New Haven, Connecticut, police department successfully increased the representation of racial minority officers from 22 percent in 1991 to 40 percent by 2000. The department recognized that its traditional methods of recruiting, such as placing ads in the newspaper, were not working effectively for groups other than whites. To overcome this problem, the department worked closely with community groups, holding focus groups to discuss the issue, for example. These sessions generated ideas about which messages were most effective with different racial and ethnic groups, and focus group members later helped with the recruitment effort. Also, police officer recruiters were carefully selected on the basis of their enthusiasm, communication skills, and ability to relate to different groups.[201]

An employer may voluntarily adopt an affirmative action plan with quotas. In 1974 the Detroit Police Department adopted a voluntary quota of promoting one African American officer for each white officer promoted. As a result, by 1992 half of all the officers at the rank of sergeant or higher were African American. Most affirmative action plans have been court ordered, as a result of discrimination suits under Title VII of the 1964 Civil Rights Act. A 1980 consent decree settling the suit against the Omaha, Nebraska, police department, for example, established a long-term goal of having 9.5 percent African American officers in the department within seven years. At the time of the suit, African Americans were only 4 percent of the sworn officers, and the figure had been declining. To achieve the 9.5 percent goal, the court ordered a three-stage recruitment plan: African Americans would be 40 percent of all new recruits until they were 6 percent of the department, 33 percent of recruits until they were 8 percent, and then 25 percent of recruits until the final 9.5 percent goal was reached. The city reached the goals of the court order ahead of schedule, and by 1992 African American officers were 11.5 percent of the police department.

In 2007, in two school desegregation cases, the Supreme Court ruled that using race alone was unconstitutional. It is likely that the Court will apply the same principle to the area of employment, meaning that the future of affirmative action plans is uncertain.[202]

Discrimination in Assignment

Discrimination also occurs in the assignment of police officers. In the South during the segregation era, African American officers were not assigned to white neighborhoods and were not permitted to arrest whites.[203] Many northern cities also confined minority officers to minority neighborhoods. Reiss found that some police departments assigned their incompetent white officers to racial minority neighborhoods.[204] Seniority rules that govern the assignment in most departments today make blatant discrimination difficult. Officers with the most seniority, regardless of race, ethnicity, or gender, have first choice for the most desirable assignments. Seniority rules can have an indirect race effect, however. In a department that has only recently hired a significant number of racial or ethnic minorities, these officers will be disproportionately assigned to high-crime areas because of their lack of seniority. Fyfe found that this seniority-based assignment pattern explained why African American officers in New York City fired their weapons more often than white officers did (although the rates were virtually the same for all officers assigned to the high-crime areas, regardless of race).[205]

There is also discrimination in assignment to special units. The Special Counsel to the Los Angeles County Sheriff Department identified two categories of desirable positions. "Coveted" positions were those that officers sought because they are interesting, high paying, or convenient (in terms of work schedule): the Special Enforcement Bureau, the Narcotics Bureau, and precinct station detective assignments. "High-profile" positions, however, are those likely to lead to promotion and career advancement. These include operations deputy, the Recruitment Training Bureau, and field training officer positions.[206]

An investigative study by the *New York Times* found that African American male officers were seriously underrepresented in the elite units of the NYPD. The 124-officer mounted patrol unit had only 3 African Americans, and there were only 2 in the 159-officer harbor patrol unit. It is well understood in the NYPD that selection for an elite unit depends on having a friend who will sponsor you—a "hook" or a "rabbi" in the slang of the NYPD. With few people in high command and in elite units, African American officers often find their career paths blocked in those areas.[207]

The assignment of African American officers to plainclothes detective work has created a new problem. In 1992 an African American transit police officer in New York City wearing plain clothes was shot and seriously wounded by a white officer who mistook him for a robber. Similar incidents have occurred in other cities. The *New York Times* report found that in New York City, virtually all of the many African American officers interviewed had at some time been stopped and questioned—sometimes at gunpoint—by white officers. Earlier (p. 18–19) we discussed the problem of police-on-police shootings, which has disproportionately affected off-duty African American officers.[208]

The Impact of Diversity

Civil rights leaders and police reformers have fought for increased employment of racial and ethnic minorities with three different goals in mind. First, employment discrimination is illegal and must be eliminated for that reason alone. Second, some reformers believe that minority officers will behave in different ways than white officers on the street and be less likely to discriminate in making arrests or using physical force.[209] Third, many experts argue that police departments should reflect the communities they serve to create a positive public image.

Officers of Color as Supervisors and Chief Executives

African American and Hispanic officers are also seriously underrepresented in supervisory ranks. In 1992 African Americans were 11.5 percent of all sworn officers in New York City but only 6.6 percent of the officers at the rank of sergeant and higher. In Los Angeles, Hispanics were 22.3 percent of all sworn officers but only 13.4 percent of those at the rank of sergeant and higher.[210]

Female African American and Hispanic officers encounter both race and gender discrimination. Women, regardless of race or ethnicity, are significantly underrepresented among all sworn officers and even more underrepresented in

Focus on an Issue
Would It Make a Difference? Assigning African American Officers to African American Neighborhoods

Some civil rights activists argue that police departments should assign African American officers exclusively to African American neighborhoods. They believe that these officers would be more sensitive to community needs, more polite and respectful to neighborhood residents, and less likely to act in a discriminatory manner.

Is this a good idea? Would it, in fact, improve the quality of policing in minority neighborhoods? The evidence does not support this proposal. First, as we have already seen, no evidence suggests that African American, Hispanic, and white officers behave in significantly different ways. Fyfe's research on deadly force found that officers assigned to high-crime precincts fired their weapons at similar rates, regardless of race. Reiss found that white and African American officers used excessive physical force at about the same rate. Black found no significant differences in the arrest patterns of white and African American officers. It is worth noting that male and female officers have also been found to behave in roughly similar ways. Thus, most experts on the police argue that situational and departmental factors, not race or gender, influence police officer behavior.[211]

Second, assigning only African American officers to African American neighborhoods, or Hispanic officers to Hispanic neighborhoods, would discriminate against the officers themselves. It would "ghettoize" them and deny them the variety of assignments and experience that helps lead to promotion. The policy would also perpetuate racial stereotypes by promoting the idea that only African American officers could handle the African American community.

Third, the proposal is based on a faulty assumption about the nature of American urban communities. Although there are all-white, all–African American, and all-Hispanic neighborhoods, there are also many mixed neighborhoods. It is impossible to draw a clear line between the "white" and the "black" communities. Under the proposed policy, which officers would be assigned to mixed neighborhoods? Moreover, the racial and ethnic composition of neighborhoods is constantly changing.[212] Today's all-white neighborhood is tomorrow's multiracial and multiethnic neighborhood. Any attempt to draw precinct boundaries based on race or ethnicity would be quickly outdated.

With respect to the first objective, increased minority employment means that the agency is complying with the law of equal employment opportunity. Obeying the law is an important consideration, regardless of any other effects of minority employment. Along these lines, failure to hire an adequate number of racial or ethnic minorities frequently results in an employment discrimination suit, which is expensive and tends to create organizational turmoil.

With respect to the second goal, there is no clear evidence that white, African American, or Hispanic police officers behave in different ways on the job. They arrest, use force, and receive citizen complaints (Table 4.5) at similar rates. For the most part, they are influenced by situational factors: the seriousness of the offense, the demeanor of the suspect, and so forth.

There is increased recognition of the importance of having officers with skills in languages other than English. Common sense suggests that officers who can

(*Continued*)

communicate effectively in Spanish or Cambodian will be better able to serve people who speak those languages.[213] At present, however, there are no studies that would confirm this hypothesis.

Diversifying a police department does have an impact on the police subculture, bringing in people with different attitudes. African American and Hispanic officers have formed their own organizations at both the local and national levels. The National Black Police Officers Association and the Guardians, for example, represent African American officers. Hispanic officers have formed the National Latino Peace Officers Association and the Hispanic American Command Officers Association. These organizations offer a different perspective on police issues from the one presented by white police officers. After the Rodney King incident, for example, members of the African American Peace Officers Association in Los Angeles stated, "Racism is widespread in the department."[214] This was a very different point of view than that expressed by white Los Angeles officers. In this respect, minority employment breaks down the solidarity of the police subculture.

The National Black Police Officers Association published a brochure titled "Police Brutality: A Strategy to Stop the Violence," urging officers to report brutality by other officers. This brochure represents a sharp break with the traditional norms of the police subculture, which emphasize protecting other officers from outside investigations.[215] The Police Foundation's national survey of police officers found that African American officers are far more likely to believe that officers in their department use excessive force than are white officers.[216] Finally, an evaluation of community policing in Chicago found

that African American officers were more receptive to change—including community policing—than were white officers.[217]

In short, minority officers do have a different perspective on policing and police problems than white officers. The extent to which these attitudes are translated into different behavior on the street is not clear, however. At the same time, differences in attitudes among officers of different race and ethnicity can cause conflict within the department. In a number of departments, race relations have been strained when African American officers file employment discrimination suits and white officers file countersuits challenging affirmative action programs. In a study of a Midwestern police department, Robin Haar found little daily interaction between white and African American officers. In particular, she asked officers who they would seek out if they had a problem or question that needed answering.[218] In short, the racial divisions that exist in society at large are reproduced within police departments.

With respect to the third goal, improved police–community relations, there is some limited evidence that increased minority employment improves public opinion about the police. A study in Detroit found that, unlike in all other surveys, African American residents rated the police department more favorably than did white residents, suggesting that this more favorable rating was the result of the significant African American representation in city government, including the police department.[219] As already mentioned, having bilingual officers on the force may improve the ability of the police to serve communities of recent immigrants and in that respect improve police–community relations with those groups.

the supervisory ranks. A 1992 survey found that white female officers were being promoted at a faster rate than either African American or Hispanic female officers. In Chicago, for example, there were 73 white females, 37 African American females, and 2 Hispanic females above the rank of sergeant in a department of 12,291 sworn officers. The data contradict the popular belief that minority women enjoy a special advantage because employers count them in two affirmative action categories. Hispanic women, in fact, were almost completely unrepresented at the rank of sergeant and higher.

Racial and ethnic minorities have been far more successful in achieving the rank of police chief executive. In recent years, African Americans have served as chief executive in many of the largest police departments in the country: New York City, Los Angeles, Chicago, Philadelphia, Atlanta, and New Orleans, among others. Several African American individuals have established distinguished careers as law enforcement chief executives. Hubert Williams served as police commissioner in Newark, New Jersey, and then became president of the Police Foundation, a private police research organization. Charles Ramsey was appointed superintendent of the Washington, DC, police department in 1998 after directing the Chicago Police Department's community policing program. After making major improvements in the department under a federal consent decree, he became Commissioner of the Philadelphia Police Department.

CONCLUSION

Significant problems persist in the relations between police and racial and ethnic communities in the United States. African Americans and Hispanics rate the police lower than do white Americans. There is persuasive evidence that minorities are more likely than white Americans to be shot and killed, arrested, and victimized by excessive physical force. Although some progress has been made in recent years in controlling police behavior, particularly with respect to the use of deadly force, significant racial and ethnic disparities remain. In addition, there is evidence of misconduct directed against racial and ethnic minorities and of police departments failing to discipline officers who are guilty of misconduct. Finally, police department employment discrimination continues.

The evidence clearly supports the argument that many American police departments have taken important and effective steps toward improving relations with people of color. Progress has been made with regard toward eliminating unjustified shootings, curbing excessive use of force, controlling racial profiling in traffic enforcement, and employing officers of color. Much remains to be done, however, and unacceptable police misconduct incidents continue to occur. As discussed in this chapter, the economic recession poses a real threat to the quality of policing in America. Because of budget constraints, many local police departments have suffered losses of personnel, which makes it difficult for them to provide adequate levels of patrol, to respond to 911 calls, and engage in innovative programs. The impact of the recession has been particularly severe in cities where poverty was already concentrated and that generally have high concentrations of communities of color. The full impact of the recession on police and racial and ethnic relations remains to be seen.

With reference to the discrimination–disparity continuum we discussed in Chapter 1, the evidence about the police suggests a combination of three of the different patterns. Some disparities are institutionalized discrimination resulting from the application of neutral criteria (as in the greater likelihood of arrest for the more serious crimes). Some represent contextual discrimination (as in the greater likelihood of arrest of minorities suspected of crimes against whites). And some are individual acts of discrimination by prejudiced individuals. There is no basis for saying that a situation of pure justice exists or that racism is a "myth," as William Wilbanks argued.

The evidence supports the conflict perspective regarding the police and racial and ethnic minorities. The data suggest that police actions such as arrest, use of deadly force, and verbal abuse reflect the broader patterns of social and economic inequality in U.S. society that we discussed in detail in Chapter 3.

Those inequalities are both racial and economic. Thus, the injustices suffered by racial and ethnic minorities at the hands of the police are a result of both discrimination against ethnic and racial minorities and the disproportionate representation of minorities among the poor.

The evidence also supports Hawkins's call for a modified conflict perspective that takes into account evident complexities and contingencies. Some of the evidence we have reviewed, for example, indicates that in certain situations, African Americans receive less law enforcement protection than do whites.

Discrimination can result from too little policing as well as excessive policing. Other evidence suggests that the race of the suspect must be considered in conjunction with the race of the complainant. Finally, the evidence indicates significant changes in some important areas of policing with respect to racial and ethnic minorities. On the positive side, the number of people shot and killed by the police has declined. On the negative side, the war on drugs has been waged most heavily against racial and ethnic minorities. In terms of employment, some slow but steady progress has been made in the employment of African Americans and Hispanics as police officers.

DISCUSSION QUESTIONS

1. What is meant by a contextual approach to examining policing, race, and ethnicity?
2. How is policing in Native American communities different from policing in the rest of the United States?
3. When does police use of force become "excessive" or "unjustified"? Give a definition of *excessive force*.

4. Are there any significant differences between how Hispanics and African Americans interact with the police? Explain.

5. Is there racial or ethnic discrimination in arrests? What is the evidence on this question?

6. Suppose that a white police officer is sitting around having drinks with some fellow officers (who are also white) and he makes some racially offensive remarks. Is that person unfit to be a police officer? Do his remarks mean that he engages in discrimination on the job?

7. This book argues that some significant progress has been made in controlling police use of deadly force. What is that evidence? Do you find it persuasive?

8. This book also argues that some progress has been made in reducing racial profiling. What evidence supports that view? Are you persuaded? Why or why not?

9. Substantial progress has been made with regard to the employment of people of color in policing. Does that make a difference in actual police operations on the street? In what ways? Explain.

10. Define the concept of *affirmative action*. Do you support or oppose affirmative action in the employment of police officers? Do you think affirmative action is more important in policing than in other areas of life? Explain.

NOTES

1. Samuel Walker and Charles M. Katz, *The Police in America: An Introduction*, 7th ed. (New York: McGraw-Hill, 2011), chap. 12.

2. Recent developments and background information on New Orleans available at http://samuelwalker.net.

3. David Bayley and Christine Nixon, *The Changing Environment for Policing, 1985–2008, New Perspectives in Policing* (Washington, DC: Department of Justice, 2010).

4. Police Executive Research Forum, *Racially Biased Policing: A Principled Response* (Washington, DC: PERF, 2001).

5. Bureau of Justice Statistics, *Policing and Homicide, 1976–98: Justifiable Homicide by Police, Police Officers Murdered by Felons*, NCJ 180987 (Washington, DC: U.S. Government Printing Office, 2001). Available at http://www.ncjrs.org; William A. Geller and Michael S. Scott, *Deadly Force: What We Know* (Washington, DC: Police Executive Research Forum, 1992).

6. Cecilia Menjivar and Cynthia L. Bejarano, "Latino Immigrants' Perceptions of Crime and Police Authorities in the United States: A Case Study from the Phoenix Metropolitan Area," *Ethnic and Racial Studies* 27 (January 2004), pp. 120–148.

7. Ronet Bachman, Heather Zaykowski, Rachel Kallmyer, Margarita Poteyeva, and Christina Lanier, *Violence Against American Indian and Alaska Native Women and the Criminal Justice Response: What is Known* (Washington, DC: Department of Justice, 2008). NCJ 223691; Stewart Wakeling, Miriam Jorgensen, Susan Michaelson, and Manley Degay, *Policing on American Indian Reservations: A Report to the National*

Institute of Justice, NCJ 188095 (Washington, DC: U.S. Government Printing Office, 2001). Available at http://www.ncjrs.org.

8. "Its Police Nearly Halved, Camden Feels Impact," *New York Times*, March 7, 2011.

9. Bureau of Justice Statistics, *Contacts Between Police and the Public: Findings from the 2002 National Survey*, NCJ 207845 (Washington, DC: U.S. Government Printing Office, 2005). Available at http://www.ncjrs.org.

10. Robert C. Davis and Nicole J. Henderson, "Willingness to Report Crimes: The Role of Ethnic Group Membership and Community Efficacy," *Crime and Delinquency* 49 (October 2003), pp. 564–580.

11. Marianne O. Nielsen, "Contextualization for Native American Crime and Criminal Justice Involvement," in *Native Americans, Crime, and Justice*, Marianne O. Nielsen and Robert A. Silverman, eds. (Boulder, CO: Westview, 1996), p. 10.

12. "Officers Killed with Impunity," *Washington Post* (July 1, 2001), p. 1.

13. On the consent decrees and their impact in Washington, DC, Cincinnati, and other jurisdictions, see Samuel Walker and Morgan Macdonald, "An Alternative Remedy for Police Misconduct: A Model State Pattern or Practice Statute," *George Mason University Civil Rights Law Review* 19 (Summer 2009), pp. 479–552.

14. Ronald Weitzer, "Racialized Policing: Residents' Perceptions in Three Neighborhoods," *Law and Society Review* 34, no. 1 (2000), pp. 129–156.

15. Patricia Y. Warren and Donald Tomaskovic-Devey, "Racial Profiling and Searches: Did the Politics of Racial Profiling Change Police Behavior?" *Criminology and Public Policy* 8, no. 2 (2009), pp. 343–369.

16. Walker and Katz, *Police in America*, chap. 2; Samuel Walker, *Popular Justice: A History of American Criminal Justice*, 2nd ed. (New York: Oxford University Press, 1998), pp. 148–49, 193–99.

17. National Advisory Commission on Civil Disorders [Kerner Commission], *Report* (New York: Bantam Books, 1968).

18. Alfredo Mirandé, *Gringo Justice* (Notre Dame, IN: University of Notre Dame Press, 1987).

19. A video documentary, *Zoot Suit Riots*, along with supporting educational material, can be found on the Public Broadcasting System website at http://www.pbs.org; Mauricio Mazon, *The Zoot-Suit Riots: The Psychology of Symbolic Annihilation* (Austin: University of Texas Press, 1984).

20. Pew Hispanic Center, *Hispanics: A People in Motion* (Washington, DC: Pew Hispanic Center, 2005).

21. Henry I. DeGeneste and John P. Sullivan, *Policing a Multicultural Community* (Washington, DC: Police Executive Research Forum, 1997), p. 15.

22. Matthew Lysakowski, Albert Antony Pearsall, III, and Jill Pope, *Policing in New Immigrant Communities* (Washington, DC: Department of Justice, 2009). Available at http://www.cops.usdoj.gov.

23. The report is no longer on the department's website, but it can be found at http://samuelwalker.net.

24. http://www.sfgov3.org/index.aspx?page=419.

25. "Audit Says Police Fall Short in Providing Translators," *New York Times*, November 19, 2010.

26. Gallup Poll data cited in Bureau of Justice Statistics, *Sourcebook of Criminal Justice Statistics*, 2003, p. 109.

27. "Discrimination in America," *Washington Post* (June 21, 2001).

28. The Police Foundation, Metropolitan Police Department, *Biased Policing Project, Final Report* (Washington, DC: The Police Foundation, 2004), p. 67.

29. Ronald Weitzer, "Racialized Policing: Residents' Perceptions in Three Neighborhoods," *Law and Society Review* 34, no. 1 (2000), pp. 129–155.

30. A comprehensive overview of public opinion trends is in Steven A. Tuch and Ronald Weitzer, "Racial Differences in Attitudes toward the Police," *Public Opinion Quarterly* 61 (1997), pp. 643–663.

31. Ronald Weitzer, "Incidents of Police Misconduct and Public Opinion, *Journal of Criminal Justice* 30 (2002), pp. 397–408.

32. Pew Hispanic Center, *Between Two Worlds: How Young Latinos Come of Age in America* (Los Angeles: Pew Hispanic Center, 2009), Figure 9.7, p. 86. Available at http://pewhispanic.org/.

33. Carl Werthman and Irving Piliavin, "Gang Members and the Police," in *The Police: Six Sociological Essays*, David J. Bordua, ed. (New York: Wiley, 1967), p. 58.

34. A. Allen Lind and Tom R. Tyler, *The Social Psychology of Procedural Justice* (New York: Plenum, 1988).

35. Wesley G. Skogan, "Citizen Satisfaction with Police Encounters," *Police Quarterly* 8 (September 2005), pp. 298–321.

36. David H. Bayley and Harold Mendelsohn, *Minorities and the Police: Confrontation in America* (New York: Free Press, 1969), p. 109.

37. Bureau of Justice Statistics, *Black Victims of Violent Crime* (Washington, DC: Department of Justice, 2007). NCJ 214258.

38. Bureau of Justice Statistics, *Criminal Victimization 2000: Changes 1999–2000 with Trends 1993–2000*, NCJ 187007 (Washington, DC: U.S. Government Printing Office, 2001). Available at http://www.ncjrs.org.

39. "From Some Parents, Warnings about Police," *New York Times* (October 23, 1997), p. A18.

40. Sandra Lee Browning, Francis T. Cullen, Liqun Cao, Renee Kopache, and Thomas J. Stevenson, "Race and Getting Hassled by the Police: A Research Note," *Police Studies* 17, no. 1 (1994), pp. 1–11.

41. Cynthia Perez McCluskey, *Policing the Latino Community* (East Lansing, MI: Julian Samora Research Institute, 1998), p. 3, 38.

42. Bureau of Justice Statistics, *Criminal Victimization in the United States 2007, Statistical Tables* (Washington, DC: Department of Justice, 2010), NCJ 227669, Tables 94, 95, 97.

43. Leigh Herbst and Samuel Walker, "Language Barriers in the Delivery of Police Services: A Study of Police and Hispanic Interactions in a Midwestern City," *Journal of Criminal Justice* 29, no. 4 (2001), pp. 329–340.

44. Lysakowski, et al., *Policing in New Immigrant Communities*; David L. Carter, "Hispanic Perceptions of Police Performance: An Empirical Assessment," *Journal of Criminal Justice* 13 (1985), pp. 487–500.

45. Samuel Walker, "Complaints against the Police: A Focus Group Study of Citizen Perceptions, Goals, and Expectations," *Criminal Justice Review* 22, no. 2 (1997), pp. 207–225.

46. Wesley G. Skogan, "Citizen Satisfaction with Police Encounters," *Police Quarterly* 8 (September 2005), pp. 298–321.

47. Bureau of Justice Statistics, *Black Victims of Violent Crime*, Table 2.

48. Stewart Wakeling, Miriam Jorgensen, Susan Michaelson, and Manley Begay, *Policing on American Indian Reservations: A Report to the National Institute of Justice*, NCJ 188095 (Washington, DC: U.S. Government Printing Office, 2001). Available at http://www.ncjrs.org.

49. Ibid., p. 9; William C. Canby, *American Indian Law* (St. Paul: West, 1998). Information on the federal Tribal Justice Initiative is available at http://www.Justice.gov/otj/.

50. Eileen M. Luna, "The Growth and Development of Tribal Police," *Journal of Contemporary Criminal Justice* 14, no. 1 (1998), pp. 75–86; Wakeling et al., *Policing on American Indian Reservations*, p. 7.

51. Bachman, et al., *Violence Against American Indians and Alaska Native Women and the Criminal Justice Response: What is Known*; Stewart Wakeling, Miriam Jorgensen, Susan Michaelson, and Manley Begay, *Policing on American Indian Reservations: A Report to the National Institute of Justice*, NCJ 188095 (Washington, DC: U.S. Government Printing Office, 2001). Available at http://www.ncjrs.org.

52. Bureau of Justice Statistics, *American Indians and Crime* (Washington, DC: Department of Justice, 1999). NCJ 173386; OJJDP, *Youth Gangs in Indian Country* (Washington, DC: Department of Justice, 2004); Eileen Luna-Firebaugh, "Violence Against Indian Women and the STOP VAIW Program," *Violence Against Women* 12 (2006), pp. 125–136.

53. Wakeling et al., *Policing on American Indian Reservations*; Clarice Fineman, "Police Problems on the Navajo Reservation," *Police Studies* 9 (Winter 1986), pp. 194–198.

54. Bureau of Justice Statistics, *Asian, Native Hawaiian, and Pacific Islander Victims of Crime* (Washington, DC: Department of Justice, 2009). NCJ 225037.

55. Arab American Anti-Discrimination Committee, *2003–2007 Report on Hate Crimes and Discrimination Against Arab Americans* (Washington, DC: ADC, 2008). Available at http://www.adc.org.

56. Ibid., pp. 29–30.

57. California Police Chiefs Association, letter to Attorney General John Ashcroft (April 10, 2002); Police Executive Research Forum, *Police Chiefs and Sheriffs Speak Out on Local Immigration Enforcement* (Washington, DC: PERF, 2008).

58. Police Executive Research Forum, *Police and Immigration: How Chiefs Are Leading their Communities Through the Challenges* (Washington, DC: Police Executive Research Forum, March 2011).

59. Search the Web for news media accounts about these two incidents.

60. Bureau of Justice Statistics, *Policing and Homicide, 1976–98*; James J. Fyfe, "Reducing the Use of Deadly Force: The New York Experience," in *Police Use of Deadly Force*, U.S. Department of Justice (Washington, DC: U.S. Government Printing Office, 1978), p. 29.

61. *Tennessee v. Garner*, 471 U.S. 1 (1985).

62. Jerry R. Sparger and David J. Giacopassi, "Memphis Revisited: A Reexamination of Police Shootings after the Garner Decision," *Justice Quarterly* 9 (June 1992), pp. 211–225. See also James J. Fyfe, "Blind Justice: Police Shootings in Memphis," *Journal of Criminal Law and Criminology* 73, no. 2 (1982), pp. 707–722.

63. William A. Geller and Kevin J. Karales, *Split-Second Decisions* (Chicago: Chicago Law Enforcement Study Group, 1981), p. 119.

64. "Officers Killed with Impunity," p. 1.

65. Bureau of Justice Statistics, *Policing and Homicide*, 1976–98.

66. Geller and Karales, *Split-Second Decisions*.

67. Lorie A. Fridell, "Deadly Force Policy and Practice: the Forces of Change," in Candace McCoy, ed., *Holding Police Accountable* (Washington, DC: Urban Institute Press, 2010), pp. 29–51. On the general movement to control discretion, Samuel Walker, *Taming the System: The Control of Discretion in Criminal Justice, 1950–1990* (New York: Oxford University Press, 1993).

68. James J. Fyfe, "Administrative Interventions on Police Shooting Discretion," *Journal of Criminal Justice* 7 (winter 1979), pp. 309–323; Jerry R. Sparger and David J. Giacopassi, "Memphis Revisited: A Reexamination of Police Shootings after the Garner Decision," *Justice Quarterly* 9 (June 1992), pp. 211–225; Bureau of Justice Statistics, *Policing and Homicide, 1976–98*.

69. New York State Task force on Police-on-Police Shootings, *Reducing Inherent Danger: Report of the Task Force on Police-on-Police Shootings* (Albany: New York State Task Force, 2010).

70. Commission to Investigate Allegations of Police Corruption [Mollen Commission], *Commission Report* (New York: City of New York, 1994), p. 48.

71. National Commission on Law Observance and Enforcement, *Lawlessness in Law Enforcement* (Washington, DC: U.S. Government Printing Office, 1931), p. 4.

72. Human Rights Watch, *Shielded from Justice: Police Brutality and Accountability in the United States* (New York: Author, 1998), p. 39.

73. Commission to Investigate Allegations of Police Corruption, *Commission Report*, p. 44, n. 4; New York City Civilian Complaint Review Board, *Status Report, January–December 2009, Statistical Appendices* (New York: CCRB, 2010), Table 2; Bureau of Justice Statistics, *Contacts Between Police and the Public*, 2005, p. 8.

74. The best review of the available studies is in Kenneth Adams, "Measuring the Prevalence of Police Abuse of Force," in *And Justice for All*, William A. Geller and Hans Toch, eds. (Washington, DC: Police Executive Research Forum, 1995), pp. 61–98; see also Anthony M. Pate and Lorie Fridell, *Police Use of Force*, 2 vols. (Washington, DC: Police Foundation, 1993).

75. Bureau of Justice Statistics, *Contacts Between Police and the Public*, 2005.

76. Bureau of Justice Statistics, *Contacts Between Police and the Public*, 2005 (Washington, DC: Department of Justice, 2007). NCJ 215243; BJS, *Contacts Between Police and the Public*, 2002.

77. Ibid.

78. Robert E. Worden, "The 'Causes' of Police Brutality: Theory and Evidence on Police Use of Force," in *And Justice for All*, Geller and Toch, eds.

79. Albert Reiss, *The Police and the Public* (New Haven, CT: Yale University Press, 1971); Donald Black, "The Social Organization of Arrest," in *The Manners and*

Customs of the Police, Donald Black, ed. (New York: Academic Press, 1980), pp. 85–108.

80. Reiss, *The Police and the Public*, pp. 149, 155.

81. New York City, Civilian Complaint Review Board, *Status Report January–December 2009, Statistical Appendices* (New York: CCRB, 2010), Table 9. Available at http://www.nyc.gov/html/ccrb/; San Jose Independent Police Auditor, *2004 Year End Report* (San Jose: Independent Police Auditor, 2005). Available at http://www.sanjoseca.gov/ipa.

82. Worden, "The 'Causes' of Police Brutality," pp. 52–53.

83. David Weisburd, Rosann Greenspan, Edwin E. Hamilton, Kellie A. Bryant, and Hubert Williams, *The Abuse of Police Authority: A National Study of Police Officers' Attitudes* (Washington, DC: Police Foundation, 2001).

84. Reiss, *The Police and the Public*, p. 151.

85. Ronald Weitzer and Steven A. Tuch, "Race and Perceptions of Police Misconduct," *Social Problems* 51, no. 4 (2004), pp. 305–325.

86. William Terrill, "Police Use of Nondeadly Force: From Determining Appropriateness to Assessing the Impact of Policy," in *Holding Police Accountable*, McCoy, ed., pp. 55–72.

87. Heather MacDonald, "Is the Criminal Justice System Racist?" *City Journal* 18 (Spring 2008).

88. Robert Tillman, "The Size of the Criminal Population: The Prevalence and Incidence of Adult Arrest," *Criminology* 25 (August 1987), pp. 561–579.

89. Federal Bureau of Investigation, *Crime in the United States* (Washington, DC: Department of Justice, annual).

90. Black, "The Social Organization of Arrest," pp. 85–108.

91. Douglas A. Smith, Christy Visher, and Laura A. Davidson, "Equity and Discretionary Justice: The Influence of Race on Police Arrest Decisions," *Journal of Criminal Law and Criminology* 75 (spring 1984), pp. 234–249; Douglas A. Smith and Christy A. Visher, "Street-Level Justice: Situational Determinants of Police Arrest Decisions," *Social Problems* 29 (December 1981), pp. 167–177.

92. Tammy Rinehart Kochel, David B. Wilson, and Stephen D. Mastrofski, "Effects of Suspect Race on Officers' Arrest Decisions," forthcoming *Criminology* (May 2011), as this edition is being written.

93. Black, "The Social Organization of Arrest."

94. David A. Klinger, "Demeanor or Crime? Why 'Hostile' Citizens Are More Likely to Be Arrested," *Criminology* 32, no. 3 (1994), pp. 475–493.

95. Federal Bureau of Investigation, *Crime in the United States, 2009* (Washington, DC: Department of Justice, 2010). Department of Health and Human Services, *Monitoring the Future* (2009).

96. Bureau of Justice Statistics, *Survey of State Criminal History Information Systems, 2008* (Washington, DC: Department of Justice, 2009).

97. Joan Petersilia, *When Prisoners Come Home: Parole and Prisoner Reentry* (New York: Oxford University Press, 2003), Ch. 6, "How We Hinder: Legal and Practical Barriers to Reintegration," pp. 105–137.

98. *United States v. City of Los Angeles*, No. 00-11-11769 (C.D. Cal. June 15, 2001) (Consent Decree). For details on federal consent decrees, see Samuel Walker,

The New World of Police Accountability (Thousand Oaks: Sage, 2005). Walker and Macdonald, "An Alternative Remedy for Police Misconduct." Additional information on consent decrees is available at http://samuelwalker.net.

99. Christopher Stone, Todd Fogelsong, and Christine M. Cole, *Policing Los Angeles Under a Consent Decree: The Dynamics of Change at the LAPD* (Cambridge: Harvard University, 2009). Available at http://samuelwalker.net.

100. Walker and Macdonald, "An Alternative Remedy for Police Misconduct."

101. Bureau of Justice Statistics, *Reducing Gun Violence: The Boston Gun Project's Operation Ceasefire* (Washington, DC: Department of Justice, 2001). Available at http://www. ncjrs.org. NCJ 188741.

102. Robin S. Engel. S. Gregory Baker, Marie Skubak Tillyer, John Eck, and Jessica Dunham, *Implementation of the Cincinnati Initiative to Reduce Violence (CIRV): Year 1 Report* (Cincinnati: University of Cincinnati, 2008); Anthony A. Braga, Glenn L. Pierce, Jack McDevitt, Brenda Bond, and Shea Cronin, "The Strategic Prevention of Gun Violence Among Gang-Involved Offenders," *Justice Quarterly* 25 (March 2008), pp. 132–162.

103. This point is argued in Samuel Walker, *Sense and Nonsense About Crime and Communities*, 7th ed. (Belmont: Cengage, 2011), pp. 128–130.

104. George L. Kelling and Catherine M. Coles, *Fixing Broken Windows* (New York: Free Press, 1996).

105. New York Civil Liberties Union, *Deflecting Blame* (New York: Author, 1998), p. 48; John E. Eck and Edward R. Maguire, "Have Changes in Policing Reduced Violent Crime? An Assessment of the Evidence," in *The Crime Drop in America*, Alfred Blumstein and Joel Wallman, eds. (New York: Cambridge University Press, 2000), pp. 224–228.

106. David Harris, *Profiles in Injustice: Why Racial Profiling Won't Work* (New York: New Press, 2001); ACLU, *Driving While Black* (New York: ACLU, 1999).

107. Bureau of Justice Statistics, *Sourcebook of Criminal Justice Statistics 2010*, Table 2.26.

108. Harris, *Profiles in Injustice*; ACLU, *Driving While Black*.

109. Police Executive Research Forum, *Racially Biased Policing*.

110. ACLU, *Driving While Black*.

111. Rights Working Group, *Faces of Racial Profiling: A Report from Communities Across America* (Washington, DC: Rights Working Group, September 2010). Available at http://www.rightsworkinggroup.org.

112. Albert J. Meehan and Michael J. Ponder, "Race and Place: The Ecology of Racial Profiling African American Motorists," *Justice Quarterly* 19 (September 2002), pp. 399–430.

113. Michael W. Smith, "Police-led Crackdowns and Cleanups: An Evaluation of a Crime Control Initiative in Richmond," *Crime and Delinquency* (2001), pp. 60–83.

114. Bureau of Justice Statistics, *Contacts between Police and the Public*, 2005.

115. Samuel Walker, *The New World of Police Accountability* (Thousand Oaks, CA: Sage, 2005); Lorie A. Fridell, *By the Numbers: A Guide for Analyzing Race Data from Traffic Stops* (Washington, DC: Police Executive Research Forum, 2004).

116. San Jose Police Department, *Vehicle Stop Demographic Study: First Report* (San Jose: San Jose Police Department, 1999).

117. Samuel Walker, "Searching for the Denominator: Problems with Police Traffic Stop Data and an Early Warning System Solution," *Justice Research and Policy* 3 (Spring 2001), pp. 63–95.

118. Bureau of Justice Statistics, *Contact Between Police and the Public: Findings from the 2002 National Survey*, Table 7.

119. L. D. Johnston, J. G. Bachman, and P. M. O'Malley, *Monitoring the Future: Questionnaire Responses from the Nation's High School Seniors, 2009* (Ann Arbor, MI: Institute for Social Research, 2009), Question C27, page 26.

120. Harris, *Profiles in Injustice.*

121. Walker, "Searching for the Denominator."

122. Internal benchmarking is explained in Walker, *The New World of Police Accountability*, pp. 111-115; Fridell, *By the Numbers*, pp. 143–160.

123. Police Executive Research Forum, *Racially Biased Policing.*

124. Ibid., pp. 51–53.

125. Sara E. Stoudtland, "The Multiple Dimensions of Trust in Resident/Police Relations in Boston," *Journal of Research in Crime and Delinquency* 38 (August 2001), pp. 226–256.

126. Current information about data collection laws and data reports is available at http://www.profilesininjustice.com.

127. Walker, *The New World of Police Accountability*; Walker and Macdonald, "An Alternative Remedy for Police Misconduct." The New Jersey consent decree and others are available on the U.S. Department of Justice website (http://www.usdoj.gov/crt/split).

128. The case is discussed in Harris, *Profiles in Injustice*, and Harris is largely responsible for popularizing the term "driving while black."

129. General Accounting Office, *U.S. Customs Service: Better Targeting of Airline Passengers for Personal Searches Could Produce Better Results*, GAO/GGD-00-38 (March 2000).

130. Harris, *Profiles in Injustice.*

131. Warren and Tomaskovic-Devey, "Racial Profiling and Searches."

132. David A. Harris, "Leveraging the Politics of Racial Profiling to Effectuate Reform," *Criminology and Public Policy* 8, no. 2 (2009), pp. 381–386.

133. This point is argued in Walker, *Sense and Nonsense About Crime and Communities*, 7th ed., pp. 139–141. It is based on the analysis by James B. Jacobs, *Drunk Driving: An American Dilemma* (Chicago: University of Chicago Press, 1989). Walker applies the argument to policies related to drugs.

134. Bureau of Justice Statistics, *Contacts Between Police and the Public, 2005* (Washington, DC: Department of Justice, 2007). NCJ 215243.

135. National Advisory Commission, *Report*, pp. 301, 304–305.

136. "Minorities Frisked More, But Arrest Rate Is Same," *New York Times*, May 13, 2010. An earlier lawsuit that challenged the NYPD practices was settled in 2003: *Daniels, et al.,* v. *City of New York*. A second lawsuit, *Floyd* v. *New York City*, is pending.

137. Heather MacDonald, "Fighting Crime Where the Criminals Are," *New York Times*, June 26, 2010.

138. Jerome Skolnick, *Justice without Trial: Law Enforcement in a Democratic Society*, 3rd ed. (New York: Macmillan, 1994), pp. 44–47.

139. Roger G. Dunham, Geoffrey P. Alpert, Megan S. Stroshine, and Katherine Bennett, "Transforming Citizens into Suspects: Factors that Influence the Formation of Police Suspicion," *Police Quarterly* 8 (September 2005), pp. 366–393.

140. Randall Kennedy, *Race, Crime, and the Law* (New York: Vintage Books, 1998), p. 137.

141. Ibid., pp. 151, 153.

142. Mervin F. White, Terry C. Cox, and Jack Basehart, "Theoretical Considerations of Officer Profanity and Obscenity in Formal Contacts with Citizens," in *Police Deviance*, 2nd ed., Thomas Barker and David L. Carter, eds. (Cincinnati: Anderson, 1991), pp. 275–297; John Van Maanen, "The Asshole," in *Policing: A View from the Street*, John Van Maanen and Peter Manning, eds. (Santa Monica, CA: Goodyear, 1978), pp. 221–238.

143. San Francisco, Office of Citizen Complaints, *Quarterly Reports, Second Quarter 2010* (San Francisco: Office of Citizen Complaints, 2010). Available at http://www.sfgov3.org/index.aspx?page=419.

144. Douglas A. Smith, Nanette Graham, and Bonney Adams, "Minorities and the Police: Attitudinal and Behavioral Questions," in *Race and Criminal Justice*, Michael J. Lynch and E. Britt Patterson, eds. (New York: Harrow & Heston, 1991), p. 31.

145. Bayley and Mendelsohn, *Minorities and the Police*, p. 144.

146. Ibid., pp. 15–18.

147. Smith et al., "Minorities and the Police," p. 28.

148. Reiss, *The Police and the Public*, p. 147.

149. David Alan Sklansky, "Not Your Father's Police Department: Making Sense of the New Demographics of Law Enforcement," *Journal of Criminal Law and Criminology* 96 (Spring 2006), pp. 1,209–1,243. Samuel Walker, "Racial-Minority and Female Employment in Policing: The Implications of 'Glacial' Change," *Crime and Delinquency* 31 (October 1985), pp. 555–572.

150. Weisburd et al., *The Abuse of Police Authority*.

151. Jerome L. Blakemore, David Barlow, and Deborah L. Padgett, "From the Classroom to the Community: Introducing Process in Police Diversity Training," *Police Studies* 18, no. 1 (1995), pp. 71–83.

152. Geoffrey P. Alpert, William C. Smith, and Daniel Watters, "Law Enforcement: Implications of the Rodney King Beating," *Criminal Law Bulletin* 28 (September–October 1992), p. 477.

153. City of New York, *Commission Report*.

154. Bureau of Justice Statistics, *Sourcebook of Criminal Justice Statistics, online edition, Table 2.21 2008*.

155. Police Foundation, Metropolitan Police Department, *Biased Policing, Final Report*, p. 81.

156. Fred A. Klyman and Joanna Kruckenberg, "A National Survey of Police–Community Relations Units," *Journal of Police Science and Administration* 7 (March 1979), p. 74.

157. U.S. Department of Justice, *Improving Police/Community Relations* (Washington, DC: Department of Justice, 1973).

158. Wesley G. Skogan and Susan M. Hartnett, *Community Policing: Chicago Style* (New York: Oxford University Press, 1997).

159. Weitzer and Tuch, "Race and Perceptions of Police Misconduct."

160. Skogan and Hartnett, *Community Policing: Chicago Style*, p. 217.

161. Wesley Skogan et al., *Community Policing and The New Immigrants: Latinos in Chicago* (Washington, DC: Department of Justice, 2002). NCJ 189908.

162. San Jose Police Department, *Vehicle Stop Demographic Study*.

163. PolicyLink, *Community-Centered Policing: A Force for Change* (Oakland, CA: Department of Justice, PolicyLink, 2001), pp. 16–20. Available at http://www.policylink.org.

164. U.S. Department of Justice, *Youth Violence*.

165. Samuel Walker, *120 Shots: What Real Police Accountability Looks Like* (2005). Available at http://samuelwalker.net.

166. National Academy of Sciences, *Fairness and Effectiveness in Policing: The Evidence* (Washington, DC: National Academy Press, 2004), p. 298.

167. Skogan and Hartnett, *Community Policing, Chicago Style*.

168. Lind and Tyler, *The Social Psychology of Procedural Justice*.

169. Bureau of Justice Statistics, *Contacts Between Police and the Public*, 2005.

170. Georgetown University website (http://www.georgetown.edu).

171. New York City Police Department, *Fact Sheet, New York City's Arab Communities*. Go to the NYPD website, "Community Affairs" page, for more recent information on outreach to immigrant communities. http://nyc.gov/html/nypd/html/community_affairs/special_outreach_programs.shtml.

172. Charlotte-Mecklenburg Police Department, International Unit, *Law Enforcement Services to a Growing International Community*. The report is no longer on the department website but is available at http://samuelwalker.net at "Innovations."

173. Samuel Walker, *Police Accountability: The Role of Citizen Oversight* (Belmont, CA: Wadsworth, 2001).

174. New York City Civilian Complaint Review Board, *Status Report, January–December 2009* (New York: Civilian Complaint Review Board, 2010), p. 16. Available at http://www.nyc.gov/html/ccrb/pdf/ccrbann2009.pdf.

175. Cecilia Menjivar and Cynthia L. Bejarano, "Latino Immigrants' Perceptions of Crime and Police Authorities in the United States: A Case Study from the Phoenix Metropolitan Area," *Ethnic and Racial Studies* 27 (January 2004), pp. 120–148.

176. Human Rights Watch, *Shielded from Justice*, pp. 63–65.

177. Police Foundation, Metropolitan Police Department, *Biased Policing Project, Final Report* (Washington, DC: Police Foundation, 2004).

178. Samuel Walker and Nanette Graham, "Citizen Complaints in Response to Police Misconduct: The Results of a Victimization Survey," *Police Quarterly* 1 (1998), pp. 65–89.

179. National Advisory Commission, *Report*. Christopher Commission, *Report of the Independent Commission*, Los Angeles: Christopher Commission, 1991, pp. 153–161. ACLU of Southern California, *The Call for Change Goes Unanswered* (Los Angeles: Author, 1992), p. 23.

180. William A. Westley, *Violence and the Police* (Cambridge, MA: MIT Press, 1970).

181. Christopher Commission, *Report of the Independent Commission*, p. 168.

182. City of New York, *Commission Report*, p. 53.

183. Pate and Fridell, *Police Use of Force*, vol. 1, p. 118. A discussion of the reasons why so few complaints are sustained is in Walker, *Police Accountability*, pp. 121–137.

184. Samuel Walker, Carol Archbold, and Leigh Herbst, *Mediating Citizen Complaints* (Washington, DC: Department of Justice, 2002).

185. Walker, *Police Accountability*, p. 6.

186. Information about different citizen oversight agencies is available at http://www.nacole.org.

187. Walker, *Police Accountability*, p. 122.

188. David Alan Sklansky, "Not Your Father's Police Department: Making Sense of the New Demographics of Law Enforcement," *Journal of Criminal Law and Criminology* 96 (Spring 2006), pp. 1,209–1,243.

189. W. Marvin Dulaney, *Black Police in America* (Bloomington, IN: Indiana University Press, 1996); President's Commission on Law Enforcement and Administration of Justice, *Task Force Report: The Police* (Washington, DC: U.S. Government Printing Office, 1967), p. 168.

190. "From Court Order to Reality: A Diverse Boston Police Force," *New York Times* (April 4, 2001), p. 1.

191. Bureau of Justice Statistics, *Local Police, 2003*.

192. Commission on Accreditation for Law Enforcement Agencies, *Standards for Law Enforcement Agencies*, 3rd ed., Standard 31–2 (Fairfax, VA: Author, 1994).

193. Samuel Walker and K. B. Turner, *A Decade of Modest Progress* (Omaha, NE: University of Nebraska at Omaha, 1992).

194. New York City, Civilian Complaint Review Board, *Status Report January–December 2009, Statistical Appendices*.

195. "From Court Order to Reality," p. 1.

196. Christopher Commission, *Report of the Independent Commission*.

197. Bureau of Justice Statistics, *Law Enforcement Management and Administrative Statistics, 2000*, Table 3a.

198. Herbst and Walker, "Language Barriers in the Delivery of Police Services."

199. Bureau of Justice Statistics, *Law Enforcement Management and Administrative Statistics, 2000*.

200. U. S. Department of Labor, Office of Federal Contract Compliance, *Employment Standards Administration* (n.d.).

201. PolicyLink, *Community-Centered Policing*, p. 33.

202. *Parents Involved in Community Schools v. Seattle*, 551 U.S. 701(2007); *Meredith v. Jefferson County*, 551 U.S. 782 (2007).

203. Gunnar Myrdal, "Police and Other Public Contacts," in *An American Dilemma* (New York: Harper & Brothers, 1944); W. Marvin Dulaney, *Black Police in America* (Bloomington, IN: Indiana University Press, 1996).

204. Reiss, *The Police and the Public*, p. 167.

205. James J. Fyfe, "Who Shoots? A Look at Officer Race and Police Shooting," *Journal of Police Science and Administration* 9, no. 4 (1981), pp. 367–382.

206. Merrick J. Bobb, Special Counsel, *9th Semiannual Report* (Los Angeles: Los Angeles County, 1998), pp. 59–61. Available at http://www.parc.info.

207. "For Black Officers, Diversity Has Its Limits," *New York Times* (April 2, 2001), p. 1; "Alone, Undercover, and Black: Hazards of Mistaken Identity," *New York Times* (November 22, 1992), p. A1. New York State Task Force on Police-on-Police Shootings, Reducing Inherent Danger: Report of the Task Force on Police-on-Police Shootings (Albany, June 2010). Available at http://samuelwalker.net, at "Innovations."

208. "Alienation Is a Partner for Black Officers," *New York Times* (April 3, 2001), p. 1; New York State Task force on Police-on-Police Shootings, *Reducing Inherent Danger: Report of the Task Force on Police-on-Police Shootings.*

209. The Kerner Commission, for example, argued that "Negro officers can also be particularly effective in controlling disorders"; National Advisory Commission, *Report*, p. 315.

210. James J. Fyfe, "Who Shoots?: A Look at Officer Race and Police Shootings," *Journal of Police Science and Administration* 9 (No. 4, 1981), pp. 367–382. Donald Black, *The Manners and Customs of the Police* (New York: Acadmic Press, 1980). Albert J. Reiss, "Police Brutality – Answers to Key Questions," *Transaction* 5 (July–August), pp. 10–19. Lawrence W. Sherman, "The Causes of Police Behavior: The Current State of Quantitative Research," *Journal of Research in Crime and Delinquency* 17 (No 1, 1980), pp. 69–100.

211. Albert Reiss, *The Police and the Public*, pp. 209–210.

212. PolicyLink, *Community-Centered Policing*, pp. 36–37.

213. "Los Angeles Force Accused from Within," *New York Times* (March 29, 1991), p. A18.

214. National Black Police Officers Association, *Police Brutality: A Strategy to Stop the Violence* (Washington, DC: Author, n.d.).

215. Weisburd et al., *The Abuse of Police Authority.*

216. Skogan and Hartnett, *Community Policing, Chicago Style.*

217. Robin N. Haarr, "Patterns of Interaction in a Police Patrol Bureau: Race and Gender Barriers to Integration," *Justice Quarterly* 14 (March 1997), pp. 53–85.

218. Frank et al., "Reassessing the Impact of Race on Citizens' Attitudes toward the Police."

219. Samuel Walker, Susan E. Martin, and K. B. Turner, "Through the Glass Ceiling? Promotion Rates for Minority and Female Police Officers." Paper presented at the American Society of Criminology, November 1994.

5

The Courts

A Quest for Justice during the Pretrial Process

> [I]t is clear to me that if America ever is to eradicate racism,
> lawyers will have to lead. We must cleanse the justice system,
> because until the justice system is truly colorblind, we cannot
> have any genuine hope for the elimination of bias in the
> other segments of American life.
>
> PHILIP S. ANDERSON, PRESIDENT, AMERICAN BAR ASSOCIATION[1]

GOALS OF THE CHAPTER

In this chapter and in Chapter 6, we discuss the treatment of racial minorities in court. The focus in this chapter is on pretrial decision making. Our goal is to determine whether people of color are more likely than whites to be tried without adequate counsel to represent them or to be denied bail or detained in jail prior to trial. In addition, we review research on prosecutors' charging and plea bargaining decisions for evidence of differential treatment of racial minorities and whites. We argue that recent reforms adopted voluntarily by the states or mandated by court decisions have reduced, but not eliminated, racial discrimination in the pretrial process.

After you have read this chapter:

- You will be able to explain the concept of "double jeopardy" as it applies to racial minorities who appear in court as criminal defendants.

- You will be able to discuss the right to counsel and explain how the U.S. Supreme Court has interpreted the right.

- You will be able to evaluate arguments regarding the quality of legal representation provided to indigent defendants.

- You will be able to assess whether affirmative action has helped or hurt African American law students.

- You will be able to explain how decisions regarding bail and charging are affected by race/ethnicity and how these decisions, in turn, influence sentence severity.

- You will be able to evaluate arguments regarding selective prosecution of African American pregnant women who abuse drugs.

AFRICAN AMERICANS IN COURT: THE CASE OF THE SCOTTSBORO BOYS

In March 1931, nine African American teenage boys were accused of raping two white girls on a slow-moving freight train traveling through Alabama. They were arrested and taken to Scottsboro, Alabama, where they were indicted for rape, a capital offense. One week later, the first case was called for trial. When the defendant appeared without counsel, the judge hearing the case simply appointed all members of the local bar to represent him and his co-defendants. An out-of-state lawyer also volunteered to assist in the defendants' defense, but the judge appointed no counsel of record.

The nine defendants were tried and convicted, and eight were sentenced to death. They appealed their convictions, arguing that their right to counsel had been denied. In 1932 the United States Supreme Court issued its ruling in the case of *Powell* v. *Alabama*,[2] one of the most famous Supreme Court cases in U.S. history. The Court reversed the defendants' convictions and ruled that due process of law required the appointment of counsel for young, inexperienced, illiterate, and indigent defendants in capital cases.

The Supreme Court's ruling in *Powell* provided the so-called Scottsboro Boys with only a short reprieve. They were quickly retried, reconvicted, and resentenced to death, despite the fact that one of the alleged victims had recanted and questions were raised about the credibility of the other victim's testimony. Once again, the defendants appealed their convictions, this time contending that their right to a fair trial by an impartial jury had been denied. All of the defendants had been tried by all-white juries. They argued that the jury selection procedures used in Alabama were racially biased. Although African Americans who were registered to vote were eligible for jury service, they were excluded in practice because state officials refused to place their names on the lists from which jurors were chosen. In 1935, the Supreme Court, noting that the exclusion of all African Americans from jury service deprived African American defendants of their right to the equal protection of the laws guaranteed by the Fourteenth Amendment, again reversed the convictions.[3]

The Supreme Court's decision was harshly criticized in the South. The Charleston *News and Courier*, for example, stated that racially mixed juries were "out of the question" and asserted that the Court's decision "can and will be evaded."[4] Southern sentiment also strongly favored yet another round of trials. Thomas Knight, Jr., the attorney who prosecuted the Scottsboro cases the second time, noted that "Approximately ninety jurors have been found saying the defendants were guilty of the offense with which they are charged and for which the penalty is death." Knight reported that he had been "retained by the State to prosecute the cases and [would] prosecute the same to their conclusion."[5]

Less than eight months after the Supreme Court's decision, a grand jury composed of 13 whites and 1 African American returned new indictments against the nine defendants. Haywood Patterson, the first defendant to be retried, again faced an all-white jury. Although there were 12 African Americans among the 100 potential jurors, 7 of the 12 asked to be excused and the prosecutor used his peremptory challenges to remove the remaining 5 African Americans. In his closing argument, the prosecutor also implied that an acquittal would force the women of Alabama "to buckle six-shooters about their middles" in order to protect their "sacred secret parts." He pleaded with the jurors to "Get it done quick and protect the fair womanhood of this great State."[6]

Patterson was convicted and sentenced to 75 years in prison. The sentence, although harsh, represented "a victory of sorts."[7] As the Birmingham *Age-Herald* noted, the decision "represents probably the first time in the history of the South that a Negro has been convicted of a charge of rape upon a white woman and has been given less than a death sentence."[8]

Three of the remaining eight defendants were tried and convicted in July 1937. One of the three, Clarence Norris, was sentenced to death; the other two received prison sentences of 75 and 99 years. Shortly thereafter, Ozie Powell pled guilty to assaulting an officer after the state agreed to dismiss the rape charge. That same day, in an unexpected and controversial move, the state dropped all charges against the remaining four defendants. In a prepared statement, Attorney General Thomas Lawson asserted that the state was "convinced beyond any question of doubt ... that the defendants that have been tried are guilty." However, "after careful consideration of all the testimony, every lawyer connected with the prosecution is convinced that the defendants Willie Roberson and Olen Montgomery are not guilty." Regarding the remaining two defendants, who were 12 and 13 years old when the crime occurred, Dawson stated that "the ends of justice would be met at this time by releasing these two juveniles on condition that they leave the State, never to return."[9]

The state's decision to drop charges against four of the nine defendants led editorial writers for newspapers throughout the United States to call for the immediate release of the defendants who previously had been convicted. The Richmond *Times-Dispatch* stated that the state's action "serves as a virtual clincher to the argument that all nine of the Negroes are innocent," and the *New York Times* called on the state to "do more complete justice later on."[10]

Charles Norris's death sentence was commuted to life imprisonment in 1938, but the Alabama Pardon and Parole Board repeatedly denied the five defendants' requests for parole. One of the defendants finally was granted parole in 1943, and by 1950 all of them had gained their freedom. Collectively, the nine Scottsboro Boys served 104 years in prison for a crime that many believe was "almost certainly, a hoax."[11]

THE SITUATION TODAY

The infamous Scottsboro Case illustrates overt discrimination directed against African American criminal defendants. However, those events took place in the 1930s and 1940s, and much has changed since then. Legislative reforms and Supreme Court decisions protecting the rights of criminal defendants, coupled with changes in attitudes, have made it less likely that criminal justice officials will treat defendants of different races differently. Racial minorities are no longer routinely denied bail and then tried by all-white juries without attorneys to assist them in their defense. They are no longer brought into court in chains and shackles. They no longer receive "justice" at the hands of white lynch mobs.

Despite these reforms, inequities persist. Racial minorities, and particularly those suspected of crimes against whites, remain the victims of unequal justice. In 1983, for example, Lenell Geter, an African American man, was charged with the armed robbery of a Kentucky Fried Chicken restaurant in Balch Springs, Texas. Despite the absence of any physical evidence to connect him to the crime and despite the prosecution's failure to establish his motive for the crime, Geter was convicted by an all-white jury and sentenced to life in prison.

Geter's conviction was particularly surprising given the fact that he had an ironclad alibi. Nine of his coworkers, all of whom were white, testified that Geter was at work on the day of the crime. His supervisor testified that there was no way Geter could have made the 50-mile trip from work to the site of the crime by 3:20 P.M., the time the robbery occurred. According to one coworker, "Unless old Captain Kirk dematerialized him and beamed him over there, he couldn't have made it back by then. He was here at work. There's no question in my mind—none at all."[12]

Prosecutors in the county where Geter was tried denied that race played a role in Geter's conviction. As one of them put it, "To say this is a conviction based on race is as far out in left field as you can get."[13] Geter's coworkers disagreed; they argued that Geter and his codefendant (who also was African American) would not have been charged or convicted if they had been white.

Events that occurred following the trial suggest that Geter's coworkers were right. Another man arrested for a series of armed robberies eventually was linked to the robbery of the Kentucky Fried Chicken restaurant. Geter's conviction and sentence were overturned after the employees who originally identified Geter picked this suspect out of a lineup. Geter served more than a year in prison for a crime he did not commit.

Like Lenell Geter, James Newsome, an African American sentenced to life in prison for the armed robbery and murder of a white man, also had an alibi. At his trial for the 1979 murder of Mickey Cohen, the owner of Mickey's Grocery Store in Chicago, Newsome's girlfriend and her two sisters testified that he was with them at the time of the murder. The prosecutor trying the case argued that Newsome's girlfriend, who was a convicted burglar, was not a credible witness. He also introduced the testimony of three eyewitnesses who identified Newsome as Cohen's killer.[14]

Despite the fact that there was no physical evidence linking Newsome to the crime, and despite the fact that Newsome's fingerprints were not found on the items in the store handled by the killer, the jury hearing the case found Newsome guilty. Although Cook County prosecutors had sought the death penalty, the jury recommended life in prison.

Newsome, who steadfastly maintained his innocence, spent the next 15 years appealing his conviction. With the help of Norval Morris, a University of Chicago Law School Professor, and two noted Chicago defense attorneys, Newsome was able to convince the Cook County Circuit Court to order that the fingerprints obtained from the crime scene be run through the police department's computerized fingerprint database to see if they matched any of those on file. The tests revealed that the fingerprints matched those of Dennis Emerson, a 45-year-old Illinois death row inmate who, at the time of Cohen's murder, was out on parole after serving 3 years for armed robbery.

Two weeks later, Newsome was released from prison. Shortly thereafter, Illinois governor Jim Edgar pardoned Newsome and ordered his criminal record expunged. Following his release, James Newsome, who spent 15 years in prison for a crime he did not commit, said, "I finally felt vindicated. I had defeated a criminal-justice giant. Fifteen years ago, they told me that I would never walk the streets again in my life. What did I do? I slayed a giant—a criminal justice giant."[15]

Like Geter, Newsome contended that race played a role in his arrest and conviction. "In the most [racially] polarized city in the world," Newsome stated, "racism was a factor. I was a suspect and I was convenient."[16]

Race also played a role in the case of Clarence Brandley, an African American who in 1981 was sentenced to death for the rape and murder of Cheryl Dee Ferguson, a white student at a high school north of Houston where Brandley worked as a janitor. Brandley and a coworker found the body and were the initial suspects in the case. Brandley's coworker, who was white, reported that during their interrogation one of the police officers stated, "One of you two is going to hang for this." Then he turned to Brandley and said, "Since you're the nigger, you're elected."[17] The police investigating the case claimed that three hairs found on the victim implicated Brandley. Although the hairs were never forensically tested, the police claimed that they were identical "in all observable characteristics" to Brandley's.

Brandley was indicted by an all-white grand jury and tried before an all-white jury, which hung 11-to-1 in favor of conviction. He was retried by a second all-white jury after the district attorney trying the case used his peremptory challenges to strike all of the prospective African American jurors. During his closing argument, the district attorney referred to Brandley as a "necrophiliac" and a "depraved sex maniac." This time, the jurors found Brandley guilty and recommended a death sentence, which the judge imposed.

Brandley spent six years on death row before a Texas district court, citing misconduct on the part of police and prosecutors, threw out his conviction. The judge, who noted that there was strong evidence that the crime was committed by two white men, stated that "the color of Clarence Brandley's skin was a substantial factor which pervaded all aspects of the State's capital prosecution against him, and was an impermissible factor which significantly influenced the investigation, trial and post-trial proceedings of [Brandley's] case."[18]

These three recent cases, of course, do not prove that there is a pattern of *systematic* discrimination directed against racial minorities in courts throughout the United States. One might argue, in fact, that these three cases are simply exceptions to the general rule of impartiality. As we explained in Chapter 1, the validity of the discrimination thesis rests not on anecdotal evidence but on the results of empirical studies of criminal justice decision making.

DECISIONS REGARDING COUNSEL AND BAIL

As we explained in Chapter 3, racial minorities are at a disadvantage in court both because of their race and because they are more likely than whites to be poor. This "double jeopardy" makes it more difficult for minority defendants to obtain competent attorneys or secure release from jail prior to trial. This, in turn, hinders their defense and may increase the odds that they will be convicted and sentenced harshly. Given these consequences, decisions regarding provision of counsel and bail obviously are important.

Racial Minorities and the Right to Counsel

The Sixth Amendment to the U.S. Constitution states, "In all criminal prosecutions, the accused shall enjoy the right to have the assistance of counsel for his defense." Historically, this meant simply that if someone had an attorney, he could bring the attorney along to defend him. The problem, of course, was that this was of no help to the majority of defendants, and particularly minority defendants, who were too poor to hire their own attorneys.

The U.S. Supreme Court, recognizing that defendants could not obtain fair trials without the assistance of counsel, began to interpret the Sixth Amendment to require the appointment of counsel for indigent defendants. The process began in 1932, when the Court ruled in *Powell* v. *Alabama*[19] that states must provide attorneys for indigent defendants charged with capital crimes (see the earlier discussion of the Scottsboro case). The Court's decision in a 1938 case, *Johnson* v. *Zerbst*,[20] required the appointment of counsel for all indigent defendants in federal criminal cases, but the requirement was not extended to the states until *Gideon* v. *Wainwright*[21] was decided in 1963. In that 1963 decision, Justice Black's majority opinion stated:

> [R]eason and reflection require us to recognize that in our adversary system of criminal justice, any person haled into court, who is too poor to hire a lawyer, cannot be assured a fair trial unless counsel is provided for him.... The right of one charged with crime to counsel may not be deemed fundamental and essential to fair trials in some countries, but it is in ours.

In subsequent decisions, the Court ruled that "no person may be imprisoned, for any offense, whether classified as petty, misdemeanor, or felony, unless he is represented by counsel,"[22] and that the right to counsel is not limited to trial but applies to all "critical stages" in the criminal justice process.[23] As a result of these rulings, most defendants must be provided with counsel from arrest and interrogation through sentencing and the appellate process. As illustrated in Box 5.1, the Supreme Court also has ruled that defendants are entitled to *effective* assistance of counsel.[24]

At the time the *Gideon* decision was handed down, 13 states had no statewide requirement for appointment of counsel except in capital cases.[25] Other states relied on members of local bar associations to defend indigents, often on a *pro bono* basis. Following *Gideon*, it became obvious that other procedures would be required if all felony defendants were to be provided attorneys.

States moved quickly to implement the constitutional requirement articulated in *Gideon*, either by establishing public defender systems or by appropriating money for court-appointed attorneys. The number of public defender systems grew rapidly. In 1951 there were only 7 public defender organizations in the United States; in 1964 there were 136; by 1973 the total had increased to 573.[26] A 1994 survey of indigent defense services among all U.S. prosecutorial districts found that 21 percent used a public defender program, 19 percent used an assigned counsel system, and 7 percent used a contract attorney system; the remaining districts (43 percent) reported that a combination of methods was used.[27] A survey of inmates incarcerated in state and federal prisons in 1997 revealed that about 73 percent of the state inmates and 60 percent of the federal inmates were represented by a public defender or assigned counsel. This survey also revealed that African Americans and Hispanics were more likely than whites to be represented by a public defender or assigned counsel. Among state prison inmates, for example, 77 percent of the African Americans, 73 percent of the Hispanics, and 69 percent of the whites reported that they were represented by a publicly funded attorney.[28]

Quality of Legal Representation   As a result of Supreme Court decisions expanding the right to counsel and the development of federal and state policies implementing these decisions, African Americans and other racial minorities are no longer routinely denied legal representation at trial or at any of the other critical stages in the process. Questions have been raised, however, about the

---

B o x 5.1   The Supreme Court and "Effective" Assistance of Counsel

In 1984 the Supreme Court articulated constitutional standards for determining whether a defendant had ineffective assistance of counsel. The Court ruled, in the case of *Strickland* v. *Washington* (466 U.S. 668 [1984], at 687), that to establish ineffectiveness, a defendant must prove:

- First, "that counsel's performance was deficient. This requires showing that counsel made errors so serious that counsel was not functioning as the 'counsel' guaranteed the defendant by the Sixth Amendment."

- Second, "that the deficient performance prejudiced the defense. This requires showing that counsel's errors were so serious as to deprive the defendant of a fair trial, a trial whose result is reliance."

The Court also stated that to establish ineffectiveness, a "defendant must show that counsel's representation fell below an objective standard of reasonableness." To establish prejudice, he or she "must show that there is a reasonable probability that, but for counsel's unprofessional errors, the result of the proceeding would have been different."

The Court revisited this issue in 2000, ruling that Terry Williams had been denied effective assistance of counsel (*Williams* v. *Taylor* 529 U.S. 420 [2000]). Williams was convicted of robbery and murder and sentenced to death after a Virginia jury concluded that he had a high probability of future dangerousness.

At the sentencing hearing, Williams's lawyer failed to introduce evidence that Williams was borderline mentally retarded and did not advance beyond sixth grade. He also failed to introduce the testimony of prison officials, who described Williams as among the inmates "least likely to act in a violent, dangerous, or provocative way." Instead, Williams's lawyer spent most of his time explaining that he realized it would be difficult for the jury to find a reason to spare Williams's life. His comments included the following: "I will admit too that it is very difficult to ask you to show mercy to a man who maybe has not shown much mercy himself.... Admittedly, it is very difficult to ... ask that you give this man mercy when he has shown so little of it himself. But I would ask that you would."

The Supreme Court ruled that Williams's right to effective assistance of counsel had been violated. According to the Court, "there was a reasonable probability that the result of the sentencing proceeding would have been different if competent counsel had presented and explained the significance of all the available evidence."

---

quality of legal representation provided to indigent defendants by public defenders. An article in the *Harvard Law Review*, for example, claimed:

> Nearly four decades after *Gideon*, the states have largely, and often outrageously, failed to meet the Court's constitutional command. The widespread, lingering deficiencies in the quality of indigent counsel have led some to wonder whether this right, so fundamental to a fair and accurate adversarial criminal process, is unenforceable.[29]

A 2003 report on Mississippi's indigent defense system reached a similar conclusion. The authors of the report, who noted that the system was "among the most poorly funded in the nation," concluded that "in Mississippi justice is available only to those with the means to pay for it. And sadly, our country's shameful history of racial discrimination is still readily apparent in the low quality representation provided to the State's poor, predominately black defendants."[30]

There is evidence suggesting that defendants share this view. In fact, one of the most oft-quoted statements about public defenders is the answer given by an unidentified prisoner in a Connecticut jail to the question of whether he had a lawyer when he went to court. "No," he replied, "I had a public defender."[31] David Neubauer similarly notes that in prison "'PD' stands not for 'public defender' but for 'prison deliverer.'"[32] Some social scientists echo this negative assessment, charging that public defenders, as part of the court-room workgroup, are more concerned with securing guilty pleas as efficiently and as expeditiously as possible than with aggressively defending their clients.[33] As Ronald Weitzer[34] notes (and as the examples in Box 5.2 confirm), "In many jurisdictions, public defenders and state-appointed attorneys are grossly underpaid, poorly trained, or simply lack the resources and time to prepare for a case—a pattern documented in cases ranging from the most minor to the most consequential, capital crimes."

Other social scientists disagree. Citing studies showing that criminal defendants represented by public defenders do not fare worse than those represented by private attorneys,[35] these researchers suggest that critics "have tended to underestimate the quality of defense provided by the public defender."[36] Paul B. Wice, in fact, concluded that the public defender is able to establish a working

---

B o x 5.2   Are Indigent Capital Defendants Represented by Incompetent Attorneys?

In "Judges and the Politics of Death," Stephen Bright and Patrick Keenan claimed, "Judges often fail to enforce the most fundamental protection of an accused, the Sixth Amendment right to counsel, by assigning an inexperienced or incompetent lawyer to represent the accused." In support of their assertion, they offered the following examples:

- A capital defendant who was represented by a lawyer who had passed the bar exam only six months earlier, had not taken any classes in criminal law or criminal procedure, and had never tried a jury or a felony trial.

- An attorney who described his client as "a little old nigger boy" during the penalty phase of the trial.

- A judge in Harris County, Texas, who responded to a capital defendant's complaints about his attorney sleeping during the trial with the assertion that, "The Constitution doesn't say the lawyer has to be awake."

- A Florida attorney who stated during the penalty phase of a capital case, "Judge, I'm at a loss. I really don't know what to do in this type of proceeding. If I'd been through one, I would, but I've never handled one except this time."

- A study of capital cases in Philadelphia that found that "even officials in charge of the system say they wouldn't want to be represented in Traffic Court by some of the people appointed to defend poor people accused of murder."

SOURCE: Stephen Bright and Patrick Keenan 1995, 800.

relationship with prosecutors and judges "in which the exchange of favors, so necessary to greasing the squeaky wheel of justice, can directly benefit the indigent defendant."[37] As part of the courtroom workgroup, in other words, public defenders are in a better position than private attorneys to negotiate favorable plea bargains and thus to mitigate punishment.

A 2000 report by the Bureau of Justice Statistics (BJS) revealed that case outcomes for state and federal defendants represented by public attorneys do not differ dramatically from those represented by private counsel.[38] There were only very slight differences in the conviction rates of defendants represented by public and private attorneys but somewhat larger differences in the incarceration rates. At the federal level, 87.6 percent of the defendants represented by public attorneys were sentenced to prison, compared with 76.5 percent of the defendants with private attorneys. The authors of the report attributed this to the fact that public counsel represented a higher percentage of violent, drug, and public-order offenders, whereas private attorneys represented a higher percentage of white-collar defendants. Felony defendants in state courts also faced lower odds of incarceration if they were represented by private attorneys (53.9 percent) rather than public defenders (71.3 percent). In both state and federal court, on the other hand, defendants represented by private attorneys got longer sentences than those represented by public defenders. At the federal level, the mean sentences were 58 months (public attorneys) and 62 months (private attorneys); at the state level, they were 31.2 months (public attorneys) and 38.3 months (private attorneys).[39]

Race, Type of Counsel, and Case Outcome   The data presented thus far do not address the question of racial discrimination in the provision of counsel. Although it is true that African American and Hispanic defendants are more likely than white defendants to be represented by public defenders, it does not necessarily follow from this that racial minorities will be treated more harshly than whites as their cases move through the criminal justice system. As we have noted, studies have not consistently shown that defendants represented by public defenders fare worse than defendants represented by private attorneys.

Most studies have not directly compared the treatment of African American, Hispanic, and white defendants represented by public defenders and private attorneys. It is possible that racial minorities represented by public defenders receive more punitive sentences than whites represented by public defenders, or that whites who hire their own attorneys receive more lenient sentences than racial minorities who hire their own attorneys. To put it another way, it is possible that hiring an attorney provides more benefits to whites than to racial minorities, and representation by a public defender has more negative consequences for racial minorities than for whites.

Malcolm D. Holmes, Harmon M. Hosch, Howard C. Daudistel, Dolores A. Perez, and Joseph B. Graves found evidence supporting these possibilities in one of the two Texas counties where they explored the interrelationships among race/ethnicity, legal resources, and case outcomes.[40] The authors of this study found that in Bexar County (San Antonio) both African American and Hispanic

T A B L E   5.1   **Race/Ethnicity and Type of Attorney in Chicago, Miami, and Kansas City**

| Race of Defendant | Percentage Represented by a Private Attorney | | |
	Chicago	Miami	Kansas City
White	22.5	34.5	37.8
African American	6.9	23.4	24.8
Hispanic	21.2	27.3	NA[a]

[a]There were only 47 Hispanic defendants in Kansas City.

defendants were significantly less likely than white defendants to be represented by a private attorney, even after such things as the seriousness of the crime, the defendant's prior criminal record, and the defendant's gender, age, and employment status were taken into account. The authors also found that defendants who retained a private attorney were more likely to be released prior to trial and received more lenient sentences than those represented by a public defender.[41] In this particular jurisdiction, then, African American and Hispanic defendants were less likely than whites to be represented by a private attorney and, as a result, they received more punitive treatment than whites.

An examination of the sentences imposed on defendants convicted of felonies in three large urban jurisdictions in 1993 and 1994 produced somewhat different results. Cassia Spohn and Miriam DeLone[42] compared the proportions of white, African American, and Hispanic defendants who were represented by a private attorney in Chicago, Miami, and Kansas City. As shown in Table 5.1, in all three jurisdictions whites were substantially more likely than African Americans to have private attorneys. In Chicago, 22.5 percent of white defendants, but only 6.9 percent of African American defendants, had a private attorney. In Miami, Hispanics also were less likely than whites to be represented by a private attorney.

Although the data presented in Table 5.1 reveal that smaller proportions of racial minorities than whites had access to the services of a private attorney, they do not provide evidence of differential treatment based on either type of attorney or race/ethnicity. In fact, when Spohn and DeLone examined the sentences imposed on racial minorities and whites in each jurisdiction, they found an interesting pattern of results. As shown in Figure 5.1, in Chicago and Kansas City only whites benefitted from having a private attorney. Among African Americans, the incarceration rates for defendants represented by private attorneys were only slightly lower than the rates for defendants represented by public defenders; among Hispanics in Chicago, the rate for defendants with private attorneys was actually somewhat *higher* than the rate for those with public defenders. In Miami, both whites and African Americans benefited from representation by private counsel, but Hispanics with private attorneys were sentenced to prison at a slightly *higher* rate than Hispanics represented by the public defender.

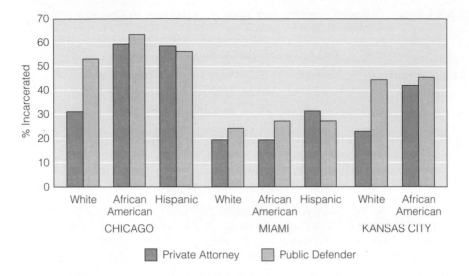

FIGURE 5.1 Race/Ethnicity, Type of Attorney, and Incarceration Rates in Chicago, Miami, and Kansas City

The incarceration rates displayed in Figure 5.1 do not take into account differences in the types of cases handled by private attorneys and public defenders. It is certainly possible that the incarceration rates for defendants represented by private attorneys generally are lower than the rates for defendants represented by public defenders, not because private attorneys are more experienced, more competent, and more zealous, but because the types of cases they handle are less serious or because the defendants they represent have less serious prior criminal records. If private attorneys, in other words, usually represent first offenders charged with relatively minor crimes and public defenders represent recidivists as well as first offenders and violent offenders as well as nonviolent offenders, we would expect the sentences imposed on defendants with private attorneys to be less severe than those imposed on defendants with public defenders, irrespective of the quality of representation provided by the attorney.

To test this possibility, Spohn and DeLone analyzed the relationship between race/ethnicity, type of attorney, and the likelihood of incarceration, controlling for several indicators of the seriousness of the crime and for the offender's prior criminal record, age, gender, and employment status. They found that, with one exception, the type of attorney had no effect on the odds of incarceration for any racial/ethnic group in any jurisdiction. The only exception was in Miami, where African Americans represented by private attorneys faced significantly lower odds of incarceration than African Americans represented by public defenders.

These results cast doubt on assertions that racial minorities are disadvantaged by their lack of access to private counsel. At least in these three jurisdictions, public defenders do not appear to "provide a lower caliber defense than what private attorneys offer."[43]

In summary, although it would be premature to conclude on the basis of research conducted to date either that decisions concerning the provision of counsel are racially neutral or that the consequences of these decisions for racial minorities are unimportant, significant changes have occurred since the 1930s. (See the "Focus on an Issue: Racial Minorities and the Legal Profession" box for a discussion of racial minorities and the legal profession.) It is clear that scenes from the infamous Scottsboro Case will not be replayed in the twenty-first century. The Supreme Court has consistently affirmed the importance of the right to counsel and has insisted that states provide attorneys to indigent criminal defendants at all critical stages in the criminal justice process. Although some critics have questioned the quality of legal services afforded indigent defendants, particularly in capital cases where the stakes are obviously very high, the findings of a number of methodologically sophisticated studies suggest that "indigent defenders get the job done and done well."[44] In short, it is no longer true that racial minorities "are without a voice"[45] in courts throughout the United States.

Racial Minorities and Bail Decision Making

Critics of the traditional money bail system, in which defendants either pay the amount set by the judge or pay a bail bondsman to post bond for them, argue that the system discriminates against poor defendants. They also charge that the system discriminates, either directly or indirectly, against racial minorities. Critics contend that historically African American and Hispanic defendants were more likely than white defendants to be detained prior to trial, either because the judge refused to set bail or because the judge set bail at an unaffordable level.[46] "As a result," according to one commentator, "the country's jails are packed to overflowing with the nation's poor—with red, brown, black, and yellow men and women showing up in disproportionate numbers."[47]

Bail Reform   Concerns about the rights of poor defendants and about the consequences of detention prior to trial led to the first bail reform movement, which emerged in the 1960s and emphasized reducing pretrial detention. Those who lobbied for reform argued that the purpose of bail was to ensure the defendant's appearance in court and that bail therefore should not exceed the amount necessary to guarantee that the defendant would show up for all court proceedings. Proponents of this view asserted that whether a defendant was released or detained prior to trial should not depend on his or her economic status or race. They also cited research demonstrating that the type and amount of bail imposed on the defendant and the time spent by the defendant in pretrial detention affected the likelihood of a guilty plea, the likelihood of conviction at trial, and the severity of the sentence.[48]

Focus on an Issue
Racial Minorities and the Legal Profession

In the early 1930s, one of the defendants in the Scottsboro case described the courtroom where he was convicted and sentenced to death as "one big smiling white face" (Carter 1969, 302). With the exception of the defendants themselves, no racial minorities were present in the courtroom.

Although the situation obviously has changed since then, racial minorities still represent a very small proportion of the lawyers and judges in the United States. Among those enrolled in law schools in 2003, only 20.6 percent were African American, Hispanic, Asian, or Native American.[49] In fact, a report on the Columbia Law School's website noted that although the number of first-year law students grew by nearly 3,000 from 1993 to 2008, the proportion of students who were African American declined by 7.5 percent and the percentage who were Hispanic declined by 11.7 percent.[50] There is even less racial diversity among practicing attorneys. In 2007, almost 90 percent of all licensed lawyers were white and only 10 percent were racial minorities: 4.9 percent were African American, 2.6 percent were Asian, and 4.3 percent were Hispanic.[51]

Racial minorities also comprise a very small proportion of the judiciary. A 2004 report by the American Bar Association revealed that only 10.1 percent of all state court judges were racial minorities. Of these judges, 5.9 percent were African American, 2.8 percent were Hispanic, 1.1 percent were Asian, and only 13 (0.1 percent) were Native American.[52] The situation is somewhat more positive at the federal level, where 11.3 of all district court judges and 6.9 percent of all court of appeals judges on the bench in 2000 were African American. Hispanics comprised 5.0 percent of the district court bench and 6.2 percent of the appellate court bench.

There were, however, very few Asian Americans or Native Americans on the federal bench.[53] Most of the racial minorities on the federal bench were men. Among district court judges, there were 54 African American men but only 16 African American women; there were 26 Hispanic men and 5 Hispanic women.[54]

The American Bar Association's 2000 report on the progress of minorities in the legal profession concluded that minority entry into the profession had stalled and that the obstacles to minority entry into the profession had grown more formidable. The report noted that the campaign to end affirmative action in law school admissions, which had spread rapidly throughout the United States, threatened "to stifle minority entry and advancement in the profession for years to come."[55] According to the American Bar Association, "the legal profession—already one of the least integrated professions in the country—threatens to become even less representative of the citizens and society it serves."[56]

ARE AFRICAN AMERICAN LAW STUDENTS HURT OR HELPED BY AFFIRMATIVE ACTION?

In 1997 Barbara Grutter, a white resident of Michigan with a 3.8 undergraduate GPA and a 161 LSAT score, was denied admission to the University of Michigan Law School. (See "In the Courts: *Grutter* v. *Bollinger*" for a more detailed discussion of this case.) She sued, claiming that she was rejected because the law school used race as a "predominant factor" and gave preference to applicants from certain minority groups. She argued that doing so violated the equal protection clause of the Fourteenth Amendment and Title VI of the Civil

Rights Act of 1964. In 2003 the United States Supreme Court ruled that "the law school's narrowly tailored use of race in admissions decisions to further a compelling interest in obtaining the educational benefits that flow from a diverse student body is not prohibited by the Equal Protection Clause or Title VI" (*Grutter* v. *Bollinger*, 288 F.3d 732 [2003]).

One year later, Richard Sander, a law professor at the University of California Los Angeles, argued in the *Stanford Law Review* that affirmative action policies hurt, not help, African American law students.[57] Sander contended that the African American students who get preferential treatment as a result of affirmative action enter law school with weaker grades and lower LSAT scores—the two best predictors of law school success—than white students. Noting that 43 percent of the African American students who entered law school in the fall of 1991 either did not graduate or did not pass the bar exam, Sander asserted that affirmative action sets African American students up for failure by placing them in schools where they cannot compete academically. He also predicted that "the number of black lawyers produced by American law schools each year and subsequently passing the bar would probably increase if those schools collectively stopped using racial preferences."[58]

Sander's methods and conclusions were called into question by social scientists and legal scholars. The harshest criticism came from David L. Chambers, Timothy T. Clydesdale, William C. Kidder, and Richard O. Lempert, who argued in the *Stanford Law Review* that Sander's conclusions were "simple, neat, and wrong."[59] They asserted that ending affirmative action would lead, not to an increase in the number of African American lawyers, as Sander had predicted, but to a 30 percent to 40 percent decline in the number of African Americans entering the legal profession.[60] Other critics stated that even if Sander's findings were correct,

his study failed to take into consideration the academic benefits of diversity, for which "there is universal celebration" on college campuses.[61]

THE PERCEPTIONS OF AFRICAN AMERICAN AND WHITE LAWYERS: DIVIDED JUSTICE?

A 1998 survey of African American and white lawyers commissioned by the *ABA Journal* and the *National Bar Association Magazine* revealed stark racial differences in perceptions of the justice system.[62] When asked about the amount of racial bias that currently exists in the justice system, more than half of the African American lawyers, but only 6.5 percent of the white lawyers, answered "very much." In fact, 29.6 percent of the white lawyers stated that they believed there was "very little" racial bias in the justice system.

Responses to other questions also varied by race:

- How does the amount of racial bias in the justice system compare with other segments of society?

	African Americans	Whites
More	22.7%	5.7%
Same	69.6	40.5
Less	5.9	45.8

- Have you witnessed an example of racial bias in the justice system in the past three years?

	African Americans	Whites
Yes	66.9%	15.1%
No	31.1	82.4

- What is your assessment of the ability of the justice system to eliminate racial bias in the future?

(Continued)

	African Americans	Whites
Hopeful	59.1%	80.7%
Pessimistic	38.2	15.1

■   Should police be allowed to create profiles of likely drug dealers or other criminals as a way to combat crime?

	African Americans	Whites
Yes	17.8%	48.6%
No	74.6	36.9

■   Should race be a factor in creating the profiles?

	African Americans	Whites
Race OK	5.5%	19.5%
Race Not OK	91.2	67.9

■   Have you seen an attempt to skew a jury racially because of the race of the defendant?

	African Americans	Whites
Yes	51.7%	22.4%
No	45.8	73.6

■   Are minority women lawyers treated less fairly than white women lawyers in hiring and promotion?

	African Americans	Whites
Yes	66.5%	10.9%
No	14.3	60.4

As these results clearly suggest, African American lawyers are substantially more likely than white lawyers to believe that the justice system is racially biased. As the author of the study noted, "Though they have made the justice system their life's work, many black lawyers believe the word 'justice' has a white spin that says 'just us.'"[63]

In the Courts: *Grutter* v. *Bollinger*

In 1997 Barbara Grutter, a white resident of Michigan with a 3.8 undergraduate GPA and a 161 LSAT score, was denied admission to the University of Michigan Law School. She filed suit, arguing the law school's admissions policies discriminated against her on the basis of race in violation of the Fourteenth Amendment and Title VI of the Civil Rights Acts of 1974.

The law school's admission policy, which was designed to achieve a diverse student body, required officials to evaluate the candidate's undergraduate GPA and LSAT score along with the quality of the undergraduate institution; the difficulty of the courses taken as an undergraduate; and the candidate's personal statement, letters of recommendation, and essay describing how he or she "would contribute to law school life and diversity." Although the policy did not define diversity solely in terms of race and ethnicity or restrict the types of diversity that would be given substantial weight in admissions decisions, it did state that the goal was to accept "a mix of students with varying backgrounds and experiences who will respect and learn from each other."[64] The policy stated explicitly that the law school was committed to "racial and ethnic diversity with special reference to the inclusion of students from groups which have been historically discriminated against, like African Americans, Hispanics, and Native Americans, who without this commitment might not be represented in our student body in meaningful numbers."[65]

Grutter claimed that she was not admitted to the University of Michigan Law School in large part because the school took the race/ethnicity of the applicant into account and, in doing so, gave African American and Hispanic applicants a significantly greater chance of admission than white students with similar credentials. She argued that the school did not have a "compelling interest" to justify the use of race as an admissions factor.

The United States Supreme Court did not agree with Grutter's arguments. The court ruled that "The Law School's narrowly tailored use of race in admissions decisions to further a compelling interest in obtaining the educational benefits that flow from a diverse student body is not prohibited by the Equal Protection Clause" or Title VI of the Civil Rights Act of 1964.[66] The Supreme Court stated that student body diversity was, in fact, a compelling state interest "that can justify using race in university admissions." The court acknowledged that it would be "patently unconstitutional" to enroll a certain number of minority students "simply to assure some specified percentage of a particular group," but stated that this was not the case with respect to the law school's admission policy. Rather, "the Law School defines its critical mass concept by reference to the substantial, important, and laudable educational benefits that diversity is designed to produce, including cross-racial understanding and the breaking down of racial stereotypes."[67]

The Supreme Court also noted that the admissions plan was "narrowly tailored," in that it considered each applicant's race/ethnicity as only one factor among many. The court reiterated that although "universities cannot establish quotas for members of certain racial or ethnic groups or put them on separate admission tracks," they can structure their admission policies to give serious consideration to all of the ways an applicant might contribute to a diverse educational environment.

Three years after the Supreme Court handed down its decision, Michigan voters enacted the Michigan Civil Rights Initiative (also known as Proposal 2), which added the following language to the Michigan Constitution:

> The University of Michigan, Michigan State University, Wayne State University, and any other public college or university, community college, or school district shall not discriminate against, or grant preferential treatment to, any individual or group on the basis of race, sex, color, ethnicity, or national origin in the operation of public employment, public education, or public contracting.

In 2008 a federal district court judge ruled that the initiative did not violate the U.S. Constitution.[68]

Arguments such as these prompted state and federal reforms designed to reduce pretrial detention. Encouraged by the results of the Manhattan Bail Project, which found that the majority of defendants released on their own recognizance did appear for trial,[69] local jurisdictions moved quickly to reduce reliance on money bail and to institute programs modeled after the Manhattan Bail Project. Many states revised their bail laws, and in 1966 Congress passed the Bail Reform Act, which proclaimed release on recognizance the presumptive bail decision in federal cases.

Then, as Samuel Walker noted, "the political winds shifted."[70] The rising crime rate of the 1970s generated a concern for crime control and led to a reassessment of bail policies. Critics challenged the traditional view that the only function of bail was to assure the defendant's appearance in court. They argued that guaranteeing public safety was also a valid function of bail and that pretrial detention should be used to protect the community from "dangerous" offenders.

These arguments fueled the second bail reform movement, which emerged in the 1970s and emphasized preventive detention. Conservative legislators and policy makers lobbied for reforms allowing judges to consider "public safety" when making decisions concerning the type and amount of bail.[71] By 1984, 34 states had enacted legislation giving judges the right to deny bail to defendants deemed dangerous.[72] Also in 1984, Congress passed a law authorizing preventive detention of dangerous defendants in federal criminal cases.[73]

The Effect of Race on Bail Decision Making   Proponents of bail reform argued that whether a defendant was released or detained prior to trial should not depend on his or her economic status or race. They argued that bail decisions should rest either on assessments of the likelihood that the defendant would appear in court or on predictions of the defendant's dangerousness.

The problem, of course, is that there is no way to guarantee that judges will not take race into account in making these assessments and predictions. As Coramae Richey Mann asserted, even the seemingly objective criteria used in making these decisions "may still be discriminatory on the basis of economic status or skin color."[74] If judges stereotype African Americans and Hispanics as less reliable and more prone to violence than whites, they will be more inclined to detain people of color and release whites, irrespective of their more objective assessments of risk of flight or dangerousness.

Studies examining the effect of race on bail decisions have yielded contradictory findings. Some researchers conclude that judges' bail decisions are based primarily on the seriousness of the offense and the defendant's prior criminal record and ties to the community; race has no effect once these factors are taken into consideration.[75] Other researchers contend that the defendant's economic status, not race, determines the likelihood of pretrial release.[76] If this is the case, one could argue that bail decision making reflects *indirect* racial discrimination because African American and Hispanic defendants are more likely than white defendants to be poor.

A number of studies document *direct* racial discrimination in bail decisions. A study by George S. Bridges of bail decision making in King County, Washington, for example, examined the effect of race/ethnicity on four bail outcomes: whether the defendant was released on his or her own recognizance; whether the court set monetary bail; the amount of bail required; and whether

T A B L E   5.2   Race/Ethnicity and Bail Outcomes in King County, Washington

	Whites	All Racial Minorities	African Americans	Hispanics	Native Americans	Asian Americans
Released on personal recognizance	25%	14%	14%	10%	8%	18%
Monetary bail set	34%	56%	46%	60%	60%	50%
Median bail amount	$10,000	$10,000	$10,000	$10,000	$10,000	$15,000
In custody prior to trial	28%	39%	36%	54%	55%	35%

SOURCE: George S. Bridges, *A Study on Racial and Ethnic Disparities in Superior Court Bail and Pre-Trial Detention Practices in Washington* (Olympia: Washington State Minority and Justice Commission, 1997), Table 1.

the defendant was held in custody pending trial.[77] As shown in Table 5.2, he found that racial minorities were less likely than whites to be released on their own recognizance and were more likely than whites to have bail set. Racial minorities also were held in pretrial detention at higher rates than whites. The detention rate was 55 percent for Native Americans, 54 percent for Hispanics, 36 percent for African American, and 28 percent for whites. There were, however, no differences in the median amount of bail required.

Bridges noted that, although "at face value these differences may seem alarming,"[78] they might be the result of legitimate factors that criminal justice officials take into consideration when establishing the conditions of pretrial release: the defendant's ties to the community, the perceived danger-ousness of the defendant, and any previous history of the defendant's failure to appear at court proceedings. When he controlled for these legally relevant variables and for the defendant's age and gender, however, he found that the race effects did not disappear. Racial minorities and men were less likely than whites and women to be released on their own recognizance and more likely than whites and women to be required to pay bail as a condition of release. For both of these decisions, the prosecutor's recommendation regarding the type and amount of bail was the strongest predictor of out-come. In contrast, race had no effect on the likelihood of pretrial detention once the bail conditions and the amount of bail set by the judge were taken into account.

Interviews with King County criminal justice officials revealed that most of them believed the racial differences in bail outcomes could be attributed to three factors: racial minorities' lack of resources and consequent inability to retain a private attorney; the tendency of judges to follow the recommendations of prosecutors; and cultural differences and language barriers that made it difficult to contact the defendant's references or verify information provided by the defendant. Because racial minorities were more likely than whites to be poor,

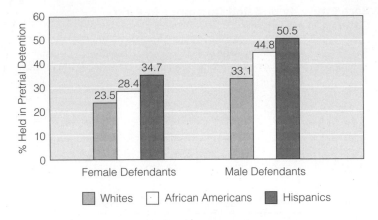

FIGURE 5.2   Race/Ethnicity, Gender, and Pretrial Detention in 75 U.S. Counties

SOURCE: Stephen Demuth and Darrell Steffensmeier, "The Impact of Gender and Race-Ethnicity in the Pretrial Release Process," *Social Problems* 51 (2004), pp. 222–242.

they were more likely to be represented by public defenders with large caseloads and limited time to prepare for bail hearings. Resource constraints similarly limited the amount of time that judges and pretrial investigators were able to devote to bail decisions, which led to reliance on the recommendations proffered by the prosecutor. Although Bridges stressed that his study produced no evidence "that disparities are the product of overt, prejudicial acts by court officials," he nonetheless concluded that "race and ethnicity matter in the disposition of criminal cases."[79] He added that this "is a serious concern for the courts in Washington" because it "implies that, despite the efforts of judges and others dedicated to fairness in the administration of justice, justice is not administered fairly."[80]

Other evidence of direct racial discrimination is found in an analysis of pretrial release outcomes for felony defendants in the nation's 75 largest counties during the 1990s.[81] As shown in Figure 5.2, Stephen Demuth and Darrell Steffensmeier found that African Americans and Hispanics were more likely than whites to be detained in jail prior to trial. Among female defendants, the detention rates were 23.5 percent (whites), 28.4 percent (African Americans), and 34.7 percent (Hispanics). Among males, the rates were 33.1 percent (whites), 44.8 percent (African Americans), and 50.5 percent (Hispanics). The pretrial detention rate for Hispanic males, in other words, was more than twice the rate for white females.

As was the case with the Washington State study, these differences did not disappear when the authors controlled for the seriousness of the charges against the defendant, the number of charges the defendant was facing, whether the defendant previously had failed to appear for a court proceeding, and the defendant's prior record and age. Demuth and Steffensmeier found that males were more likely than females and that African Americans and Hispanics were more likely than whites to be detained in jail prior to trial. They also found that white females faced a significantly smaller likelihood of pretrial detention than any of the other groups, particularly Hispanic males and African American males.[82]

Findings from this study also provided some clues as to the reasons why defendants were held in jail prior to trial. For African Americans, the increased likelihood of detention was because they were almost two times more likely than whites to be held on bail; African Americans, in other words, were less likely than whites to be able to pay bail and secure their release. For Hispanics, however, the increased likelihood of detention reflected not only their inability to pay bail but also the fact that they were more likely than whites to have to pay bail for release and the amount they were required to pay was higher than the amount that similarly situated whites were required to pay.[83] The authors also found that both female and male white defendants were more likely than their racial/ethnic counterparts to be released prior to trial and that this was largely because of their greater ability to make bail. As they noted, "white defendants of both sexes apparently have greater financial capital or resources either in terms of their personal bankroll/resources, their access to family or social networks willing to post bail, or their greater access to bail bondsmen for purposes of making bail."[84]

There also is evidence that defendant race interacts with other variables related to bail severity. Margaret Farnworth and Patrick Horan,[85] for example, found that the amount of bail imposed on white defendants who retained private attorneys was less than the amount imposed on African American defendants who retained private attorneys. Theodore G. Chiricos and William D. Bales similarly found that the likelihood of pretrial detention was greatest for African American defendants who were unemployed.[86]

Bail and Case Outcomes   Concerns about discrimination in bail decision making focus on two facts: African American and Hispanic defendants who are presumed to be innocent are jailed prior to trial *and* those who are detained prior to trial are more likely to be convicted and receive harsher sentences than those who are released pending trial. These concerns focus, in other words, on the possibility that discrimination in bail decision making has "spillover" effects on other case processing decisions.

An analysis of pretrial release of felony defendants by the BJS attests to the validity of these concerns.[87] Using data from 1994 to 2004, the BJS compared the conviction rates for released and detained defendants in the 75 largest counties in the United States. They found that 78 percent of those who were detained prior to trial, but only 60 percent of those who were released, were convicted. Felony defendants who were released also were less likely than those who were detained to be convicted of a felony: the rates were 46 percent for those who were released but 69 percent for those who were detained.

Although these data suggest that pretrial release does have important spillover effects on case outcomes, the higher conviction and imprisonment rates for defendants who were detained pending trial could result from the fact that defendants who are held in jail prior to trial tend to be charged with more serious crimes, have more serious prior criminal histories, and have a past history of nonappearance at court proceedings. A BJS study of felony defendants processed in state courts in 2006, for example, found that defendants charged with murder had the lowest release rate and that defendants with more serious prior records or a history of nonappearance were more likely to be detained prior to trial.[88] Given these findings, it is possible that the relationship between pretrial status and case outcomes would disappear once controls for case seriousness and prior criminal record were taken into consideration.

Data collected for a study of sentencing outcomes in Chicago, Miami, and Kansas City during 1993 and 1994 were used to explore this possibility.[89] Spohn and DeLone found that the offender's pretrial status was a strong predictor of the likelihood of imprisonment, even after other relevant legal and extralegal variables were taken into account. In all three cities, offenders who were released prior to trial faced substantially lower odds of a prison sentence than did offenders who were detained pending trial. Further analysis of sentences imposed by judges in Chicago and Kansas City revealed that pretrial detention had a similar effect on incarceration for each racial/ethnic group and for males and females.[90] As shown in Table 5.3, among both males and females, African American, Hispanic, and white defendants who were detained prior to trial faced substantially greater odds of incarceration than African American, Hispanic, and white defendants who were released pending trial. In Chicago, the highest incarceration rates were found for African American (73 percent), Hispanic (72 percent), and white (63 percent) males who were detained prior to trial; the lowest rates for were found for white (7 percent), African American (11 percent), and Hispanic (11 percent) females who were released pending trial.

T A B L E 5.3   The Effect of Pretrial Detention on Incarceration Rates for Typical Felony Offenders in Chicago and Kansas City

	% Sentenced to Prison	
	Detained Prior to Trial	Released Prior to Trial
Chicago		
African American male	73	23
Hispanic male	72	22
White male	63	16
African American female	53	11
Hispanic female	55	11
White female	42	7
Kansas City		
African American male	29	16
White male	24	13
African American female	13	6
White female	10	5

NOTE: These probabilities were calculated for defendants who were 30 years old, were charged with one count of possession of narcotics with intent, had one prior felony conviction, were not on probation at the time of the current offenses, were represented by a public defender, and pled guilty.

The results of this study suggest that defendants who were detained prior to trial received more punitive sentences than those who were released and that the highest incarceration rates were for African Americans and Hispanics who were detained prior to trial. In Chicago this "detention penalty" is compounded by the fact that African Americans were significantly more likely than whites to be detained prior to trial. Because they were detained more often than whites in the first place, African American defendants were more likely than whites to suffer both the pains of imprisonment prior to trial and the consequences of pretrial detention at sentencing.

A study of pretrial detention and case outcomes in three U.S. district courts found a similar pattern of results.[91] Spohn compared pretrial detention rates and sentences for African American and white offenders who were convicted of drug trafficking offenses in the Southern District of Iowa, the District of Minnesota, and the District of Nebraska. She found that 67.7 percent of the African American offenders but only 43.3 percent of the white offenders were held in custody until their sentencing hearing. These differences did not disappear when she controlled for offender characteristics, including measures of the offender's dangerousness and community ties, access to financial resources, the offender's criminal history, and the seriousness of the crime. Even after these legally relevant predictors of pretrial detention were taken into consideration, African Americans faced higher odds of pretrial detention than did whites.[92] Spohn also found that the likelihood of pretrial custody was substantially higher for African American male offenders than for other offenders. The odds of pretrial detention for African American males were twice those for white males, and the differences between African American males and either African American females or white females were even larger. In fact, African American males were 3.7 times more likely than white females and 3 times more likely than African American females to be held in custody before trial. There also were large differences between white females and white males, but the difference between white females and African American females was not statistically significant. Thus, African American males were treated more harshly than all other offenders, but white females were not treated any differently than African American females.[93]

To determine whether the race of the offender had *indirect* and/or *cumulative* effects on sentence severity through its effect on pretrial detention, Spohn estimated a model of sentence length, controlling for the offender's pretrial status and for the offender and case characteristics identified by prior research as predictors of sentences imposed under the federal sentencing guidelines. Her analysis revealed that offenders who were in custody at the time of the sentence hearing received sentences that averaged almost 8 months (b = 7.95) longer than those imposed on offenders who were not detained before the hearing.[94]

Spohn speculated that the pattern of results she uncovered might reflect judges of the federal bail statute, which allows them to take the offender's dangerousness into consideration when deciding between pretrial release and detention. As she noted,

> If, as prior research has shown, judges stereotype black drug traffickers and male drug traffickers as more dangerous and threatening than whites or females engaged in drug trafficking, their interpretation of the legally relevant criteria may lead to higher rates of pretrial detention for black offenders and for male offenders.[95]

Although the findings are somewhat contradictory, it thus appears that the reforms instituted since the 1960s have not produced racial equality in bail decision making. It is certainly true that racial minorities are no longer routinely jailed prior to trial because of judicial stereotypes of dangerousness or because they are too poor to obtain their release. Nevertheless, there is evidence that judges in some jurisdictions continue to take race into account in deciding on the type and amount of bail. There also is evidence that race interacts with factors such as prior record or employment status to produce higher pretrial detention rates for African American defendants than for white defendants. Given the consequences of pretrial detention, these findings are an obvious cause for concern.

CHARGING AND PLEA BARGAINING DECISIONS

> Regrettably, the evidence is clear that prosecutorial discretion is systematically exercised to the disadvantage of black and Hispanic Americans. Prosecutors are not, by and large, bigoted. But as with police activity, prosecutorial judgment is shaped by a set of self-perpetuating racial assumptions.[96]

Thus far we have examined criminal justice decisions concerning appointment of counsel and bail for evidence of racial discrimination. We have shown that, despite reforms mandated by the Supreme Court or adopted voluntarily by the states, inequities persist. African Americans and Hispanics who find themselves in the arms of the law continue to suffer discrimination in these important court processing decisions.

In this section, we examine prosecutors' charging and plea bargaining decisions for evidence of differential treatment of minority and white defendants. We argue that there is compelling evidence of racial *disparity* in charging and plea bargaining. We further contend that this disparity frequently reflects racial *discrimination*.

Prosecutors' Charging Decisions

Prosecutors exercise broad discretion in deciding whether to file formal charges against individuals suspected of crimes and in determining the number and seriousness of the charges to be filed. According to the Supreme Court, "So long as the prosecutor has probable cause to believe that the accused committed an offense defined by statute, the decision whether or not to prosecute, and what charge to file or bring before a grand jury, generally rests entirely in his discretion."[97] As Justice Jackson noted in 1940, "the prosecutor has more control over life, liberty, and reputation than any other person in America."[98]

The power of the prosecutor is reflected in the fact that in most states, from one-third to one-half of all felony cases are dismissed by the prosecutor prior to a determination of guilt or innocence.[99] Prosecutors can reject charges at the initial screening, either because they believe the suspect is innocent or, more typically, because they believe the suspect is guilty but a conviction would be unlikely.

Prosecutors also can reject charges if they feel it would not be in the "interest of justice" to continue the case—because the crime is too trivial; because of a perception that the suspect has been punished enough; or because the suspect has agreed to provide information about other, more serious, cases.[100] Finally, prosecutors can reject charges as felonies but prosecute them as misdemeanors.

If a formal charge is filed by the prosecutor, it still can be reduced to a less serious felony or to a misdemeanor during plea bargaining. It also can be dismissed by the court on a recommendation by the prosecutor. This usually happens when the case "falls apart" prior to trial. A witness may refuse to cooperate or may fail to appear at trial, or the judge may rule that the confession or other essential evidence is inadmissible. Unlike the prosecutor's initial decision to reject the charge, the decision to dismiss a charge already filed requires official court action.

The Effect of Race on Charging Decisions   Although the prosecutor's discretion is broad, it is not unlimited. The Supreme Court, in fact, has ruled that the decision to prosecute may not be "deliberately based upon an unjustifiable standard such as race, religion, or other arbitrary classification."[101] The prosecutor, in other words, cannot legitimately take the race of the suspect into account in deciding whether to file charges or in deciding on the seriousness of the charge to be filed.

Relatively few studies have examined the effects of race and ethnicity on prosecutorial charging decisions, and those few studies conducted reach contradictory conclusions.[102] Some researchers found either that race/ethnicity did not affect charging decisions at all or that race/ethnicity played a very minor role in the decision of whether to prosecute.[103] Two recent studies, one of charging decisions in federal courts and one of charging outcomes in state courts, illustrate this conclusion. Lauren Shermer and Brian Johnson examined U.S. attorneys' decisions to reduce the severity of the charges that defendants were facing in U.S. district courts.[104] They found that males were less likely than females to receive charge reductions but that neither race/ethnicity nor age affected the likelihood of charge reduction. Further analysis revealed that race, ethnicity, gender, and age did not interact to affect charge reductions in the predicted way; that is, young male African American and Hispanic offenders were *not* less likely than older white male offenders to receive a reduction in the charges. Although they were careful to point out that they only examined one aspect of charging in federal courts, Shermer and Johnson concluded that the results of their study "are encouraging in that they support a general lack of systematic bias in the charge reduction decisions of federal prosecutors."[105] Travis Franklin found a similar pattern of results using state court data to examine whether the prosecutor dismissed the case against the defendant (after charges were initially filed).[106] Race did not affect the likelihood of dismissal, and black males were no less likely than black females, white males, or white females to have the charges against them dismissed. Both of these recent and methodologically sophisticated studies, then, found no evidence of racial/ethnic bias in prosecutors' decisions to reduce or dismiss the charges. (For a discussion of a case of *reverse discrimination* in a prosecutor's charging decision, see Box 5.3, "In the Media: Mike Nifong and the Duke Lacrosse Case.")

B o x   5.3   In the Media: Mike Nifong and the Duke Lacrosse Case

---

Gunnar Myrdal, a Swedish social scientist and the author of a book examining the "Negro Problem" in the Unites States in the late 1930s and early 1940s, found substantial discrimination against African Americans in the decision of whether to charge. As Myrdal noted:

> State courts receive indictments for physical violence against Negroes in an infinitesimally small proportion of the cases. It is notorious that practically never have white lynching mobs been brought to court in the south, even when the killers are known to all in the community and are mentioned by name in the local press. When the offender is a Negro, indictment is easily obtained, and no such difficulty at the start will meet the prosecution of the case.[107]

Discrimination of a different type surfaced in a recent, and highly publicized, case involving three members of the Duke University lacrosse team. In April of 2006, Durham County (North Carolina) District Attorney Mike Nifong filed first degree forcible rape, first degree sexual offense, and kidnapping charges against the players, all of whom were white, after an African American woman who had been hired as a stripper for a team party claimed that she had been repeatedly raped. The charges were filed in spite of the fact that the complainant's story changed several times and that DNA tests failed to connect any of the accused to the alleged sexual assault.

In the weeks and months following the filing of charges, District Attorney Nifong gave dozens of interviews to local and national media. He stated repeatedly that he was "confident that a rape occurred,"[108] and he called the players "a bunch of hooligans" whose "daddies could buy them expensive lawyers."[109] Professors at Duke University were even blunter, emphasizing the race of the victim and the suspects and implying that justice would not be served. For example, William Chafe, a professor of history, published an op-ed piece in which he argued that there were similarities between the Duke case and the case involving whites who kidnapped, beat, and murdered an African American boy named Emmett Till in 1950s Mississippi:

> Sex and race have always interacted in a vicious chemistry of power, privilege and control. Emmett Till was brutalized and lynched in Mississippi in 1954 for allegedly speaking with too easy familiarity to a white woman storekeeper.... What has all this to do with America today? Among other things, it helps to put into context what occurred in Durham two weeks ago. The mixture of race and sex that transpired on Buchanan Boulevard is not new.[110]

The case against the three Duke University students began to unravel during the summer and fall of 2006. In mid-December it was revealed that Nifong had withheld exculpatory DNA evidence (that is, evidence that proved none of the three men accused of the assaults was involved) from defense lawyers, and on December 22, Nifong dropped the rape charges, but not the sexual offense and kidnapping charges. Six days later the North Carolina Bar Association filed ethics charges against Nifong, alleging that he had engaged in "conduct that involves dishonesty, fraud, deceit or misrepresentation, as well as conduct that is prejudicial to the administration of justice."[111] In January of 2007, Nifong asked to be taken off the case, which was then turned over to the North Carolina Attorney General, Roy Cooper. After conducting his own investigation, Cooper dropped all of the remaining charges on April 11. Cooper stated that his office "believed these three individuals are innocent of these charges." He also alleged that the charges resulted from a "tragic rush to accuse and a failure to verify serious allegations" and showed "the enormous consequences of overreaching by a prosecutor."[112]

Nifong resigned from his position as Durham County District Attorney on June 18. Two days earlier, he had been disbarred after a disciplinary hearing committee of the North Carolina Bar ruled that he had committed numerous violations of the state's rules of professional conduct. In August, Nifong was held in criminal contempt of court and sentenced to one day in jail for his actions in the case.

As this case illustrates, prosecutors have an ethical obligation to "do justice." Their charging decisions cannot be motivated by "personal or political advantages or disadvantages which might be involved" or by "a desire to enhance [their conviction records]."[113]

Several studies concluded that prosecutors' charging decisions *are* affected by race. For example, a study that examined the decision to reject or dismiss charges against felony defendants in Los Angeles County revealed a pattern of discrimination in favor of female defendants and against African American and Hispanic defendants.[114] The authors controlled for the defendant's age and prior criminal record, the seriousness of the charge against the defendant, and whether the defendant used a weapon in committing the crime. As shown in Table 5.4, they found that Hispanic males were most likely to be prosecuted fully, followed by African American males, white males, and females of all ethnic groups.

The authors of this study speculated that prosecutors took both race and gender into account in deciding whether to file charges in "marginal cases." They reasoned that strong cases would be prosecuted and weak cases would be dropped, regardless of the race or gender of the suspect. In marginal cases, however,

> prosecutors may simply feel less comfortable prosecuting the dominant rather than the subordinate ethnic groups. They might feel the dominant groups are less threatening. Or they might believe they can win convictions more often against blacks and Hispanics than against Anglos.[115]

T A B L E 5.4   The Effect of Race and Gender on Prosecutors' Charging Decisions

	Adjusted Means[a]		
Group	Rejected at Screening	Dismissed by Court	Fully Prosecuted
African American male	46%	34%	39%
African American female	57	42	30
Hispanic male	46	33	42
Hispanic female	54	43	31
White male	54	33	26
White female	59	42	19

[a]Means have been adjusted for the effect of four independent variables: age of the defendant, prior record of the defendant, seriousness of the charge, and whether the defendant used a weapon.

SOURCE: Table adapted from Cassia Spohn, John Gruhl, and Susan Welch, "The Impact of the Ethnicity and Gender of Defendants on the Decision to Reject or Dismiss Felony Charges," *Criminology* 25 (1987), pp. 175–191.

Similar results surfaced in a study of prosecutors' charging decisions in King County, Washington.[116] When the authors of this study examined the prosecutor's decision to file felony charges (rather than file misdemeanor charges or decline to prosecute the case), they found that prosecutors were substantially more likely to file felony charges against racial minorities than against whites. These differences were especially pronounced for violent crimes and drug offenses. Moreover, the racial disparities did not disappear when the authors controlled for the seriousness of the crime, the defendant's prior criminal record, and the defendant's age and gender. Even taking these factors into account, Native Americans were 1.7 times more likely than whites to be charged with a felony, and African Americans were 1.15 times more likely than whites to face felony charges.[117]

Robert D. Crutchfield and his co-authors stressed that these racial differences were not "necessarily the result of individuals making biased decisions."[118] Rather, the differences probably reflected race-linked legal, economic, and social factors that prosecutors take into account in deciding whether to charge, as well as officials' focus on drug offenses involving crack cocaine. As we have repeatedly emphasized, however, this type of subtle or indirect discrimination is problematic. It is difficult to disentangle the effects of race/ethnicity, social class, employment history, and family situation. Even if criminal justice officials are justified in taking these social and economic factors into account, doing so will necessarily produce unintended race effects.

Prosecutorial Discretion in the Context of Mandatory Minimum Sentences and Habitual Offender Laws

An important component of prosecutorial discretion is found in the context of mandatory minimum sentences and habitual offender laws. In many jurisdictions, prosecutors have discretion whether to file charges that trigger mandatory minimum sentences, three-strikes-and-you're-out provisions, and habitual offender sentencing requirements. If such charges are filed, the judges' discretion at sentencing is reduced or, in some jurisdictions, eliminated entirely. By determining whether defendants will face charges that trigger these sentence enhancements, prosecutors in essence influence the sentences that judges impose.

There is compelling evidence that prosecutors do exercise their discretion in these types of cases. A study by the U.S. Sentencing Commission, for example, showed that only about half of all federal offenders who were potentially subject to mandatory minimums actually received a mandatory minimum sentence, and there are a number of studies at the state level that reveal that mandatory minimums, sentencing enhancements for use of a firearm, and habitual offender provisions are applied to only a small proportion of eligible defendants.[119]

There also is evidence that race and ethnicity influence prosecutors' decisions in these situations. Both David Bjerk[120] and Jill Farrell[121] found that racial minorities were more likely than whites to be sentenced under mandatory minimum sentences, and two studies[122] found that eligible racial minorities were substantially more likely than eligible whites to be sentenced as habitual offenders. A somewhat different pattern of results was found by Jeffery Ulmer and his colleagues, who used data from Pennsylvania (which operates under sentencing guidelines) to examine cases that were eligible to receive a mandatory minimum sentence.[123] The outcome of interest was whether the prosecutor filed a motion to apply the mandatory sentence. Their analysis controlled for the severity of the offense, the offender's prior criminal record, the type of offense, whether the defendant went to trial or pled guilty, and the defendant's race, ethnicity, gender, and age. They found, consistent with the research discussed earlier, that prosecutors applied the mandatory minimums to a small fraction of eligible offenders. They also found that Hispanics, but not African Americans, were more likely than whites to receive mandatory minimums, and that young Hispanic males were singled out for mandatory application, particularly in drug trafficking cases.[124] The authors of this study concluded that "legally relevant factors, case processing concerns (i.e., rewarding guilty pleas), and social statuses (i.e., gender, ethnicity and age) shape prosecutors' perceptions of blameworthiness and community protection and thus their decisions to apply mandatories."[125]

The Effect of Offender Race and Victim Race on Charging Decisions

The research discussed thus far suggests that the race/ethnicity of the offender affects prosecutors' charging decisions. There also is evidence that charging decisions vary depending on the race of the offender and the race of the victim. Gary D. LaFree,[126] for example, found that African Americans arrested for raping white women were more likely to be charged with felonies than were either African Americans arrested for raping African American women or whites arrested for raping white women. One study found that defendants arrested for murdering whites in Florida were more likely to be indicted for first-degree murder than those arrested for murdering African Americans.[127] Another study of prosecutors' charging decisions in death penalty cases found that homicide cases involving African American defendants and white victims were more likely than similar cases involving other offender–victim racial combinations to result in first-degree murder charges.[128] The prosecutor in the Midwestern jurisdiction where this study was conducted was also more likely to file a notice of aggravating circumstances and to proceed to a capital trial if the defendant was an African American who was accused of killing a white.

Research on sexual assault case processing decisions in Detroit reached a different conclusion. Cassia Spohn and Jeffrey Spears[129] used data on sexual assaults bound over for trial in Detroit Recorder's Court to examine the effect of offender race, victim race, and other case characteristics on the decision to dismiss the charges against the defendant (versus the decision to fully prosecute the case). Building on previous research demonstrating that African Americans who murder or rape whites receive more punitive treatment than other victim–offender racial combinations, they hypothesized that black-on-white sexual assaults would be more likely than either black-on-black or white-on-white sexual assaults to result in the dismissal of all charges. They found just the opposite: the likelihood of charge dismissal was significantly *greater* for cases involving African American offenders and white victims than for the other two groups of offenders. They also found that African Americans prosecuted for assaulting whites were less likely to be convicted than whites charged with sexually assaulting whites.[130]

Spohn and Spears concluded that their "unexpected findings" suggest that African American–on–white sexual assaults with weaker evidence are less likely to be screened out during the preliminary stages of the process.[131] Police and prosecutors, in other words, may regard sexual assaults involving African American men and white women as inherently more serious than intraracial sexual assaults; consequently, they may be more willing to take a chance with a reluctant victim or a victim whose behavior at the time of the incident was questionable. According to the authors of this study:

> The police may be willing to make an arrest and the prosecutor may be willing to charge, despite questions about the procedures used to obtain physical evidence or about the validity of the defendant's confession. If this is true, then cases involving black offenders and white victims will be *more* likely than other types of cases to 'fall apart' before or during trial.[132]

A study of charging decisions in California reached a similar conclusion. Joan Petersilia found that white suspects were *more* likely than African American or Hispanic suspects to be formally charged.[133] Her analysis of the reasons given for charge rejection led her to conclude that the higher dismissal rates for non-white suspects reflected the fact that "blacks and Hispanics in California are more likely than whites to be arrested under circumstances that provide insufficient evidence to support criminal charges."[134] Prosecutors were more reluctant to file charges against racial minorities than against whites, in other words, because they viewed the evidence against racial minorities as weaker and the odds of convicting them as lower.

Race, Drugs, and Selective Prosecution   The results of Petersilia's study in Los Angeles and Spohn and Spears's study in Detroit provide evidence suggestive of a pattern of *selective prosecution*—that is, cases involving racial minorities, or certain types of racial minorities, are singled out for prosecution, whereas similar cases involving whites are either screened out very early in the process or never enter the system in the first place.

This argument has been made most forcefully with respect to drug offenses. In *Malign Neglect*, for example, Michael Tonry[135] argues, "Urban black Americans have borne the brunt of the War on Drugs." More specifically, he charges that "the recent blackening of America's prison population is the product of malign neglect of the war's effects on black Americans."[136] Jerome Miller similarly asserts that "from the first shot fired in the drug war African-Americans were targeted, arrested, and imprisoned in wildly disproportionate numbers."[137]

There is ample evidence that the war on drugs is being fought primarily in African American and Hispanic communities. In 2009, for example, racial minorities comprised nearly three-fourths of all offenders prosecuted in federal district courts for drug trafficking: 26 percent of these offenders were white,

---

B o x 5.4   The U.S. Attorney General and Racial Neutrality in Prosecution

In January 1999, Janet Reno, then Attorney General for the United States, issued a memorandum on "Ensuring Racial Neutrality in Prosecution Practices" to all United States Attorneys.[138] Excerpts from the memo included the following:

- "Each United States Attorney should examine his or her office's practices and procedures and take all necessary measures to ensure the use of race-neutral policies in the exercise of prosecutorial discretion within a district. Absent compelling, specific law enforcement imperatives there is ordinarily no justification for differing policies and practices within a district with respect to similarly situated defendants. Moreover, any race-neutral policy that has a disparate racial impact should be carefully reviewed to determine whether the disparity is justified by law enforcement necessity and not the product of conscious or unconscious racial bias."

- "Care must be taken to ensure that race plays no part in the Government's decision whether to file a substantial assistance motion or the amount of any recommended reduction."

- "As the chief federal law enforcement officer in the district, the United States Attorney should take a leadership role in ensuring that all agencies within the district are aware of issues of racial disparity.... [O]ur constant vigilance will ensure that there is no perception of racial disparity in the discharge of our duties. The public recognition that our policies are administered in a race-neutral fashion is as important as the reality that we do so administer them."

---

31 percent were African American, and 40 percent were Hispanic.[139] These figures are inconsistent with national data on use of drugs, which reveal that whites are more likely than either African Americans or Hispanics to report having "ever" used a variety of drugs, including cocaine, PCP, LSD, and marijuana.[140]

Some commentators cite evidence of a different type of selective prosecution in drug cases (see Box 5.4 for the U.S. Attorney General's memorandum regarding racial neutrality in federal prosecution). Noting that the penalties for use of crack cocaine mandated by the federal sentencing guidelines are substantially harsher than the penalties provided under many state statutes, these critics suggest that state prosecutors are more likely to refer crack cases involving racial minorities to the federal system for prosecution. Richard Berk and Alec Campbell,[141] for example, compared the racial makeup of defendants arrested for sale of crack cocaine in Los Angeles to the racial makeup of defendants charged with sale of crack cocaine in state and federal courts. They found that the racial makeup of arrestees was similar to the racial makeup of those charged with violating state statutes. However, African Americans were overrepresented in federal cases; in fact, over a four-year period, no whites were prosecuted for the sale of crack cocaine in federal court.

This issue was addressed by the Supreme Court in 1996. The five defendants in the case of U.S. v. Armstrong et al.[142] alleged that they were selected for prosecution in federal court (the U.S. District Court for the Central District of California) rather than in state court because they were African American.

They further alleged that this decision had serious potential consequences. Christopher Armstrong, for example, faced a prison term of 55 years to life under federal statutes, compared to 3 to 9 years under California law. Another defendant, Aaron Hampton, faced a maximum term of 14 years under California law but a mandatory life term under federal law.

Following their indictment for conspiring to possess with intent to distribute more than 50 grams of crack cocaine, the defendants filed a motion for discovery of information held by the U.S. Attorney's office regarding the race of people prosecuted by that office. In support of their motion, they offered a study showing that all of the defendants in the crack cocaine cases closed by the Federal Public Defender's Office in 1991 were African American.

The U.S. District Court ordered the U.S. Attorney's office to provide the data requested by the defendants. When federal prosecutors refused to do so, noting that there was no evidence that they had refused to prosecute white or Hispanic crack defendants, U.S. District Judge Consuelo Marshall dismissed the indictments. The 9th Circuit U.S. Court of Appeals affirmed Judge Marshall's dismissal of the indictments. The appellate court judges stated that they began with "the presumption that people of all races commit all types of crimes—not with the premise that any type of crime is the exclusive province of any particular racial or ethnic group."[143] They stated that the defendant's evidence showing that all 24 crack defendants were African American required some response from federal prosecutors.

The U.S. Supreme Court disagreed. In an 8-to-1 decision that did not settle the issue of whether the U.S. Attorney's Office engaged in selective prosecution, the Court ruled that federal rules of criminal procedure regarding discovery do not require the government to provide the information requested by the defendants. Although prosecutors *are* obligated to turn over documents that are "material to the preparation of the … defense," this applies *only* to documents needed to mount a defense against the government's "case-in-chief" (in other words, the crack cocaine charges) and not to documents needed to make a selective prosecution claim. Further, the Court ruled that "For a defendant to be entitled to discovery on a claim that he was singled out for prosecution on the basis of his race, he must make a threshold showing that the Government declined to prosecute similarly situated suspects of other races."[144]

Justice Stevens, the lone dissenter in the case, argued that the evidence of selective prosecution presented by the defendants "was sufficiently disturbing to require some response from the United States Attorney's Office." According to Stevens:

> If a District Judge has reason to suspect that [the United States Attorney for the Central District of California], or a member of her staff, has singled out particular defendants for prosecution on the basis of their race, it is surely appropriate for the Judge to determine whether there is a factual basis for such a concern.[145] (See Box 5.5 for a discussion of prosecutorial decisions in the case of the Jena Six.)

Box 5.5   Selective Prosecution: The Case of the Jena Six

In September of 2006 an African American student at Jena (Louisiana) High School defied tradition and sat under a large oak tree in the center of campus that was "reserved" for whites. The next day, three hangman's nooses were found dangling from the tree. This led to a series of altercations involving white and African American students and, eventually, to the beating of a white student, Justin Barker, by six African American youths who also attended the school. Barker was treated at a local hospital and released. The white students who admitted hanging the nooses were suspended from school for three days.

Although the incident was widely regarded as nothing more than a "schoolyard brawl,"[146] the six students, five of whom were juveniles at the time of the incident, were expelled from school and charged, not with assault, but with attempted second-degree murder and conspiracy to commit second-degree murder. All but one of the students—Jesse Ray Beard, who was 14 at the time of the incident—were charged as adults and were facing sentences of up to 100 years in prison.

Rapides Parish District Attorney Reed Walters, who initially justified the murder charges by classifying the tennis shoes the African American students were wearing during the incident as "deadly weapons," reduced the charges against Mycah Bell, who was 16 when the incident occurred, to aggravated second-degree battery and conspiracy to commit aggravated second-degree battery just before the case was to go to trial. He was convicted of these charges by an all-white jury, but a Louisiana Appellate threw out the conviction, ruling that Bell's case should have been heard in juvenile court. Bell pled guilty to simple battery in juvenile court and was sentenced to serve 18 months in a juvenile facility. In 2009 the remaining five defendants pleaded no contest to misdemeanour simple battery and were sentenced to seven days unsupervised probation and ordered to pay fines of $500.

Walters's decisions to charge the Jena Six with felonies in adult court and to not file charges against the students who hung the nooses were widely criticized. In September of 2007 Walters answered those criticisms in an op-ed piece for the *New York Times*.[147] Although he acknowledged that hanging the nooses was "abhorrent and stupid," he nonetheless argued that "it broke no law." He also contended that the attack on Justin Barker was not a "schoolyard fight," but rather was a brutal and unprovoked attack on an individual who had nothing to do with the noose incident. According to Walters,

> I can understand the emotions generated by the juxtaposition of the noose incident with the attack on Mr. Barker and the outcomes for the perpetrators of each. In the final analysis, though, I am bound to enforce the laws of Louisiana as they exist today, not as they might in someone's vision of a perfect world.[148]

Walters's explanation did not placate his critics. In 2007 the *Harvard Civil Rights–Civil Liberties Law Review* devoted an entire issue to the case of the Jena Six, with a focus on the actions of the prosecuting attorney. Andrew E. Taslitz and Carole Steiker, who wrote the lead article for the issue, argued that Walters's decisions and the racial conflict they sparked "provide important windows into how race operates in the American criminal justice system."[149] According to these authors,

> The racialized meaning of modern actions also affects public attitudes toward crime, the content of resulting legislation, the ways in which judicial and prosecutorial discretion are exercised, and the nature of what are likely to be effective solutions to the problems of racial bias and disparity. Once again, these meanings may do their work at a subconscious level, yet their influence cannot be denied. All Americans, but especially those with power to change the criminal justice system, have a duty to expose the subconscious and institutional influences at work in their own choices (and in those of other criminal justice system actors) and to correct racism's pernicious effects.[150]

Stevens added that the severity of federal penalties imposed for offenses involving crack cocaine, coupled with documented racial patterns of enforcement, "give rise to a special concern about the fairness of charging practices for crack offenses." His concerns are echoed by U.S. District Court Judge Consuelo B. Marshall, who observed, "We do see a lot of these [crack] cases and one does ask why some are in state court and some are being prosecuted in federal court … and if it's not based on race, what's it based on?"[151]

Prosecution of Pregnant Women Who
Abuse Drugs: Racial Discrimination?

In 1989 Jennifer Clarise Johnson, a 23-year-old African American crack addict, became the first woman in the United States to be convicted for exposing a baby to illegal drugs during pregnancy. The Florida court gave Johnson 15 to 20 years probation and required her to enter drug treatment and report subsequent pregnancies to her probation officer. According to the prosecutor who filed charges against Johnson, "We needed to make sure this woman does not give birth to another cocaine baby."[152]

Other prosecutions and convictions in other state courts followed; by 1992 more than 100 women in 24 states had been charged with abusing an unborn child through illegal drug use during pregnancy.

Many of these cases were appealed and, until 1997, all of the appeals resulted in the dismissal of charges. Then in October 1997, the South Carolina Supreme Court became the first court in the United States to rule that a viable fetus could be considered a person under child abuse laws and that a pregnant woman who abused drugs during the third trimester of pregnancy therefore could be charged with child abuse or other, more serious, crimes.[153] Two months later, Talitha Renee Garrick, a 27-year-old African American woman who admitted that she smoked crack cocaine an hour before she gave birth to a stillborn child, pled guilty to involuntary manslaughter in a South Carolina courtroom.

Do Prosecutors "Target" Pregnant African American Women?   A number of commentators contend that prosecutors' charging decisions in these types of cases reflect racial discrimination. Humphries and colleagues, for example, asserted, "The overwhelming majority of prosecutions involve poor women of color."[154] Dorothy Roberts[155] similarly argued that "Poor Black women are the primary targets of prosecutors, not because they are more likely to be guilty of fetal abuse, but because they are Black and poor."[156]

To support her allegations, Roberts cited evidence documenting that most of the women who have been prosecuted have been African American; she notes that the 52 women prosecuted through 1990 included 35 African Americans, 14 whites, 2 Hispanics, and 1 Native American. Ten out of 11 cases in Florida, and 17 out of 18 cases in South Carolina, were brought against African American women.[157] According to Roberts, these glaring disparities create a presumption of racially selective prosecution.

Randall Kennedy, an African American professor of law at Harvard University and the author of *Race, Crime, and the Law*, acknowledged that Roberts's charges of selective prosecution and racial misconduct "are surely plausible." As he noted, "Given the long and sad history of documented, irrefutable racial discrimination in the administration of criminal law ... no informed observer should be shocked by the suggestion that some prosecutors treat black pregnant women more harshly than identically situated white pregnant women."[158]

Kennedy claimed, however, that Roberts's contention that prosecutors target women "*because* they are black and poor,"[159] although plausible, is not persuasive. He noted that Roberts relied heavily on evidence from a study designed to estimate the prevalence of alcohol and drug abuse among pregnant women in Pinellas County, Florida. This study revealed that there were similar rates of substance abuse among African American and white women but that African American women were 10 times more likely than white women to be reported to public health authorities (as Florida law required).

Kennedy argued that the Florida study does not provide conclusive evidence of racial bias. He noted, in fact, that the authors of the study themselves suggested that the disparity in reporting rates might reflect either the fact that newborns who have been exposed to cocaine exhibit more severe symptoms at birth or the fact that African American pregnant women are more likely than white pregnant women to be addicted to cocaine (rather than to alcohol, marijuana, or some other drug). Kennedy asserted that Roberts failed to address these alternative hypotheses and simply insisted "'racial prejudice and stereotyping must be a factor' in the racially disparate pattern of reporting..."[160]

Kennedy also contended that Roberts's analysis failed to consider the problem of underprotection of the law. Imagine, he asked, what the reaction would be if the situation were reversed and prosecutors brought child abuse charges solely against drug-abusing white women. "Would that not rightly prompt suspicion of racially selective devaluation of black babies on the grounds that withholding prosecution deprives black babies of the equal *protection* of the laws?"[161]

What do you think? Do prosecutors "target" pregnant women who are poor and African American? What would the reaction be (among whites? among African Americans?) if only white women were prosecuted?

Race and Plea Bargaining Decisions

There has been relatively little research focusing explicitly on the effect of race on prosecutors' plea bargaining decisions. Few studies have asked if prosecutors take the race of the defendant into consideration in deciding whether to reduce or drop charges in exchange for a guilty plea. Moreover, the studies that have been conducted have reached contradictory conclusions.

Research reveals that prosecutors' plea bargaining decisions are strongly determined by the strength of evidence against the defendant, by the defendant's prior criminal record, and by the seriousness of the offense.[162] Prosecutors are more willing to offer concessions to defendants who commit less serious crimes and have less serious prior records. They also are more willing to alter charges when the evidence against the defendant is weak or inconsistent.

A number of studies conclude that white defendants are offered plea bargains more frequently and get better deals than racial minorities. A study of the charging process in New York, for example, found that race did not affect charge reductions if the case was disposed of at the first presentation. Among defendants who did not plead guilty at the first opportunity, however, African Americans received less substantial reductions than whites.[163] An analysis of 683,513 criminal cases in California concluded that "Whites were more successful in getting charged reduced or dropped, in avoiding 'enhancements' or extra charges, and in getting diversion, probation, or fines instead of incarceration."[164]

An analysis of plea bargaining under the federal sentencing guidelines also concluded that whites receive better deals than racial minorities.[165] This study, which was conducted by the United States Sentencing Commission, examined sentence reductions for offenders who provided "substantial assistance" to the government. According to §5K1.1 of the *Guidelines Manual*, if an offender assists in the investigation and prosecution of another person who has committed a crime, the prosecutor can ask the court to reduce the offender's sentence. Because the guidelines do not specify either the types of cooperation that "count" as substantial assistance or the magnitude of the sentence reduction that is to be given, this is a highly discretionary decision.

The Sentencing Commission estimated the effect of race/ethnicity on both the probability of receiving a substantial assistance departure and the magnitude of the sentence reduction. They controlled for other variables such as the seriousness of the offense, use of a weapon, the offender's prior criminal record, and other factors deemed relevant under the sentencing guidelines. They found that African Americans and Hispanics were less likely than whites to receive a substantial assistance departure; among offenders who did receive a departure, whites received a larger sentence reduction than either African Americans or Hispanics.[166] According to the Commission's report, "the evidence consistently indicated that factors that were associated with either the making of a §5K1.1 motion and/or the magnitude of the departure were not consistent with principles of equity."[167]

Similar results were reported by Celesta A. Albonetti,[168] who examined the effect of guideline departures on sentence outcomes for drug offenders. She found that guideline departures (most of which reflected prosecutors' motions to reduce the sentence in return for the offenders' "substantial assistance") resulted in larger sentence reductions for white drug offenders than for African American or Hispanic drug offenders. A guideline departure produced a 23 percent reduction in the probability of incarceration for white offenders, compared with a 14 percent reduction for Hispanic offenders and a 13 percent reduction for African American offenders.[169] Albonetti concluded that her findings "strongly suggest that the mechanism by which the federal guidelines permit the exercise of discretion operates to the disadvantage of minority defendants."[170]

Two studies found that race did not affect plea bargaining decisions in the predicted way. An examination of the guilty plea process in nine counties in Illinois, Michigan, and Pennsylvania revealed that defendant race had no effect on four measures of charge reduction.[171] The authors of this study concluded that "the allocation of charge concessions did not seem to be dictated by blatantly discriminatory criteria or punitive motives."[172] A study of charge reductions in two jurisdictions found that racial minorities received more *favorable* treatment than whites. In one county, African Americans received more favorable charge reductions than whites; in the other county, Hispanics were treated more favorably than whites.[173] The authors of this study speculated that these results might reflect devaluation of minority victims. As they noted, "if minority victims are devalued because of racist beliefs, such sentiments could, paradoxically, produce more favorable legal outcomes for minority defendants." The authors also suggested that the results might reflect overcharging of minority defendants by the police; prosecutors may have been forced "to accept pleas to lesser charges from black defendants because of the initial overcharging."[174]

In sum, although the evidence concerning the effect of race on prosecutors' charging and plea bargaining decisions is both scanty and inconsistent, a number of studies have found that African American and Hispanic suspects are more likely than white suspects to be charged with a crime and prosecuted fully. There also is evidence supporting charges of selective prosecution of racial minorities, especially for drug offenses. The limited evidence concerning the effect of race on plea bargaining is even more contradictory. Given the importance of these initial charging decisions, these findings "call for the kind of scrutiny in the pretrial stages that has been so rightly given to the convicting and sentencing stages."[175]

CONCLUSION

The court system that tried and sentenced the Scottsboro Boys in 1931 no longer exists, in the South or elsewhere. Reforms mandated by the U.S. Supreme Court or adopted voluntarily by the states have eliminated much of the blatant racism directed against racial minorities in court. African American and Hispanic criminal defendants are no longer routinely denied bail and then tried by all-white juries without attorneys to assist them in their defense. They are not consistently prosecuted and convicted with less-than-convincing evidence of guilt.

Implementation of these reforms, however, has not produced equality of justice. As shown in the preceding sections of this chapter, there is evidence that defendant race/ethnicity continues to affect decisions regarding bail, charging, and plea bargaining. Some evidence suggests that race has a direct and obvious effect on these pretrial decisions; other evidence suggests that the effect of race is indirect and subtle. It is important to note, however, that discriminatory treatment during the pretrial stage of the criminal justice process can have profound consequences for racial minorities at trial and sentencing. If racial minorities are more likely than whites to be represented by incompetent attorneys or detained in jail prior to trial, they may, as a result of these differences, face greater odds of conviction and harsher sentences. Racially discriminatory charging decisions have similar "spillover" effects at trial.

DISCUSSION QUESTIONS

1. Some commentators have raised questions about the quality of legal representation provided to the poor. They also have suggested that racial minorities, who are more likely than whites to be poor, are particularly disadvantaged. Is this necessarily the case? Are racial minorities represented by public defenders or assigned counsel treated more harshly than those represented by private attorneys? If you were an African American, Hispanic, or Native American defendant and could choose whether to be represented by a public defender or a private attorney, which would you choose? Why?

2. Racial minorities comprise a very small proportion of the lawyers and judges in the United States. What accounts for this? What difference, if any, would it make if more of the lawyers representing criminal defendants were racial minorities?

3. Do you agree or disagree with the Supreme Court's decision (*Grutter* v. *Bollinger*) in the case in which the University of Michigan Law School's admission procedures were challenged? What is the basis for your agreement or disagreement?

4. Assume that racial minorities *are* more likely than whites to be detained prior to trial. Why is this a matter for concern? What are the consequences of pretrial detention? How could the bail system be reformed to reduce this disparity?

5. Randall Kennedy, the author of *Race, Crime, and the Law*, argues (p. 10) that it is sometimes difficult to determine "whether, or for whom, a given disparity is harmful." Regarding the prosecution of pregnant women who abuse drugs, he states that "Some critics attack as racist prosecutions of pregnant drug addicts on the grounds that such prosecutions disproportionately burden blacks." But, he asks, "on balance, are black communities *hurt* by prosecutions of pregnant women for using illicit drugs harmful to their unborn babies or *helped* by intervention which may at least plausibly deter conduct that will put black unborn children at risk?" How would you answer this question?

6. Why did the case of the Jena Six spark so much controversy? Did Reed Walters, the district attorney, overcharge the six African American students? Should the white students who hung the nooses in the tree have been charged with hate crimes?

7. Assume that there is evidence that prosecutors in a particular jurisdiction offer more favorable plea bargains to racial minorities than to whites—that is, they are more willing to reduce the charges or to recommend a sentence substantially below the maximum permitted by law if the defendant is a racial minority. What would explain this seemingly "anomalous" finding?

8. What evidence would the defendants in *U.S.* v. *Armstrong et al.*, the Supreme Court case in which five black defendants challenged their prosecution for drug offenses in federal rather than state court, need to prove that

they had been the victims of unconstitutional selective prosecution? How would they obtain this evidence? Has the Supreme Court placed an unreasonable burden on defendants alleging selection prosecution?

NOTES

1. Philip S. Anderson, "Striving for a Just Society," *ABA Journal* (February 1999), p. 66.
2. *Powell* v. *Alabama*, 287 U.S. 45 (1932).
3. *Norris* v. *Alabama*, 294 U.S. 587 (1935).
4. Dan T. Carter, *Scottsboro: A Tragedy of the American South* (Baton Rouge: Louisiana State University Press, 1969), p. 326.
5. Ibid., p. 328.
6. Ibid., pp. 344–345.
7. Ibid., p. 347.
8. Birmingham *Age-Herald*, January 24, 1936 (quoted in Carter, *Scottsboro*, p. 347).
9. Carter, *Scottsboro*, pp. 376–377.
10. Ibid., p. 377.
11. Randall Kennedy, *Race, Crime, and the Law* (New York: Vintage Books, 1997), p. 104.
12. Peter Applebome, "Facts Perplexing in Texas Robbery," *New York Times*, December 19, 1983, p. 17.
13. Ibid., p. 17.
14. *Chicago Tribune*, August 9, 1995, Section 5, pp. 1–2.
15. Ibid., p. 2.
16. Ibid.
17. Available at The Justice Project website at http://www.justice.policy.net/cjreform/profiles.
18. Kennedy, *Race, Crime, and the Law*, p. 127.
19. *Powell* v. *Alabama*, 287 U.S. 45 (1932).
20. *Johnson* v. *Zerbst*, 304 U.S. 458 (1938).
21. *Gideon* v. *Wainwright*, 372 U.S. 335 (1963).
22. *Argersinger* v. *Hamlin*, 407 U.S. 25 (1972).
23. A defendant is entitled to counsel at every stage "where substantial rights of the accused may be affected" that require the "guiding hand of counsel" (*Mempa* v. *Rhay*, 389 U.S. 128, [1967]). These critical stages include arraignment, preliminary hearing, entry of a plea, trial, sentencing, and the first appeal.
24. *Strickland* v. *Washington*, 466 U.S. 668 (1984).
25. Anthony Lewis, *Gideon's Trumpet* (New York: Vintage Books, 1964).
26. Lisa J. McIntyre, *The Public Defender: The Practice of Law in the Shadows of Repute* (Chicago: University of Chicago Press, 1987).

27. Bureau of Justice Statistics, *Defense Counsel in Criminal Cases* (Washington, DC: U.S. Department of Justice, 2000), Table 5.

28. Ibid., Tables 16 and 19.

29. "Notes: Gideon's Promise Unfulfilled: The Need for Litigated Reform of Indigent Defense," *Harvard Law Review* 113 (2000), pp. 2,062–2,079.

30. Legal Defense and Educational Fund, National Association for the Advancement of Colored People, *Assembly Line Justice: Mississippi's Indigent Defense Crisis* (New York: NAACP), p. 2.

31. Jonathan D. Casper, "Did You Have a Lawyer When You Went to Court? No, I Had a Public Defender," *Yale Review of Law & Social Action* 1 (1971), pp. 4–9.

32. David W. Neubauer, *America's Courts and the Criminal Justice System*, 7th ed. (Belmont, CA: Wadsworth, 2002), p. 186.

33. See, for example, Abraham S. Blumberg, "The Practice of Law as a Confidence Game: Organizational Cooptation of a Profession," *Law & Society Review* 1 (1967), pp. 15–39; David Sudnow, "Normal Crimes: Sociological Features of the Penal Code in the Public Defender's Office," *Social Problems* 12 (1965), pp. 255–277.

34. Ronald Weitzer, "Racial Discrimination in the Criminal Justice System: Findings and Problems in the Literature," *Journal of Criminal Justice* 24 (1996), p. 313.

35. Jonathan D. Casper, *Criminal Courts: The Defendant's Perspective* (Englewood Cliffs, NJ: Prentice-Hall, 1978); Richard D. Hartley, "Type of Counsel and Its Effects on Criminal Court Outcomes in a Large Midwestern Jurisdiction: Do You Get What You Pay For?" Diss. University of Nebraska at Omaha, 2005; Martin A. Levin, *Urban Politics and the Criminal Courts* (Chicago: University of Chicago Press, 1977); Lisa J. McIntyre, *The Public Defender: The Practice of Law in the Shadow of Repute* (Chicago: University of Chicago Press, 1987); Dallin H. Oaks and Warren Lehman, "Lawyers for the Poor," in *The Scales of Justice*, Abraham S. Blumberg, ed. (Chicago: Aldine, 1970); Lee Silverstein, *Defense of the Poor* (Chicago: American Bar Foundation, 1965); Gerald R. Wheeler and Carol L. Wheeler, "Reflections on Legal Representation of the Economically Disadvantaged: Beyond Assembly Line Justice," *Crime and Delinquency* 26 (1980), pp. 319–332.

36. Jerome Skolnick, "Social Control in the Adversary System," *Journal of Conflict Resolution* 11 (1967), p. 67.

37. Paul B. Wice, *Chaos in the Courthouse: The Inner Workings of the Urban Municipal Courts* (New York: Praeger, 1985).

38. Bureau of Justice Statistics, *Defense Counsel in Criminal Cases* (Washington, DC: U.S. Department of Justice, 2000).

39. Ibid.

40. Malcolm D. Holmes, Harmon M. Hosch, Howard C. Daudistel, Dolores A. Perez, and Joseph B. Graves, "Ethnicity, Legal Resources, and Felony Dispositions in Two Southwestern Jurisdictions," *Justice Quarterly* 13 (1996), pp. 11–30.

41. Ibid., p. 24.

42. The findings reported in this chapter are unpublished. For a discussion of the overall conclusions of this study, see Cassia Spohn and Miriam DeLone, "When Does Race Matter? An Examination of the Conditions Under Which Race Affects Sentence Severity," *Sociology of Crime, Law, and Deviance* 2 (2000), pp. 3–37.

43. Weitzer, "Racial Discrimination in the Criminal Justice System," p. 313.

44. Roger A. Hanson and Brian J. Ostrom, "Indigent Defenders Get the Job Done and Done Well," in *Criminal Justice: Law and Politics*, 6th ed., George Cole, ed. (Belmont, CA: Wadsworth, 1993).

45. Gunnar Myrdal, *An American Dilemma: The Negro Problem and Modern Democracy* (New York: Harper and Brothers, 1944), p. 547.

46. Ibid., p. 548.

47. Haywood Burns, "Black People and the Tyranny of American Law," *The Annals of the American Academy of Political and Social Sciences* 407 (1973), pp. 156–166.

48. Celesta A. Albonetti, "An Integration of Theories to Explain Judicial Discretion," *Social Problems* 38 (1991), pp. 247–266; Ronald A. Farrell and Victoria L. Swigert, "Prior Offense Record as a Self-Fulfilling Prophecy," *Law & Society Review* 12 (1978), pp. 437–453; Caleb Foote, "Compelling Appearance in Court: Administration of Bail in Philadelphia," *University of Pennsylvania Law Review* 102 (1954), pp. 1,031–1,079; Joan Petersilia, *Racial Disparities in the Criminal Justice System* (Santa Monica, CA: Rand Corporation, 1978); Gerald R. Wheeler and Carol L. Wheeler, "Reflections on Legal Representation of the Economically Disadvantaged."

49. American Bar Association, "Lawyer Demographics." Available at http://www.abanet.org/legaled/statistics.html.

50. "A Disturbing Trend in Law School Diversity." Available at http://blogs.law.columbia.edu/salt.

51. Bureau of Labor Statistics, Employed Persons by Detailed Occupation, Sex, Race, and Hispanic or Latino Ethnicity, Employment and Earnings, Current Population Survey (2008), http://www.bls.gov/cps/cpsa2007.pdf.

52. American Bar Association, National Database on Judicial Diversity in State Courts. Available at http://www.abanet.org/judind/diversity/national.html.

53. American Bar Association, "Commission on Racial and Ethnic Diversity in the Profession," *Miles to Go 2000: Progress of Minorities in the Legal Profession* (Chicago: American Bar Association, 2000), Table 42 and Table 46.

54. Ibid., Table 44.

55. Ibid., p. 28.

56. Ibid., p. 29.

57. Richard H. Sander, "A Systematic Analysis of Affirmative Action in American Law Schools," *Stanford Law Review* 57 (2004), pp. 367–585.

58. Ibid., p. 474.

59. David L. Chambers, Timothy T. Clydesdale, William C. Kidder, and Richard O. Lempert, "The Real Impact of Eliminating Affirmative Action in American Law Schools: An Empirical Critique of Richard Sander's Study," *Stanford Law Review* 57 (2005), pp. 1,855–1,898.

60. Ibid., p. 1,857.

61. John Hechinger, "Critics Assail Study of Race, Law Students," *Wall Street Journal* November 5, 2004. Available at http://www.wsj.com.

62. American Bar Association, "Race and the Law: Special Report," February (1999): 42–70.

63. Terry Carter, "Divided Justice," *ABA Journal*, February (1999), pp. 42–45.

64. The University of Michigan Law School, *Report and Recommendations of the Admissions Committee*. Available at http://www.law.umich.edu/admissionspolicy.pdf.

65. Ibid.

66. *Grutter* v. *Bollinger*, 288 F.3d 732 (2003).

67. Ibid.

68. Case No. 06-15024. United States District Court, Eastern District of Michigan.

69. Wayne Thomas, *Bail Reform in America* (Berkeley, CA: University of California Press, 1976).

70. Samuel Walker, *Taming the System: The Control of Discretion in Criminal Justice, 1950–1990* (New York: Oxford University Press, 1993).

71. J. Austin, B. Krisberg, and P. Litsky, "The Effectiveness of Supervised Pretrial Release," *Crime and Delinquency* 31 (1985), pp. 519–537; John S. Goldkamp, "Danger and Detention: A Second Generation of Bail Reform," *The Journal of Criminal Law and Criminology* 76 (1985), pp. 1–74; Walker, *Taming the System*.

72. Goldkamp, "Danger and Detention."

73. This law was upheld by the U.S. Supreme Court in *United States* v. *Salerno*, 481 U.S. 739 (1987).

74. Coramae Richey Mann, *Unequal Justice: A Question of Color* (Bloomington, IN: Indiana University Press, 1993), p. 168.

75. R. Stryker, Ilene Nagel, and John Hagan, "Methodology Issues in Court Research: Pretrial Release Decisions for Federal Defendants," *Sociological Methods and Research* 11 (1983), pp. 460–500; Charles M. Katz and Cassia Spohn, "The Effect of Race and Gender on Bail Outcomes: A Test of an Interactive Model," *American Journal of Criminal Justice* 19 (1995), pp. 161–184.

76. S. H. Clarke and G. G. Koch, "The Influence of Income and Other Factors on Whether Criminal Defendants Go To Prison," *Law & Society Review* 11 (1976), pp. 57–92.

77. George S. Bridges, *A Study on Racial and Ethnic Disparities in Superior Court Bail and Pre-Trial Detention Practices in Washington* (Olympia, WA: Washington State Minority and Justice Commission, 1997).

78. Ibid., p. 54.

79. Ibid., p. 98.

80. Ibid.

81. Stephen Demuth and Darrell Steffensmeier, "The Impact of Gender and Race-Ethnicity in the Pretrial Release Process," *Social Problems* 51 (2004), pp. 222–242.

82. Ibid., Tables 2 and 4.

83. Ibid., p. 233.

84. Ibid., p. 238.

85. Margaret Farnworth and Patrick Horan, "Separate Justice: An Analysis of Race Differences in Court Processes," *Social Science Research* 9 (1980), pp. 381–399.

86. Theodore G. Chiricos and William D. Bales, "Unemployment and Punishment: An Empirical Assessment," *Criminology* 29 (1991), pp. 701–724.

87. Bureau of Justice Statistics, *Pretrial Release of Felony Defendants, 1990–2004* (Washington, DC: U.S. Department of Justice, 2007), Table 5.

88. Bureau of Justice Statistics, *Felony Defendants in Large Urban Counties, 2006* (Washington, DC: U.S. Department of Justice, 2010), Tables 5 and 8.

89. Spohn and DeLone, "When Does Race Matter?" Table 2.

90. Spohn and DeLone, unpublished data.

91. Cassia Spohn, "Race, Sex and Pretrial Detention in Federal Court: Indirect Effects and Cumulative Disadvantage," *University of Kansas Law Review* 57 (2009), pp. 879–902.

92. Ibid., p. 889.

93. Ibid., pp. 895–897.

94. Ibid., p. 893.

95. Ibid., pp. 898–899.

96. Leadership Conference on Civil Rights, *Justice on Trial: Racial Disparities in the American Criminal Justice System* (Washington, DC: Leadership Conference on Civil Rights, 2000).

97. *Bordenkircher* v. *Hayes*, 434 U.S. 357, 364 (1978).

98. Kenneth Culp Davis, *Discretionary Justice* (Baton Rouge: Louisiana State University Press, 1969), p. 190.

99. Barbara Boland (INSLAW Inc.), *The Prosecution of Felony Arrests* (Washington, DC: Bureau of Justice Statistics, 1983); Kathleen B. Brosi, *A Cross-City Comparison of Felony Case Processing* (Washington, DC: Institute for Law and Social Research, 1979); Vera Institute of Justice, *Felony Arrests: Their Prosecution and Disposition in New York City's Courts* (New York: Longman, 1981).

100. Charles E. Silberman, *Criminal Violence, Criminal Justice* (New York: Random House, 1978), p. 271.

101. *Bordenkircher* v. *Hayes*, supra, 434 U.S. 357, at 364 (1978).

102. For a review of this research, see Marvin Free, "Race and Presentencing Decisions in the United States: A Summary and Critique of the Research," *Criminal Justice Review* 27 (2002), pp. 203–232. Free reviewed 24 studies of prosecutorial charging decisions; his review revealed that 15 of them found that race (and, in some cases, ethnicity) did not affect charging outcomes.

103. Celesta A. Albonetti, "Criminality, Prosecutorial Screening, and Uncertainty: Toward a Theory of Discretionary Decision Making in Felony Case Processing," *Criminology* 24 (1986), pp. 623–644; Dawn Beichner and Cassia Spohn, "Prosecutorial Charging Decisions in Sexual Assault Cases: Examining the Impact of a Specialized Prosecution Unit," *Criminal Justice Policy Review* 16 (2005), pp. 461–498; Travis W. Franklin, "The Intersection of Defendants' Race, Gender, and Age in Prosecutorial Decision Making," *Journal of Criminal Justice* 38 (2010), pp. 185–192; Martha A. Myers, *The Effects of Victim Characteristics in the Prosecution, Conviction, and Sentencing of Criminal Defendants*, unpublished Ph.D. dissertation (Bloomington, IN: Indiana University, 1977); Laureen O'Neil Schermer and Brian D. Johnson, "Criminal Prosecutions: Examining Prosecutorial Discretion and Charge Reductions in U.S. Federal District Courts," *Justice Quarterly* 27 (2010), pp. 394–430; Cassia Spohn and David Holleran, "Prosecuting Sexual Assault: A Comparison of Charging Decisions in Sexual Assault Cases Involving Strangers, Acquaintances, and Intimate Partners," *Justice Quarterly* 18 (2001), pp. 651–688.

104. Schermer and Johnson, "Criminal Prosecutions."

105. Ibid., p. 422.

106. Franklin, "The Intersection of Defendant's Race, Gender, and Age in Prosecutorial Decision Making."

107. Myrdal, *An American Dilemma*, pp. 552–553.

108. "Duke Suspends Lacrosse Team from Play amid Rape Allegations," *USA Today*, March 28, 2006.

109. "Duke Rape Suspects Speak Out," *60 Minutes*, October 15, 2006.

110. William Chafe, "Race and Sex," *Durham Chronicle*, March 31, 2006, at A7.

111. "Duke DA Answers Critics: Denies Unethical Conduct, Wants Some Charges Dropped," ABC News Online (http://abcnews.go.com), February 28, 2007.

112. A. Beard, "Prosecutors Drop Charges in Duke Case," *Associated Press*, April 11, 2007.

113. American Bar Association, *Standards for Criminal Justice: The Prosecution Function*. Standard 3-3.9(d). Available at http://www.abanet.org/crimjust/standards/pfunc_toc.html.

114. Cassia Spohn, John Gruhl, and Susan Welch, "The Impact of the Ethnicity and Gender of Defendants on the Decision To Reject or Dismiss Felony Charges," *Criminology* 25 (1987), pp. 175–191.

115. Ibid., p. 186.

116. Robert D. Crutchfield, Joseph G. Weis, Rodney L. Engen, and Randy R. Gainey, *Racial and Ethnic Disparities in the Prosecution of Felony Cases in King County* (Olympia, WA: Washington State Minority and Justice Commission, 1995).

117. Ibid., p. 32.

118. Ibid., p. 58.

119. David Bjerk, "Making the Crime Fit the Penalty: the Role of Prosecutorial Discretion Under Mandatory Minimum Sentencing," *Journal of Law and Economics* 48 (2005), pp. 591–625; Timothy S. Bynum, "Prosecutorial Discretion and the Implementation of a Legislative Mandate," in *Implementing Criminal Justice Policies*, Merry Morash, ed. (Beverly Hills, CA: Sage, 1982), pp. 47–59; Charles Crawford, "Gender, Race, and Habitual Offender Sentencing in Florida," *Criminology* 38 (2000), pp. 263–280; Charles Crawford, Ted Chiricos, and Gary Kleck, "Race, Racial Threat and Sentencing of Habitual Offenders," *Criminology* 36 (1998), pp. 481–513; Jill Farrell, "Mandatory Minimum Firearm Penalties: A Source of Sentencing Disparity," *Justice Research and Policy* 5 (2003), pp. 95–115; Paul Hofer, "Federal Sentencing for Violent and Drug Trafficking Crimes Involving Firearms: Recent Changes and Prospects for Improvement," *American Criminal Law Review* 37 (2000), pp. 41–73; Paula Kautt and Miriam DeLone, "Sentencing Outcomes Under Competing But Coexisting Sentencing Interventions: Untying the Gordian Knot," *Criminal Justice Review* 31 (2006), pp. 105–131; Colin Loftin, Milton Heumann, and David McDowall, "Mandatory Sentencing and Firearms Violence: Evaluating an Alternative to Gun Control," *Law & Society Review* 17 (1983), pp. 287–318; Jeffery T. Ulmer, Megan C. Kurlychek, and John H. Kramer, "Prosecutorial Discretion and the Imposition of Mandatory Minimum Sentences," *Journal of Research in Crime and Delinquency* 44 (2007), pp. 427–458.

120. Bjerk, "Making the Crime Fit the Penalty."

121. Farrell, "Mandatory Minimum Firearm Penalties."

122. Crawford, "Gender, Race, and Habitual Offender Sentencing in Florida"; Crawford et al., "Race, Racial Threat and Sentencing of Habitual Offenders."

123. Ulmer et al., "Prosecutorial Discretion and the Imposition of Mandatory Minimum Sentences."

124. Ibid., Tables 2 and 3.

125. Ibid., p. 452.

126. Gary D. LaFree, "The Effect of Sexual Stratification by Race on Official Reactions to Rape," *American Sociological Review* 45 (1980), pp. 842–854.

127. Michael L. Radelet, "Racial Characteristics and the Imposition of the Death Penalty," *American Sociological Review* 46 (1981), pp. 918–927.

128. Jon Sorensen and Donald H. Wallace, "Prosecutorial Discretion in Seeking Death: An Analysis of Racial Disparity in the Pretrial Stages of Case Processing in a Midwestern County," *Justice Quarterly* 16 (1999), pp. 559–578.

129. Cassia Spohn and Jeffrey Spears, "The Effect of Offender and Victim Characteristics on Sexual Assault Case Processing Decisions," *Justice Quarterly* 13 (1996), pp. 649–679.

130. Ibid., pp. 661–662.

131. Ibid., p. 673.

132. Ibid., p. 674.

133. Joan Petersilia, *Racial Disparities in the Criminal Justice System* (Santa Monica, CA: Rand, 1983).

134. Ibid., p. 26.

135. Michael Tonry, *Malign Neglect: Race, Crime, and Punishment in America* (New York: Oxford University Press, 1995), p. 105.

136. Ibid., p. 115.

137. Jerome Miller, *Search and Destroy: African-American Males in the Criminal Justice System* (Cambridge: Cambridge University Press, 1996), p. 80.

138. Available at http://www.usdoj.gov/ag/readingroom/.

139. United States Sentencing Commission, *2009 Sourcebook of Federal Sentencing Statistics* (Washington, DC: United States Sentencing Commission, 2010), Table 34.

140. U.S. Department of Health and Human Services, Substance Abuse and Mental Health Services Administration, *National Household Survey on Drug Abuse: Population Estimates 1994* (Rockville, MD: U.S. Department of Health and Human Services, 1995).

141. Richard Berk and Alec Campbell, "Preliminary Data on Race and Crack Charging Practices in Los Angeles," *Federal Sentencing Reporter* 6 (1993), pp. 36–38.

142. *U.S. v. Armstrong et al.*, 517 U.S. 456 (1996).

143. 48 F.3d 1508 (9th Cir. 1995).

144. *U.S. v. Armstrong et al.*, 517 U.S. 456 (1996).

145. Ibid., (Stevens, J., dissenting).

146. Andrew E. Taslitz and Carol Steiker, "Introduction to the Symposium: The Jena Six, the Prosecutorial Conscience, and the Dead Hand of History," *Harvard Civil Rights–Civil Liberties Law Review* 44 (2009), pp. 275–296.

147. Reed Walters, "Op-Ed, Justice in Jena," *New York Times*, September 26, 2007, at A27.

148. Ibid.

149. Taslitz and Steiker, "Introduction to the Symposium," p. 295.

150. Ibid.

151. Leadership Conference on Civil Rights, *Justice on Trial*, p. 14.

152. Drew Humphries, John Dawson, Valerie Cronin, Phyllis Keating, Chris Wisniewski, and Jennine Eichfeld, "Mothers and Children, Drugs and Crack: Reactions to Maternal Drug Dependency," in *The Criminal Justice System and Women*, 2nd ed., Barbara Raffel Price and Natalie J. Sokoloff, eds. (New York: McGraw-Hill, 1995), p. 169.

153. *Whitner* v. *State of South Carolina* (1996).

154. Ibid., p. 173.

155. Dorothy Roberts, "Punishing Drug Addicts Who Have Babies: Women of Color, Equality, and the Right of Privacy," *Harvard Law Review* 104 (1991), pp. 1,419–1,454.

156. Ibid., p. 1,432.

157. Ibid., p. 1,421, n. 6.

158. Kennedy, *Race, Crime, and the Law*, p. 354.

159. Ibid., p. 359.

160. Ibid., p. 360.

161. Ibid., p. 363.

162. Lynn M. Mather, *Plea Bargaining or Trial?* (Lexington, MA: Heath, 1979).

163. Ilene Nagel Bernstein, Edward Kick, Jan T. Leung, and Barbara Schultz, "Charge Reduction: An Intermediary State in the Process of Labelling Criminal Defendants," *Social Forces* 56 (1977), pp. 362–384.

164. Weitzer, "Racial Discrimination in the Criminal Justice System," p. 313.

165. Linda Drazga Maxfield and John H. Kramer, *Substantial Assistance: An Empirical Yardstick Gauging Equity in Current Federal Policy and Practice* (Washington, DC: United States Sentencing Commission, 1998).

166. Ibid., pp. 14–19.

167. Ibid., p. 21.

168. Celesta A. Albonetti, "Sentencing Under the Federal Sentencing Guidelines: Effects of Defendant Characteristics, Guilty Pleas, and Departures on Sentence Outcomes for Drug Offenses, 1991–92," *Law & Society Review* 31 (1997), pp. 789–822.

169. Ibid., p. 813.

170. Ibid., p. 818.

171. Peter F. Nardulli, James Eisenstein, and Roy B. Flemming, *The Tenor of Justice: Criminal Courts and the Guilty Plea Process* (Chicago: University of Chicago Press, 1988).

172. Ibid., p. 238.

173. Malcolm D. Holmes, Howard C. Daudistel, and Ronald A. Farrell, "Determinants of Charge Reductions and Final Dispositions in Cases of Burglary and Robbery," *Journal of Research in Crime and Delinquency* 24 (1987), pp. 233–254.

174. Ibid., pp. 248–249.

175. Spohn, Gruhl, and Welch, "The Impact of the Ethnicity and Gender of Defendants on the Decision To Reject or Dismiss Felony Charges," p. 189.

6

✳

Justice on the Bench?

Trial and Adjudication in Criminal Court

In our courts, when it's a white man's word against a black man's,
the white man always wins. They're ugly but those are the facts of
life. The one place where a man ought to get a square deal is a
courtroom, be he any color of the rainbow, but people have a
way of carrying their resentments right into a jury box.
—HARPER LEE, *TO KILL A MOCKINGBIRD*[1]

GOALS OF THE CHAPTER

In this chapter we focus on trial and adjudication in criminal court. We begin
with an examination of race and the jury selection process. We focus on both
the procedures used to select the jury pool and the process of selecting the jurors
for a particular case. We also discuss the role that race plays in exonerations in
rape cases and the issue of "playing the race card" in a criminal trial. We end the
chapter by summarizing the scholarly debate surrounding the issue of racially
based jury nullification.

After you have read this chapter:

1. You should be able to discuss the role of the jury and explain how the U.S.
   Supreme Court has interpreted the requirement that jurors be chosen from a
   random cross-section of the population.
2. You should be able to explain how race and ethnicity continue to be taken
   into consideration during the jury selection process.

3. You should be able to evaluate competing arguments regarding the peremptory challenge and whether it should be eliminated.

4. You should be able to explain the concept of jury nullification and assess competing arguments regarding the legitimacy of race-based nullification.

5. You should be able to clarify why Randall Kennedy asserts that playing the race card in a criminal trial is "virtually always morally and legally wrong."

RACE/ETHNICITY AND THE CRIMINAL TRIAL

In 1997 Orange County (California) Superior Court Judge Everett Dickey reversed Geronimo Pratt's 1972 conviction for first-degree murder, assault with intent to commit murder, and robbery.[2] Pratt, a decorated Vietnam War veteran and a leader in the Black Panther Party, was accused of killing Caroline Olsen and shooting her ex-husband Kenneth Olsen on the Lincoln Park tennis court in Santa Monica. Pratt, who claimed he had been in Oakland on Panther business at the time of the crime, was convicted based in large part on the testimony of another member of the Black Panther Party, Julius Butler. It was later revealed that Butler had been a paid police informant and that police and prosecutors in Los Angeles conspired to keep this information from the jury hearing Pratt's case.

Over the next 25 years, Pratt's lawyers filed a series of appeals, arguing that Pratt's conviction "was based on false testimony knowingly presented by the prosecution."[3] Their requests for a rehearing were repeatedly denied by California courts, and the Los Angeles District Attorney's Office refused to reopen the case. Then, in May 1997, Judge Dickey granted Pratt's petition for a writ of habeas corpus and reversed his conviction. Citing errors by the district attorney who tried the case, Judge Dickey stated, "The evidence which was withheld about Julius Butler and his activities could have put the whole case in a different light, and failure to timely disclose it undermines confidence in the verdict."[4]

Pratt, who spent 25 years in prison—including 8 years in solitary confinement—was released on June 10, 1997. In April 2000 Pratt's lawsuit for false imprisonment and violation of his civil rights was settled out of court: the City of Los Angeles agreed to pay Pratt $2.75 million, and the federal government agreed to pay him $1.75 million. Pratt's attorney, Johnnie Cochran, Jr., described the settlement as "unprecedented" and praised Pratt for "the relentless pursuit of justice." Cochran also stated that the settlement puts "to rest a matter that has dragged on for more than three decades."[5]

Trial and Adjudication in the Twenty-First Century

We began the previous chapter with a discussion of the Scottsboro case, a case involving nine young African American males who were convicted of raping two white girls in the early 1930s. We noted that the defendants were tried by all-white juries and that the Supreme Court overturned their convictions because of the systematic exclusion of African Americans from the jury pool.

However, the Scottsboro Boys were tried in the 1930s, and much has changed since then. Race relations have improved, and decisions handed down by the Supreme Court have made it increasingly difficult for court systems to exclude African Americans from jury service. Nevertheless, "racial prejudice still sometimes seems to sit as a 'thirteenth juror.'"[6] As the Geronimo Pratt case reveals, the court system is not racially neutral. All-white juries continue to convict African American defendants on less-than-convincing evidence. All-white juries continue to acquit whites who victimize African Americans despite persuasive evidence of guilt. And police and law enforcement officials sometimes bend the law in their zeal to obtain a conviction. Consider the following recent cases:

1991: Four white Los Angeles police officers were charged in the beating of Rodney King, an African American man stopped for a traffic violation. A videotape of the incident, which showed the officers hitting King with their batons and kicking him in the head as he lay on the ground, was introduced as evidence at the trial. Los Angeles exploded in riots after a jury composed of 10 whites, 1 Asian American, and 1 Hispanic American acquitted the officers on all charges. A poll conducted in the aftermath of the jury verdict revealed that 45 percent of African Americans but only 12 percent of whites attributed the not guilty verdicts to racism and lack of African American participation on the juries rather than to errors by the prosecutor or inadequate evidence of the officers' guilt.[7]

2005: Walter Rideau, a 62-year-old African American whom *Life* magazine once called "the most rehabilitated prisoner in America," walked out of a Calcasieu (Louisiana) Parish jail a free man after a jury that included four African Americans found him guilty of manslaughter rather than murder. Rideau, who had previously been sentenced to death three times by all-white, all-male juries, spent 44 years in prison for the 1961 murder of a white female bank teller, a crime he did not deny. Each of his convictions and death sentences were overturned by federal courts. His first conviction was overturned by the U.S. Supreme Court, which referred to his trial as "kangaroo court proceedings." A federal appellate court overturned his second conviction and death sentence because the prosecutor removed potential jurors who said they would be hesitant, but not completely unwilling, to sentence Rideau to death. In 2000 a federal appellate court overturned his third conviction because of racial discrimination in the selection of the grand jury. Following this decision, the state of Louisiana decided to retry Rideau a fourth time, despite the fact that many of the prosecution witnesses were dead or otherwise unable to testify. The Calcasieu Parish District Attorney (with the approval of the judge in the case) had the testimony of the state's witnesses in the earlier trial read to the new jury. The jury found him guilty of manslaughter, which under Louisiana law carried a maximum penalty of 21 years in prison. Theodore M. Shaw, president of the NAACP Legal Defense and Educational Fund, which represented Rideau in the most recent case, stated, "This was not a case about innocence. It was about fairness and redemption—fairness, because even the guilty are entitled to a trial untainted by racial discrimination and misconduct, and redemption, because in a real sense the teenager who committed the tragic crime died while incarcerated for 44 years and was reborn as the man who paid the price and struggled for redemption."[8]

2010: Johannes Mehserle, a white former Bay Area Rapid Transit (BART) police officer, was convicted of involuntary manslaughter for killing Oscar Grant, a 22-year-old African American who was unarmed and lying face down on an outdoor train platform in Oakland (California) on New Year's Day of 2009. Mehserle, who was charged with second-degree murder, maintained that he shot Grant by mistake when he pulled his gun, rather than his Taser, from its holster. The jury's verdict meant that the jury did not believe that Mehserle intended to shoot Grant, but instead believed that his behavior was so negligent as to constitute a crime. After the jury's verdict was revealed, the U.S. Department of Justice's civil rights division announced that it was launching an investigation into whether Mehserle violated Grant's civil rights. In a letter to U.S. Attorney General Eric Holder urging him to open the investigation, U.S. Representative Barbara Lee wrote, "While I understand this is a state criminal matter, certain issues surrounding this case seem to invite further examination by the Civil Rights Division of the Department of Justice. Given the ongoing tensions between African-American communities, communities of color and law enforcement, care must be taken to ensure that civil rights statutes are properly enforced and positive relationships between these communities and law enforcement are forged."[9]

SELECTION OF THE JURY POOL

Three facts about jury discrimination are largely undisputed. First, the all-white jury has been a staple of the American criminal justice system for most of our history. Second, the Supreme Court has long condemned discrimination in jury selection. And third, race discrimination in jury selection remains a pervasive feature of our justice system to this day. The interesting question is how all of these facts can be true at the same time.
—DAVID COLE, *NO EQUAL JUSTICE*[10]

The jury plays a critically important role in the criminal justice system. Indeed, "the jury is the heart of the criminal justice system."[11] Although it is true that most cases are settled by plea and not by trial, many of the cases that do go to trial involve serious crimes in which defendants are facing long prison terms or even the death penalty. In these serious—and highly publicized—cases, the jury serves as the conscience of the community and, in the words of the United States Supreme Court, as "an inestimable safeguard against the corrupt or overzealous prosecutor and against the compliant, biased, or eccentric judge."[12] As the Court has repeatedly emphasized, the jury also serves as "the criminal defendant's fundamental 'protection of life and liberty against race or color prejudice.'"[13]

Racial Discrimination in Selection of the Jury Pool

The Supreme Court first addressed the issue of racial discrimination in jury selection in its 1880 decision of *Strauder* v. *West Virginia*.[14] The Court ruled that a West Virginia statute limiting jury service to white males violated the equal protection clause of the Fourteenth Amendment and therefore was unconstitutional. The Court concluded that the statute inflicted two distinct harms. The first was a harm that affected the entire African American population. According to the Court,

> The very fact that colored people are singled out and expressly denied by a statute all right to participate in the administration of the law, as jurors, because of their color ... is practically a brand upon them affixed by the law, an assertion of their inferiority, and a stimulant to that race prejudice which is an impediment to securing to individuals of the race that equal justice which the law aims to secure to all others.[15]

The Court stated that the West Virginia statute inflicted a second harm that primarily hurt African American defendants, who were denied even the *chance* to have people of their own race on their juries. "How can it be maintained," the Justices asked, "that compelling a man to submit to trial for his life by a jury drawn from a panel from which the State has expressly excluded every man of his race, because of his color alone, however well qualified in other respects, is not a denial to him of equal legal protection?"[16] The Court added that this was precisely the type of discrimination the equal protection clause was designed to prevent.

After *Strauder* v. *West Virginia*, it was clear that states could not pass laws excluding African Americans from jury service. This ruling, however, did not prevent states, and particularly Southern states, from developing techniques designed to preserve the all-white jury. In Delaware, for example, local jurisdictions used lists of taxpayers to select "sober and judicious" persons for jury service. Under this system, African American taxpayers were eligible for jury service but were seldom, if ever, selected for the jury pool. The state explained this result by noting that few of the African Americans in Delaware were intelligent, experienced, or moral enough to serve as jurors. As the Chief Justice of the Delaware Supreme Court concluded: "That none but white men were selected is in nowise remarkable in view of the fact—too notorious to be ignored—that the great body of black men residing in this State are utterly unqualified by want of intelligence, experience, or moral integrity to sit on juries."[17]

The U.S. Supreme Court refused to accept this explanation. In *Neal* v. *Delaware*, decided two years after *Strauder*, the court ruled that the practice had systematically excluded African Americans from jury service and was therefore a case of purposeful—and unconstitutional—racial discrimination.[18] Justice Harlan, writing for the Court, stated that it was implausible "that such uniform exclusion of [Negroes] from juries, during a period of many years, was solely because ... the black race in Delaware were utterly disqualified, by want of intelligence, experience, or moral integrity."[19]

These early court decisions did not eliminate racial discrimination in jury selection, particularly in the South. Gunnar Myrdal's analysis of the "Negro problem" in the United States in the late 1930s and early 1940s concluded that the typical jury in the South was composed entirely of whites.[20] He noted that some courts had taken steps "to have Negroes on the jury list and call them in occasionally for service."[21] He added, however, that many Southern courts, and particularly those in rural areas, had either ignored the constitutional requirement or had developed techniques "to fulfill legal requirements without using Negro jurors."[22] As a result, as Seymour Wishman noted, "For our first hundred years, blacks were explicitly denied the right to be jurors, which meant that if a black defendant was not lynched on the spot, an all-white jury would later decide what to do with him."[23]

Since the mid-1930s, the Supreme Court has made it increasingly difficult for court systems to exclude African Americans from the jury pool. It consistently has struck down the techniques used to circumvent the requirement of racial neutrality in the selection of the jury pool. The Court, for example, ruled that it was unconstitutional for a Georgia county to put the names of white potential jurors on white cards, the names of African American potential jurors on yellow cards, and then "randomly" draw cards to determine who would be summoned.[24] Similarly, the Court struck down the "random" selection of jurors from tax books in which the names of white taxpayers were in one section and the names of African American taxpayers were in another.[25] As the Justices stated in *Avery* v. *Georgia*, "the State may not draw up its jury lists pursuant to neutral procedures but then resort to discrimination at other stages in the selection process."[26]

The states' response to the Supreme Court's increasingly vigilant oversight of the jury selection process was not always positive.[27] The response in some southern jurisdictions "was a new round of tokenism aimed at maintaining as much of the white supremacist status quo as possible while avoiding judicial intervention."[28] These jurisdictions, in other words, included a token number of racial minorities in the jury pool in an attempt to head off charges of racial discrimination. The Supreme Court addressed this issue as late as 1988.[29] The Court reversed the conviction of Tony Amadeo, who was sentenced to death for murder in Putnam County, Georgia, after it was revealed that the Putnam County district attorney asked the jury commissioner to limit the number of African Americans and women on the master lists from which potential jurors were chosen.

The Exclusion of Mexican-Americans from Jury Service

The cases discussed thus far focus on *racial discrimination* in the selection of the jury pool. The issue of whether Hispanics—or, in the case of Texas, Mexican Americans—were similarly protected by the Equal Protection Clause of the Fourteenth Amendment proved more contentious and was not settled until 1954, a full 74 years after the Court ruled in *Strauder* that states could not ban African Americans from jury service by statute.

In a series of cases challenging the exclusion of Mexican Americans from jury service, Texas appellate courts consistently ruled against those challenging the system.[30] In early cases, the Texas courts ruled that the lack of Mexican-American jurors did not reflect purposeful discrimination but, rather, a lack of qualified candidates. For example, in *Lugo* v. *Texas*,[31] which was decided in 1939, the Court of Criminal Appeals heard testimony from the sheriff of San Patricio County that only two Mexican Americans had been summoned for jury duty (and neither of them served) in his 15 years as sheriff. However, the court ruled that this did not constitute evidence of intentional discrimination, noting that the sheriff also testified that "most of the Mexican population of this county are unable to speak intelligently in English and are unable to read and write the English language."

In later cases, the appellate courts in Texas shifted gears, arguing that there was no discrimination against the "Mexican race" because, first, the Equal Protection Clause recognized only two races or "classes" of people—whites and blacks—and, second, Mexican Americans were part of the white race and therefore were not discriminated against when juries were made up entirely of whites. As the court stated in *Hernandez* v. *State,* "Mexican people ... are not a separate race but are white people of Spanish descent. In contemplation of the Fourteenth Amendment, Mexicans are therefore members of and within the classification of the white race, as distinguished from the members of the Negro race."[32]

The Texas courts insisted that Mexican Americans were not a racial group, but a nationality group, and, as such, the Equal Protection Clause did not apply to them. As Clare Sheridan has pointed out, "The irony of absorbing Mexican Americans into the category 'white' was that it denied them equal protection as a group."[33]

The United States Supreme Court weighed in on these issues in 1954. The case involved Pete Hernandez, who was indicted for murder by a grand jury in Jackson County, Texas; he was convicted and sentenced to life imprisonment. Hernandez's lawyers challenged the composition of both the grand jury that indicted him and the petit jury that was selected for his trial, arguing that the selection process, which systematically excluded persons of Mexican descent from jury service, violated the Fourteenth Amendment. There was evidence that no Mexican Americans had been on a jury in Jackson County for at least a quarter century, despite the fact that there were Mexican Americans who were qualified to serve.

Lawyers for the state of Texas argued that Mexican Americans were "whites of Spanish descent" and that Hernandez therefore had an impartial jury, composed of members of his own race (in other words, whites). The Texas Court of Criminal Appeals agreed, concluding that Mexican Americans were a nationality, not a race, and that the Equal Protection Clause was not designed to ensure equal rights to those of different nationalities. The court stated that Hernandez was seeking "special privileges" that other whites did not have. According to the court's ruling, "It is apparent, therefore, that appellant seeks to have this court recognize and classify Mexicans as a special class within the white race and to recognize that special class as entitled to special privileges in the organization of grand and petit juries in this state."[34]

The United States Supreme Court disagreed with the Texas Court of Criminal Appeals' analysis. Writing for the majority, Chief Justice Earl Warren said, "The State of Texas would have us hold that there are only two classes—white and Negro—within the contemplation of the Fourteenth Amendment. The decisions of this Court do not support that view."[35] According to the Court's decision:

> Throughout our history differences in race and color have defined easily
> identifiable groups which have at times required the aid of the courts
> in securing equal treatment under the laws. But community prejudices are
> not static, and from time to time other differences from the community
> norm may define other groups which need the same protection. Whether
> such a group exists within a community is a question of fact. When the
> existence of a distinct class is demonstrated, and it is further shown that the
> laws, as written or as applied, single out that class for different treatment not
> based on some reasonable classification, the guarantees of the Constitution
> have been violated. The Fourteenth Amendment is not directed solely
> against discrimination due to a "two-class theory"—that is, based upon
> differences between "white" and Negro.[36]

The Supreme Court overturned Hernandez's conviction and, in doing so, stated that the fact that there were no Mexican Americans on juries for over 25 years could not be due to chance. As the majority stated, "it taxes our credulity to say that mere chance resulted in there being no members of this class among the over six thousand jurors called in the past 25 years. The result bespeaks discrimination, whether or not it was a conscious decision on the part of any individual jury commissioner."[37]

Techniques for Increasing Racial Diversity

Although the Supreme Court decisions discussed in the previous two sections have made it more difficult for states to discriminate overtly on the basis of race or ethnicity, the procedures used to select the jury pool are not racially neutral. Many states obtain the names of potential jurors from lists of registered voters, automobile registrations, or property tax rolls. The problem with this seemingly objective method is that in some jurisdictions racial minorities are less likely than whites to register to vote or to own automobiles or taxable property. As a result, racial minorities are less likely than whites to receive a jury summons. Further compounding the problem is the fact that "for a number of reasons, from skepticism and alienation to the inability to take time off from their jobs, minorities and the poor are also less likely to respond to those summonses they receive."[38] The result is a jury pool that overrepresents white middle- and upper-class persons and underrepresents racial minorities and those who are poor. (See Box 6.1 for the requirements for serving on a jury in Massachusetts.)

B o x   6.1   Excerpts from Massachusetts Jury Selection Statute

Juror Service

Juror service in the participating counties shall be a duty which every person who qualifies under this chapter shall perform when selected. All persons selected for juror service on grand and trial juries shall be selected at random from the population of the judicial district in which they reside. All persons shall have equal opportunity to be considered for juror service. All persons shall serve as jurors when selected and summoned for that purpose except as hereinafter provided. No person shall be exempted or excluded from serving as a grand or trial juror because of race, color, religion, sex, national origin, economic status, or occupation. Physically handicapped persons shall serve except where the court finds such service is not feasible. This court shall strictly enforce the provisions of this section.

Disqualification from Juror Service

As of the date of receipt of the juror summons, any citizen of the United States, who is a resident of the judicial district or who lives within the judicial district more than fifty per cent of the time, whether or not he is registered to vote in any state or federal election, shall be qualified to serve as a grand or trial juror in such judicial district unless one of the following grounds for disqualification applies:

1. Such person is under the age of eighteen years.

2. Such person is seventy years of age or older and indicates on the juror confirmation form an election not to perform juror service.

3. Such person is not able to speak and understand the English language.

4. Such person is incapable by reason of a physical or mental disability of rendering satisfactory juror service.

5. Such person is solely responsible for the daily care of a permanently disabled person living in the same household and the performance of juror service would cause a substantial risk of injury to the health of the disabled person.

6. Such person is outside the judicial district and does not Intend to return to the judicial district at any time during the following year.

7. Such person has been convicted of a felony within the past seven years or is defendant in pending felony cases or is in the custody of a correctional institution.

8. Such person has served as a grand or trial juror in any state or federal court within the previous three calendar years or the person is currently scheduled to perform such service.

SOURCE: 234A M.6.L.A. § et seq.

B o x 6.2   The Advantages of "Jurymandering"

In advocating for race-conscious jury selection, Hiroshi Furukai and Darryl Davies state,
... jury studies show that a number of legal and non-legal factors operate
together to cause the under-representation of racial minorities on the jury. Relying
on current color-blind jury selection procedures—in effect leaving the racial composition of the jury to chance—almost always leads to racially disproportionate representation. One way to guarantee a mixed jury is through a race-conscious selection
policy, or its equivalent, the 'jurymandering' method. Jurymandering is the use of an
affirmative mechanism, such as a racial quota, to engineer mixed juries that may not
occur under current jury selection procedures.

SOURCE: Hiroshi Furukai and Darryl Davies, "Affirmative Action in Jury Selection," *Virginia Journal of Social
Policy & the Law* 4 (1996), p. 653.

State and federal jurisdictions have experimented with a number of techniques for increasing the racial diversity of the jury pool. When officials in Hennepin County (St. Paul), Minnesota, which is 9 percent nonwhite, discovered that
most grand juries were all white, they instituted a number of reforms designed to
make jury service less burdensome. They doubled the pay for serving, provided
funding to pay jurors' daycare expenses, and included a round-trip bus pass with
each jury summons.[39] As a result of these measures, the number of racial minorities selected for grand juries increased.

A more controversial approach involves "race-conscious jury selection"[40] or
"jurymandering."[41] (See Box 6.2, for an argument in favor of jurymandering.)
Some jurisdictions, for example, send a disproportionate number of summonses
to geographic areas with large populations of racial minorities. Others attempt to
select a more representative jury pool by subtracting the names of white prospective jurors until the proportion of racial minorities in the pool matches the proportion in the population. A more direct effort to ensure racial diversity involves
setting aside a certain number of seats for racial minorities. Although no jurisdiction has applied this approach to the selection of trial jurors, judges in Hennepin
County are required to select two minority grand jurors for every grand jury.[42]

A somewhat different approach was tried in a U.S. District Court. In 2005, a
federal district court judge in Boston ordered court administrators to send a new
summons to another person in the same zip code if a summons was returned as
undeliverable.[43] Judge Nancy Gertner took this step in an attempt to increase the
pool of African American jurors available for a federal death penalty case involving
two African American men. Massachusetts pioneered the use of resident lists rather
than lists of registered voters in an attempt to increase the racial diversity of the jury
pool. However, defense attorneys in the case argued that resident lists are more
likely to be inaccurate in areas with the highest percentage of African Americans,
resulting in a large number of summonses returned as undeliverable. According to
Patricia Garin, one of the defense attorneys, Gertner's remedy, although unlikely to
make juries truly representative of the community, was "a step in the right direction" and would increase the chances that people of color would serve on juries.[44]

Opinions regarding these techniques are divided. Randall Kennedy argued that "officials should reject proposals for race-dependent jury reforms."[45] Although he acknowledged that these proposals are well-intentioned, Kennedy maintained that they would have unintended consequences (for example, jurors selected because of their race might believe they are expected to act as representatives of their race during deliberations) and would be difficult to administer (for example, officials would be required to determine the race of potential jurors and defendants, which would inevitably result in controversies over racial identification). Kennedy also suggested that the more direct techniques may be unconstitutional. As he noted, "Over the past decade, the U.S. Supreme Court has become increasingly hostile to race-dependent public policies, even when they have been defended as efforts to include historically oppressed racial minorities in networks of economic opportunity and self-government."[46]

Although the Supreme Court has not yet addressed this issue, in 1998 the U.S. Court of Appeals for the Sixth Circuit ruled that subtracting whites from jury panels so that all panels matched the racial makeup of the community violated the equal protection rights of white jurors.[47] Four years later, the U.S. Court of Appeals for the Second Circuit handed down a similar ruling. This case involved the prosecution of an African American charged with the death of an Orthodox Jewish student. The judge in the case believed that it was important to seat a jury that was racially and religiously diverse. When one of the empaneled jurors was excused as a result of illness, the judge removed a second white juror from the panel and filled the two slots with an African American and a Jewish juror, neither of whom was next in line on the list of alternate jurors. In *United States* v. *Nelson*,[48] the court recognized the motivations that led to the judge's decision, noting that they were "undoubtedly meant to be tolerant and inclusive rather than bigoted and exclusionary," but nonetheless ruled that "that fact cannot justify the district court's race-conscious actions. The significance of a jury in our polity as a body chosen apart from racial and religious manipulations is too great to permit categorization by race or religion even from the best of intentions."[49]

Those who disagree with these court rulings contend that race-conscious plans that create representative jury pools should be allowed because they reduce the likelihood that people of color will be tried by all-white juries. Albert Alschuler, an outspoken advocate of racial quotas for juries, asserted that "few statements are more likely to evoke disturbing images of American criminal justice than this one: 'the defendant was tried by an all-white jury.'"[50] He and other critics of jury selection procedures contend that lack of participation by racial minorities on juries that convict the African Americans and Hispanics who fill court dockets in many jurisdictions leads to questions regarding the legitimacy of their verdicts. (See Box 6.3 for anecdotal evidence of racial bias during jury deliberations.) Advocates of race-conscious plans also argue that the inclusion of greater numbers of racial minorities will counteract the cynicism and distrust that minorities feel toward their government. As David Cole, a professor at Georgetown University Law Center, wrote, "If the criminal justice system is to be accepted by the black community, the black community must be represented on juries. The long history of excluding blacks from juries is one

---

B o x   6.3   Racial Bias and Jury Selection: A Juror's Perspective

In an article on "Unconscious Bias and the Impartial Jury" that appeared in the *Connecticut Law Review*, Janet Bond Arterton, a U.S. District Court Judge for the District of Connecticut, discussed a note that she received from a juror at the conclusion of a case involving an all-white jury and three African American plaintiffs. The juror wrote:

"I would like to convey to you, in confidence, a few thoughts about my experience. I recall walking into the Jury Assembly room last Thursday, and being stunned by the singular 'whiteness' of the crowd. Out of almost 120 people reporting, one—yes, one—was a person of color. While it is my feeling that concern for quotas along racial lines can sometimes be excessive these days, no one could argue that the juries formed that day were a fair representation of our society. Couple that with the fact that the case involved three principals who are African-American, and the selection process seems all the more problematic.

"Personally, I have no qualms with our decision in the case. We were able to size up the credibility of witnesses and their testimony without a great deal of soul-searching or in-depth deliberation. I believe this was fortunate, considering the makeup and predisposition of the jury. During deliberations, matter-of-fact expressions of bigotry and broad-brush platitudes about 'those people' rolled off the tongues of a vocal majority as naturally and unabashedly as if they were discussing the weather.... Had just one African-American been sitting in that room, the content of the discussion would have been quite different. And had the case been more balanced—one that hinged on fine distinction or subtle nuances—a more diverse jury might have made a material difference in the outcome."

SOURCE: Honorable Janet Bond Arterton, "Unconscious Bias and the Impartial Jury," *Connecticut Law Review* 40 (2008), pp. 1,023–1,033.

---

important reason why blacks as a class are more skeptical than whites about the fairness of the criminal justice system."[51]

THE PEREMPTORY CHALLENGE: RACIAL PROFILING IN THE COURTROOM?

The Supreme Court consistently has ruled that the jury should be drawn from a representative cross-section of the community and that race is not a valid qualification for jury service. These requirements, however, apply only to the selection of the jury pool. They do not apply to the selection of individual jurors for a particular case. In fact, the Court has repeatedly stated that a defendant is not entitled to a jury "composed in whole or in part of persons of his own race."[52] Thus, prosecutors and defense attorneys can use their peremptory challenges—"challenges without cause, without explanation, and without judicial scrutiny"[53]—as they see fit (for evidence of this, see Box 6.4). They can use their peremptory challenges in a racially discriminatory manner.

It is clear that lawyers do take the race of the juror into consideration during the jury selection process. Prosecutors assume that racial minorities will side with minority defendants, and defense attorneys assume that racial minorities will be more inclined than whites to convict white defendants. As a result of these

---

B o x 6.4   Selecting a Jury: Stereotypes and Prejudice

A 1973 Texas prosecutor's manual for jury selection provided the following advice:

- You are not looking for a fair juror, but rather a strong, biased and sometimes hypocritical individual who believes that defendants are different from them in kind, rather than degree. You are not looking for any member of a minority group which may subject him to oppression—they almost always empathize with the accused. You are not looking for free thinkers or flower children.

- Observation is worthwhile…. Look for physical afflictions. These people usually sympathize with the accused.

- I don't like women jurors because I can't trust them. They do, however, make the best jurors in cases involving crimes against children.

- Extremely overweight people, especially women and young men, indicates a lack of self-discipline and often times instability. I like the lean and hungry look.

- If the veniremen have not lived in the county long, ask where they were born and reared. People from small towns and rural areas generally make good State's jurors. People from the east or west coasts often make bad jurors.

- Intellectuals such as teachers, etc. generally are too liberal and contemplative to make good State's jurors.

- Ask veniremen their religious preference. Jewish veniremen generally make poor State's jurors. Jews have a history of oppression and generally empathize with the accused. Lutherans and Church of Christ veniremen usually make good State's jurors.

SOURCE: Albert W. Alschuler, "The Supreme Court and the Jury: Voir Dire, Peremptory Challenges, and the Review of Jury Verdicts," *University of Chicago Law Review* 56 (1989), p. 153. [Online]. Available at: http://www.lexis-nexis.com/universe.

---

assumptions, both prosecutors and defense attorneys have used their peremptory challenges to strike racial minorities from the jury pool. Kennedy, in fact, characterized the peremptory challenge as "a creature of unbridled discretion that, in the hands of white prosecutors and white defendants, has often been used to sustain racial subordination in the courthouse."[54]

Dramatic evidence of this surfaced during an electoral campaign in Philadelphia. In April 1997 Lynne Abraham, Philadelphia's District Attorney, released a 1986 videotape made by Jack McMahon, a former assistant district attorney, and her electoral opponent. In the hour-long training video, McMahon advised fellow prosecutors that "young black women are very bad for juries" and that "blacks from the low-income areas are less likely to convict." He also stated, "There's a resentment for law enforcement. There's a resentment for authority. And as a result, you don't want *those people* on your jury"[55] (emphasis added). A Philadelphia defense attorney characterized the videotape as "an abuse of the office," noting, "It was unconstitutional then, and it's unconstitutional now. You don't teach young attorneys to exclude poor people, or black people or Hispanic people."[56]

These comments notwithstanding, there is compelling evidence that prosecutors do use their peremptory challenges to strike racial minorities from the jury pool. As a result, African American and Hispanic defendants are frequently tried by all-white juries. In 1964, for example, Robert Swain, a 19-year-old African

American, was sentenced to death by an all-white jury for raping a white woman in Alabama. The prosecutor had used his peremptory challenges to strike all six African Americans on the jury panel. In 1990, the State used all of its peremptory challenges to eliminate African Americans from the jury that would try Marion Barry, the African American mayor of Washington, DC, on drug charges.

The Supreme Court and the Peremptory Challenge:
From Swain to Batson

The Supreme Court initially was reluctant to restrict the prosecutor's right to use peremptory challenges to excuse jurors on the basis of race. In 1965 the Court ruled in *Swain* v. *Alabama* that the prosecutor's use of peremptory challenges to strike all six African Americans in the jury pool did not violate the equal protection clause of the Constitution.[57] The Court reasoned,

> The presumption in any particular case must be that the prosecutor is using the State's challenges to obtain a fair and impartial jury.... The presumption is not overcome and the prosecutor therefore subjected to examination by allegations that in the case at hand all Negroes were removed from the jury or that they were removed because they were Negroes.[58]

The Court went on to observe that the Constitution did place some limits on the use of the peremptory challenge. The Justices stated that a defendant could establish a *prima facie* case of purposeful racial discrimination by showing that the elimination of African Americans from a particular jury was part of a pattern of discrimination in that jurisdiction.

The problem, of course, was that the defendants in *Swain*, and in the cases that followed, could not meet this stringent test. As Seymour Wishman observed, "A defense lawyer almost never has the statistics to prove a pattern of discrimination, and the state under the *Swain* decision is not required to keep them."[59] The ruling, therefore, provided no protection to the individual African American or Hispanic defendant deprived of a jury of his or her peers by the prosecutor's use of racially discriminatory strikes. As Supreme Court Justice William Brennan later wrote:

> With the hindsight that two decades affords, it is apparent to me that *Swain*'s reasoning was misconceived.... *Swain* holds that the state may presume in exercising peremptory challenges that only white jurors will be sufficiently impartial to try a Negro defendant fairly.... Implicit in such a presumption is profound disrespect for the ability of individual Negro jurors to judge impartially. It is the race of the juror, and nothing more, that gives rise to the doubt in the mind of the prosecutor.[60]

Despite harsh criticism from legal scholars and civil libertarians, who argued that *Swain* imposed a "crushing burden ... on defendants alleging racially discriminatory jury selection,"[61] the decision stood for 21 years. It was not until 1986 that the Court, in *Batson* v. *Kentucky*, rejected *Swain*'s systematic exclusion requirement and ruled "that a defendant may establish a *prima facie* case of purposeful discrimination in selection of the petit jury solely on evidence concerning the prosecutor's exercise of peremptory challenges at the defendant's trial."[62] The justices added that once the defendant makes a *prima facie* case of racial discrimination, the burden shifts to the state to provide a racially neutral explanation for excluding African American jurors. (See Box 6.5 for a discussion of the use of the peremptory challenge to exclude African American jurors in cases involving white defendants.)

Interpreting and Applying the *Batson* Standard   Although *Batson* seemed to offer hope that the goal of a representative jury was attainable, an examination of cases decided since 1986 suggests otherwise. State and federal appellate courts have ruled, for example, that leaving one or two African Americans on the jury precludes any inference of purposeful racial discrimination on the part of the

---

B o x   6.5   White Defendants and the Exclusion of Black Jurors

The Equal Protection Clause of the Fourteenth Amendment declares that "No State shall ... deny to any person within its jurisdiction the equal protection of the law." Enacted in the wake of the Civil War, the Fourteenth Amendment was designed to protect the rights of the newly freed slaves. As Congressman Stevens, one of the amendment's sponsors, stated, "Whatever law punishes a white man for a crime shall punish the black man precisely in the same way and to the same degree. Whatever law protects the white man shall afford 'equal' protection to the black man" (Mason & Beaney, 1972, 379).

The Supreme Court has interpreted the equal protection clause to prohibit prosecutors from using their peremptory challenges in a racially discriminatory manner— that is, to forbid prosecutors from striking African Americans or Hispanics from the pool of potential jurors in cases involving African American and Hispanic defendants. But what about cases involving white defendants? Are prosecutors prohibited from using their challenges to strike racial minorities when the defendant is white?

The Supreme Court has ruled that white defendants can challenge the exclusion of racial minorities from the jury. In 1991, for example, the Court ruled that "a criminal defendant may object to the race-based exclusion of jurors effected through peremptory challenges regardless of whether the defendant and the excluded juror share the same race" (*Powers* v. *Ohio*, 499 U.S. 400 [1991]). This case involved a white criminal defendant on trial for homicide who objected to the prosecutor's use of peremptory challenges to remove African Americans from the jury. In 1998, the Court handed down a similar decision regarding the grand jury, ruling that whites who are indicted by grand juries from which African Americans have been excluded can challenge the constitutionality of the indictment (*Campbell* v. *Louisiana,* 523 U.S. 392 [1998]).

In both of these cases, the Court stated that a white defendant has the right to assert a violation of equal protection on behalf of excluded African American jurors. According to the Court, the discriminatory use of peremptory challenges by the prosecution, "casts doubt upon the integrity of the judicial process and places the fairness of the criminal proceeding in doubt." And, although an individual juror does not have the right to sit on any particular jury, "he or she does possess the right not to be excluded from one on account of race." As the Court stated, "Both the excluded juror and the criminal defendant have a common interest in eliminating racial discrimination from the courtroom." Because it is unlikely that the excluded juror will challenge the discriminatory use of the peremptory challenge, the defendant can assert this right on his or her behalf (*Powers* v. *Ohio*, 499 U.S. 400 [1991]).

What do you think? Should a white defendant be allowed to challenge the prosecutor's use of peremptory challenges to exclude African Americans and other racial minorities from his or her jury?

prosecutor,[63] and that striking only one or two jurors of the defendant's race does not constitute a "pattern" of strikes.[64]

Trial and appellate courts have also been willing to accept virtually any explanation offered by the prosecutor to rebut the defendant's inference of purposeful discrimination.[65] As Kennedy[66] noted, "judges tend to give the benefit of the doubt to the prosecutor." Kennedy cited as an example *State* v. *Jackson*, a case in which the prosecutor used her peremptory challenges to strike four African Americans in the jury pool. According to Kennedy,

> The prosecutor said that she struck one black prospective juror because she was unemployed and had previously served as a student counselor at a university, a position that bothered the prosecution because it was "too liberal a background." The prosecution said that it struck another black prospective juror because she, too, was unemployed, and, through her demeanor, had displayed hostility or indifference. By contrast, two whites who were unemployed were seated without objection by the prosecution.[67]

Although Kennedy acknowledged that "one should give due deference to the trial judge who was in a position to see directly the indescribable subtleties," he stated that he "still has difficulty believing that, had these prospective jurors been white, the prosecutor would have struck them just the same." Echoing these concerns, Brian J. Serr and Mark Maney conclude, "The cost of forfeiting truly peremptory challenges has yielded little corresponding benefit, as a myriad of 'acceptable' explanations and excuses cloud any hope of detecting racially based motivations."[68] (For a more detailed discussion of the peremptory challenge, see "Focus on an Issue: Should We Eliminate the Peremptory Challenge?")

The validity of their concerns is illustrated by a 1995 Supreme Court case, *Purkett* v. *Elem*.[69] Jimmy Elem, an African American on trial for robbery in Missouri, objected to the prosecutor's use of peremptory challenges to strike two African American men from the jury panel. The prosecutor provided the following racially neutral explanation for these strikes:

> I struck [juror] number twenty-two because of his long hair. He had long curly hair. He had the longest hair of anybody on the panel by far. He appeared to me to not be a good juror for that fact, the fact that he had long hair hanging down shoulder length, curly, unkempt hair. Also, he had a mustache and a goatee type beard. And juror number twenty-four also has a mustache and goatee type beard. Those are the only two people on the jury ... with the mustache and goatee type beard.... And I don't like the way they looked, with the way the hair is cut, both of them. And the mustaches and the beards look suspicious to me.[70]

The U.S. Court of Appeals for the Eighth Circuit ruled that the prosecutor's reasons for striking the jurors were not legitimate race-neutral reasons because they were not plausibly related to "the person's ability to perform his or her duties as a juror." Thus, the trial court had erred in finding no intentional discrimination.

The Supreme Court reversed the Circuit Court's decision, ruling that *Batson* v. *Kentucky* required only "that the prosecution provide a race-neutral justification for the exclusion, not that the prosecution show that the justification is plausible." Noting that neither beards nor long, unkempt hair is a characteristic peculiar to any race, the Court stated that the explanation offered by the prosecutor, although it may have been "silly or superstitious," was race-neutral. The trial court, in other words, was required to evaluate the *genuineness* of the prosecutor's explanation, not its *reasonableness*. As the Court noted, "At this step of the inquiry, the issue is the facial validity of the prosecutor's explanation. Unless a discriminatory intent is inherent in the prosecutor's explanation, the reason offered will be deemed race neutral."

The two dissenting judges—Justice Stevens and Justice Breyer—were outraged. They argued that the Court in this case actually overruled a portion of the opinion in *Batson* v. *Kentucky*. They stated that, the majority's conclusions notwithstanding, Batson clearly required that the explanation offered by the prosecutor must be "related to the particular case to be tried." According to Justice Stevens,

> In my opinion, it is disrespectful to the conscientious judges on the Court of Appeals who faithfully applied an unambiguous standard articulated in one of our opinions to say that they appear "to have seized on our admonition in *Batson* … that the reason must be 'related to the particular case to be tried.'" Of course, they "seized on" that point because *we told them to*. The Court of Appeals was following *Batson's* clear mandate. To criticize those judges for doing their jobs is singularly inappropriate.[71]

Justice Stevens went on to say, "Today, without argument, the Court replaces the *Batson* standard with the surprising announcement that any neutral explanation, no matter how 'implausible or fantastic,' even if it is 'silly or superstitious,' is sufficient to rebut a *prima facie* case of discrimination."

Critics of *Batson* and its progeny maintain that until the courts articulate and apply a more meaningful standard or eliminate peremptory challenges altogether (see In the Courts: *Miller-El* v. *Dretke*), "peremptory strikes will be color-blind in theory only."[72]

Focus on an Issue
Should We Eliminate the Peremptory

In theory, the peremptory challenge is used to achieve a fair and impartial jury. The assumption is that each side will "size up" potential jurors and use its challenges "to eliminate real or imagined partiality or bias that may be based only on a hunch, an impression, a look, or a gesture" (Way 1980, 344). Thus, a prosecutor may routinely strike "liberal" college professors, whereas a defense attorney may excuse "prosecution-oriented" business executives. The result of this process, at least in principle, is a jury that will decide the case based on the evidence alone.

The reality is that both sides use their peremptory challenges to "stack the deck" (Levine 1992, 51). The prosecutor attempts to pick a jury that will be predisposed to convict, whereas the defense attorney attempts to select jurors who will be inclined to acquit. In other words, rather than choosing open-minded jurors who will withhold judgment until they have heard all of the evidence, each

(Continued)

attorney attempts to pack the jury with sympathizers. According to one attorney, "Most successful lawyers develop their own criteria for their choices of jurors. Law professors, experienced lawyers, and a number of technical books suggest general rules to help select *favorable jurors*" [emphasis added] (Wishman 1986, 105).

DO PROSECUTORS USE PEREMPTORY CHALLENGES IN A RACIALLY DISCRIMINATORY MANNER?

The controversy over the use of the peremptory challenge has centered on the prosecution's use of its challenges to eliminate African Americans from juries trying African American defendants. It centers on what Justice Marshall called "the shameful practice of racial discrimination in the selection of juries" (*Batson* v. *Kentucky*, 479 U.S. 79 [1986]). Critics charge that the process reduces minority participation in the criminal justice system and makes it difficult, if not impossible, for racial minorities to obtain a "jury of their peers." They assert that peremptory challenges "can transform even a representative venire into a white, middle-class jury," thereby rendering "meaningless the protections provided to the venire selection process by *Strauder* and its progeny" (Serr & Maney 1988, 7–8).

There is substantial evidence that prosecutors exercise peremptory challenges in a racially discriminatory manner. A study of challenges issued in Calcasieu Parish, Louisiana, from 1976 to 1981, for example, found that prosecutors excused African American jurors at a disproportionately high rate (Turner, Lovell, Young, & Denny 1986, 61–69). Although the authors also found that defense attorneys tended to use their challenges to excuse whites, they concluded that "Because black prospective jurors are a minority in many jurisdictions, the exclusion of most black prospective jurors by prosecution can be accomplished more easily than the similar exclusion of Caucasian

prospective jurors by defense" (Turner et al. 1986, 68; Hayden, Senna, & Seigel 1978).

African American defendants challenging their convictions by all-white juries also have produced evidence of racial bias. One defendant, for example, showed that Missouri prosecutors challenged 81 percent of the African American jurors available for trial in 15 cases with African American defendants (*United States* v. *Carter*, 528 F. 2d 844, 848 [CA 8 1975]). Another defendant presented evidence indicating that in 53 Louisiana cases involving African American defendants, federal prosecutors used more than two-thirds of their challenges against African Americans, who comprised less than one-fourth of the jury pool (*United States* v. *McDaniels*, 379 F. Supp. 1,243 [ED La. 1974]). A third defendant showed that South Carolina prosecutors challenged 82 percent of the African American jurors available for 13 trials involving African American defendants (*McKinney* v. *Walker*, 394 F. Supp. 1,015, 1,017–1,018 [SC 1974]). Evidence such as this supports Justice Marshall's contention (in a concurring opinion in *Batson* v. *Kentucky*) that "Misuse of the peremptory challenge to exclude black jurors has become both common and flagrant" (*Batson* v. *Kentucky*, 106 Sct. 1712, 1726 [1986] [Marshall, J., concurring]).

ARE ALL-WHITE JURIES INCLINED TO CONVICT AFRICAN AMERICAN DEFENDANTS?

Those who question the prosecutor's use of peremptory challenges to eliminate African Americans from the jury pool argue that African American defendants tried by all-white juries are disproportionately convicted. They assert that white jurors take the race of the defendant and the race of the victim into account in deciding whether to convict the defendant.

Researchers have examined jury verdicts in actual trials and in mock jury studies for evidence of racial bias. Harry Kalven and Hans Zeisel (1966), for example, asked the presiding judge in more than 1,000 cases if he or she agreed with the jury's verdict. Judges who disagreed with the verdict were asked to explain the jury's behavior. Judges disagreed with the jury's decision to convict the defendant in 22 cases; in four of these cases they attributed the jury's conviction to prejudice against African American defendants involved in interracial sexual assault. Kalven and Zeisel also found that juries were more likely than judges to acquit African American defendants who victimized other African Americans.

Sheri Johnson (1985) argued, "Mock jury studies provide the strongest evidence that racial bias frequently affects the determination of guilt." She reviewed nine mock jury studies in which the race of the defendant was varied while other factors were held constant. According to Johnson, white "jurors" in all of the studies were more likely to convict minority-race defendants than they were to convict white defendants (1,626).

One mock jury study found evidence of racial bias directed at both the defendant and the victim (Klein & Creech 1982, 21). In this study, white college students read two transcripts of four crimes in which the race of the male defendant and the race of the female victim were varied; they then were asked to indicate which defendant was more likely to be guilty. For the crime of rape, the probability that the defendant was guilty ranged from 70 percent for crimes with black offenders and white victims, to 68 percent for crimes with white offenders and white victims, 52 percent for crimes with black offenders and black victims, and 33 percent for crimes with white offenders and black victims (Klein & Creech 1982, 24).

SHOULD THE PEREMPTORY CHALLENGE BE ELIMINATED?

Defenders of the peremptory challenge, although admitting that there is inherent

tension between peremptory challenges and the quest for a representative jury, argue that the availability of peremptories ensures an *impartial* jury. Defenders of the process further argue that restricting the number of peremptory challenges or requiring attorneys to provide reasons for exercising them would make selection of an impartial jury more difficult. Those who advocate elimination of the peremptory challenge assert that prosecutors and defense attorneys can use the challenge for cause to eliminate biased or prejudiced jurors. They argue that because prosecutors exercise their peremptory challenges in a racially discriminatory manner, African American defendants are often tried by all-white juries predisposed toward conviction.

In a concurring opinion in the Batson case, Justice Marshall called on the Court to ban the use of peremptory challenges by the prosecutor and to allow states to ban their use by the defense (*Batson* v. *Kentucky*, 106 Sct. 1712, 1726 [1986] [Marshall, J., concurring]). Marshall argued that the remedy fashioned by the Court in *Batson* was inadequate to eliminate racial discrimination in the use of the peremptory challenge. He noted that a black defendant could not attack the prosecutor's discriminatory use of peremptory challenges at all unless the abuse was "so flagrant as to establish a *prima facie* case," and that prosecutors, when challenged, "can easily assert facially neutral reasons for striking a juror" (*Batson* v. *Kentucky*, at 1727).

Other commentators, who acknowledge that the solution proposed in Batson is far from ideal and that reform is needed, propose more modest reforms. Arguing that the *chances* for abolition of the peremptory challenge are slim, they suggest that a more feasible alternative would be to limit the number of challenges available to each side. As one legal scholar noted, "Giving each side fewer challenges will make it more difficult to eliminate whole groups of people from juries"

(Continued)

(Note, *Batson* v. *Kentucky* 1988, 298). Another argued that courts must "enforce the prohibition against racially discriminatory peremptory strikes more consistently and forcefully than they have done thus far" (Kennedy 1997, 230). Another, more radical, suggestion is to allow each side to designate one or two prospective jurors who cannot be challenged peremptorily (see, for example, Ramirez 1998, 161).

Those who lobby for reform of the peremptory challenge maintain that the system would be fairer without them. As Morris B. Hoffman (2000) put it, "Imagine a jury selection process that sends the message to all 50 prospective jurors in the courtroom that this is a rational process. That we have rules for deciding who is fair and not fair, just as we have rules for deciding who prevails in the end and who does not."

In the Courts: *Miller-El* v. *Dretke* and *Snyder* v. *Louisiana*

Miller-El v. *Dretke* (537 US 322 [2005])

In 1986 Thomas Joe Miller-El was convicted and sentenced to death by a Dallas County (Texas) jury composed of 11 whites and 1 African American. The jury found Miller-El, an African American, guilty of killing a hotel employee and severely wounding another during the course of a robbery. During jury selection, Miller-El challenged the prosecutor's use of peremptory strikes against 10 of the 11 African Americans eligible to serve on the jury. He claimed that the strikes were based on race, citing as proof both the prosecutor's questioning of potential jurors in his trial and the fact that the Dallas County District Attorney had a history of excluding African Americans from criminal juries. The Texas courts that heard his appeal ruled against him, stating that there was no evidence that the jurors were struck because of their race and that the race-neutral reasons given by the prosecutor were "completely credible and sufficient" (*Miller-El* v. *State,* 748 S. W. 2d 459 [1988]).

Following a round of appeals in the federal courts, all of which agreed with the state courts' conclusions, Miller-El's case reached the United States Supreme Court. In June 2005 the Supreme Court reversed Miller-El's conviction, ruling 6–3 that there was strong evidence of racial

prejudice during jury selection and that the state court's conclusions were therefore "unreasonable as well as erroneous" (*Miller-El* v. *Dretke*, 537 US 322, 336 [2005]). Justice David H. Souter, writing for the majority, said, "The prosecutors' chosen race-neutral reasons for the strikes do not hold up and are so far at odds with the evidence that pretext is the fair conclusion, indicating the very discrimination the explanations were meant to deny." To support their conclusion, the justices cited the following evidence:

- Out of 20 African American members of the 108-person jury panel for Miller-El's trial, only 1 served. Nine of the 20 were excused for cause; of the remaining 11 African Americans, 10 were peremptorily struck by the prosecution. As the court noted, "Happenstance is unlikely to produce this disparity."

- The "racially neutral" reasons given by the prosecution to explain the strikes of African Americans applied just as well to whites who were not struck and, in some cases, mischaracterized the testimony of African Americans regarding such things as their willingness to impose the death penalty. In fact, the court stated that one of the African Americans who was struck expressed strong support of the death penalty and, therefore, should have been "an ideal juror in the eyes of a prosecutor seeking a death sentence." The fact that he was struck, and that whites who expressed less support for the death penalty were not, "supports a conclusion that race was significant in determining who was challenged and who was not." According to Justice Souter, "it blinks reality" to deny that some of the African America jurors were struck because of their race.

- Prosecutors repeatedly used their right to reshuffle the cards bearing potential jurors' names to reseat the African Americans at the back of the panel, where they were less likely to be questioned during the *voir dire* (and more likely to be dismissed without being questioned). The prosecution did not offer a racially neutral reason for shuffling the jury. Justice Souter wrote, "At least two of the jury shuffles conducted by the state make no sense except as efforts to delay consideration of black jury panelists."

- The questions posed to African American and white jurors during *voir dire* were different. Before asking potential jurors about their feelings regarding the death penalty, for example, prosecutors gave them a description of the death penalty. Ninety-four percent of the white jurors heard a bland description ("We anticipate that we will be able to present to a jury the quantity and type of evidence necessary to convict him of capital murder"), whereas more than half of the African American jurors heard a graphic description that described the method of execution in detail ("at some point Mr. Thomas Joe Miller-El—the man sitting right down there—will be taken ... to the death house and placed on a gurney and injected with a lethal substance until he is dead). The

Court concluded that the graphic script was used "to make a case for excluding black panel members opposed to or ambivalent about the death penalty." Race, according to the court, "was the major consideration when the prosecution chose to follow the graphic script."

The Supreme Court concluded that the evidence proffered by Miller-El, which clearly documented that prosecutors were selecting and rejecting potential jurors because of race, "is too powerful to conclude anything but discrimination."

Less than one month after the Supreme Court handed down its decision, Dallas District Attorney Bill Hill announced that the state would retry Miller-El and would seek the death penalty. Instead, in March of 2008, Thomas Joe Miller-El pled guilty to murder and aggravated robbery; he was sentenced to life in prison on the murder charge and to 20 years on the aggravated robbery charge. In exchange for the district attorney's agreement to not seek the death penalty, Miller-El waived his right to appeal his sentence.

Snyder v. Louisiana (552 U.S. 472 [2008])

Like Thomas Joe Miller-El, Allen Snyder, an African American, was convicted of first-degree murder and sentenced to death by an all-white jury. In this case, 36 prospective jurors survived the first stages of the jury selection process. Five of the 36 were African American and the prosecutor used 5 of his 12 peremptory challenges to eliminate them from the jury panel. On appeal, the Louisiana Supreme Court affirmed Snyder's conviction and Snyder then filed for a writ of certiorari with the United States Supreme Court. While his petition was pending before the Court, *Miller-El v. Dretke* was decided.

In *Snyder v. Louisiana*, the Supreme Court reiterated that "The Constitution forbids striking even a single prospective juror for a discriminatory purpose." The Court concluded that the prosecutor's decision to strike one juror, Jeffrey Brooks,

(Continued)

had been racially motivated. The justices noted that when the defense attorney objected to the strike of Mr. Brooks, a college senior, the prosecutor offered two "race-neutral" reasons for the strike:

> I thought about it last night. Number 1, the main reason is that he looked very nervous to me throughout the questioning. Number 2, he's one of the fellows that came up at the beginning [of voir dire] and said he was going to miss class. He's a student teacher. My main concern is for that reason, that being that he might, to go home quickly, come back with guilty of a lesser verdict so there wouldn't be a penalty phase. Those are my two reasons.

In ruling that the prosecutor's rationale did not meet the requirements of *Batson*, the Supreme Court focused on the second reason proffered. The Court stated that the scenario outlined by the prosecutor was "highly speculative," noting that if Mr. Brooks had wanted to ensure a quick resolution of the case, he would not necessarily have rejected a first-degree murder charge. Rather, if the majority of jurors had initially voted to convict Snyder of first-degree murder, "Mr. Brooks' purported inclination might have led him to agree in order to speed the deliberations." The Court also noted that the prosecutor did not excuse a white juror who was self-employed and who stated that serving on the jury would be a personal and financial hardship. According to the justices, "If the prosecution had been sincerely concerned that Mr. Brooks would favor a lesser verdict than first-degree murder in order to shorten the trial, it is hard to see why the prosecution would not have had at least as much concern regarding Mr. Laws." The Supreme Court concluded that "the prosecution's pretextual explanation gives rise to an inference of discriminatory intent."

As these two recent cases reveal, the issue of racial discrimination in the use of the peremptory challenge has not been laid to rest.

RACE AND JURY SELECTION IN THE TWENTY-FIRST CENTURY

In August of 2010 the Equal Justice Initiative, a non-profit legal organization headquartered in Montgomery, Alabama, released a report entitled, *Illegal Racial Discrimination in Jury Selection: A Continuing Legacy*.[73] The report, which detailed the results of an investigation of jury selection procedures in eight southern states (Alabama, Arkansas, Florida, Georgia, Louisiana, Mississippi, South Carolina, and Tennessee), was highly critical of the role that race continued to play in the jury selection process in the twenty-first century. In fact, Bryan A. Stevenson, Executive Director of the Initiative, began the executive summary of the report by noting,

> Today in America, there is perhaps no arena of public life or governmental administration where racial discrimination is more widespread, apparent, and seemingly tolerated than in the selection of juries. Nearly 135 years after Congress enacted the 1875 Civil Rights Act to eliminate racially discriminatory jury selection, the practice continues, especially in serious criminal and capital cases.[74]

The authors of the report were particularly critical of the prosecutor's use of the peremptory challenge, which they argued led to dramatic underrepresentation of racial minorities on juries in criminal cases. In support of this, they presented the following statistics:

- From 2005 to 2009 prosecutors in Houston County, Alabama, used their peremptory challenges to remove 80 percent of the African Americans qualified for jury service in cases in which the death penalty was eventually imposed. Although the county is 27 percent African American, half of the juries in these cases were all-white and the remainder had only one African American juror.[75]

- Prosecutors in the Chattahoochee (Georgia) Judicial Circuit used 83 percent of their peremptory challenges to strike African American potential jurors.[76]

- The "racially neutral" reasons that prosecutors give for striking African Americans from the jury often reflect stereotypes about African Americans' demeanor, appearance, and behavior. For example, in a South Carolina case the prosecutor stated that he struck an African American because he "shucked and jived" as he walked, and a Louisiana court allowed the prosecutor to strike an African American juror because he "looked like a drug dealer."[77]

- Racially tainted jury selection procedures led to the reversal of convictions in 80 cases in Alabama, 33 convictions in Florida, 12 convictions in Louisiana, and 10 convictions in Mississippi and Arkansas.[78] In fact, as recently as 2008, the United States Supreme Court reversed a criminal conviction in a death penalty case in Louisiana because the prosecutor used the peremptory challenge to eliminate all five of the potential African American jurors.[79]

- Although more than 100 criminal defendants in Tennessee have challenged their convictions based on prosecutors' use of race in exercising peremptory challenges, appellate courts in that state have never reversed a conviction because of racial discrimination in jury selection, due in large part to the fact that courts there "tend to accept at face value prosecutors' explanations for striking jurors of color."[80]

- Most district attorneys in the United States—and in the eight southern states examined for the report—are white. When the report was written, there were no African American district attorneys in Arkansas, Florida, or Tennessee.[81]

Noting that racially discriminatory jury selection procedures violate the constitutional rights of African American potential jurors and call into question "the credibility, reliability, and integrity of the criminal justice system,"[82] the authors of the report called for "coordinated efforts to eliminate illegal exclusion and discrimination in jury selection."[83] More specifically, they recommended, among other things, (1) more consistent enforcement of antidiscrimination laws designed to preclude racially biased jury selection; (2) that the *Batson* rule banning racially discriminatory use of peremptory challenges be applied retroactively to death row inmates or other offenders facing long prison sentences whose claims have not been reviewed because they were tried prior to 1986; (3) prosecutors who engage in racially biased jury selection should be held accountable and should not be able to participate in the retrial of any person whose conviction was overturned as a result of discrimination in jury selection; and (4) jurisdictions should enact or strengthen policies designed to ensure that racial minorities are fairly represented in the jury pool.[84] As the Executive Director of the Initiative concluded, the problem of illegal bias in jury selection "has persisted for far too long, and respect for the law cannot be achieved until it is eliminated and equal justice for all becomes a reality."[85]

In summary, there is incontrovertible evidence that the reforms implemented since the Scottsboro boys were tried, convicted, and sentenced to death by all-white juries have *reduced* racial discrimination in the jury selection process. Decisions handed down by the Supreme Court have made it difficult, if not impossible, for courts to make "no pretense of putting Negroes on jury lists, much less calling or using them in trials."[86] However, as the Equal Justice Initiative report and the other evidence presented in this chapter makes clear, the jury selection process remains racially biased. There is compelling evidence that prosecutors continue to use the peremptory challenge to exclude African American and Hispanic jurors from cases with African American and Hispanic defendants and that appellate courts continue to rule that their "racially neutral" explanations adequately meet the standards articulated in *Batson*. Supreme Court decisions notwithstanding, the peremptory challenge remains an obstacle to impartiality.

In the next section, we turn our attention to the issue of wrongful convictions, noting that race and mistaken eyewitness identification combine to produce an especially high rate of exonerations of African Americans accused of rape. This is followed by a discussion of "playing the race card in a criminal trial."

EXONERATING THE INNOCENT: RAPE, RACE, AND MISTAKEN EYEWITNESS IDENTIFICATION

During the past two decades, the issue of wrongful convictions has appeared on the national political agenda. Highly publicized exonerations of individuals convicted of murder, sexual assault, and other serious crimes have led to questions about the accuracy and fairness of the procedures used to investigate and adjudicate criminal cases. These concerns are based in part on the fact that a large number of the exonerees, many of whom were facing sentences of death or life in prison, were freed as a result of DNA tests that either were unavailable or were deemed unnecessary when their cases were being investigated and tried; this, in turn, has led some critics to suggest that the documented cases of wrongful conviction are only "the tip of the iceberg."[87] Concerns about false convictions also are based on research showing not only that a disproportionate number of those exonerated have been racial minorities but also that the disparity is particularly

---

B o x 6.6   Exonerating the Innocent: The Role of DNA

In 1989 a Cook County (Chicago) Circuit Judge vacated Gary Dotson's conviction for rape and dismissed the charges against him. Dotson thus became the first prisoner in the United States to be exonerated by DNA identification technology. As the technology improved and became more widely available, the number of DNA exonerations increased, from 1 or 2 a year in the early 1990s, to about 6 per year in the mid-1990s, to an average of 20 per year from 2000 to 2009. By the end of 2009, there had been 259 post-conviction DNA exonerations—152 (58.9 percent) of the exonerees were African American, 71 (27.5 percent) were white, and 21 (8.1 percent) were Hispanic.

SOURCE: The Innocence Project, Benjamin N. Cardozo School of Law, Yeshiva University. Available at http://www .innocenceproject.org/know/.

---

stark in cases of interracial sexual assault.[88] Together, these concerns have raised questions about the legitimacy and integrity of the criminal justice process (see Box 6.6 for additional evidence of the overrepresentation of racial minorities among those who have been exonerated as a result of DNA evidence).

A recent analysis of 340 exonerations in the United States from 1989 to 2003 revealed that DNA exonerations were especially prevalent in rape cases.[89] These cases also were characterized by eyewitness misidentification. In fact, in 107 of the 121 exonerations for rape, the defendant was the victim of eyewitness misidentification, and in 105 of these cases the defendant was eventually cleared by DNA evidence. About half (102 of 205) of the exonerations in murder cases also involved eyewitness misidentification, but only 39 of the 205 defendants were cleared as a result of DNA evidence.[90]

Rape, Race, and Misidentification

Although the percentages of African Americans, Hispanics, and whites who were exonerated for all crimes were similar to the percentages of each group incarcerated in state prisons, this was not the case for rape. In 2002, 58 percent of all people incarcerated for rape were white, 29 percent were African American, and 13 percent were Hispanic. Among defendants who were convicted of rape but later exonerated, the percentages were reversed: 64 percent were African American, 28 percent were white, and 7 percent were Hispanic. African Americans, in other words, comprised only 29 percent of all persons incarcerated for rape but 64 percent of all defendants exonerated for rape.[91]

The authors of this study suggested that the key to the explanation for the overrepresentation of African Americans among defendants falsely convicted for rape "is probably the race of the victim."[92] As they pointed out, the race of the victim was known in 52 of the 69 exonerations of African Americans for rape. In 78 percent of these cases, the victim was white. As they noted, "Inter-racial rape is uncommon, and rapes of white women by black men in particular account for well under 10 percent of all rapes. But among rape exonerations for which we know the race of both parties, almost exactly half (39/80) involve a black man who was falsely convicted of raping a white woman."[93]

The authors, who admitted that there were many possible explanations for this finding, stated that the "most obvious explanation for this racial disparity is probably also the most powerful: the perils of cross-racial identification."[94] Almost all of the exonerations in the interracial rape cases included in their study were based at least in part on eyewitness misidentification.

There is substantial evidence that cross-racial eyewitness identifications, and particularly eyewitness identifications of African Americans by whites, are unreliable.[95] What seems to happen, then, is that a white victim of a rape case mistakenly identifies an African American as the perpetrator of the crime, the defendant is found guilty at trial based at least in part on the eyewitness identification, and the defendant is exonerated when DNA evidence reveals that he was not the man who committed the crime.

PLAYING THE "RACE CARD" IN
A CRIMINAL TRIAL

In 1994 O. J. Simpson, an African American actor and former All-American football star, was accused of murdering his ex-wife, Nicole Brown Simpson, and Ronald Goldman, a friend of hers. On October 4, 1995, a jury composed of eight African American women, two white women, one Hispanic man, and one African American man acquitted Simpson of all charges. Many commentators attributed Simpson's acquittal at least in part to the fact that his attorney, Johnnie L. Cochran, Jr., had "played the race card" during the trial. In fact, another of Simpson's attorneys, Robert Shapiro, charged that Cochran not only played the race card but he also "dealt it from the bottom of the deck."[96]

Cochran was criticized for attempting to show that Mark Fuhrman, a Los Angeles police officer who found the bloody glove that linked Simpson to the crime, was a racist who planted the evidence in an attempt to frame Simpson. He also was harshly criticized for suggesting during his closing argument that the jurors would be justified in nullifying the law by acquitting Simpson. Cochran encouraged the jurors to take Fuhrman's racist beliefs into account during their deliberations. He urged them to "send a message" to society that "we are not going to take that anymore."[97]

Although appeals to racial sentiment—that is, "playing the race card"—are not unusual in U.S. courts, they are rarely used by defense attorneys representing African Americans accused of victimizing whites. Much more typical are *prosecutorial* appeals to bias. Consider the following examples:

- An Alabama prosecutor, who declared, "Unless you hang this Negro, our white people living out in the country won't be safe."[98]
- A prosecutor in North Carolina, who dismissed as implausible the claim of three African American men that the white woman they were accused of

raping had consented to sex with them. The prosecutor stated that "the average white woman abhors anything of this type in nature that had to do with a black man."[99]

- A prosecutor in a rape case involving an African American man and a white woman who asked the jurors, "Gentlemen, do you believe that she would have had intercourse with this black brute?"[100]

- A prosecutor in a case involving the alleged kidnapping of a white man by two African American men, who said in his closing argument that "not one *white* witness has been produced" to rebut the victim's testimony [emphasis added].[101]

- A prosecutor who stated, during the penalty phase of a capital case involving Walter J. Blair, an African American man charged with murdering a white woman, "Can you imagine [the victim's] state of mind when she woke up at 6 o'clock that morning, staring into the muzzle of a gun held by this black man?"[102]

All of these appeals to racial sentiment, with the exception of the last, resulted in reversal of the defendants' convictions. A federal court of appeals, for example, ruled in 1978 that the North Carolina prosecutor's contention that a white woman would never consent to sex with an African American man was a "blatant appeal to racial prejudice." The court added that when such an appeal involves an issue as "sensitive as consent to sexual intercourse in a prosecution for rape ... the prejudice engendered is so great that automatic reversal is required."[103]

A federal court of appeals, however, refused to reverse Walter Blair's conviction and death sentence. Its refusal was based on the fact that Blair's attorney failed to object at trial to the prosecutor's statement. The sole dissenter in the case suggested that the court should have considered whether the defense attorney's failure to object meant that Blair had been denied effective assistance of counsel. He also vehemently condemned the prosecutor's statement, which he asserted "played upon white fear of crime and the tendency of white people to associate crime with blacks."[104]

According to Harvard law professor Randall Kennedy, playing the race card in a criminal trial is "virtually always morally and legally wrong." He asserted that doing so encourages juries to base their verdicts on irrelevant considerations and loosens the requirement that the state prove the case beyond a reasonable doubt. As he noted, "Racial appeals are not only a distraction but a menace that can distort interpretations of evidence or even seduce jurors into believing that they should vote in a certain way irrespective of the evidence."[105] (Further evidence of this is presented in Box 6.7, which discusses the role that racial and cultural stereotypes played in recent cases involving defendants and victims of Hmong descent.) As the case discussed in the "Focus on an Issue: The Lynching of an Innocent Man and Defiance of the U.S. Supreme Court" makes clear, appeals to racial bias also can seduce individuals into believing that they have a right to take matters into their own hands.[106]

B o x 6.7   Racial and Cultural Stereotypes in the Courtroom

A basic tenet of criminal law is that individuals are entitled to equal treatment at trial and that juries should not be asked to convict someone because of that person's race, color, creed, or national origin. As the United States Court of Appeals for the Second Circuit ruled in 1973, use of racial stereotyping "negates the defendant's right to be tried on the evidence in the case and not on extraneous issues … [and] helps further embed the already too deep impressions in public consciousness that there are two standards for justice in the United States. One for Whites and the other for Blacks" (*United States ex rel. Haynes* v. *McKendrick*, 481 F.2d 152 (2d. Cir. 1973).

In an article published in the *Hamline Law Review*, William E. Martin and Peter N. Thompson illustrate the use of racial stereotyping in cases of sexual assault tried in Minnesota courts that involved victims and defendants of Hmong descent. In three different cases, prosecutors were allowed to introduce testimony regarding cultural stereotypes to discredit the defendant's consent defenses (that is, the defendants in these cases asserted that the victim had consented to the sexual acts). In one case, for example, the prosecutor introduced expert testimony to establish that cultural values would preclude Hmong women from consenting to have sex with a person other than her spouse. At trial this prosecutor argued that the jurors should consider the expert witnesses' testimony that in the Hmong culture,

> … it is not proper for a women to initiate sex, even with her husband. It is not proper for a woman to touch a man. It is not proper for a woman to kiss a man, and especially in public. There are cultural taboos you heard, even about being alone with a man not of your own class. Ask yourself if the woman you saw here is the kind of vixen that this defendant describes. The kind of vixen she would have to be [to be] so outside her own culture in behavior.

The defendant appealed his conviction, arguing that the use of cultural stereotypes was improper; his attorney compared the state's contention that a Hmong woman would not initiate sex to the oft-made but discredited argument that a white woman would never consent to sex with a black man because of cultural norms.

The Minnesota Court of Appeals upheld the defendant's conviction, noting that the prosecutor attempted to differentiate the victim and the defendant "by their social status and educational level not by social or cultural factors." However, as Martin and Thompson pointed out, even if the argument was an appeal to class bias or social status bias, it was nonetheless improper. Federal courts have ruled that appeals to class prejudice, like appeals to racial bias, will not be allowed in the courtroom.

The authors of this article criticize the decisions of the Minnesota court, arguing that "the fundamental values of our trial system require that persons be tried for the acts they commit, not for the supposed cultural characteristics that determine who they are."

SOURCE: William E. Martin and Peter N. Thompson, "Judicial Tolerance of Racial Bias in the Minnesota Justice, System," *Hamline Law Review* 25 (2001–2002), pp. 236–270, pp. 253–259.

Focus on an Issue
The Lynching of an Innocent Man and of the U.S. Supreme Court

On January 23, 1906, Nevada Taylor, a 21-year-old white woman who worked as a bookkeeper for a shop in Chattanooga, Tennessee, was sexually assaulted after she got off the trolley near the home she shared with her father and her brothers and sisters (Curriden & Phillips 1999). Taylor did not see her attacker and initially could describe him only as about her height and dressed in a black outfit and a hat. When asked by Hamilton County Sheriff Joseph Shipp if her attacker was "a white man or a Negro," she first said that she did not know, that she had not gotten a good look at him. She then changed her mind, stating that she believed the man was black (Curriden & Phillips 1999, 31).

The next day, the *Chattanooga News* reported the attack in a story with the headline "Brutal Crime of Negro Fiend." According to the *News*, "The fiendish and unspeakable crime committed in St. Elmo last night by a Negro brute, the victim being a modest, pretty, industrious and popular girl, is a sample of the crimes which heat southern blood to the boiling point and prompt law abiding men to take the law into their own hands and mete out swift and horrible punishment" (Curriden & Phillips 1999, 33).

There were no clues as to the identity of the suspect, other than a leather strap found at the scene of the crime. A reward of $375—more money than many people in Chattanooga earned in a year—was offered for information leading to the arrest of Taylor's attacker. Two days later, a man by the name of Will Hixson called Sheriff Shipp, asked if the reward was still available, and stated that he had seen a black man near the trolley station on the evening in question. He told Sheriff Shipp that he thought he could identify the man, and later that afternoon he fingered Ed Johnson.

Ed Johnson denied the allegations, stating that he had been at work at the Last Chance Saloon that afternoon and evening. He gave the sheriff the names of witnesses, most of whom were black, who could vouch for him. Despite the fact that there was no evidence, other than Hixson's identification, linking him to the crime and that he had an alibi, Johnson was arrested and charged with the rape of Nevada Taylor.

As news of Johnson's arrest spread, a mob began to gather at the jail. Within hours, more than 1,500 people had congregated, and many of them were urging the jailers to turn Johnson over to them. When informed by Hamilton County Criminal Court Judge Sam D. McReynolds that Johnson was no longer in Chattanooga, that he had been transported to Knoxville for safekeeping until trial, the crowd dispersed. As Curriden & Phillips (1999, 50) noted, the leaders of the mob "had put Sheriff Shipp and Judge McReynolds on notice: convict and punish this Negro quickly or they would be back."

Seventeen days after the attack on Nevada Taylor, a jury of 12 white men found Ed Johnson, who had steadfastly insisted that he was innocent, guilty of rape. The trial was replete with references to the fact that Johnson was black and his victim was white. The prosecutor, for example, asked Taylor to point out "the Negro brute" who assaulted her. Taylor pointed to Ed Johnson, who was the only black person in the courtroom. The prosecutor trying the case concluded his final argument by stating that the jurors should "Send that black brute to the gallows and prove to the world that in Chattanooga and Hamilton County the law of the country does not countenance such terrible crimes, has not ceased to mete out the proper punishment for such horrible outrages" (Curriden & Phillips 1999, 118).

The judge in the case also allowed the people in the audience—and the jurors—to express their opinions about the case and about Ed Johnson. When Johnson testified, the pro-prosecution spectators booed and heckled him. The audience cheered when prosecutors made a point and hissed and jeered when the defense objected. At one point in the trial, one of the jurors leaped to his feet, pointed at Johnson, and yelled, "If I could get at him, I'd tear his heart out right now" (Curriden & Phillips 1999, Chap. 5).

(Continued)

Judge McReynolds sentenced Ed Johnson to die and scheduled his execution for March 13, 1906. When Johnson's attorneys announced that they did not intend to appeal his conviction, two prominent local African American attorneys stepped in and filed a motion for a new trial. Noah Parden and Styles Hutchins believed that the evidence did not support a conviction and that there had been numerous violations of Johnson's constitutional rights. After their motion for a new trial was denied, they appealed to the Tennessee Supreme Court, which ruled that there had been "no serious errors" in the case.

Parden and Hutchins then appealed to the U.S. District Court, arguing that Johnson had not received a fair trial. District Court Judge C. D. Clark ruled that although "there was great haste in this trial" and "counsel were to an extent terrorized on account of the fear of a mob," the district court had no authority to intervene. The problem, according to Judge Clark, was that the right to a fair trial guaranteed by the Sixth Amendment did not apply to state-court cases. Nonetheless, Judge Clark did issue a stay of execution to allow Johnson's lawyers to appeal to the U.S. Supreme Court (Curriden & Phillips 1999, 168).

In a precedent-setting decision, the Supreme Court decided to intervene in the case. On March 18, 1906, Supreme Court Justice John M. Harlan sent a telegram to Judge Clark announcing that the court would hear Johnson's appeal. The Court also sent a telegram to Sheriff Shipp and Judge McReynolds informing them that Johnson's execution was to be stayed pending the outcome of his appeal.

The citizens of Chattanooga were outraged that "people in Washington, DC" were interfering in the case and telling them how to run their court system. The *Chattanooga News* issued what amounted to a call to arms, predicting that mob violence would result if "by legal technicality the case is prolonged and the culprit finally escapes" (Curriden & Phillips 1999, 197).

On March 19, the newspaper's prediction of violence came true. A mob gathered at the jail and, led by 25 determined men, bashed in the doors of the jail, grabbed Johnson from his cell, and dragged him through town to the bridge that spanned the Tennessee River. The leaders of the mob urged Johnson to confess. Instead, he repeated his claim of innocence, stating, "I am going to tell the truth. I am not guilty." His words enraged the crowd, and as they prepared to hang him from the bridge, Ed Johnson uttered his last words, "God bless you all. I am innocent" (Curriden & Phillips 1999, 210–214).

Although the citizens of Chattanooga blamed the lynching of Ed Johnson on the interference of the federal courts, the justices of the Supreme Court, and especially Justices Harlan and Holmes, were outraged that their order staying the execution had been ignored. President Theodore Roosevelt also condemned the lynching, which he called "contemptuous of the court" and "an affront to the highest tribunal in the land that cannot go by without proper action being taken." As Justice Harlan told the *Washington Post*, "the mandate of the Supreme Court has for the first time in the history of the country been openly defied by a community" (Curriden & Phillips 1999, 222).

The events that transpired next shocked the citizens of Chattanooga. In May 1906, the U.S. Department of Justice charged Sheriff Shipp, his deputies, and the ringleaders of the lynch mob with contempt of court. In December of that year, the Supreme Court announced that it had jurisdiction in the case and that the justices, sitting as a trial court, would determine the fate of the defendants. According to Curriden & Phillips (1999, 284), the Supreme Court was sending a message "that its authority was supreme" and that defiance of its orders "would not and could not be tolerated."

Although charges were eventually dropped against 17 of the 26 defendants and three of the remaining nine were found not guilty, the Supreme Court found Sheriff Shipp, one of his deputies, and four members of the lynch mob guilty of contempt of court. Shipp and two members of the mob were sentenced to 90 days in prison; the others received sentences of 60 days. Noah Parden, the lawyer who filed the appeal with the Supreme Court, told the *Atlanta Independent* that the court's actions sent an important message. "We are at a time," he said, "when many of our people have abandoned the respect for the rule of law due to the racial hatred deep in their hearts and souls, and nothing less than our civilized society is at stake" (Curriden & Phillips 1999, 336).

Ninety-four years later, Hamilton County Criminal Court Judge Doug Meyer overturned Johnson's conviction. "It really is hard for us in the White community to imagine how badly Blacks were treated at that time," said Judge Meyer. "Something I don't believe the White community really understands is that, especially at that time, the object was to bring in a Black body, not necessarily the person who had committed the crime. And I think that's what happened in this case. There was a rush to find somebody to convict and blame."[107] The attorney who filed the petition to overturn Johnson's conviction was Leroy Phillips, one of the co-authors of *Contempt of Court.*

Race-Conscious Jury Nullification: Black Power in the Courtroom?

In a provocative essay published in the *Yale Law Journal* shortly after O. J. Simpson's acquittal, Paul Butler, an African American professor of law at George Washington University Law School, argued for "racially based jury nullification"[108]—that is, he urged African American jurors to refuse to convict African American defendants accused of nonviolent crimes, regardless of the strength of the evidence mounted against them. According to Butler, "it is the moral responsibility of black jurors to emancipate some guilty black outlaws."[109]

Jury nullification, which has its roots in English common law, occurs when a juror believes that the evidence presented at trial establishes the defendant's guilt but nonetheless votes to acquit. The juror's decision may be motivated either by a belief that the law under which the defendant is being prosecuted is unfair or by an objection to the application of the law to a particular defendant. In the first instance, a juror might refuse to convict a defendant tried in federal court for possession of more than 50 grams of crack cocaine, based on her belief that the draconian penalties mandated by the law are unfair. In the second instance, a juror might vote to acquit a father charged with child endangerment after his 2-year-old daughter, who was not restrained in a child safety seat, was thrown from the car and killed when he lost control of his car on an icy road. In this case, the juror does not believe that the law itself is unfair, but, rather, that the defendant has suffered enough and that nothing will be gained by additional punishment.

Jurors clearly have the power to nullify the law and to vote their conscience. If a jury votes unanimously to acquit, the double jeopardy clause of the Fifth

Amendment prohibits reversal of the jury's decision. The jury's decision to acquit, even in the face of overwhelming evidence of guilt, is final and cannot be reversed by the trial judge or by an appellate court. In most jurisdictions, however, jurors do not have to be told that they have the right to nullify the law.[110]

Butler's position on jury nullification is that the "black community is better off when some nonviolent lawbreakers remain in the community rather than go to prison."[111] Arguing that there are far too many African American men in prison, Butler suggested that there should be "a presumption in favor of nullification"[112] in cases involving African American defendants charged with *nonviolent, victimless* crimes like possession of drugs. Butler claimed that enforcement of these laws has a disparate effect on the African American community and does not "advance the interest of black people."[113] He also suggested that white racism, which "creates and sustains the criminal breeding ground which produces the black criminal,"[114] is the underlying cause of much of the crime committed by African Americans. He thus urged African American jurors to "nullify without hesitation in these cases."[115]

Butler did not argue for nullification in all types of cases. In fact, he asserted that defendants charged with violent crimes such as murder, rape, and armed robbery should be convicted if there is proof beyond a reasonable doubt of guilt. He contended that nullification is not morally justifiable in these types of cases because "people who are violent should be separated from the community, for the sake of the nonviolent."[116] Violent African American offenders, in other words, should be convicted and incarcerated to protect potential innocent victims. Butler was willing to "write off" these offenders based on his belief that the "black community cannot afford the risks of leaving this person in its midst."[117]

The more difficult cases, according to Butler, involve defendants charged with nonviolent property offenses or with more serious drug-trafficking offenses. He discussed two hypothetical cases, one involving a ghetto drug dealer and the other involving a thief who burglarizes the home of a rich family. His answer to the question "Is nullification morally justifiable here?" is "It depends."[118] Although he admitted that "encouraging people to engage in self-destructive behavior is evil" and that therefore most drug dealers should be convicted, he argued that a juror's decision in this type of case might rest on the particular facts in the case. Similarly, although he is troubled by the case of the burglar who steals from a rich family because the behavior is "so clearly wrong," he argued that the facts in the case—for example, a person who steals to support a drug habit—might justify a vote to acquit. Nullification, in other words, may be a morally justifiable option in both types of cases.

Randall Kennedy's Critique

Randall Kennedy[119] raised a number of objections to Butler's proposal, which he characterized as "profoundly misleading as a guide to action."[120] Although he acknowledged that Butler's assertion that there is racial injustice in the administration of the criminal law is correct, Kennedy nonetheless objected to Butler's portrayal of the criminal justice system as a "one-dimensional system that is

totally at odds with what black Americans need and want, a system that unequiv-
ocally represents and unrelentingly imposes 'the white man's law.'"[121] Kennedy
faulted Butler for his failure to acknowledge either the legal reforms implemented as a result of struggles *against* racism or the significant presence of African
American officials in policymaking positions and the criminal justice system.
The problems inherent in the criminal justice system, according to Kennedy,
"require judicious attention, not a campaign of defiant sabotage."[122]

Kennedy objected to the fact that Butler expressed *more* sympathy for nonviolent African American offenders than for "the law-abiding people compelled
by circumstances to live in close proximity to the criminals for whom he is willing to urge subversion of the legal system."[123] He asserted that law-abiding African Americans "desire *more* rather than *less* prosecution and punishment for *all*
types of criminals,"[124] and suggested that, in any case, jury nullification "is an
exceedingly poor means for advancing the goal of a racially fair administration
of criminal law."[125] He claimed that a highly publicized campaign of jury nullification carried on by African Americans will not produce the social reforms that
Butler demands. Moreover, such a campaign might backfire. Kennedy suggested
that it might lead to increased support for proposals to eliminate the requirement
that the jury be unanimous in order to convict, restrictions on the right of
African Americans to serve on juries, or widespread use of jury nullification by
white jurors in cases involving white-on-black crime.

According to Kennedy, the most compelling reason to oppose Butler's call for
racially based jury nullification is that it is based on "an ultimately destructive sentiment of racial kinship that prompts individuals of a given race to care more about
'their own' than people of another race."[126] He objected to the implication that it is
proper for African American jurors to be more concerned about the fate of African
American defendants than white defendants, more disturbed about the plight of
African American communities than white communities, and more interested in
protecting the lives and property of African American than white citizens. "Along
that road," according to Kennedy, "lies moral and political disaster." Implementation of Butler's proposal, Kennedy insisted, would not only increase but also legitimize "the tendency of people to privilege in racial terms 'their own.'"[127]

CONCLUSION

In Chapter 5, we concluded that the reforms implemented during the past few decades have substantially reduced racial discrimination during the pretrial stages of the
criminal justice process. Our examination of the jury selection process suggests that
a similar conclusion is warranted. Reforms adopted voluntarily by the states
or mandated by appellate courts have made it increasingly unlikely that African
American and Hispanic defendants will routinely be tried by all-white juries.

An important caveat, however, concerns the use of racially motivated
peremptory challenges. As the recent report by the Equal Justice Initiative
demonstrates, the peremptory challenge stands in the way of a racially neutral
jury selection process. Supreme Court decisions notwithstanding, prosecutors

still manage to use the peremptory challenge to eliminate African Americans and Hispanics from juries trying African American and Hispanic defendants. More troubling, prosecutors' "racially neutral" explanations for strikes alleged to be racially motivated, with few exceptions, continue to be accepted at face value. Coupled with anecdotal evidence that prosecutors are not reluctant to "play the race card" in a criminal trial, these findings regarding jury selection suggest that the process of adjudication, like the pretrial process, is not free of racial bias.

Based on the research reviewed in this chapter and the previous one, we conclude that contemporary court processing decisions are not characterized by *systematic* discrimination against racial minorities. This may have been true at the time that the Scottsboro Boys and Ed Johnson were tried, but it is no longer true. As we have shown, the U.S. Supreme Court has consistently affirmed the importance of protecting the rights of criminal defendants and has insisted that the race and ethnicity of the defendant not be taken into consideration in making case processing decisions. Coupled with reforms adopted voluntarily by the states, these decisions make systematic racial discrimination unlikely.

We are not suggesting, however, that these reforms have produced an equitable, or color-blind, system of justice. We are not suggesting that contemporary court processing decisions reflect *pure justice*. Researchers have demonstrated that court processing decisions in some jurisdictions reflect racial discrimination, whereas decisions in other jurisdictions are racially neutral. Researchers also have shown that African Americans and Hispanics who commit certain types of crimes are treated more harshly than whites and that being unemployed, having a prior criminal record, or being detained prior to trial may have a more negative effect on court outcomes for people of color than for whites.

These findings lead us to conclude that discrimination against African Americans and other racial minorities is not universal but is confined to certain types of cases, certain types of settings, and certain types of defendants. We conclude that the court system of today is characterized by *contextual discrimination*.

DISCUSSION QUESTIONS

1. The Supreme Court has repeatedly asserted that a defendant is not entitled to a jury "composed in whole or in part of persons of his own race." Although these rulings establish that states are not *obligated* to use racially mixed juries, they do not *prohibit* states from doing so. In fact, a number of policy makers and legal scholars have proposed reforms that use racial criteria to promote racial diversity on American juries. Some have suggested that the names of majority race jurors be removed from the jury list (thus ensuring a larger proportion of racial minorities); others have suggested that a certain number of seats on each jury be set aside for racial minorities. How would you justify these reforms to a state legislature? How would an opponent of these reforms respond? Overall, are these good ideas or bad ideas?

2. Evidence suggesting the prosecutors use their peremptory challenges to preserve all-white juries in cases involving African American or Hispanic defendants has led some commentators to call for the elimination of the peremptory challenge. What do you think is the strongest argument in favor of eliminating the peremptory challenge? In favor of retaining it?

3. Given that the Supreme Court is unlikely to rule that the peremptory challenge violates the right to a fair trial and is therefore unconstitutional, are there any remedies or reforms that could be implemented?

4. Should a white defendant be allowed to challenge the prosecutor's use of peremptory challenges to exclude African Americans and other racial minorities from his or her jury? Why or why not?

5. Why do you think the U.S. Supreme Court decided to intervene in the Ed Johnson case (see "Focus on an Issue: The Lynching of an Innocent Man")?

6. In this chapter, we present a number of examples of lawyers who "played the race card" in a criminal trial. Almost all of them involved prosecutors who appealed to the potential racist sentiments of white jurors. But what about defense attorneys representing African American defendants who attempt to appeal to the potential racist sentiments of African American jurors? Does this represent misconduct? How should the judge respond?

7. Why does Paul Butler advocate "racially based jury nullification"? Why does Randall Kennedy disagree with him?

NOTES

1. Harper Lee, *To Kill a Mockingbird* (New York: Warner Books, 1960), p. 220.
2. For an excellent discussion of this case, see Jack Olsen, *Last Man Standing: The Tragedy and Triumph of Geronimo Pratt* (New York: Doubleday, 2000).
3. Ibid., p. 367.
4. Ibid., p. 465.
5. Jeremy Engel, "Federal Judge Approves $4.5 Million Settlement in Pratt Case," *Metropolitan News-Enterprise, Capitol News Service,* May 1, 2000.
6. James P. Levine, *Juries and Politics* (Pacific Grove, CA: Brooks/Cole Publishing, 1992).
7. Hiroshi Fukurai and Darryl Davies, "Affirmative Action in Jury Selection: Racially Representative Juries, Racial Quotas, and Affirmative Juries of the Hennepin Model and the Jury *de Medietate Linguae,*" *Virginia Journal of Social Policy & the Law* 4 (1996), pp. 645–682.
8. NAACP Legal Defense and Educational Fund, "Justice Prevails in Louisiana: Rideau Is Free," January 15, 2005. Available at http://www.naacpldf.org.
9. Josh Richman, "Lee Calls for Federal Inquiry of Mehserle Trial," *Oakland Tribune,* July 17, 2010.

10. David Cole, *No Equal Justice: Race and Class in the American Criminal Justice System* (New York: The New Press, 1999), p. 103.

11. Ibid., p. 101.

12. *Duncan* v. *Louisiana*, 391 U.S. 145 (1968).

13. *McCleskey* v. *Kemp*, 481 U.S. 279 (1987) (quoting *Strauder* v. *West Virginia*, 100 U.S. 303 [1880]).

14. *Strauder* v. *West Virginia*, 100 U.S. 303 (1880).

15. Ibid., pp. 307–308.

16. Ibid., p. 309.

17. *Neal* v. *Delaware*, 103 U.S. 370, 394 (1881), at 393–394 (1881).

18. Ibid.

19. Ibid., p. 397.

20. Gunnar Myrdal, *An American Dilemma: The Negro Problem and Modern Democracy* (New York: Harper, 1944), p. 549.

21. Ibid.

22. Ibid.

23. Seymour Wishman, *Anatomy of a Jury: The System on Trial* (New York: Times Books, 1986), p. 54.

24. *Avery* v. *Georgia*, 345 U.S. 559 (1953).

25. *Whitus* v. *Georgia*, 385 U.S. 545 (1967).

26. *Avery* v. *Georgia*, 345 U.S. 559 (1953), at 562.

27. Randall Kennedy, *Race, Crime, and the Law* (New York: Vintage, 1997), p. 179.

28. Ibid.

29. *Amadeo* v. *Zant*, 486 U.S. 214 (1988).

30. For a thorough discussion of these cases, see Ian F. Haney Lopez, "Race, Ethnicity, Erasure: The Salience of Race to LatCrit Theory," *University of California Law Review* 85 (1997), pp. 1,166–1,170.

31. *Lugo* v. *Texas*, 124 S.W. 2d 344 (1939).

32. *Hernandez* v. *Texas*, 251 W.W. 2d 531, at 535.

33. Clare Sheridan, "'Another White Race': Mexican Americans and the Paradox of Whiteness in Jury Selection," *Law and History Review* 21 (2003), pp. 109–144, p. 121.

34. *Hernandez* v. *Texas*, 251 W.W. 2d 531, at 535.

35. *Hernandez* v. *Texas*, 347 U.S. 475 (1954), at 477.

36. Ibid., at 478.

37. Ibid., at 482.

38. Cole, *No Equal Justice*, pp. 104–105. For an empirical investigation of the effect of the racial composition of the neighborhood on the likelihood that racial minorities would appear when summoned, see Ralph B. Taylor, Jerry H. Ratcliffe, Lillian Dote, and Brian A. Lawton, "Roles of Neighborhood Race and Status in the Middle Stages of Juror Selection," *Journal of Criminal Justice* 35 (2007), pp. 391–403.

39. Michael Higgins, "Few Are Chosen," *ABA Journal* (1999), pp. 50–51.

40. Fukurai and Davies, "Affirmative Action in Jury Selection," p. 653.

41. Kennedy, *Race, Crime, and the Law*, p. 239.

42. Albert W. Alschuler, "Racial Quotas and the Jury," *Duke Law Journal* 44 (1995), p. 44.

43. Denise Lavoie, "Judge Rules on Racial Makeup of Juries," *Newsday.Com*, October 2, 2005. Available at http://www.newsday.com/news/nationwide.

44. Ibid.

45. Kennedy, *Race, Crime, and the Law*, p. 253.

46. Ibid., p. 255.

47. *U.S.* v. *Ovalle*, 136 F.3d 1,092 (6th Cir. 1998).

48. *United States* v. *Nelson*, 277 F.3d 164, 169–172 (2d Cir. 2002).

49. Ibid., at 207–208.

50. Alschuler, "Racial Quotas and the Jury," p. 704.

51. Cole, *No Equal Justice*, p. 126.

52. *Strauder* v. *West Virginia*, 100 U.S. 303 (1880), at 305; *Batson* v. *Kentucky*, 476 U.S. 79 (1986), at 85.

53. *Swain* v. *Alabama*, 380 U.S. 202, 212 (1965).

54. Kennedy, *Race, Crime, and the Law*, p. 214.

55. "Former Prosecutor Accused of Bias in Election Year," *New York Times* (March 31, 1997).

56. Ibid.

57. *Swain* v. *Alabama*, 380 U.S. 202 (1965).

58. Ibid., at 222.

59. Wishman, *Anatomy of a Jury*, p. 115.

60. Justice Brennan dissenting from denial of certiorari in *Thompson* v. *United States*, 105 S.Ct. at 445.

61. Brian J. Serr and Mark Maney, "Racism, Peremptory Challenges, and the Democratic Jury: The Jurisprudence of a Delicate Balance," *Journal of Criminal Law and Criminology* 79 (1988), p. 13.

62. *Batson* v. *Kentucky*, 476 U.S. 79 (1986), at 96.

63. *United States* v. *Montgomery*, 819 F.2d at 851. The Eleventh Circuit, however, rejected this line of reasoning in *Fleming* v. *Kemp* [794 F.2d 1478 (11th Cir. 1986)] and *United States* v. *David* [803 F.2d 1567 (11th Cir. 1986)].

64. *United States* v. *Vaccaro*, 816 F.2d 443, 457 (9th Cir. 1987); *Fields* v. *People*, 732 P.2d 1,145, 1,158 n.20 (Colo. 1987).

65. Serr and Maney, "Racism, Peremptory Challenges, and the Democratic Jury," pp. 43–47.

66. Kennedy, *Race, Crime, and the Law*, p. 211.

67. Ibid., p. 213.

68. Serr and Maney, "Racism, Peremptory Challenges, and the Democratic Jury," p. 63.

69. *Purkett* v. *Elem*, 115 S.Ct. 1,769 (1995). Available at http://www.lexis-nexis.com/universe.

70. Ibid.

71. Ibid. (Stevens, J., dissenting).

72. Cole, *No Equal Justice*, p. 124

73. Equal Justice Initiative, *Illegal Racial Discrimination in Jury Selection: A Continuing Legacy* (Montgomery, AL: Equal Justice Institute, 2010).

74. Ibid., p. 4.

75. Ibid., p. 14.

76. Ibid.

77. Ibid., p. 18.

78. Ibid., p. 19.

79. *Snyder* v. *Louisiana*, 552 U.S. 472 (2008).

80. Equal Justice Initiative, *Illegal Racial Discrimination in Jury Selection*, p. 22.

81. Ibid., p. 42

82. Ibid., p. 38

83. Ibid., p. 44.

84. Ibid., pp. 43–50.

85. Ibid., p. 4.

86. Myrdal, *An American Dilemma*, pp. 547–548.

87. Samuel R. Gross, Kristen Jacoby, Daniel J. Matheson, Nicholas Montgomery, and Sujata Patil, "Exonerations in the United States 1989 Through 2003," *Journal of Criminal Law & Criminology* 95 (2005), pp. 523–553, p. 531.

88. Ibid.

89. Ibid., p. 529.

90. Ibid.

91. Ibid., p. 547.

92. Ibid.

93. Ibid., p. 548.

94. Ibid.

95. See, for example, Christian A. Meissner and John C. Brigham, "Thirty Years of Investigating the Own-Race Bias in Memory for Faces: A Meta-Analytic Review," *Psychology, Public Policy, and Law* 7 (2001), pp. 3–35; John R. Rutledge, "They All Look Alike: The Inaccuracy of Cross-Racial Identifications," *American Journal of Criminal Law* 28 (2001), pp. 207–228.

96. "Shapiro Lashes out at Cochran over 'Race Card,'" *USA Today*, October 4, 1995.

97. Kennedy, *Race, Crime, and the Law*, pp. 286–290.

98. *Moulton* v. *State*, 199 Ala. 411 (1917).

99. *Miller* v. *North Carolina*, 583 F.2d 701 (CA 4 1978).

100. *State* v. *Washington*, 67 So. 930 (La. Sup. Ct., 1915).

101. *Withers* v. *United States*, 602 F.2d 124 (CA 6 1976).

102. *Blair* v. *Armontrout*, 916 F.2d 1310 (CA 8 1990).

103. *Miller* v. *North Carolina*, 583 F.2d 701 (CA 4 1978), 708.

104. *Blair* v. *Armontrout*, 916 F.2d 1310 (CA 8 1990), 1,351.

105. Kennedy, *Race, Crime, and the Law*, pp. 256–257.

106. For an excellent and detailed account of this case, see Mark Curriden and Leroy Phillips, Jr., *Contempt of Court: The Turn-of-the-Century Lynching that Launched a Hundred Years of Federalism* (New York: Faber and Faber, 1999).

107. "Black Man Lynched By Mob After Getting Stay Of Execution In Rape Case 94 Years Ago Is Cleared," *Jet Magazine*, March 20, 2000. Available at http://www.jetmag.com.

108. Paul Butler, "Racially Based Jury Nullification: Black Power in the Criminal Justice System," *Yale Law Journal* 105 (1995), pp. 677–725.

109. Ibid., p. 679.

110. See, for example, *United States* v. *Dougherty*, 473 F.2d 1,113 (D.C.Cir., 1972).

111. Butler, "Racially Based Jury Nullification," p. 679.

112. Ibid., p. 715.

113. Ibid., p. 714.

114. Ibid., p. 694.

115. Ibid., p. 719.

116. Ibid., p. 716.

117. Ibid., p. 719.

118. Ibid., p. 719.

119. Kennedy, *Race, Crime, and the Law*, pp. 295–310.

120. Ibid., p. 299.

121. Ibid., p. 299.

122. Ibid., p. 301.

123. Ibid., p. 305.

124. Ibid., pp. 305–306.

125. Ibid., p. 301.

126. Ibid., p. 310.

127. Ibid., p. 310.

7

Race and Sentencing

In Search of Fairness and Justice

We must confront another reality. Nationwide, more than
40 percent of the prison population consists of African
American inmates. About 10 percent of African American
men in their mid-to-late 20s are behind bars. In some cities,
more than 50 percent of young African American men are
under the supervision of the criminal justice system ... Our
resources are misspent, our punishments too severe,
our sentences too long.
—JUSTICE ANTHONY KENNEDY, SPEAKING AT THE AMERICAN BAR
ASSOCIATION, AUGUST 2003

GOALS OF THE CHAPTER

In this chapter, we address the issue of racial disparity in sentencing. Our purpose
is not simply to add another voice to the debate over the *existence* of racial discrimination in the sentencing process. Although we do attempt to determine
whether racial minorities are sentenced more harshly than whites, we believe
that this is a theoretically unsophisticated and incomplete approach to a complex
phenomenon. It is overly simplistic to assume that racial minorities will receive
harsher sentences than whites regardless of the nature of the crime, the seriousness of the offense, the culpability of the offender, or the characteristics of the
victim. The more interesting question is "When does race matter?" It is this
question that we attempt to answer.

After you have read this chapter:

1. You should be able to explain why racial disparity in sentencing does not necessarily signal the presence of racial discrimination in sentencing and to discuss the five explanations for racial disparities in sentencing.

2. You should be able to clarify why crime seriousness and prior criminal record are not necessarily racially neutral factors.

3. You should be able to discuss and evaluate the conclusions of recent reviews of research investigating the effects of race/ethnicity on sentencing.

4. You should be able to answer the question "When does race (and ethnicity) matter in sentencing?"

5. You should be able to explain why some researchers argue that race/ethnicity, age, and sex are a "volatile combination" in the context of sentencing decisions.

6. You should be able to discuss differences in research findings regarding sentences imposed on whites and those imposed on African Americans, Hispanics, Asian Americans, and Native Americans.

7. You should be able to explain how the race of the victim affects sentencing decisions.

8. You should be able to discuss the focal concerns perspective and explain how judges' focal concerns may lead to unwarranted disparities in sentencing.

9. You should be able to explain the difference between direct and indirect race effects.

10. You should be able to evaluate competing arguments regarding similarities and differences in the sentencing decisions of African American and white judges.

11. You should be able to discuss the crack–powder cocaine disparity, explain its relationship to racial/ethnic disparities in sentencing, and explain how it was recently modified by Congress.

RACE AND SENTENCING: IS THE UNITED STATES MOVING FORWARD OR BACKWARD?

In 2004 the United States celebrated the fiftieth anniversary of *Brown* v. *Board of Education*, the landmark Supreme Court case that ordered desegregation of public schools. Also in 2004 the Sentencing Project issued a report entitled "Schools and Prisons: Fifty Years after *Brown* v. *Board of Education*."[1] The report noted that, whereas many institutions in society had become more diverse and more responsive to the needs of people of color in the wake of the *Brown* decision, the American criminal justice system had taken "a giant step back-ward."[2] To illustrate this, the report pointed out that in 2004 there were *nine times* as many African Americans in prison or jail as on the day the *Brown* decision was handed down—the number increased from 98,000 to 884,500. The report also noted that 1 of every 3 African American males and 1 of every 18 African American females born today could expect to be imprisoned at some point in his or her lifetime.[3] The authors of the report concluded that "such an outcome should be shocking to all Americans."[4]

Other statistics confirm that racial minorities—and especially young African American and Hispanic men—are substantially more likely than whites to be serving time in jail or prison. In 2009, for example, African Americans comprised 12.9 percent of the U.S. population but 39.4 percent of all jail and prison inmates. Hispanics were 15.8 percent of the U.S. population but 20.7 percent of inmates incarcerated in jails and prisons. In contrast, non-Hispanic whites made up 65.1 percent of the total population but only 34.4 percent of the jail and prison population.[5]

Explanations for the disproportionate number of African American and Hispanic males under the control of the criminal justice system are complex. As discussed in more detail in Chapter 9, a number of studies have concluded that most—but not all—of the racial disparity in incarceration rates can be attributed to racial differences in offending patterns and prior criminal records. Young African American and Hispanic males, in other words, face greater odds of incarceration than young white males primarily because they commit more serious crimes and have more serious prior criminal records. As the National Research Council's Panel on Sentencing Research concluded in 1983, "Factors other than racial discrimination in the sentencing process account for most of the disproportionate representation of black males in U.S. prisons."[6] Although there is recent evidence that the proportion of the racial disparity in incarceration unexplained by racial differences in arrest rates is increasing, most scholars would contend that this conclusion is still valid today.[7]

Not all of the racial disparity, however, can be explained away in this fashion. Critics contend that at least some of the overincarceration of racial minorities is the result of racially discriminatory sentencing policies and practices. As one commentator noted, "A conclusion that black overrepresentation among prisoners is not primarily the result of racial bias does not mean that there is no racism in the system."[8] The National Academy of Sciences Panel similarly concluded that evidence of racial discrimination in sentencing may be found in some jurisdictions or for certain types of crimes.

Underlying this controversy are questions concerning discretion in sentencing. To be fair, a sentencing scheme must allow the judge or jury discretion to shape sentences to fit individuals and their crimes. The judge or jury must be free to consider all *relevant* aggravating and mitigating circumstances. To be consistent, on the other hand, a sentencing scheme requires the even-handed application of objective standards. The judge or jury must take only relevant considerations into account and must be precluded from determining sentence severity based on prejudice or whim.

Critics of the sentencing process argue that judges, juries, and other members of the courtroom workgroup sometimes exercise their discretion inappropriately. Although they acknowledge that some degree of sentence disparity is to be expected in a system that attempts to individualize punishment, these critics suggest that there is *unwarranted* disparity in the sentences imposed on similarly situated offenders convicted of similar crimes. More to the point, they assert that judges impose harsher sentences on African American, Hispanic, and Native American offenders than on white offenders.

Other scholars contend that judges' sentencing decisions are not racially biased. They argue that disparity in sentencing is the result of legitimate differences among individual cases and that racial disparities disappear once these differences are taken into consideration. These scholars argue, in other words, that judges' sentencing decisions are both fair and consistent.

RACIAL DISPARITY IN SENTENCING

There are two types of clear and convincing evidence of racial *disparity* in sentencing. The first is evidence derived from national statistics on prison admissions and prison populations. These statistics, which we discuss in detail in Chapter 9, reveal that the incarceration rates for African Americans and Hispanics are much higher than the rate for whites. In June 2009, for example, 4,749 of every 100,000 African American men, 1,822 of every 100,000 Hispanic men, and 708 of every 100,000 white men were incarcerated in a state or federal prison or local jail. Stated another way, the incarceration rate for African American men was 6.5 times greater than the rate for white men; the incarceration rate for Hispanic men was 2.6 times greater than the rate for white men. The incarceration rates for women, although much lower than the rates for men, revealed a similar pattern: 333 of every 100,000 for African Americans, 142 of every 100,000 for Hispanics, and 91 of every 100,000 for whites. Among males between the ages of 25 and 29 the disparities were even larger: 10,501 of every 100,000 African Americans, 3,954 of every 100,000 Hispanics, and 1,569 of every 100,000 whites were incarcerated.[9]

The second type of evidence comes from studies of judges' sentencing decisions. These studies, which are the focus of this chapter, reveal that African American and Hispanic defendants are more likely than whites to be sentenced to prison; those who are sentenced to prison receive longer terms than whites. Consider the following statistics:

- Black and Hispanic offenders sentenced under the federal sentencing guidelines in U.S. District Courts from 1997 to 2000 received harsher sentences than white offenders. The incarceration rate was 93 percent for Hispanics, 85 percent for African Americans, and 74 percent for whites; in contrast, the incarceration rate for Asian Americans (71 percent) was lower than the rate for all other groups, including whites. Among those sentenced to prison, African Americans received the longest sentences, Asian

Americans received the shortest sentences, and Hispanics and whites fell in the middle.[10]

- Among offenders convicted of drug offenses in federal district courts in 1997 and 1998, the mean sentence length was 82 months for African Americans and 52 months for whites. For offenses with mandatory minimum sentences, the mean sentences were 136 months (African Americans) and 82 months (whites).[11]

- Fifty-eight percent of the African American offenders convicted of violent crimes in state courts in 2006 were sentenced to prison, compared with 52 percent of the white offenders. The figures for offenders convicted of drug offenses were 43 percent for African Americans and 31 percent for whites. The mean maximum sentence imposed on offenders sentenced to prison for violent offenses was 108 months for African Americans and 99 months for whites.[12]

- African American and Hispanic offenders convicted of felonies in Chicago, Miami, and Kansas City faced greater odds of incarceration than whites. In Chicago 66 percent of the African Americans, 59 percent of the Hispanics, and 51 percent of the whites were incarcerated. In Miami 51 percent of the African Americans, 40 percent of the Hispanics, and 35 percent of the whites were incarcerated. In Kansas City the incarceration rates were 46 percent (African Americans), 40 percent (Hispanics), and 36 percent (whites).[13]

Five Explanations for Racial Disparities in Sentencing

These statistics provide compelling evidence of *racial disparity* in sentencing. They indicate that the sentences imposed on African American and Hispanic offenders are different than—that is, harsher than—the sentences imposed on white offenders. These statistics, however, do not tell us *why* this occurs. They do not tell us whether the racial disparities in sentencing reflect racial discrimination and, if so, whether that discrimination is institutional or contextual. We suggest that there are at least five possible explanations for racial disparity in sentencing, only four of which reflect racial discrimination. Box 7.1 summarizes these explanations.

First, the differences in sentence severity could result from the fact that African Americans and Hispanics commit more serious crimes and have more serious prior criminal records than whites. Studies of sentencing decisions consistently have demonstrated the importance of these two "legally relevant" factors (but see Box 7.2 for an alternative interpretation of the legal relevance of crime seriousness and prior record). Offenders who are convicted of more serious offenses, who use a weapon to commit the crime, or who seriously injure the victim receive harsher sentences, as do offenders who have serious, more recent, or multiple prior felony convictions. The more severe sentences imposed on African Americans and Hispanics, then, might reflect the influence of these legally prescribed factors, rather than the effect of racial prejudice or unconscious bias on the part of judges.

B o x 7.1   Five Explanations for Racial Disparities in Sentencing

African Americans and Hispanics are sentenced more harshly than whites for the following reasons:

1. They commit more serious crimes and have more serious prior criminal records than whites.
   Conclusion: Racial disparity but not racial discrimination

2. They are more likely than whites to be poor; being poor is associated with a greater likelihood of pretrial detention and unemployment, both of which may lead to harsher sentences.
   Conclusion: Indirect (i.e., economic) discrimination

3. They are more likely to be subject to facially neutral laws and policies that prescribe more severe sentences or sentence enhancements:
   Conclusion: Institutional discrimination

4. Judges are biased or have prejudices against racial minorities.
   Conclusion: Racial discrimination

5. The disparities occur in some contexts but not in others.
   Conclusion: Subtle (i.e., contextual) racial discrimination

---

Second, the differences could result from economic discrimination. As explained in Chapter 5, poor defendants are not as likely as middle- or upper-class defendants to have a private attorney or be released prior to trial. They also are more likely to be unemployed. All of these factors may be related to sentence severity. Defendants represented by private attorneys or released prior to trial may receive more lenient sentences than those represented by public defenders or held in custody prior to trial. Defendants who are unemployed may be sentenced more harshly than those who are employed. Because African American and Hispanic defendants are more likely than white defendants to be poor, economic discrimination amounts to *indirect* racial discrimination.

Third, the differences might result from the application of facially neutral laws and policies that have racially disparate effects. For example, many jurisdictions prescribe harsher sentences for offenses involving crack cocaine than for offenses involving powder cocaine. These laws, which are based on assertions that crack cocaine is a more dangerous drug than powder cocaine, are racially neutral laws; the harsher sentences are imposed on all offenders convicted of offenses involving crack cocaine, regardless of the offender's race. However, the fact that African Americans are more likely than whites to be charged with and convicted of crack cocaine offenses means that they receive longer sentences than similarly situated white offenders charged with possessing, manufacturing, or delivering powder cocaine. Sentencing guidelines, habitual offender statutes, and three-strikes-and-you're-out laws, all of which prescribe harsher penalties for offenders with more serious prior criminal histories, similarly could produce racially disparate results. If, in other words, African Americans and Hispanics are more likely than whites to have accumulated prior criminal histories that make them eligible for harsher sentences under sentencing guidelines or for sentence enhancements, the application of these policies, which are racially neutral on their face, might result in systematically more punitive sentences for racial minorities. As discussed in Chapter 1, this would be evidence of institutional discrimination.

Fourth, the differences could result from overt racial discrimination or unconscious racial bias on the part of judges, prosecutors, and other participants in the sentencing process. Judges might take the race or ethnicity of the offender into account in determining the appropriate sentence, and prosecutors might consider the offender's race or ethnicity in deciding whether to plea bargain and in making sentence recommendations to the judge. If so, this implies that judges and prosecutors who are confronted with similarly situated African American, Hispanic, and white offenders treat racial minorities more harshly than whites. It also implies that these criminal justice officials, the majority of whom are white, stereotype African American and Hispanic offenders as more violent, more dangerous, and less amenable to rehabilitation than white offenders. Alternatively, the differential treatment of racial minorities could result from more implicit—or unconscious—racial bias that leads criminal justice officials to treat racial minorities differently than whites (for a more detailed discussion of this possibility, see Box 7.5).

Fifth, the sentencing disparities could reflect both equal treatment and discrimination, depending on the nature of the crime, the racial composition of the victim–offender dyad, the type of jurisdiction, the age and gender of the offender, and so on. It is possible, in other words, that racial minorities who commit certain types of crimes (such as forgery) are treated no differently than whites who commit these crimes, whereas those who commit other types of crimes (such as sexual assault) are sentenced more harshly than their white counterparts. Similarly, it is possible that racial discrimination in sentencing of offenders convicted of sexual assault is confined to the South or to cases involving black offenders and white victims. It is possible, in other words, that the type of discrimination found in the sentencing process is contextual discrimination.

EMPIRICAL RESEARCH ON RACE
AND SENTENCING

Researchers have conducted dozens of studies to determine which of the five explanations for racial disparity in sentencing is more correct and to untangle the complex relationship between race and sentence severity. In fact, as Marjorie Zatz has noted, this issue "may well have been the major research inquiry for studies of sentencing in the 1970s and early 1980s."[14] The studies that have been conducted vary enormously in theoretical and methodological sophistication. They range from simple bivariate comparisons of incarceration rates for whites and racial minorities, to methodologically more rigorous multivariate

Box 7.2   Are Crime Seriousness and Prior Criminal Record
"Legally Relevant" Variables?

Most policy makers and researchers assume that the seriousness of the conviction charge and the offender's prior criminal record are legally relevant to the sentencing decision. They assume that judges who base sentence severity primarily on crime seriousness and prior record are making legitimate, and racially neutral, sentencing decisions. But are they?

Some scholars argue that crime seriousness and prior criminal record are "race-linked" variables. If, for example, sentencing schemes consistently mandate the harshest punishments for the offenses for which racial minorities are most likely to be arrested (such as robbery and drug offenses involving crack cocaine), the imposition of punishment is not necessarily racially neutral.

Similarly, if prosecutors routinely file more serious charges against racial minorities than against whites who engage in the same type of criminal conduct, or offer less attractive plea bargains to racial minorities than to whites, the more serious conviction charges for racial minorities will reflect these racially biased charging and plea bargaining decisions. An African American defendant who is convicted of a more serious crime than a white defendant, in other words, may not necessarily have engaged in more serious criminal conduct than his or her white counterpart.

Prior criminal record also may be race-linked. If police target certain types of crimes (for example, selling illegal drugs) or patrol certain types of neighborhoods (for example, inner-city neighborhoods with large African American or Hispanic populations) more aggressively, racial minorities will be more likely than whites to "accumulate" a criminal history that then can be used to increase the punishment for the current offense. Racially biased charging and convicting decisions would have a similar effect.

If crime seriousness and prior criminal record are, in fact, race-linked in the ways outlined here, it is misleading to conclude that sentences based on these two variables are racially neutral. Similarly, it is misleading to conclude that the absence of "a race effect" once these two variables are taken into account signals the absence of racial discrimination in sentencing.

analyses designed to identify direct race effects, to more sophisticated designs incorporating tests for indirect race effects and for interaction between race and other predictors of sentence severity. The findings generated by these studies and the conclusions drawn by their authors also vary.

Reviews of Recent Research

Studies conducted from the 1930s through the 1960s generally concluded that racial disparities in sentencing reflected overt racial discrimination. For example, the author of one of the earliest sentencing studies, which was published in 1935, claimed that "equality before the law is a social fiction."[15] Reviews of these early studies,[16] however, found that most of them were methodologically flawed. They usually used simple bivariate statistical techniques, and they failed to control adequately for crime seriousness and prior criminal record.

The conclusions of these early reviews, coupled with the findings of its own review of sentencing research,[17] led the National Research Council's Panel on

Sentencing Research to state in 1983 that the sentencing process was not characterized by "a widespread systematic pattern of discrimination." Rather, "some pockets of discrimination are found for particular judges, particular crime types, and in particular settings."[18] Zatz, who reviewed the results of four waves of race and sentencing research conducted from the 1930s through the early 1980s, reached a somewhat different conclusion.[19] Although she acknowledged that "it would be misleading to suggest that race/ethnicity is *the* major determinant of sanctioning," Zatz nonetheless asserted that "race/ethnicity is a determinant of sanctioning, and a potent one at that."[20]

The three most recent reviews of research on race and sentencing confirm Zatz's assertion. Theodore G. Chiricos and Charles Crawford reviewed 38 studies published between 1979 and 1991 that included a test for the direct effect of race on sentencing decisions in noncapital cases.[21] Unlike previous reviews, they distinguished results involving the decision to incarcerate or not from those involving the length of sentence decision. Chiricos and Crawford also considered whether the effect of race varied depending on structural or contextual conditions. They asked whether the impact of race would be stronger "in southern jurisdictions, in places where there is a higher percentage of Blacks in the population or a higher concentration of Blacks in urban areas, and in places with a higher rate of unemployment."[22] Noting that two-thirds of the studies that they examined had been published subsequent to the earlier reviews (which generally concluded that race did not play a prominent role in sentencing decisions), Chiricos and Crawford stated that their assessment "provides a fresh look at an issue that some may have considered all but closed."[23]

The authors' assessment of the findings of these 38 studies revealed "significant evidence of a *direct* impact of race on imprisonment."[24] This effect, which persisted even after the effects of crime seriousness and prior criminal record were controlled, was found only for the decision to incarcerate or not; it was not found for the decision on length of sentence. The authors also identified a number of structural contexts that conditioned the race/imprisonment relationship. African American offenders faced significantly greater odds of incarceration than white offenders in the South, in places where African Americans comprised a larger percentage of the population, and in places where the unemployment rate was high.

Cassia Spohn's[25] review of noncapital sentencing research that used data from the 1980s and 1990s also highlighted the importance of attempting to identify "the structural and contextual conditions that are most likely to result in racial discrimination."[26] Spohn reviewed 40 studies examining the relationship between race, ethnicity, and sentencing. This included 32 studies of sentencing decisions at the state level and 8 studies at the federal level. Consistent with the conclusions of Chiricos and Crawford, Spohn reported that many of these studies found a *direct race effect*. At both the state and federal levels, there was evidence that African Americans and Hispanics were more likely than whites to be sentenced to prison; at the federal level, there was also evidence that African Americans received longer sentences than whites.[27]

B o x 7.3   Race, Ethnicity, and Sentencing Decisions: Contextual Effects

Spohn's review of recent studies analyzing the effect of race and ethnicity on state and federal sentencing decisions identified four themes, or patterns, of contextual effects. These studies revealed the following:

1. Racial minorities are sentenced more harshly than whites if they are young and male,

    are unemployed,

    are male and unemployed,

    are young, male, and unemployed,

    have lower incomes, or

    have less education.

2. Racial minorities are sentenced more harshly than whites if they are detained in jail prior to trial,

    are represented by a public defender rather than a private attorney,

    are convicted at trial rather than by plea,

    have more serious prior criminal records.

3. Racial minorities who victimize whites are sentenced more harshly than other race-of-offender / race-of-victim combinations.

4. Racial minorities are sentenced more harshly than whites if they are

    convicted of less serious crimes or

    convicted of drug offenses or more serious drug offenses.

SOURCE: Cassia Spohn, "Thirty Years of Sentencing Reform: The Quest for a Racially Neutral Sentencing Process," in *Criminal Justice 2000: Policies, Process, and Decisions of the Criminal Justice System* (Washington, DC: U.S. Department of Justice, 2000).

Noting that "[e]vidence concerning direct racial effects ... provides few clues to the circumstances under which race matters,"[28] Spohn also evaluated the 40 studies included in her review for evidence of indirect or contextual discrimination. Although she acknowledged that some of the evidence was contradictory—for example, some studies revealed that racial disparities were confined to offenders with less serious prior criminal records, whereas others reported such disparities only among offenders with more serious criminal histories—Spohn nonetheless concluded that the studies revealed four "themes," or "patterns," of contextual effects. Box 7.3 summarizes these themes.

The first theme or pattern revealed was that the combination of race/ethnicity and other legally irrelevant offender characteristics produces greater sentence disparity than race/ethnicity alone. That is, the studies demonstrated that certain types of racial minorities—males, the young, the unemployed, the less educated—are singled out for harsher treatment. Some studies found that each of these offender characteristics, including race/ethnicity, had a direct effect on sentence outcomes but that the combination of race/ethnicity and one or more of the other characteristics was a more powerful predictor of sentence severity than any characteristic individually. Other studies found that race/ethnicity had an effect only if the offender was male, young, and/or unemployed.[29]

The second pattern of indirect/interaction effects was that a number of process-related factors conditioned the effect of race/ethnicity on sentence severity.[30] Some of the studies revealed, for example, that pleading guilty, hiring a private attorney, or providing evidence or testimony in other cases resulted in greater sentence discounts for white offenders than for African American or Hispanic offenders. Other studies showed that racial minorities paid a higher penalty—in terms of harsher sentences—for being detained prior to trial or for having a serious prior criminal record. As Spohn noted, these results demonstrate that race and ethnicity influence sentence outcomes through their relationships with earlier decisions and suggest that these process-related determinants of sentence outcomes do not operate in the same way for racial minorities and whites.

The third theme or pattern concerned an interaction between the race of the offender and the race of the victim. Consistent with research on the death penalty (which is discussed in Chapter 8), two studies found that African Americans who sexually assaulted whites were sentenced more harshly than either African Americans who sexually assaulted other African Americans or whites who sexually assaulted whites. Thus, "punishment is contingent on the race of the victim as well as the race of the offender."[31]

The final pattern of indirect/interaction effects, which Spohn admitted was "less obvious" than the other three,[32] was that the effect of race/ethnicity was conditioned by the nature of the crime. Some studies found that racial discrimination was confined to less serious—and thus more discretionary—crimes. Other studies revealed that racial discrimination was most pronounced for drug offenses or, alternatively, that harsher sentencing of racial minorities was found only for the most serious drug offenses.[33]

The most recent review of research on race and sentencing is Ojmarrh Mitchell's meta-analysis of published and unpublished studies that included controls for offense seriousness and prior criminal record.[34] Mitchell's quantitative analysis focused on the direction and size of the effect (the "effect size") of race on sentencing. His analysis revealed that 76 percent of the effect sizes from the non-federal studies and 73 percent of the effect sizes from the federal studies indicated that African Americans were sentenced more harshly than whites, especially for drug offenses and especially for imprisonment decisions. The effect sizes were smaller in studies that used more precise controls for offense seriousness and criminal history; they were larger in jurisdictions that did not utilize structured sentencing guidelines. Moreover, the analysis revealed that the amount of unwarranted disparity in sentencing had not changed appreciably since the 1970s. Mitchell concluded that his findings "undermine the so-called 'no discrimination thesis,'" given that "independent of other measured factors, on average African Americans were sentenced more harshly than whites."[35]

The fact that a majority of the studies reviewed by Chiricos and Crawford, by Spohn, and by Mitchell found that African Americans (and Hispanics) were more likely than whites to be sentenced to prison, even after taking crime seriousness and prior criminal record into account, suggests that racial discrimination in sentencing is not a thing of the past. Although the contemporary sentencing process may not be characterized by "a widespread systematic pattern of discrimination,"[36] it is not racially neutral.

WHEN DOES RACE/ETHNICITY MATTER?

Research conducted during the past two decades clearly demonstrates that race/ethnicity interacts with or is conditioned by (1) other legally irrelevant offender characteristics such as sex and employment status, (2) process-related factors such as pretrial detention, (3) the race of the victim, and (4) the nature and seriousness of the crime. A comprehensive review of these studies is beyond the scope of this book. Instead, we summarize the findings of a few key studies. We begin by summarizing the results of a study that found both direct and indirect racial/ethnic effects. This is followed by a discussion of studies that focus explicitly on sentence outcomes for Hispanic Americans, illegal immigrants, Asian Americans, and Native Americans. Next we review the findings of a series of studies that explore the intersections among race, ethnicity, sex, age, employment status, and sentence severity. We also review studies that examine differential treatment of interracial and intraracial crime. We then discuss the findings of studies examining the effect of race on sentencing for different types of offenses and the findings of a number of studies that focus explicitly on the relationship between race and sentence severity for drug offenders. Our purpose is to illustrate the subtle and complex ways in which race influences the sentencing process.

Race/Ethnicity and Sentencing: Direct and Indirect Effects

A number of methodologically sound studies have concluded that African American and Hispanic offenders are sentenced more harshly than whites. Cassia Spohn and Miriam DeLone, for example, compared the sentences imposed on African American, Hispanic, and white offenders convicted of felonies in Chicago, Kansas City, and Miami in 1993 and 1994.[37] They controlled for the legal and extralegal variables that affect judges' sentencing decisions: the offender's age, sex, and prior criminal record; whether the offender was on probation at the time of the current offense; the seriousness of the conviction charge; the number of conviction charges; the type of attorney representing the offender; whether the offender was detained or released prior to trial; and whether the offender pled guilty or went to trial.

Spohn and DeLone found evidence of racial discrimination in the decision to incarcerate or not in two of the three jurisdictions. Although race had no effect on the likelihood of incarceration in Kansas City, both African Americans and Hispanics were more likely than whites to be sentenced to prison in Chicago, and Hispanics (but not African Americans) were more likely than whites to be incarcerated in Miami. The data presented in Figure 7.1 illustrate these results more clearly. The authors used the results of their multivariate analyses

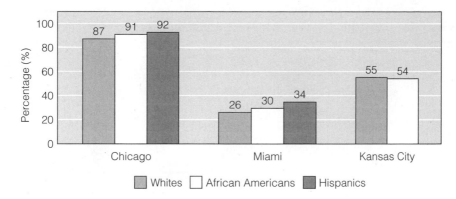

FIGURE 7.1 Estimated Probabilities of Incarceration for Offenders Convicted of Burglary

to calculate the estimated probability of imprisonment for a "typical" white, African American, and Hispanic offender who was convicted of burglary in each of the three cities.[38]

These estimated probabilities confirm that offender race had no effect on the likelihood of incarceration in Kansas City; 55 percent of the whites and 54 percent of the African Americans convicted of burglary were sentenced to prison. In Chicago, however, there was about a 4 percentage-point difference between white offenders and African American offenders and between white offenders and Hispanic offenders. In Miami the difference between white offenders and Hispanic offenders was somewhat larger; even after the other legal and extralegal variables were taken into consideration, 34 percent of the Hispanics, but only 26 percent of the whites, received a prison sentence.

Consistent with the explanations presented in Box 7.1, Spohn and DeLone also found evidence of economic discrimination. When they analyzed the likelihood of pretrial detention, controlling for crime seriousness, the offender's prior criminal record, and other factors associated with the type and amount of bail required by the judge, they found that African Americans and Hispanics faced significantly higher odds of pretrial detention than whites in Chicago and Miami, and that African Americans were more likely than whites to be detained in Kansas City. They also found that pretrial detention was a strong predictor of the likelihood of incarceration following conviction in all three cities. Thus, African American and Hispanic defendants were more likely than whites to be detained prior to trial, and those who were detained were substantially more likely than those who were released to be incarcerated.

This study, then, demonstrated that race/ethnicity affected the likelihood of incarceration differently in these three cities. In Chicago race/ethnicity had both a direct effect on incarceration (African Americans and Hispanics were more likely than whites to be sentenced to prison) and an indirect effect on incarceration through pretrial detention (African Americans and Hispanics were more likely than whites to be detained prior to trial and pretrial detention increased the odds of a prison sentence). In Miami, on the other hand, ethnicity, but not

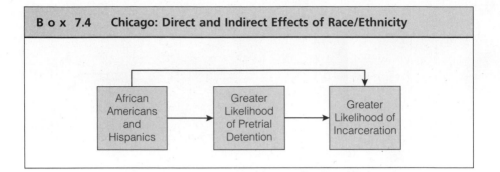

B o x 7.4   **Chicago: Direct and Indirect Effects of Race/Ethnicity**

race, had a direct effect on the likelihood of a prison sentence (Hispanics were more likely than whites to be sentenced to prison), but both race and ethnicity had an indirect effect on incarceration through pretrial detention. And in Kansas City, race did not have a direct effect on incarceration but did influence the likelihood of a prison sentence through its effect on pretrial detention. The pattern of results found for Chicago is illustrated in Box 7.4.

The authors of this study were careful to point out that the race effects they uncovered, although statistically significant, were "rather modest"[39] and that the seriousness of the offense and the offender's prior criminal record were the primary determinants of sentence outcomes. They noted, however, that the fact that offender race/ethnicity had both direct and indirect effects, coupled with the fact that female offenders and those who were released prior to trial received substantially more lenient sentences than male offenders and those who were detained before trial, suggests that "judges' sentencing decisions are not guided *exclusively* by factors of explicit legal relevance."[40] They concluded that judges' sentencing decisions reflect "stereotypes of dangerousness and culpability that rest, either explicitly or implicitly, on considerations of race, gender, pretrial status, and willingness to plead guilty."[41]

Are Hispanics Sentenced More Harshly Than All Other Offenders?

A study of sentencing decisions in the state of Pennsylvania, where judges use sentencing guidelines, compared the relative harshness of sentences imposed on Hispanic and African American offenders. Arguing that "Hispanic defendants may seem even more culturally dissimilar and be even more disadvantaged" than African Americans, Darrell Steffensmeier and Stephen Demuth hypothesized that Hispanic offenders would be sentenced more harshly than either white offenders or African Americans offenders.[42] They based this hypothesis on a number of factors, including the perceived threat posed by growing numbers of Hispanic immigrants; stereotypes that link Hispanics with drug trafficking and that characterize them as "lazy, irresponsible, low in intelligence, and dangerously criminal"; and the relative powerlessness of Hispanic Americans in the political arena.[43] As the authors noted, "We expect that the specific social and historical context involving Hispanic Americans exacerbates perceptions of their cultural dissimilarity and the 'threat' they pose in ways that will contribute to their harsher treatment in criminal courts."[44]

When they looked at the raw data, Steffensmeier and Demuth found that Hispanics were sentenced to prison more often than either African Americans or whites. The incarceration rates for nondrug offenses were 46.2 percent (whites), 62.9 percent (African Americans), and 66.8 percent (Hispanics). The differences were even larger for drug offenses: 52.3 percent (whites), 69.9 percent (African Americans), and 87.4 percent (Hispanics).[45] These differences diminished, but did not disappear, when the authors controlled for the seriousness of the offense, the offender's criminal history, the mode of conviction, and the offender's age. In non-drug cases, African Americans were 6 percent more likely and Hispanics were 18 percent more likely than whites to be incarcerated. In drug cases, there was a 7 percentage-point difference in the probabilities of incarceration for African Americans and whites and a 26 percentage-point difference in the probabilities for Hispanics and whites.[46] For both types of crimes, then, African Americans faced higher odds of incarceration than whites, and Hispanics faced higher odds of incarceration than both whites and African Americans.

Steffensmeier and Demuth stated that their findings were consistent with hypotheses "drawn from the writings on prejudice and intergroup hostility suggesting that the specific social and historical context facing Hispanic Americans will exacerbate perceptions of their cultural dissimilarity and the 'threat' they pose."[47] They illustrated this with comments made by a judge in a county with a rapidly growing Hispanic population:

> We shouldn't kid ourselves. I have always prided myself for not being prejudiced but it is hard not to be affected by what is taking place. The whole area has changed with the influx of Hispanics and especially Puerto Ricans. You'd hardly recognize the downtown from what it was a few years ago. There's more dope, more crime, more people on welfare, more problems in school.[48]

This judge's comments suggest that "unconscious racism"[49] may infect the sentencing process. Concerns about the changes in the racial/ethnic makeup of a community, coupled with stereotypes linking race and ethnicity to drug use and drug-related crime and violence, may interact to produce harsher treatment of racial minorities by criminal justice officials who have always "prided themselves for not being prejudiced." As David F. Greenberg notes, individuals who have ambivalent attitudes about race "may engage in automatic invidious stereotyping and may act on the basis of these stereotypes."[50] (See Box 7.5 for a discussion of a study investigating unconscious racial bias among judges.)

Are Illegal Immigrants Sentenced Differently than U.S. Citizens?

Do stereotypes of illegal immigrants as dangerous and crime-prone influence the sentences imposed on them? Anecdotal evidence suggests that they do. Consider

Box 7.5   Judges and Unconscious Racial Bias: Can Judges Control the "Bigot in the Brain"?

The first study to explicitly test for unconscious racial bias in judges was published in 2008–2009 in the *Notre Dame Law Review* (Rachlinski, Johnson, Wistrich, and Guthrie 2008–2009). The authors of the study pointed out that there is evidence suggesting that explicit, or overt, racial bias has declined markedly over time. Noting that racial disparities in punishment have persisted even as explicit bias has declined, the authors suggested that one possible explanation might be implicit, or unconscious racial bias, which they defined as "stereotypical associations so subtle that people who hold them might not even be aware of them" (Rachlinski et al. 2008–2009, 1196).

Rachlinski and his colleagues recruited 128 judges from three different jurisdictions to participate in a study designed to answer two questions: do judges hold implicit racial biases and, if so, do those biases produce racially biased decisions. To answer the first question, they used the Implicit Association Test (IAT), which is a test developed by psychologists to measure whether participants associate good or bad stereotypes with white or black faces. They found that judges, like most other individuals, "harbor implicit racial biases" (Rachlinski et al. 2008–2009, 1208). Seventy-four of the 85 white judges, and 14 of the 43 African American judges, demonstrated a "white preference," but the white judges expressed significantly stronger white preferences than did the African American judges. The remainder of the African American judges either expressed no preference at all or expressed a black preference.

To answer the second question about the effect of implicit bias on behavior, the authors asked the judges to read three hypothetical cases and to indicate what they believed to be the most appropriate disposition in each case. What they found was that when the race of the defendant was clearly identified (as it was in only one of the hypothetical cases), the white judges treated white defendants and African American defendants the same. In fact, the higher the judge's white preference score on the IAT, the more favorably the judge treated the African American defendant.

According to the authors, the findings of their study "demonstrate that the white judges were attempting to compensate for unconscious racial biases in their decision making. These judges were, we believe, highly motivated to avoid making biased judgments" (Rachlinski et al., 1223). The authors noted that most of the judges reported that they knew that the study was designed to assess racial bias— that is, they were aware of the potential for biased decision making and had "the cognitive skills necessary to avoid its influence" (1225).

Rachlinski and his colleagues were careful to point out that they were not concluding that judges would be able "to avoid bias on a continual basis in their own courtrooms" (1225). They noted that judges may not have the time or the information necessary to avoid unconscious bias. As they put it, judges who have implicit biases but who, "due to time pressure or other distractions, do not actively engage in an effort to control the 'bigot in the brain'" are apt to make racially biased decisions (1225).

the comments of a federal district judge, who justified a sentence at the top of the guideline range by stating on the record:

> You are not a citizen of this country. This country was good enough to allow you to come in here to confer on you … a number of the benefits of this society, form of government, and its opportunities and you

repay that kindness by committing a crime like this. We have got enough criminals in the United States without importing any.[51]

There also is empirical evidence that an offender's citizenship status influences sentence outcomes. For example, there are a number of studies[52] of federal sentencing that included the offender's citizenship status as a control variable in models of sentence length and other sentencing decisions. These studies demonstrated that offenders who were not citizens of the United States received harsher sentences than U.S. citizens did.

The first study to systematically investigate the effect of citizenship status on federal sentencing outcomes was conducted by Scott Wolfe and his colleagues at Arizona State University.[53] They used data on offenders adjudicated in federal district courts in 2006 to explore the sentences imposed on U.S. citizens, illegal aliens, and resident-legal aliens. When they examined the descriptive data, they found that the incarceration rate was higher for illegal aliens (99 percent) and resident-legal aliens (89 percent) than for citizens (85 percent). In contrast, the mean sentence imposed on U.S. citizens was longer than the average sentence imposed on the two groups of non-citizens: it was 74.36 months for citizens, 52.65 months for resident-legal aliens, and only 34.79 months for illegal aliens. They also found that illegal aliens were substantially more likely than U.S. citizens to be Hispanic, to not have a high school degree, to be charged with an immigration offense, and to be held in custody prior to trial.[54]

The authors then controlled for the offender's offense seriousness score, prior record score, and other offender and case characteristics that have been shown to affect sentencing outcomes in federal courts. They found that both categories of non-citizens were significantly more likely than citizens to be sentenced to prison, but that there were no differences in the prison sentences imposed on resident-legal aliens and citizens. Moreover, the sentences imposed on illegal aliens were 5 percent shorter than those imposed on U.S. citizens. They also found that the offender's ethnicity affected the length of the sentence for both U.S. citizens and illegal aliens; however, the effect of ethnicity was negative for U.S. citizens (Hispanic citizens received shorter prison sentences than white citizens), but positive for illegal aliens (Hispanic illegal aliens received longer prison sentences than white illegal aliens).[55]

To explain their finding that illegal aliens had higher odds of incarceration than U.S. citizens but received shorter prison sentences than citizens, the authors suggested that it may reflect the fact that illegal aliens are likely to face deportation once they have served their prison sentences. Federal judges, in other words, imprison illegal aliens to ensure their appearance at removal proceedings but impose shorter sentences to expedite their deportation. According to the authors, there is "an incentive for judges to impose a sentence at the low end of the guideline range (or even to depart downward) in these types of cases, as doing so reduces the cost of imprisoning illegal aliens who eventually will be subject to removal proceedings."

The authors concluded that their findings provide evidence that judges believe that non-citizens, and particularly illegal aliens, are more dangerous and blameworthy than U.S. citizens. This was reflected in the fact that conviction for immigration offenses, a drug offense, or a violent offense had a more pronounced effect on the likelihood of incarceration for illegal aliens than for citizens. The authors speculated that federal judges may take into account "that illegal alien offenders who are convicted of such offenses have brought violence, drug trafficking and further immigration problems into a country already fraught with crime."

The results of this study, then, demonstrate the power of popular perceptions that increasing numbers of immigrants are associated with increases in crime rates. The existence of a substantial body of evidence challenging these perceptions notwithstanding, the stereotype of the crime-prone immigrant appears to affect federal judges' sentencing decisions.

Are Asian Americans Sentenced More Leniently than All Other Offenders?

Noting that sentencing scholars have devoted "conspicuously little attention" to the sentences imposed on Asian Americans, Brian Johnson and Stephanie Betsinger compared outcomes for African Americans, Hispanics, Asian Americans, and whites who were convicted in federal district courts from 1997 to 2000.[56] They argued that it was important to include Asian Americans in studies of sentencing disparity given their popular image as "the model minority." According to the authors, the negative image of Asian Americans that was predominant in the period prior to World War II was altered during the post-war period. As they noted, "Whatever the reasons for the historic transformation, by the mid-1960s, the popular press had begun to highlight the success stories of Asian Americans, identifying them as the 'model minority'"—a group characterized by positive traits such as a strong work ethic, high levels of educational achievement, and social and economic success.[57]

Johnson and Betsinger began their analysis by examining sentence outcomes for each of four groups: Asian Americans, whites, African Americans, and Hispanics. They found that Hispanics had the highest incarceration rate (93 percent), followed by African Americans (85 percent), whites (74 percent), and Asian Americans (71 percent). They found a similar pattern when they examined the length of the sentence: Hispanics received the longest sentences and Asians received the shortest sentences. Although this suggests leniency in the sentencing of Asian Americans, the authors pointed out that the Asian offenders differed in important ways from offenders in the other three groups—Asians had less serious criminal histories, were less likely to be detained prior to sentencing, were less likely to be convicted of drug offenses and more likely to be convicted of fraud offenses, and were more likely to be college graduates.[58]

The racial/ethnic differences in sentence severity did not disappear when Johnson and Betsinger controlled for these variables and for other legally relevant factors. Even after taking these factors into account, Asian offenders were significantly less likely to be incarcerated; they were 35 percent less likely than whites to be sentenced to prison, 37 percent less likely than African Americans to be sentenced to prison, and 80 percent less likely than Hispanics to be sentenced to prison. Even larger differences were found when the authors compared the likelihoods of incarceration for young males in each of the four groups. Compared to young Asian males, the odds of incarceration were 18 percent greater for young white males, 42 percent higher for young African American males, and 106 percent greater for young Hispanic males. The differences were also larger when the authors examined drug offenses separately; there were no significant differences in the odds of incarceration for Asian and white offenders convicted of drug offenses, but African Americans and Hispanics were more than twice as likely as Asians to be incarcerated for drug offenses.[59]

The findings of this study, which was the first study to comprehensively compare sentence outcomes for Asian Americans with those for other racial/ethnic groups, confirm that race and ethnicity matter, even in a jurisdiction with rigid sentencing guidelines. They also provide support for the notion that Hispanic Americans receive harsher sentences than other racial groups and provide a first look at the more lenient treatment of Asian Americans. As the authors of the study stated, their results suggest that "federal punishments are race graded in important ways."[60] Noting that Asian Americans, as an aggregate group, can be regarded as an American success story on a variety of dimensions, Johnson and Betsinger concluded that

> It may be, then, that economic equality is a precursor to social justice—
> that is, striving to improve the relative socioeconomic standing of
> other racial and ethnic minority groups may have important ripple
> effects that translate into more favorable societal stereotypes and greater
> equality of punishment within the American justice system itself.[61]

Native Americans and Sentencing Disparity: Disparity in State and Federal Courts

Although there is a growing body of sentencing research that includes Hispanic Americans, most studies investigating the effect of race on sentence outcomes focus exclusively on African Americans and whites. As we have seen, there are very few studies that include other racial minorities, such as Asian Americans or Native Americans.

There are reasons to expect harsher sentences for Native Americans than for whites, since negative stereotypes of members of this group are common. For example, Iris Marion Young[62] asserted that "Native Americans are viewed in terms of narrow ethnocentric stereotypes (for example, drunken savage)," and Carol Chiago Lujan[63] contended that the stereotype of the "drunken Indian" makes Native Americans more vulnerable to arrest for alcohol-related offenses and that stereotypical perceptions of reservation life as unstable and conducive to crime may lead to longer sentences for Native Americans. Similarly, Keith Wilmot and Miriam DeLone noted that forces such as colonialism "have lead to distinct public perceptions about the crime-proneness and threatening nature of Native Americans,"[64] and that these perceptions may also affect the sentencing decisions of judges confronted with Native American offenders.

The few studies that do examine sentence outcomes for Native Americans have produced mixed results. Some studies found that Native Americans and whites are sentenced similarly once crime seriousness, prior record, and other legally relevant variables are taken into account.[65] Other studies concluded that Native Americans adjudicated in federal[66] and state[67] courts are sentenced more harshly than similarly situated whites or that Native Americans serve significantly more of their prison sentence before parole or release than whites do.[68]

One study used data on offenders incarcerated in Arizona state correctional facilities in 1990 to compare sentence lengths for Native Americans and whites.[69] Alvarez and Bachman found that whites received longer sentences than Native Americans for homicide, but Native Americans received longer sentences than whites for burglary and robbery.

Alvarez and Bachman speculated that these findings may reflect the fact that homicide tends to be intraracial, whereas burglary and robbery are more likely to be interracial. Whites may have received longer sentences for homicide, in other words, because their victims were also likely to be white, whereas the victims of Native Americans usually were other Native Americans. As the authors note, "Because the lives of American Indian victims may not be especially valued by U.S. society and the justice system, these American Indian defendants may receive more lenient sentences for their crime." Similarly, Native Americans convicted of burglary or robbery may have received harsher sentences than whites convicted of these crimes because their victims were more likely to be "higher-status Caucasians."[70] Alvarez and Bachman concluded that their study demonstrates "the need for more crime-specific analyses to investigate discriminatory practices in processing and sentencing minority group members, especially American Indians."[71]

The most methodologically sophisticated study of Native American sentencing disparities is Wilmot and DeLone's[72] study of sentences imposed on white, Native American, African American, Hispanic, and Asian offenders. This study was conducted using data from Minnesota, which has operated under presumptive sentencing guidelines since 1980. Using data on offenders convicted in 2001, the authors of this study found that Native American offenders were treated more harshly than white offenders on five of the six sentencing outcomes examined. For example, the pronounced prison sentence (that is, the prison sentence that the offender would serve if he/she were sentenced to prison) was longer for Native Americans (and African Americans) than for whites, and Native Americans were 10 percent more likely than whites to receive an executed prison sentence (that is, to be sentenced to prison rather than to jail or probation).[73] These differences were found even after the seriousness of the offense, the offender's prior record, the type of crime, and other legally relevant factors were taken into consideration.

Wilmot and DeLone ended their paper with a call for the development of a theoretical perspective on criminal justice decision making (including sentencing) that takes into account the unique aspects of Native American cultural and historical experiences. Noting that such perspectives already exist for African Americans and Hispanics, the authors concluded that "Such theories allow for the formation of racially and ethnically specific hypotheses that highlight the contextual circumstances under which no differences between racial groups is expected, as well as the situations in which racial and ethnic groups will be expected to experience discrimination in ways that are similar and dissimilar across different racial and ethnic groups."[74]

Race/Ethnicity, Gender, Age, and Employment: A Volatile Combination?

In an article exploring the "convergence of race, ethnicity, gender, and class on court decision making," Zatz urged researchers to consider the ways in which offender (and victim) characteristics jointly affect case outcomes.[75] As she noted, "Race, gender, and class are the central axes undergirding our social structure. They intersect in dynamic, fluid, and multifaceted ways."[76]

The findings of a series of studies conducted by Darrell Steffensmeier and his colleagues at Pennsylvania State University illustrate these "intersections." Research published by this team of researchers during the early 1990s concluded that race,[77] gender,[78] and age[79] each played a role in the sentencing process in Pennsylvania. However, it is interesting to note, especially in light of its later research findings,[80] that the team's initial study of the effect of race on sentencing concluded that race contributed "very little" to our understanding of judges' sentencing decisions.[81] Although the incarceration (jail or prison) rate for African Americans was 8 percentage points higher than the rate for whites, there was only a 2 percentage-point difference in the rates at which African Americans and whites were sentenced to prison. Race also played "a very small role in decisions about sentence length."[82] The average sentence for African American defendants was only 21 days longer than the average sentence for white defendants. These findings led Kramer and Steffensmeier to conclude that "if defendants' race affects judges' decisions in sentencing ... it does so very weakly or intermittently, if at all."[83]

This conclusion is called into question by Steffensmeier, Ulmer, and Kramer's more recent research,[84] which explores the ways in which race, gender, and age interact to influence sentence severity. They found that each of the three legally irrelevant offender characteristics had a significant direct effect on both the likelihood of incarceration and the length of the sentence: African Americans were sentenced more harshly than whites, younger offenders were sentenced more harshly than older offenders, and males were sentenced more harshly than females. More importantly, they found that the three factors interacted to produce substantially harsher sentences for one particular category of offenders—young, African American males—than for any other age–race–gender combination. According to the authors, their results illustrate the "high cost of being black, young, and male."[85]

Although the research conducted by Steffensmeier and his colleagues provides important insights into the judicial decision-making process, their findings also suggest the possibility that factors other than race, gender, and age may interact to affect sentence severity. If, as the authors suggest, judges impose harsher sentences on offenders perceived to be more deviant, more dangerous, and more likely to recidivate, and if these perceptions rest, either explicitly or implicitly, on "stereotypes associated with membership in various social categories,"[86] then offenders with constellations of characteristics other than "young, black, and male" may also be singled out for harsher treatment.

The validity of this assertion is confirmed by the results of a replication and extension of the Pennsylvania study. Cassia Spohn and David Holleran examined the sentences imposed on offenders convicted of felonies in Chicago, Miami, and Kansas City.[87] Their study included Hispanics and African Americans and tested for interactions between race, ethnicity, gender, age, and employment status. They found that none of the four offender characteristics had a significant effect on the length of the sentence in any of the three jurisdictions but that each of the characteristics had a significant effect on the decision to incarcerate or not in at least one of the jurisdictions. As shown in Part A of Table 7.1, in Chicago, African American offenders were 12.1 percent more likely than white offenders to be sentenced to prison; Hispanics were 15.3 percent more likely than whites to be incarcerated. In Miami, the difference in the probabilities of incarceration for Hispanic offenders and white offenders was 10.3 percent. Male offenders were more than 20 percent more likely than female offenders to be sentenced to prison in Chicago and Kansas City, and unemployed offenders faced significantly higher odds of incarceration than employed offenders (+9.3 percent) in Kansas City. In all three jurisdictions, offenders aged 21–29 were about 10 percent more likely than offenders aged 17–20 to be sentenced to prison.[88] Race, ethnicity, gender, age, and employment status, then, each had a direct effect on the decision to incarcerate or not.

Like Steffensmeier and his colleagues, Spohn and Holleran found that various combinations of race/ethnicity, gender, age, and employment status were better predictors of incarceration than any variable alone. As shown in Part B of Table 7.1, young African American and Hispanic males were consistently more likely than middle-aged white males to be sentenced to prison. These offenders, however, were not the only ones singled out for harsher treatment. In Chicago, young African American and Hispanic males and middle-aged African American males faced higher odds of incarceration than middle-aged white males. In Miami, young African American and Hispanic males and older Hispanic males were incarcerated more often than middle-aged white males. In Kansas City, both young African American males and young white males faced higher odds of incarceration than middle-aged whites. These results led Spohn and Holleran to conclude that "in Chicago and Miami the combination of race/ethnicity and age is a more powerful predictor of sentence severity than either variable individually, while in Kansas City age matters more than race."[89]

Other, more recent, research confirms these findings.[90] One study, for example, analyzed the effects of race/ethnicity and sex on sentences imposed on drug offenders in three U.S. District Courts.[91] This study found that African American and Hispanic females received more lenient sentences than their male

T A B L E 7.1   Do Young, Unemployed African American and Hispanic Males Pay a Punishment Penalty?

Differences in the Probabilities of Incarceration:
The Effect of Race, Ethnicity, Gender, Age, and Employment Status

A. Probability Differences	Chicago	Miami	Kansas City
African Americans versus whites	+12.1%	not significant	not significant
Hispanics versus whites	+15.3%	+10.3%	(not applicable)
Males versus females	+22.8%	not significant	+21.1%
Unemployed versus employed	not significant	(not applicable)	+9.3%
Age 21–29 versus age 17–20	+10.0%	+9.5%	+10.8%

Differences in the Probabilities of Incarceration: Male Offenders Only

B. Probability Differences between Whites aged 30–39 and	Chicago	Miami	Kansas City
African Americans, 17–29	+18.4%	+14.7%	+12.7%
Hispanics, 17–29	+25.1%	+18.2%	(not applicable)
Whites, 17–29	not significant	not significant	+14.4%
African Americans, 30–39	+23.3%	not significant	not significant
Hispanics, 30–39	not significant	+18.5%	(not applicable)

C. Probability Differences between Employed Whites and			
Unemployed African Americans	+16.9%	(not applicable)	+13.0%
Unemployed Hispanics	+23.5%	(not applicable)	(not applicable)
Unemployed Whites	not significant	(not applicable)	not significant
Employed African Americans	not significant	(not applicable)	not significant
Employed Hispanics	not significant	(not applicable)	(not applicable)

SOURCE: Cassia Spohn and David Holleran, "The Imprisonment Penalty Paid by Young, Unemployed Black and Hispanic Male Offenders," *Criminology* 38 (2000), Tables 3, 5, 6.

counterparts, but there were no differences in the sentences imposed on white females and males. Further analysis revealed that black male drug offenders received longer sentences than all other offenders, with the exception of Hispanic males. A second study[92] of federal sentencing decisions explored the independent and joint effects of race/ethnicity, gender, and age, finding that young (ages 18–20) Hispanic and African American males received significantly harsher sentences than young white males. This study also found that young Hispanic females received sentences that were more similar to those imposed on male defendants than on female defendants, but that African American females were treated similar to or more leniently than white females.

The findings of the studies discussed above confirm Richard Quinney's assertion, which he made 35 years ago, that "judicial decisions are not made uniformly. Decisions are made according to a host of extra-legal factors, including the age of the offender, his race, and social class."[93] Their findings confirm that dangerous or problematic populations are defined "by a mix of economic *and* racial ... references."[94] African American and Hispanic offenders who are also male, young, and unemployed may pay a higher punishment penalty than white offenders or other types of African American and Hispanic offenders.

Why Do Young, Unemployed Racial Minorities Pay a Punishment Penalty?   The question, of course, is *why* young, unemployed racial minorities are punished more severely than other types of offenders—why "today's prevailing criminal predator has become a euphemism for young, black males."[95]

A number of scholars suggest that certain categories of offenders are regarded as more dangerous and more problematic than others and thus more in need of formal social control. Steven Spitzer, for example, used the term "social dynamite"[96] to characterize that segment of the deviant population that is viewed as particularly threatening and dangerous; he asserted that social dynamite "tends to be more youthful, alienated and politically volatile" and contended that those who fall into this category are more likely than other offenders to be formally processed through the criminal justice system.[97] Building on this point, Steven Box and Chris Hale argued that unemployed offenders who are also young, male, and members of a racial minority will be perceived as particularly threatening to the social order and thus will be singled out for harsher treatment.[98] Judges, in other words, regard these types of "threatening" offenders as likely candidates for imprisonment "in the belief that such a response will deter and incapacitate and thus defuse this threat."[99]

Steffensmeier and his colleagues advanced a similar explanation for their finding "that young black men (as opposed to black men as a whole) are the defendant subgroup most at risk to receive the harshest penalty."[100] They interpreted their results using the "focal concerns" perspective on sentencing. According to this perspective, judges' sentencing decisions reflect their assessment of the blameworthiness or culpability of the offender; their desire to protect the community by incapacitating dangerous offenders or deterring potential offenders; and their concerns about the practical consequences, or social costs, of sentencing decisions. Because judges rarely have enough information to accurately determine an offender's culpability or dangerousness, they develop a "perceptual shorthand" based on stereotypes and attributions that are themselves linked to offender characteristics such as race, gender, and age (see Box 7.6 for a discussion of the ways in which a prior criminal record affect perceptions of offenders by potential employers). Thus, according to these researchers,

> Younger offenders and male defendants appear to be seen as more of a threat to the community or not as reformable, and so also are black offenders, particularly those who also are young and male. Likewise, concerns such as "ability to do time" and the costs of incarceration appear linked to race-, gender-, and age-based perceptions and stereotypes.[101]

| Box 7.6 | The Mark of a Criminal Record |

It is clear that racial disparities in the treatment of defendants at various stages of the criminal justice system have spillover effects and collateral consequences. As noted earlier in this chapter, if African Americans and Hispanics are more likely than whites to be arrested, prosecuted, convicted, and sentenced to prison, they will accumulate more serious prior criminal histories than whites. As a result, they may be treated differently than whites in areas outside the criminal justice system—for example, they may find it more difficult to locate suitable housing or find appropriate employment.

The effect of having a criminal record was examined in an innovative study by Devah Pager. Her work on "The Mark of a Criminal Record" used the so-called "audit strategy." In this design, which was used first to study the effects of race and ethnicity on job prospects, the backgrounds and resumes of job applicants from different racial/ethnic groups are carefully constructed to be identical. The matched pairs (who differ only by race or ethnicity) present themselves to potential employers, and differences in outcomes are then assumed to be due to differences in race or ethnicity. This work enjoys a long tradition in applied economics, where research consistently documents that African Americans do worse than matched white job applicants and Hispanics fare worse than matched white applicants.

Pager used the audit strategy to independently assess the impact of a criminal record by matching prospective job applicants on race and varying the presence or absence of a criminal background. In a carefully controlled experiment conducted in Milwaukee, Wisconsin, Pager had matched pairs of African American and white job seekers send their resumes to prospective employers. These pairs had identical resumes with regard to age, length of time in the job market, prior type of job, and education. However, one member of each race-matched pair indicated that he had been to prison.

Use of this strategy allowed Pager to test for differences within and between racial groups. Using callbacks from employers as the dependent variable, she found significant differences within race for the impact of a prison sentence. African American job applicants without a criminal record were nearly three times as likely to get a callback as were African American job applicants with a criminal record (14 percent versus 5 percent). The effects of a criminal record were not quite as stark for whites, as applicants without a criminal record were twice as likely to get a callback (34 percent versus 17 percent). However, the between race results remain the major finding from Pager's research, as white applicants **with** a criminal record were more likely to receive job callbacks than were African American applicants who did not have a criminal record.

These findings reinforce the effect of criminal stigma for job seeking, an effect that varies with race but is often trumped by race.

SOURCE: Devah Pager, "The Mark of a Criminal Record," *American Journal of Sociology* 108 (2003), pp. 937–975; Devah Pager, *Marked: Race, Crime, and Finding Work in an Era of Mass Incarceration* (Chicago: University of Chicago Press, 2009).

The conclusions proffered by Spohn and Holleran, who noted that their results are consistent with the focal concerns perspective on sentencing, are very similar. They suggested that judges, who generally have limited time in which to make decisions and have incomplete information about offenders, "may resort to stereotypes of deviance and dangerousness that rest on considerations of race, ethnicity, gender, age, and unemployment."[102] Young, unemployed African American and Hispanic males, in other words, are viewed as more dangerous, more threatening, and less amenable to rehabilitation; as a result, they are sentenced more harshly.

Differential Treatment of Interracial and Intraracial Sexual Assault

There is compelling historical evidence that interracial and intraracial crimes were treated differently. Gunnar Myrdal's examination of the southern court system in the 1930s, for example, revealed that African Americans who victimized whites received the harshest punishment, whereas African Americans who victimized other African Americans were often "acquitted or given a ridiculously mild sentence...."[103] Myrdal also noted that "it is quite common for a white criminal to be set free if his crime was against a Negro."[104]

These patterns are particularly pronounced for the crime of sexual assault. As Susan Brownmiller has noted, "No single event ticks off America's political schizophrenia with greater certainty than the case of a black man accused of raping a white woman."[105] Evidence of this can be found in pre–Civil War statutes that prescribed different penalties for African American and white men convicted of sexual assault. As illustrated in Box 7.7, these early laws also differentiated between the rape of a white woman and the rape of an African American woman.

B o x 7.7   Pre–Civil War Statutes on Sexual Assault: Explicit Discrimination against African American Men Convicted of Raping White Women

Virginia Code of 1819
The penalty for the rape or attempted rape of a white woman by a slave, African American, or mulatto was death; if the offender was white, the penalty was 10–21 years.

Georgia Penal Code of 1816
The death penalty was prescribed for rape or attempted rape of a white woman by slaves or free persons of color. A term of not more than 20 years was the penalty for rape of a white woman by a white man. A white man convicted of raping an African American woman could be fined or imprisoned at the court's discretion.

Pennsylvania Code of 1700
The penalty for the rape of a white woman by an African American man was death; the penalty for attempted rape was castration. The penalty for a white man was 1–7 years in prison.

Kansas Compilation of 1855
An African American man convicted of raping a white woman was to be castrated at his own expense. The maximum penalty for a white man convicted of raping a white woman was 5 years in prison.[106]

Differential treatment of interracial and intraracial sexual assaults continued even after passage of the Fourteenth Amendment, which outlawed explicit statutory racial discrimination. In the first half of the twentieth century, African American men accused of, or even suspected of, sexually assaulting white women often faced white lynch mobs bent on vengeance. As Jennifer Wriggins noted, "The thought of this particular crime aroused in many white people an extremely high level of mania and panic."[107] In a 1907 Louisiana case, the defense attorney stated:

> Gentlemen of the jury, this man, a nigger, is charged with breaking into the house of a white man in the nighttime and assaulting his wife, with the intent to rape her. Now, don't you know that, if this nigger had committed such a crime, he never would have been brought here and tried; that he would have been lynched, and if I were there I would help pull on the rope.[108]

African American men who escaped the mob's wrath were almost certain to be convicted, and those who were convicted were guaranteed a harsh sentence. Many, in fact, were sentenced to death; 405 of the 453 men executed for rape in the United States from 1930 to 1972 were African Americans.[109] According to Brownmiller, "Heavier sentences imposed on blacks for raping white women is an incontestable historic fact."[110] As we show, it is not simply a historic fact. Research conducted during the past three decades illustrates that African American men convicted of raping white women continue to be singled out for harsher treatment.

Offender–Victim Race and Sentences for Sexual Assault

Researchers analyzing the impact of race on sentencing for sexual assault (and other crimes with victims) have argued that focusing only on the race of the defendant and ignoring the race of the victim will produce misleading conclusions about the overall effect of race on sentencing. They contend that researchers may incorrectly conclude that race does not affect sentence severity if only the race of the defendant is taken into consideration. Table 7.2 presents a hypothetical example to illustrate how this might occur. Assume that 460 of 1,000 African American men (46 percent) and 440 of 1,000 white men (44 percent) convicted of sexual assault in a particular jurisdiction were sentenced to prison. A researcher who focused only on the race of the offender would therefore conclude that the incarceration rates for the two groups were nearly identical.

Assume now that the 1,000 cases involving African American men included 800 cases with African American victims and 200 cases with white victims and that 320 of the 800 cases with African American victims and 140 of the 200 cases with white victims resulted in a prison sentence. As shown in Table 7.2, although the overall incarceration rate for African American offenders is 46 percent, the rate for crimes involving African American men and white women is 70 percent, whereas the rate for crimes involving African American men and African American women is only 40 percent. A similar pattern—an incarceration

T A B L E 7.2   Incarceration of Offenders Convicted of Sexual Assault: A Hypothetical Example of the Effect of Offender–Victim Race

Example: 2,000 men convicted of sexual assault. Analysis reveals that incarceration rate for African Americans is very similar to the rate for whites.

1,000 convicted African American offenders	460 incarcerated = 46% incarceration rate
1,000 convicted white offenders	440 incarcerated = 44% incarceration rate

Problem: Similarities are masking differences based on the race of the victim.

1,000 African American Offenders	460 incarcerated (46%)
800 cases with African American victims	320 incarcerated (40%)
200 cases with white victims	140 incarcerated (70%)
1,000 White Offenders	440 incarcerated (44%)
300 cases with African American victims	90 incarcerated (30%)
700 cases with white victims	350 incarcerated (50%)

Thus, the incarceration rate varies from 30% (for whites who assaulted African Americans) to 70% (for African Americans who assaulted whites).

rate of 50 percent for cases with white victims but only 30 percent for cases with African American victims—is found for sexual assaults involving white offenders. The similar incarceration rates for African American and white offenders in this hypothetical example mask large differences based on the race of the victim.

The findings of empirical research suggest that this scenario is not simply hypothetical. Gary D. LaFree, for example, examined the impact of offender–victim race on the disposition of sexual assault cases in Indianapolis.[111] He found that African American men who assaulted white women were more likely than other offenders to be sentenced to prison. They also received longer prison sentences than any other offenders. LaFree concluded that his results highlighted the importance of examining the racial composition of the offender–victim pair. Because the law was applied *most* harshly to African Americans charged with raping white women but *least* harshly to African Americans charged with raping African American women, simply examining the overall disposition of cases with African American defendants would have produced misleading results.

Anthony Walsh[112] reached a similar conclusion. When he examined the sentences imposed on offenders convicted of sexual assault in a metropolitan Ohio county, he found that neither the offender's race nor the victim's race influenced the length of the sentence. In addition, the incarceration rate for white defendants was *higher* than the rate for African American defendants. Further analysis, however, revealed that African Americans convicted of assaulting whites received more severe sentences than those convicted of assaulting members of their own race. This was true for those who assaulted acquaintances and for those who assaulted strangers. As Walsh noted, "The leniency extended to blacks who sexually assault blacks provides a rather strong indication of disregard for minority victims of sexual assault."[113]

Somewhat different results were reported by Cassia Spohn and Jeffrey Spears,[114] who analyzed a sample of sexual assaults bound over for trial in Detroit Recorder's Court. Unlike previous research, which controlled only for offender–victim race and other offender and case characteristics, the authors of this study also controlled for a number of victim characteristics in addition to race. They controlled for the age of the victim, the relationship between the victim and the offender, evidence of risk-taking behavior on the part of the victim, and the victim's behavior at the time of the incident. They compared the incarceration rates and the maximum sentences imposed on three combinations of offender–victim race: African American–African American, African American–white, and white–white.

In contrast to the results reported by LaFree and Walsh, Spohn and Spears found that the race of the offender–victim pair did not affect the likelihood of incarceration. The prison sentences imposed on African Americans who assaulted whites, however, were significantly longer than the sentences imposed on whites who assaulted whites or African Americans who assaulted African Americans. The average sentence for African American–on–white crimes was more than four years longer than the average sentence for white-on-white crimes and more than three years longer than the average sentence for African American–on–African American crimes. These results, according to the authors, reflected discrimination based on the offender's race and the victim's race.[115]

To explain the fact that offender–victim race affected the length of sentence but had no effect on the decision of whether to incarcerate, the authors suggested that judges confronted with offenders convicted of sexual assault may have relatively little discretion in deciding whether to incarcerate. As they noted, "Because sexual assault is a serious crime … the 'normal penalty' may be incarceration. Judges may have more latitude, and thus more opportunities to consider extralegal factors such as offender/victim race, in deciding on the length of the sentence."[116]

Spohn and Spears also tested a number of hypotheses about the interrelationships among offender race, victim race, and the relationship between the victim and the offender. Noting that previous research has suggested that crimes between intimates are perceived as less serious than crimes between strangers, they hypothesized that sexual assaults involving strangers would be treated more harshly than assaults involving intimates or acquaintances regardless of the offender's race or the victim's race. Contrary to their hypothesis, they found that the offender–victim relationship came into play only when both the offender and the victim were African American. African Americans convicted of assaulting African American strangers received harsher sentences than African Americans convicted of assaulting African American intimates or acquaintances; they were more likely to be incarcerated, and those who were incarcerated received longer sentences.[117]

The data presented in Figure 7.2 illustrate these differences. The authors used the results of their multivariate analysis of sentence length to calculate

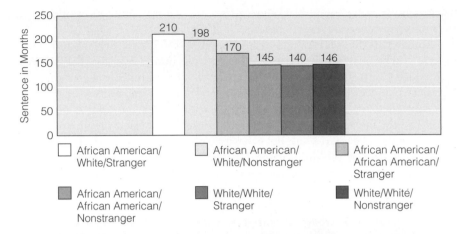

FIGURE 7.2 Offender's Race, Victim's Race, Relationship, and Length of Sentence

SOURCE: "The Effect of Offender and Victim Characteristics on Sexual Assault Case Processing Decisions," Cassia Spohn and Jeffrey Spears, *Justice Quarterly* 3 (1996), copyright © The Academy of Criminal Justice Sciences (Taylor & Francis Ltd, http://www.tandf.co.uk/journals) on behalf of Academy of Criminal Justice Sciences.

adjusted sentence means for each of the six combinations of offender race, victim race, and the relationship between the victim and the offender. These adjusted rates take all of the other independent variables into account. They show that three types of offenders received substantially longer sentences than the other three types. The harshest sentences were imposed on African Americans who victimized whites (strangers or nonstrangers) and on African Americans who victimized African American strangers. More lenient sentences were imposed on African Americans who assaulted African American nonstrangers and on whites who assaulted whites (strangers or nonstrangers).

As the authors noted, these results suggest that judges consider the offender's race, but not the relationship between the victim and offender, in determining the appropriate sentence for offenders convicted of assaulting whites. Regardless of the relationship between the victim and the offender, African Americans who victimized whites received longer sentences than whites who victimized whites. However, judges do consider the relationship between the victim and offender in determining the appropriate sentence for African Americans convicted of sexually assaulting other African Americans. Judges apparently believe that African Americans who sexually assault African Americans who are strangers to them deserve harsher punishment than those who sexually assault African American friends, relatives, or acquaintances.

Considered together, the results of these studies demonstrate that in sexual assault cases criminal punishment is contingent on the race of the victim as well as the race of the offender. The harshest penalties are imposed on African Americans who victimize whites, and the most lenient penalties are imposed on African Americans who victimize other African Americans. (See Box 7.8 for information on different groups' perceptions of the severity of sanctions.)

B o x   7.8   Perceptions of the Severity of Sanctions: Do African Americans Evaluate Prison Differently than Whites?

Studies of sentencing decisions assume that prison is a harsher punishment than probation, a county jail sentence, or other alternatives to incarceration. But is this necessarily this case? Is it possible that some people would rather serve time in prison than be subjected to electronic monitoring, ordered to perform community service, or placed on intensive supervision probation? More to the point, is it possible that African Americans would evaluate the severity of these sanctions differently than whites?

To answer these questions, Peter Wood and David May asked 113 probationers to rate the severity of prison and a number of alternatives to incarceration.[118] Respondents were given descriptions of 10 alternative sanctions and then were asked to indicate how many months of the alternative they would be willing to do to avoid serving a sentence of 4, 8, or 12 months of imprisonment in a medium-security facility. The authors used these responses to calculate the percentage of respondents who would choose each prison term rather than any duration of the alternative sanction. They found that African Americans were much more likely than whites to choose prison rather than an alternative; this was true for each of the alternative sentences. For example,

- 22.2 percent of African Americans, but only 13.2 percent of whites, said that they would rather serve 4 months in prison than any time on electronic monitoring; 17 percent of African Americans, but only 11.5 percent of whites, said that they would rather serve a year in prison than any time on electronic monitoring.

- Six times as many African Americans as whites said that they would rather spend time in prison than be placed on intensive supervision probation (ISP). For example, 26.8 percent of African Americans said that they would rather serve a year in prison than any time on ISP; for whites, the figure was only 3.8 percent.

- The percentage of African Americans who said they would rather spend 8 months in prison than any time in county jail was 24.1 percent, compared to 13.5 percent of whites.[119]

Wood and May also asked the respondents about their reasons for wanting to avoid alternative sanctions. Like their evaluations of the sanctions themselves, these varied depending on the race of the respondent. Twice as many African Americans as whites reported that a "very important reason" for avoiding alternative sanctions was that the officials in charge of these programs were too hard on participants—they wanted to catch them and send them back to prison. Similarly, 38.9 percent of African Americans, but only 18.9 percent of whites, said that abuse by officials overseeing the programs was a very important reason for avoiding them. African Americans also were more likely than whites to believe that serving time in prison is less of a hassle and that the program rules for alternative sanctions were too hard to follow. Because African Americans believe that the risk of revocation is high, they are "less willing to gamble on alternatives and more likely to choose prison instead."[120]

According to the authors of this study, their findings raise questions about the deterrent value of imprisonment for African Americans. Although they admitted that they did not know whether African Americans' preference for prison over alternative sanctions was due to a belief that doing time in prison was easier or that the risk of revocation made alternatives too risky, the authors did conclude that "a brief prison term may be more of a deterrent for whites than for blacks."[121]

The Effect of Race on Sentencing for Various Types of Crimes

The studies summarized thus far highlight the importance of testing for interaction between offender race/ethnicity and other factors, such as the age, gender, and employment status of the offender, the race of the victim, and the relationship between the victim and the offender. The importance of testing for interactions between offender race and other predictors of sentencing is also demonstrated by the results of studies examining the effect of race on sentence severity for various types of crimes. Some researchers, building on Harry Kalven and Hans Zeisel's "liberation hypothesis,"[122] assert that African Americans will be sentenced more harshly than whites only in less serious cases.

The liberation hypothesis, which Kalven and Zeisel developed to explain jury decision making, suggests that jurors deviate from their fact-finding mission in cases in which the evidence against the defendant is weak or contradictory. Jurors' doubts about the evidence, in other words, liberate them from the constraints imposed by the law and free them to consider their own sentiments or values. When Kalven and Zeisel examined jurors' verdicts in rape cases, they found that jurors' beliefs about the victim's behavior at the time of the attack (for example, whether the victim was intoxicated or under the influence of drugs, whether the victim was walking alone late at night or in a bar by herself) were much more likely to influence their verdicts if the victim was raped by an unarmed acquaintance than if the victim was raped by a stranger armed with a gun or a knife.

Applied to the sentencing process, the liberation hypothesis suggests that in more serious cases the appropriate sentence is strongly determined by the seriousness of the crime and by the defendant's prior criminal record. In these types of cases, judges have relatively little discretion and thus few opportunities to consider legally irrelevant factors such as race. In less serious cases, on the other hand, the appropriate sentence is not clearly indicated by the features of the crime or the defendant's criminal record, which may leave judges more disposed to bring extralegal factors to bear on the sentencing decision.

Consider, for example, a case of sexual assault in which the offender, who has a prior conviction for armed robbery, raped a stranger at gunpoint. This case clearly calls for a severe sentence; all defendants who fall into this category, regardless of their race or their victim's race, will be sentenced to prison for close to the maximum term.

The appropriate sentence for a first-time offender who assaults an acquaintance with a weapon other than a gun, however, is not necessarily obvious. Some defendants who fall into this category will be incarcerated, but others will not. This opens the door for judges to consider the race of the defendant or the race of the victim in determining the appropriate sentence.

The Liberation Hypothesis and Offenders Convicted
of Violent Felonies

Cassia Spohn and Jerry Cederblom used data on defendants convicted of violent felonies in Detroit to test the hypothesis that racial discrimination in sentencing is confined to less serious criminal cases.[123] Although they acknowledged that all of the cases included in their data file are by definition "serious cases," they argued that some are more serious than others: murder, rape, and robbery are more serious than assault; crimes in which the defendant used a gun are more serious than those in which the defendant did not use a gun; and crimes in which the defendant had a prior felony conviction are more serious than those in which the defendant did not have prior convictions.

As shown in Table 7.3, which summarizes the results of their analysis of the likelihood of incarceration (controlling for other variables linked to sentence severity), the authors found convincing support for their hypothesis. With only one exception, race had a significant effect on the decision to incarcerate only in less serious cases (but see Box 7.9 for evidence of racial stereotyping in homicide cases). African Americans convicted of assault were incarcerated at a higher rate than whites convicted of assault; there were no racial differences for the three

T A B L E 7.3   The Effect of Race on the Likelihood of Incarceration for Various Types of Cases in Detroit

	Effect of Race on Incarceration: Statistically Significant?
Most serious conviction charge	
Murder	No
Robbery	No
Rape	No
Other sex offenses	No
Assault	Yes
Prior criminal record	
Violent felony conviction	No
No violent felony conviction	Yes
Relationship between offender and victim	
Strangers	No
Acquaintances	Yes
Use of a weapon	
Offender used a gun	No
Offender did not use a gun	Yes
Injury to victim	
Offender injured victim	Yes
Offender did not injure victim	Yes

SOURCE: Adapted from Cassia Spohn and Jerry Cederblom, "Race and Disparities in Sentencing: A Test of the Liberation Hypothesis," *Justice Quarterly* 8 (1991), pp. 305–327.

more serious offenses. Similarly, race affected the likelihood of incarceration for
defendants with no violent felony convictions, but not for those with a prior
conviction; for defendants who victimized acquaintances, but not for those
who victimized strangers; and for defendants who did not use a gun to commit
the crime, but not for those who did use a gun.

Spohn and Cederblom concluded that their results provided support for Kalven and Zeisel's liberation hypothesis, at least with respect to the decision to
incarcerate. They also concluded that their findings offered important insights
into judges' sentencing decisions. According to the authors,

> When the crime is serious and the evidence strong, judges' sentencing
> decisions are determined primarily by factors of explicit legal relevance—
> the seriousness of the conviction charge, the number of conviction
> charges, the nature of the defendant's prior criminal record, and so on.
> Sentencing decisions in less serious cases, however, reflect the influence of
> extralegal as well as legal factors.[124]

B o x 7.9   Racial Stereotyping in Homicide Cases

The assumption that offender race will not affect sentence outcomes in the most
serious felonies because of limited judicial discretion in these cases is called into
question by the results of a study examining sentences imposed on male homicide
offenders sentenced to a term of years (rather than a life or death sentence) in Philadelphia.[125] Because either life without parole or death were the only sentence
options allowed in cases of first- or second-degree murder, and because judges
adhered closely to these guidelines, the study focused on offenders convicted of
third-degree murder, voluntary manslaughter, involuntary manslaughter, and homicide by vehicle.

Kathleen Auerhahn suggested that the offender's race and ethnicity would
not have a direct effect on the length of the sentence. Rather, she hypothesized
that harsher treatment would be reserved for African American and Hispanic
defendants who more closely matched stereotypes of dangerousness and threat—
that is, those who were also young and held in custody prior to trial. Her results
were consistent with this hypothesis; the race/ethnicity of the offender did not
have a direct effect on sentence length, but the combination of being young,
African American or Hispanic, and detained prior to trial did lead to longer sentences. In other words, all three characteristics were needed to trigger more punitive sentences.

Auerhahn concluded that her findings provided

> convincing evidence that sentencing judges make attributions about offenders
> based on their conformity to a criminal stereotype, and sentence them more
> harshly because of it ... conformity to the stereotype may trigger attributions
> about the defendant's character, disposition, or blameworthiness, as well as
> assumptions about the potential for future criminality in that stereotypes may
> be seen as the embodiment of stable characteristics on the part of decision
> makers.[126]

Racial Discrimination in the Sentencing of
Misdemeanor Offenders?

Most of the research on sentencing examines the sentences imposed on offenders convicted of felonies. There is relatively little research testing for racial discrimination in the sentencing of individuals convicted of misdemeanor offenses. Because the lower courts where misdemeanor cases are handled usually have huge caseloads and informal, nonadversarial procedures for delivering what is often referred to as "assembly-line justice," one might predict that the likelihood of racially disparate decisions would be even greater in these courts than in the more formal felony courts.

Research by Michael J. Leiber and Anita N. Blowers addressed this issue.[127] They used data from an urban jurisdiction in a southeastern state to test for racial differences in a series of outcomes in misdemeanor cases. One of the dependent variables they examined was whether the case was assigned "priority status." This case-screening decision, which was made based on the defendant's prior criminal record or the facts in the case, identified cases that warranted priority prosecution. Two other dependent variables were whether the defendant was convicted and whether the defendant was sentenced to jail or prison.

When they examined the case prioritization variable, they found that cases involving assaults, cases in which the victim was a stranger to the offender, and cases involving offenders with prior criminal histories were more likely to be prioritized. They also found that cases involving African Americans were significantly more likely than those involving whites to be prioritized. Regarding the conviction and incarceration variables, they found that more serious cases had greater odds of conviction and incarceration and that the race of the offender did not affect either of these decisions. However, both decisions were affected by the status of the case; cases labeled as priority status cases were more likely to result in convictions and sentences to jail or prison.[128] The effect of race on these decisions, in other words, was indirect rather than direct. Cases involving African Americans were more likely to be prioritized and, as a result, were more likely than cases involving whites to result in conviction and incarceration. In these misdemeanor cases, then, African Americans were treated more harshly than whites when the case was characterized as serious rather than nonserious.

The results of these studies demonstrate that the criteria used by judges to determine the appropriate sentence will vary depending on the nature of the crime and the defendant's prior criminal record. More to the point, they demonstrate that *the effect of race on sentence severity will vary*. Judges impose harsher sentences on African Americans than on whites under some circumstances and for some types of crime; they impose similar sentences under other circumstances and for other types of crime. The fact that race does not affect sentence severity for *all* cases, in other words, does not mean that judges do not discriminate in *any* cases.

Sentencing and the War on Drugs

The task of assessing the effect of race on sentencing is complicated by the war on drugs, which critics contend has been fought primarily in minority communities. Michael Tonry, for example, argued that "urban black Americans have borne the brunt of the War on Drugs."[129] More specifically, he charged that "the recent blackening of America's prison population is the product of malign neglect of the war's effects on black Americans."[130] Miller similarly asserted that, "The racial discrimination endemic to the drug war wound its way through every stage of the processing—arrest, jailing, conviction, and sentencing."[131] Marc Mauer's criticism is even more pointed. He asserted that "... the drug war has exacerbated racial disparities in incarceration while failing to have any sustained impact on the drug problem."[132]

Assertions such as these suggest that racial minorities will receive more punitive sentences than whites for drug offenses. This expectation is based in part on theoretical discussion of the "moral panic" surrounding drug use and the war on drugs.[133] Moral panic theorists argue that society is characterized by a variety of common-sense perceptions about crime and drugs that result in community intolerance for such behaviors and increased pressure for punitive action.[134] Many theorists argue that this moral panic can become ingrained in the judicial ideology of sentencing judges, resulting in more severe sentences for those—that is, African Americans and Hispanics—believed to be responsible for drug use, drug distribution, and drug-related crime.[135]

Racial Disparities in Sentences Imposed for Drug Offenses

As demonstrated in earlier chapters and summarized in what follows, there is ample evidence that the war on drugs has been fought primarily in minority communities (see also Box 7.10, Drug-Free School Zones). In 2000 Human Rights Watch, a New York–based watchdog organization, issued a report titled *Punishment and Prejudice*.[136] The report analyzed nationwide prison admission statistics and presented the results of the first state-by-state analysis of the impact of drug offenses on prison admissions for African Americans and whites. The authors of the report alleged that the war on drugs, which is "ostensibly color blind," has been waged "disproportionately against black Americans." As they noted, "The statistics we have compiled present a unique—and devastating—picture of the price black Americans have paid in each state for the national effort to curtail the use and sale of illicit drugs." In support of this conclusion, the report noted that:

- African Americans constituted 62.6 percent of all drug offenders admitted to state prisons in 1996; in certain states, the disparity was much worse—in Maryland and Illinois, for example, African Americans comprised 90 percent of all persons admitted to state prisons for drug offenses.

- Nationwide, the rate of drug admissions to state prison for African American men was 13 times greater than the rate for white men; in 10 states, the rates for African American men were 26 to 57 times greater than those for white men.

- Drug offenders accounted for 38 percent of all African American prison admissions but only 24 percent of all white prison admissions; in New Hampshire, drug offenders accounted for 61 percent of all African American prison admissions.

- The disproportionate rates at which African Americans are sentenced to prison for drug offenses "originate in racially disproportionate rates of arrest." From 1979 to 1998, the percentage of drug users who were African American did not vary appreciably; however, among those arrested for drug offenses, the percentage of African Americans increased significantly. In 1979 African Americans comprised 10.8 percent of all drug users and 21.8 percent of all drug arrests; in 1998, African Americans comprised 16.9 percent of all drug users and 37.3 percent of all drug arrests.

The authors of the report stated that their purpose was "to bring renewed attention to extreme racial disparities in one area of the criminal justice system—the incarceration of drug law offenders." They also asserted that, although the high rates of incarceration for all drug offenders were a cause for concern, "the grossly disparate rates at which blacks and whites are sent to prison for drug offenses raise a clear warning flag concerning the fairness and equity of drug law enforcement across the country, and underscore the need for reforms that would minimize these disparities without sacrificing legitimate drug control objectives."

Critics of the report's conclusions, which they branded "inflammatory," argued that the statistics presented did not constitute evidence of racial discrimination. "There will be inevitably, inherently, disparities of all sorts in the enforcement of any kind of law," said Todd Graziano, a senior fellow in legal studies at the Heritage Foundation. Critics noted that because the illegal drug trade flourishes in inner-city, minority neighborhoods, the statistics presented in the report could simply indicate that African Americans commit more drug crimes than whites.

There are now a number of studies that focus on racial disparities in sentences imposed on drug offenders. In this section, we summarize the results of three studies comparing the sentences imposed on African American, Hispanic, and white drug offenders. All of these studies used data on offenders sentenced since the initiation of the war on drugs. The first two studies[137] used data on offenders sentenced in state court; the second[138] analyzed data on offenders sentenced under the Federal Sentencing Guidelines.

Sentencing of Drug Offenders in State Courts

Steffensmeier and Demuth's study of sentence outcomes in Pennsylvania focused on differential treatment of white, black, and Hispanic drug offenders.[139] Arguing that "the specific social and historical context involving Hispanic Americans exacerbates perceptions of their cultural dissimilarity and the 'threat' they pose," the authors of this study hypothesized that *Hispanic drug offenders* would be singled out for the harshest treatment.[140] They found evidence in support of their hypothesis when they examined the raw data: the incarceration rate for Hispanics (87.4 percent) was substantially higher than the rates for African Americans (69.9 percent) or whites (52.3 percent), and Hispanics received somewhat longer sentences than African Americans or whites.[141]

These differences did not disappear when the authors controlled for the offender's age and for a number of case characteristics (offense type and severity, criminal history, number of convictions, whether the conviction was by plea or trial). Hispanics were 26 percentage points and African Americans were 7 percentage points more likely than whites to be incarcerated; Hispanics also received sentences that averaged 8 months longer than the sentences imposed on whites.[142] These findings led the authors to conclude that Hispanic defendants in Pennsylvania faced "real and meaningful" disadvantages at sentencing. They also concluded that the results of their study raise questions "about the equal application of law and the wherewithal of the sentencing guidelines in reducing sentencing disparities of any kind, including race and ethnicity."[143]

Research conducted in Washington State also examined the effect of race on sentencing decisions in drug cases. Sara Steen, Rodney L. Engen, and Randy R. Gainey interviewed criminal justice officials about their perceptions of typical drug cases and drug offenders and the factors they used to differentiate among drug cases.[144] They found that decision makers used three offender characteristics—gender, prior record, and whether the offender was using or dealing drugs—to construct a stereotype of a dangerous drug offender. Males with prior felony convictions who were convicted of drug-delivery offenses involving cocaine, heroin, or methamphetamine were perceived as more dangerous and threatening than other types of drug offenders.

As shown in Table 7.4, Steen and her colleagues also found that African Americans were more likely than whites to have the characteristics of the stereotypical dangerous drug offender. African Americans were more likely than whites to be male, to be drug dealers rather than drug users, and to have prior felony convictions. African Americans also were more likely than whites to have *all* of the characteristics of a dangerous drug offender; 16 percent of the African Americans, but only 6 percent of the whites, were male offenders with prior felony convictions who were convicted of drug dealing. According to the authors, "this disproportionality, along with cultural stereotypes, makes decision makers more inclined to expect this 'worst case' behavior from black offenders (especially black males) than from white offenders."[145] As a result, whites who match the stereotype of a dangerous drug offender will be seen as atypical, and their behavior will be subjected to more judicial scrutiny; African Americans who match the stereotype, however, will be perceived as typical and their cases will be handled in a routine fashion.

The results of the authors' analysis of the decision whether to incarcerate revealed that African Americans were substantially more likely than whites to be incarcerated and that offenders whose characteristics matched those of the dangerous drug offenders had higher odds of incarceration than offenders whose characteristics were at odds with the stereotype. Males were 56 percent more likely than females to be incarcerated, and the odds of incarceration were 23 times greater for dealers than for nondealers and 8 times greater for offenders

TABLE 7.4   Race and the Stereotype of a Dangerous Drug Offender: Percentage of Whites and African Americans Having Characteristics Stereotypical of a Dangerous Drug Offender

	Whites (%)	African Americans (%)
Offender is male	74	82
Offender is a drug dealer	14	27
Offender has at least one prior felony conviction	48	68
Offender Groups		
Offender is a male dealer with prior felony convictions	6	16
Offender is a male dealer without prior felony convictions	5	6
Offender is a male nondealer with prior felony convictions	32	41
Offender is a male nondealer with no prior felony convictions	31	18
Offender is a female dealer	3	4
Offender is a female nondealer with prior felony convictions	9	8
Offender is a female nondealer without prior felony convictions	14	6

with prior felony convictions than for those without prior felonies. When the authors partitioned the data by the race of the offender, they found that although being a drug dealer had a significant effect on the likelihood of incarceration for both white offenders and African American offenders, it had a significantly larger effect for whites than for African Americans. Being a dealer increased the odds of incarceration 27 times for white offenders, compared to 9 times for African American offenders.[146] Further analysis revealed that fitting the stereotype of a dangerous drug offender (that is, a male dealer with prior felony convictions) also affected the likelihood of incarceration for white offenders more than for African American offenders.[147]

The authors interpreted their finding that matching the stereotype of a dangerous drug offender had a more pronounced effect on the severity of the sentence for whites than for African Americans as reflecting "greater leniency in the sentencing of less-threatening white offenders, compared to blacks, as opposed to greater punitiveness in the sentencing of the most threatening white offenders."[148] All offenders—whites as well as African Americans—who matched the stereotype of a dangerous offender were sentenced to jail or prison. Probation was not an option for these dangerous offenders. Among less serious offenders, however, judges sent whites to jail or prison less often than African Americans. The authors concluded that their results suggested that "decision makers are more likely to define low-level black offenders as a threat to public safety, and therefore deserving of incarceration, than similarly situated white offenders."[149] (For additional discussion of dangerous drugs and dangerous drug offenders, see "Focus on an Issue: Penalties for Crack and Powder Cocaine.")

The findings of this state-level study provide clues regarding the contexts in which race and ethnicity matter in sentencing drug offenders. They suggest that decision makers' beliefs about the dangerousness of and degree of threat posed by white and African American offenders are intertwined with their assumptions about crime and criminality. As Steen and her colleagues noted, "stereotypes about both crimes and criminals affect the way cases are perceived and decisions are made."[150]

Box 7.10   Drug-Free School Zones: A Racially Neutral Policy?

Dematric Young was 20 years old when he was convicted of selling a small amount of cocaine to an undercover narcotics agent in North Lubbock, Texas. Young sold the drugs from his room in the Sunset Motel, a rundown place in a largely Hispanic neighborhood that, unknown to him, was located within 1,000 feet of Cavazos Junior High School. The normal sentence for Young's crime under Texas law would have been about 10 years. Because Young sold the drugs in a "drug-free school zone," he was sentenced to serve 38 years in prison.[151]

The Texas law under which Young was sentenced was modeled after the Federal Drug-Free School Zones Act (21 U.S.C. § 860 [1984]), which was enacted "to reduce the presence of drugs in the schools by threatening those who distributed drugs near schools with heavy penalties." The law, which doubles the maximum sentences for drug offenses that occur within the protected zones, is applicable to offenders who are convicted of distributing, possessing with intent to distribute, or manufacturing a controlled substance in or on, or within 1,000 feet of, the real property comprising a public or private elementary, vocational, or secondary school; a public or private college, junior college, or university; a playground; or housing facility owned by a public housing authority or within 100 feet of a public or private youth center, swimming pool, or video arcade facility.

Laws similar to this have been enacted in most states. Although they are designed to prevent the sale of drugs to children by moving drug dealing away from schools, critics contend that the statutes are irrational in that they assume that all drug sales near a school involve children or are more dangerous to children than drug sales that occur farther away from schools. Critics also argue that the laws transform entire urban areas—indeed, entire cities—into school zones and that this is most likely to occur in the inner-city neighborhoods populated by poor African Americans and Hispanics. A study of New Bedford, Massachusetts, for example, found that "most of the urban core falls within the enhanced-penalty area" and that more than three-fourths of all drug-dealing cases within the city limits occurred within school zones. This study also found that the drug dealers who were arrested within the school zones were not selling drugs to children and that most of them were arrested when school was not in session.[152]

A report by the Justice Policy Institute reached similar conclusions about the impact of the drug-free school zone law in New Jersey.[153] Noting that the New Jersey law used a broad definition of "schools" that included day care centers and vocational training centers, the report concluded that "in New Jersey's poorest urban centers, minority offenders find themselves blanketed in drug free school zones." The report also noted that "a more suburban county, with fewer African American and Hispanic residents and a less dense distribution of 'schools' might experience less enforcement of school-zone laws, placing fewer Whites at risk of arrest and imprisonment."

As these reports suggest, drug-free school zone statutes, which are racially neutral on their face, may have racially discriminatory effects.

Sentencing of Drug Offenders in Federal Courts

Cassia Spohn and Lisa Sample build on Steen and her colleagues' study of the dangerous drug offender in state court using data on drug offenders convicted in three U.S. District Courts.[154] They extended the study conducted by Steen and her colleagues by (1) using data on federal, rather than state, drug offenders; (2) including Hispanics as well as African Americans in the analyses; (3) using a definition of the dangerous drug offender that reflects the nature of the drug caseload in the federal court system; and (4) examining whether the effects of stereotypes of dangerousness varied by type of drug.

Because there were only 23 drug offenders in their data file who were convicted of an offense other than drug trafficking, Spohn and Sample could not differentiate between offenders convicted of drug delivery and those convicted of simple possession. Instead, they defined the dangerous drug offender in *federal court* as a male offender with a prior conviction for drug trafficking who used a weapon during the current crime. They hypothesized that offenders who perfectly matched the stereotype—that is, males with prior trafficking convictions who used a weapon—would receive longer sentences than all other offenders. They also predicted that the effect of matching the stereotype of a dangerous drug offender would not vary by race/ethnicity and that the effect of being a dangerous drug offender would vary by the type of drug involved in the case and by the race/ethnicity of the offender. They hypothesized that the effect of being a dangerous drug offender would be confined to crack cocaine cases for African American offenders and to methamphetamine cases for white and Hispanic offenders.

As shown in Table 7.5, Spohn and Sample found that African American offenders were more likely than either white offenders or Hispanic offenders to have the characteristics of a dangerous drug offender; they also found that white offenders were more likely than Hispanic offenders to match the characteristics of a dangerous drug offender. Forty-four percent of the African Americans but only 23 percent of the whites and 12 percent of the Hispanics had a prior drug trafficking conviction, and 25 percent of the African Americans but only 21 percent of the whites and 12 percent of the Hispanics used a weapon during the commission of the crime. Consistent with these findings, African Americans were overrepresented in the most serious category of the offender groups. Fourteen percent of the African American offenders, but only 5 percent of the white offenders and 2 percent of the Hispanic offenders, were male offenders with prior drug trafficking convictions who used weapons in the current offense.

Although Spohn and Sample found partial support for their hypothesis that offenders who perfectly matched the stereotype of a dangerous drug offender would be sentenced most harshly, their results were inconsistent with their hypothesis that the effect of matching this stereotype would not vary by race/ethnicity. They found that there were no significant differences in the sentences imposed on the most dangerous offenders and the five categories of less dangerous offenders for whites or Hispanics. That is, matching the stereotype of the dangerous drug offender did not result in harsher sentences for whites or

T A B L E 7.5   Race, Ethnicity, and Characteristics of the Dangerous Drug Offender

	Whites (N = 705)		African Americans (N = 443)		Hispanics (N = 544)	
	%	N	%	N	%	N
Offender Characteristics						
Male	.77	545	.86	380	.90	492
Prior Drug Trafficking Conviction	.23	164	.44	194	.12	66
Used a Weapon During Offense	.21	148	.25	109	.12	67
Offender Groups						
Male Prior Conviction Weapon	.05	39	.14	0	.02	10
Male Prior Conviction No Weapon	.14	97	.27	4	.10	53
Male No Prior Conviction Weapon	.13	89	.10		.10	54
Male No Prior Conviction No Weapon	.45	320	.36		.69	375
Female Prior Conviction or Weapon	.06	43	.04		.01	6
Female No Prior Conviction No Weapon	.17	117	.10		.08	46

SOURCE: Cassia Spohn and Lisa Sample. "The Dangerous Drug Offender in Federal Court: Stereotyping Blacks and Crack Cocaine," *Crime and Delinquency*, Table 1. July 8, 2008. Reprinted by permission of SAGE Publications.

Hispanics. There were, on the other hand, significant differences in the prison sentences imposed on the most dangerous African American offenders and offenders in all five categories of less dangerous African American offenders. Partitioning the data by type of drug further clarified these relationships. Matching the stereotype of the dangerous drug offender had no effect on sentence severity for white or Hispanic offenders in either methamphetamine cases or cases involving other types of drugs. In contrast, fitting the dangerousness stereotype significantly affected the length of the prison sentence for African American offenders convicted of offenses involving crack cocaine, but had no effect on sentence length for African American offenders convicted of offenses involving other types of drugs. At least in these three U.S. District Courts, images of dangerousness and threat affected the length of the prison sentence only for African American offenders who were convicted of trafficking in crack cocaine.

The authors of this study concluded that their finding of within-race differences in sentencing only for African Americans convicted of trafficking in crack cocaine suggests that judges' attributions of dangerousness and threat reflect a complex interplay among offender characteristics, crime seriousness, and type of drug. They speculated that the linkage between African Americans and crack cocaine may create a more vivid and powerful metaphor of dangerousness in the minds of judges. If, in other words, judges regard crack as a particularly harmful drug and believe that the typical crack offender is African American, they may believe that it is appropriate to impose especially punitive sentences on offenders who accumulate more of the characteristics of a dangerous offender.

Spohn and Sample noted that although the results of their study conflicted with the substantive findings from Washington State, they were nonetheless consistent with Steen and her colleagues' conclusion that "the meaning of race ... will vary depending on other offender and offense characteristics, and that differences in treatment within race may therefore be as large as differences between races."[155]

Does It Make a Difference? A Comparison of the Sentencing Decisions of African American, Hispanic, and White Judges

Historically, most state and federal judges have been white males. Although the nation's first African American judge was appointed in 1852, by the mid-1950s there were only a handful of African Americans presiding over state or federal courts. During the 1960s and 1970s, civil rights leaders lobbied for increased representation of African Americans at all levels of government, including the courts. By 1990 there were nearly 500 African American judges on the bench nationwide.

Those who champion the appointment of racial minorities argue that African American and Hispanic judges could make a difference. They contend that increasing the number of racial minorities on state and federal courts will alter the character of justice and the outcomes of the criminal justice system. Because the life histories and experiences of African Americans and Hispanics differ dramatically from those of whites, the beliefs and attitudes they bring to the bench also will differ. Justice A. Leon Higginbotham Jr., an African American who retired from the U.S. Court of Appeals for the Third Circuit in 1993, wrote, "The advantage of pluralism is that it brings a multitude of different experiences to the judicial process."[156] More to the point, he stated that "someone who has been a victim of racial injustice has greater sensitivity of the court's making sure that racism is not perpetrated, even inadvertently."[157] Judge George Crockett's assessment of the role of the African American judge was even more pointed: "I think a black judge ... has got to be a reformist—he cannot be a member of the club. The whole purpose of selecting him is that the people are dissatisfied with the status quo and they want him to shake it up, and his role is to shake it up."[158]

Assuming that African American judges agree with Judge Crockett's assertion that their role is to "shake it up," how would this affect their behavior on the bench? One possibility is that African American (and Hispanic) judges might attempt to stop—or at least slow—the flow of young African American (and Hispanic) men into state and federal prisons. If African American judges view the disproportionately high number of young African American males incarcerated in state and federal prisons as a symptom of racial discrimination, they might be more willing than white judges to experiment with alternatives to incarceration for offenders convicted of nonviolent drug and property crimes. Susan Welch and her colleagues make an analogous argument. Noting that African American judges tend to view themselves as liberal rather than conservative, they speculate that African American judges might be "more sympathetic to criminal defendants than whites judges are, since liberal views are associated with support for the underdog and the poor, which defendants disproportionately are."[159] Other scholars similarly suggest that increasing the number of African American judges would reduce racism in the criminal justice system and produce more equitable treatment of African American and white defendants.[160]

Statements made by African American judges suggest that they might bring a unique perspective to the courts. Michael David Smith's[161] survey of African American judges throughout the United States revealed that these judges believed that their presence on the bench reduced racial discrimination and promoted equality of justice. A Philadelphia judge, for instance, stated that the mere presence of African American judges "has done more than anything I know to reduce police brutality and to reduce illegal arrests and things of that sort."[162] Moreover, nearly half of the respondents stated that African American judges should exercise their powers to protect the rights of African American defendants. One Michigan judge remarked that African American judges should state that "everybody's going to get equal justice," by saying that, "you're going to give blacks something that they haven't been getting in the past."[163]

Deicision Making by African American and White Federal Judges

As more African Americans have been appointed or elected to state and federal trial courts, it has become possible to compare their decisions with those of white judges. Two studies examined the consequences of the affirmative action policies of President Carter, who appointed a record number of African Americans to the federal courts. (Carter appointed 258 judges to the federal district courts and courts of appeals; 37, or 14 percent, were African Americans. In contrast, African Americans accounted for only 6 of the 71 [7.2 percent] persons appointed to the U.S. District Courts by President George W. Bush and only 10 of the 132 [6.8 percent] persons appointed to the U.S. District Courts by President Geroge H. W. Bush. Fifty-three [17.4 percent] of President Clinton's 229 appointees were African American and 18 [5.9 percent] were Hispanic.)[164]

Thomas G. Walker and Deborah J. Barrow[165] compared decisions handed down by the African American and white district court judges appointed by President Carter. The question they asked was, "Did it make a difference that President Carter appointed unprecedented numbers of women and minorities to the bench as opposed to filling vacancies with traditional white, male candidates?"[166] The authors found no differences in criminal cases or in four other types of cases. In criminal cases African American judges ruled in favor of the defense 50 percent of the time; white judges ruled in favor of the defense 48 percent of the time. These similarities led the authors to conclude that black judges do not view themselves as advocates for the disadvantaged or see themselves as especially sympathetic to the policy goals of minorities.

Jon Gottschall[167] examined decisions in the U.S. Courts of Appeals in 1979 and 1981. He compared the decisions of African American and white judges in terms of "attitudinal liberalism," which he defined as "a relative tendency to vote in favor of the legal claims of the criminally accused and prisoners in criminal and prisoner's rights cases and in favor of the legal claims of women and racial minorities in sex and race discrimination cases."[168]

In contrast to Walker and Barrow, Gottschall found that the judge's race had a "dramatic impact" on voting in cases involving the rights of criminal defendants and prisoners. African American male judges voted to support the legal claims of defendants and prisoners 79 percent of the time, as compared to only 53 percent for white male judges. African American judges, however, did not vote more liberally than white judges in race or sex discrimination cases. Gottschall concluded, "Affirmative action for blacks does appear to influence voting on the courts of appeals in cases involving the rights of the accused and prisoners, where black voting is markedly more liberal than is that of whites."[169]

A more recent study[170] of the decisions of judges appointed to the U.S. Courts of Appeals found that judges who were both members of a racial minority group and female decided cases differently than other judges. Arguing that "female members of a racial minority occupy a unique place within society,"[171] Todd Collins and Laura Moyer hypothesized that female minority judges would support more liberal (that is, more pro-defendant) outcomes in cases involving the rights of criminal defendants. Consistent with their hypothesis, they found that minority female judges voted in favor of the defendant in 33.9 percent of the cases; the comparable figures for white males, white females, and minority males were 20 percent, 23 percent, and 24.7 percent, respectively. Further analysis revealed that these differences persisted even after the authors added other judge characteristics and characteristics of the circuit to the model. The authors concluded that the results of their analysis suggest that "minority women may have a distinctive identity that differs significantly from Caucasian women and minority males."[172]

An Alternative Approach: Racial Representation of the Bench   Because the United States Sentencing Commission does not provide data on the identity of the judge who imposed the sentence on an offender adjudicated in one of the U.S. District Courts, researchers have been unable to compare the sentencing decisions of white, African American, and Hispanic judges on the federal bench. Two studies used an alternative approach to this issue.[173] Rather than examining the race of the sentencing judge, these studies compared sentences for offenders of different races/ethnicities who were sentenced in jurisdictions with different proportions of white, African American, and Hispanic court workers, including judges. The purpose of these studies, in other words, was to determine "whether racially representative courts yield more racially equitable case outcomes."[174]

Both of the studies using this approach produced similar, although not identical, results. Farrell and her colleagues found that defendants were less likely to be sentenced to prison in jurisdictions with greater representation of African American judges and prosecutors, but were more likely to be sentenced to prison in districts with greater numbers of African American public defenders and probation officers. They also found that although African American offenders were more likely than white offenders to be sentenced to prison, the disparity was reduced when African American offenders were sentenced in districts with increased representation of African American prosecutors (in contrast, the disparity in incarceration rates did not decline as the percentage of judges who were African American increased).[175] These findings led the authors to conclude that "greater representation of workers of color in the justice system can contribute to more equitable treatment of racial groups. Specifically, equity would be improved with greater representation of blacks among prosecutors."[176]

Max Schanzenbach's[177] approach differed somewhat from the approach Farrell and her colleagues used. Whereas the latter researchers included variables measuring the percentages of judges, prosecutors, public defenders, and probation officers who were African American, Schanzenbach focused only on the effects of the percentages of judges who were African American and Hispanic. When he examined sentences imposed on offenders convicted of more serious crimes, he found that as the proportion of the bench that was Hispanic increased, the probability of incarceration decreased for African American and Hispanic offenders; he also found that representation of African Americans on the bench had no effect on the likelihood of incarceration for African American offenders but did result in a lower likelihood for Hispanic offenders. For non-serious crimes, on the other hand, the percentage of African American judges did reduce the odds of incarceration for African American offenders. These results led Schanzenbach to conclude that, at least for serious crimes, appointing more African American judges to the bench would not reduce racial disparities in sentencing.

Decision Making by African American and White State Court Judges

Research comparing the sentencing decisions of African American and white state court judges also has yielded mixed results. Most researchers have found few differences and have concluded that the race of the judge is not a strong predictor of sentence severity.[178] Two early studies, for example, found few differences in the sentencing behavior of African American and white judges. Engle[179] analyzed Philadelphia judges' sentencing decisions. He found that although the judge's race had a statistically significant effect, nine other variables were stronger predictors of sentence outcomes. He concluded that the race of the judge exerted "a very minor influence" overall.[180] Thomas M. Uhlman's[181] study of convicting and sentencing decisions in "Metro City" reached a similar conclusion. African American judges imposed somewhat harsher sentences than white judges, but the differences were relatively small. And both African American and white judges imposed harsher sentences on African American defendants than on white defendants. Moreover, there was more "behavioral diversity" among the African American judges than between African American and white judges. Some of the African American judges imposed substantially harsher sentences than the average sentence imposed by all judges, whereas other African

American judges imposed significantly more lenient sentences. These findings led Uhlman to conclude that "Black and white judges differ little in determining both guilt and the punishment a defendant 'deserves' for committing a crime in Metro City."[182]

A later study of sentencing decisions in "Metro City" reached a different conclusion. Susan Welch, Michael Combs, and John Gruhl[183] found that African American judges were more likely than white judges to send white defendants to prison. Further analysis led them to conclude that this difference reflected African American judges' tendency to incarcerate African American and white defendants at about the same rate and white judges' tendency to incarcerate African American defendants more often than white defendants. They also found, however, that African American judges, but not whites judges, favored defendants of their own race when determining the length of the prison sentence.

These results led them to conclude that "black judges provide more than symbolic representation."[184] According to these authors, "To the extent that they equalize the criminal justice system's treatment of black and white defendants, as they seem to for the crucial decision to incarcerate or not, [black judges] thwart discrimination against black defendants. In fact, the quality of justice received by both black and white defendants may be improved."[185]

A study of sentencing decisions by African American and white judges on the Cook County (Chicago) Circuit Court reached a similar conclusion.[186] Spears found that African American judges sentenced white, African American, and Hispanic offenders to prison at about the same rate, whereas white judges sentenced both African American and Hispanic offenders to prison at a significantly higher rate than white offenders. In fact, compared to white offenders sentenced by white judges, African American offenders sentenced by white judges had a 13 percent greater probability of imprisonment; for Hispanic offenders sentenced by white judges, the difference was 15 percent. Like the "Metro City" study, then, this study found that white judges sentenced racial minorities more harshly than whites and concluded that having African American judges on the bench "does provide more equitable justice."[187]

Spohn's[188] analysis of the sentences imposed on offenders convicted of violent felonies in Detroit Recorder's Court produced strikingly different results and led to very different conclusions. Like Engle and Uhlman, Spohn uncovered few meaningful differences between African American and white judges. She found that African American judges were somewhat more likely than white judges to sentence offenders to prison, but that judicial race had no effect on the length of sentence. Like Engle, she concluded that "the effect of judicial race, even where significant, was clearly overshadowed by the effect of the other independent variables."[189] Spohn also tested for interaction between the race of the judge, the race of the offender, and the race of the victim—that is, she attempted to determine, first, if African American and white judges treated African American and white offenders differently and, second, if African American and white judges imposed different sentences on African American offenders who victimized other African Americans, African American offenders who victimized whites, white offenders who victimized other whites, and white offenders who victimized African Americans.

Spohn's research highlighted the similarities in the sentences imposed by African American and by white judges. African American judges sentenced 72.9 percent of African American offenders to prison, whereas white judges incarcerated 74.2 percent, a difference of less than 2 percentage points. The adjusted figures for white offenders were 65.3 percent (African American judges) and 66.5 percent (white judges), again a difference of less than 2 percentage points. More important, these data reveal that both African American and white judges sentenced African American defendants more harshly than white defendants. For both African American and white judges, the adjusted incarceration rates for African American offenders were 7 percentage points higher than for white offenders. Moreover, African American judges sentenced offenders to prison at about the same rate as white judges, regardless of the racial makeup of the offender–victim pair.

These findings led Spohn to conclude that there was "remarkable similarity"[190] in the sentencing decisions of African American and white judges. They also led her to question the assumption that discrimination against African American defendants reflects prejudicial or racist attitudes on the part of white criminal justice officials. As she noted, "Contrary to expectations, both black and white judges in Detroit imposed harsher sentences on black offenders. Harsher sentencing of black offenders, in other words, cannot be attributed solely to discrimination by white judges."[191] Spohn suggested that her findings contradicted the widely held assumption that African Americans do not discriminate against other African Americans and conventional wisdom about the role of African American judges. She concluded "that we should be considerably less sanguine in predicting that discrimination against black defendants will decline as the proportion of black judges increases."[192]

To explain her unexpected finding that both African American and white judges sentenced African American defendants more harshly than white defendants, Spohn suggested that African American and white judges might perceive African American offenders as more threatening and more dangerous than white offenders. Alternatively, she speculated that at least some of the discriminatory treatment of African American offenders might be the result of concern for the welfare of African American victims. African American judges, in other words, "might see themselves not as representatives of black defendants but as advocates for black victims. This, coupled with the fact that black judges might see themselves as potential victims of black-on-black crime, could help explain the harsher sentences imposed on black offenders by black judges."[193]

Spohn acknowledged that because we do not know with any degree of certainty what goes through a judge's mind during the sentencing process, these explanations were highly speculative. As she put it, "We cannot know precisely how the race of the offender is factored into the sentencing equation. Although the data reveal that both black and white judges sentence black offenders more harshly than white offenders, the data do not tell us *why* this occurs."[194]

Decision Making by Hispanic and White Judges   Although most research examining the effect of judicial characteristics on sentencing has focused on the race of the sentencing judge, there is one study that compares the sentencing decisions of white and Hispanic judges in two southwestern jurisdictions.[195] Malcolm D. Holmes and his colleagues found that Hispanic judges sentenced white and Hispanic offenders similarly, whereas white judges sentenced Hispanics more harshly than whites. In fact, the sentences imposed on Hispanic offenders by Hispanic and white judges were very similar to the sentences imposed by Hispanic judges on white offenders. What was different, according to these researchers, was that white judges sentenced white offenders more leniently. Thus, "Anglo judges are not so much discriminating against Hispanic defendants as they are favoring members of their ethnic groups."[196]

Reasons for Similarities in Decision Making

Although there is some evidence that African American and Hispanic judges sentence racial minorities and whites similarly, and that white judges give preferential treatment to white offenders, the bulk of the evidence suggests that judicial race/ethnicity makes very little difference. The fact that African American, Hispanic, and white judges decide cases similarly is not particularly surprising. Although this conclusion challenges widely held presumptions about the role of African American and Hispanic criminal justice officials, it is not at odds with the results of other studies comparing African American and white decision makers. As noted in Chapter 4, studies have documented similarities in the behavior of African American and white police officers.

Similarities in judicial decision making can be attributed in part to the judicial recruitment process, which produces a more or less homogeneous judiciary. Most judges recruited to state courts are middle or upper class and were born and attended law school in the state in which they serve. Even African American and white judges apparently share similar background characteristics. Studies indicate that "both the black and white benches appear to have been carefully chosen from the establishment center of the legal profession."[197] The judicial recruitment process may screen out candidates with unconventional views.

These similarities are reinforced by the judicial socialization process, which produces a subculture of justice and encourages judges to adhere to prevailing norms, practices, and precedents. They also are reinforced by the courtroom work group—judges, prosecutors, and defense attorneys who work together day after day to process cases as efficiently as possible. Even unconventional or maverick judges may be forced to conform. As one African American jurist noted, "No matter how 'liberal' black judges may believe themselves to be, the law remains essentially a conservative doctrine, and those who practice it conform."[198]

Focus on an Issue
Penalties for Crack and Powder Cocaine

Federal sentencing guidelines for drug offenses differentiate between crack and powder cocaine. In fact, until very recently, the guidelines treated crack cocaine as being 100 times worse than powder cocaine. Until 2010 possession of 500 grams of powder cocaine, but only 5 grams of crack, triggered a mandatory minimum sentence of five years. Critics charged that this policy, although racially neutral on its face, discriminated against African American drug users and sellers, who prefer crack cocaine to powder cocaine. More than 90 percent of the offenders sentenced for crack offenses in federal courts are African American. Those who defend the policy, however, suggested that it is not racially motivated; rather, as Randall Kennedy, an African American professor at Harvard Law School, contended, the policy is a sensible response "to the desires of law-abiding people—including the great mass of black communities—for protection against criminals preying on them."[199]

Concerns about the racial implications of the crack–powder disparity led some federal judges to attempt to circumvent the mandatory minimum sentences for offenders convicted of offenses involving crack cocaine. For example, in 1993 Judge Lyle Strom, the chief judge of the United States District Court in Nebraska, sentenced four African American crack dealers to significantly shorter prison terms than called for under the guidelines. In explanation, Strom wrote, "Members of the African American race are being treated unfairly in receiving substantially longer sentences than Caucasian males who traditionally deal in powder cocaine."[200]

Strom's decision was overturned by the Eighth Circuit Court of Appeals in 1994. The three-judge panel ruled that even if the guidelines are unfair to African Americans, that is not enough to justify a more lenient sentence than called for under the guidelines. Other federal appellate courts have upheld the 100-to-1 rule, holding that the rule does not violate the equal protection clause of the Fourteenth Amendment (see, for example, *U.S.* v. *Thomas*, 900 F.2d 37 [4th Cir. 1990]; *U.S.* v. *Frazier*, 981 F.2d 92 [3rd Cir. 1992]; and *U.S.* v. *Latimore*, 974 F2d 971 [8th Cir. 1992].

In 1996 the U.S. Supreme Court ruled 8–1 that African Americans who allege that they have been singled out for prosecution under the crack cocaine rule must first show that whites in similar circumstances were not prosecuted.[201] The case was brought by five African American defendants from Los Angeles, who claimed that prosecutors were systematically steering crack cocaine cases involving African Americans to federal court, where the 100-to-1 rule applied, but steering cases involving whites to state court, where lesser penalties applied. The Court stated that a defendant who claimed he or she was a victim of selective prosecution "must demonstrate that the federal prosecutorial policy had a discriminatory effect and that it was motivated by a discriminatory purpose."

The United States Sentencing Commission repeatedly recommended that the penalties for crack and powder cocaine offenses be equalized. In 1995 the Commission recommended that the 100-to-1 ratio be changed to a 1-to-1 ratio. Both Congress and former President Clinton rejected this amendment. In May 2002 the Commission "unanimously and firmly" reiterated its earlier position that "the various congressional objectives can be achieved more effectively by decreasing substantially the 100-to-1 drug quantity ratio."[202] The Commission recommended increasing the quantity levels that trigger the mandatory minimum penalties for crack cocaine. They recommended that the 5-year mandatory minimum threshold be increased to at least 25 grams and that the 10-year mandatory minimum threshold be increased to at least 250 grams. The Commission also recommended that Congress repeal the mandatory minimum sentence for simple possession of crack cocaine.

The Commission's 2002 report also noted that the majority (85 percent in 2000) of offenders subject to the harsh penalties for drug offenses involving crack cocaine were African American. Although the commissioners acknowledged that this did not necessarily prove that "the current penalty structure promotes unwarranted disparity based on race," they cautioned that "even the perception of racial disparity [is] problematic because it fosters disrespect for and lack of confidence in the criminal justice system."[203]

In 2010 Congress finally acted to reduce the crack/powder cocaine disparity. Under the Fair Sentencing Act, which President Obama signed into law in August of 2010, the amount of crack cocaine necessary to trigger a 5-year mandatory minimum sentence was increased from 5 grams to 28 grams; the amount necessary to trigger a 10-year sentence was increased from 50 grams to 280 grams. Because the amounts of powder cocaine that led to a 5-year (500 grams) or a 10-year (1,000 grams) sentence did not change, the disparity under the 2010 law is 18-to-1 rather than 100-to-1. (For a discussion of another type of race-linked sentencing statute, see "In the Courts: The Constitutionality of Hate-Crime Sentencing Enhancements—*Wisconsin* v. *Mitchell* (508 U.S. 47 [1993])."

Marc Mauer, who is the Executive Director of The Sentencing Project, has suggested that one way to avoid the enactment of facially neutral but racially disparate policies such as the crack/powder cocaine sentencing disparity is to require "racial impact statements" whenever new sentencing legislation is proposed.[204] Arguing that it would be better to assess the racial dimensions of proposed policy changes before new legislation is enacted, Mauer called for the adoption of a policy requiring policy makers to evaluate the potential racial effects of laws prior to their adoption. As he noted, "the adoption of racial impact statements offers a means by which policymakers can avoid some of the mistakes of the past and develop crime policy that is both constructive and fair."[205]

At the time that this book went to press, the Sentencing Commission had not yet decided whether the changes in the laws regarding crack cocaine should be retroactive. How was this issue resolved?

In the Courts: The Constitutionality of Hate-Crime Sentencing Enhancements—*Wisconsin* v. *Mitchell* (508 U.S. 47 [1993])

In 1989 Todd Mitchell, a 19-year-old African American, and a group of his friends accosted Gregory Reddick, a 14-year-old white boy, beat him severely, and stole his tennis shoes. Mitchell and his friends had just watched the movie *Mississippi Burning*, which depicts Ku Klux Klan terrorism against African Americans in the South during the 1960s. They were standing outside an apartment complex in Kenosha, Wisconsin, discussing the movie, when Reddick walked by. Mitchell asked his friends, "Do you feel hyped up to move on some white people?" He then pointed to Reddick and said, "There goes a white boy.... Go get him!" The beating put Reddick in a coma for four days and he suffered permanent brain damage.

Mitchell was convicted of aggravated battery, an offense that ordinarily carries a maximum sentence of two years in prison. The jury, however, found that Mitchell had intentionally selected his victim because of the boy's race, in violation of Wisconsin's hate-crime statute. That law, which increased the maximum sentence for Mitchell's crime to seven years, enhances the maximum penalty for an offense whenever the defendant "intentionally selected the person against whom the crime ... is committed ... because of the race, religion, color, disability, sexual orientation, national origin, or ancestry of that person."[206] The judge sentenced Mitchell to four years in prison for the aggravated battery.

Mitchell challenged his conviction and sentence, arguing that the hate-crime statute infringed on his First Amendment right to freedom of speech. The Wisconsin Supreme Court agreed, holding that the statute "violates the First Amendment directly by punishing what the legislature has deemed to be offensive thought." The court rejected the state's claim that the statute punished only conduct (that is, the intentional selection of a victim on the basis of race) and stated that "the Wisconsin legislature cannot criminalize bigoted thought with which it disagrees."

In 1993 the United States Supreme Court upheld the hate-crime statute and ruled that Mitchell's First Amendment rights were not violated by the application of the sentencing enhancement provision. Writing for a unanimous court, Chief Justice Rehnquist stated that the primary responsibility for determining penalties for criminal behavior rests with the legislature, which can differentiate among crimes based on their seriousness and the degree of harm they inflict on victims and on society. Justice Rehnquist noted that this was the case with the hate-crime statute: the Wisconsin legislature had decided that bias-inspired conduct was more harmful and thus had enhanced the penalties for these types of crimes. Although he acknowledged that "a defendant's abstract beliefs, however obnoxious to most people, may not be taken into consideration by a sentencing judge," Rehnquist stated that trial judges are not barred from considering the defendant's racial animus toward his victim. (The decision in this case is available online at http://straylight.law.cornell.edu/. Search for *Wisconsin* v. *Mitchell*.)

CONCLUSION

Despite dozens of studies investigating the relationship between defendant race and sentence severity, a definitive answer to the question, "Are racial minorities sentenced more harshly than whites?" remains elusive. Although a number of studies have uncovered evidence of racial discrimination in sentencing, others have found that there are no significant racial differences.

The failure of research to produce uniform findings of racial discrimination in sentencing has led to conflicting conclusions. Some researchers assert that racial discrimination in sentencing has declined over time and contend that the predictive power of race, once relevant legal factors are taken into account, is quite low. Other researchers claim that discrimination has not declined or disappeared but simply has become more subtle and difficult to detect. These researchers argue that discrimination against racial minorities is not universal but is confined to certain types of cases, certain types of settings, and certain types of defendants.

We assert that the latter explanation is more convincing. We suggest that although the sentencing process in most jurisdictions today is not characterized by overt or systematic racism, racial discrimination in sentencing has not been eliminated. We argue that sentencing decisions in the 1990s reflect *contextual discrimination*. Judges in some jurisdictions continue to impose harsher sentences on racial minorities who murder or rape whites and more lenient sentences on racial minorities who victimize members of their own racial/ethnic group. Judges in some jurisdictions continue to impose racially biased sentences in less serious cases; in these "borderline cases" racial minorities get prison, whereas whites get probation. Judges, in other words, continue to take race into account, either explicitly or implicitly, when determining the appropriate sentence.

The problem is compounded by the existence of institutional discrimination. This type of discrimination is exemplified by facially neutral sentencing policies—the crack/powder cocaine sentencing disparity, the drug-free school zones, and habitual offender or three-strikes-and-you're-out laws—that have disparate effects on racial minorities and whites. Because these laws are applicable more often to African American and Hispanics than to whites, their effects are to increase racial disparities in incarceration rates and to exacerbate the collateral consequences of incarceration for racial minorities and the communities in which they live.

It thus appears that although flagrant racism in sentencing has been eliminated, equality under the law has not been achieved. Today, whites who commit crimes against racial minorities are not beyond the reach of the criminal justice system, African Americans suspected of crimes against whites do not receive "justice" at the hands of white lynching mobs, and racial minorities who victimize other racial minorities are not immune from punishment. Despite these significant changes, inequities persist. Racial minorities who find themselves in the arms of the law continue to suffer discrimination in sentencing.

DISCUSSION QUESTIONS

1. Why is evidence of racial disparity in sentencing not necessarily evidence of racial discrimination in sentencing? What are the alternative explanations? Which of these explanations is most convincing?

2. Some researchers argue that racial stereotypes affect the ways in which decision makers, including criminal justice officials, evaluate the behavior of racial minorities. Do an Internet search for race-linked stereotypes. What are the stereotypes most commonly associated with African Americans? Hispanics? Native Americans? Asian Americans? How might these stereotypes affect judges' sentencing decisions?

3. Do you agree or disagree with the argument (see Box 7.2) that crime seriousness and prior criminal record are not necessarily legally relevant variables?

4. Based on Spohn's (2000) review of research on race and sentencing, how would you answer the question, "When does race matter?" Prepare a PowerPoint presentation that summarizes these effects.

5. Research reveals that young, unemployed African American and Hispanic males pay a higher punishment penalty than other types of offenders. What accounts for this?

6. Spohn and Spears's study of sentencing decisions in sexual assault cases revealed that judges imposed the harshest sentences on African Americans who sexually assaulted whites (strangers or nonstrangers) and on African Americans who sexually assaulted African American strangers. They imposed much more lenient sentences on African Americans who sexually assaulted African American friends, relatives, and acquaintances and on whites who victimized other whites (strangers or nonstrangers). How would you explain this pattern of results?

7. As discussed in Box 7.8, African Americans are more likely than whites to be willing to serve time in prison rather than be sentenced to some alternative to incarceration such as electronic monitoring or intensive supervision probation. What accounts for these racial differences in perceptions of the severity of sanctions?

8. Under the Fair Sentencing Act of 2010, the disparity in amounts of crack and powder cocaine necessary to trigger a mandatory minimum sentence of 5 (or 10) years was reduced from 100-to-1 to 18-to-1. Does this "solve" the problem, or is the 18-to-1 disparity still racially discriminatory?

9. Those who champion the appointment/election of racial minorities to the bench argue that African American and Hispanic judges could make a difference. Why? Does research comparing the sentencing decisions of white judges to those of African American or Hispanic judges confirm or refute this assumption?

10. Do you agree with the Supreme Court's decision (*Wisconsin* v. *Mitchell*) upholding sentencing enhancements for hate crimes? Why or why not?

NOTES

1. The Sentencing Project, "Schools and Prisons: Fifty Years after *Brown* v. *Board of Education.*" Available at http://www.sentencingproject.org/pdfs/brownvboard.pdf.

2. Ibid., p. 5.

3. Ibid.

4. Ibid., p. 5.

5. Bureau of Justice Statistics, *Prison and Jail Inmates at Midyear* 2009 (Washington, DC: U.S. Department of Justice, 2010), Table 17.

6. Alfred Blumstein, Jacqueline Cohen, Susan E. Martin, and Michael Tonry, *Research on Sentencing*: The *Search for Reform*, Volume I (Washington, DC: National Academy Press, 1983).

7. See, for example, Bruce Western, *Punishment and Inequality in America* (New York: Russell Sage Foundation, 2006). For a different perspective, see Michelle Alexander, *The New Jim Crow: Mass Incarceration in the Age of Colorblindness* (New York: The New Press, 2010). Alexander argues (p. 16) that "The fact that more than half of the young black men in any large American city are currently under the control of the criminal justice system (or saddled with criminal records) is not—as many argue—just a symptom of poverty or poor choices, but rather evidence of a new racial caste system at work." For recent research comparing finds that the racial disparity in incarceration rates that is unexplained by racial disparity in arrest rates has increased, see Michael Tonry and Matthew Melewski, "The Malign Effects of Drug Control Policies on Black Americans," *Crime and Justice* 37 (2008), pp. 1–44.

8. Michael Tonry, *Malign Neglect: Race, Crime, and Punishment in America* (New York: Oxford University Press, 1995), p. 49.

9. Bureau of Justice Statistics, *Prison and Jail Inmates at Midyear* 2009 (Washington, DC: U.S. Department of Justice, 2010), Tables 17 and 19.

10. Brian D. Johnson and Sara Betsinger, "Punishing the 'Model Minority': Asian-American Criminal Sentencing Outcomes in Federal District Courts," *Criminology* 47 (2009): 1045–1090.

11. Paula Kautt and Cassia Spohn, "*Crack-ing* Down on Black Drug Offenders? Testing for Interactions Among Offenders' Race, Drug Type, and Sentencing Strategy in Federal Drug Sentences," *Justice Quarterly* 19 (2000): 2–35.

12. Bureau of Justice Statistics, *Felony Sentences in State Courts*, 2006 (Washington, DC: U.S. Department of Justice, 2009), Tables 3.4 and 3.6.

13. Cassia Spohn and Miriam DeLone, "When Does Race Matter? An Analysis of the Conditions Under Which Race Affects Sentence Severity," *Sociology of Crime, Law, and Deviance* 2 (2000): 3–37.

14. Marjorie Zatz, "The Changing Forms of Racial/Ethnic Biases in Sentencing," *Journal of Research in Crime and Delinquency* 25 (1987): 69–92, p. 69.

15. Thorsten Sellin, "Race Prejudice in the Administration of Justice," *American Journal of Sociology 41* (1935): 212–217, p. 217.

16. John Hagan, "Extra-legal Attributes and Criminal Sentencing: An Assessment of a Sociological Viewpoint," *Law & Society Review 8* (1974): 357–383; Gary Kleck, "Racial Discrimination in Sentencing: A Critical Evaluation of the Evidence with

Additional Evidence on the Death Penalty," *American Sociology Review 43* (1981): 783–805.

17. John Hagan and Kristin Bumiller, "Making Sense of Sentencing: A Review and Critique of Sentencing Research," in *Research on Sentencing: The Search for Reform,* Alfred Blumstein, Jacqueline Cohen, Susan Martin, and Michael Tonry, eds. (Washington, DC: National Academy Press, 1983).

18. Blumstein, Cohen, Martin, and Tonry, *Research on Sentencing: The Search for Reform,* p. 93.

19. Zatz, "The Changing Forms of Racial/Ethnic Biases in Sentencing."

20. Ibid., p. 87.

21. Theodore G. Chiricos and Charles Crawford, "Race and Imprisonment: A Contextual Assessment of the Evidence," in *Ethnicity, Race, and Crime: Perspectives Across Time and Place,* Darnell F. Hawkins, ed. (Albany: State University of New York Press, 1995).

22. Ibid., p. 282.

23. Ibid., p. 300.

24. Ibid., p. 300.

25. Spohn, "Thirty Years of Sentencing Reform: A Quest for a Racially Neutral Sentencing Process," in *Policies, Processes, and Decisions of the Criminal Justice System, vol. 3, Criminal Justice* 2000 (Washington, DC: U.S. Department of Justice, 2000).

26. Hagan and Bumiller, "Making Sense of Sentencing," p. 21.

27. Spohn, "Thirty Years of Sentencing Reform," pp. 455–456.

28. Ibid., p. 458.

29. Ibid., pp. 460–461.

30. Ibid., pp. 466–467.

31. Ibid., p. 469.

32. Ibid., p. 461.

33. Ibid., pp. 469–473.

34. Ojmarrh Mitchell. "A Meta-Analysis of Race and Sentencing Research: Explaining the Inconsistencies," *Journal of Quantitative Criminology* 21 (2005), pp. 439–466.

35. Ibid., p. 462.

36. Blumstein et al., *Research on Sentencing,* vol. 1, p. 93.

37. Cassia Spohn and Miriam DeLone, "When Does Race Matter? An Analysis of the Conditions Under Which Race Affects Sentence Severity," *Sociology of Crime, Law and Deviance* 2 (2000), pp. 3–37.

38. These estimated probabilities are adjusted for the effects of the other legal and extralegal variables included in the multivariate analysis. See Spohn and DeLone, "When Does Race Matter?" for a description of the procedures used to calculate the probabilities.

39. Spohn and DeLone, "When Does Race Matter?" p. 29.

40. Ibid.

41. Ibid., p. 30.

42. Darrell Steffensmeier and Stephen Demuth, "Ethnicity and Judges' Sentencing Decisions: Hispanic–Black–White Comparison," *Criminology* 39 (2001), pp. 145–178.

43. Ibid.

44. Ibid., p. 153.

45. Ibid., Table 2.

46. Ibid., Table 3.

47. Ibid., p. 170.

48. Ibid., p. 168.

49. David F. Greenberg, "'Justice' and Criminal Justice," in *Crime Control and Criminal Justice: The Delicate Balance*, Darnell F. Hawkins, Samuel L. Meyers Jr., and Randolph N. Stone, eds. (Westport, CT: Greenwood, 2002), p. 330.

50. Ibid., p. 331.

51. *United States* v. *Onwuemene* (1999). As cited in N. V. Demleitner and J. Sands, "Non-citizen Offenders and Immigration Crimes: New Challenges in the Federal System," *Federal Sentencing Reporter* 14 (2002), pp. 247–254.

52. See, for example, Celesta A. Albonetti, "Sentencing Under the Federal Sentencing Guidelines: Effects of Defendant Characteristics, Guilty Pleas, and Departures on Sentence Outcomes for Drug Offenses, 1991–1992," *Law & Society Review* 31 (1997), pp. 789–822; Stephen Demuth, "The Effect of Citizenship Status on Sentencing Outcomes in Drug Cases," *Federal Sentencing Reporter* 14 (2002), pp. 271–275; Richard D. Hartley, Sean Maddan, and Cassia Spohn, "Prosecutorial Discretion: An Examination of Substantial Assistance Departures in Federal Crack-Cocaine and Powder-Cocaine Cases," *Justice Quarterly* 24 (2007), pp. 382–407; Brian D. Johnson, Jeffery T. Ulmer, and John H. Kramer, "The Social Context of Guidelines Circumvention: The Case of Federal District Courts," *Criminology* 46 (2008), pp. 737–784; Cassia Spohn and Robert Fornango, "U.S. Attorneys and Substantial Assistance Departures: Testing for Inter-Prosecutor Disparity," *Criminology* 47 (2009), pp. 813–842.

53. Scott Wolfe, David Pyrooz, and Cassia Spohn, "Unraveling the Effect of Offender Citizenship Status on Federal Sentencing Outcomes," *Social Science Research* (in press).

54. Ibid., Table 1.

55. Ibid., Tables 2 and 3.

56. Johnson and Betsinger, "Punishing the Model Minority," p. 1,046.

57. Ibid., p. 1,051.

58. Ibid., pp. 1,065–1,066.

59. Ibid., Tables 3, 4, and 5.

60. Ibid., p. 1,078.

61. Ibid., p. 1,078.

62. Iris Marion Young, *Justice and the Politics of Difference* (Princeton, NJ: Princeton University Press, 1990), p. 59.

63. Carol Chiago Lujan, "Stereotyping by Politicians: Or 'The Only Real Indian Is the Stereotypical Indian,'" in *Images of Color, Images of Crime*, Coramae Richey Mann and Marjorie Zatz, eds. (Los Angeles: Roxbury, 1998).

64. Keith Wilmot and Miriam DeLone, "Sentencing of Native Americans: A Multistage Analysis Under the Minnesota Sentencing Guidelines," Journal of Ethnicity in Criminal Justice 8 (2010), pp. 151–180.

65. Steve Feimer, Frank Pommersheim, and Steve Wise, "Marking Time: Does Race Make a Difference? A Study of Disparate Sentencing in South Dakota," *Journal of*

Crime and Justice 13 (1990), pp. 86–102; Frank Pommersheim and Steve Wise, "Going to the Penitentiary: A Study of Disparate Sentencing in South Dakota," *Criminal Justice and Behavior* 16 (1989), pp. 155–165.

66. B. Swift and G. Bickel, *Comparative Parole Treatment of American Indians and Non-Indians at United States Federal Prisons* (Washington, DC: Bureau of Social Science Research, 1974.)

67. Alexander Alvarez and Ronet D. Bachman, "American Indians and Sentencing Disparity: An Arizona Test," *Journal of Criminal Justice* 24 (1996), pp. 549–561; Edwin L. Hall and Albert A. Simkins, "Inequality in the Types of Sentences Received by Native Americans and Whites," *Criminology* 13: 199–222.

68. Ronet D. Bachman, Alexander Alvarez, and C. Perkins, "The Discriminatory Imposition of the Law: Does It Affect Sentence Outcomes for American Indians?" in *Native Americans, Crime, and Justice*, Marianne O. Nielsen and Robert A. Silverman, eds. (Boulder, CO: Westview Press, 1996); Timothy S. Bynum and Raymond Paternoster, "Discrimination Revisited: An Exploration of Frontstage and Backstage Criminal Justice Decision Making," *Sociology and Social Research* 69 (1984), pp. 90–108.

69. Alvarez and Bachman, "American Indians and Sentencing Disparity."

70. Ibid., p. 558.

71. Ibid.

72. Wilmot and DeLone, "Sentencing of Native Americans."

73. Ibid., Tables 2 and 3.

74. Ibid., p. 174.

75. Marjorie Zatz, "The Convergence of Race, Ethnicity, Gender, and Class on Court Decisionmaking: Looking Toward the 21st Century," in *Policies, Processes, and Decisions of the Criminal Justice System*, vol. 3, *Criminal Justice* 2000 (Washington, DC: U.S. Department of Justice, 2000).

76. Ibid., p. 540.

77. John H. Kramer and Darrell Steffensmeier, "Race and Imprisonment Decisions," *The Sociological Quarterly* 34 (1993), pp. 357–376.

78. Darrell Steffensmeier, John Kramer, and Cathy Streifel, "Gender and Imprisonment Decisions," *Criminology* 31 (1993), pp. 411–446.

79. Darrell Steffensmeier, John Kramer, and Jeffery Ulmer, "Age Differences in Criminal Sentencing," *Justice Quarterly* 12 (1995), pp. 701–719.

80. Darrell Steffensmeier, Jeffery Ulmer, and John Kramer, "The Interaction of Race, Gender, and Age in Criminal Sentencing: The Punishment Cost of Being Young, Black, and Male," *Criminology* 36 (1998), pp. 363–397.

81. Kramer and Steffensmeier, "Race and Imprisonment Decisions," p. 370.

82. Ibid., p. 368.

83. Ibid., p. 373.

84. Ibid.

85. Ibid., p. 789.

86. Ibid., p. 768.

87. Cassia Spohn and David Holleran, "The Imprisonment Penalty Paid by Young Unemployed Black and Hispanic Male Offenders," *Criminology* 38 (2000), pp. 281–306.

88. Ibid., pp. 291–293.

89. Ibid., p. 301.

90. See, for example, Pauline K. Brennan and Cassia Spohn, "The Joint Effects of Offender Race/Ethnicity and Sex on Sentence Length Decisions in Federal Courts," *Race and Social Problems* 1 (2009), pp. 200–217; Theodore R. Curry and Guadalupe Corral-Camacho, "Sentencing Young Minority Males for Drug Offenses: Testing for Conditional Effects Between Race/Ethnicity, Gender, and Age during the U.S. War on Drugs," *Punishment & Society* 10 (2008), pp. 253–276; Jill K. Doerner and Stephen Demuth, "The Independent and Joint Effects of Race/Ethnicity, Gender, and Age on Sentencing Outcomes in U.S. Federal Courts," *Justice Quarterly* 27 (2010), pp. 1–27; Tina L. Freiburger and Carly M. Hilinski, "An Examination of the Interactions of Race and Gender on Sentencing Decisions Using a Trichotomous Dependent Variable," *Crime & Delinquency*, Online First, published on February 24, 2009; and Hartley, Maddan, and Spohn, "Prosecutorial Discretion."

91. Brennan and Spohn, "The Joint Effects of Offender Race/Ethnicity and Sex on Sentence Length Decisions in Federal Courts."

92. Doerner and Demuth, "The Independent and Joint Effects of Race/Ethnicity, Gender, and Age on Sentencing Outcomes in U.S. Federal Courts."

93. Quinney, *The Social Reality of Crime*, p. 142.

94. Dario Melossi, "An Introduction: Fifty Years Later, Punishment and Social Structure in Contemporary Analysis," *Contemporary Crises* 13 (1989), pp. 311–326.

95. Gregg Barak, "Between the Waves: Mass-Mediated Themes of Crime and Justice," *Social Justice* 21 (1994), pp. 133–147.

96. Steven Spitzer, "Toward a Marxian Theory of Deviance," *Social Problems* 22 (1975), pp. 638–651.

97. Ibid., p. 646.

98. Steven Box and Chris Hale, "Unemployment, Imprisonment, and Prison Over-crowding," *Contemporary Crises* 9 (1985), pp. 209–228.

99. Ibid., p. 217.

100. Steffensmeier, Ulmer, and Kramer, "The Interaction of Race, Gender, and Age in Criminal Sentencing," p. 789.

101. Ibid., p. 787.

102. Spohn and Holleran, "The Imprisonment Penalty Paid by Young, Unemployed Black and Hispanic Male Offenders," p. 301.

103. Gunnar Myrdal, *An American Dilemma: The Negro Problem and Modern Democracy* (New York: Harper and Brothers, 1944), p. 551.

104. Ibid., p. 553.

105. Susan Brownmiller, *Against Our Will: Men, Women, and Rape* (New York: Bantam Books, 1975).

106. Jennifer Wriggins, "Rape, Racism, and the Law," *Harvard Women's Law Journal* 6 (1983), pp. 103–141.

107. Wriggins, "Rape, Racism, and the Law."

108. Ibid., p. 109.

109. Marvin E. Wolfgang and Marc Reidel, "Race, Judicial Discretion, and the Death Penalty," *Annals of the American Academy* 407 (1973), pp. 119–133; Marvin E.

Wolfgang and Marc Reidel, "Rape, Race, and the Death Penalty in Georgia," *American Journal of Orthopsychiatry* 45 (1975), pp. 658–668.

110. Brownmiller, *Against Our Will*, p. 237.

111. Gary D. LaFree, *Rape and Criminal Justice: The Social Construction of Sexual Assault* (Belmont, CA: Wadsworth, 1989).

112. Anthony Walsh, "The Sexual Stratification Hypothesis and Sexual Assault in Light of the Changing Conceptions of Race," *Criminology* 25 (1987), pp. 153–173.

113. Ibid., p. 167.

114. Cassia Spohn and Jeffrey Spears, "The Effect of Offender and Victim Characteristics on Sexual Assault Case Processing Decisions," *Justice Quarterly* 13 (1996), pp. 649–679.

115. Ibid., p. 663.

116. Ibid., p. 675.

117. Ibid., p. 665.

118. Peter B. Wood and David C. May, "Racial Differences in Perceptions of the Severity of Sanctions: A Comparison of Prison with Alternatives," *Justice Quarterly* 20 (2003), pp. 605–631.

119. Ibid., p. 618.

120. Ibid., pp. 623–624.

121. Ibid., p. 628.

122. Harry Kalven Jr. and Hans Zeisel, *The American Jury* (Boston: Little, Brown: 1966).

123. Cassia Spohn and Jerry Cederblom, "Racial Disparities in Sentencing: A Test of the Liberation Hypothesis," *Justice Quarterly* 8 (1991), pp. 305–327.

124. Ibid., p. 323.

125. Kathleen Auerhahn, "Just Another Crime? Examining Disparity in Homicide Sentencing," *The Sociological Quarterly* 48 (2007), pp. 277–313.

126. Ibid., pp. 299–300.

127. Michael J. Leiber and Anita N. Blowers, "Race and Misdemeanor Sentencing," *Criminal Justice Policy Review* 14 (2003), pp. 464–485.

128. Ibid., pp. 475–477.

129. Michael Tonry, *Malign Neglect: Race, Crime, and Punishment in America* (New York: Oxford University Press, 1995), p. 105.

130. Ibid., p. 115.

131. Jerome G. Miller, *Search and Destroy: African-American Males in the Criminal Justice System* (Cambridge, England: Cambridge University Press, 1996), p. 83.

132. Marc Mauer, *Race to Incarcerate* (New York: The New Press, 1999), p. 143.

133. William J. Chambliss, "Crime Control and Ethnic Minorities: Legitimizing Racial Oppression by Creating Moral Panics," in *Ethnicity, Race, and Crime: Perspectives Across Time and Place*, Darnell F. Hawkins, ed. (Albany, NY: State University of New York Press, 1995); Tonry, *Malign Neglect*.

134. Phillip Jenkins, "'The Ice Age': The Social Construction of a Drug Panic," *Justice Quarterly* 11 (1994), pp. 7–31.

135. For a review of this research, see Theodore G. Chiricos and Miriam DeLone, "Labor Surplus and Punishment: A Review and Assessment of Theory and Evidence," *Social Problems* 39 (1992), pp. 421–446.

136. Human Rights Watch. *Punishment and Prejudice: Racial Disparities in the War on Drugs* 12, no. 2 (G), May 2000. Available at http://www.hrw.org/reports/2000/usa/.

137. Darrell Steffensmeier and Stephen Demuth, "Ethnicity and Judges' Sentencing Decisions: Hispanic–Black–White Comparison," *American Sociological Review* 65 (2006), pp. 145–178; Sara Steen, Rodney L. Engen, and Randy R. Gainey, "Images of Danger and Culpability: Racial Stereotyping, Case Processing, and Criminal Sentencing," *Criminology* 45 (2005), pp. 435–468. For other state-level studies, see Theodore G. Chiricos and William D. Bales, "Unemployment and Punishment: An Empirical Assessment," *Criminology* 29 (1991), pp. 701–724; John H. Kramer and Darrell Steffensmeier, "Race and Imprisonment Decisions"; Martha Myers, "Symbolic Policy and the Sentencing of Drug Offenders," *Law & Society Review* 23 (1989), pp. 295–315; Cassia Spohn and Jeffrey Spears, "Sentencing of Drug Offenders in Three Cities: Does Race/Ethnicity Make a Difference?" in *Crime Control and Criminal Justice: The Delicate Balance*, Darnell F. Hawkins, Samuel L. Meyers, Jr., and Randolph N. Stone, eds. (Westport, CT: Greenwood, 2002); James D. Unnever, "Direct and Organizational Discrimination in the Sentencing of Drug Offenders," *Social Problems* 30 (1982), pp. 212–225.

138. Cassia Spohn and Lisa Sample, "The Dangerous Drug Offender in Federal Court: Intersections of Race, Ethnicity, and Culpability," *Crime & Delinquency* (2009). Published in Online First on July 8, 2008 as doi:10.1177/00111287083928. For another study of sentencing decisions involving drug offenders adjudicated in federal courts, see Albonetti, "Sentencing Under the Federal Sentencing Guidelines."

139. Steffensmeier and Demuth, "Ethnicity and Judges' Sentencing Decisions."

140. Ibid., p. 153.

141. Ibid., Table 2.

142. Ibid., Table 3.

143. Ibid., p. 167.

144. Steen, Engen, and Gainey, *Images of Danger and Culpability*. pp. 441–444.

145. Ibid., p. 444.

146. Ibid., Table 2.

147. Ibid., p. 454.

148. Ibid., p. 460.

149. Ibid., p. 461.

150. Ibid., p. 464.

151. John Gould, "Zone Defense: Drug–Free School Zones Were Supposed to Keep Dealers Away From Kids. But What Happens When the Zones Engulf Whole Cities," *Washington Monthly*, June 11, 2002.

152. William Brownsberger and Susan Aromaa, "An Empirical Study of the School Zone Law in Three Cities in Massachusetts." Available online at http://www.jointogether.org/sa/files/pdf/schoolzone.pdf.

153. Vincent Schiraldi and Jason Ziedenberg, *Costs and Benefits? The Impact of Drug Imprisonment in New Jersey* (Washington, DC: Justice Policy Institute, 2003).

154. Spohn and Sample, "The Dangerous Drug Offender in Federal Court."

155. Steen et al., "Images of Danger and Culpability," p. 435.

156. Linn Washington, *Black Judges on Justice: Perspectives from the Bench* (New York: The New Press, 1994), p. 11.

157. Ibid., pp. 11–12.

158. George Crockett, "The Role of the Black Judge," in *The Criminal Justice System and Blacks*, D. Georges-Abeyie, ed. (New York: Clark Boardman, 1984), p. 393.

159. Susan Welch, Michael Combs, and John Gruhl, "Do Black Judges Make a Difference?" *American Journal of Political Science* 32 (1988), pp. 126–136.

160. Crockett, "The Role of the Black Judge"; Welch, Combs, and Gruhl, "Do Black Judges Make a Difference?"

161. Michael David Smith, *Race Versus Robe: The Dilemma of Black Judges* (Port Washington, NY: Associated Faculty Press, 1983).

162. Cited in Smith, *Race Versus Robe*, p. 80.

163. Cited in Smith, *Race Versus Robe*, p. 81.

164. Cassia Spohn, *How Do Judges Decide? The Search for Fairness and Equity in Sentencing* (Thousand Oaks, CA: Sage, 2009).

165. Thomas G. Walker and Deborah J. Barrow, "The Diversification of the Federal Bench: Policy and Process Ramifications," *Journal of Politics* 47 (1985), pp. 596–617.

166. Ibid., pp. 613–614.

167. Jon Gottschall, "Carter's Judicial Appointments: The Influence of Affirmative Action and Merit Selection on Voting on the U.S. Courts of Appeals," *Judicature* 67 (1983), pp. 165–173.

168. Ibid., p. 168.

169. Ibid., p. 173.

170. Todd Collins and Laura Moyer, "Gender, Race, and Intersectionality on the Federal Appellate Bench," *Political Research Quarterly* 61 (2008), pp. 219–227.

171. Ibid., p. 219.

172. Ibid., p. 225.

173. Amy Farrell, Geoff Ward, and Danielle Rousseau, "Race Effects of Representation among Federal Court Workers: Does Black Workforce Representation Reduce Sentencing Disparities," *Annals of the American Academy of Political and Social Science* 623 (2009), pp. 121–133; Max Schanzenbach, "Racial and Sex Disparities in Prison Sentences: The Effect of District-Level Judicial Demographics," *Journal of Legal Studies* 34 (2005), pp. 57–88.

174. Farrell et al., "Race Effects of Representation among Federal Court Workers," p. 124. For an example of a study of state court sentencing using this approach, see Ryan D. King, Kecia R Johnson, and Kelly McGeever, "Demography of the Legal Profession and Racial Disparities in Sentencing," *Law & Society Review* 44 (2010), pp. 1–33.

175. Ibid., pp. 130–131.

176. Ibid., p. 132.

177. Schanzenbach, "Racial and Sex Disparities in Prison Sentences."

178. Charles Donald Engle, *Criminal Justice in the City: A Study of Sentence Severity and Variation in the Philadelphia Court System* (Ph.D. dissertation, Temple University, 1971); Cassia Spohn, "Decision Making in Sexual Assault Cases: Do Black and Female Judges Make a Difference?" *Women & Criminal Justice* 2 (1990), pp. 83–105;

Thomas M. Uhlman, "Black Elite Decision Making: The Case of Trial Judges," *American Journal of Political Science* 22 (1978), pp. 884–895.

179. Engle, *Criminal Justice in the City*.

180. Ibid., pp. 226–227.

181. Thomas M. Uhlman, *Racial Justice: Black Judges and Defendants in an Urban Trial Court* (Lexington, MA: Lexington Books, 1979).

182. Ibid., p. 71.

183. Welch, Combs, and Gruhl, "Do Black Judges Make a Difference?"

184. Ibid., p. 134.

185. Ibid.

186. Jeffrey W. Spears, *Diversity in the Courtroom: A Comparison of the Sentencing Decisions of Black and White Judges and Male and Female Judges in Cook County Circuit Court* (Ph.D. dissertation, University of Nebraska at Omaha, 1999).

187. Ibid., p. 135.

188. Cassia Spohn, "The Sentencing Decisions of Black and White Judges: Expected and Unexpected Similarities," *Law & Society Review* 24 (1990), pp. 1,197–1,216.

189. Ibid., p. 1,206.

190. Ibid., p. 1,211.

191. Ibid., p. 1,212–1,213.

192. Ibid., p. 1,213.

193. Ibid., p. 1,214.

194. Ibid.

195. Malcolm D. Holmes, Harmon M. Hosch, Howard C. Daudistel, Dolores A. Perez, and Joseph B. Graves, "Judges' Ethnicity and Minority Sentencing: Evidence Concerning Hispanics," *Social Science Quarterly* 74 (1993), pp. 496–506.

196. Ibid., p. 502.

197. Uhlman, "Black Elite Decision Making," p. 893.

198. Bruce McM. Wright, "A Black Broods on Black Judges," *Judicature* 57 (1973), pp. 22–23.

199. Randall Kennedy, "Changing Images of the State: Criminal Law and Racial Discrimination: A Comment," *Harvard Law Review* 107 (1994), pp. 1,255 and 1,278. See also Randall Kennedy, *Race, Crime, and the Law* (New York: Vintage Books, 1997).

200. *Omaha World Herald*, April 17, 1993, p. 1.

201. *U.S. v. Armstrong*, 116 S.Ct. 1480, (1996).

202. United States Sentencing Commission, *Report to the Congress: Cocaine and Federal Sentencing Policy* (Washington, DC: U.S. Sentencing Commission, 2002), p. viii.

203. Ibid.

204. Marc Mauer, "Racial Impact Statements as a Means of Reducing Unwarranted Sentencing Disparities," *Ohio State Journal of Criminal Law* 5 (2007–2008), pp. 19–46.

205. Ibid., pp. 31–32.

206. Wis. Stat. §939.6435[1][b]

8

✳

The Color of Death
Race and the Death Penalty

> We may not be capable of devising procedural or substantive
> rules to prevent the more subtle and often unconscious forms
> of racism from creeping into the system ... discrimination
> and arbitrariness could not be purged from the administration
> of capital punishment without sacrificing the equally essential
> component of fairness—individualized sentencing.
>
> SUPREME COURT JUSTICE HARRY BLACKMUN[1]

In January 2003 Illinois Governor George Ryan ignited national debate by
announcing that he had commuted the sentences of all of the state's 167
death row inmates to life in prison.[2] He justified his unprecedented and highly
controversial decision, which came three years after he announced a moratorium
on executions, by stating that "our capital system is haunted by the demon of
error: error in determining guilt and error in determining who among the guilty
deserves to die." Governor Ryan, who left office two days after making the
announcement, also stated that he was concerned about the effects of race and
poverty on death penalty decisions. He acknowledged that his decision would be
unpopular but stated that he felt he had no choice but to strike a blow in "what
is shaping up to be one of the great civil rights struggles of our time."

Similar views were expressed by Supreme Court Justice Harry A. Blackmun,
who announced in February 1994 that he would "no longer tinker with the
machinery of death."[3] In an opinion dissenting from the Court's order denying
review in a Texas death penalty case, Blackmun charged the Court with coming
"perilously close to murder" and announced that he would vote to oppose all
future death sentences. He also stated that the death penalty was applied in an

345

arbitrary and racially discriminatory manner. "Rather than continue to coddle the Court's delusion that the desired level of fairness has been achieved and the need for regulation eviscerated," Blackmun wrote, "I feel morally and intellectually obligated simply to concede that the death penalty experiment has failed."[4]

Governor Ryan and Justice Blackmun are not alone in their assessment of the system of capital punishment in the United States. Legal scholars, civil libertarians, and state and federal policy makers also have questioned the fairness of the process by which a small proportion of convicted murderers is sentenced to death and an even smaller proportion is eventually executed.[5] As a lawyer who defends defendants charged with capital crimes put it, "You are dealing with a group of people who are in this situation not so much because of what they did, but because of who they are. And who they are has a lot to do with the color of their skin and their socio-economic status."[6] Echoing Justice Blackmun, these critics contend that "the most profound expression of racial discrimination in sentencing occurs in the use of capital punishment."[7]

As these comments demonstrate, controversy continues to swirl around the use of the death penalty in the United States. Although issues other than race and class animate this controversy, these issues clearly are central. The questions asked and the positions taken by those on each side of the controversy mimic to some extent the issues that dominate discussions of the non-capital sentencing process. Supporters of capital punishment contend that the death penalty is administered in an even-handed manner on those who commit the most heinous murders. They also argue that the restrictions contained in death penalty statutes and the procedural safeguards inherent in the process preclude arbitrary and discriminatory decision making. Opponents contend that the capital sentencing process, which involves a series of highly discretionary charging, convicting, and sentencing decisions, is fraught with race- and class-based discrimination. Moreover, they argue that the appellate process is unlikely to uncover, much less remedy, these abuses.

GOALS OF THE CHAPTER

In this chapter we address the issue of racial discrimination in the application of the death penalty. We begin with a discussion of Supreme Court decisions concerning the constitutionality of the death penalty. We follow this with a discussion of racial differences in attitudes toward capital punishment. We then present statistics on death sentences and executions and summarize the results of empirical studies examining the effect of race on the application of the death penalty. The next section discusses *McCleskey* v. *Kemp*,[8] the Supreme Court case that directly addressed the question of racial discrimination in the imposition of the death penalty. We conclude with a discussion of recent calls for a moratorium on the death penalty and legislation intended to reform the capital sentencing process.

After you have read this chapter:

1. You should be able to discuss the implications of Supreme Court decisions concerning the constitutionality of the death penalty.

2. You should understand that there are significant racial differences in attitudes toward capital punishment and you should be able to summarize and synthesize the results of empirical studies examining the effect of race on the application of the death penalty.

3. You should be able to explain the issues addressed in *McCleskey* v. *Kemp*,[9] the Supreme Court case that directly confronted the question of racial discrimination in the imposition of the death penalty.

4. You should be able to evaluate the pros and cons of recent calls for a moratorium on the death penalty and legislation intended to reform the capital sentencing process.

THE CONSTITUTIONALITY
OF THE DEATH PENALTY

The Eighth Amendment to the United States Constitution prohibits "cruel and unusual punishments." The determination of which punishments are cruel and unusual, and thus unconstitutional, has been left to the courts. According to the Supreme Court,

> Punishments are cruel when they involve torture or lingering death; but the punishment of death is not cruel, within the meaning of that word as used in the Constitution. It implies there something inhuman and barbarous, something more than the mere extinguishment of life.[10]

Whatever the arguments may be against capital punishment, both on moral grounds and in terms of accomplishing the purposes of punishment—and they are forceful—the death penalty has been employed throughout our history, and, in a day when it is still widely accepted, it cannot be said to violate the constitutional concept of cruelty.[11]

Although the Supreme Court consistently has stated that punishments of torture violate the Eighth Amendment, the Court has never ruled that the death penalty itself is a cruel and unusual punishment.

Furman v. *Georgia*

In 1972 the Supreme Court ruled in *Furman* v. *Georgia* that the death penalty, as it was being administered under then-existing statutes, was unconstitutional.[12] The 5–4 decision, in which nine separate opinions were written, did not hold that the death penalty per se violated the Constitution's ban on cruel and unusual punishment. Rather, the majority opinions focused on the procedures by which convicted defendants were selected for the death penalty. The justices ruled that because the statutes being challenged offered no guidance to juries charged with deciding whether to sentence convicted murderers or rapists to death, there was a substantial risk that the death penalty would be imposed in an arbitrary and discriminatory manner.

Although all of the majority justices were concerned about the arbitrary and capricious application of the death penalty, the nature of their concerns varied. Justices Brennan and Marshall wrote that the death penalty was inherently cruel and unusual punishment. Whereas Justice Brennan argued that the death penalty violated the concept of human dignity, Justice Marshall asserted that the death penalty served no legitimate penal purpose. These justices concluded that the death penalty would violate the Constitution under any circumstances.

The other three justices in the majority concluded that capital punishment as it was then being administered in the United States was unconstitutional. These justices asserted that the death penalty violated both the Eighth Amendment's ban on cruel and unusual punishment and the Fourteenth Amendment's requirement of equal protection under the law. Justice Douglas stated that the procedures used in administering the death penalty were "pregnant with discrimination." Justice Stewart focused on the fact that the death penalty was "so wantonly and so freakishly imposed." Justice White found "no meaningful basis for distinguishing the few cases in which [the death penalty] is imposed from the many cases in which it is not."[13]

The central issue in the *Furman* case was the meaning of the Eighth Amendment's prohibition of cruel and unusual punishment, but the issue of racial discrimination in the administration of the death penalty was raised by three of the five justices in the majority. Justices Douglas and Marshall cited evidence of discrimination against defendants who were poor, powerless, or African American. Marshall, for example, noted that giving juries "untrammeled discretion" to impose a sentence of death was "an open invitation to discrimination."[14] Justice Stewart, although asserting that "racial discrimination has not been proved," stated that Douglas and Marshall "have demonstrated that, if any basis can be discerned for the selection of these few to be sentenced to die, it is the constitutionally impermissible basis of race."[15]

The Impact of Furman   The impact of the *Furman* decision was dramatic. The Court's ruling "emptied death rows across the country" and "brought the process that fed them to a stop."[16] Many commentators argued that *Furman* reflected the Supreme Court's deep-seated concerns about the fairness of the death penalty process; they predicted that the Court's next step would be the abolition of capital punishment. The Court defied these predictions, deciding to regulate capital punishment rather than abolish it.

Also as a result of the *Furman* decision, the death penalty statutes in 39 states were invalidated. Most of these states responded to *Furman* by adopting new statutes designed to narrow discretion and thus avoid the problems of arbitrariness and discrimination identified by the justices in the majority. These statutes were of two types. Some required the judge or jury to impose the death penalty if a defendant was convicted of first-degree murder. Others permitted the judge or jury to impose the death penalty on defendants convicted of certain crimes, depending on the presence or absence of aggravating and mitigating circumstances. These "guided-discretion" statutes usually also required a bifurcated trial in which the jury first decided guilt or innocence and then decided whether to impose the death penalty. They also provided for automatic appellate review of all death sentences.

Post-*Furman* Decisions

The Supreme Court ruled on the constitutionality of the new death penalty statutes in 1976. The Court held that the mandatory death penalty statutes enacted by North Carolina and Louisiana were unconstitutional,[17] both because they provided no opportunity for consideration of mitigating circumstances and because the jury's power to determine the degree of the crime (conviction for first-degree murder or for a lesser included offense) opened the door to the type of "arbitrary and wanton jury discretion"[18] condemned in *Furman*. The justices stated that the central problem of the mandatory statutes was their treatment of all defendants "as members of a faceless, undifferentiated mass to be subjected to the blind infliction of the penalty of death."[19]

In contrast, the Supreme Court ruled that the guided discretion death penalty statutes adopted by Georgia, Florida, and Texas did not violate the Eighth Amendment's prohibition of cruel and unusual punishment.[20] In *Gregg* v. *Georgia* the Court held that Georgia's statute—which required the jury to consider and weigh 10 specified aggravating circumstances (see Box 8.1), allowed the jury to consider mitigating circumstances, and provided for automatic appellate review—channeled the jury's discretion and thereby reduced the likelihood that the jury would impose arbitrary or discriminatory sentences.[21] According to the Court,

> No longer can a jury wantonly and freakishly impose the death sentence; it is always circumscribed by the legislative guidelines. In addition, the review function of the Supreme Court of Georgia affords additional assurance that the concerns that prompted our decision in *Furman* are not present to any significant degree in the Georgia procedure applied here.[22]

Since 1976, the Supreme Court has handed down additional decisions on the constitutionality of the death penalty. With the exception of *McCleskey* v. *Kemp*, which we address later, these decisions do not focus on the question of racial discrimination in the application of the death penalty. The Court has ruled that the death penalty cannot be imposed on a defendant convicted of the raping of either an adult[23] or a child,[24] and that the death penalty can be imposed on an offender convicted of felony murder if the offender played a major role in the crime and displayed "reckless indifference to the value of human life."[25] In 2002 the Court ruled that the execution of someone who is mentally handicapped is cruel and unusual punishment in violation of the Eighth Amendment,[26] and in 2005 the Court ruled 5–4 that the Eighth and Fourteenth Amendments forbid the imposition of the death penalty on offenders who were younger than 18 when their crimes were committed.[27] In 2008 the Court took up the issue of lethal injection, ruling that Kentucky's three-drug protocol for administering lethal injection did not amount to cruel and unusual punishment

---

B o x 8.1   Georgia's Guided Discretion Death Penalty Statute

Under Georgia law, if the jury finds at least one of the following aggravating circumstances it may, but need not, recommend death:[28]

1. The offense was committed by a person with a prior record of conviction for a capital felony or by a person who has a substantial history of serious assaultive criminal convictions.

2. The offense was committed while the offender was engaged in the commission of another capital felony, or aggravated battery, or burglary, or arson in the first degree.

3. The offender knowingly created a great risk of death to more than one person in a public place by means of a weapon or device which would normally be hazardous to the lives of more than one person.

4. The offender committed the offense of murder for himself or another, for the purpose of receiving money or any other thing of monetary value.

5. The murder of a judicial officer, former judicial officer, district attorney or solicitor, or former district attorney or solicitor during or because of the exercise of his official duty.

6. The offender caused or directed another to commit murder or committed murder as an agent or employee of another person.

7. The offense was outrageously or wantonly vile, horrible, or inhuman in that it involved torture, depravity of mind, or an aggravated battery to the victim.

8. The offense was committed against any peace officer, corrections employee, or fireman while engaged in the performance of his official duties.

9. The offense was committed by a person in, or who has escaped from, the lawful custody of a peace officer or place of lawful confinement.

10. The murder was committed for the purpose of avoiding, interfering with, or preventing a lawful arrest or custody in a place of lawful confinement of himself or another.

---

under the Eighth Amendment.[29] In recent years the Supreme Court has also overturned a number of death sentences due to ineffective assistance of counsel.[30]

ATTITUDES TOWARD CAPITAL PUNISHMENT

In *Gregg* v. *Georgia*, the seven justices in the majority noted that both the public and state legislatures had endorsed the death penalty for murder. The Court stated that "it is now evident that a large proportion of American society continues to regard it as an appropriate and necessary criminal sanction." Public opinion data indicates that the Court was correct in its assessment of the level of support for the death penalty. In 1976, the year that *Gregg* was decided, 66 percent of the respondents to a nationwide poll said that they favored the death penalty for persons convicted of murder.[31] By 1997, three-fourths of those polled voiced support for the death penalty. Although the exoneration of death row inmates and subsequent decisions to impose a moratorium on executions (discussed later) led to a decline in support, in October 2009, 65 percent of Americans still reported that they favored the death penalty for people convicted of murder.[32]

The reliability of these figures has not gone unchallenged. In fact, Supreme Court Justices themselves have raised questions about the reliability and meaning of public opinion data derived from standard "do you favor or oppose?" polling questions. Justice Marshall observed in his concurring opinion in *Furman* that Americans were not fully informed about the ways in which the death penalty was used or about its potential for abuse. According to Marshall, the public did not realize that the death penalty was imposed in an arbitrary manner or that "the burden of capital punishment falls upon the poor, the ignorant, and the underprivileged members of society."[33] Marshall suggested that public opinion data demonstrating widespread support for the death penalty should therefore be given little weight in determining whether capital punishment is consistent with "evolving standards of decency." In what has become known as the "Marshall Hypothesis,"[34] he stated that "the average citizen" who knew "all the facts presently available regarding capital punishment would ... find it shocking to his conscience and sense of justice."[35]

Researchers also have raised questions about the poll results,[36] suggesting that support for the death penalty is not absolute but depends on such things as the circumstances of the case, the character of the defendant, or the alternative punishments that are available. William Bowers, for example, challenged the conclusion that "Americans solidly support the death penalty" and suggested that the poll results have been misinterpreted.[37] He argued that instead of reflecting a "deep-seated or strongly held commitment to capital punishment," expressed public support for the death penalty "is actually a reflection of the public's desire for a genuinely harsh but meaningful punishment for convicted murderers."[38]

In support of this proposition, Bowers presented evidence from surveys of citizens in a number of states and from interviews with capital jurors in three states. He found that support for the death penalty plummeted when respondents were given an alternative of life in prison without parole plus restitution to the victim's family; moreover, a majority of the respondents in every state preferred this alternative to the death penalty. Bowers also found that about three-quarters of the respondents, and 80 percent of jurors in capital cases, agreed that "the death penalty is too arbitrary because some people are executed and others are sent to prison for the very same crimes." Bowers concluded that the results of his study "could have the critical effect of changing the perspectives of legislators, judges, the media, and the public on how people think about capital punishment."[39]

Consistent with Bowers's results, recent public opinion polls reveal that most Americans believe that innocent people are sometimes convicted of murder. These polls also suggest that respondents' beliefs about the likelihood of wrongful convictions affect their views of the death penalty. A National Omnibus Poll

T A B L E   8.1   Factors Related to Reduction in Support for the Death Penalty

Percent of respondents favoring the death penalty who said that the factor, if proven true, would reduce their support for the death penalty	%
Execution of innocent people	27
It takes too long to go through the whole appeals process in death penalty cases and only a few of those sentenced to death are actually executed	26
Receiving the death penalty often depends on race, economics, and geography	22
The high cost of the death penalty	22
Exonerations of those wrongfully convicted	21
Sentence of life without parole	12
Religious leaders' opposition	11

SOURCE: Adapted from Richard C. Dieter, *A Crisis in Confidence: Americans' Doubts About the Death Penalty* (Washington, DC: Death Penalty Information Center, 2007), p. 8.

conducted by RT Strategies in 2007 for the Death Penalty Information Center found that 87 percent of the respondents believed that innocent people have been executed.[40] Of those who stated that they believed this, 55 percent said that it had negatively affected their view of the death penalty. Respondents who favored the death penalty were given a list of factors and asked whether each one, if proven true, might lessen their support for the death penalty. As shown in Table 8.1, 27 percent of the respondents stated that knowing that innocent people had been executed would reduce their support for the death penalty. A similar percentage said that knowing the fact that the appeals process takes too long and that too few are executed would reduce their support. Twenty-two percent of the respondents stated that their level of support would be reduced by a finding that receiving the death penalty depended on race, social class, and geography or by information regarding the high cost of administering the death penalty. The results of the survey led the authors of the report to conclude that "the public is losing confidence in the death penalty" and that Americans "are deeply concerned about the risk of executing the innocent, about the fairness of the process, and about the inability of capital punishment to accomplish its basic purpose."[41]

It is also clear that there are significant racial differences in support for the death penalty. A 2007 Gallup poll, for example, found that 70 percent of whites but only 40 percent of African Americans expressed support for the death penalty.[42] In fact, as shown in Figure 8.1, since 1972 the percentage of respondents who report that they support the death penalty has been consistently higher among whites than among African Americans. Other research shows that whereas 35.9 percent of whites surveyed in 2000 stated that they strongly favored the death penalty for persons convicted of murder, 34.2 percent of African Americans reported that they were strongly opposed to the use of the death penalty.[43] Beliefs about the fairness of the death penalty and estimates of the number of innocent people convicted of murder also vary by race and ethnicity.

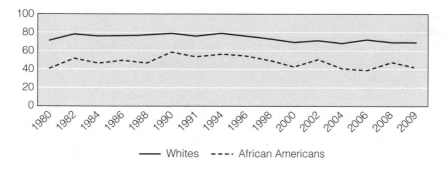

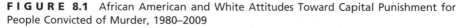

——— Whites   ---- African Americans

FIGURE 8.1 African American and White Attitudes Toward Capital Punishment for People Convicted of Murder, 1980–2009

SOURCE: Data from Bureau of Justice Statistics, *Sourcebook of Criminal Justice Statistics Online,* Tables 2.50 and 2.52.

Fifty-nine percent of whites but only 32 percent of African Americans stated that they believed the death penalty was applied fairly.[44] African American respondents estimated that 22 of every 100 persons convicted of murder were innocent. In contrast, the estimate was 15 of every 100 for Hispanic respondents, and 10 of every 100 for white respondents.[45]

Researchers have advanced a number of explanations to account for these consistent racial differences. Some attribute African American opposition to perceptions of racial bias in the application of the death penalty.[46] Others contend that white support is associated with racial prejudice.[47] One study, for example, found that antipathy to African Americans (which was measured by two items asking respondents to indicate their attitudes toward living in a majority–African American neighborhood or having a family member marry an African American) and belief in racial stereotypes (believing that African Americans are lazy, unintelligent, violent, and poor) predicted white respondents' support for the death penalty.[48] As the authors noted, "Simply put, many White people are both prejudiced against Blacks and are more likely to favor capital punishment."[49] The authors concluded that their finding of an association between racial prejudice and support for the death penalty suggests "that public sentiment may be an unacceptable indicator of contemporary standards of appropriate punishment for persons convicted of homicide."[50]

A more recent study by James D. Unnever and Francis T. Cullen similarly found that one-third of the racial difference in support for the death penalty could be explained by "white racism."[51] The authors also noted that the fact that substantial differences remained even after white racism was taken into account suggests that "African Americans may have a distinct history with the death penalty" that encompasses both the epidemic of lynching that occurred throughout the South in the early 1900s and discriminatory use of the death penalty for crimes such as rape.[52] Unnever and Cullen's findings suggest that when policy makers justify their support for the death penalty by referencing "the will of the people," they are ignoring a "discomforting reality." That is, "that strong or high levels of support for capital punishment are largely rooted in the views of that segment of the public holding racist views toward African Americans."[53]

There also is evidence of geographic variation in support for the death penalty and that these variations can be explained by features of the social context, such as the homicide rate, the political climate, and the size of the minority population.[54] Eric Baumer and his colleagues found that support for the death penalty in 268 jurisdictions ranged from less than 50 percent to more than 90 percent. As they noted, this finding of geographic variation in support for the death penalty "challenges conventional wisdom and popular portrayals that support for capital punishment in the United States is universally high."[55] They also found that support for the death penalty was higher among respondents who lived in areas with high homicide rates, among people who lived in politically conservative jurisdictions, and among respondents who lived in areas with higher percentages of African Americans in the population. Community contextual characteristics, in other words, shaped citizens' attitudes toward the death penalty. This suggests that attitudes toward capital punishment are determined not only by individual characteristics, including race/ethnicity, but also by the characteristics of the communities in which people live.

RACE AND THE DEATH PENALTY:
THE EMPIRICAL EVIDENCE

The Supreme Court's decisions regarding the constitutionality of the death penalty have been guided by a number of assumptions. In the *Furman* decision, the five justices in the majority assumed that the absence of guidelines and procedural rules in then-existing death penalty statutes opened the door to arbitrary, capricious, and discriminatory decision making. In *Gregg*, the Court affirmed the guided discretion statutes on their face and assumed that the statutes would eliminate the problems condemned in *Furman*. The Court assumed that racial discrimination was a potential problem under the statutes struck down in *Furman*, but would not be a problem under the statutes approved in *Gregg* and the companion cases.

In this section we address the validity of these assumptions. We begin by presenting statistics on the application of the death penalty. We then discuss the results of pre-*Furman* and post-*Furman* studies investigating the relationship between race and the death penalty. We also examine recent research on the federal capital sentencing process.

Statistical Evidence of Racial Disparity

There is clear evidence of racial disparity in the application of the death penalty. Despite the fact that African Americans make up only 13 percent of the U.S. population, they have been a much larger proportion of offenders sentenced to death and executed, both historically and during the post-*Gregg* era. There also is compelling evidence that those who murder whites, and particularly African

Americans who murder whites, are sentenced to death and executed at disproportionately high rates. For example, the state of Georgia, which generated both *Furman* and *Gregg*, carried out 18 executions between 1976 and 1994. Twelve of those executed were African Americans; 6 of the 12 were sentenced to death by all-white juries. Sixteen of the 18 persons executed had killed whites.[56]

The pattern found in Georgia casts doubt on the Supreme Court's assertion in *Gregg* that the disparities that prompted their decision in *Furman* will not be present "to any significant degree"[57] under the guided discretion procedures. Other evidence also calls this into question. Consider the following statistics:

- Of the 3,261 people under sentence of death in the United States in January 2010, 1,351 (41.4 percent) were African Americans, 383 (11.7 percent) were Hispanic, and 1,448 (44.4 percent) were white.[58]

- Of the 58 females on death row in 2008, 15 (25.9 percent) were African American.[59]

- In 2010 African Americans made up approximately half of the death row populations in Alabama, Delaware, Georgia, Mississippi, North Carolina, Ohio, and South Carolina; they constituted nearly two-thirds (or more) of those on death row in Arkansas, Colorado, Connecticut, Louisiana, and Pennsylvania.[60]

- Thirty-one of the 59 offenders sentenced to death by the federal courts from 1993 through 2009 were African American, 23 were white, 4 were Hispanic, and 1 was Native American.[61]

- Of the 1,188 prisoners executed from 1976 through 2009, 666 (56 percent) were white, 415 (35 percent) were African American, 85 (7 percent) were Hispanic, and 22 (2 percent) were Native American or Asian.[62]

- Of the 1,757 victims of those executed from 1977 through 2009, 1,368 (77.9 percent) were white, 255 (14.5 percent) were African American, 95 (5.4 percent) were Hispanic, and 39 (2.3 percent) were Native Americans or Asians. During this period, approximately 50 percent of all murder victims were African Americans.[63]

- From 1977 through 2009, 53 percent of the prisoners executed were whites convicted of killing other whites, 21 percent were African Americans convicted of killing whites, 11 percent were African Americans convicted of killing other African Americans, and only 1.3 percent were whites convicted of killing African Americans.[64]

- Among those executed from 1930 through 1972 for the crime of rape, 89 percent (405 of the 455) were African Americans.[65] During this period, Louisiana, Mississippi, Oklahoma, Virginia, West Virginia, and the District of Columbia executed 66 African American men, but not a single white man, for the crime of rape.[66]

- Among those sentenced to death for rape in North Carolina from 1909 to 1954, 56 percent of the African Americans, but only 43 percent of the whites, were eventually executed.[67]

- Twenty percent of the whites, but only 11 percent of the African Americans, sentenced to death for first-degree murder in Pennsylvania between 1914 and 1958 had their sentences commuted to life in prison.[68]

These statistics clearly indicate that African Americans have been sentenced to death and executed "in numbers far out of proportion to their numbers in the population."[69] They document racial disparity in the application of the death penalty, both prior to *Furman* and following *Gregg*.[70] As we have noted frequently throughout this book, however, disparities in the treatment of racial minorities and whites do not necessarily constitute evidence of racial discrimination. Racial minorities may be sentenced to death at a disproportionately high rate, not because of discrimination in the application of the death penalty, but because they are more likely than whites to commit homicide, the crime most frequently punished by death. As illustrated by the hypothetical examples presented in Box 8.2, the appropriate comparison is not the number of African Americans and whites sentenced to death during a given year or over time. Rather, the appropriate comparison is the percentage of death-eligible homicides involving African Americans and whites that result in a death sentence.

The problem with the hypothetical examples presented in Box 8.2 is that there are no national data on the number of death-eligible homicides or on the race of those who commit or who are arrested for such crimes. Gary Kleck, noting that most homicides are intraracial, used the number of African American and white homicide *victims* as a surrogate measure.[71] He created an indicator of "execution risk" by dividing the number of executions (for murder) of persons of a given race in a given year by the number of homicide victims of that race who died in the previous year.[72] Using data from 1930 through 1967, Kleck

---

B o x 8.2   Discrimination in the Application of the Death Penalty: A Hypothetical Example

Example 1

- 210 death-eligible homicides with African American offenders: 70 offenders (30 percent) receive the death penalty.
- 150 death-eligible homicides with white offenders: 50 offenders (30 percent) receive the death penalty.
- Conclusion: No evidence of discrimination, despite the fact that a disproportionate number of African Americans are sentenced to death.

Example 2

- 210 death-eligible homicides with African American offenders: 90 offenders (43 percent) receive the death penalty.
- 150 death-eligible homicides with white offenders: 30 offenders (20 percent) receive the death penalty.
- Conclusion: Possibility of discrimination because African Americans are more than twice as likely to be sentenced to death.

found that the risk of execution was somewhat greater for whites (10.43 executions per 1,000 homicides) than for African Americans (9.72 executions per 1,000 homicides) for the United States as a whole, but that African Americans faced a greater likelihood of execution than whites in the South (10.47 for African Americans versus 8.39 for whites).[73] He concluded that the death penalty "has not generally been imposed for murder in a fashion discriminatory toward blacks, except in the South."[74]

None of the statistics cited here, including the execution rates calculated by Kleck, prove that the death penalty has been imposed in a racially discriminatory manner, in the South or elsewhere, either before the *Furman* decision or after the *Gregg* decision. As we pointed out earlier, conclusions of racial discrimination in sentencing rest on evidence indicating that African Americans are sentenced more harshly than whites after other legally relevant predictors of sentence severity are taken into account.

Even if it can be shown that African Americans face a greater risk of execution than whites, we cannot necessarily conclude that this reflects racial prejudice or racial discrimination. The difference might be the result of legitimate legal factors—the heinousness of the crime or the prior criminal record of the offender, for example—that juries and judges consider in determining whether to sentence the offender to death. If African Americans are sentenced to death at a higher rate than whites because they commit more heinous murders than whites or because they are more likely than whites to have a prior conviction for murder, then we cannot conclude that criminal justice officials or juries are making racially discriminatory death penalty decisions.

The data presented in Table 8.2 provide some evidence in support of this possibility. Among prisoners under sentence of death in 2008, African Americans were more likely than either Hispanics or whites to have a prior felony conviction. African Americans and Hispanics also were more likely than whites to have been on parole when they were arrested for the capital offense. There were, on the other hand, very few differences in the proportions of whites and African Americans who had a prior homicide conviction.

Just as the presence of racial disparity does not necessarily signal the existence of racial discrimination, the absence of disparity does not necessarily

T A B L E   8.2   Criminal History Profile of Prisoners under Sentence of Death In the United States, 2008

	Race of Prisoner		
	African American	Hispanic	White
Prior felony conviction (%)	71.1	61.7	61.8
Prior homicide conviction (%)	8.7	6.5	8.4
On parole at time of capital offense (%)	16.3	19.8	13.2

SOURCE: Department of Justice, Bureau of Justice Statistics, *Capital Punishment 2008—Statistical Tables* (Washington, DC: U.S. Government Printing Office, 2009), Table 8.

indicate the absence of discrimination. Even if it can be shown that African Americans generally face the same risk of execution as whites, we cannot conclude that the capital sentencing process operates in a racially neutral manner. Assume, for example, that the crimes for which African Americans are sentenced to death are less serious than those for which whites are sentenced to death. If this is the case, apparent equality of treatment may be masking race-linked assessments of crime seriousness. Moreover, as we noted in our discussion of the noncapital sentencing process, it is important to consider not only the race of the offender but the race of the victim as well. If African Americans who murder whites are sentenced to death at a disproportionately high rate, but African Americans who murder other African Americans are sentenced to death at a disproportionately low rate, the overall finding of "no difference" in the death sentence rates for African American and white offenders may be masking significant differences based on the race of the victim. As Guy Johnson wrote in 1941,

> If caste values and attitudes mean anything at all, they mean that offenses by or against Negroes will be defined not so much in terms of their intrinsic seriousness as in terms of their importance in the eyes of the dominant group. Obviously, the murder of a white person by a Negro and the murder of a Negro by a Negro are not at all the same kind of murder from the standpoint of the upper caste's scale of values ... instead of two categories of offenders, Negro and white, we really need four offender-victim categories, and they would probably rank in seriousness from high to low as follows: (1) Negro versus white, (2) white versus white, (3) Negro versus Negro, and white versus Negro.[75]

Evidence in support of Johnson's rankings is presented in Box 8.3, which focuses on the "anomalous" cases in which whites have been executed for crimes against African Americans. According to Michael L. Radelet, "the scandalous paucity of these cases, representing less than two-tenths of 1 percent of known executions, lends further support to the evidence that the death penalty in this country has been discriminatorily applied."[76]

There is now a substantial body of research investigating the relationship between race and the death penalty. Most, but not all, of the research tests for both race-of-defendant and race-of-victim effects. Some of these studies are methodologically sophisticated, both in terms of the type of statistical analysis used and the number of variables that are taken into consideration in the analysis. Other studies use less sophisticated statistical techniques and include fewer control variables.

We summarize the results of these studies—presenting the results of the pre-*Furman* studies first and then the results of the post-*Gregg* studies. Our purpose is to assess the validity of the Supreme Court's assumptions that race played a role in death penalty decisions prior to *Furman*, but that the guided discretion statutes enacted since 1976 have removed arbitrariness and discrimination from the capital sentencing process.

B o x   8.3   Executions of Whites for Crimes against African Americans: Exceptions to the Rule?

Between 1608 and the mid-1980s, there were about 16,000 executions in the United States.[77] Of these, only 30, or about two-tenths of 1 percent, were executions of whites for crimes against African Americans. Historically, in other words, there has been one execution of a white for a crime against an African American for every 533 recorded executions.

Michael Radelet believes that these white offender–black victim cases, which would appear to be "theoretically anomalous" based on the proposition that race is an important determinant of sentencing, are not really "exceptions to the rule."[78] Although he acknowledges that each case is in fact anomalous if *race alone* is used to predict the likelihood of a death sentence, Radelet suggests that these cases are consistent with a more general theoretical model that uses the *relative social status* of defendants and victims to explain case outcomes. These cases, in other words, are consistent with "the general rule that executions almost always involve lower status defendants who stand convicted for crimes against victims of higher status."[79]

Radelet's examination of the facts in each case revealed that 10 of the 30 cases involved white men who murdered slaves, and 8 of these 10 involved men convicted of murdering a slave who belonged to someone else. The scenario of one case, for example, read as follows:

> June 2, 1985. Texas. James Wilson (a.k.a. Rhode Wilson). Wilson had been on bad terms with a powerful white farmer, and had threatened to kill him on several occasions. One day Wilson arrived at the farm with the intention of carrying out the threats. The farmer was not home, so Wilson instead murdered the farmer's favorite slave (male).[80]

According to Radelet, cases such as this are really "economic crimes" in which the true victim is not the slave himself, but the slave's owner. As he notes, "Slaves are property, the wealth of someone else, and their rank should be measured accordingly." James Wilson, in other words, was sentenced to death not because he killed a slave, but because he destroyed the property of someone of higher status than himself. Similarly, the death sentences imposed on the two men who killed their own slaves were meant to discourage such brutality, which might threaten the legitimacy of the institution of slavery.

The twenty remaining cases of whites who were executed for crimes against African Americans involved either

- an African American victim of higher social status than his white murderer (five cases);
- a defendant who was a marginal member of the white community—a tramp, a recent immigrant, a hard drinker (four cases);
- a defendant with a long record of serious criminality (seven cases); or
- murders that were so heinous that they resulted in "an unqualified disgust and contempt for the offender unmitigated by the fact of his or the victim's race."[81]

Based on his analysis of these 30 cases, Radelet concluded that "it was not primarily outrage over the violated rights of the black victim or the inherent value of the victim's life that led to the condemnation."[82] Rather, the 30 white men executed for crimes against African Americans were sentenced to death because their crimes threatened the institution of slavery, involved a victim of higher social status than the defendant, or involved a defendant who was a very marginal member of the community. As Radelet noted, "The data show that the criminal justice system deems the executioner's services warranted not simply for those who *do something*, but who also *are someone*."[83]

Pre-*Furman* Studies

We noted in our discussion of the Supreme Court's decision in *Furman* v. *Georgia* that three of the five justices in the majority mentioned the problem of racial discrimination in the application of the death penalty. Even two of the dissenting justices—Chief Justice Burger and Justice Powell—acknowledged the existence of historical evidence of discrimination against African Americans. Justice Powell also stated, "If a Negro defendant, for instance, could demonstrate that members of his race were being singled out for more severe punishment than others charged with the same offense, a constitutional violation might be established."[84]

Several studies suggest that African Americans, and particularly African Americans who murdered or raped whites, were "singled out for more severe punishment" in the pre-*Furman* era.[85] Most of these studies were conducted in the South. Researchers found, for example, that African Americans indicted for murdering whites in North Carolina from 1930 to 1940 faced a disproportionately high risk of a death sentence,[86] that whites sentenced to death in nine southern and border states during the 1920s and 1930s were less likely than African Americans to be executed,[87] and that African Americans sentenced to death in Pennsylvania were less likely than whites to have their sentences commuted to life in prison and more likely than whites to be executed.[88]

Harold Garfinkel's[89] study of the capital sentencing process in North Carolina during the 1930s revealed the importance of taking both the race of the offender and the race of the victim into account. Garfinkel examined three separate decisions: the grand jury's decision to indict for first-degree murder; the prosecutor's decision to go to trial on a first-degree murder charge (in those cases in which the grand jury returned an indictment for first-degree murder); and the judge or jury's decision to convict for first-degree murder (and thus to impose the mandatory death sentence).

As shown in Figure 8.2, which summarizes the movement of death-eligible cases from one stage to the next, there were few differences based on the race of the offender. In fact, among defendants charged with first-degree murder, white offenders were *more* likely than African American offenders to be convicted of first-degree murder and thus to be sentenced to death; 14 percent of the whites, but only 9 percent of the African Americans, received a death sentence.

In contrast, there were substantial differences based on the race of the victim, particularly in the decision to convict the defendant for first-degree murder. Only 5 percent of the defendants who killed African Americans were convicted of first-degree murder and sentenced to death, compared to 24 percent of the defendants who killed whites.

The importance of considering both the race of the offender and the race of the victim is further illustrated by the data presented in Figure 8.3. Garfinkel's analysis revealed that African Americans who killed whites were more likely than any of the other race-of-offender / race-of-victim groups to be indicted for, charged with, or convicted of first-degree murder. Again, the differences were particularly pronounced at the trial stage of the process. Among offenders

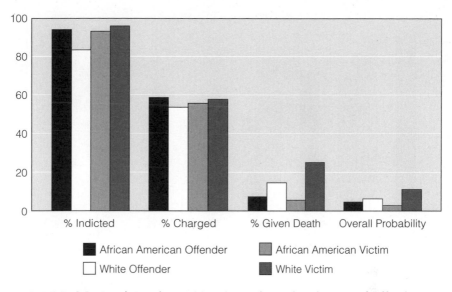

FIGURE 8.2 Death Penalty Decisions in North Carolina, by Race of Offender and Victim, 1930–1940

SOURCE: Data obtained from Harold Garfinkel, "Research Note on Inter- and Intra-Racial Homicides," *Social Forces* 27 (1949), Tables 2 and 3.

charged with first-degree murder, the rate of conviction for first-degree murder ranged from 43 percent for African Americans who killed whites, to 15 percent for whites who killed whites, to 5 percent for blacks who killed blacks, to 0 percent for whites who killed blacks. The overall probability of a death sentence (that is, the probability that an indictment for homicide would result in a death sentence) revealed similar disparities. African Americans who killed whites had a substantially higher overall probability of a death sentence than any of the other three groups.

The results of Garfinkel's study suggest that there were pervasive racial differences in the administration of capital punishment in North Carolina during the 1930s. Although Garfinkel did not control for the possibility that the crimes committed by African Americans and the crimes committed against whites were more serious, and thus more likely to deserve the death penalty, the magnitude of the differences "cast[s] doubt on the possibility that legally relevant factors are responsible for these differences."[90]

Studies of the use of capital punishment for the crime of rape also reveal overt and pervasive discrimination against African Americans in the pre-*Furman* era. These studies reveal that "the death penalty for rape was largely used for punishing blacks who had raped whites."[91] One analysis of sentences for rape in Florida from 1940 through 1964, for example, revealed that 54 percent of the African Americans convicted of raping whites received the death penalty, compared to only 5 percent of the whites convicted of raping whites. Moreover, none of the eight whites convicted of raping African Americans was sentenced to death.[92]

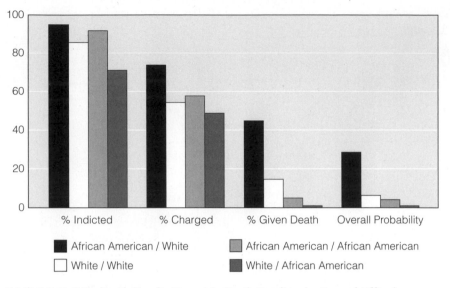

F I G U R E 8.3 Death Penalty Process in North Carolina, by Race of Offender and Victim

SOURCE: Date obtained from Harold Garfinkel, "Research Note on Inter- and Intra-Racial Homicides," *Social Forces* 27 (1949), Tables 2 and 3.

Marvin E. Wolfgang and Marc Reidel's[93] study of the imposition of the death penalty for rape in 12 southern states from 1945 through 1965 uncovered a similar pattern. As shown in Table 8.3, they found that 13 percent of the African Americans, but only 2 percent of the whites, were sentenced to death.

T A B L E 8.3   Race and the Death Penalty for Rape in the South, 1945–1965

	Sentenced to Death		Not Sentenced to Death	
	N	%	N	%
Race of offender				
African American	110	13	713	87
White	9	2	433	98
Race of offender/victim				
African American / white	113	36	204	64
All other combinations	19	2	902	98

SOURCE: Marvin E. Wolfgang and Marc Reidel, "Race, Judicial Discretion, and the Death Penalty," *Annals of the American Academy* 407 (1973), pp. 119–133, p. 129, Tables 1 and 2.

Further analysis revealed that cases in which African Americans were convicted of raping whites were 18 times more likely to receive a death penalty than were cases with any other racial combinations.

These differences did not disappear when Wolfgang and Reidel controlled for commission of a contemporaneous felony or for other factors associated with the imposition of the death penalty. According to the authors, "All the nonracial factors in each of the states analyzed 'wash out,' that is, they have no bearing on the imposition of the death penalty in disproportionate numbers upon blacks. The only variable of statistical significance that remains is race."[94]

Critics of the pre-*Furman* research note that most researchers did not control for the defendant's prior criminal record, for the heinousness of the crime, or for other predictors of sentence severity. Kleck, for example, although admitting that additional controls probably would not eliminate "the huge racial differentials in use of the death penalty" for rape, asserted that the more modest differences found for homicide might disappear if these legal factors were taken into consideration.[95]

A handful of more methodologically sophisticated studies of capital sentencing in the pre-*Furman* era controlled for these legally relevant factors. An analysis of death penalty decisions in Georgia, for example, found that African American defendants and defendants who murdered whites received the death penalty more often than other equally culpable defendants.[96] These results were limited, however, to borderline cases in which the appropriate sentence (life in prison or death) was not obvious.

An examination of the capital sentencing process in pre-*Furman* Texas also found significant racial effects.[97] Paige H. Ralph and her colleagues controlled for legal and extralegal factors associated with sentence severity. They found that offenders who killed during a felony had a higher probability of receiving the death penalty, as did nonwhite offenders and offenders who killed whites. In fact, their analysis revealed that the race of the victim was the most important extralegal variable; those who killed whites were 25.2 percent more likely to be sentenced to death than those who killed nonwhites. The authors concluded, "Overall we found a significant race-linked bias in the death sentencing of non-Anglo-American murderers; the victim's race, along with legal factors taken together, emerged as the pivotal element in sentencing."[98]

The results of these studies, then, reveal that the Supreme Court was correct in its assumption of the potential for racial discrimination in the application of the death penalty in the pre-*Furman* era. The death penalty for rape was primarily reserved for African Americans who victimized whites (for a discussion of gendered racism in capital sentencing, see Box 8.4). The evidence with respect to homicide, although less consistent, also suggests that African Americans, and particularly African Americans who murdered whites, were sentenced to death at a disproportionately high rate. We now turn to an examination of the capital sentencing process in the post-*Gregg* period.

**B o x 8.4   African American Female Executions—Gendered
Racism in Capital Sentencing**

In an article published in *Criminal Justice Review* in 2008, David V. Baker contends
that criminal justice researchers have largely ignored the use of capital punishment
for African American women. In an attempt to remedy this, Baker examines the
"contextual peculiarities giving rise to Black female executions since the earliest
periods of American history."[99]

Baker presents data that illustrate the situations that gave rise to the execution
of African American slave women during the colonial and antebellum periods. He
notes that "slave women mostly strangled, clubbed, stabbed, burned, shot, poisoned,
or hacked to death their White masters, mistresses, overseers, and even their owner's
children."[100] These crimes were prompted by mistreatment, including sexual abuse,
at the hands of their owners. According to Baker, "The historical record makes clear
that slave women fought back viciously against the sexualized brutality of White
masters," either by killing their owners or members of their owner's family or by
intentionally aborting pregnancies that resulted from sexual abuse by their owners.
Slave women often were assisted by slave men or, occasionally, by white co-
conspirators. However, Baker notes that slave women were given harsher punishments than slave men; they were often burned at the stake while their male co-
conspirators were hanged.

Post-*Gregg* Studies

In *Gregg* v. *Georgia* the Supreme Court upheld Georgia's guided discretion death
penalty statute and stated that "the concerns that prompted our decision in *Furman* are not present to any significant degree in the Georgia procedure applied
here."[101] The Court, in essence, predicted that race would not affect the capital
sentencing process in Georgia or in other states with similar statutes. Critics of
the Court's ruling were less optimistic. Wolfgang and Reidel, for example,
noted that the post-*Furman* statutes narrowed but did not eliminate discretion.
They suggested that "it is unlikely that the death penalty will be applied with
greater equity when substantial discretion remains in these post-*Furman*
statutes."[102]

Other commentators predicted that the guided discretion statutes would
simply shift discretion, and thus the potential for discrimination, to earlier stages
in the capital sentencing process. They suggested that discretion would be transferred to charging decisions made by the grand jury and the prosecutor. Thus,
according to Bowers and Glenn L. Pierce, "under post-*Furman* capital statutes,
the extent of arbitrariness and discrimination, if not their distribution over stages
of the criminal justice process, might be expected to remain essentially
unchanged."

Compelling evidence supports this hypothesis. (See also Box 8.5.) Studies
conducted during the past three decades document substantial discrimination in
the application of the death penalty under post-*Furman* statutes. In fact a 1990
report by the U.S. General Accounting Office (GAO) concluded that there

---

B o x   8.5   Discrimination in the Georgia Courts: The Case of Wilburn Dobbs

Statistical evidence of racial disparities in the use of the death penalty, although important, cannot illustrate the myriad ways in which racial sentiments influence the capital sentencing process. Consider the case of Wilburn Dobbs, an African American on death row in Georgia for the murder of a white man.[103] The judge trying his case referred to him in court as "colored" and "colored boy," and two of the jurors who sentenced him to death admitted after trial that they used the racial epithet "nigger." Moreover, the court-appointed lawyer assigned to his case, who also referred to Dobbs as "colored," stated on the morning of trial that he was "not prepared to go to trial" and that he was "in a better position to prosecute the case than defend it." He also testified before the federal court hearing Dobbs's appeal that he believed that African Americans were uneducated and less intelligent than whites and admitted that he used the word "nigger" jokingly.[104]

The federal courts that heard Dobbs's appeals ruled that neither the racial atti- tudes of the trial judge or the defense attorney nor the racial prejudice of the jurors required that Dobbs's death sentence be set aside. The Court of Appeals, for instance, noted that although several of the jurors made statements reflecting racial prejudice, none of them "viewed blacks as more prone to violence than whites or as morally inferior to whites."[105]

The Court's reasoning in this case led Stephen Bright to conclude that "racial discrimination which would not be acceptable in any other area of American life today is tolerated in criminal courts."[106]

---

was "a pattern of evidence indicating racial disparities in the charging, sentenc- ing, and imposition of the death penalty after the *Furman* decision."[107]

The GAO evaluated the results of 28 post-*Gregg* empirical studies of the capital sentencing process. They found that the race of the victim had a statisti- cally significant effect in 23 of the 28 studies; those who murdered whites were more likely to be charged with capital murder and to be sentenced to death than those who murdered African Americans. The authors of the report noted that the race of the victim affected decisions made at all stages of the criminal justice process. They concluded that these differences could not be explained by the defendant's prior criminal record, by the heinousness of the crime, or by other legally relevant variables.

With respect to the effect of the race of the defendant, the GAO report concluded that the evidence was "equivocal."[108] The report noted that about half of the studies found that the race of the defendant affected the likelihood of being charged with a capital crime or receiving the death penalty; most, but not all, of these studies found that African Americans were more likely than whites to be sentenced to death. The authors of the report also stated that although some studies found that African Americans who murdered whites faced the highest odds of receiving the death penalty, "the extent to which the finding was influenced by race of victim rather than race of defendant was unclear."[109]

A more recent review of research on the capital sentencing process reached a somewhat different conclusion. David C. Baldus and George Woodworth reviewed post-*Furman* research, concluding that there was not systematic evidence of discrimination against black defendants.[110] The authors suggested three possible explanations for this change from the pre-*Furman* period. First, the change might reflect the fact that prosecutors are striving for equal treatment.[111] Alternatively, it might reflect greater racial diversity among judges, prosecutors, and defense attorneys and/or the fact that defendants facing capital charges are provided with more competent defense attorneys than they were in the past. Consistent with the results of the GAO report, Baldus and Woodworth reported that a number of the studies they reviewed continued to find a race-of-victim effect. They concluded that "while the discriminatory application of the death penalty continues to occur in some places, it does not appear to be inherent to the system; in other words, it is not an inevitable feature of all American death-sentencing systems."[112]

A comprehensive review of the post-*Gregg* research is beyond the scope of this book.[113] Instead, we summarize the results of three studies. The first, a study of the capital sentencing process in Georgia,[114] is one of the most sophisticated studies conducted to date. It also figured prominently in the Supreme Court's decision in *McCleskey* v. *Kemp*. The second is a study of capital sentencing patterns in eight states,[115] and the third is a study of death sentencing for California homicides during the 1990s.[116] We then discuss recent research on the federal capital sentencing process. We end this section by summarizing the results of a study of race and the probability of execution in the post-*Gregg* period.

Race and the Death Penalty in Georgia   David Baldus and his colleagues analyzed the effect of race on the outcomes of more than 600 homicide cases in Georgia from 1973 through 1979.[117] Their examination of the raw data revealed that the likelihood of receiving a death sentence varied by both the race of the offender and the race of the victim. The first column of Table 8.4 shows that 35 percent of the African Americans charged with killing whites were sentenced to death, compared with only 22 percent of the whites who killed whites, 14 percent of the whites who killed African Americans, and 6 percent of the African Americans who killed other African Americans.

Baldus and his co-authors also discovered that the race of the victim played an important role in both the prosecutor's decision to seek the death penalty and the jury's decision to impose the death penalty (see columns 2 and 3, Table 8.4). The victim's race was a particularly strong predictor of the prosecutor's decision to seek or waive the death penalty. In fact, Georgia prosecutors were nearly four times more likely to request the death penalty for African American offenders convicted of killing whites than for African American offenders convicted of killing African Americans. The effect of the race of the victim was less pronounced when the offender was white; prosecutors sought the death penalty in 38 percent of the cases with white offenders and white victims but only 21 percent of the cases with white offenders and black victims.

T A B L E 8.4   Death Penalty Decisions in Post-*Gregg* Georgia

	Overall Death Sentencing Rate	Prosecutor's Decision To Seek Death Penalty	Jury's Decision To Impose Death Penalty
Offender and Victim Race			
Black / White	.35 (45/130)	.58 (72/125)	.58 (45/77)
White / White	.22 (51/230)	.38 (85/224)	.56 (51/91)
Black / Black	.06 (17/232)	.15 (34/231)	.40 (14/35)
White / Black	.14 (2/14)	.21 (3/14)	.67 (2/3)

SOURCE: David C. Baldus, George G. Woodworth, and Charles A. Pulaski, Jr., *Equal Justice and the Death Penalty* (Boston Northeastern University Press, 1990), Tables 30 and 34.

The authors of this study then controlled for more than 200 variables that might explain these disparities; they included detailed information on the defendant's background and prior criminal record, information concerning the circumstances and the heinousness of the crime, and measures of the strength of evidence against the defendant. They found that inclusion of these controls did not eliminate the racial differences. Although the race of the offender was only a weak predictor of death penalty decisions once these legal factors were taken into consideration, the race of the victim continued to exert a strong effect on both the prosecutor's decision to seek the death penalty and the jury's decision to impose the death penalty. In fact those who killed whites were more than four times as likely to be sentenced to death as those who killed African Americans.

Further analysis revealed that the effects of race were not uniform across the range of homicide cases included in the analysis. Not surprisingly, race had little effect on decision making in the least aggravated cases, in which virtually no one received the death penalty, or in the most heinous cases, in which a high percentage of murderers, regardless of their race or the race of their victims, were sentenced to death. Rather, race played a role primarily in the mid-range of cases where decision makers could decide either to sentence the offender to life in prison or impose the death penalty. In these types of cases, the death-sentencing rate for those who killed whites was 34 percent compared with only 14 percent for those who killed African Americans.

These findings led Baldus and his colleagues to conclude that the race of the victim was "a potent influence in the system"[118] and that the state of Georgia was operating a "dual system" for processing homicide cases. According to the authors, "Georgia juries appear to tolerate greater levels of aggravation without imposing the death penalty in black victim cases; and, as compared to white victim cases, the level of aggravation in black victim cases must be substantially greater before the prosecutor will even seek a death sentence."[119]

Anthony Amsterdam's[120] analysis was even blunter. Noting that 9 of the 11 murderers executed in Georgia between 1973 and 1988 were African American and that 10 of the 11 had killed white victims, Amsterdam asked, "Can there be the slightest doubt that this revolting record is the product of some sort of racial bias rather than a pure fluke?"[121]

Some commentators would be inclined to answer this question in the affirmative. They would argue that the statistics included in the Baldus study are not representative of death penalty decisions in the United States as a whole; rather, they are peculiar to southern states such as Georgia, Texas, Florida, and Mississippi. A study by Samuel R. Gross and Robert Mauro addressed this possibility.

Death Penalty Decisions in Eight States   Gross and Mauro examined death penalty decisions in the post-*Gregg* era (1976 to 1980) in eight states—Arkansas, Florida, Georgia, Illinois, Mississippi, North Carolina, Oklahoma, and Virginia.[122] They found that the risk of a death sentence was much lower for defendants charged with killing African Americans than for defendants charged with killing whites in each of the eight states included in their study. In Georgia and Mississippi, for example, those who killed whites were nearly 10 times as likely to be sentenced to death as those who killed African Americans. The ratios for the other states included in the study were 8:1 (Florida), 7:1 (Arkansas), 6:1 (Illinois, Oklahoma, and North Carolina), and 5:1 (Virginia).

The authors also discovered that African Americans who killed whites faced the greatest odds of a death sentence. Figure 8.4 presents the percentages of death sentences by race of suspect and race of victim for the three states with the largest number of death-eligible cases. In Georgia, 20.1 percent of the African Americans who killed whites were sentenced to death, compared with only 5.7 percent of the whites who killed whites, 2.9 percent of the whites who killed African Americans, and less than 1 percent (0.8 percent) of the African Americans who killed African Americans. There were similar disparities in Florida and Illinois. In fact, in these three states only 32 of the 4,731 cases with African American defendants and African American victims resulted in a death sentence, compared with 82 of the 621 cases involving African American defendants and white victims.

These racial disparities did not disappear when Gross and Mauro controlled for other legally relevant predictors of sentence severity. According to the authors,

> The major factual finding of this study is simple: there has been racial discrimination in the imposition of the death penalty under post-*Furman* statutes in the eight states that we examined. The discrimination is based on the race of the victim, and it is a remarkably stable and consistent phenomenon.... The data show "a clear pattern, unexplainable on grounds other than race."[123]

Like the Baldus study, then, this study of the capital sentencing process in eight states showed that the race of the victim was a powerful predictor of death sentences.

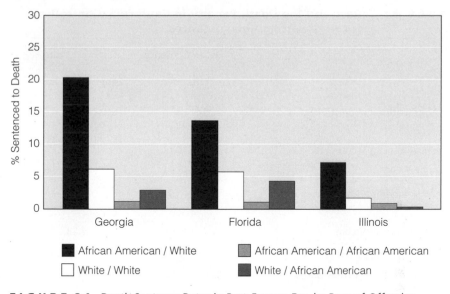

FIGURE 8.4 Death Sentence Rates in Post-*Furman* Era, by Race of Offender and Victim

SOURCE: Data obtained from Samuel R. Gross and Robert Mauro, *Death and Discrimination: Racial Disparities in Capital Sentencing* (Boston: Northeastern University Press, 1989).

Race and the Death Penalty in California The two studies described previously provide compelling evidence of victim-based racial discrimination in the use of the death penalty in the years immediately following the *Gregg* decision. Recent research in states such as Maryland,[124] North Carolina,[125] Virginia,[126] Ohio,[127] and California[128] provides equally compelling evidence of racial disparities in the capital sentencing process during the 1990s and early 2000s.

Research conducted in California illustrates this more recent trend. In 2005 California had the largest death row population in the United States, with 648 inmates under sentence of death.[129] Of those inmates on death row, 39 percent were white, 36 percent were African American, 20 percent were Hispanic, 3 percent were Asian, and 2 percent were Native American.

To determine whether these figures reflected racial/ethnic bias in the imposition of the death penalty in California, Pierce and Radelet examined the characteristics of all offenders sentenced to death in the state from 1990 through 2003 (for homicides committed from 1990 to 1999). They found that offenders who killed whites were 3.7 times more likely to be sentenced to death than offenders who killed African Americans; those who killed whites were 4.7 times more likely to be sentenced to death than those who killed Hispanics.[130] To address the possibility that these differences were because the murders of whites were more aggravated or more heinous than the murders of nonwhites, the authors divided the homicides in their sample into three categories: those with no aggravating circumstances, those with one aggravating circumstance, and those with two aggravating circumstances. As the authors noted, "If homicides that victimize

T A B L E 8.5   Race and the Death Penalty in California, Controlling for Aggravating Circumstances

	Death Sentence Rate per 100 Offenders	Ratio of White Victim Rate / Other Victim Rate
No Aggravating Circumstances		
White Victim	0.775	—
African American Victim	0.102	7.60
Hispanic Victim	0.070	11.07
One Aggravating Circumstance		
White Victim	4.560	—
African American Victim	1.999	2.28
Hispanic Victim	1.583	2.88
Two Aggravating Circumstances		
White Victim	24.286	—
African American Victim	12.162	2.00
Hispanic Victim	14.773	1.64

SOURCE: Glenn L. Pierce and Michael L. Radelet, "The Impact of Legally Inappropriate Factors on Death Sentencing for California Homicides, 1990–1999," *Santa Clara Law Review* 46 (2005), Table 6.

whites are indeed more aggravated than other homicides, death sentencing rates will be similar across each category of victim's race/ethnicity for each level of aggression."[131]

The results presented in Table 8.5 do not support the hypothesis that those who kill whites are sentenced to death more often because their crimes are more heinous. Although the death sentencing rate increased for each of the three groups as the number of aggravating circumstances increased, for each level of aggravation, those who killed whites were substantially more likely than those who killed African Americans or Hispanics to be sentenced to death. These findings were confirmed by the results of a multivariate analysis, which simultaneously controlled for the number of aggravating circumstances, the race/ethnicity of the victim, and the population density and racial makeup of the county in which the crime occurred. The authors found that those who killed African Americans or Hispanics were significantly less likely than those who killed whites to be sentenced to death. They concluded that "the data clearly show that the race and ethnicity of homicide victims is associated with the imposition of the death penalty."[132]

Race and the Probability of Execution   The research discussed thus far focused on the likelihood that a defendant would be charged with a capital crime and, if so, the probability of a death sentence. In an article entitled, "Who Survives on Death Row?" David Jacobs and his colleagues addressed a different question—that is, what factors affect whether an offender who has been sentenced to death will be executed?[133]

This is an important question, given that only about 10 percent of offenders on death row ultimately are executed. Most death-sentenced offenders eventually are resentenced to life in prison or some other sentence as a result of a successful appeal, are pardoned as a result of a clemency proceeding, are freed as a result of evidence of their innocence, or die of natural causes while on death row. Yet there is very little research designed to identify the individual and contextual factors that determine who, among all those sentenced to death, ultimately will be executed. As Jacobs and his colleagues noted, "whether victim race continues to explain the fate of condemned prisoners after they have been sentenced remains a complete mystery."[134]

The authors of this study used data on offenders sentenced to death from 1973 to 2002 to examine the ways in which "offender attributes and the political and social context of the states affect post-sentencing execution likelihood." When they examined the characteristics of those who were executed, they found that 55.5 percent were white, 34.9 percent were African American, and 9.7 percent were Hispanic; among cases for which the race of the victim was known, 80.3 percent of the offenders who were executed had white victims and only 19.7 percent had nonwhite victims.[135]

The results of the authors' multivariate analysis revealed that African Americans who killed whites had significantly greater odds of execution than did other death-sentenced offenders and that Hispanics also faced a somewhat higher probability of execution if their victims were white. The authors concluded that "the post-sentencing capital punishment process continues to place greater value on white lives," and that "despite efforts to transcend an unfortunate racial past, residues of this fierce discrimination evidently still linger, at least when the most morally critical decision about punishment is decided."[136]

Race and the Death Penalty in the Post-*Gregg* Era   The results of the death penalty studies conducted in the post-*Gregg* era provide compelling evidence that the issues raised by the Supreme Court in *Furman* have not been resolved. The Supreme Court's assurances in *Gregg* notwithstanding, racial discrimination in the capital sentencing process did not disappear as a result of the guided-discretion statutes enacted in the wake of the *Furman* decision. Methodologically sophisticated studies conducted in southern and nonsouthern jurisdictions, and in the 1990s as well as the 1970s and 1980s, consistently conclude that the race of the victim affects death sentencing decisions. Many of these studies also conclude that the race of the defendant, or the racial makeup of the offender/victim pair, influences the capital sentencing process.

According to Austin Sarat, professor of jurisprudence and political science at Amherst College, "the post-*Furman* effort to rationalize death sentences has utterly failed; it has been replaced by a policy that favors execution while trimming away procedural protection for capital defendants. This situation only exacerbates the incompatibility of capital punishment and legality."[137] Scott W. Howe, a professor of criminal law at Chapman University School for Law,

similarly contends that widespread evidence of racial disparity in capital sentencing undermines "confidence in the neutrality of capital selection nationwide....
The studies, considered as a group, imply racial discrimination."[138] (See Box 8.6
for a discussion of the effect of the race and gender of the victim on the capital
sentencing process.)

Race and the Federal Capital Sentencing Process

As noted earlier, state legislatures moved quickly to revise their death penalty
statutes in the wake of the 1972 *Furman* decision. The federal government, however, did not do so until 1988, when passage of the Anti-Drug Abuse Act made
the death penalty available for certain serious drug-related offenses. The number

---

**B o x   8.6   The Death Penalty and the Race and Gender of the Victim:
Are Those Who Kill White Women Singled Out for
Harsher Treatment?**

Research on the application of the death penalty reveals that those who kill whites
are more likely than those who kill African Americans to be sentenced to death.
There also is evidence that those who kill females are more likely than those who kill
males to receive the death penalty. This raises the question, Are those who kill white
women sentenced to death at a disproportionately high rate?

    To answer this question, Marian R. Williams and Jefferson E. Holcomb analyzed
data on homicides in Ohio for the years 1981 to 1994.[139] When they looked at the
raw data, they found that white females made up only 15 percent of all homicide
victims but 35 percent of all death sentences. Cases in which the offender was a
white male and the victim was a white female made up 12 percent of all homicides
but 28 percent of all death sentences; cases in which the offender was an African
American male and the victim was a white female made up 2 percent of homicide
cases but 8 percent of death sentences.[140]

    Multivariate analysis confirmed these findings. The authors controlled for the
race, gender, and age of the victim and the offender; whether a gun was used;
whether the victim and offender were strangers; whether the homicide involved
another felony or multiple victims; and the location of the crime. They found that
homicides with female victims were more than twice as likely as those with male victims to result in a death sentence, and that homicides with white victims were about
one and a half times more likely as those with African American victims to result in a
death sentence. Further analysis revealed that offenders who victimized white
females had significantly higher odds of being sentenced to death than offenders
who victimized African American females, African American males, or white males.[141]

    Williams and Holcomb concluded that the results of their study, which they
acknowledged provided only a preliminary test of their hypothesis, suggested "that
the central factor in understanding existing racial disparity in death sentences may be
the severity with which those who kill White females are treated relative to other
gender-race victim combinations."[142] This suggests that criminal justice officials and
jurors who make death penalty decisions believe that homicides involving white
women are especially heinous and that those people who kill white women are
therefore more deserving of death sentences than those who kill men or women
of color.

of federal offenses for which the death penalty is an option increased substantially as a result of legislation passed during the mid-1990s. The Federal Death Penalty Act of 1994 added over 40 federal offenses to the list of capital crimes, and the Antiterrorism and Effective Death Penalty Act of 1996 added an additional four offenses.[143]

The Department of Justice has adopted a set of standards and procedures—commonly known as the "death penalty protocol"—to govern death penalty decisions in federal cases. According to this protocol, a U.S. attorney cannot seek the death penalty without prior written authorization from the attorney general. The steps in the capital case review process are as follows:[144]

- U.S. attorneys are required to submit all cases involving a charge for which the death penalty is a legally authorized sanction, regardless of whether the attorney recommends seeking the death penalty, to the Capital Case Unit of the Criminal Division for review.

- The Capital Case Unit reviews the case and prepares an initial analysis and recommendation regarding the death penalty.

- The case is forwarded to the attorney general's Capital Case Review Committee, which is composed of senior U.S. Justice Department lawyers—the members of the committee meet with the U.S. attorney and defense counsel responsible for the case, review documents submitted by all parties, and make a recommendation to the attorney general.

- The attorney general makes the final decision regarding whether to seek the death penalty.

According to the U.S. Department of Justice, these procedures are designed to ensure that the federal capital sentencing process is fair and equitable: "Both the legal rules and the administrative procedures that currently govern federal capital cases incorporate extensive safeguards against any influence of racial or ethnic bias or prejudice."[145]

The U.S. Department of Justice has conducted two studies of the federal capital sentencing process. The first study, which was released in 2000, revealed that from 1995 to 2000, U.S. attorneys forwarded for review 682 death-eligible cases. Eighty percent of the defendants in these cases were racial minorities: 324 (48 percent) were African American; 195 (29 percent) were Hispanic; and 29 (4 percent) were Native American, Asian, and other races.[146] This study also revealed, however, that participants in the review process were less likely to recommend (or to seek) the death penalty if the defendant was a racial minority. As shown in Table 8.6, U.S. attorneys recommended the death penalty in 36 percent of the cases involving white defendants, compared with 25 percent of those involving African American defendants and 20 percent of those involving Hispanic defendants. There was a similar pattern of results for the Capital Case Unit's recommendation (to the attorney general) to request the death penalty, the attorney general's decision to authorize the U.S. attorney to file a notice of intent to seek the death penalty, and the U.S. Department of Justice's final decision to seek the death penalty.

T A B L E 8.6   Race/Ethnicity and the Federal Death Penalty: 1995–2000

		Race of the Defendant			
	Total	White	African American	Hispanic	Other
Number (% of total) of cases submitted for review	682	134 (20%)	324 (48%)	195 (29%)	29 (4%)
Rate at which U.S. attorneys recommended seeking the death penalty	.27	.36	.25	.20	.52
Rate at which the Review Committee recommended seeking the death penalty	.30	.40	.27	.25	.50
Rate at which the attorney general approved filing of notice of intent to seek the death penalty	.27	.38	.25	.20	.46
Rate at which the U.S. Department of Justice sought the death penalty	.23	.33	.22	.16	.41

SOURCE: U.S. Department of Justice, *The Federal Death Penalty System: A Statistical Survey (1988–2000)*. (Washington, DC: U.S. Department of Justice), pp. 10–11.

The data presented in Table 8.6 demonstrate that although the U.S. Justice Department's study did not find racial bias in the decisions that followed the U.S. attorney's initial decision to submit the case for review, it did find that a significant majority of the cases that were submitted for review involved African American and Hispanic defendants. The attorney general at the time, Janet Reno, stated that she was "sorely troubled" by these findings, adding that "we must do all we can in the federal government to root out bias at every step." Reno's concerns were echoed by then-Deputy Attorney General of the United States (and now Attorney General of the United States) Eric Holder, an African American prosecutor who oversaw the study. He said that he was "both personally and professionally disturbed by the numbers."[147] Publication of the report also led President Clinton to grant a six-month reprieve to Juan Raul Garza, a Mexican American from Texas who was scheduled to be executed in January of 2001. In granting the reprieve, Clinton stated that "the examination of possible racial and regional bias should be completed before the United States goes forward with an execution in a case that may implicate the very questions raised by the Justice Department's continuing study."[148]

Attorney General Reno ordered the Department of Justice to gather additional data about the federal capital sentencing process. The results of this study, which was overseen by Janet Reno's successor, John Ashcroft, were released in 2001.[149] Unlike the first study, which examined only those cases that were charged as capital crimes and submitted for review, this study included an analysis of cases in which the facts would have supported a capital charge but the defendants were not charged with a capital crime (and thus the case was not submitted for review). The results of the second study were generally similar to those of the first. Within the larger pool of cases examined in the follow-up study, which included 973 defendants, 17 percent (166) were white, 42 percent (408) were African American, and 36 percent (350) were Hispanic. Consistent with the results of the 2000 study, "potential capital cases involving Black or Hispanic defendants were less likely to result in capital charges and submission of the case to the review procedure ... likewise [these cases] were less likely to result in decisions to seek the death penalty."[150]

The 2001 report, which noted that the proportion of racial minorities in federal capital cases was substantially greater than the proportion of racial minorities in the general population, concluded that "the cause of this disproportion is not racial or ethnic bias, but the representation of minorities in the pool of potential federal capital cases."[151] The report attributed the overrepresentation of African Americans and Hispanics in the federal capital case pool to a number of factors, including the fact that federal law enforcement officers focused their attention on drug trafficking and related criminal violence. According to the report,

> In areas where large-scale, organized drug trafficking is largely carried out by gangs whose memberships is drawn from minority groups, the active federal role in investigating and prosecuting these crimes results in a high proportion of minority defendants in federal cases, including a high proportion of minority defendants in potential capital cases arising from the lethal violence associated with the drug trade. This is not the result of any form of bias, but reflects the normal factors that affect the division of federal and state prosecutorial responsibility.[152]

Opponents of the death penalty criticized the 2001 report, and the Justice Department's interpretation of the data, on a number of grounds. The American Civil Liberties Union (ACLU), for example, asserted that there were a number of problems with the study, which it characterized as "fatally flawed."[153] The ACLU noted that the report did not address questions regarding the prosecution of cases in the federal system rather than the state system or examine whether race/ethnicity played a role in these decisions or in U.S. attorneys' decisions to enter into plea bargains. The ACLU asserted that Attorney General Ashcroft reached a "premature" conclusion that "racial bias has not played a role in who is on federal death row in America," adding that "This remarkable conclusion is not only inaccurate, but also dangerous, because it seeks to give Americans the impression that our justice system is fair when in fact there is substantial evidence that it is not."[154]

On June 11, 2001, Timothy McVeigh, who was convicted of a number of counts stemming from the 1995 Oklahoma City bombing, became the first federal offender since 1963 to be put to death. The execution of Juan Raul Garza, a Texas marijuana distributor who was sentenced to death in 1993 for the murder of three other drug traffickers, followed eight days later. A third federal offender, Louis Jones, who was sentenced to death for kidnapping and murdering a white female soldier, was executed in March of 2003. By October of 2010 there were

60 offenders on federal death row: 27 were African American, 24 were white, 8 were Hispanic, and 1 was Native American.[155]

Explanations for Disparate Treatment

Researchers have advanced two interrelated explanations for the higher death penalty rates for homicides involving African American offenders and white victims and the lower rates for homicides involving African American offenders and African American victims.

The first explanation builds on conflict theory's premise that the law is applied to maintain the power of the dominant group and to control the behavior of individuals who threaten that power.[156] It suggests that crimes involving African American offenders and white victims are punished most harshly because they pose the greatest threat to "the system of racially stratified state authority."[157] Some commentators further suggest that in the South the death penalty may be imposed more often on African Americans who kill whites "because of a continuing adherence to traditional southern norms of racial etiquette."[158]

The second explanation for the harsher penalties imposed on those who victimize whites emphasizes the race of the victim rather than the racial composition of the victim–offender dyad. This explanation suggests that crimes involving African American victims are not taken seriously and/or that crimes involving white victims are taken very seriously. It also suggests that the lives of African American victims are devalued relative to the lives of white victims. Thus, crimes against whites will be punished more severely than crimes against African Americans regardless of the offender's race. Some commentators suggest that these beliefs are encouraged by the media, which plays up the murders of wealthy whites but ignores those involving poor African Americans and Hispanics. The publicity accorded crimes involving middle-class and wealthy white victims also influences prosecutors to seek the death penalty more often in these types of cases than in cases involving poor racial minorities. According to David Baldus, "If the victim is black, particularly if he's an unsavory character, a drug dealer, for example, prosecutors are likely to say, 'No jury would return a death verdict.'"[159]

Most researchers have failed to explain adequately *why* those who victimize whites are treated more harshly than those who victimize African Americans. Gross and Mauro[160] suggest that the explanation, at least in capital cases, may hinge on the degree to which jurors are able to identify with the victim. The authors argue that jurors take the life-or-death decision in a capital case very seriously. To condemn a murderer to death thus requires something more than sympathy for the victim. Jurors will not sentence the defendant to death unless they are particularly horrified by the crime, and they will not be particularly horrified by the crime unless they can identify or empathize with the victim. According to Gross and Mauro:

> In a society that remains segregated socially if not legally, and in which the great majority of jurors are white, jurors are not likely to identify

with black victims or to see them as family or friends. Thus jurors are more likely to be horrified by the killing of a white than of a black, and more likely to act against the killer of a white than the killer of a black.[161]

Bright[162] offers a somewhat different explanation. He contends that the unconscious racism and racial stereotypes of prosecutors, judges, and jurors, the majority of whom are white, "may well be 'stirred up'" in cases involving an African American offender and a white victim.[163] In these types of cases, in other words, officials' and jurors' beliefs that African Americans are violent or morally inferior, coupled with their fear of African Americans, might incline them to seek or to impose the death penalty. Bright also asserts that black-on-white murders generate more publicity and evoke greater horror than other types of crimes. As he notes, "Community outrage, … the social and political clout of the family in the community, and the amount of publicity regarding the crime are often far more important in determining whether death is sought than the facts of the crime or the defendant's record and background."[164]

McCLESKY v. *KEMP:* THE SUPREME COURT AND RACIAL DISCRIMINATION IN THE APPLICATION OF THE DEATH PENALTY

Empirical evidence of racial discrimination in the capital sentencing process has been used to mount constitutional challenges to the imposition of the death penalty. African American defendants convicted of raping or murdering whites have claimed that the death penalty is applied in a racially discriminatory manner in violation of both the equal protection clause of the Fourteenth Amendment and the cruel and unusual punishment clause of the Eighth Amendment.

These claims have been consistently rejected by state and federal appellate courts. The case of the Martinsville Seven, a group of African American men who were sentenced to death for the gang rape of a white woman, was the first case in which defendants explicitly argued that the death penalty was administered in a racially discriminatory manner.[165] It also was the first case in which lawyers presented statistical evidence to prove systematic racial discrimination in capital cases. As explained in more detail in "In the Courts: The Case of the Martinsville Seven," the defendants' contention that the Virginia rape statute had "been applied and administered with an evil eye and an unequal hand"[166] was repeatedly denied by Virginia appellate courts.

The question of racial discrimination in the application of the death penalty also has been addressed in federal court. In a series of decisions, the U.S. Court of Appeals ruled, first, that the empirical studies used to document systematic racial discrimination did not take every variable related to capital sentencing into account and, second, that the evidence presented did not demonstrate that the appellant's *own* sentence was the product of discrimination.[167]

In the Courts: The Case of the Martinsville Seven

Just after dark on January 8, 1949, Ruby Floyd, a 32-year-old white woman, was assaulted and repeatedly raped by several men as she walked in a predominately black neighborhood in Martinsville, Virginia.[168] Within a day and a half, seven African American men had been arrested; when confronted with incriminating statements made by their co-defendants, all of them confessed. Two months later, a grand jury composed of four white men and three African American men indicted each defendant on one count of rape and six counts of aiding and abetting a rape by the other defendants.

The defendants were tried in the Seventh Judicial Circuit Court, located in Martinsville. Before the legal proceedings began, Judge Kennon Caithness Whittle, who presided over all of the trials, called the prosecutors and defense attorneys into his chambers to remind them of their duty to protect the defendants' right to a fair trial and to plead with them to "downplay the racial overtones" of the case. He emphasized that the case "must be tried as though both parties were members of the same race."[169]

Although prosecutors took Judge Whittle's admonitions to heart and emphasized the seriousness of the crime and the defendants' evident guilt rather than the fact that the crime involved the rape of a white woman by African American men, the "racial overtones" of the case inevitably surfaced. Defense attorneys, for example, moved for a change of venue, arguing that inflammatory publicity about the case, coupled with widespread community sentiment that the defendants were guilty and "ought to get the works,"[170] meant that the defendants could not get a fair trial in Martinsville. Judge Whittle, who admitted that it might be difficult to find impartial jurors and acknowledged that some jurors might be biased against the defendants because of their race, denied the motion, asserting that "no mass feeling about these defendants"[171] had surfaced. Later, prosecutors used their peremptory challenges to exclude the few African Americans who remained in the jury pool after those who opposed the death penalty had been excused for cause. As a result, each case was decided by an all-white jury. The result of each day-long trial was the same: all seven defendants were found guilty of rape and sentenced to death. On May 3, 1949, less than four months after the assault on Ruby Floyd, Judge Whittle officially pronounced sentence and announced that four of the defendants were to be executed on July 15, the remaining three on July 22. Noting that this gave the defendants more than 60 days to appeal, he stated, "If errors have been made I pray God they may be corrected."[172]

The next 19 months witnessed several rounds of appeals challenging the convictions and death sentences of the Martinsville Seven. The initial petition submitted by attorneys for the NAACP Legal Defense Fund, which represented the defendants on appeal, charged the trial court with four violations of due process. Although none of the charges focused directly on racially discriminatory practices, allegations of racial prejudice were interwoven with a number of the arguments. Appellants noted, for example, that prior to 1866 Virginia law specified that the death penalty for rape

---

The Supreme Court directly addressed the issue of victim–based racial discrimination in the application of the death penalty in the case of *McCleskey* v. *Kemp*.[179] Warren McCleskey, an African American, was convicted and sentenced to death in Georgia for killing a white police officer during the course of an armed robbery. McCleskey claimed that the Georgia capital sentencing process was administered in a racially discriminatory manner. In support of his claim, he

could be imposed only on African American men convicted of raping white women and that even after the law was repealed virtually all of those sentenced to death for rape had been African American. They also stated that the trial judge's questioning of prospective jurors about capital punishment and subsequent exclusion of those who were opposed to the imposition of the death penalty sent the unmistakable message that "only one penalty would be appropriate for the offenders."[173]

These appeals failed at both the state and federal level. The Virginia Supreme Court of Appeals voted unanimously to affirm the convictions. Chief Justice Edward W. Hudgins, who wrote the opinion, vehemently denied appellants' assertions that the death penalty was reserved for blacks, noting that there was not "a scintilla of evidence" to support it.[174] Hudgins also chastised the defendants' attorneys for even raising the issue, contending that it was nothing more than "an abortive attempt to inject into the proceedings racial prejudice."[175]

The defendants appealed the decision to the U.S. Supreme Court, but the Court declined to review the case. This prompted the NAACP attorneys to adopt a radically different strategy for the next round of appeals. Rather than challenging the defendants' convictions and death sentences on traditional due process grounds, the attorneys mounted a direct attack on the discriminatory application of the death penalty in Virginia. Martin Martin and Samuel Tucker, the NAACP attorneys who argued in support of the defendants' *habeas corpus* petition, presented statistical evidence documenting a double standard of justice in Virginia rape cases. Noting that 45 African Americans, but not a single white, had been executed for rape since 1908, Tucker stated that African Americans were entitled to the same protection of the law as whites and concluded "if you can't equalize upward [by executing more whites], we must equalize downward."[176]

In an opinion that foreshadowed the Supreme Court's decision in *McCleskey* v. *Kemp* a quarter of a century later, Judge Doubles, who was presiding over the Hustings Court of the City of Richmond, denied the petition. Judge Doubles stated that there was no evidence of racial discrimination in the actions of the six juries that sentenced the Martinsville Seven to death or in the performance of other juries in similar cases. He then concluded that even if one assumed that those juries had been motivated by racial prejudice, "the petitioners could not demonstrate that an official policy of discrimination, rather than the independent actions of separate juries, resulted in the death verdicts."[177] As a result, there was no constitutional violation.

The case then was appealed to the Virginia Supreme Court and, when that appeal failed, to the U.S. Supreme Court. In January of 1951, the Supreme Court again declined to review the case. Last-minute efforts to save the Martinsville Seven failed. Four of the men were executed on February 2, the remaining three on February 5. "After two years, six trials, five stays of execution, ten opportunities for judicial review, and two denials of executive clemency, the legal odyssey of the Martinsville Seven had ended."[178]

offered the results of the study conducted by Baldus and his colleagues.[180] As noted earlier, this study found that African Americans convicted of murdering whites had the greatest likelihood of receiving the death penalty.

The Supreme Court rejected McCleskey's Fourteenth and Eighth Amendment claims. Although the majority accepted the validity of the Baldus study, they nonetheless refused to accept McCleskey's argument that the disparities

documented by Baldus signaled the presence of unconstitutional racial discrimination. Justice Powell, writing for the majority, argued that the disparities were
"unexplained" and stated that "At most, the Baldus study indicates a discrepancy
that appears to correlate with race."[181] The Court stated that the Baldus study
was "clearly insufficient to support an inference that any of the decisionmakers
in McCleskey's case acted with discriminatory purpose."[182]

The Court also expressed its concern that accepting McCleskey's claim
would open a Pandora's box of litigation. "McCleskey's claim, taken to its logical conclusion," Powell wrote, "throws into serious question the principles that
underlie our entire criminal justice system ... if we accepted McCleskey's claim
that racial bias impermissibly tainted the capital sentencing decision, we would
soon be faced with similar claims as to other types of penalty."[183] A ruling in
McCleskey's favor, in other words, would open the door to constitutional challenges to the legitimacy not only of the capital sentencing process but also of
sentencing in general.

The four dissenting justices were outraged. Justice Brennan, who was joined
in dissent by Justices Blackmun, Marshall, and Stevens, wrote, "The Court today
holds that Warren McCleskey's sentence was constitutionally imposed. It finds
no fault with a system in which lawyers must tell their clients that race casts a
large shadow on the capital sentencing process." Brennan also characterized the
majority's concern that upholding McCleskey's claim would encourage other
groups—"even women"[184]—to challenge the criminal sentencing process "as a
fear of too much justice" and "a complete abdication of our judicial role."[185]

Legal scholars were similarly outraged. Anthony Amsterdam, who was the
lead attorney in a 1968 U.S. Court of Appeals case in which an African American
man challenged his death sentence for the rape of a white woman,[186] wrote,

> I suggest that any self-respecting criminal justice professional is obliged
> to speak out against this Supreme Court's conception of the criminal
> justice system. We must reaffirm that there can be no justice in a system
> which treats people of color differently from white people, or treats
> crimes against people of color differently from crimes against white
> people.[187]

Randall Kennedy's analysis was similarly harsh. He challenged Justice
Powell's assertion that the Baldus study indicated nothing more "than a discrepancy that appears to correlate with race," which he characterized as "a statement
as vacuous as one declaring, say, that 'at most' studies on lung cancer indicate a
discrepancy that appears to correlate with smoking."[188] Bright characterized the
decision as "a badge of shame upon America's system of justice,"[189] while Gross
and Mauro concluded that "The central message of the *McCleskey* case is all too
plain; de facto racial discrimination in capital sentencing is legal in the United
States."[190] (See Box 8.7 for a discussion of the possible remedies for racial discrimination in the application of the death penalty.)

**B o x   8.7   Racial Discrimination in Capital Sentencing: The Problem
of Remedy**

A number of commentators have suggested that the Court's reluctance to accept
McCleskey's claim reflected its anxiety about the practical consequences of ruling
that race impermissibly affected the capital sentencing process.[191] The Court's decision, in other words, reflected its concern about the appropriate remedy if it found a
constitutional violation.

The remedies that have been suggested include the following:

1. Abolish the death penalty and vacate all existing death sentences nationwide.
   - The problem with this remedy, of course, is that it is impractical, given the
     level of public support for the death penalty and the current emphasis on
     crime control. As Gross and Mauro note "Although abolition is a perfectly
     practical solution to the problems of capital punishment … it is not a seri-
     ous option in America now."[192]

2. Vacate all death sentences in each state where there is compelling evidence of
   racial disparities in the application of the death penalty.
   - Although this state-by-state approach would not completely satisfy the
     abolitionists, according to Kennedy, it would place "a large question mark
     over the legitimacy of any death penalty system generating unexplained
     racial disparities of the sort at issue in *McCleskey*.[193]

3. Limit the class of persons eligible for the death penalty to those who commit
   the most heinous, the most aggravated homicides. As Justice Stevens suggested in his dissent in *McCleskey*, the Court could narrow the class of death-
   eligible defendants to those "categories of extremely serious crimes for
   which prosecutors consistently seek, and juries consistently impose, the death
   penalty without regard to the race of the victim or the race of the
   offender."[194]
   - Although not an "ideal" solution for a number of reasons, this would,
     as Baldus and his colleagues contend, impart "a greater degree of rational-
     ity and consistency into state death-sentencing systems than any of the
     other procedural safeguards that the Supreme Court has heretofore
     endorsed."[195]

4. Reinstate mandatory death sentences for certain crimes.
   - This remedy would, of course, require the Supreme Court to retract its
     invalidation of mandatory death penalty statutes.
   - Kennedy contends that this would not solve the problem, since prosecutors
     could refuse to charge the killers of African Americans with a capital crime
     and juries could decline to convict those who killed African Americans of
     crimes that triggered the mandatory death sentence.[196]

5. Opt for the "level-up solution,"[197] which would require courts to purposely
   impose more death sentences on those who murdered African Americans.
   - According to Kennedy, states in which there are documented racial
     disparities in the use of the death penalty could be given a choice:
     either condemn those who kill African Americans to death at the same
     rate as those who kill whites or "relinquish the power to put anyone to
     death."[198]

The Execution of Warren McCleskey   The Court's decision in *McCleskey* v. *Kemp* did not mark the end of Warren McCleskey's odyssey through the appellate courts. He filed another appeal in 1987, alleging that the testimony of a jailhouse informant, which was used to rebut his alibi defense, was obtained illegally. Offie Evans testified at McCleskey's trial in 1978 that McCleskey admitted to and boasted about killing the police officer. McCleskey argued that the state placed Evans in the jail cell next to his and instructed Evans to try to get him to talk about the crime. He contended that because he did not have the assistance of counsel at the time he made the incriminating statements, they could not be used against him.

In 1991 the Supreme Court denied McCleskey's claim, asserting that the issue should have been raised in his first appeal.[199] The Court stated that McCleskey would have been allowed to raise a new issue if he had been able to demonstrate that the alleged violation resulted in the conviction of an innocent person. However, according to the Court, "the violation, if it be one, resulted in the admission at trial of truthful inculpatory evidence which did not affect the reliability of the guilt determination. The very statement that McCleskey now embraces confirms his guilt."[200]

After a series of last-minute appeals, requests for clemency, and requests for commutation were denied, Warren McCleskey was strapped into the electric chair at the state prison in Jacksonville, Georgia. He was pronounced dead at 3:13 A.M., September 26, 1991.

Justice Thurgood Marshall, one of three dissenters from the Supreme Court's decision not to grant a stay of execution, wrote, "In refusing to grant a stay to review fully McCleskey's claims, the court values expediency over human life. Repeatedly denying Warren McCleskey his constitutional rights is unacceptable. Executing him is inexcusable."[201]

The Aftermath of *McCleskey:* Calls for Reform or Abolition of the Death Penalty

Opponents of the death penalty viewed the issues raised in *McCleskey* v. *Kemp* as the only remaining challenge to the constitutionality of the death penalty. They predicted that the Court's decision, which effectively closed the door to similar appeals, would speed up the pace of executions. Data on the number of people executed since 1987 provide support for this. Although only 25 people were executed in 1987, 11 in 1988, 16 in 1989, 23 in 1990, and 14 in 1991, the numbers began to increase in 1992. As shown in Figure 8.5, 31 people were put to death in 1992, and the number of executions reached a post-*McCleskey* high of 98 in 1999. Beginning in 2000 the number of executions began to decline, reaching a low of 37 in 2008.[202]

The increase in executions since 1991 no doubt reflects the impact of two recent Supreme Court decisions sharply limiting death-row appeals. As noted above, in 1991 the Court ruled that with few exceptions death row inmates and other state prisoners must raise constitutional claims on their first appeals.[203]

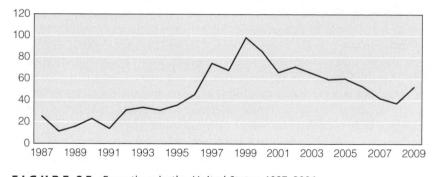

FIGURE 8.5 Executions in the United States, 1987–2004

SOURCE: Death Penalty Information Center, Facts about the Death Penalty. Available at http://www.deathpenaltyinfo. org/documents/FactSheet.pdf.

This ruling, coupled with a 1993 decision stating that "late claims of innocence" raised by death row inmates who have exhausted other federal appeals do not automatically qualify for a hearing in federal court,[204] severely curtailed the ability of death row inmates to pursue multiple federal court appeals.

The Racial Justice Act

The U.S. House of Representatives responded to the Supreme Court's ruling in *McCleskey* v. *Kemp* by adding the Racial Justice Act to the Omnibus Crime Bill of 1994. A slim majority of the House voted for the provision, which would have allowed condemned defendants to challenge their death sentences by showing a *pattern* of racial discrimination in the capital sentencing process in their jurisdictions. Under this provision, in other words, the defendant would not have to show that criminal justice officials acted with discriminatory purpose in his or her case; rather, the defendant could use statistical evidence indicating that a disproportionate number of those sentenced to death in the jurisdiction were African Americans or had killed whites. Once this pattern of racial discrimination had been established, the state would be required to prove that its death penalty decisions were racially neutral. The state might rebut an apparent pattern of racial discrimination in a case involving an African American convicted of killing a white police officer, for example, by showing a consistent pattern of seeking the death penalty for defendants, regardless of race, who were accused of killing police officers.

Opponents of the Racial Justice Act argued that it would effectively abolish the death penalty in the United States. As Senator Orrin Hatch remarked, "The so-called Racial Justice Act has nothing to do with racial justice and everything to do with abolishing the death penalty."[205] The provision was a source of heated debate before it was eventually eliminated from the 1994 Omnibus Crime Bill.

In 1998 Kentucky became the first state to enact a Racial Justice Act. This was followed by the adoption of a similar law in North Carolina in 2009; passage of the North Carolina law was motivated in part by the fact that over a five-year period five African American men on death row were exonerated after having spent a total of 60 years in prison. As of 2010 these are the only states that have adopted such laws.

Both the Kentucky and the North Carolina laws permit the defense to introduce statistical evidence of racial bias in the capital sentencing process. In both states the defense has the burden of proof and the state can rebut the evidence with its own statistical data. A judge determines whether the data prove that the death penalty was sought or imposed on the basis of race.

The North Carolina law allowed defendants who were on death row at the time of the law's adoption to file racial bias claims. By the August 2010 deadline, 152 of the 159 inmates had filed such a claim.[206] Included among those who filed claims was Kenneth Bernard Rouse, an African American who was tried by an all-white jury and sentenced to death for the murder of a 63-year-old white woman. Although Rouse cited these facts in his claim, he also presented more specific

---

B o x 8.8   Death and Discrimination in Texas

On June 5, 2000, the U.S. Supreme Court set aside Victor Saldano's death sentence after lawyers for the state of Texas admitted that the decision had been based in part on the fact that he is Hispanic.[208] Saldano kidnapped Paul Green at gunpoint from a grocery store parking lot, took him to an isolated area, shot him five times, and stole his watch and wallet. At his sentencing hearing, a psychologist testified about Saldano's "future dangerousness." He noted that blacks and Hispanics were overrepresented in prison and stated that the fact that Saldano was Hispanic was an indicator of his future dangerousness. The Texas Court of Criminal Appeals upheld Saldano's death sentence, stating that allowing his ethnicity to be used as an indicator of dangerousness was not a "fundamental error."

In his appeal to the U.S. Supreme Court, Saldano disagreed with that conclusion. He stated that it is "fundamentally unfair for the prosecution to use racial and ethnic stereotypes in order to obtain a death penalty." The Texas Attorney General conceded Saldano's point. He admitted that the state had erred and joined Saldano in asking the Supreme Court to order a new sentencing hearing. After the Court's decision was announced, a spokesperson for the Texas Attorney General's Office stated that an audit had uncovered eight additional cases that might raise similar issues regarding testimony linking race and ethnicity to assessments of future dangerousness.

Questions about the fairness of the Texas death penalty process have been raised in other forums. During the summer of 2000, for example, the *Chicago Tribune* published a two-part series that focused on the 131 executions that were carried out during Texas Governor George W. Bush's tenure.[209] (Since 1977, Texas has executed 218 people, which is more than three times the number executed by any other state.[210]) The report noted that in 40 of the 131 cases the defense attorney either presented no mitigating evidence at all or called only one witness during the sentencing hearing. In 43 of the cases, the defendant was represented by an attorney who had been (or was subsequent to the trial) publicly sanctioned for misconduct by the State Bar of Texas. One attorney, for example, who had been practicing for only 17 months, was appointed to represent Davis Losada, who was accused of rape and murder. Losada was found guilty and sentenced to death after the attorney delivered a "disjointed

evidence of racial bias. His petition claimed that when his lawyer interviewed one of the jurors in his case, the juror used a racial epithet to describe African Americans and said that "Black men rape white women so that they can brag to their friends about having done so."[207] According to Rouse's attorney, "If the Racial Justice Act covers anything, it covers Kenneth Rouse."

THE DEATH PENALTY IN THE
TWENTY-FIRST CENTURY

Opponents of the death penalty assumed that the Supreme Court's decision in *McCleskey* v. *Kemp*, coupled with the defeat of the Racial Justice Act by Congress, sounded a death knell for attempts to abolish the death penalty. They

and brief argument" in which he told the jury: "The System. Justice. I don't know. But that's what y'all are going to do." He later admitted that he had a conflict of interest in the case (he previously had represented the key witness against his client), and in 1994 he was disbarred for stealing money from his clients.

Other problems cited in the *Tribune* report included the use of unreliable evidence, such as testimony by jail-house informants; the use of questionable testimony from a psychiatrist, nicknamed "Dr. Death," regarding the potential dangerousness of capital offenders; and the refusal of the Texas Court of Criminal Appeals to order new trials or sentencing hearings despite allegations of fundamental violations of defendants' rights. The report noted that since Governor Bush took office in 1995, the Court of Criminal Appeals affirmed 270 capital convictions, granted new trials eight times, and ordered new sentencing hearings only six times.

In September of 2000 the Texas Civil Rights Project issued a comprehensive report on "The Death Penalty in Texas" that identified many of the same problems.[211] The authors of the report stated that there were "six areas where the probability of error and the probability of wrongful execution grow dramatically": appointment of counsel to represent indigent defendants; the prosecutor's decision to seek the death penalty; the jury selection process; the sentencing process; the appellate process; and the review of cases by the Board of Pardons and Parole. The report emphasized that the issue was not "a possible break at one juncture, but a probable break at two or more critical junctures." To remedy these deficiencies, the Texas Civil Rights Project recommended that Governor Bush call for a moratorium on the death penalty in Texas. They also recommended that Governor Bush appoint a commission to review the convictions of those currently on death row; the commission would be charged with determining whether the defendant's rights to due process had been violated and whether race and/or social class affected the death penalty process.[212] According to the report, "[i]f the State of Texas is going to continue to take the lives of people, then it needs to repair the system ..." The report concluded that "The frightening truth of the matter is that Texas is at greater risk than at anytime [sic] since it resumed executions in 1982 of killing innocent people."[213]

predicted that these decisions would dampen—if not extinguish—the controversy surrounding the death penalty. Contrary to their predictions, however, the controversy did not die down. In fact a series of events at the turn of the century pushed the issue back on the public agenda:

- In February of 1997 the American Bar Association (ABA) went on record as being formally opposed to the current capital sentencing system and called for an immediate moratorium on executions in the United States. The ABA report cited the following concerns: lack of adequate counsel in death penalty cases; restrictions on access to appellate courts; and racial disparities in the administration of capital punishment.[214]

- In January of 2000 George Ryan, the governor of Illinois, issued a moratorium on the use of the death penalty in that state. His decision was motivated by the fact that since the death penalty was reinstated in Illinois, 12 people were executed but 13 were exonerated. Governor Ryan, who called for a "public dialogue" on "the question of the fairness of the application of the death penalty in Illinois," stated that he favored a moratorium because of his "grave concerns about our state's shameful record of convicting innocent people and putting them on death row."[215] Three years later, Governor Ryan commuted the sentences of all of the state's 167 death row inmates to life in prison. In March of 2011, Illinois Governor Patrick Quinn signed into law a bill repealing the death penalty.

- In May of 2000 the New Hampshire legislature voted to repeal the death penalty. One legislator—a Republican and a longtime supporter of the death penalty—justified his vote for repeal by saying, "There are no millionaires on death row. Can you honestly say that you're going to get equal justice under the law when, if you've got the money, you are going to get away with it."[216] Although the legislation was subsequently vetoed by the governor, it was the first time in more than two decades that a state legislature had voted to repeal the death penalty.

- In October of 2000 the Texas Civil Rights Project (TCRP) released a report on the death penalty in Texas (see Box 8.8: Death and Discrimination in Texas). The report identified six critical issues, including the competency of attorneys appointed to represent defendants charged with capital murder, that "decrease due process for low-income death penalty defendants and increase the probability of wrongful convictions." The report called on then-Governor George Bush to institute a moratorium on the death penalty pending the results of two studies, one of which would determine whether race and social class influenced the use of the death penalty in Texas.[217]

- In 2004 the New York State Court of Appeals ruled that the state's death penalty statute was unconstitutional. Efforts to reinstate the death penalty through legislation were unsuccessful.

- In 2007 New Jersey became the first state in the nation to pass legislation abolishing the death penalty since the use of capital punishment was reinstated by *Gregg* v. *Georgia* in 1976. Two years later, New Mexico also enacted legislation abolishing the death penalty.

▪ In October 2009 the American Law Institute voted to disavow the framework for capital punishment that it had created in 1962 as part of the Model Penal Code, "in light of the current intractable institutional and structural obstacles to ensuring a minimally adequate system for administering capital punishment." A study commissioned by the institute said that experience proved that the goal of individualized decisions about who should be executed and the goal of systemic fairness for minorities and others could not be reconciled.[218]

As these examples illustrate, concerns about the fairness and accuracy of the capital sentencing process led many to conclude that it was time to rethink the death penalty. This period of "rethinking" spawned two distinct movements, one for reform of the capital sentencing process and one for abolishing the death penalty.

The Movement to Reform the Death Penalty

Advocates of reform contend that the capital sentencing process can be "fixed." While acknowledging that the system is not infallible, they argue that the enactment of reforms designed to ensure that innocent persons are not convicted and sentenced to death will remedy the situation. The reforms that have been proposed include increasing access to post-conviction DNA testing and providing funding to pay for DNA tests requested by indigent inmates; banning the execution of the mentally retarded; and establishing standards on qualifications and experience for defense counsel in death penalty cases.

Typical of this approach is the Innocence Protection Act of 2004 (HR 5107), a package of criminal justice reforms that President George W. Bush signed into law on October 30, 2004. The act was part of the larger Justice for All Act, which had broad bipartisan support in the U.S. Senate and House of Representatives; this bill enhanced protection for victims of federal crimes, increased federal resources available to state and local governments to combat crimes with DNA technology, and provided safeguards designed to prevent wrongful convictions and executions. The Innocence Protection Act (Title VI of the Justice for All Act) has three important provisions. The first provision allows a person convicted of a federal crime to obtain DNA testing to support a claim of innocence, prohibits the destruction of DNA evidence in federal criminal cases while a defendant remains incarcerated, and provides funding to states to help defray the costs of post-conviction DNA testing. The second provision authorizes a grant program to improve the quality of legal representation provided to indigent defendants in state capital cases. The third provision increases the maximum amount of damages that can be awarded in cases of unjust imprisonment to $100,000 per year in capital cases.[219]

One of the act's main supporters in the Senate, Patrick Leahy (Democrat from Vermont), characterized the Innocence Protection Act as "the most

---

B o x   8.9   The Death Penalty and Wrongful Convictions

Opponents of the death penalty consistently note the possibility that an individual will be sentenced to death for a crime that he or she did not commit. Hugo A. Bedau and Michael L. Radelet[220] have identified 350 cases in which defendants were wrongfully convicted of a homicide for which they could have received the death penalty or of a rape in which the death penalty was imposed. Of those individuals, 139 were sentenced to die; 23 eventually were executed. Another 22 people came within 72 hours of being executed.

These wrongful convictions include a number of people sentenced to death in the post-*Furman* era. In 1987, for example, Walter McMillian, an African American man who was dating a white woman, was charged with the death of an 18-year-old white female store clerk in Alabama. In spite of testimony from a dozen witnesses, who swore he was at home on the day of the murder, and despite the lack of any physical evidence, McMillian was convicted after a one-and-a-half-day trial. His conviction hinged on the testimony of Ralph Myers, a 30-year-old with a long criminal record. The jury recommended life in prison without parole, but the judge hearing the case, citing the "vicious and brutal killing of a young lady in the full flower of adulthood,"[221] sentenced McMillian to death.

Six years later, Myers recanted his testimony. He said he had been pressured by law enforcement officials to accuse McMillian and to testify against him in court. McMillian was freed in March of 1993, after prosecutors conceded that his conviction was based on perjured testimony and that evidence had been withheld from his lawyers. He had spent six years on death row for a crime he did not commit.

A similar fate awaited Rolando Cruz, a Hispanic American who, along with co-defendant Alejandro Hernandez, was convicted of the 1983 kidnapping, rape, and murder of 10-year-old Jeanine Nicarico in DuPage County (Illinois) Circuit Court. Cruz was twice convicted and condemned to death for the crime, but both verdicts were overturned by appellate courts because of procedural errors at trial. He spent nearly 10 years on death row before he was acquitted at a third trial in November 1995. Hernandez also was convicted twice and sentenced to death once before his case was dropped following the acquittal of Cruz.[222]

This case attracted national attention for what many believed was the "railroading" of Cruz and Hernandez. Prosecutors presented no physical evidence or

---

significant step we have taken in many years to improve the quality of justice in this country." Leahy added that DNA testing, which he called the "miracle forensic tool of our lifetimes," had revealed the flaws in the death penalty process. He also stated that the bill's provisions regarding provision of counsel represent "a modest step toward addressing one of the most frequent causes of wrongful convictions in capital cases, the lack of adequate legal counsel."[226]

A similar approach was taken by the bipartisan commission appointed by Illinois Governor George Ryan after he halted executions in January of 2000. The commission's report, which was issued in April of 2002, recommended 85 changes in the capital sentencing process in Illinois. Included were proposals to prohibit the imposition of the death penalty based solely on the testimony of a single eyewitness, a jail–house informant, or an accomplice; videotape interrogations of suspects; establish an independent forensics laboratory; and establish

eyewitness testimony linking the two to the crime but relied almost exclusively on the testimony of jailhouse informants, who stated that the defendants had admitted the crime, and on questionable testimony regarding a dream about the crime that Cruz allegedly described to sheriff's deputies. They also ignored compelling evidence that another man, Brian Dugan, had committed the crime. According to one commentator, "The crime had been 'solved' by cobbling together a shabby case against Rolando Cruz and Alex Hernandez of Aurora and presenting it to a jury that convicted them and sent them to Death Row."[223]

On November 3, 1995, Judge Ronald Mehling, who was presiding at Cruz's third trial, acquitted Cruz of the charges. In a strongly worded address from the bench, Mehling stated that the murder investigation was "sloppy" and that the government's case against Cruz was "riddled with lies and mistakes." He also sharply criticized prosecutors for their handling of the "vision statement" and suggested that investigators had lied about the statement and about other evidence. "What troubles me in this case," Mehling said, "is what the evidence does not show."[224] Cruz was set free that day; Hernandez was released several weeks later.

One year later, a grand jury handed down a 47-count indictment against three of the prosecutors and four of the sheriff's deputies involved in the case. The indictment charged the deputies with repeated acts of perjury and alleged that prosecutors knowingly presented perjured testimony and buried the notes of an interview with Dugan that could have exonerated Cruz.[225] The defendants, dubbed the "DuPage Seven," were acquitted of all charges in 1999. Lawyers for Rolando Cruz, Alejandro Hernandez, and Stephen Buckley (a third defendant who had been charged in the crime) then filed a federal civil rights suit. In October of 2000 the DuPage County State's Attorney agreed to pay the defendants an out-of-court settlement of $3.5 million.

These two cases are not isolated incidents. In April of 2002 Ray Krone, who was convicted and sentenced to death for the murder of a cocktail waitress in 1991, became the 100th former death-row prisoner to be exonerated since 1973. Krone was freed after DNA tests revealed that he was not the killer. In 2005 Derrick Jamison became the 121st death-row inmate to be exonerated. He was freed and all charges were dismissed after it came to light that prosecutors in the case had withheld critical eyewitness statements and other evidence from his attorneys.

a state panel to review prosecutors' decisions to seek the death penalty. The report also proposed eliminating several categories of capital crimes, including murder committed in the course of a felony. The co–chairman of the commission, Thomas P. Sullivan, a former federal prosecutor, stated that the options were to "repair or repeal" the death penalty. "Fix the capital punishment system or abolish it," he said. "There is no other principled recourse."[227]

The Movement to Abolish the Death Penalty

In contrast to those who advocate reform of the capital sentencing system, proponents of abolishing the death penalty contend that the system is fatally flawed. To support their position, these "new abolitionists"[228] cite mounting evidence of wrongful conviction of those on death row (see Box 8.9), as well as evidence that the death penalty is administered in an arbitrary and discriminatory manner. Like former Supreme Court Justice Harry Blackmun, they argue that it is futile to continue to "tinker with the machinery of death."

Whereas traditional abolitionists base their opposition to the death penalty on the immorality of state killing, the sanctity of human life, or the inherent cruelty of death as a punishment, the new abolitionists claim that the death penalty "has not been, and cannot be, administered in a manner that is compatible with our legal system's fundamental commitments to fair and equal treatment."[229] They contend that the implementation of procedural rules, such as those proposed by the advocates of reform, has not solved—indeed, cannot solve—the problems inherent in the capital sentencing process: the post-*Furman* reforms notwithstanding, "the death penalty remains fraught with arbitrariness, discrimination, caprice, and mistake."[230] Like Justice Blackmun, the advocates of abolition insist that "no combination of procedural rules or substantive regulations ever can save the death penalty from its inherent constitutional deficiencies."[231]

Concerns about fairness and discrimination in the capital sentencing process prompted death penalty opponents to call not for procedural reforms but for a moratorium on executions in the United States. Although these resolutions typically call for a cessation of executions until reforms designed to ensure due process and equal protection have been implemented, Sarat maintains that they "amount to a call for the abolition, not merely the cessation, of capital punishment."[232]

Sarat contends that the reforms needed to "fix" the capital sentencing process—provision of competent counsel for all capital defendants, expansion of death row inmates' rights to appeal, guaranteed access to DNA testing, and review of prosecutors' decisions to seek the death penalty—while feasible, are "hardly a likely or near-term possibility."[233] He notes, for example, that one of the reasons the American Bar Association cites in its call for a moratorium on the death penalty is the "longstanding patterns of racial discrimination ... in courts around the country." To address this problem, the ABA calls for the development of "effective mechanisms" to eliminate racial discrimination in capital cases. Similarly, the National Death Penalty Moratorium Act, which was introduced in both houses of Congress in 2001 but which did not pass, would have set up a National Commission on the Death Penalty; the commission would have been charged with "establishing guidelines and procedures which ... ensure that the death penalty is not administered in a racially discriminatory manner."[234] The problem, according to Sarat, is that it is not clear that any such "mechanisms," "guidelines," or "procedures" exist. As he contends,

> The pernicious effects of race in capital sentencing are a function of the persistence of racial prejudice throughout society combined with the wide degree of discretion necessary to afford individualized justice in capital prosecutions and capital trials. Prosecutors with limited resources may be inclined to allocate resources to cases that attract the greatest public attention, which often will mean cases where the victim was white and his or her assailant black. Participants in the legal system—

whether white or black—demonize young black males, seeing them as more deserving of death as a punishment because of their perceived danger. These cultural effects are not remediable in the near term ...[235]

Because it may be impossible to ensure that the capital sentencing process is operated in a racially neutral manner, in other words, Sarat and others who embrace the new abolitionism maintain that the only solution is to abolish the death penalty.

CONCLUSION

The findings of research examining the effect of race on the capital sentencing process are consistent. Study after study has demonstrated that those who murder whites are much more likely to be sentenced to death than those who murder African Americans. Many of these studies also have shown that African Americans convicted of murdering whites receive the death penalty more often than whites who murder other whites. These results come from studies conducted before *Furman*, in the decade following the *Gregg* decision, and in the 1980s, 1990s, and beyond. They come from studies conducted in both southern and nonsouthern jurisdictions and from studies examining prosecutors' charging decisions as well as jurors' sentencing decisions.

These results suggest that racial disparities in the application of the death penalty reflect racial discrimination. Some might argue that these results signal contextual, rather than systematic, racial discrimination. As noted earlier, although research consistently has revealed that those who murder whites are sentenced to death at a disproportionately high rate, not all studies have found that African American offenders are more likely than white offenders to be sentenced to death.

We contend that the type of discrimination found in the capital sentencing process falls closer to the systematic end of the discrimination continuum presented in Chapter 1. Racial discrimination in the capital sentencing process is not limited to the South, where historical evidence of racial bias would lead one to expect differential treatment, but is applicable to other regions of the country as well. It is not confined to one stage of the decision-making process, but affects decisions made by prosecutors as well as juries. It also is not confined to the pre-*Furman* period, when statutes offered little or no guidance to judges and juries charged with deciding whether to impose the death penalty or not, but is found, too, under the more restrictive guided discretion statutes enacted since *Furman*. Moreover, this effect does not disappear when legally relevant predictors of sentence severity are taken into consideration.

With respect to the capital sentencing process, then, empirical studies suggest that the Supreme Court was overly optimistic in predicting that the statutory reforms adopted since *Furman* would eliminate racial discrimination. To the contrary, these studies document "a clear pattern unexplainable on grounds other than race."[236]

DISCUSSION QUESTIONS

1. Do you agree or disagree with the so-called "Marshall Hypothesis"—that is, that the average citizen who knew "all the facts presently available regarding capital punishment would … find it shocking to his conscience and sense of justice"?

2. In *Gregg* v. *Georgia* the Supreme Court assumed that racial discrimination would not be a problem under the guided-discretion statutes enacted in the wake of the *Furman* decision. Does the empirical evidence support or refute this assumption?

3. Explain why Michael Radelet believes that the handful of executions of whites for crimes against African Americans are not really "exceptions to the rule."

4. The procedures adopted by the U.S. Department of Justice to govern death penalty decisions in federal cases (the so-called "death penalty protocol") are designed to ensure that the federal capital sentencing process is fair and equitable. But studies conducted by the Department of Justice revealed that racial minorities were overrepresented in federal capital criminal cases and among those sentenced to death in U.S. District Courts. How did the Department of Justice interpret these findings? Why did the American Civil Liberties Union conclude that the 2001 study was "fatally flawed"?

5. In the case of the Martinsville Seven a series of state and federal court rulings rejected the defendants' allegations regarding racial discrimination in the application of the death penalty; Judge Doubles, for instance, ruled that there was no evidence of racial discrimination in the actions of the six juries that sentenced the seven men to death. In *McCleskey* v. *Kemp*, the U.S. Supreme Court similarly ruled that there was insufficient evidence "to support an inference that any of the decisionmakers in McCleskey's case acted with discriminatory purpose." Assume that you are the lawyer representing an African American offender who has been sentenced to death. What types of evidence would you need to convince the appellate courts that decision makers in your client's case had "acted with discriminatory purpose"? Is it realistic to assume that any offender can meet this burden of proof?

6. Consider the five remedies for racial discrimination in capital sentencing (Box 8.6). Which do you believe is the appropriate remedy? Why?

7. In 1994 Supreme Court Justice Harry Blackmun stated that it was futile to continue to "tinker with the machinery of death." Although those who advocate abolishing the death penalty agree with this assessment, advocates of reform contend that the death penalty can be "fixed." Summarize their arguments.

8. Do you agree or disagree with our conclusion that "the type of discrimination found in the capital sentencing process falls closer to the systematic end of the discrimination continuum presented in Chapter 1"? Why?

NOTES

1. *Callins* v. *Collins*, 510 U.S. 1,141 (1994), at 1,154–1,155.
2. Jeff Flock, "'Blanket Commutation' Empties Illinois Death Row," CNN, January 13, 2003. Available at: http://www.cnn.com/2003/LAW/01/11/illinois.death.row/html.
3. *Callins* v. *Collins*, 510 U.S. 1,141 (1994), at 1,145.
4. Ibid.
5. For a discussion of the "new abolitionist policies," see Austin Sarat, "Recapturing the Spirit of *Furman*: The American Bar Association and the New Abolitionist Politics," *Law and Contemporary Problems* 61 (1998), pp. 5–28; and Austin Sarat, *When the State Kills: Capital Punishment and the American Condition* (Princeton: Princeton University Press, 2001), Ch. 9.
6. Cited in Sarat, "Recapturing the Spirit of *Furman*," p. 14.
7. Clyde E. Murphy, "Racial Discrimination in the Criminal Justice System," *North Carolina Central Law Journal* 17 (1988), pp. 171–190.
8. *McCleskey* v. *Kemp*, 481 U.S. 279 (1987).
9. Ibid.
10. *In re Kemmler,* 136 U.S. 436,447 (1890).
11. *Trop* v. *Dulles*, 356 U.S. 86, 99 (1958).
12. *Furman* v. *Georgia*, 408 U.S. 238 (1972).
13. Ibid., at 257 (Douglas, J., concurring); at 310 (Stewart, J., concurring); at 313 (White, J., concurring).
14. Ibid., at 257 (Marshall, J., concurring).
15. Ibid., at 310 (Stewart, J., concurring).
16. Samuel R. Gross and Robert Mauro, *Death & Discrimination: Racial Disparities in Capital Sentencing* (Boston: Northeastern University Press, 1989), p. 215.
17. *Woodson* v. *North Carolina*, 428 U.S. 280 (1976); *Roberts* v. *Louisiana*, 428 U.S. 325 (1976).
18. *Woodson* v. *North Carolina*, 428 U.S. 280 (1976), at 303.
19. Ibid., at 305.
20. Georgia Code Ann., §27-2534.1 (Supp. 1975).
21. *Gregg* v. *Georgia*, 428 U.S. 153 (1976); *Proffitt* v. *Florida*, 428 U.S. 242 (1976); *Jurek* v. *Texas*, 428 U.S. 262 (1976).
22. *Gregg* v. *Georgia,* 428 U.S. 153 (1976).
23. Ibid., at 206–207.
24. *Coker* v. *Georgia*, 433 U.S. 584, 592 (1977).
25. *Kennedy* v. *Louisiana*, 554 U.S. 334 (2008).
26. *Tison* v. *Arizona*, 107 S.Ct. 1,676 (1987).
27. *Atkins* v. *Virginia*, 536 U.S. 304 (2002).
28. *Roper* v. *Simmons*, 543 U.S. 551 (2005).
29. *Baze* v. *Rees*, 128 S.Ct. 1,520 (2008).

30. See, for example, *Porter* v. *McCollum*, 130 S.C. 447 (2009) and *Sears* v. *Upton*, 130 S.C. 3,259 (2010).

31. National Opinion Research Center, *General Social Surveys*, 1972–94, *General Social Surveys*, 1996 (Storrs, CT: The Roper Center for Public Opinion Research, University of Connecticut, 1997).

32. Data on public attitudes toward the death penalty since 1936 can be found at http://www.gallup.com/poll/1606/death-penalty.aspx.

33. *Furman* v. *Georgia*, 408 U.S. 238, at 365–66 (1972), (Marshall, J., concurring).

34. Raymond Paternoster, *Capital Punishment in America* (New York: Lexington Books, 1991), p. 72.

35. *Furman* v. *Georgia*, 408 U.S. 238, at 369, (1972), (Marshall J., concurring).

36. See, for example, Robert M. Bohm, "American Death Penalty Opinion, 1936–1986: A Critical Examination of the Gallup Polls," in *The Death Penalty in America: Current Research*, Robert M. Bohm, ed. (Cincinnati, OH: Anderson, 1991); William Bowers, "Capital Punishment and Contemporary Values: People's Misgivings and the Court's Misperceptions," *Law & Society Review* 27 (1993), pp. 157–175; James Alan Fox, Michael L. Radelet, and Julie L. Bonsteel, "Death Penalty Opinion in the Post-*Furman* Years," *New York University Review of Law and Social Change* 18 (1990–91); Philip W. Harris, "Over-Simplification and Error in Public Opinion Surveys on Capital Punishment, *Justice Quarterly* 3 (1986), pp. 429–455; Austin Sarat and Neil Vidmar, "Public Opinion, the Death Penalty, and the Eighth Amendment: Testing the Marshall Hypothesis," in *Capital Punishment in the United States*, Hugo A. Bedau and Chester M. Pierce, eds. (New York: AMS Publications, 1976).

37. Bowers, "Capital Punishment and Contemporary Values," p. 162.

38. Ibid.

39. Ibid., p. 172.

40. Richard C. Dieter, *A Crisis of Confidence: Americans' Doubts About the Death Penalty* (Washington, DC: Death Penalty Information Center, 2007), p. 5.

41. Ibid., p. 1.

42. http://www.gallup.com/poll/28243/racial-disagreement-over-death-penalty-has-varied-historically.aspx.

43. Mark Peffley and jon Hurwitz, "Persuasion and Resistance: Race and the Death Penalty in America," *American Journal of Political Science* 51 (2007), pp. 996–1,012.

44. Bureau of Justice Statistics, *Sourcebook of Criminal Justice Statistics 2003,* Table 2.54.

45. Taylor, "Support for Death Penalty Still Very Strong in spite of Widespread Belief that Some Innocent People are Convicted of Murder," (2001, August 17). *The Harris Poll*, 41, Table 6.

46. Tom W. Smith, "A Trend Analysis of Attitudes Toward Capital Punishment, 1936–1974," in *Studies of Social Change Since 1948: Vol. 2*, James E. Davis, ed. (Chicago: National Opinion Research Center, 1975): pp. 257–318.

47. Steven E. Barkan and Steven F. Cohn, "Racial Prejudice and Support for the Death Penalty by Whites," *Journal of Research in Crime and Delinquency* 31 (1994), pp. 202–209; James D. Unnever and Francis T. Cullen, "The Racial Divide in Support for the Death Penalty: Does White Racism Matter?" *Social Forces* 85 (2007), pp. 1,281–1,301; Robert L. Young, "Race, Conceptions of Crime and Justice, and Support for the Death Penalty," *Social Psychological Quarterly* 54 (1991), pp. 67–75.

48. Barkan and Cohn, "Racial Prejudice and Support for the Death Penalty by Whites."

49. Ibid., p. 206.

50. Ibid., p. 207.

51. Unnever and Cullen, "The Racial Divide in Support for the Death Penalty."

52. Ibid., pp. 1,292–1,293.

53. Ibid., p. 1,293.

54. Eric P. Baumer, Steven F. Messner, and Richard Rosenfeld, "Explaining Structural Variation in Support for Capital Punishment: A Multilevel Analysis," *American Journal of Sociology* 108 (2003), pp. 844–875. For a discussion of regional differences in support by whites for the death penalty, see Steven E. Barkan and Steven F. Cohn, "Contemporary Regional Differences in Support by Whites for the Death Penalty: A Research Note," *Justice Quarterly* 27 (2010), pp. 458–471.

55. Ibid., p. 856,

56. Stephen B. Bright, "Discrimination, Death, and Denial: The Tolerance of Racial Discrimination in Infliction of the Death Penalty," *Santa Clara Law Review* 35 (1995), pp. 901–950.

57. *Gregg* v. *Georgia*, 428 U.S. 153 (1976), at 207.

58. NAACP Legal Defense Fund, *Death Row, U.S.A., Winter 2010* (New York: NAACP LDF, 2010).

59. U.S. Department of Justice, Bureau of Justice Statistics, *Capital Punishment, 2008— Statistical Tables* (Washington, DC: U.S. Government Printing Office, 2009), Table 13.

60. NAACP Legal Defense and Educational Fund, *Death Row U.S.A., Winter 2010,* pp. 35–36.

61. Ibid., p. 36.

62. Ibid., p. 10.

63. Ibid.

64. Ibid.

65. U.S. Department of Justice, Bureau of Justice Statistics, *Capital Punishment 1991* (Washington, DC: U.S. Government Printing Office), p. 8.

66. Marvin E. Wolfgang and Marc Riedel, "Race, Judicial Discretion, and the Death Penalty," *The Annals of the American Academy of Political and Social Science* 407 (1973), pp. 119–133, p. 123.

67. Elmer H. Johnson, "Selective Factors in Capital Punishment," *Social Forces* 36 (1957), p. 165.

68. Marvin E. Wolfgang, Arlene Kelly, and Hans C. Nolde, "Comparisons of the Executed and the Commuted Among Admissions to Death Row," *Journal of Criminal Law, Criminology, and Police Science* 53 (1962), p. 301.

69. Gary Kleck, "Racial Discrimination in Criminal Sentencing: A Critical Evaluation of the Evidence With Additional Evidence on the Death Penalty," *American Sociological Review* 46 (1981), p. 793.

70. For example, according to Raymond Fosdick, who studied U.S. police departments shortly before the country's entry into World War I, southern police departments

had three classes of homicide. One official told Fosdick, "If a nigger kills a white man, that's murder. If a white man kills a nigger, that's justifiable homicide. If a nigger kills another nigger, that's one less nigger." See Raymond Fosdisk, *American Police Systems* (Montclair, NJ: Patterson Smith Reprint Series, 1972), p. 45 (originally published in 1920).

71. Gary Kleck, "Racial Discrimination in Criminal Sentencing," p. 793.

72. Ibid.

73. Ibid., p. 796.

74. Ibid., p. 798.

75. Guy Johnson, "The Negro and Crime," *Annals of the American Academy* 217 (1941), p. 98.

76. Michael L. Radelet, "Executions of Whites for Crimes Against Blacks: Exceptions to the Rule?" *The Sociological Quarterly* 30 (1989), p. 535.

77. Ibid., pp. 529–544, p. 531.

78. Ibid., p. 533.

79. Ibid., p. 536.

80. Ibid., p. 538.

81. Ibid., pp. 534–535.

82. Ibid., p. 536.

83. Ibid., p. 536 (emphasis in original).

84. *Furman* v. *Georgia*, 408 U.S. 238 (1972), The ANNALS of the American Academy of Political and Social Sciences 217 (1941), pp. 93–104; at 449 (Powell, J., dissenting).

85. Harold Garfinkel, "Research Note on Inter- and Intra-Racial Homicides," *Social Forces* 27 (1949), pp. 369–381; Guy Johnson, "The Negro and Crime"; Charles S. Mangum, Jr., *The Legal Status of the Negro* (Chapel Hill, NC: North Carolina Press, 1940); Paige H. Ralph, Jonathan R. Sorensen, and James W. Marquart, "A Comparison of Death-Sentenced and Incarcerated Murderers in Pre-*Furman* Texas," *Justice Quarterly* 9 (1992), pp. 185–209; Wolfgang, Kelly, and Nolde, "Comparison of the Executed and Commuted Among Admissions to Death Row"; Marvin E. Wolfgang and Marc Reidel, "Race, Judicial Discretion, and the Death Penalty," *Annals of the American Academy* 407 (1973), pp. 119–133; Marvin E. Wolfgang and Marc Reidel, "Rape, Race, and the Death Penalty in Georgia," *American Journal of Orthopsychiatry* 45 (1975), pp. 658–668.

86. Guy Johnson, "The Negro and Crime."

87. Charles S. Mangum Jr., *The Legal Status of the Negro*. Chapel Hill, NC: North Carolina Press, 1940.

88. Wolfgang, Kelly, and Nolde, "Comparisons of the Executed and Commuted Among Admissions to Death Row."

89. Garfinkel, "Research Note on Inter- and Intra-Racial Homicides."

90. William Bowers and Glenn L. Pierce, "Arbitrariness and Discrimination Under Post-*Furman* Capital Statutes," *Crime and Delinquency* 74 (1980), pp. 1,067–1,100.

91. Kleck, "Racial Discrimination in Criminal Sentencing," p. 788.

92. Florida Civil Liberties Union, *Rape: Selective Electrocution Based on Race* (Miami: Florida Civil Liberties Union, 1964).

93. Wolfgang and Reidel, "Race, Judicial Discretion, and the Death Penalty."

94. Ibid., p. 133.

95. Kleck, "Racial Discrimination in Criminal Sentencing," p. 788.

96. David C. Baldus, George Woodworth, and Charles A. Pulaski, *Equal Justice and the Death Penalty: A Legal and Empirical Analysis* (Boston: Northeastern University Press, 1990).

97. Ralph, Sorensen, and Marquart, "A Comparison of Death-Sentenced and Incarcerated Murderers in Pre-*Furman* Texas."

98. Ibid., p. 207.

99. David V. Baker, "Black Female Executions in Historical Context," *Criminal Justice Review* 33 (2008), pp. 64–88, p. 64.

100. Ibid., p. 66.

101. Ibid., pp. 206–207.

102. Wolfgang and Reidel, "Rape, Race, and the Death Penalty in Georgia," p. 667.

103. Case described in Stephen B. Bright, "Discrimination, Death, and Denial: The Tolerance of Racial Discrimination in the Infliction of the Death Penalty," *Santa Clara Law Review* 35 (1995), pp. 901–950, pp. 912–915.

104. Ibid., pp. 912–913.

105. *Dobbs* v. *Zant*, 963 F.2d 1,403, 1,407 [11th Cir. 1991], cited in Bright, "Discrimination, Death, and Denial," n. 7.

106. Ibid., p. 914.

107. U.S. General Accounting Office, *Death Penalty Sentencing: Research Indicates Pattern of Racial Disparities* (Washington, DC: General Accounting Office, 1990), p. 5.

108. Ibid., p. 6.

109. Ibid.

110. David C. Baldus and George Woodworth, "Race Discrimination and the Legitimacy of Capital Punishment: Reflections on the Interaction of Fact and Perception," *DePaul Law Review* (2004), pp. 1,411–1,496.

111. Ibid., p. 1,421.

112. Ibid., p. 1,479.

113. Studies that find either a race-of-victim or race-of-defendant effect include (but are not limited to): Stephen Arkin, "Discrimination and Arbitrariness in Capital Punishment: An Analysis of Post-*Furman* Murder Cases in Dade County, Florida, 1973–1976," *Stanford Law Review* 33 (1980), pp. 75–101; William Bowers, "The Pervasiveness of Arbitrariness and Discrimination Under Post-*Furman* Capital Statutes," *Journal of Criminal Law & Criminology* 74 (1983), pp. 1,067–1,100; Bowers and Pierce, "Arbitrariness and Discrimination Under Post-*Furman* Capital Statutes"; Sheldon Ekland-Olson, "Structured Discretion, Racial Bias, and the Death Penalty: The First Decade After *Furman* in Texas, *Social Science Quarterly* 69 (1988), pp. 853–873; Thomas Keil and Gennaro Vito, "Race and the Death Penalty in Kentucky Murder Trials: An Analysis of Post-*Gregg* Outcomes," *Justice Quarterly* (1990), pp. 189–207; Raymond Paternoster, "Prosecutorial Discretion in Requesting the Death Penalty: A Case of Victim-Based Racial Discrimination," *Law & Society Review* 18 (1984), pp. 437–478; Michael L. Radelet, "Racial Characteristics and the Imposition of the Death Penalty," *American Sociological Review* 46 (1981), pp. 918–927; Michael L. Radelet and Glenn L. Pierce, "Race and Prosecutorial Discretion in Homicide Cases,"

Law & Society Review 19 (1985), pp. 587–621; and Dwayne M. Smith, "Patterns of Discrimination in Assessments of the Death Penalty: The Case of Louisiana," *Journal of Criminal Justice* 15 (1987), pp. 279–286.

114. Baldus, Woodworth, and Pulaski, *Equal Justice and the Death Penalty.*

115. Gross and Mauro, *Death & Discrimination.*

116. Glenn L. Pierce and Michael L. Radelet, "The Impact of Legally Inappropriate Factors on Death Sentencing for California Homicides, 1990–99," *Santa Clara Law Review* 46 (2005).

117. Baldus, Woodworth, and Pulaski, *Equal Justice and the Death Penalty.*

118. Ibid., p. 185.

119. David Baldus, Charles Pulaski, and George Woodworth, "Comparative Review of Death Sentences: An Empirical Study of the Georgia Experience," *The Journal of Criminal Law & Criminology* 74 (1983), pp. 709–710.

120. Anthony Amsterdam, "Race and the Death Penalty," *Criminal Justice Ethics* 7 (1988), pp. 2, 84–86.

121. Ibid., p. 85.

122. Gross and Mauro, *Death & Discrimination*, Chs. 4 and 5.

123. Ibid., pp. 109–110.

124. Raymond Paternoster and Robert Brame, "Reassessing Race Disparities in Maryland Capital Cases," *Criminology* 46 (2008): 971–1007.

125. Isaac Unah and Jack Boger, "Race and the Death Penalty in North Carolina: An Empirical Analysis: 1993–1997." Available online at http://www.deathpenaltyinfo.org.

126. Rachel King, "Broken Justice: The Death Penalty in Virginia." Available online at http://www.aclu.org/DeathPenalty/DeathPenalty.cfm?ID=14388&c=17.

127. Andrew Welsh-Huggins, "Death Penalty Unequal," Associated Press, May 7, 2005.

128. Pierce and Radelet, "The Impact of Legally Inappropriate Factors on Death Sentencing for California Homicides, 1990–1999."

129. NAACP Legal Defense and Educational Fund, Inc., *Death Row, USA, Summer 2005.*

130. Pierce and Radelet, "The Impact of Legally Inappropriate Factors on Death Sentencing for California Homicides, 1990–1999," Table 4.

131. Ibid.

132. Ibid.

133. David Jacobs, Jason T. Carmichael, Zhenchao Qian, and Stephanie L. Kent, "Who Survives on Death Row? An Individual and Contextual Analysis," *American Sociological Review* 72 (2007), pp. 610–632.

134. Ibid., p. 610.

135. Ibid., Table 1.

136. Ibid., p. 629.

137. Sarat, "Recapturing the Spirit of *Furman*," p. 27.

138. Scott W. Howe, "The Futile Quest for Racial Neutrality in Capital Selection and the Eighth Amendment Argument for Abolition Based on Unconscious Racial Discrimination," *William & Mary Law Review* 45 (2004), pp. 2,083–2,166.

139. Marian R. Williams and Jefferson E. Holcomb, "The Interactive Effects of Victim Race and Gender on Death Sentence Disparity Findings," *Homicide Studies* 8 (2004), pp. 350–376.

140. Ibid., Table 2 and p. 366.

141. Ibid., Tables 3 and 4.

142. Ibid., p. 370.

143. U.S. Department of Justice, *The Federal Death Penalty System: A Statistical Survey (1988–2000)* (Washington, DC: U.S. Department of Justice, 2000), p.4.

144. U.S. Department of Justice, *The Federal Death Penalty System: Supplementary Data, Analysis, and Revised Protocols for Capital Case Review* (Washington, DC: U.S. Department of Justice, 2001), pp. 6–7.

145. Ibid., p. 5.

146. U.S. Department of Justice, *The Federal Death Penalty System: A Statistical Survey (1988–2000)*, p. 9.

147. Marc Lacey and Raymond Bonner, "Reno Troubled by DP Stats," *New York Times*, September 12, 2000, A17.

148. American Civil Liberties Union, *Federal Death Row: Is It Really Color-Blind? Analysis of June 6 Department of Justice Report on the Death Penalty.* Available at: http://www.aclu.org/Congress/10614la.htm.

149. U.S. Department of Justice, *The Federal Death Penalty System: Supplementary Data, Analysis, and Revised Protocols for Capital Case Review.*

150. Ibid., p. 9.

151. Ibid., p. 3.

152. Ibid.

153. American Civil Liberties Union, *Federal Death Row.*

154. Ibid.

155. Death Penalty Information Center, The Federal Death Penalty. Available at http://www.deathpenaltyinfo.org/federal-death-penalty.

156. Richard Quinney, *The Social Reality of Crime* (Boston: Little, Brown, 1970); Austin Turk, *Criminality and Legal Order* (New York: Rand McNally, 1969).

157. Darnell F. Hawkins, "Beyond Anomalies: Rethinking the Conflict Perspective on Race and Criminal Punishment," *Social Forces* 65 (1987), p. 726.

158. Keil and Vito, "Race and the Death Penalty in Kentucky Murder Trials," p. 204.

159. Quoted in Stephen Wissink, "Race and the Big Needle," *Spectator Online.* Available at: http://www.spectatoronline.com/2001-03-07/news_cover.html.

160. Gross and Mauro, *Death & Discrimination.*

161. Ibid., p. 113.

162. Bright, "Discrimination, Death, and Denial," pp. 903–905.

163. Ibid., p. 904–905.

164. Ibid., p. 921.

165. For an excellent and detailed discussion of this case, see Eric W. Rise, *The Martinsville Seven: Race, Rape, and Capital Punishment* (Charlottesville: University Press of Virginia, 1995).

166. Ibid., p. 122.

167. Ibid.

168. Ibid., p. 30.

169. Ibid., p. 32.

170. Ibid., p. 35.

171. Ibid., p. 48.

172. Ibid., p. 85.

173. *Hampton* v. *Commonwealth*, 58 S.E.2d 288, 298 (Va. Sup. Ct., 1950).

174. Ibid.

175. Rise, *The Martinsville Seven*, p. 121.

176. Ibid., p. 124.

177. Ibid., p. 148.

178. See, for example, *Maxwell* v. *Bishop*, F.2d 138 (8th Cir. 1968); *Spinkellink* v. *Wainwright*, 578 F.2d 582 (5th Cir. 1978); *Shaw* v. *Martin*, 733 F.2d 304 (4th Cir. 1984); and *Prejean* v. *Blackburn*, 743 F.2d 1,091 (5th Cir. 1984).

179. *McCleskey* v. *Kemp*, 481 U.S. 279, 107 S.Ct. 1,756 (1987).

180. David C. Baldus, George W. Woodworth, Charles A. Pulaski, "Monitoring and Evaluating Contemporary Death Penalty Systems: Lessons From Georgia," *University of California at Davis Law Review* 18 (1985), pp. 1,375–1,407.

181. *McCleskey v. Kemp*, 107 S.Ct 1,756 (1987), at 1,777.

182. Ibid., at 1,769.

183. *McCleskey* v. *Kemp*, 481 U.S. 279 (1987), at 315 (Brennan, J., dissenting).

184. Ibid., at 316–317.

185. Ibid.

186. *Maxwell* v. *Bishop*, 398 F.2d 138 (CA 8 1968).

187. Amsterdam, "Race and the Death Penalty," p. 86.

188. Randall Kennedy, *Race, Crime, and the Law* (New York: Vintage Books, 1998).

189. Bright, "Discrimination, Death, and Denial," p. 947.

190. Gross and Mauro, *Death & Discrimination*, p. 212.

191. Baldus, Woodworth, and Pulaski., *Equal Justice and the Death Penalty*, pp. 384–387; Gross and Mauro, *Death & Discrimination*, Ch. 11; Kennedy, *Race, Crime, and the Law*, pp. 340–345.

192. Gross and Mauro, *Death & Discrimination*, p. 216.

193. Kennedy, *Race, Crime, and the Law*, p. 341.

194. *McCleskey* v. *Kemp*, 107 S.Ct., 1,756 (1987) at 1,806 (Stevens, J., dissenting).

195. Baldus, Woodworth, and Pulaski, *Equal Justice and the Death Penalty*, p. 385.

196. Kennedy, *Race, Crime, and the Law*, p. 343.

197. Ibid., p. 344.

198. Ibid.

199. *McCleskey* v. *Zant*, 111 S. Ct. 1,454 (1991).

200. Ibid.

201. *New York Times*, September 26, 1991, p. A10.

202. Death Penalty Information Center, Facts About the Death Penalty. Available at http://www.deathpenaltyinfo.org/documents/FactSheet.pdf.

203. *McCleskey* v. *Zant*, 111 S.Ct 1,454 (1991).

204. *Herrera* v. *Collins*, 113 S.Ct. 853 (1993).

205. Congressional Record, S 4,602 (April 21, 1994).

206. Nathan Koppel, "Death Penalty Goes on Trial in North Carolina," *The Wall Street Journal*, September 20, 2010.

207. Ibid.

208. *Saldano* v. *Texas*, 99–8,119.

209. *Chicago Tribune*, "Flawed Trials Lead to Death Chamber," June 11, 2000; "Gatekeeper Court Keeps Gates Shut," June 12, 2000.

210. U.S. Department of Justice, Bureau of Justice Statistics, *Sourcebook of Criminal Justice Statistics, 1999* (Washington, DC: Government Printing Office, 2000).

211. Texas Civil Rights Project, *The Death Penalty in Texas: Due Process and Equal Justice … or Rush to Execution?* (Austin, TX: Texas Civil Rights Project, 2000).

212. Ibid., p. iv.

213. Ibid., p. ii.

214. American Bar Association, "Whatever You Think About the Death Penalty, A System That Will Take Life Must First Give Justice: A Report from the IR&R Death Penalty Committee," 24 *W.T.R. Hum. Rts.* 22.

215. Press Release, January 31, 2000. Available online at http://www.state.il.us/gov/press/00/Jan/morat.htm.

216. John Kifner, "A State Votes to End Its Death Penalty," *New York Times*, May 19, 2000, A8.

217. Press Release, Sept. 20, 2000. Available online at http://www.igc.org/tcrp/press/HRR/death_penalty.htm.

218. Adam Liptak, "Group Gives Up Death Penalty Work," *New York Times*, January 4, 2010.

219. Public Law No. 108–405.

220. Hugo A. Bedau and Michael L. Radelet, "Miscarriages of Justice in Potentially Capital Cases," *Stanford Law Review* 40 (1987), pp. 21–179.

221. *Omaha World Herald*, March 3, 1993.

222. Information about this case was obtained from articles appearing in the *Chicago Tribune* from 1995 to 1998.

223. Eric Zorn, "Dark Truths Buried in Nicarico Case May Yet See Light," *Chicago Tribune*, October 18, 1995, Section 2, p. 1.

224. *Chicago Tribune*, November 4, 1995, Section 1, pp. 1–2.

225. *Chicago Tribune*, April 9, 1998, DuPage section, p. 1.

226. Comments taken from U.S. Senator Patrick Leahy's website, http://leahy.senate.gov/press/200410/103004A.html.

227. Jodi Wilgoren, "Few Death Sentences or None Under Overhaul Proposed by Illinois Panel," *New York Times* online, April 16, 2002.

228. Austin Sarat, *When the State Kills*, pp. 246–260.

229. Ibid., p. 251.

230. *Callins* v. *Collins*, 510 U.S. 1,141 (1994), at 1,144 (Blackmun, J., dissenting).

231. Ibid., at 1,145.

232. Sarat, *When the State Kills*, p. 255.

233. Ibid., p. 256.

234. National Death Penalty Moratorium Act of 2001, S. 223, H.R. 1038.

235. Sarat, *When the State Kills*, p. 257.

236. Gross and Mauro, *Death & Discrimination*, pp. 109–110.

9

✳

Corrections in America

A Portrait in Color

Corrections versus College: A Different View of America

According to Black Star Project Executive Director, Phillip Jackson, in 2007 there were 321 African American men enrolled at Northwestern University (1.7 percent of the student body) but four times that number—1,207—imprisoned at Western Illinois Correctional Center (60 percent of the prison population). Similarly, 41 black men were enrolled at the Art Institute of Chicago (less than 2 percent of the student body), but 1,183 black men were imprisoned at the Illinois River Correctional Center (60 percent of that prison's population). Additionally, 115 black men were enrolled at Bradley University (1.9 percent of the student body), but 1,093 African American men were imprisoned at the Danville Correctional Center (60 percent of the prison's population).[1]

The picture presented here is representative of the entire country. Four times as many whites attend college than are under correctional supervision. However, there are more African Americans and Hispanics under some form of correctional supervision than there are attending college. The differences are particularly stark when focusing on males—nearly 20 percent of African American males and 8 percent of Hispanic males are under correctional supervision, whereas less than 3 percent of white males are under correctional supervision. College attendance estimates, however, indicate that fewer than 4 percent of African American and Hispanic males were attending college in 2003, whereas twice as many white males were attending college as there were under correctional supervision.[2]

Jackson concludes that "the low number of Black students applying to and enrolling in American colleges and universities is shocking." It not only presents an alarming picture of where we are today, but "it predicts an absolutely disastrous future in the next 10 to 20 years for the Black community. Instead of more Black doctors, lawyers, educators, accountants, business managers, technologists, social workers, and engineers, the Black community will have more government-dependent, unskilled, and unemployed workers."[3]

GOALS OF THE CHAPTER

This chapter describes various disparities in the ethnic and racial makeup of American correctional populations. It examines which groups are overrepresented in situations of incarceration and supervision in the community. The extent of minority overrepresentation also is explored in relation to gender distinctions, federal versus state populations, and recidivism, with an emphasis on historical fluctuations. The juxtaposition of Native American philosophies and methods of correction with the mainstream American criminal justice system is also explored.

After you have read this chapter:

1. You will have a good picture of who is in prison and of the racial and ethnic composition of the prison population.
2. You will be able to discuss intelligently the differences between prison and jail, between probation and parole, and between federal and state prisons.
3. You will understand the special problems involving Native Americans and the corrections system.
4. You will be familiar with the unique issues related to women of color in prison.
5. You will be able to discuss what difference it makes when corrections personnel (prison guards, parole officers) are people of color.
6. Because prison is often the end result of social and economic inequalities, you will have a new perspective on the issues covered in Chapter 3.

The descriptive information in this chapter is supplemented by a discussion of current research on discrimination in the correctional setting. Finally, the inmate social system, which reflects key aspects of prison life, is discussed. This section will focus on the influence of minority group status on prison subcultures and religion.

THE INCARCERATED: PRISON AND JAIL
POPULATIONS

Describing incarcerated populations in the United States is a complicated task. The answer to the question, "Who is locked up?" depends on what penal institution and which inmates we are discussing. Prison and jail population figures are descriptive counts taken on one particular day, often at midyear. These figures are used for the purpose of describing disparity and are not standardized rates (see discussion later in this chapter). There are a number of important distinctions between prisons and jails, male and female inmates, and state and federal populations. In addition, important changes occur over time.

Prisons and jails are not the same: they serve different functions in the criminal justice system. These differences may result in different levels of minority overrepresentation, so jails and prisons are discussed separately. Gender differences are also important when discussing incarceration; therefore, we also explore the issues of the racial and ethnic composition of male and female prisoner populations. State and federal prison populations must be examined separately because of the differences in state and federal crime.[4]

Minority Overrepresentation

In 2009 more than 1.6 million people were incarcerated in federal and state prison and local jails.[5] Looking at this population through the lens of race and ethnicity of incarcerated inmates, our primary observation about the prison population in the United States (Table 9.1, column 1) is that African Americans are strikingly overrepresented compared with their presence in the general

---

Focus on an Issue
Indigenous Justice Paradigm

In "Crime and Punishment: Traditional and Contemporary Tribal Justice," Ada Pecos Melton observes that in many contemporary tribal communities "a dual justice system exists, one based on an American paradigm of justice and the other based on an indigenous paradigm."[6] The American justice paradigm is characterized by an adversarial system and stands apart from most religious tenants. Crimes are viewed as actions against the state, with little attention to the needs of the victim or community. The focus is on the defendant's individual rights during adjudication. Punishing the offender is generally governed by a retributive philosophy and removal from society.

In contrast, tribal justice is based on a holistic philosophy and is not easily divorced from the religious and spiritual realms of everyday life. Melton attempts to distill the characteristic elements of a number of diverse American tribal justice ideologies into an indigenous justice

paradigm. The holistic philosophy is the key element of this paradigm and supports a "circle of justice" where "the center of the circle represents the underlying problems and issues that need to be resolved to attain peace and harmony for the individuals and the community." The corresponding values of restorative and reparative justice prescribe the actions the offender must perform to be forgiven. These values reflect the importance of the victim and the community in restoring harmony.

The influence of the American paradigm of justice on Native American communities has a long and persistent history.[7] However, the values of restorative and reparative justice are emerging in a number of programs off the reservation. In particular, the restorative justice practices of the Navajo Nation have influenced a number of new-offender rehabilitation programs, including many supported by the Presbyterian Church.

T A B L E 9.1   Racial and Ethnic Profile of State Prison, Federal Prison, and Jail Populations, by Race and Gender, at Midyear, 2009

	Combined	Female	Male
White (non-Hispanic)	39.4	45.8	32.6
African American (non-Hispanic)	34.2	32.2	40.1
Hispanic	20.6	13.1	21.4
Other (Native American, Alaskan Native, Asian, and Pacific Islander)	5.9	8.9	5.9

SOURCE: Heather West, *Prison Inmates at Midyear 2009—Statistical Tables* (Bureau of Justice Statistics, 2010), computed from Table 16.

population. African Americans comprise less than 15 percent of the U.S. population but nearly 40 percent of all incarcerated offenders. Hispanics also are overrepresented but not as markedly, representing roughly 15 percent of the U.S. population; however they represent just over 20 percent of the incarcerated population. Conversely, whites (non–Hispanic) are underrepresented compared with their presence in the population—they are more than 70 percent of the general population but just more than one-third (34.2 percent) of the incarcerated population.[8]

In recent years Hispanics have been the fastest-growing minority group being imprisoned. They were 10.5 percent of the prison population in 1985, 15.5 percent in 1995, 16.4 percent in 2000, and 20.6 percent in 2009. These increases reflect a rate twice as high as the increase for African American and white inmates.[9] Little information is available about the number of Asian, Pacific Islander, Alaska Native, and Native American prisoners because they are generally represented in a category collapsed into "Other." The representation of Asians and Pacific Islanders does not appear substantially greater than their representation in the general population. However, Native American and Alaska Natives are overrepresented compared with their representation in the U.S. population.

Given the changes in racial categories in the U.S. census forms in 2000, prison statistics are starting to reflect the percentage of prisoners who identify themselves as being of two or more races. Although the number seems small at this point, future researchers should note that increased attention to this group is warranted.

Racial and Ethnic Female Prisoners

The picture of the racial and ethnic composition of prison populations changes slightly when focusing on gender (Table 9.1; columns 2 and 3). Because women make up 9.5 percent of the incarcerated persons, up from 5.7 percent in 1990, we should not generalize patterns from predominantly male populations to females. For example, although prison populations have increased markedly in the last several years, the increase for female inmates is more rapid than for male inmates from 1995 to 2009. Over this nearly 15-year period, female prison populations have increased by more than 50 percent, whereas male populations increased by only one-third of a percent.[10]

Among female prisoners, similarities and differences exist when comparing their racial and ethnic makeup to the overall (predominately male) prison population. Although people of color represent more than half of the women incarcerated in federal and state prisons, white, non-Hispanic women make up the largest group of female prisoners (45.8 percent). This is the reverse of the male population, in which the largest racial group is African American males (40.1 percent). The percentage of female inmates who identify themselves as African American indicates an overrepresentation of African American females in prison compared with the general population, but the proportion of this overrepresentation is different than the number for the African American male population (32.2 percent compared with 40.1 percent). Notably, the percentage of female prisoners who are Hispanic is lower than the percentage of male prisoners who are Hispanic (13.1 percent compared with 21.4 percent).

Federal Racial and Ethnic Prisoners

Although state prison populations account for the majority (nearly 90 percent) of incarcerated offenders, a look at the racial and ethnic percentages of federal populations alone is warranted. Just as state and federal laws differ, so will their prison populations because they present different offenses and unique sentencing practices (see Chapter 7). An important implication for federal prisoners is that they can expect to serve more of their original sentence than do state inmates (up to 50 percent more).[11] Also, federal prison populations are increasing at rates higher than state populations, with higher rates of change in court commitments to federal prison than to state prisons.

Comparisons between state and federal prison populations with regard to racial composition are a challenge. The U.S. Bureau of Justice Statistics (BJS) sources used to estimate the racial and ethnic composition of federal and state prison populations (Table 9.1) reflect the convention of using racial and ethnic status combined (white, non-Hispanic; African American, non-Hispanic; Hispanic, other); however, the Federal Bureau of Prisons uses the convention of measuring race and ethnicity as separate concepts (more like the U.S. census).

The descriptive profile of the federal inmate population presented in Table 9.2 suggests an important correction in the magnitude of racial and ethnic differences in state versus federal prison populations. African Americans do not appear as severely overrepresented in the federal prison population as they do in the profile of state and federal prison populations combined. In short, in the federal population alone, African Americans represent less than 40 percent of the population, whereas state and federal populations combined reveal roughly 46 percent are African American.

**T A B L E 9.2   Racial and Ethnic Profile of Federal
Prison Population, 2009**

Race	Percent
White	57.2
African American	39.3
Other	3.5
Ethnicity (of any race)	
Hispanic	32.2
Non-Hispanic	67.8

SOURCE: Bureau of Justice Statistics, *Sourcebook of Criminal Justice Statistics, 2009*
(Washington, DC: U.S. Department of Justice, 2009). Available at http://www.albany.edu/
sourcebook/pdf/t600222009.pdf.

Perhaps the most startling contrast appears with the Hispanic population.
When Hispanics are identified as being of any race, they represent nearly one-
third (32 percent) of the federal prison population, compared to less than 20 percent of the combined prison population.

These data suggest that the overrepresentation of Hispanics in federal prison
populations is hidden in the description of the racial and ethnic composition.
Also the underrepresentation of whites in prison is inflated by the extraction of
Hispanics (who are predominantly white) from the calculation of demographic
percentages.

These differences in disparity among racial and ethnic groups are explained
in large part by different patterns of offending. Whites are relatively more likely
to commit and be convicted of federal offenses. African Americans, conversely,
are relatively more likely to be arrested and convicted for index crimes, which
are generally state offenses. Hispanics are consistently overrepresented among
convicted drug offenders at the federal level and among immigration law
offenders.[12]

Security Level of Facilities

When convicted offenders are committed to federal prison, they undergo a
classification process that determines, among other things, what type of institution (or security level) they should be assigned to as inmates. Federal Bureau of
Prison statistics offer a picture of male inmates of color by security level of the
prison they are assigned to, presented in Figure 9.1.[13] Roughly the same percentages of inmates, regardless of race, are found in the low- and minimum-
security settings (about 25 percent and 10 percent, respectively). However, a
larger percentage of African American inmates are in the highest two security
levels compared to the white inmates. Thus, although the typical federal prison
inmate is white, the typical inmate in the high-security facilities is African
American.

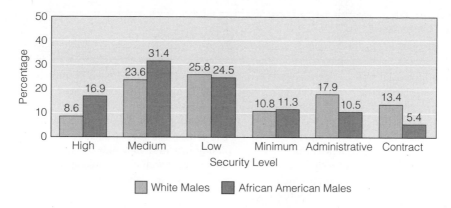

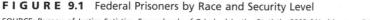

FIGURE 9.1 Federal Prisoners by Race and Security Level

SOURCE: Bureau of Justice Satistics, *Sourcebook of Criminal Justice Statistics* 2002 (Washington, DC: Government Printing Office, 2003). Available at www.albany.edu/sourcebook/.

Conclusion

The impact of overrepresentation in incarceration settings varies in magnitude and quality. The racial and ethnic profile of prison inmates is to some extent conditioned by how the concepts of race and ethnicity are measured. One of the important implications of the more extreme overrepresentation of Hispanic offenders in federal prison is that offenders sentenced to federal prison serve longer sentences with more time served than those offenders sentenced to state prisons, given that federal prisoners can expect to serve 50 percent more of their original sentence than do state inmates. In short, this detrimental impact of conditions of imprisonment on Hispanics would not have been known if we only examined the demographic profile offered in Table 9.1.

Race, Ethnicity, and Recidivism

The concept of recidivism can take on different meanings in different settings. Generally, the term is used to refer to offenders who return to offending after experiencing a criminal conviction and the corresponding punishment. Four key distinctions in the research on offender recidivism center on the point in the system we measure as the return to criminal behavior: (1) rearrest for a new crime (either felony or misdemeanor), (2) reconviction (in state or federal court), (3) resentence to prison, and (4) revocation of parole (technical or new offense violation). In a study of recidivism among prisoners released from 15 states, racial differences did emerge in the findings. A group of 272,111 offenders released in 1994 were followed for three years after their release. Findings indicate that compared to white ex-offenders, African Americans were more likely to be rearrested (72.9 percent compared to 62.7 percent), reconvicted (51.1 percent compared to 43.3 percent), resentenced (28.5 percent compared to 22.6 percent), and revoked (54.2 percent compared to 51.9 percent). Conversely, non-Hispanics were more likely than Hispanics to be rearrested (71.4 percent

---

Focus on an Issue

Correctional Personnel: Similarities and Differences on the Basis of Race

---

Currently, federal and state prisons have fairly equitable representation of African American citizens among correctional officers and supervisors, as compared with the general population. Hispanic representation among correctional personnel is still lacking.[14] Important goals include ensuring fair employment practices in government hiring and ensuring there are minority decision makers to cause a beneficial (and perhaps less discriminatory) impact on the treatment of minority populations.

A review of the research in the area of attitudes and beliefs of correctional officers toward inmates and punishment ideologies suggests that respondents' views do appear to differ in many ways on the basis of race. In particular, the author notes that African American officers appear to have more positive attitudes toward inmates than do white officers; however, others have found that black officers expressed a preference for greater distance between officers and inmates than did white officers.[15] Additionally, neither white nor African American correction officers seem able to correctly identify the self-reported needs of prison inmates.

Ideologically, African American officers were more often supportive of rehabilitation than their white counterparts. African American officers also appear to be more ambivalent about the current punitive nature of the criminal justice system, indicating that the court system is often too harsh.

In short, current research does not offer a definitive answer to the question of whether minority correctional officers make different decisions. Assuming that differential decision making by correction officers could be both a positive and negative exercise of discretion, at what point are differential decisions beneficial to inmates, and at what point are they unprofessional or unjust? What research could be done to resolve the issue of the presence or absence of differential decision making by correctional officers on the basis of race?

---

compared to 64.6 percent), reconvicted (50.7 percent compared to 43.9 percent), and revoked (57.3 percent compared to 51.9 percent). There were no significant differences between Hispanics and non-Hispanics in terms of the likelihood of being resentenced (24.7 percent compared to 26.8 percent).[16]

Historical Trends

The overrepresentation of African Americans in state and federal prisons is not a new phenomenon. Figure 9.2 illustrates the changing demographic composition of the prison population from 1926 to 2009. Reviewing this figure we can document a disproportionate number of African Americans in the prison population since 1926 (the beginning of national-level data collection on prison populations). The racial disparity has increased in recent years, however. In 1926 African Americans represented 9 percent of the population and 21 percent of the prison population. Over time, the proportion of the prison population of African Americans increased steadily, reaching 30 percent in the 1940s, 35 percent in 1960, 44 percent in 1980, peaking at slightly more than 50 percent in the

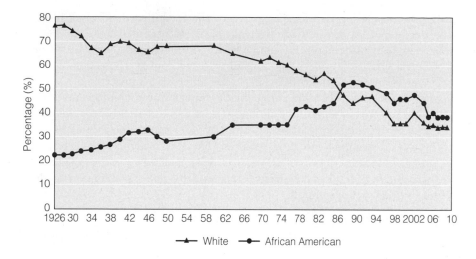

FIGURE 9.2 Admissions to State and Federal Prisons by Race, 1926 to 2010

SOURCES: Bureau of Justice Statistics, *Race of Prisoners Admitted to State and Federal Institutions, 1926-86* (Washington, DC: Government Printing Office, 1991); Bureau of Justice Statistics, *Correctional Populations in the United States, 1996* (Washington, DC: Government Printing Office, 1997); Bureau of Justice Statistics, *Correctional Populations in the United States, 1996* (Washington, DC: Government Printing Office, 1998); Allen J. Beck, *Prison and Jail Inmates, 1999*; Allen J. Beck and Jennifer C. Karberg, *Prison and jail Inmates at Midyear 2000*; Allen J. Beck, Jennifer C. Karberg, Paige M. Harrison, *Prison and Jail Inmates at Midyear 2001*; Paige M. Harrison and Allen J. Beck, *Prison and Jail Inmates at Midyear 2004*. Available at www.ojp.usdoj/bjs/.

mid-1990s, and leveling off at about 45 percent in the late 1990s to the present. The representation of African Americans in the general population has never exceeded 15 percent. The African American prisoner population ratio to white prisoner population ratio was 2.5:1.0 in 1926, but it has reached the current ratio of 3:1.[17]

Impact of the War on Drugs

Dramatic increases in the overrepresentation of African Americans in the prison population have occurred in a context of generally increasing prison population totals and rising incarceration rates since the early 1970s. The incarceration binge seems to be slowing in the first years of the twenty-first century, but it remains at a level of approximately 2 million people incarcerated in state and federal jails and prisons. Although the incarceration binge surely has multiple sources, it may reflect an impact of the war on drugs. Michael Tonry, for example, argues that the war on drugs has had a particularly detrimental effect on African American males. Evidence of this impact, he argues, can be seen by focusing on the key years affected by the war on drugs: 1980 to 1992. During this period, the number of white males incarcerated in state and federal prison increased by 143 percent; for African American males the number increased by 186 percent.[18]

Statisticians for the BJS argue that the sources of growth for prison populations differ for white and African American inmates. Specifically, drug offenses and violent offenses account for the largest source of growth among state prison inmates. During the 10-year period from 1985 to 1995, "the increasing number of drug offenders accounted for 42 percent of the total growth of black inmates and 26 percent of the growth among white inmates." Similarly, the number of African American inmates serving time for violent offenses increased by 37 percent, whereas growth among white inmates was at a higher 47 percent.[19]

As we discussed in Chapters 3 and 4, the differential impact of the war on drugs may result more from the enforcement strategies of law enforcement than from higher patterns of minority drug use. Critics argue that although the police are reactive in responding to robbery, burglary, and other index offenses, they are proactive in dealing with drug offenses. There is evidence to suggest that they target minority communities—where drug dealing is more visible and where it is thus easier to make arrests—and tend to give less attention to drug activities in other neighborhoods.

Incarceration Rates

Another way to describe the makeup of U.S. prisons is to examine incarceration *rates*. The information offered by incarceration rates expands the picture of the prison inmate offered in population totals and percentages (as outlined previously). Incarceration rates offer the most vivid picture of the overrepresentation of African Americans and Hispanics in prison populations. Rates allow for the standardization of population figures that can be calculated over a particular target population. For example, the general incarceration rate in 2009 was 758 per 100,000 population.[20] This number can be further explored by calculating rates that reflect the number of one race group in the prison population relative to the number of that population in the overall U.S. population.

As shown in Table 9.3, over the last two decades African Americans and Hispanics have been substantially more likely than whites to be incarcerated. Although rates for all groups are increasing over time, the current rate for African American males remains the highest, at more than 7 times the rate for white males. Hispanic male rates were 2.5 times as high as the rate for white males but lower than the rate for African American males. Note that female rates of

T A B L E 9.3   Incarceration Rates by Race/Ethnicity and Gender

	Male			Female		
	White	African American	Hispanic	White	African American	Hispanic
1990	339	2,376	817	19	125	43
1995	461	3,250	1,174	27	176	57
2000	683	4,777	1,715	63	380	117
2005	709	4,682	1,856	88	347	144
2009	708	4,749	1,822	91	333	142

SOURCE: Heather West, *Prison Inmates at Midyear 2009—Statistical Tables* (Bureau of Justice Statistics, 2010), Table 18.

T A B L E 9.4   Incarceration Rates by Race/Ethnicity, Age, and Gender, 2009 (per 100,000 Population U.S. Residents by Race/ Ethnicity, Age, and Gender)

Age	Male				Female			
	Total	White	African American	Hispanic	Total	White	African American	Hispanic
Total	1398	708	4749	1822	131	91	333	142
18–19	1529	776	4403	1938	100	70	210	140
20–24	2939	1389	8889	3937	261	194	595	329
25–29	3298	1569	10501	3954	292	222	733	314
30–34	3278	1673	10995	3650	349	260	896	302
35–39	2915	1587	10068	3090	361	263	895	300
40–44	2593	1475	8668	2735	301	214	730	248
45–49	18.3	972	6387	2327	170	115	405	191
50–54	1061	568	3914	1583	82	63	155	132
55–59	644	383	2203	1159	40	25	60	86
60–64	349	227	1134	758	21	9	49	36
65 or older	127	87	454	243	5	3	5	9

SOURCE: Heather West, *Prison Inmates at Midyear 2009—Statistical Tables* (Washington, DC: Bureau of Justice Statistics, 2010), Table 19.

incarceration are substantially lower than male rates, but they are increasing at faster rates over time. In 2009 African American female rates of incarceration were more than 3 times higher than the rate for white females. The rate for Hispanic females was 1.5 times the rate for white females; it was lower than the rate for African American females.

These total incarceration rates fail to reveal the stark differences that occur among racial and gender groups by age. In Table 9.4 young African American males (ages 20 to 40) have incarceration rates 2.5 times higher than the aggregate rate for African American males and 4 times higher than white males in those age groups. Notably, in 2009 nearly 13 percent of all young black males, ages 25 to 29, were in prison or jail. The incarceration rates for Hispanic and white males also increase for the younger age groups but in less drastic proportions compared to African Americans. Moreover, less than 4 percent of young Hispanic males (ages 25 to 29) and less than 2 percent of young white males (ages 25 to 29) were incarcerated in prisons and jails.[21]

The information in Table 9.4 for females by race and age indicate drastically lower incarceration rates compared to males, but similar patterns emerge within race by age and within age by race. Notably, incarceration rates for African American females are 1.5 to 2.5 times higher than the total incarceration rate for the ages 20 to 40. African American women have the highest incarceration rates by race, regardless of age, with the exception of Hispanic women age 55–59. Incarceration rates also peak during those years for white and Hispanic

---

B o x   9.1   International Comparisons

In the international arena, the United States consistently has the highest incarceration rate in the world. According to the International Centre for Prison Studies, which reviewed incarceration rates in 216 countries in 2010, the United States has 748 people incarcerated in jails and prisons for every 100,000 people in the general population; in distant second is the Russian Federation at 585 per 100,000 population. America's neighbors have markedly lower rates, with Canada and Mexico at 117 and 202 people per 100,000 population incarcerated, respectively. Notably, more than half of the world's countries (57 percent) have incarceration rates of less than 150 per 100,000 population. European countries have among the lowest rates, with England/Wales at 155; France, 96; Germany, 88; Switzerland, 79; Sweden, 78; Norway, 71; Denmark, 71; Finland, 60; and Lichtenstein at 28 per 100,000 population.[22]

In 2001 The Sentencing Project also calculated that the incarceration rate for African American males in the United States was more than four times the rate of South Africa in the last years of apartheid—that is, in 1993 the incarceration rate for African American males was 3,822 per 100,000 compared to the rate of 815 per 100,000 for South African males. In 2001 the incarceration rate for African American males in the United States soared to 4,848 per 100,000.

The racial disparity in the nation's prison populations is revealed even more dramatically by The Sentencing Project, which estimates that at some point in their lives, African American males have a 29 percent chance of serving time in prison or jail. Hispanic males have a lower lifetime risk at 16 percent, whereas white males have a 4 percent chance of being incarcerated at some time during their lives.[23]

---

women, with incarceration rates for white women surpassing Hispanic women from ages 30–40. (See Box 9.1 for information on incarceration rates in other parts of the world.)

JAILS AND MINORITIES

The Role of Jail

Jail populations are significantly different from prison populations. Because jails serve a different function in the criminal justice system, they are subject to different dynamics in terms of admissions and releases. The Annual Survey of Jails reveals that just more than half of inmates are being detained while awaiting trial, whereas just less than half of the daily population of all jail inmates are convicted offenders. Those awaiting trial are in jail because they were denied bail or were unable to raise bail. The other inmates are convicted offenders who have been sentenced to serve time in jail. Although the vast majority of these inmates have been convicted of misdemeanors, some convicted felons are given a "split sentence" involving jail followed by probation. Also, a small number of inmates have been sentenced and are in jail awaiting transfer to state or federal prison facilities.

T A B L E 9.5   **Percentage of Jail Inmates by Race and Ethnicity, One-Day Count, 2009**

Race/Ethnicity	Percentage
White (non-Hispanic)	42.5
African American (non-Hispanic)	39.2
Hispanic	16.2
Other (Native Americans, Alaska Natives, Asians, Pacific Islanders)	1.9

SOURCE: Todd D. Minton. *Jail Inmates at Midyear 2009—Statistical Tables* (Washington, DC: U.S. Department of Justice, 2010).

Because of the jail's role as a pretrial detention center, there is a high rate of turnover among the jail population. The data used in Table 9.5 represent a static one-day count, as opposed to an annual total of all people who pass through the jail system. Thus, *daily* population of jails is lower than prisons, but the *annual* total of people incarcerated is higher.

Minority Overrepresentation

Racial and ethnic minorities are consistently overrepresented in the nation's local jail populations; at midyear 2009 nearly 6 of 10 people in local jails were racial and ethnic minorities. As Table 9.5 indicates, whereas whites make up the largest proportion of inmates in jails around the country (roughly 43 percent), African Americans are notably overrepresented compared to their representation in the general population. Hispanics represent a slightly higher percentage of the jail population than the general population. These numbers change slightly from year to year; sometimes African Americans make up the largest proportion of jail inmates, so that over time there are roughly the same number of African Americans and whites in jail. The overrepresentation of Hispanics has been higher in some years than 2009 (see 1996), indicating a more serious disparity than that reflected in Table 9.5. Overall, the picture of disparity depicted by these jail numbers is essentially similar to the reflection of race and ethnicity in prison populations. (See "Focus on an Issue: Jails on Tribal Lands" for specific information about tribal jails.) Because of the jail's function as a pretrial detention center, jail population is heavily influenced by bail decisions. If more people were released on nonfinancial considerations, the number of people in jail would be lower. This raises the questions of racial discrimination in bail setting, which we discussed in Chapter 5. As noted in that chapter, there is evidence that judges impose higher bail—or are more likely to deny bail altogether—if the defendant is a racial minority.

COMMUNITY CORRECTIONS

More than 7.6 million people were under correctional supervision in the United States in 2009.[24] Over 5 million of these offenders were supervised in the community on the status of parole or probation. Does the pattern of racial and ethnic disparity present in incarceration facilities remain in community corrections?

Parole: Early Release from Prison

Parole is a form of early release from prison under supervision in the community. Prison inmates are released to one of two forms of parole: discretionary parole or

---

Focus on an Issue
Jails on Tribal Lands

In 2008 more than 75,400 Native Americans were under correctional supervision (prison, jail, probation, and parole) in the United States (federal, state, local, and tribal authorities combined). Most, 62 percent, were under community supervision (47,000). The population of Native Americans under correctional supervision increasd by 5.8 percent from 2007 to 2008. The U.S. population is approximately 1 percent Native American, and 1.2 percent of inmates in custody in prisons and jails across the United States in 2007 were Native American. Between 2000 and 2008, the survey of jails and prisons indicated that the number of Native Americns grew by 4.4 percent annually.[25] The incarceration rate for Native Americans in prison and jail facilities was 21 percent higher than the incarceration rate for all races combined (921 per 100,000 Native Americans compared to 759 per 100,000 U.S. residents).

The picture of jails on tribal lands is presented by the Bureau of Justice Statistics, in "Jails in Indian Country, 2008." The statutory meaning of "Indian country" (18 U.S.C. 1,151) is all lands within an Indian reservation, dependent Indian Communities, and Indian Trust allotments.[26] Currently, nearly 300 Native

American land areas / reservations exist across 33 states. Federal regulations limit the jurisdiction and incarceration powers of tribal governments by identity of the victim and offender, the severity of the crime, and location of the crime. Tribal sentencing authority is limited to one year, a $5,000 fine per offense, or both (25 U.S.C. 1,153).[27]

More than 12,500 people were admitted to jails in the first six months of 2008, with a total of 2,135 people on the census date, June 30. This population is smaller than the number of Native Americans held in locally operated city/county jails, which was estimated at 9,000 for the year 2008.

These offenders were incarcerated in 82 tribal confinement facilities; however, 0.5 percent of the tribal inmate population is held in 33 jails. The largest Native American tribal jail populations are found in Arizona, with additional large institutions in New Mexico and North Dakota. In 2008, 63 percent of inmates being held were convicted offenders, predominantly for misdemeanor offenses. Overall, 40 percent of offenders were held for a violent offense, with 15 percent charged with either simple assault or domestic violence offenses.[28]

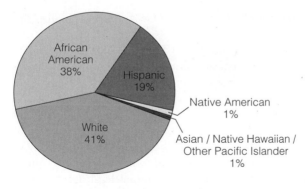

F I G U R E 9.3 State Parole Populations by Race and Ethnicity, 2008

SOURCE: Glaze Lauren and Thomas Bonczar, *Probation and Parole in the United States, 2008* (Washington, DC: U.S. Department of Justice, 2010), Appendix Table 15.

mandatory parole. The U.S. Department of Justice defines discretionary parole as a decision made by a parole board to "conditionally release prisoners based on a statutory or administrative determination of eligibility," whereas mandatory parole "occurs in jurisdictions using determinate sentencing statutes. Inmates are conditionally released from prison after serving a portion of their original sentence minus any good time earned."[29] It is not surprising, therefore, that parole populations are similar in racial and ethnic distribution to federal and state prison populations. In 2008 (Figure 9.3) slightly more whites than African Americans were released on parole (41 percent compared to 38 percent). The percentage of the parolee population that is African American has declined over the past 15 years from 45 percent in 1995. Hispanics make up the other roughly 20 percent of parolees. Although African Americans and Hispanics are still overrepresented in parole populations compared to their presentation in the population, the proportions of parolees that are African American and Hispanic are different from the percentages of incarcerated inmates that are African American and Hispanic. Does this evidence suggest that the positive transition to parole is more commonly reserved for white inmates than African American and Hispanic inmates? Given the positive impact of supervised transition back into society to reduce the occurrence of recidivism, are African American and Hispanic inmates who are released from prison after completing their entire sentence without the benefit of parole experiencing a type of discrimination? (See Chapter 1 for types of discrimination.)

Recent research by Kathryn D. Morgan and Brent Smith examining parole decision making in one southern state found that the significant predictors for setting the parole hearing were seriousness of the original offense, time served, total disciplinary reports, and recommendations from the institutional parole officer; granting the release decision was significantly impacted only by prison personnel recommendations. Race did not have a direct impact on either decision, when controlling for the expected legal/institutional variables.[30] This finding is similar to the sentencing research (Chapter 7) that finds that extra-legal variables are the strongest predictors of a decision to incarcerate and length of prison sentence.

However, as suggested in the works of Marjorie S. Zatz and Cassia Spohn, the interaction of race with these decision-making factors is also important to consider.[31] When partitioning the sample, Morgan and Smith found little evidence or facial patterns in the influences on the parole release decision, but the eligibility for parole release decision does suggest that time since last disciplinary report may have an impact for African American inmates but not for white inmates.

In an analysis of parole timing decisions in one state, Beth M. Huebner and Timothy S. Bynum look at the impact of race in combination with a number of institutional factors. Their analysis found that parole board members were influenced by "measures of the current offense, institutional behavior and the official parole guidelines score." In addition to these institutional/legal factors, race emerged as a direct and indirect predictor of the parole timing decision. In short, African American "offenders spent a longer time in prison awaiting parole compared with white offenders, and the racial and ethnic differences were maintained net of legal and individual demographic and community characteristics" and "increases with time" Huebner and Bynum place these decisions by the parole board members in a familiar theoretical context: they characterize the parole decisions as being influenced by members' perceptions of how the dangerousness of the typical black male drug offender impacts community safety (focal concerns theory and perceptual shorthand were discussed in Chapter 7). Additionally, they draw on social context of the social threat perspective (Chapters 2 and 3) and the legal organizational context (legal variables having the most influence on decision making, Chapter 7) to discuss their findings.[32]

Success and Failure on Parole

A parolee "succeeds" on parole if he or she completes the terms of supervision without violations. A parolee can "fail" in one of two ways: by being arrested for another crime or by violating one of the conditions of parole release (using drugs, possessing a weapon, violating curfew, and so on). In either case, parole authorities can revoke parole and send the person back to prison.

Parole revocation, therefore, is nearly equivalent to the judge's power to sentence an offender in the first place because it can mean that the offender will return to prison. The decision to revoke parole is discretionary; parole authorities may choose to overlook a violation and not send the person back to prison. This use of discretion opens the door for possible discrimination.

Most parolees are released from state prisons. Currently, nearly 80 percent of inmates will be released to parole supervision rather than simply being released at the expiration of their sentence. Recent data indicate that 42 percent of all parolees at the state level successfully completed parole. The success rate varied somewhat by racial/ethnic groups: 40.0 percent of whites, 39.0 percent of African Americans, 50.6 percent of Hispanics, and 42.2 percent of other races. The percentage of parole violators by race within one study year indicates that the majority of those violating parole were African American (51.8 percent), with whites representing less than one-third of violators (27.5 percent) and Hispanics representing approximately one-fifth of violators (18.3 percent).[33]

B o x 9.2   Supervision in the Community: An Uneven Playing Field?

Both parole and probation involve supervision in the community under a set of specific provisions for client behavior. One of the most common provisions is the requirement of employment. Not being able to attain or retain employment may lead to a violation of supervision conditions and unsuccessful discharge of an individual from probation or parole. Essentially, a person could be sent to prison for being unemployed. It is possible that the employment provision creates uneven hardships for minorities. In 2010 the unemployment rate for U.S. citizens, regardless of race, was 9.3 percent.[34] This rate, of course, varies by race and ethnicity: the rate for whites is 8.4 percent; African Americans, 15.4 percent; and Hispanics, 12.7 percent. Unemployment rates also vary by age; youth between the ages of 16 and 24 have higher unemployment rates than the general population. Young people have unemployment rates two to three times higher, with the highest unemployment rates found for young (16 to 19) African Americans at 45.8 percent and young Hispanics at 30 percent; the lowest was for young white males, at 20.8 percent.[35] In short, ethnic- and race-specific unemployment rates vary substantially, showing the disadvantaged status of minorities in the labor market. If employment is a nearly universal expectation for probation and parole, does this aspect of the general economy adversely affect defendants and inmates of color when judges make decisions about who is suitable for probation or when parole boards make decisions about who is suitable to be granted parole? If yes, could this be seen as a form of institutional discrimination? (See chapter 1 for discussion of types of discrimination.)

A small number of federal inmates are still eligible for parole consideration. Recent data on federal parole reveal that approximately 78 percent of federal parole discharges were from successful completion of parole conditions. Once again, these rates vary by minority group status. Whites and other races had the highest successful completion rate of 76 percent, followed by Hispanics at 68 percent and African Americans with the lowest at 53 percent. Similarly, African Americans had the highest return-to-prison rates (36 percent), with all other groups exhibiting a return rate of lower than 20 percent.[36] (See Box 9.2 for a discussion of supervision of people on parole in the community.)

Probation: A Case of Sentencing Discrimination?

Probation is an alternative to incarceration, a sentence to supervision in the community. The majority of all the people under correctional supervision are on probation, totaling more than 4.2 million people.[37]

The racial demographics in Figure 9.4 offer a picture of the probation population with race and ethnicity presented separately. These figures indicate that African Americans are overrepresented (29 percent) in the probation population relative to their presence in the general population. Correspondingly, whites are underrepresented at 56 percent of all probationers and Hispanics are represented at roughly the same as their representation in the population.

It is immediately apparent that the racial disparity for probation is not as great as it is for the prison population, however. Given that probation is a less severe

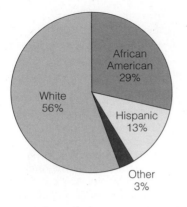

FIGURE 9.4 Probation Population by Race and Ethnicity, 2008

SOURCE: Glaze Lauren and Thomas Bonczar, *Probation and Parole in the United States, 2008.* (Washington, DC: U.S. Department of Justice, 2010), Appendix Table 5

sentence than prison, this difference may indicate that the advantage of receiving the less severe sentence of probation is more likely to be reserved for whites. In a study of sentencing in California, Joan Petersilia found that 71 percent of whites convicted of a felony were granted probation, compared with 67 percent of African Americans and 65 percent of Hispanics.[38] Similarly, Spohn and other colleagues found that in "borderline cases" in which judges could impose either a long probation sentence or a short prison sentence, whites were more likely to get probation and African Americans were more likely to get prison. (See the discussion of discrimination in sentencing in Chapter 7 and Figure 9.4.)

Community Corrections: A Native American Example

The phenomenon of drug courts in American criminal justice emerged in the late 1980s. Primarily, these specialized courts emerged in response to the growing concern over drug-related cases that were clogging the courts and filling up our jails and prisons and the perception that traditional "War on Drugs" strategies of attacking supply and incarcerating users to control demand was not producing the desired results.

The Drug Courts Program Office of the U.S. Department of Justice defines the drug court approach as departing "from the standard court approach by systematically bringing drug treatment to the criminal justice population entering the court system ... In the drug court, ... treatment is anchored in the authority of the judge who holds the defendant or offender personally and publicly accountable for treatment progress." Essentially, local teams of judges, law enforcement officials, prosecuting attorneys, defense attorneys, probation officers, and treatment providers are using "the coercive powers of the court to force abstinence and alter behavior with a combination of intensive judicial supervision, escalating sanctions, mandatory drug testing and strong aftercare programs."[39]

Starting in 1997, attempts have been made to adapt the drug court curriculum to tribal court settings. Currently, more than 40 programs exist in more than

13 states. A number of adaptations need to be made to incorporate the drug court model to the tribal court setting, but the basic philosophy of therapeutic jurisprudence is a strong complement to many elements of indigenous justice philosophy. First, the naming of drug courts has undergone a transition to the title of "Tribal Healing to Wellness Courts." This renaming and the subsequent adaptation of procedures are designed to meet the cultural needs of individual Native communities and their long-established traditional Native concepts of justice.

The Tribal Law and Policy Institute notes that the "Tribal Healing to Wellness Courts return to a more traditional method of Justice for Indian people by 1) creating an environment that focuses on the problems underlying the criminal act rather than the acts itself and 2) stressing family, extended family and community involvement in the healing process." In short, advocates argue that the Tribal Healing to Wellness Courts are "a modern revitalization of Native principles of Justice—truth, honor, respect, harmony, balance, healing, wellness, apology or contrition, restitution, rehabilitation and an holistic approach." The hope is that the court will function to "restore harmony and balance to individuals, the families and the communities which have been devastated by alcohol and drug use."[40]

Tribal Healing to Wellness Courts involve a number of tribal members in the court process, including tribal elders and medicine men, to accomplish the goals of treatment and community service. Usually, part of the treatment component is the mandatory attendance at community activities reflecting traditional, cultural heritage values. Such activities include "traditional healing ceremonies, talking circles, peacemaking, sweats, sweat lodge, visits with medicine men, sun dance and vision quest," depending on the practices of the individual Native community. Beyond the typical community service requirement of drug courts are the requirements of spending time with elders, tribal storytellers, or both.

All of the methods and procedures adopted by Tribal Healing to Wellness Courts are firmly grounded in traditional dispute resolution mechanisms and traditional spiritual components to promote healing to wellness. The most common issue dealt with in the Tribal Courts is the problem of alcohol abuse. Records indicate that more than 90 percent of the criminal cases that come before tribal courts have an alcohol or substance abuse component. The substance abuse issues are present not just for some adults but also for some children, so some tribes have adopted courts for both groups. Juveniles also have the problem of inhalant use.[41]

The development of the Tribal Healing to Wellness Courts is often limited by the sentencing authority granted to the tribal courts. These courts have limited jurisdiction to nonmajor crimes on tribal lands and limited influence in off-reservation crimes. The Tribal Law and Policy Institute notes, however, that some Tribal Healing to Wellness Courts have agreements with state court systems to transfer jurisdiction to them when tribal members are involved in substance abuse–related offenses.

Focus on an Issue
Civil Rights of Convicted Felons

Individuals convicted of felonies in the United States may experience a range of sentences from incarceration to probation. Such sentences in effect limit the civil rights of the convicted. No longer do we live in a society that views the convicted felon from the legal status of civil death, literally a slave of the state, but some civil rights restrictions endure after the convicted offender serves a judicially imposed sentence. *Collateral consequences* is a term used to refer to the statutory restrictions imposed by a legislative body on a convicted felon's rights. Such restrictions vary by state but include restrictions on employment, carrying firearms, holding public office, and voting.

The Sentencing Project highlights the negative nature of restricting the rights of convicted felons to vote with this dramatic statement:

> Nationally, an estimated 5.3 million Americans are denied the right to vote because of laws that prohibit voting by people with felony convictions. Felony disenfranchisement is an obstacle to participation in democratic life which is exacerbated by racial disparities in the criminal justice system, resulting in an estimated 13% of Black men unable to vote.[42]

Forty-eight states and the District of Columbia restrict the rights of imprisoned people to vote; more than half of states restrict the right to vote for offenders on probation and roughly two-thirds of states limit this right while on parole.[43] In most states the right to vote can be restored (automatically or by petition) after completion of the sentence (or within a fixed number of years). However, in eight states the legal prohibition on voting is permanent. The Sentencing Project reports that although some states allow for the restoration of voting rights to felony offenders who have served out their sentences, the

process is not always easy. In the state of Nebraska, the ex-offender has his/her voting rights restored automatically after two years, but in some states the ex-offender has to apply to the Pardons Board for reinstatement.[44]

In the state of Alabama ex-offenders are required to provide a DNA sample to the Alabama Department of Forensic Sciences as part of the process of regaining the right to vote.[45] Additional restrictions on convicted felons were created with the passage of the USA PATRIOT Act. Under these provisions, ex-offenders are unable to attain certain commercial driver's licenses and are banned from transporting materials designated as hazardous waste.

Given the current increases in incarceration rates across the country, the additional penalty of disenfranchisement for convicted felons becomes an increasing concern. In short, the permanence of this measure may have unanticipated consequences. Because there is an overrepresentation of African American males in U.S. prisons, "significant proportions of the black population in some states have been locked out of the voting booth." For example, in the state of Florida, which denies voting rights permanently to convicted felons, nearly one-third of the African American male population is not eligible to vote.[46] It has been argued that laws such as these, that have the effect of barring a substantial portion of the minority population from voting, fail to promote a racially diverse society. Is this a form of institutional discrimination (see Chapter 1)? Should we change laws that have a racial impact, even if the intent is not racially motivated?

In 2009 Representative John Conyers and Senator Russell Feingold introduced federal legislation to restore voting rights to convicted felons for federal elections. If passed, the Democracy Restoration Act

(DRA) will restore federal election rights to over 5 million Americans. Do you support this legislation? Would restoring the vote to these Americans impact presidential elections? Should convicted offenders be allowed to earn back their right to vote as recognition of their efforts at rehabilitation?

THEORETICAL PERSPECTIVES ON THE RACIAL DISTRIBUTION OF CORRECTIONAL POPULATIONS

Several theoretical arguments are advanced to explain the overwhelming overrepresentation of African Americans in the correctional system. The most fundamental question is whether prison populations reflect discrimination in the criminal justice system or other factors. One view is that the overrepresentation reflects widespread discrimination; the alternative view is that the overrepresentation results from a disproportionate involvement in criminal activity on the part of minorities. Coramae Richey Mann argues that there is systematic discrimination based on color, whereas William Wilbanks contends that the idea of systematic discrimination is a "myth."[47] The work of Alfred Blumstein offers a benchmark to explore the results of such research. Focusing on 1979 prison population data, Blumstein sought to isolate the impact of discrimination from other possible factors. The key element of his research is the following formula:[48]

X = ratio of expected black-to-white incarceration rates based only on arrest disproportionality/ratio of black-to-white incarceration rates actually observed.

Essentially, this formula compares the expected black–white disparity (X) in state prison populations based on recorded black–white disparity in arrest rates (numerator) over the observed black–white disparity in incarceration rates (denominator). Thus, accepting the argument that arrest rates are not a reflection of discrimination, Blumstein's formula calculates the portion of the prison population left unexplained by the disproportionate representation of African Americans at the arrest stage. In short, this figure is the amount of actual racial disproportionality in incarceration rates that is open to an explanation or charge of discrimination.

Overall, Blumstein found that 20 percent of the racial disparity in incarceration rates is left unexplained by the overrepresentation of African Americans at the arrest stage. Crime-specific rates indicate that results vary by crime type:

All offenses	20.0 percent
Homicide	2.8 percent
Aggravated assault	5.2 percent
Robbery	15.6 percent
Rape	26.3 percent
Burglary	33.1 percent
Larceny / auto theft	45.6 percent
Drugs	48.9 percent

Arguably, the main implication of this list is that the level of unexplained disproportionality is "directly related to the discretion permitted or used in handling each of the offenses, which tends to be related to offense seriousness—the less serious the offenses (and the greater discretion), the greater the amount of the disproportionality in prison that must be accounted for on grounds other than differences in arrest."[49]

This observation is particularly salient in the context of drug offenses. Recall the arguments from Chapter 4 that contend that drug arrest decisions are subject to more proactive enforcement than most offenses. Combine this observation with the fact that during the surge of incarceration rates from 1980 to 1996, the offense with the greatest impact on new commitments to prison was drug offenses. In short, the offense category indicated to suffer from the broad use of discrimination and the most opportunity for discrimination is the fastest-growing portion of new commitments to prison. Thus, Blumstein's findings, although generally not an indictment of the criminal justice system, suggest an ominous warning for the presence of discrimination during the era of the war on drugs.

Patrick Langan reexamined Blumstein's argument, contending that he relied on an inappropriate data set. Langan argued that prison admissions offered a more appropriate comparison to arrest differentials than prison populations. Langan also incorporated victim identification data as a substitute for arrest data to circumvent the biases associated with arrest. In addition to altering Blumstein's formula, he looked at three years of data (1973, 1979, 1982) across five offense types (robbery, aggravated assault, simple assault, burglary, and larceny). Even after making these modifications, Langan confirmed Blumstein's findings; about 20 percent of the racial overrepresentation in prison admissions was left unexplained.[50]

In an updated analysis with 1990 prison population data, Blumstein found that the amount of unexplained variation in racially disproportionate prison populations on the basis of arrest data increased from 20 percent to 24 percent. In addition, the differentials discussed earlier on the basis of discretion and seriousness increased for drug crimes and less-serious crimes, becoming smaller for homicide and robbery only. This seems to confirm the argument that the war on drugs has increased the racial disparities in prison populations.[51]

Tonry challenges Blumstein's work on several grounds. He argues, first, that it is a mistake to assume that official Uniform Crime Report arrest statistics accurately reflect offending rates. As discussed in Chapter 4, there is evidence of race discrimination in arrests. This is particularly true with respect to drug arrests, which account for much of the dramatic increase in the prison populations in recent years. Second, Tonry points out that Blumstein's analysis used national-level data. Aggregating in this fashion can easily mask evidence of discrimination in certain areas of the country.

Tonry's third criticism is that Blumstein's approach could easily hide "offsetting forms of discrimination that are equally objectionable but not observable in the aggregate."[52] One example would be sentencing African American offenders with white victims more harshly, while at the same time punishing African American offenders with African American victims less harshly (see Chapter 7 for a more detailed discussion). The former represents a bias against African

American offenders, and the latter is a bias against African American victims. If we aggregate the data, as Blumstein did, neither pattern is evident.

Darnell F. Hawkins and Kenneth A. Hardy speak to the possibility of regional differences by looking at state-specific imprisonment rates. These authors find a wide variation across the 50 states in the extent of the differential in African American imprisonment rates left unexplained by disproportionate African American arrest rates. The "worst state" was New Mexico, with only 2 percent of the difference explained by the expected impact of arrest. At the other end of the continuum, Missouri was the "best state," with 96 percent of the incarceration rates of African Americans explained by differential arrest rates. Hawkins and Hardy conclude that "Blumstein's figure of 80 percent would not seem to be a good approximation for all states."[53]

Crutchfield, Bridges, and Pitchford further address the question of whether differential imprisonment rates by race reflect differential offending or differential enforcement with a state and regional level analysis. They use data arrest data (for all index crimes combined and violent crimes only) as well as imprisonment data. In comparison to Blumstein and Langan, who find that "little unwarranted racial disparity in imprisonment rates exists in the United States," Cruthfield et al. find that, "in some areas the unwarranted disparities are substantial and ... the statistical relationship between arrest and imprisonment rates is quite weak." Starting with the assumption that arrest figures reflect a reliable indicator of criminal involvement by race, they find that "there is considerable variation among states in the degree to which levels of criminal involvement among Blacks actually explain observed Black imprisonment numbers." Roughly two-thirds of imprisonment disparity is explained by index crime arrest disparity in national data. Crutchfield et al. note that "40% of states explain less of their observed Black imprisonment via Black involvement in serious crimes than can be explained for the aggregated national observed black imprisonment rate." While Mississippi, Indiana, and Nevada explain almost all of their observed disparity in imprisonment rate with arrest data, Alaska explains less than 1 percent of its differential imprisonment rate with the index crime arrest data. Additionally, Texas and New Jersey explain less than half of their disparities with index crime arrest data. In the analysis of violent imprisonment data, nearly 90 percent of the discrepancy is explained by differential arrest at the national level. In this analysis one-third of states had lower amounts of observed numbers of imprisonment explained by arrest numbers than the national average. Overall, contextual differences by jurisdiction do still seem to influence differential imprisonment rates across the United States in addition to the differential offense patterns in arrest numbers.[54]

Doing additional work in this area, J. Sorensen, R. Hope, and D. Stemen explore regional differences in the racial disproportionality of state prison admissions. They find that the Midwestern states have a higher level of racial disproportionality in imprisonment rates, even when controlling for race-specific arrest rates. Their findings indicate that the Midwest has 67.4 percent of racial disproportionality in state prison admissions, followed by 64.3 percent in the Northeast, 61 percent in the South, and 60.2 percent in the West. After looking at possible explanations for this region disparity, Sorensen et al. conclude that these "differences among regions are due to differential involvement in serious crime by race resulting from a higher concentration of ... Blacks relative to whites in the urban areas of the Midwest."[55]

Crutchfield and colleagues offer a suitable conclusion to the review of these studies by stating that "racial patterns in imprisonment are substantively important for criminologists, and the perpetuation of unwarranted racial disparities in imprisonment is a critical matter for public policy."[56] These works seem to suggest a combination of differential offending by race and differential enforcement by race. Remember that Chapters 2 and 3 discuss a number of theoretical explanations that help explain the racial gap in offending; Chapters 4–7 discuss a number of theoretical explanations for differential enforcement.

In a similar attempt to look past systematic racial discrimination in the criminal justice system, researchers have begun to explore the intricacies of contextual discrimination. A review by Theodore G. Chiricos and Charles Crawford reveals that researchers have started to study the social context's impact on the racial composition of imprisonment rates by investigating such issues as the population's racial composition, the percentage of unemployed African Americans, and the region.[57]

The first two issues reflect the theoretical argument that communities and thus decision makers will be apprehensive under certain conditions and become more punitive. Specific conditions of apprehension (or threat) are related to racial mass. For example, large concentrations of African Americans will be associated with a higher fear of crime and a need to be more punitive. Raymond J. Michalowski and Michael A. Pearson found that racial composition of African Americans in a state was positively associated with general incarceration rates. However, the impact of racial composition on race-specific incarceration rates is less clear.[58] Hawkins and Hardy discovered that states with smaller percentages of African Americans were associated with more racial disparity in incarceration rates that could be accounted for by arrest rates.[59] In contrast, Bridges and Crutchfield found that states with higher percentages of African Americans in the general population were associated with lower levels of racial disparity in incarceration rates.[60] Miriam DeLone and Theodore Chiricos argue that this inconsistency is the result of an improper level of analysis. They argue that looking at state-level imprisonment and racial composition rates can be deceiving. The proper level of analysis is the level of the sentencing court. In their study of county-level incarceration rates, they found that higher levels of African Americans led to higher levels of general incarceration and African American incarceration rates.[61]

Race-specific unemployment rates reflect the idea that idle (or surplus) populations are crime prone and in need of deterrence. This line of reasoning requires more punitive response, with higher incarceration rates when the perceived crime-prone population is idle.[62] Generally, this "threat" is measured by the unemployment rate of the perceived crime-prone population—young, African American males. DeLone and Chiricos have found that at the county level, high young African American male unemployment rates are not associated with higher general incarceration rates but are predictive of higher young African American male incarceration rates.[63] (Box 9.3 details other explanations for the racial distribution of the prison population.)

**B o x   9.3   Additional Explanations for the Racial Distribution
of U.S. Prison Populations**

Historically, some have argued that prison replaced the social control of slavery in the South after the end of the Civil War. Given the criminalization of vagrancy and the operation of the convict lease system, a *de facto* slavery system was invoked on those African Americas who did not leave the South and who refused to offer their labor to former plantation owners who needed it.[64]

Others have argued that prison has always been used to supplement the needs of capitalism as a mechanism to control surplus populations in times of high unemployment. Specifically, African American males, who have the highest unemployment rates, have been viewed as socially dangerous surplus populations.[65]

In the context of the war on drugs, some have argued that the increasing African American male prison populations are a response to a moral panic about drugs that stems from the association of crime and drug use with this population almost exclusively.[66]

Adjustment to Prison

Research on the adjustment of men to life in prison has been available for many years, beginning with Donald Clemmer's *The Prison Community* and including Gresham Sykes's *The Society of Captives* and John Irwin and Donald Cressey's "Thieves, Convicts, and Inmate Culture."[67] James B. Jacobs argues that without exception these studies disregarded the issue of race, although the prison populations in the institutions under study were racially diverse. Consequently, according to Jacobs, the prevailing concept of the "prison subculture" needs to be revised. Jacobs further argues that race is the defining factor of the prison experience. Racial and ethnic identity defines the social groupings in prisons, the operation of informal economic systems, the organization of religious activities, and the reasons for inmate misconduct. In other words, white inmates tend to associate with white inmates, African American inmates associate with African Americans, and so on. In this respect, the racial and ethnic segregation in prison mimics society on the outside.[68]

Goodstein and MacKenzie support Jacob's observations and argue that their own "exploratory study of race and inmate adjustment to prison demonstrates that the experience of imprisonment differs for African Americans and whites." They report that although African Americans may develop more antiauthoritarian attitudes, and are more likely to challenge prison officials, they appear to have fewer conflicts with fellow inmates.[69]

Kevin N. Wright explored the relationship between "race and economic marginality" to explain adjustment to prison. He explored the apparently common-sense assumption that African Americans, because of their experience in the "modern urban ghetto" (see information on the underclass in Chapter 3), will be more "resilient" to the pains of imprisonment. He found that "ghetto life supposedly socializes the individual to engage in self-protection against the hostile social environment of the slum and the cold and unpredictable prison setting." Using multiple indicators of adaptation to the prison environment, Wright found that although economic marginality does appear to influence the ease of adjustment to prison, this appears to be the case regardless of race.[70]

Other research on male prison populations also indicates that race may not always explain institutional behavior. Research on the effects of race on levels of institutional misconduct reveals an inconsistent picture. Although some researchers find nonwhites overrepresented in inmate misconduct, Joan Petersilia, Paul Honig, and Charles Hubay's study of three state prison systems found three different patterns in relationships between race and rule infractions. In Michigan there was no relationship between race and rule infractions; in California whites had significantly higher rule infractions; and in Texas, African Americans had significantly higher rule infractions.[71]

Timothy Flanagan finds similarly inconsistent results. He argues that inmates' age at commitment, history of drug use, and current incarceration offense are most predictive of general misconduct rates. He does, however, find that race is an important predictor for older inmates with no drug history and sentenced for an offense other than homicide. Flanagan recommends that race (among other predictors) is a variable that is inappropriate to use in assisting with the security classification of inmates as a result of its low predictive power in relation to institutional misconduct.[72]

Research of federal prison inmates by Miles D. Harer and Darrell J. Steffensmeier offers support for the importation model of prison violence, indicating that

---

Focus on an Issue
Mortality in Prisons and Jails

Inmate mortality rates are available for state prison and local jail populations. For all causes, regardless of race, 141 per 100,000 inmates die in jails per year and 251 per 100,000 inmates die in prison per year. The average annual figures from 2000–2007 indicate that there are significant racial/ethnic differences for all causes combined, as well as for suicide rates, with few differences for homicide rates. Both suicide and homicide rates have declined steadily since the 1980s. Currently, the rates for suicide are 42 and 16 per 100,000 inmates (jail and prison, respectively), with the rates for homicide at 3 and 4 per 100,000 inmates (jail and prison, respectively).[73]

Suicide rates are substantially higher for whites in jail and prison than for African Americans inmates (68 per 100,000 jail inmates and 26 per 100,000 prison inmates, respectively, compared to 16 per 100,000 jail inmates and 7 per 100,000 state inmates, respectively). Hispanic inmates have a somewhat lower rate than whites (34 per 100,000 jail inmates and 18 per 100,000 prison inmates) but higher than for African American inmates.

The homicide rate average from 2000–2007 in local jails was reported at 3 per 100,000 population and does not vary across racial/ethnic groups. However, the homicide rates for state prison inmates are higher than the overall rate of 4 per 100,000 population for Hispanics (5 per 100,000 inmates) and whites (5 per 100,000 inmates) and less than the overall rate for African American inmates (3 per 100,000 inmates).

African American inmates are significantly more likely to receive disorderly conduct reports for violence than white inmates are, but they are more likely to have lower levels of alcohol and drug misconduct reports than whites.[74] This picture reflects the differential levels of violence and drug behavior between African Americans and whites conveyed in arrest figures and assumed to characterize the general behavior patterns of these groups in American society (see Chapter 2).

Many correctional observers say that even with the numerical dominance of African Americans in correctional facilities, they are still at a disadvantage in terms of the allocation of resources. For example, Thomas argues that race operates in prison culture to guide behavior, allocate resources, and elevate white groups to a privileged status even when they are not numerically dominant.[75]

Hostility Among Released Inmates

Do the deprivations of prison have a lasting effect on the released inmate? Andy Hochstetler, Matt DeLisi, and Travis C. Pratt offer a contemporary look at the feelings of hostility among released male inmates in an effort to understand how the strains of imprisonment affect the mental health of the released offender and potentially the negative impact on his reintegration.[76] Their results indicate that hostility among released prisoners can be explained well by the released inmate's level of social support. They hypothesize that social support is the key mediating factor between race, age, self-control (control of temper, impulsivity, risk taking, self-centeredness), and perceptions of prison discomfort (sense of deprivation, loss of privacy, boredom, stress, and so on) in predicting low or high levels of hostility. They find that race does not have a directly predictive effect on hostility, but rather that the impact of race is conditioned by social support. These findings suggest that whatever strains exist in the nonwhite released inmate's experiences they can be mediated by strong social support from family and friends, resulting in less hostility and arguably more chance at successful noncriminal reintegration into society.[77] In a similar vein, the discomfort of prison as a source of postrelease hostility can be at least partially neutralized by the presence of social support. These findings support a long-standing push by criminologists to get policy makers to recognize the importance of social support mechanisms to successful prisoner reentry.[78]

Race and Religion

Religion often emerges as a source of solidarity among prison inmates and as a mechanism for inmates to adjust to the frustrations of the prison environment. Although religion may be seen as a benign or even a rehabilitative influence, some religious activities in prison have been met with criticism by correctional officials and accepted only with federal court intervention. Concern arises when religious tenants seem to espouse the supremacy of one racial group over another.

Jacobs argues that the Black Muslim movement in U.S. prisons was a response to active external proselytizing by the church.[79] The most influential Muslim movement was the Nation of Islam, founded by Elijah Muhammad. Darlene Conley and Julius Debro point out that although the Nation of Islam was not particularly competitive with Christianity in the nonprison population, "it had special appeal to incarcerated Black males. In contrast to the various religious denominations, which preached religious repentance and submission and obedience to the U.S. justice system … the Nation of Islam preached Black pride and resistance to white oppression."[80] Prison administrators overtly resisted the movement for several years. The American Correctional Association issued a policy statement in 1960 refusing to recognize the legitimacy of the Muslim religion, based on arguments that it was a "cult" that disrupted prison operations. Jacobs notes that "prison officials saw in the Muslims not only a threat to prison authority, but also a broader revolutionary challenge to American society"[81] that led to challenges of the white correctional authority.

Consequently, prison officials tried to suppress Muslim religious activities by such actions as banning the Koran. This led to lawsuits asserting the Muslim's right to the free exercise of religion. In 1962, however, the U.S. Supreme Court (*Fulwood* v. *Clemmer*) ordered the District of Columbia Department of Corrections to "stop treating the Muslims differently from other religious groups."[82] This decision paved the way for the Black Muslim movement to be seen as a legitimate religion and taken seriously as a vehicle of prison change through such avenues as litigation.

One example of the rise and subsequent influence of Native American religious groups can be found in Nebraska. The Native American Cultural and Spiritual Awareness group is composed of Native American inmates who seek to build solidarity and appreciation of Native American values. This group also pursues change in the prison environment through litigation. The element of inmate-on-inmate violence and guard assaults characteristic of other groups are not apparent here.[83]

As the direct result of litigation, Native American inmates won the right to have a sweat lodge on prison grounds and medicine men and women visit to perform religious ceremonies. The significance of this concession is that it happened four years before federal legislation dictated the recognition and acceptance of Native American religions.

Other religious movements have come to concern prison officials and social commentators because of their apparent assertions of racial supremacy. The impact of such values in a closed environment like a prison is obvious, but concerns have surfaced that the impact of these subcultures may reach outside prison walls. Are groups emerging that promote tenets of racial hatred under the guise of religions?

The Five Percent and Asatru movements are two groups that have prison officials concerned. The former group is made up of African Americans, and the latter is made up of whites, each emphasizing tenets of racial purity. Currently, six states censor the teachings of the Five Percenters, whereas other states label all followers as gang members. The movement began in Harlem in 1964 and has spread across the country, claiming thousands of followers. Teachings include the rejection of "history, authority and organized religion" while calling themselves a nation of Gods (men) and Earths (women). Although the group advocates peace and rejects drinking alcohol and using drugs, correctional officials have linked Five Percenters to violence in some state institutions. Similar to the Nation of Islam, their beliefs stress that "blacks were the original beings and must separate from white society."[84]

The Asatru followers practice a form of pagan religion based on principles of pre-Christian Nordic traditions. This religion was officially recognized in Iceland in 1972 and professes nine noble virtues, including courage, honor, and perseverance. However, prison officials claim that as this group has grown in popularity in American prisons, so has racial violence. Some critics charge that "while Asatru is a genuine religion to some followers, these modern pagan groups have been a breeding ground for right-wing extremists" and that they attract white supremacists. Some state prison systems have taken steps to ban Asatru groups, stating security concerns. Some Asatru followers have surfaced in connection with acts of racial violence. Most notably, perhaps, is the recent case of John William King, a white male convicted of the dragging death of an African American man in Jasper, Texas. While serving a prison sentence prior to this crime, King is said to have joined an Odinist group, an Asatru variant. From this affiliation he has tattoos depicting an African American man lynched on a cross and the words "Aryan Pride."[85]

Prison Gangs

Prison gangs are an integral part of understanding the prison environment and the inmate social system. The U.S. Department of Justice describes prison gangs this way

> self-perpetuating criminal entities that can continue their operations outside the confines of the penal system. Typically, a prison gang consists of a select group of inmates who have an organized hierarchy and who are governed by an established code of conduct. Prison gangs vary in both organization and composition, from highly structured gangs such as the Aryan Brotherhood and Nuestra Familia to gangs with a less formalized structure such as the Mexican Mafia (La Eme). Prison gangs generally have fewer members than street gangs and OMGs and are structured along racial or ethnic lines. Nationally, prison gangs pose a threat because of their role in the transportation and distribution of narcotics. Prison gangs are also an important link between drug-trafficking organizations (DTOs), street gangs and OMGs, often brokering the transfer of drugs from DTOs to gangs in many regions. Prison gangs typically are more powerful within state correctional facilities rather than within the federal penal system.[86]

Little systematic information on prison gangs (or security threat groups) is available; however, from the states that do document such subcultures we know that they cover the racial and ethnic spectrum. Some of these gangs have networks established between prisons; across states; and most recently, with street gangs.

The Florida and Texas prison systems offer examples of the variety of prison gangs present in prisons today. The Florida Department of Corrections documented six major prison gangs; one was white, two were African American, and three were Hispanic.[87] The Texas prison system documented eight well-established prison gangs; two were white, two were African American, and four were Hispanic. Following are some representative examples.

Aryan Brotherhood

The Aryan Brotherhood is one of the largest prison gangs and is made up of white males. This group originated in 1967 in the San Quentin State Prison in California. They are present in numerous federal and state facilities. Their membership is dominated by inmates with white supremacist and neo-Nazi ideologies. Identifying tattoos/marks include shamrocks, double lightning bolts, and swastikas. The group is implicated in criminal enterprises in prison (both violence and contraband) and in illegal activities on the outside. This group is thought to be involved in a number of inmate and staff homicides. Although the group maintains economic arrangements with the Mexican Mafia, they are long-time enemies with such groups as the La Nuestra Familia and African American prison gangs such as the Black Guerilla Family.[88]

Black Guerilla Family

The Black Guerilla Family is made up of African American males. It was founded in the San Quentin Prison in California in 1966 by a former Black Panther. This group is distinguished by a predominant political ideology: Marxist/Maoist/Leninist communism. Its goals are to struggle to maintain dignity in prison, eradicate racism, and overthrow the U.S. government. Rival gangs are the Aryan Brotherhood, Texas Syndicate, and the Mexican Mafia. However, the group does form alliances with such groups as the Black Liberation Army and black street gangs.

Mandingo Warriors

The Mandingo Warriors is made up of African American males. It came into existence after most of the Hispanic and white groups formed. These members are involved in prison violence and the *sub rosa* economic system but appear to be less organized than the other race/ethnic groups.[89]

Mexican Mafia

The Mexican Mafia (nickname La Eme) was formed in the late 1950s in the youth offenders' facilities of California by former Los Angeles street gang members. The members are male and Mexican American. This group is often identified as the most active gang in the federal prison system. They are described as having a philosophy of ethnic pride and act to control the drug trafficking in the institutions. They have active relationships with the Aryan Brotherhood and urban Latino street gangs. They have intense rivalries with the Black Guerilla Family and black street gangs.[90]

Neta

Neta is a gang composed of Puerto Rican members, reportedly established in 1970 in the Rio Pedras Prison, Puerto Rico. Florida correctional personnel characterize their actions as a cultural organization a façade for criminal behavior. Members are characterized as strongly patriotic and revolutionary with a philosophy of Puerto Rican independence from American rule. Members usually wear beads that are red, white, and blue (the colors of the Puerto Rican flag). The gang emblem is a heart pierced by two crossing Puerto Rican flags with a shackled right hand with the middle and index fingers crossed. They have entrenched themselves in the drug trade and participate in extortion, and they have been suspected of performing "hits" for other prison gangs.[91]

Texas Syndicate

The Texas Syndicate has its origins in the California Department of Corrections. Once released, these individuals returned to Texas and entered the Texas Department of Corrections as the result of continuing criminal activity. The membership is predominately Hispanic, with the occasional acceptance of white inmates. This group is structured along paramilitary lines, has a documented history of prison violence, and will enforce rule breaking with death. A spinoff associated with this group is the predominantly white gang Dirty White Boys.[92]

Although little information exists on Native American or Asian / Pacific Islander street gangs, criminal justice personnel remain cautious about their emergence as the presence of street gangs or organized crime is a known avenue of prison gang formation. Indications of Native American prison gangs are found in some Canadian prisons. Asian inmates are often presented as the image of the model prisoner, but more study of these issues is warranted.

One of the management issues associated with dealing with gangs in prison is the tension created by integrating prison populations that prefer to be racially segregated. While self-sought racial segregation is a dominant feature of most residential areas in the United States there are legal issues that structure such segregation decisions in the prison and jail environment. See "In the Courts: Racial and Ethnic Segregation in Prison: By Law or by Choice?" for additional insight into this issue.

Women in Prison

Studies addressing the imprisonment of women are less numerous than those for men, but they are increasing in number. Within this growing body of research,

---

In the Courts: Racial and Ethnic Segregation in Prison: By Law or by Choice?

A series of court decisions have declared de jure racial segregation in prisons to be unconstitutional. As late as the 1970s, prisons in the South and even some in states such as Nebraska segregated prisoners according to race as a matter of official policy. Although such policies have been outlawed, inmates often self-segregate along racial and ethnic lines as a matter of choice. Most recently, the racial segregation policies of the California Department of Corrections (DOC) have been under judicial review.[93]

In 2005 the U.S. Supreme Court in *Johnson* v. *California* ruled that the DOC could not use racial classifications in prison to assign mandatory segregated housing based on race. The DOC was using a race / ethnic–based classification that required mandatory residential segregation for an inmate's stay in the reception center and for the initial pairing (60 days) of the two-inmate room assignment. The DOC argues that this policy prevents violence within facilities because of the extensive nature of race-based security threat groups (gangs such as the Aryan Brotherhood, Mexican Mafia, and Black Guerilla Family). In short, correctional administrators were arguing that "separate, but equal" treatment of inmates was justified to prevent violence among inmates. Administrators note that all racial/ethnic groups are segregated at the initial phases of admission; "the DOC policy further subdivided ethnic groups so that Chinese Americans were separated from Japanese Americans and Northern California Hispanics from Southern California Hispanics." Administrators also noted that no other areas in the facilities were segregated, such as the dining hall and the recreation yards.

The U.S. Supreme Court's opinion striking down this policy was written by Justice Sandra Day O'Connor, where she states for the majority that in the implementation of policies such as these "there is simply no way of determining ... what classifications are in fact motivated by illegitimate notions of racial inferiority or simple racial politics. We therefore apply strict scrutiny to all racial classifications to 'smoke out' illegitimate uses of race by assuring that [government] is pursuing a goal important enough to warrant use of a highly suspect tool."[94]

Justice O'Connor also stated in her opinion that "when government officials are permitted to use race as a proxy for gang membership and violence without demonstrating compelling government interest ... society as a whole suffers." She further contends that the Federal Bureau of Prisons supports the assertion that "racial integration leads to less violence in institutions and better prepares inmates for reentry into society." The courts' recommendation is that "race-neutral" remedies be pursued to handle the problems associated with inmate violence. Correctional administrators should strive to avoid policies that may breed racial intolerance.

Given the clear judicial message that correctional administrators cannot pursue "separate, but equal" policies of race / ethnic–based segregation to reduce prison violence, the issue remains—to what extent should integration be *required work*, housing, recreation, and education assignments? Should administrators allow inmates to make decisions on the basis of personal preference, even if these decisions result in self-segregation? Racial tensions are a serious problem in most prisons; forcing white and African American inmates to share cells, when they are actively hostile to each other, could bring these tensions to a boil. In one instance, a white inmate felt so threatened by the politicized racial atmosphere in his prison that he filed suit asking a federal court to reverse the integration requirement and return to segregation.

However, if correctional administrators bowed to the wishes of inmates on this matter they would create two problems. First, they would be actively promoting racial segregation, which is illegal. Second, they would undermine their own authority by acknowledging that inmates could veto policy they did not like.

What is the best strategy for administrators in this difficult situation? You decide.

the issue of race is not routinely addressed either. When race is assessed the comparisons are generally limited to African Americans and whites. The evidence is mixed on the issue of whether race effects the adjustment of women to prison life.

Doris L. MacKenzie explains the behaviors (conflicts and misconduct reports) of women in prison on the basis of age and attitudes (anxiety, fear of victimization). She comments that the four prisons she examined are similar in racial composition, but she does not comment on whether she explored differences by race in relation to attitudes and aggressive behavior. Such research ignores the possibility that race may influence one's perception of prison life, tendencies toward aggression, age of inmate, or length of time in prison.[95] MacKenzie and others do, in later works, address race in the demographic description of the incarcerated women. In a study of one women's prison in Louisiana, for example, they found that nonwhite women were severely overrepresented among all prisoners and even more likely to be serving long sentences. Their findings indicate unique ·adjustment problems for long-term inmates, but they fail to incorporate race into their explanatory observations about institutional misconduct. This omission seems contrary to the observation that nonwhite women are more likely to have longer sentences.[96] Race has specifically been recognized as a factor in research addressing the issue of sexual deprivation among incarcerated women. Robert G. Leger identifies racial dimensions to several key explanatory factors in the participation of female prisoners in lesbianism. First, the demographic information reveals that most lesbian relationships are intraracial and that no distinctions emerged by race in participation in the gay or straight groups. Second, once dividing the group by the characteristics of previous confinements (yes or no) and age at first lesbian experience, the pattern of even representation of whites and African Americans changed. African American females were overrepresented in the group indicating previous confinement, and the information about age at first arrest indicates that African American females are more likely to have engaged in their first lesbian act prior to their first arrest.[97]

CONCLUSION

The picture of the American correctional system is most vivid in black and white, but it also has prominent images of brown. Such basic questions as "Who is in prison?" and "How do individuals survive in prison?" cannot be divorced from the issues of race and ethnicity. The most salient observation about minorities and corrections is the striking overrepresentation of African Americans in prison populations. In addition, this overrepresentation is gradually increasing in new court commitments and population figures. Explanations for this increasing overrepresentation are complex.

The most obvious possibility is that African American criminality is increasing. This explanation has been soundly challenged by Tonry's work, which compares the stability of African American arrest rates since the mid-1970s to the explosive African American incarceration rates of the same period. He argues that a better explanation may be the racial impact of the war on drugs.[98]

Blumstein's analysis offers another clue to the continuing increase in the African American portion of the prison population, which links discretion and the war on drugs. His work suggests that the racial disparities in incarceration rates for drug offenses are not well explained by racial disparities in drug arrest rates. Thus, the war on drugs and its impact on imprisonment may be fostering the "malign neglect" Tonry charges.[99]

DISCUSSION QUESTIONS

1. What does this chapter offer in terms of resolving the issue of whether African Americans have differentially high offending rates compared to whites, or that African Americans are subject to differentially high processing rates (possibly discriminatory) by the criminal justice system? What must a researcher do to advance a description of disparity to an argument of discrimination (hint: causation)? In the case of prison populations, how do you advance from the demographic description of the overrepresentation of African Americans in prison to a causal analysis of discrimination by the criminal justice system? In the case of the demographic makeup of the probation population (less racial disparity than jail and prison) does this reflect sentencing discrimination, thus saving the more favorable sentences for whites? Or is the presence of less extreme disparity, which is similar to the disparities in arrest figures (see Chapter 2)—a balancing out of discrimination?

2. In what ways is the indigenous justice paradigm in conflict with the principles of the traditional, adversarial American criminal justice system? In what ways do the principles of Native American justice complement more mainstream correctional initiatives? Are these values more compatible with some offenses than others? More appropriate for some types of offenders than others?

3. In what way are Blumstein and colleagues' findings about the wide variation of unexplained racial disparity in prison populations according to type of offense similar to the liberation hypothesis discussed in the chapter on sentencing (Chapter 7)? In what way should the findings of Crutchfield and colleagues impact criminal justice policy makers?

4. Should post-prison reintegration programs be race neutral? Were the factors that lead to offending and incarceration race neutral? In what ways should issues of race and ethnicity be considered when creating policies to facilitate inmate readjustment to society upon release?

5. Do you think prison gang formation is influenced most by external forces and the gang affiliations offenders bring to prison from the street or by the internal forces of the prison environment, such as racial composition? What arguments can you offer to support your position?

NOTES

1. http://blackstarproject.org/action/index.php?option=com_content&view=article&id=27:the-future-of-the-black-community-looks-dim-as-fewer-black-students-enroll-in-american-colleges-and-universities&catid=3:editorials&Itemid=15.

2. Estimates calculated from U.S. Department of Justice, News Release: *National Correctional Population Reaches New High* (August 26, 2001). Available at: http://www.ojp.usdoj/bjs/abstract/oous000.htm; Allen J. Beck and Paige M. Harrison, *Prisoners in 2000* (Washington, DC: U.S. Department of Justice, 2001). Available at: http://www.ojp.usdoj.gov/bjs/.

3. http://blackstarproject.org/.

4. Harry E. Allen and Clifford E. Simonson, *Corrections in America: An Introduction*, 7th ed. (Englewood Cliffs, NJ: Prentice-Hall, 1995).

5. Heather West, *Prison Inmates at Midyear 2009—Statistical Tables* (Washington, DC: Bureau of Justice Statistics, 2010). Computed from Table 16.

6. Ada Pecos Melton, "Crime and Punishment: Traditional and Contemporary Tribal Justice" in *Images of Color, Images of Crime*, Coramae Richey Mann and Marjorie S. Zatz, eds. (Los Angeles: Roxbury Publishing Company, 1998).

7. See Marjorie S. Zatz, Carol Chiago Lujan, and Zoann K. Snyder-Joy, "American Indians and Criminal Justice: Some Conceptual and Methodological Considerations," in *Race and Criminal Justice* for a review of these issues.

8. West, *Prison Inmates at Midyear 2009*.

9. Ibid.

10. Ibid.

11. Bureau of Justice Statistics, *Comparing State and Federal Inmates, 1991* (Washington, DC: Government Printing Office, 1993).

12. Ibid.

13. Bureau of Justice Statistics, *Sourcebook 2002*, 2003, pg 518. Note that the administrative classification is made up of special populations needing medical treatment or in pretrial detention.

14. American Correctional Association, *1993 Directory of Juvenile and Adult Correctional Departments, Institutions, Agencies, and Paroling Authorities* (Laurel, MD: American Correctional Association, 1993).

15. John A. Arthur, "Correctional Ideology of Black Correctional Officers," *Federal Probation* 58 (1994), pp. 57–65.

16. Patrick A. Langan and David J. Levin. "Recidivism of Prisoners Released in 1994," *Bureau of Justice Statistics Report*, 2002 (Washington DC).

17. Margaret Werner Cahalan, *Historical Corrections Statistics in the United States, 1850–1984* (Washington, DC: Government Printing Office, 1986), pp. 65–66.

18. Michael Tonry, *Malign Neglect* (New York: Oxford University Press, 1995).

19. Ibid.

20. West, *Prison Inmates at Midyear 2009.*

21. Ibid.

22. International Centre for Prison Studies, World Prison Brief, Available at: http://www.kcl.ac.uk/depsta/law/research/icps/worldbrief.

23. Marc Mauer, *Americans Behind Bars: A Comparison of International Rates of Incarceration* (Washington, DC: The Sentencing Project, 1990).

24. Lauren Glaze and Thomas Bonczar, *Probation and Parole in the United States, 2008* (Washington, DC: U.S. Department of Justice, 2010); Todd D. Minton, *Jail Inmates at Midyear 2009—Statistical Tables* (Washington, DC: U.S. Department of Justice, 2010).

25. Todd D. Minton, *Jails in Indian Country, 2008* (Washington, DC: U.S. Department of Justice, 2009). Available at www.ojp.usdoj.gov/bjs/pub/pdf/jic08.pdf.

26. Ibid., p. 8.

27. Ibid., p. 8.

28. Ibid.

29. Timothy A. Hughes, Doris James Wilson, and Allen J. Beck, *Trends in State Parole, 1990–2000* (Washington, DC: U.S. Department of Justice, 2001), p. 2. Available at: www.ojp.usdoj.gov/bjs/.

30. Kathryn D. Morgan and Brent Smith, "The Impact of Race on Parole Decision-Making," *Justice Quarterly* 25 (2008), pp. 411–435.

31. Marjorie S. Zatz, "The Changing Form of Racial/Ethnic Biases in Sentencing," *Journal of Research in Crime and Delinquency* 25 (1987), pp. 69–92; Cassia Spohn, "Thirty Years of Sentencing Reform: A Quest for a Racially Neutral Sentencing Process," in *Policies, Processes, and Decisions of the Criminal Justice System*, Vol. 3, *Criminal Justice 2000* (Washington, DC: U.S. Department of Justice, 2000).

32. Beth M. Huebner and Timothy S. Bynum, "The Role of Race and Ethnicity in Parole Decisions," *Criminology* 46 (2008), pp. 907–937.

33. Timothy A. Hughes, Doris James Wilson, and Allen J. Beck, *Trends in State Parole, 1990–2000* (Washington, DC: U.S. Department of Justice, 2001), p. 2. Available at: http://www.ojp.usdoj.gov/bjs/.

34. Keep in mind 2008 was a time of recession and high unemployment. However, the proportional differences by race are consistent with non-recession years, but the actual percentages are lower. Source: Bureau of Labor Statistics. News Release: *The Employment Situation—November 2010*. U.S. Department of Labor. Table A-1. Available at: http://www.bls.gov/news.release/pdf/empsit.pdf.

35. Bureau of Labor Statistics. News Release: *The Employment Situation—November 2010*. U.S. Department of Labor. Tables A-2, A-3. Available at: http://www.bls.gov/news.release/pdf/empsit.pdf.

36. The Sentencing Project, *Facts about Prison and Prisoners* (Washington, DC: The Sentencing Project, 2001). Available at: http://www.sentencingproject.org.

37. Lauren Glaze and Thomas Bonczar, *Probation and Parole in the United States, 2008.*

38. Joan Petersilia, *Racial Disparities in the Criminal Justice System* (Santa Monica, CA: Rand, 1983), p. 28.

39. Tribal Law and Policy Institute, *Healing to Wellness Courts: A Preliminary Overview of Tribal Drug Courts* (Washington, DC: Office of Justice Programs, 1999).

40. Ibid.

41. Ibid.

42. The Sentencing Project, *Expanding the Vote: State Felony Disenfranchisement Reform, 1997–2008* (Washington, DC: The Sentencing Project, 2008). Available at: http://www.sentencingproject.org.

43. Maine and Vermont are the only states that do not disenfranchise convicted felons. The Sentencing Project, *Felony Disenfranchisement Laws in the United States* (2008). Available at: http://www.sentencingproject.org/doc/publications/fd_bs_fdlawsinus.pdf.

44. *Nebraska Lawmakers Restore Felons' Voting Rights*, March 11, 2005 Available at: http://www.cnsnews.com.

45. Sentencing Project, *Felony Disenfranchisement Laws*.

46. *Omaha World Herald*, March 3, 1999, p. 22.

47. Coramae Richey Mann, *Unequal Justice: A Question of Color* (Bloomington, IN: Indiana University Press, 1993); William Wilbanks, *The Myth of the Racist Criminal Justice System* (Monterey, CA: Brooks/Cole, 1987); Alfred Blumstein, "On the Disproportionality of United States' Prison Populations," *The Journal of Criminal Law and Criminology* 73 (1982), pp. 1,259–1,281.

48. Blumstein, "On the Disproportionality of United States' Prison Populations."

49. Ibid., 1274.

50. Patrick Langan, "Racism on Trial: New Evidence to Explain the Racial Composition of Prisons in the United States," *Journal of Criminal Law and Criminology* 76 (1985), pp. 666–683.

51. Alfred Blumstein, "Racial Disproportionality in U.S. Prisons Revisited," *University of Colorado Law Review* 64 (1993), pp. 743–760.

52. Tonry, *Malign Neglect*, pp. 67–68.

53. Darnell F. Hawkins and Kenneth A. Hardy, "Black–White Imprisonment Rates: A State-by-State Analysis," *Social Justice* 16 (1989), pp. 75–94.

54. Robert D. Crutchfield, George S. Bridges, and Susan R. Pitchford, "Analytical and aggregation biases in analyses of imprisonment: Reconciling discrepancies in studies of racial disparity," *Journal of Research in Crime and Delinquency*, 31 (1994), pp. 166–182.

55. J. Sorensen, R. Hope, and D. Stemen, "Racial Disproportionality in State Prison Admissions: Can Regional Variation be Explained by Differential Arrest Rates?" *Journal of Criminal Justice* 31 (2003), pp. 73–84.

56. Ibid., p. 179.

57. Theodore G. Chiricos and Charles Crawford, "Race and Imprisonment: A Contextual Assessment of the Evidence," in *Ethnicity, Race, and Crime*, Darnell F. Hawkins, ed. (Albany: State University of New York Press, 1995).

58. Raymond J. Michalowski and Michael A. Pearson, "Punishment and Social Structure at the State Level: A Cross-Sectional Comparison of 1970 and 1980," *Journal of Research in Crime and Delinquency* 27 (1990), pp. 52–78.

59. Hawkins and Hardy, "Black–White Imprisonment Rates: A State-by-State Analysis."

60. George S. Bridges and Robert D. Crutchfield, "Law, Social Standings, and Racial Disparities in Imprisonment," *Social Forces* 66 (1988), pp. 699–724.

61. Miriam A. DeLone and Theodore G. Chiricos, "Young Black Males and Incarceration: A Contextual Analysis of Racial Composition," paper presented at the Annual Meetings of the American Society of Criminology, 1994.

62. Dario Melossi, "An Introduction: Fifty Years Later, Punishment and Social Structure in Comparative Analysis," *Contemporary Crises* 13 (1989), pp. 311–326.

63. DeLone and Chiricos, "Young Black Males and Incarceration."

64. W. E. B. Du Bois, "The Spawn of Slavery: The Convict-Lease System in the South," *The Missionary Review of the World* 14 (1901), pp. 737–745; Martha A. Myers, *Race, Labor, and Punishment in the South* (Columbus, OH: Ohio State University Press, 1999).

65. Raymond J. Michalowski and Susan J. Carlson, "Unemployment, Imprisonment, and Social Structures of Accumulation: Historical Contingency in the Rusche-Kirchheimer Hypothesis," *Criminology* 37 (1999), pp. 217–250. For a review of this literature, see Theodore G. Chiricos and Miriam A. DeLone, "Labor Surplus and Punishment: A Review and Assessment of Theory and Evidence," *Social Problems* 39 (1992), pp. 421–446.

66. Theodore G. Chiricos, "The Moral Panic of the Drug War," in *Race and Criminal Justice*, Michael J. Lynch and E. Britt Patterson, eds. (New York: Harrow and Heston, 1995).

67. Donald Clemmer, *The Prison Community* (New York: Holt, Reinhart, and Winston, 1940); Gresham M. Sykes, *The Society of Captives* (Princeton: Princeton University Press, 1958); John Irwin and Donald Cressey, "Thieves, Convicts, and Inmate Culture," *Social Problems* 10 (1962), pp. 142–155.

68. James Jacobs, *New Perspectives on Prison and Imprisonment* (Ithaca, NY: Cornell University Press, 1983).

69. Lynne Goldstein and Doris Layton MacKenzie, "Racial Differences in Adjustment Patterns of Prison Inmates—Prisonization, Conflict, Stress, and Control," in *The Criminal Justice System and Blacks*, Daniel Georges-Abeyie, ed. (New York: Clark Boardman Company, Ltd, 1984).

70. Kevin N. Wright, "Race and Economic Marginality," *Journal of Research in Crime and Delinquency* 26 (1989), pp. 67–89.

71. Joan Petersilia, Paul Honig, and Charles Hubay, *The Prison Experiences of Career Criminals* (Santa Monica, CA: Rand Corporation, 1980).

72. Timothy Flanagan, "Correlates of Institutional Misconduct Among Prisoners," *Criminology* 21 (1983), pp. 29–39.

73. Margaret Noonan, *Mortality in Local Jails, 2000–2007* (Washington, DC: Bureau of Justice Statistics, 2010); Christopher J. Mumola and Margaret Noonan. *Suicide and Homicide in State Prisons and Local Jails, 2001–2007* (Washington, DC: U.S. Department of Justice, 2010).

74. Miles D. Harer and Darrell J. Steffensmeier, "Race and Prison Violence," *Criminology* 34 (1996), pp. 323–355.

75. Jim Thomas, "Racial Codes in Prison Culture: Snapshots in Black and White," in *Race and Criminal Justice*, Michael Lynch and Britt Patterson, eds. (New York: Harrow and Heston, 1991).

76. Andy Hochstetler, Matt DeLisi, and Travis C. Pratt, "Social Support and Feelings of Hostility Among Released Inmates," *Crime and Delinquency* 56 (2010), pp. 588–607.

77. Francis Cullen, "Social Support as an Organizing Concept for Criminology," Presidential Address to the Academy of Criminal Justice Sciences, *Justice Quarterly* 11 (1994), pp. 527–560.

78. Jerome Travis and Christy Visher, *Prisoner Reentry and Crime in America* (New York: Cambridge University Press, 2005).

79. Jacobs, *New Perspectives on Imprisonment*.

80. Darlene Conley and Julius Debro, "Black Muslims in California Prisons: The Beginning of a Social Movement for Black Prisoners in the United States," in *Race, Class, Gender, and Justice in the Unites States*, Charles E. Reasons, Darlene J. Conley, and Julius Debro, eds. (Boston: Allyn and Bacon, 2002), p. 279.

81. Jacobs, *New Perspective on Imprisonment*, p. 65.

82. Ibid.

83. Elizabeth S. Grobsmith, *Indians in Prison* (Lincoln, NE: University of Nebraska Press, 1994).

84. *Omaha World Herald*, Sunday, December 6, 1998, 19-A.

85. *Omaha World Herald*, Sunday February 28, 1999, p. 1.

86. Available at: http://www.justice.gov/criminal/gangunit/gangs/prison.html.

87. Florida Department of Corrections, "Gang and Security Groups Awareness, 2005." Available at: http://www.dc.state.fl.us/pub/gangs.

88. Ibid.

89. Robert Fong, Ronald Vogel, and Salvador Buentello, "Prison Gang Dynamics: A Look Inside the Texas Department of Corrections," in *Corrections: Dilemmas and Directions*, Peter J. Benekos and Alida V. Merlo, eds. (Cincinnati: Anderson Publishing Co. and Academy of Criminal Justice Sciences, 1992).

90. Ibid.

91. Ibid.

92. Florida Department of Corrections, "Gang and Security Groups Awareness, 2005." Available at: www.dc.state.fl.us/pub/gangs.

93. Jacobs, *New Perspectives on Prisons and Imprisonment*.

94. *Johnson v. California*, 543 U.S. 499 (2005).

95. Doris L. MacKenzie, "Age and Adjustment to Prison: Interactions with Attitudes and Anxiety," *Criminal Justice and Behavior* 14 (1987), pp. 427–447.

96. Doris L. MacKenzie, James Robinson, and Carol Campbell, "Long-Term Incarceration of Female Offenders: Prison Adjustment and Coping," *Criminal Justice and Behavior* 16 (1989), pp. 223–238.

97. Robert G. Leger, "Lesbianism Among Women Prisoners: Participants and Nonparticipants," *Criminal Justice and Behavior* 14 (1987), pp. 448–467.

98. Tonry, *Malign Neglect*.

99. Blumstein, "On the Disproportionality of United States' Prison Populations."

10

✳

Minority Youth and Crime
Minority Youth in Court

> Youth in general, and young minority males in particular, often
> are demonized by legislators, the media, scholars, and the
> public at large. These attacks reinforce stereotypes and place a
> particularly heavy burden on young Black and Latino males.
> —LINDA S. BERES AND THOMAS D. GRIFFITH, "DEMONIZING YOUTH"[1]

In June 2001 Lionel Tate, an African American boy who was 12 years old when he killed a 6-year-old family friend while demonstrating a wrestling move he had seen on television, was sentenced to life in prison without the possibility of parole. Tate, who claimed that the death was an accident, was tried as an adult in Broward County, Florida; he was convicted of first degree murder. One month later, Nathaniel Brazill, a 14-year-old African American, was sentenced by a Florida judge to 28 years in prison without the possibility of parole. Brazill was 13 years old when he shot and killed Barry Grunow, a popular 30-year-old seventh grade teacher at a middle school in Lake Worth, Florida. Although Brazill did not deny that he fired the shot that killed his teacher, he claimed that he had only meant to scare Grunow and that the shooting was an accident. Like Tate, Brazill was tried as an adult; he was convicted of second degree murder.

These two cases raised a storm of controversy regarding the prosecution of children as adults. Those on one side argue that children who commit adult crimes, such as murder, should be treated as adults; they should be prosecuted as adults and sentenced to adult correctional institutions. As Marc Shiner, the prosecutor in Brazill's case, put it, "This was a heinous crime committed by a young man with a difficult personality who should be behind bars. Let us not

443

forget a man's life has been taken away."[2] Those on the other side contend that prosecuting children as adults is "unwarranted and misguided." They assert that children who commit crimes of violence usually suffer from severe mental and emotional problems and that locking kids up in adult jails does not deter crime or rehabilitate juvenile offenders. Although they acknowledge that juvenile offenders should be punished for their actions, they claim that incarcerating them in adult prisons for the rest of their lives "is an outrage."[3] According to Vincent Schiraldi, president of the Justice Policy Institute, "In adult prisons, Brazill will never receive the treatment he needs to reform himself. Instead, he will spend his time trying to avoid being beaten, assaulted, or raped in a world where adults prey on, rather than protect, the young."[4]

Nathaniel Brazill is still incarcerated in the Brevard Correctional Institution. Assuming that none of his pending appeals are successful, he will not be released until 2028, when he will be 41 years old.[5] Lionel Tate's conviction, on the other hand, was overturned by a Florida appellate court in 2003. The court ruled that Tate should be retried because his competency to stand trial was not evaluated before he went to trial. The state decided not to retry Tate and instead offered him a plea agreement—Tate pled guilty to second degree murder in exchange for a sentence to time served (which was about 3 years), plus 1 year of house arrest and 10 hours of probation.[6] He was released from prison in January 2004. In May 2005 he was back in jail in Fort Lauderdale, Florida, after he allegedly robbed a pizza delivery man at gunpoint. Because he was on probation at the time of the crime, Tate faced a potential life sentence on the robbery charge.[7] In 2006 he was sentenced to 30 years in prison on a gun possession charge and in 2008 he was sentenced to 10 years in prison for the robbery.

GOALS OF THE CHAPTER

The prosecution of children as adults, and the potential for racial bias in the decision to "waive" youth to adult court, is one of the issues we address in this chapter. We also discuss racial/ethnic patterns in victimization of juveniles and in offending by juveniles, the treatment of juveniles by the police, and police use of gang databases. We end the chapter with a discussion of the treatment of minority youth by the juvenile justice system.

After you have read this chapter:

1. You will have explored the myths and realities about victimization of and crime by minority youth.

2. You will have examined the relationship between the police and racial and ethnic minority youth.

3. You will have reviewed recent research on racial disparities in the juvenile justice system.

YOUNG RACIAL MINORITIES AS VICTIMS AND OFFENDERS

Juveniles as Victims of Crime

In Chapter 2 we showed that, regardless of age, African Americans have higher personal theft and violent victimization rates than other racial / ethnic groups and that Hispanics generally have higher victimization rates than non-Hispanics. However, information concerning the racial and ethnic trends in victimization for juveniles is scarce. In this section we examine National Crime Victimization (NCVS) data, supplemented by National Incident Based Reporting System (NIBRS) data and Supplemental Homicide Reports (SHR) from the FBI. We first discuss property victimization, followed by violent victimization and homicide victimization.

Property Crime Victimization   Using information from the 1996 and 1997 NCVS, the Office of Juvenile Justice and Delinquency Prevention released a brief on "Juvenile Victims of Property Crime."[8] Their findings indicated that one of every six juveniles (defined as youth aged 12 to 17) had been the victim of property crime.[9] This rate was 40 percent higher than the property crime victimization rate for adults.[10]

Table 10.1 offers a comparison of juvenile and adult property crime victimization rates for this time period by race and ethnicity. A ratio of juvenile to adult rates higher than 1:1 indicates that the juvenile victimization rate is higher than the adult rate. The ratio of 1:1.4 for whites, for example, indicates that the property crime victimization rate for white juveniles is higher than the property crime victimization rate for white adults; moreover, as indicated by the asterisk, the difference in the rates for adults and juveniles is statistically significant. This pattern is found for all three racial categories. Hispanic property crime victimization rates, however, do not vary significantly between juveniles and adults, but non-Hispanic rates do vary.

Looking at the victimization rates for juveniles only in Table 10.1, we see that African American youth have the highest property crime victimization rate, followed by white youth, then "other race" (American Indian / Alaska Native and Asian / Pacific Islander) youth. With regard to ethnicity, non-Hispanic juveniles report a higher rate of property crime victimization than Hispanic juveniles. The racial pattern of property crime victimization among juveniles, in other words, mirrors the overall pattern for all ages combined (see Chapter 2); both comparisons show the highest rates for African Americans. The victimization rates of Hispanic and non-Hispanic juveniles (higher rates for non-Hispanics), on the other hand, differ from the rates for all age groups combined (higher rates for Hispanics).[11]

The FBI also collects information about crime victims through the NIBRS. These data do not represent the entire U.S. population, but they do provide substantial information on the victims of crime in the jurisdictions covered. Using this information, researchers estimate that juveniles with the following

T A B L E   10.1   **Juvenile and Adult Property Victimization Rates by Race and Ethnicity (1996 and 1997 Combined)**

	Property Crime Rate (Per 1,000 Population)		Property Crime Ratio (Juvenile/ Adults)
	Juvenile	Adult	
Victim Race			
White	162	114	1:1.4*
African American	194	151	1:1.3*
Other	155	108	1:1.4*
Victim Ethnicity			
Hispanic	143	133	1:1.1
Non-Hispanic	170	117	1:1.5*

*Juvenile rate divided by adult rate; significant difference at the 0.05 level or below.
SOURCE: Office of Juvenile Justice and Delinquency Prevention, "Juvenile Victims of Property Crimes" (Washington, DC: U.S. Department of Justice, 2000).

characteristics have a relatively high risk for property crime victimization: "African American juveniles, juveniles in urban areas, and juveniles in the West."[12] In short, these victimization patterns closely mirror "the higher risk for adults in these categories."[13]

Violent Crime   In general, violent victimization rates are somewhat higher for younger age groups than for older age groups. For example, in 2009 the violent victimization rate for youth from 12 to 15 years old was 36.8 victimizations for every 1,000 persons in that age group, and the rate for youth 16 to 19 years old was 30.3 victimizations for every 1,000 persons in that age group. In contrast, the rate for individuals who were 20 to 24 years old was 28.1 per 1,000, and the rate for those who were 25 to 34 years old was 21.5 per 1,000. The rates for simple assault were 25.9 for those who were 12 to 15, 19.3 for those who were 16 to 19, 16.3 for those who were 20 to 24, and 13.4 for those who were 25 to 34.[14]

The most recent data on violent victimization by age, race, and gender are for 2007. These data reveal that the overall violent victimization rate, which in years past was higher for African Americans than for whites, is now very similar for these two groups. For example, in 2000 the violent victimization rates for youth ages 12 to 15 were 66.7 for African Americans and 58.7 for whites; in 2007 the rates were 46.1 for African Americans and 42.1 for whites.[15] Thus, the victimization rates for both groups declined from 2000 to 2007, but the rate for African Americans fell more sharply than did the rate for whites.

Data on violent victimization rates broken down by age, race, and gender reveal that *young African American males* have a greater likelihood than other offenders of being victims of robbery but that the rates for overall violence are very similar for young African American males and for offenders other than white females.[16] These data reveal that in 2007 the violent victimization rate for youth between the ages of 12 and 15 was 46.1 for African American males, 47.9 for white males, 46.2 for African American females, and 36.1 for white females. For violent crime in general, then, the rates for African American males, African American females, and white males differed by less than two percentage points. In contrast, the robbery victimization rate for African American males (9.1) was considerably larger than the rate for white males (5.4) and was more than 10 times the rate for white females (0.9) and African American females (0.0).

A 2003 report by the Bureau of Justice Statistics revealed that African American and Hispanic youth were more likely than white youth to be victims of crimes committed with weapons.[17] This was true for crimes committed with any weapon and for crimes committed with a firearm, and it was true for youth between the ages of 12 and 14 as well as youth between the ages of 15 and 17. Among the 15- to 17-year-olds, for example, the rate of violent victimizations with a firearm for white youth was only half the rate for Hispanic youth; the rate for African American youth was even higher than the rate for Hispanic youth.

The question, of course, is why African American and Hispanic youth are more likely than whites to be the victims of violent crime. To answer this question, Janet L. Lauritsen used 1995 data from the National Crime Victimization Survey to explore the effects of individual, family, and community characteristics on the risk for nonlethal violence among youth.[18] She disaggregated violent incidents into incidents perpetrated by strangers and those perpetrated by non-strangers, and she distinguished incidents that occurred in the youth's own neighborhood from those that occurred elsewhere. She found that youth living in single-parent families had higher risks for violence than those living in two-parent families, and that the risk for violence was much higher for youth living in the most disadvantaged communities.[19]

According to Lauritsen, "because family and community characteristics vary among racial and ethnic groups in the United States, it is important to consider differences in victimization risk across racial and ethnic groups."[20] As shown in Table 10.2, when she examined the risk for violence by race and gender, she found that young males faced a substantially higher risk of violence than young females; this was true for both stranger and non-stranger violence and for all violence as well as violence that took place in the youth's own neighborhood. She also found that,

- white, African American, and Hispanic males had roughly equal risks of non-stranger violence, but young white males had a lower risk of victimization for stranger violence in their own neighborhoods than African American and Hispanic young males; and

- African American girls faced much higher risks of non-stranger violence than either Hispanic or white girls, and both African American girls and Hispanic

T A B L E   10.2   Risk for Stranger and Non-Stranger Violence for African American, Hispanic, and White Youth

	Stranger Violence		Non-Stranger Violence	
	All Violence	Neighborhood Violence	All Violence	Neighborhood Violence
Males	34.9	20.2	25.0	14.4
African American	35.8	27.1	25.5	17.1
Hispanic	43.4	31.2	24.4	13.1
White	33.2	16.6	25.0	14.0
Females	19.8	10.1	23.1	12.8
African American	24.3	14.2	30.1	22.7
Hispanic	22.7	14.1	16.3	10.3
White	18.2	8.5	22.7	11.0

SOURCE: Janet L. Lauritsen, "How Families and Communities Influence Youth Victimization" (Washington, DC: U.S Department of Justice, 2003). Adapted from Table 5.

girls were more likely than white girls to be victimized by a stranger in their neighborhoods (see also Box 10.1, which discusses in more detail the victimization of young African American girls).

To determine whether these patterns could be explained by other factors, Lauritsen used analytical techniques that simultaneously controlled for individual, family, and community characteristics. She found that the amount of time the youth spent at home and the length of time the youth had lived in his/her current home had a negative effect on risk of violent victimization, and that youths who lived in single-parent families faced a greater risk than those who lived in two-parent families. She also found that youth who lived in communities with higher percentages of female-headed families and higher percentages of residents under the age of 18 had higher likelihoods of violent victimization.[21]

The most interesting finding from this analysis was that the racial and ethnic differences in risk for violent victimization disappeared when the characteristics of the youth's family and community were taken into account. The racial and ethnic differences discussed earlier, in other words, "are primarily a reflection of community and family differences rather than the result of being part of a particular racial or ethnic group."[22] Thus, African American and Hispanic youth have greater risks for violent victimization than white youth because they are more likely than white youth to spend time away from home, to live in single-parent families, to have less-stable living arrangements, and to live in disadvantaged communities. As Lauritsen noted, "the sources of risk are similar for all adolescents, regardless of their race or ethnicity."[23]

In *Getting Played: African American Girls, Urban Inequality, and Gendered Violence*, Jody Miller examines the victimization experiences of African American girls living in disadvantaged neighborhoods in St. Louis, Missouri. She uses in-depth interviews with young African American women and men to investigate "the social contexts in which violence against young women in disadvantaged communities emerges, with an emphasis on the situations that produce and shape such events."[24]

Miller focuses on young girls' victimization experiences in their neighborhoods, their schools, and their relationships. Noting that most of the youth interviewed for her study lived in extremely disadvantaged neighborhoods in which drug dealing, street gangs, and violence were commonplace, Miller demonstrates that young girls faced particular risks in these male-dominated neighborhoods. They witnessed violence against other women that occurred in public view, were subjected to sexual come-ons by young men and sexual harassment by adult men, and faced an ongoing risk of sexual assault and sexual coercion. In response to these dangers, girls adopted gendered risk-avoidance strategies: they avoided public places, especially at night, and they relied on others, especially male relatives and friends, for protection. They also criticized girls who engaged in risky behavior or wore provocative clothing, arguing that doing so heightened girls' risk of victimization. According to Miller, "the public nature of violence against women ... created a heightened vigilance and awareness among girls of their own vulnerability, but it also resulted in coping strategies that included victim-blaming as a means of psychologically distancing themselves from such events."[25]

Miller also discusses sexual harassment of girls at school, noting that a majority of the girls she interviewed reported experiencing inappropriate sexual comments or being grabbed or touched in ways that made them feel uncomfortable. She stated that these types of harassment were "an everyday feature of the cultural milieu at school" and were not taken seriously by school personnel.[26] Miller also notes that the girls who were subjected to this type of treatment had a limited arsenal of effective responses. Avoidance was not an option in schools where youths were constantly in contact with one another and standing up for oneself carried significant risks. As she put it, "Their attempts to defend themselves were read by young men as disrespect, and the incidents quickly escalated into hostile confrontations when young women challenged young men's sexual and gender entitlements. Thus, young women were in a lose-lose situation."[27]

One of the most troubling findings of Miller's study is the high rate of sexual violence experienced by the girls. She found that half of the girls, whose mean age was only 16, had experienced some form of sexual coercion or sexual assault and that a third reported multiple experiences with sexual victimization. In contrast, the boys who were interviewed did not see their behaviors as sexual violence but as persuasion. Miller notes that much of the sexual violence, including gang rape, took place at unsupervised parties, where drugs and alcohol were readily available. As she explained, "Such social contexts not only made young women more vulnerable to sexual mistreatment but also enhanced the likelihood that girls would be viewed as either willing participants or deserving victims."[28]

Miller concludes that her research "points to the clear need to address violence against girls in disadvantaged communities in a systematic fashion."[29] Although she acknowledges that "there are no simple answers or easy solutions," she nonetheless suggests that the problem can be ameliorated by "remedies that attend to the root causes of urban disadvantage" and by "improving institutional support for challenging gender inequalities and strengthening young women's efficacy."[30] She recommends that policy makers consider ways to make disadvantaged neighborhoods safer, that police adopt community policing strategies designed to engender trust and confidence in the police, that school personnel take a more proactive approach to addressing sexual harassment, and that community service agencies develop ways of providing stable adult role models and mentors for youth at risk.

Homicide Victimization   In 2005, 1 in every 10 murder victims was under
the age of 18; 4.9 percent of the victims were under age 14, and 5.1 percent
were between 14 and 17.[31] Although homicide events are fairly rare (16,397 in
2005), racial patterns and trends by age are available. The Supplemental Homicide Reports (SHR) collected by the FBI indicate there are important racial patterns to be found in homicide trends. As discussed in Chapter 2, African
Americans generally are overrepresented both as homicide victims and offenders.
Although the highest homicide rates regardless of race and age are found among
18- to 24-year-olds, youth between the ages of 14 and 17 have rates that are
similar to those for the 25-and-older age group.[32]

The homicide victimization rates for 14- to 17-year-olds, which are presented in Table 10.3, indicate that homicide rates declined dramatically from
1990 to 2005. For each of the four groups—white males, white females, African
American males, and African American females—the rates peaked in 1995,
declined substantially by 2000, and remained relatively steady from 2000 to
2005. Aside from the changes over time, the most startling finding revealed by
the data presented in Table 10.3 concerns the differences in homicide victimization rates by race. Regardless of gender, African American juveniles have substantially higher victimization rates than white juveniles. Throughout the time
period, the rate for African American females was approximately four times
greater than the rate for white females, and the rate for African American males
was six to seven times greater than the rate for white males. In fact until 2005 the
homicide victimization rates for African American females were higher than the
rates for white males.

It thus seems clear that African American youth are overrepresented as crime
victims in the United States. African American juveniles have the highest
property crime victimization rates of any group, and African American males
and females are substantially more likely than white males and females to be
homicide victims. As the study conducted by Lauritsen revealed, these racial
and ethnic differences can be attributed primarily to race / ethnicity–linked
differences and the characteristics of the families and the communities in which
the youth live.

**T A B L E   10.3   Juvenile Homicide Victimization Rates (per 100,000
population, ages 14–17) by Race and Gender**

	1990	1995	2000	2005
White male	7.5	8.6	4.1	4.4
White female	2.5	2.7	1.4	1.1
African American male	59.0	63.2	25.8	26.4
African American female	10.3	11.9	4.5	4.0

SOURCE: James Allen Fox and Marianne W. Zawitz, *Homicide Trends in the United States*, (Washington, DC: U.S.
Department of Justice, 2010). Available at: http://bjs.ojp.usdoj.gov/content/homicide/homtrnd.cfm.

Juveniles as Offenders

Creating a profile of the juvenile offender is not an easy task. Much of the available data relies on arrest statistics and/or the perceptions of crime victims. Some critics argue that the portrait of the offender based on these data is biased (because of racial differences in reporting and racial bias in decisions to arrest) and suggest that the picture of the typical offender should be taken from a population of adjudicated offenders. We discuss this alternative picture of the juvenile offender in the section on juveniles in the correctional system, which appears later in this chapter.

Juvenile Arrests   Table 10.4 presents UCR arrest data for persons under the age of 18. The racial differences in these arrest statistics are similar to those for offenders in all age groups. The overrepresentation of African American youth for violent crimes is notable. In 2009 African Americans made up 51.2 percent of all arrests of youth for violent Index Crimes. Among young offenders arrested for homicide and robbery, African Americans constituted 58.0 percent and 67.3 percent, respectively, of all arrestees. African American juveniles also were overrepresented among arrests for serious property (Part 1 / Index) crimes, but the proportions are smaller than for violent crime (33.2 percent for serious property crime versus 51.2 percent for violent crime).

Native American youth make up less than 1 percent of the juvenile population; they were slightly overrepresented in juvenile arrest figures for Index offenses (1.2 percent of all arrestees), especially motor vehicle theft (1.5 percent of all arrestees). Asian / Pacific Islander youth, who make up less than 3 percent of the U.S. population, were not overrepresented for any Part 1 / Index offenses.

The data presented in Table 10.4 reveal more variability in the race of juveniles arrested for the less serious Part 2 offenses. White juveniles were overrepresented for driving under the influence, liquor law violations, and drunkenness; they represented about 90 percent of arrestees in each category. African Americans made up fewer than 9 percent of juveniles arrested for these offenses. A similar pattern is found for vandalism, where the racial makeup of arrestees is consistent with the racial makeup of the general population. African American juveniles were overrepresented among arrestees for a number of these less serious offenses, including gambling (92.7 percent), prostitution (58.4 percent), offenses involving stolen property (43.6 percent), disorderly conduct (41.4 percent), other assaults (39.2 percent), weapons offenses (33.2 percent), fraud (36.0 percent), embezzlement (33.3 percent), and drug abuse violations (25.6 percent).

Native American / American Indian youth were overrepresented for three of the liquor-related Part 2 offenses: DUI, liquor law violations, and drunkenness. They made up 3.1 percent of all arrests for liquor law violations, 1.8 percent of all arrests for driving under the influence, and 1.9 percent of all arrests for drunkenness. Asian / Pacific Islander youth were overrepresented only for the status offense of running away and were significantly underrepresented for offenses such as liquor and drug abuse violations.

T A B L E   10.4   Percent Distribution of Arrests by Race, under 18 Years of Age, 2009

	% White	% African American	% American Indian	% Asian
Total	65.9	31.3	1.2	1.6
Part 1 / Index crimes				
Murder and nonnegligent manslaughter	40.4	58.0	0.9	0.7
Forcible rape	63.4	34.5	0.8	1.3
Robbery	31.1	67.3	0.4	1.2
Aggravated assault	55.4	42.4	1.0	1.2
Burglary	60.9	37.3	0.9	1.0
Larceny-theft	65.0	31.8	1.2	2.0
Motor vehicle theft	54.0	43.2	1.5	1.4
Arson	76.7	20.6	1.3	1.4
Violent crime	46.4	51.6	0.8	1.2
Property crime	63.9	33.2	1.2	1.7
Part 2 crimes				
Other assaults	58.6	39.2	1.1	1.1
Forgery and counterfeiting	66.4	32.2	0.5	0.9
Fraud	61.9	36.0	1.1	1.0
Embezzlement	63.8	33.3	0.2	2.7
Stolen property; buying, receiving, possessing	54.0	43.6	0.8	1.0
Vandalism	78.4	19.2	1.2	1.2
Weapons: carrying, possessing, etc.	60.7	37.3	0.8	1.2
Prostitution and commercialized vice	36.7	58.4	0.4	1.5
Sex offenses (except forcible rape and prostitution)	71.2	26.6	0.8	1.4
Drug abuse violations	72.4	25.6	0.9	1.1
Gambling	6.8	92.7	0.0	0.5
Offenses against family and children	73.9	24.3	1.3	0.4
DUI	92.0	5.1	1.8	1.2
Liquor laws	89.4	6.2	3.1	1.3
Drunkenness	88.5	8.7	1.9	0.8
Disorderly conduct	56.8	41.4	1.0	0.8
Vagrancy	71.5	27.3	0.4	0.7
All other offenses (except traffic)	69.2	28.0	1.1	1.8
Suspicion	42.3	57.1	0.0	0.6
Curfew and loitering law violations	60.8	37.1	1.0	1.2
Runaways	66.6	26.7	2.2	5.4

SOURCE: Sourcebook of Criminal Justice Statistics, Table 4.10. Available at: http://www.albany.edu/sourcebook/pdf/t4102009.pdf.

TABLE 10.5   **Self-Reported Violent Behavior, by Race and Ethnicity: Mean Percent Who Reported Engaging in Each Type of Violence**

	Serious Fighting	Caused Injury	Pulled Knife or Gun	Shot or Stabbed	Serious Violence Scale
Asian	.115*	.032*	.014*	.013	.17*
African American	.210*	.102*	.086*	.031*	.43*
Hispanic	.236*	.119*	.066*	.030*	.45*
Native American	.402*	.166*	.079	.009	.66*
White	.179	.074	.032	.012	.30

*Group mean is significantly different from mean for white adolescents (P ≤ .05).

SOURCE: Thomas L. McNulty and Paul E. Bellair, "Explaining Racial and Ethnic Differences in Serious Adolescent Violent Behavior," *Criminology* 41 (2003), pp. 709–748, Appendix 1 and Table 1.

Self-Reported Violent Behavior   Data on juvenile offending also comes from surveys in which youth are asked to self-report delinquent acts. The National Longitudinal Survey of Adolescent Health, for example, gathered data from students attending 132 schools throughout the United States.[33] Youth between the ages of 11 and 20 were asked to indicate the number of times in the past 12 months they engaged in four types of serious violent behavior: getting into a serious fight, hurting someone badly enough to need bandages or care from a doctor or nurse, pulling a knife or gun on someone, and shooting or stabbing someone.

Thomas McNulty and Paul E. Bellair used these data to examine racial and ethnic differences in violent behavior. As shown in Table 10.5, there were significant differences between white adolescents and each of the four other groups on the first two items. Asians were less likely than whites to have been in a serious fight or to have injured someone else; African Americans, Hispanics, and Native Americans, on the other hand, were more likely than whites to have engaged in these types of violent behavior. Asians also were less likely than whites to have pulled a knife or gun on someone else, but African Americans and Hispanics were more likely than whites to have pulled a gun or knife on someone or to have shot or stabbed another person.[34] McNulty and Bellair used these data to create a serious violence scale, which focused on the breadth of violent activity (that is, whether the respondent engaged in the activity or not). The scale ranged from zero (respondent had not engaged in any of the types of violent behavior) to four (respondent had engaged in all four types of violence).[35] They found that Native American adolescents were the most likely to have engaged in violent behavior (mean = .66), followed by Hispanics (.45), African Americans (.43), whites (.30), and Asians (.17). Overall, then, there were large and statistically significant differences between white youth and youth in each of the other four groups. Asians were less likely than whites to have engaged in violent behavior; Native Americans, Hispanics, and African Americans were more likely than whites to have participated in violence.

Somewhat different results emerged from a study of violent offending among eighth-grade students in 11 cities throughout the United States.[36] Dana Peterson and her co-authors used self-report data to examine the prevalence of violent offending and, for active offenders, their levels of offending (that is, the average number of offenses committed by offenders who reported engaging in the behavior). When they examined annual prevalence rates (that is, the percentage of youth who reported engaging in the behavior during the previous 12 months), they found that African American youth were more likely than White or Asian youth to have engaged in serious violence but that the percentages of African American, Hispanic, and Native American youth who reported involvement in serious violence were very similar (32 percent for African Americans, 30 percent for Hispanics, and 35 percent for Native Americans). Moreover, the authors also found that there were "no statistically significant race differences in levels of offending once offending begins."[37]

Peterson and her colleagues concluded that the results of their study "call into question the extent to which violent juvenile offending can be characterized as a minority male problem."[38] These researchers did find that males and racial minorities were overrepresented among violent offenders, but the differences were not as great as arrest data from the Uniform Crime Reports would suggest. As they put it, "Although there may be a 'racial gap' in terms of self-reported violence prevalence, no racial gap appears in frequency of violent offending among active offenders."[39]

Homicide Offenders   Data on homicide offenders reveal that offending peaks at around age 18, that males are overrepresented as offenders, that roughly 50 percent of all homicides are committed by offenders known to the victim (non-strangers), and that the victim and the offender come from the same age group and racial category. The Supplemental Homicide Reports (SHR) collected by the FBI can be used to calculate approximate rates of homicide offending by age, race, and gender. We consider these approximate rates because the data come from reports filled out by police agencies investigating homicides, rather than from convicted offenders. As a consequence, these data may reflect a number of biases and should be viewed with caution.

The SHR data indicate that offending rates vary by age group and that the pattern is similar to that found for victimization rates: the 18-to-24-year-old group has the highest offending rate, followed by the 14-to-17-year-old group, with those 25 and older having the lowest offending rates.[40] Figure 10.1 displays homicide offending rates from 1980 to 2005 for white males, white females, African American males, and African American females aged 14 to 17.[41] Two trends are apparent. First, over time, the homicide offending rate for African American males has been substantially higher than the rates for the other three groups. In 2005, for example, the rate for young African American males (64.1) was 8 times the rate for young white males (7.9), 16 times the rate for young African American females (4.0), and more than 60 times the rate for young white females (0.7). The second trend revealed by the data is that the homicide offending rates for each group peaked in either 1990 or 1995 and declined

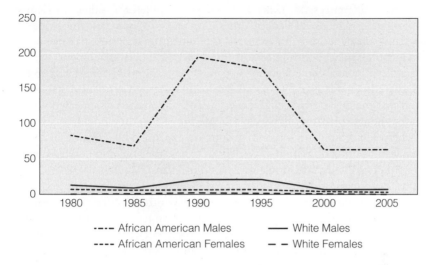

FIGURE 10.1 Homicide Offending Rates for Youth age 14 to 17 by Race and Gender

SOURCE: James Allen Fox and Marianne W. Zawitz, *Homicide Trends in the United States*, (Washington, DC: U.S. Department of Justice, 2010). Available at: http://bjs.ojp.usdoj.gov/content/homicide/homtrnd.cfm.

dramatically after 1995. The rate for African American males, for example, was 194.0 in 1990, 178.6 in 1995, 63.2 in 2000, and 64.1 in 2005. For white males the rates fell from 22.0 (1990 and 1995) to 7.9 (2005).

The intraracial pattern identified in Chapter 2 for all homicides—that is, most homicides involve victims and offenders of the same race—is found for juvenile homicides as well. However, interracial homicides are more common among young perpetrators.[42]

Explaining Racial and Ethnic Differences in Violent Behavior   The data discussed thus far reveal that there are racial and ethnic differences in violent behavior among juveniles. Data on homicide indicate that African American males have the highest offending rate and self-report data on other types of violence reveal that Asians and whites have lower rates of offending than Native Americans, Hispanics, and African Americans.

Researchers have advanced a number of explanations for these racial and ethnic differences. Although a detailed discussion of these explanations is beyond the scope of this book, they generally focus on the effects of community social disorganization,[43] individual and family level risk factors,[44] weakened family attachments and weak bonds to school and work,[45] and involvement with delinquent peers and gangs.[46] Most studies focus on *either* individual/family influences or community level risk factors such as social disorganization. There are very few studies that examine the causes of violent crime across these levels of analysis.

An exception to this is the recent study by McNulty and Bellair (discussed earlier); this study found that Asians were significantly less likely than whites to engage in serious violent behavior and that Native Americans, Hispanics, and African Americans were more likely than whites to report they had committed violent acts.[47]

To explain these differences, McNulty and Bellair controlled for individual factors (for example, gender, age, use of alcohol/drugs, easy access to a gun, and prior violent behavior), family characteristics (for example, type of family structure, parents' education and income), social bonds indicators (for example, family attachment, school bonding, grades in school), involvement in gangs, exposure to violence, and community characteristics (for example, social disorganization and residential stability). They found that the racial/ethnic differences in violent behavior disappeared when they included these explanatory factors in a single model. As they noted, "statistical differences between whites and minority groups are explained by variation in community disadvantage (for blacks), involvement in gangs (for Hispanics), social bonds (for Native Americans), and situational variables (for Asians)."[48]

The authors of this study concluded that their results had important implications for implementing policies designed to reduce youth violence. They noted, however, that "the implementation of social programs is unlikely to alter contemporary patterns of racial and ethnic group involvement in violent behavior without amelioration of the fundamental social and economic inequalities faced by minority group members."[49]

Similar results were found by Paula J. Fite, Porche Wynn, and Dustin A. Pardini,[50] who used data from the Pittsburgh youth survey to examine discrepancies in violent arrest rates between African American and white male juveniles. They found that 38.4 percent of the African American boys, but only 24.6 percent of the white boys, were arrested for a violent offense as juveniles. They also found, however, that race was significantly correlated with 10 of the 14 risk factors they were examining, including conduct problems, low academic achievement, family socioeconomic status, poor parent-child communication, peer delinquency, neighborhood disadvantage and neighborhood problems.

The authors used statistical techniques that allowed them to determine whether these risk factors could explain the relationship between race and likelihood of arrest as a juvenile. As they noted, "If race is no longer a significant predictor of arrests after the inclusion of the risk factors in the model, then it suggests that race only indirectly affects arrest through its relation with one or more risk factors in the model."[51] In fact, their results were consistent with this: once the risk factors were added to the model, race was no longer a predictor of arrest for a violent crime.

Further analysis revealed that several of the risk factors had a significant effect on the likelihood of a violence-related arrest. The odds of arrest were higher for youth with conduct problems, low academic achievement, problems in communicating with parents, delinquent peers, and neighborhood problems. These five risk factors accounted for 70 percent of the relationship between race and arrest for a violent offense.[52]

In terms of policy implications, the authors of this study concluded that interventions designed to reduce juvenile arrests should focus on young boys exhibiting early signs of conduct problems such as fighting, stealing, and vandalizing property. Noting that low academic achievement also was associated with an increased risk of arrest, they suggested that "programs designed for children exhibiting co-occurring conduct disorder symptoms and academic problems will likely have the greatest impact on disproportionate minority arrest rates."[53]

> **B o x 10.2   Race, Crime, and the Media**
>
> In a 2001 review of over 70 studies focusing on crime in the news, Lori Dorfman and Vincent Schiraldi, of the Berkeley Media Studies Group, asked the following questions: Does news coverage reflect actual crime trends? How does news coverage depict minority crime? Does news coverage disproportionately depict youth of color as perpetrators of crime?[54]
>
> The authors of the report concluded that "the studies taken together indicate that depictions of crime in the news are not reflective of the rate of crime generally, the proportion of crime that is violent, the proportion of crime committed by people of color, or the proportion of crime that is committed by youth. The problem is not the inaccuracy of individual stories, but the cumulative choices of what is included in the news—or not included—presents the public with a false picture of higher frequency and severity of crime than is actually the case."[55]
>
> Dorfman and Schiraldi noted that although crime dropped 20 percent from 1990 to 1998, crime news coverage increased by over 80 percent.[56] Moreover, 75 percent of the studies found that minorities were overrepresented as perpetrators;[57] over 80 percent of the studies found that more attention was paid to white victims than to minority victims.[58] The authors concluded that the studies revealed that a "misinformation synergy" occurs in the way crime news is presented in the media.[59] The result is a message that crime is constantly on the increase, the offenders are young, minority males, and their victims are white.

JUVENILES OF COLOR AND THE POLICE

The racial/ethnic patterns found in data on arrests of juveniles raise questions about the general pattern of relations between the police and juveniles. We discussed this subject in Chapter 4. It is useful to review the major points here.

First, juveniles have a high level of contact with the police, and juveniles of color have particularly high rates of contact. Several factors explain this pattern. Most importantly, young people tend to be out on the street more than adults. This is simply a matter of lifestyle related to the life cycle. Low-income juveniles are even more likely to be out in public than middle-class youth. Middle-class and wealthy people have more opportunities for indoor recreation: family rooms, large back yards, and so on. A study of juvenile gangs in the 1960s found that gang members regarded the street corner as, in effect, their private space.[60] At the same time, juveniles are more likely to be criminal offenders than middle-age people. Criminal activity peaks between ages 14 and 24. For this reason, the police are likely to pay closer attention to juveniles—and to stop and question them on the street—than to older people (for further discussion of this, see Focus on An Issue: The Use of Gang Databases).

Second, in large part because of the higher levels of contact, juveniles consistently have less favorable attitudes toward the police. Age and race, in fact, are the two most important determinants of public attitudes, with both young people and African Americans having the most negative view of the police. As Chapter 4 explains, the attitudes of Hispanics are less favorable than non-Hispanic whites but not as negative as those of African Americans. When age and race are combined, the result is that young African Americans have the most negative attitudes toward the police.[61]

Attitudes—and behavior that reflects negative attitudes—can have a significant impact on arrest rates. In his pioneering study of arrest patterns, Donald Black found that the demeanor of the suspect was one of the important determinants of officers' decision to make an arrest. With other factors held constant, individuals who are less respectful or more hostile are more likely to be arrested. Black then found that African Americans were more likely to be less respectful of the police, and consequently were more likely to be arrested. Thus the general state of poor relations leads to hostility in individual encounters with the police, which in turn results in higher arrest rates.[62]

A study published in 2003 used data from the National Incident-Based Reporting System (NIBRS) to assess whether the likelihood of arrest varied by the race of the juvenile in incidents involving murder, a violent sex offense, robbery, aggravated assault, simple assault, or intimidation.[63] (These incidents were selected because they were the ones in which there was interaction between the offender and the victim, and victims were asked to describe the characteristics of the offender.) Carl E. Pope and Howard N. Snyder found that white juveniles were significantly more likely than African American juveniles to be arrested: whites made up 69.2 percent of all juvenile offenders (based on victim's perceptions) but 72.7 percent of all juvenile offenders who were arrested. The results of a multivariate analysis that controlled for other incident characteristics (for example, the number of victims; the age, sex, and race of the victim; the relationship between the victim and the offender; and the offender's sex) revealed that the likelihood of arrest did not vary for white and nonwhite juveniles. This was true for each state and for each of the types of offenses examined. According to Pope and Snyder, "Overall, the NIBRS data offer no evidence to support the hypothesis that police are more likely to arrest nonwhite juvenile offenders than white juvenile offenders, once other incident attributes are taken into consideration."[64]

Focus on an Issue
The Use of Gang Databases

In the late 1980s California became the first state to create a computerized database of suspected gang members. Originally known as GREAT (Gang Reporting, Evaluation, and Trafficking System), by 2000 CalGang contained the names of over 300,000 suspected gang members. In fact the CalGang database included more names than there were students in the University of California system.[65]

As concerns about youth violence mounted during the early 1990s, other jurisdictions followed California's example. Laws authorizing law enforcement agencies to compile databases of gang members were enacted in Colorado, Florida, Illinois, Georgia, Tennessee, Texas, Minnesota, Ohio, and Virginia. The FBI also maintains a database, the Violent Gang and Terrorist

Organization File, which became operational in 1995.[66]

The criteria for inclusion in a gang database—which typically includes information about the individual (name, address, physical description and/or photograph, tattoos, gang moniker), the gang (type and racial makeup), and a record of all police encounters with the individual—are vague. The Texas statute, for example, states that an individual can be included in the gang database if two or more of the following conditions are met: (1) self-admission by the individual of criminal street gang membership; (2) an identification of the individual as a criminal street gang member by an informant or other individual of unknown reliability; (3) a corroborated identification of the individual by an informant or other individual of unknown reliability; (4) evidence that the individual frequents a documented area of a criminal street gang, associates with known criminal street gang members, and uses criminal street gang dress, hand signals, tattoos, or symbols; or (5) evidence that the individual has been arrested or taken into custody with known criminal street gang members for an offense or conduct consistent with criminal street gang activity.[67] Critics of the use of gang databases point to the third criterion, which allows entry of "associates" of gang members without evidence of actual gang membership, as especially problematic. According to a former California attorney general, the CalGang database mixes "verified criminal history and gang affiliations with unverified intelligence and hearsay evidence, including reports on persons who have committed no crime."[68]

Other critics suggest that the gang databases, which are racially neutral on their face, are racially biased. One observer, for example, stated that "it's not a crackdown on gangs; it's a crackdown on blacks."[69] Statistics on the composition

of gang databases confirm this. In 1997 in Orange County, California, for example, Hispanics, who made up only 27 percent of the county population, made up 74 percent of the youth in the database; in fact 93 percent of those included in the database were people of color. In 1993 African Americans made up 5 percent of Denver's population but 47 percent of those in the gang database; Hispanics made up 12 percent of the population but 33 percent of the gang database.[70] In Schaumburg, Illinois (a suburb of Chicago), African Americans made up 3.7 percent of the village's population but 22 percent of gang members in the database.[71]

Gang database supporters counter that these statistics simply reflect the composition of criminal street gangs. The fact that most of the individuals whose names appear on gang databases are African American, Hispanic, and Asian, in other words, is due not to racially discriminatory policing but to the fact that most of those who belong to street gangs are racial minorities. Critics, however, maintain that the vagueness of the criteria for inclusion in the database, coupled with accounts by youth of color of repeated stops and frequent questions about gang membership and the extremely high percentages of African Americans and Hispanics in gang databases in cities like Los Angeles and Denver, "support claims that the number of racial minorities who are not gang members but are included in the database is disproportionate."[72]

THE USE OF GANG DATABASES: POLICE HARASSMENT AND SENTENCE ENHANCEMENTS

Critics' concerns about racial and ethnic disparities in gang databases focus on the potential for police harassment, as well as the fact that in many states inclusion in a

(Continued)

gang database may result in harsher sentences. Two incidents in California illustrate the potential for police harassment. The first took place in Garden Grove. In 1993, three Asian teens were stopped by Garden Grove police officers at a strip mall that the officers claimed was frequented by gang members. The officers questioned the youths, took down information on them that was later entered into the gang database, and took photographs of them without their permission.[73] The second incident took place in Union City. In 2002 Union City police officers called a "gang intervention meeting" at a local high school. They rounded up 60 students, most of whom were Hispanic and Asian, and sent them to separate classrooms based on their race / ethnicity. The students were then searched, interrogated, and photographed; the information was collected; and the photographs of the students were entered into the gang database.[74] Both of these cases resulted in suits filed by the ACLU of Northern California. In the first case, a settlement was reached in which the police department agreed to take photographs only if they had reasonable suspicion of criminal activity and written consent. The settlement in the second case is similar; it required police to destroy the photographs and other material collected during the sweep and prohibits further photographing of students for the gang database.

There also is evidence that inclusion in a gang database may lead to harsher treatment for youth convicted of crimes. In Arizona, for example, the prosecutor may increase the charges from a misdemeanor to a felony if the offense was committed for the benefit of a gang; if the youth is adjudicated delinquent, the prosecutor may request a sentence enhancement for gang-related activity.[75] In 2000, 60 percent of California voters approved Proposition 21, The Gang Violence and Juvenile Crime Prevention Act, which increased the sentence enhancements for gang-related crimes. If the crime is serious, 5 years are added to the sentence; if the crime is violent, 10 years are added. Proposition 21 also makes it easier to prosecute juveniles who are alleged gang members as adults, allows the police to use wiretaps against known or suspected gang members, and adds gang-related murder to the list of special circumstances that make offenders eligible for the death penalty."

If, as critics contend, inclusion in a gang database is more likely for youth of color, these gang-related sentence enhancements, which are racially neutral on their face, may have racially discriminatory effects. As Marjorie S. Zatz and Richard P. Krecker noted, "if ascriptions of gang membership did not carry penalties, defining gang membership in racialized ways might be innocuous…. But allegations of gang membership do carry added penalties, at least in Arizona." Noting that Hispanic boys and girls were more likely than whites to be identified as gang members, and thus more likely to be subject to the penalty enhancements, they asked, how does this differ "in effect even if not in intent, from saying that the severity of sanctions is increased for Latinos?"[76]

RACE / ETHNICITY AND THE JUVENILE
JUSTICE SYSTEM

One particularly troubling aspect of juvenile justice as it has been constructed throughout the 20th Century is its disproportionate involvement, in an aggregate social sense, with youths from the lowest socioeconomic strata, who at least in the latter half of the 20th Century overwhelmingly have been children of color.[77]

Although most research on the effect of race on the processing of criminal defendants has focused on adults, researchers have also examined the juvenile justice system for evidence of racial discrimination. Noting that the juvenile system, with its philosophy of *parens patriae*,[78] is more discretionary and less formal than the adult system, researchers suggest that there is greater potential for racial discrimination in the processing of juveniles than in the processing of adults. In cases involving juveniles, in other words, criminal justice officials are more concerned about rehabilitation than retribution, and they have discretion to decide whether to handle the case formally or informally. As a result, they have more opportunities than those who handle cases involving adults to take extralegal factors such as race / ethnicity and gender into consideration during the decision-making process.

Focus on an Issue
The Past, Present, and Future of the Juvenile Court

The traditional view of the emergence of the juvenile court in America pictures the "child savers" as a liberal movement of the late nineteenth century, made up of benevolent, civic-minded, middle-class Americans who worked to help delinquent, abused, and neglected children who were suffering due to the negative impact of the rapid growth of industrialization. Although the emergence of the juvenile court is most often described as the creation of a welfare agency for the humane treatment of children,[79] Anthony Platt highlighted the movement's social control agenda as well. According to Anthony Platt, the "child saving movement" did little to humanize the justice system for children, but rather "helped create a system that

subjected more and more juveniles to arbitrary and degrading punishments."[80]

Platt contended that the attention of the juvenile court was originally focused on a select group of at-risk youth: court personnel originally focused on the children of urban, foreign-born, poor families for their moral reclamation projects.[81] Barry Feld argued that in modern times the juvenile court continues to intervene disproportionately in the lives of minority youth.[82] He asserted that the persistent overrepresentation of minority youth at all stages of the system is largely the consequence of the juvenile court's unstable foundation of trying to reconcile social welfare and social control agendas. This conceptual contradiction allows "public officials to couch their get-tough policy

(Continued)

changes in terms of 'public safety' rather than racial oppression."[83]

Feld argued that the social welfare and social control aims of the juvenile court are irreconcilable, and that attempts to pursue and reconcile these two competing agendas have left the contemporary juvenile court in crisis. He called it "a conceptually and administratively bankrupt institution with neither a rationale nor a justification."[84] He also contended that the juvenile court today offers a "second-class criminal court for young people" and does not function as a welfare agency.[85] Feld suggested that the distinction between adult and juvenile courts should be eliminated and that social welfare agencies should be used to address the needs of youth. His suggestion would make age a mitigating factor in our traditional, adjudicatory (adult) court system.

Would this policy suggestion ease the oppressive element of the juvenile court's intervention in the lives of racial and ethnic minorities? Why or why not?

There is compelling evidence that racial minorities are overrepresented in the juvenile justice system. In 2005, for example, African Americans made up about 15 percent of the U.S. population aged 10 to 17 but 33 percent of all youth under juvenile court jurisdiction. Whites constituted approximately 80 percent of the youth population but only 64 percent of all offenders in juvenile court. African American juveniles were involved in 41 percent of person offense cases (murder, rape, robbery, and assault), 29 percent of property offense cases, 24 percent of drug offense cases, and 34 percent of public-order offenses.[86] Stated another way, the total delinquency case rate for African American juveniles in 2005 (108.4) was more than twice the rate for white juveniles (44.4) and for Native American juveniles (53.3); the delinquency case rate for Asian juveniles was only 17.2.[87]

There also is evidence of racial disparity in the treatment of juvenile offenders. As shown in Table 10.6, which presents nationwide data on juvenile court outcomes in 2005, African Americans were treated more harshly than whites at several stages in the juvenile justice process. African Americans were more likely than whites to be detained prior to juvenile court disposition and to be petitioned to juvenile court for further processing. Among those adjudicated delinquent, African Americans were more likely than whites to be placed in a juvenile facility but somewhat less likely than whites to be placed on probation. White youth, on the other hand, were more likely than African American youth to be adjudicated delinquent. The data presented in Table 10.6 also reveal that Native Americans are treated more harshly than whites at all stages of the process; in fact, Native Americans are more likely than African Americans to be adjudicated delinquent, waived to adult court, and placed on probation.

Much of the criticism of the treatment of racial minorities by the juvenile justice system focuses on the fact that racial minorities are more likely than whites to be detained in secure facilities prior to adjudication and sentenced to secure confinement following adjudication. Since 1988 the Juvenile Justice and Delinquency Prevention Act has required states to determine whether the

TABLE 10.6   Juvenile Court Case Outcomes, 2005

	Whites	African Americans	Native Americans	Asians
Delinquent Cases				
Detained prior to juvenile court disposition	18%	26%	20%	22%
Petitioned to juvenile court	53%	62%	56%	59%
Petitioned Cases				
Adjudicated delinquent	68%	62%	70%	69%
Waived to adult court	0.7%	0.8%	1.3%	0.4%
Adjudicated Cases				
Placed out of home	21%	26%	26%	22%
Placed on probation	62%	56%	58%	64%

SOURCE: National Center for Juvenile Justice, *Juvenile Court Statistics 2005* (Washington, DC: Office of Juvenile Justice and Delinquency Prevention, 2008).

proportion of minorities in confinement exceeds their proportion of the population. If there is disproportionate minority confinement, the state must develop and implement policies to reduce it. As shown in Table 10.6, 26 percent of African American and Native American youth who were adjudicated delinquent received an out-of-home placement disposition; for white youth, the figure was 21 percent. Among youth adjudicated delinquent for drug offenses, 29 percent of African American youth received an out-of-home placement, compared with 18 percent of Native American youth, 17 percent of Asian youth, and 15 percent of white youth.[88]

Although most of the statistics on disproportionate minority confinement compare African American and white youth, there is some state-level evidence that Hispanic and Native American youth are overrepresented in juvenile detention facilities. In Santa Cruz County, California, for example, Hispanics comprised 33 percent of the population ages 10 through 17 but made up 64 percent of the youths incarcerated in the Juvenile Hall on any given day in 1997 and 1998.[89] A study in Colorado revealed that Hispanic youths were overrepresented at all stages in the juvenile justice system, and a study in North Dakota found that Native American youth made up 8 percent of the juvenile population but 21 percent of secure detention placements and 33 percent of secure correctional placements.[90]

A report by the Building Blocks for Youth initiative, a national project to address unfairness in the juvenile justice system and to promote non-discriminatory and effective policies, also addressed this issue.[91] The authors of the report, *And Justice for Some*, concluded that minority youth—and especially African American youth—receive harsher treatment than white youth throughout the juvenile justice system. The differences were particularly pronounced at the beginning stages of involvement with the juvenile justice system (that is, in terms of decisions regarding intake and detention) and at the end of the process (that is, in terms of decisions regarding out-of-home placement in a secure facility). With respect to detention prior to adjudication, the report found that minority youth were overrepresented, especially for drug offenses. White youth made up 66 percent of all youth referred to juvenile courts for drug offenses but only 44 percent of those detained. African American youth made up 32 percent of the drug offenders referred to juvenile court but 55 percent of those detained.[92] There was a similar pattern for out-of-home placement: in every offense category, and especially for drug offenses, minority youth were more likely than white youth to be committed to a locked institution.[93] Mark Soler, head of the Building Blocks for Youth initiative, stated that the report painted "a devastating picture of a system that has totally failed to uphold the American promise of 'equal justice for all.'"

The figures presented in Table 10.6 and the statistics on disproportionate minority confinement do not take racial differences in crime seriousness, prior juvenile record, or other legally relevant criteria into consideration. If racial minorities are referred to juvenile court for more serious offenses or have more serious criminal histories than whites, the observed racial disparities in case processing might diminish or disappear once these factors were taken into consideration. Like research on sentencing in adult court, studies of juvenile court outcomes consistently reveal that judges base their decisions primarily on the seriousness of the offense and the offender's prior record.[94] Thus, "real differences in rates of criminal behavior by black youths account for part of the disparities in justice administration."[95]

Research conducted during the past 20 years reveals that racial differences in past and current involvement in crime do not account for all of the differential treatment of racial minorities in juvenile court. Carl Pope and William H. Feyerherm, for example, reviewed 46 studies published in the 1970s and 1980s.[96] They found that two thirds of the studies they examined found evidence that racial minorities were treated more harshly, even after offense seriousness, prior record, and other legally relevant factors were taken into account. A recent review of 34 studies published from 1989 to 2001 found a similar pattern of results.[97] Eight of the 34 studies found that race and/or ethnicity had direct effects on juvenile court outcomes; 17 reported that the effects of race / ethnicity were contextual (that is, present at only some decision points or for some types of offenders); only one study reported no race effects.[98] An analysis that focused explicitly on disproportionate minority confinement reached the same conclusion. According to David Huizinga and Delbert S. Elliot, "Even if the slightly higher rates for more serious offenses among minorities were given more importance than is statistically indicated, the relative proportions of whites and minorities involved in delinquent behavior could not account for the observed differences in incarceration rates."[99]

The studies conducted to date also find evidence of what is referred to as "cumulative disadvantage"[100] or "compound risk."[101] That is, they reveal that small racial differences in outcomes at the initial stages of the process "accumulate and become more pronounced as minority youths are processed further into the juvenile justice system."[102] The Panel on Juvenile Crime, for example, calculated the likelihood that a youth at one stage in the juvenile justice process would reach the next stage (the transitional probability), as well as the proportion of the total population under age 18 that reached each stage in the juvenile justice process (the compound probability).[103] The panel did this separately for African American and white youth and then used these probabilities to calculate the African American–to–white relative risk and the African American–to–white compound risk. As shown in Table 10.7, 7.2 percent of the African American population under age 18, but only 3.6 percent of the white population under age 18, was arrested. African Americans, in other words, were twice as likely as whites to be arrested. Of those arrested, 69 percent of the African Americans and 58 percent of the whites were referred to juvenile court. Taking these differences into account resulted in a compound probability—that is, the proportion of the total youth population referred to juvenile court—of 5.0 percent for African American youth and 2.1 percent for white youth. Thus African Americans were 2.38 times more likely than whites to be referred to juvenile court. These differences in outcomes, as Table 10.7 shows, meant that at the end of the process African Americans were more than three times as likely as whites to be adjudicated delinquent and confined in a residential facility. As the panel pointed out, "at almost every stage in the juvenile justice process the racial disparity is clear, but not extreme. However, because the system operates cumulatively the risk is compounded and the end result is that black juveniles are three times as likely as white juveniles to end up in residential placement."[104]

In the sections that follow, we summarize the findings of five recent, methodologically sophisticated studies. The first is a comparison of outcomes for African Americans and whites in Florida. The second is an analysis of

TABLE 10.7   Juvenile Justice Outcomes for African Americans and Whites: Compound Risk

| Outcome | Transitional Probability[a] | | Compound Probability[b] | | Black to White Risk | |
	African Americans	Whites	African Americans	Whites	Relative Risk[c]	Compound Risk[d]
Arrested	.072	.036	.072	.036	2.00:1.00	2.00:1.00
Referred to juvenile court	.690	.580	.050	.021	1.19:1.00	2.38:1.00
Case handled formally	.620	.540	.031	.011	1.15:1.00	2.82:1.00
Adjudicated delinquent / found guilty	.550	.590	.0168	.0067	0.93:1.00	2.51:1.00
Residential placement	.320	.260	.0053	.0017	1.23:1.00	3.12:1.00

[a]The transitional probability = the proportion of youth at one stage who proceed to the next stage.
[b]The compound probability = the proportion of the population under age 18 that reach each stage in the process.
[c]The relative risk = the ratio of the black transitional probability to the white transitional probability.
[d]The compound risk = the ratio of the black compound probability to the white compound probability.
SOURCE: Adapted from The Panel on Juvenile Justice, *Juvenile Crime Juvenile Justice* (Washington, DC: National Academy Press, 2001), Figure 6.3 and Table 6.5.

outcomes for African American, Hispanic, and white youth in Pennsylvania. The third, which also examines the treatment of juveniles in Pennsylvania, is an exploration of the degree to which outcomes are affected by the urbanization of the jurisdiction and the youth's family situation. The fourth study is an examination of outcomes for white and African American youth in Georgia, which analyzes the degree to which admitting guilt affects adjudication and disposition. The fifth study uses data from Nebraska to explore the extent to which black males aged 16 to 17 are treated differently than other youth. We also discuss evidence concerning racial disparities in waivers to adult criminal court.

Race / Ethnicity and Juvenile Court Outcomes in Five Jurisdictions

Processing Juveniles in Florida   Donna M. Bishop and Charles S. Frazier examined the processing of African American and white juveniles in Florida.[105] In contrast to previous researchers, most of whom focused on a single stage of the juvenile justice process, these researchers followed a cohort of 54,266 youth through the system from intake through disposition. They examined the effect of race on five stages in the process: (1) the decision to refer the case to juvenile court for formal processing (rather than close the case without further action or handle the case informally); (2) the decision to place the youth in detention prior to disposition; (3) the decision to petition the youth to juvenile court; (4) the decision to adjudicate the youth delinquent (or hold a waiver hearing in anticipation of transferring the case to criminal court); and (5) the decision to commit the youth to a residential facility or transfer the case to criminal court.

Table 10.8 displays the outcomes for African American and white youth, as well as the proportion of African Americans in the cohort at each stage in the process. These data indicate that African Americans were substantially more likely than whites to be recommended for formal processing (59.1 percent versus 45.6 percent), petitioned to juvenile court (47.3 percent versus 37.8 percent), and either incarcerated in a residential facility or transferred to criminal court (29.6 percent versus 19.5 percent). As the cohort of offenders proceeded through the juvenile justice system, the proportion that was African American increased

T A B L E   10.8   **Race and Juvenile Justice Processing in Florida, 1979–1981**

	Recommended for Formal Processing	Detained	Petitioned to Juvenile Court	Adjudicated Delinquent	Incarcerated/ Transferred
African Americans	59.1%	11.0%	47.3%	82.5%	29.6%
Whites	45.6	10.2	37.8	80.0	19.5
Proportion					
African American	34.0	30.0	32.4	33.3	43.1

SOURCE: Adapted from Donna M. Bishop and Charles E. Frazier, "The Influence of Race in Juvenile Justice Processing," *Journal of Research in Crime and Delinquency* 25 (1988), pp. 242–263, p. 250.

from 34.0 percent (among those recommended for formal processing) to 43.1 percent (among those committed to a residential facility or transferred to criminal court). As Bishop and Frazier pointed out, however, these differences could reflect the fact that the African American youths in their sample were arrested for more serious crimes and had more serious prior criminal records than white youths. If this were the case, the differences would reflect racial disparity but not racial discrimination.

When the authors controlled for crime seriousness, prior record, and other predictors of juvenile justice outcomes, they found that the racial differences did not disappear. Rather, African Americans were more likely than whites to be recommended for formal processing, referred to juvenile court, and adjudicated delinquent. They also received harsher sentences than whites. These findings led Bishop and Frazier to conclude that "... race is a far more pervasive influence in processing than much previous research has indicated."[106]

A follow-up study using more recent (1985–1987) Florida data produced similar results.[107] As shown in Figure 10.2, Frazier and Bishop found that outcomes for "typical" white and nonwhite youth varied significantly. They defined a typical youth as "a 15-year-old male arrested for a misdemeanor against person (e.g., simple battery), with a prior record score consistent with having one prior referral for a misdemeanor against property (e.g., criminal mischief)."[108] Compared to his white counterpart, the typical nonwhite youth was substantially more likely to be recommended for formal processing, held in secure detention prior to disposition, and committed to a residential facility or transferred to

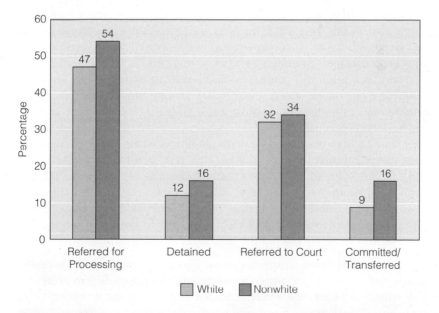

FIGURE 10.2 Juvenile Court Outcomes for "Typical" Florida Youth, 1985–1987

SOURCE: Adapted from Charles E. Frazier and Donna M. Bishop, "Reflections on Race Effects in Juvenile Justice," in *Minorities in Juvenile Justice*, Kimberly Kempf Leonard, Carl E. Pope, and William H. Feyerherm (Thousand Oaks, CA: Sage, 1995).

criminal court. They also found that being detained had a significant effect on subsequent outcomes; youth who were detained were significantly more likely than those who were released to be referred to juvenile court and, if adjudicated delinquent, to be committed to a residential facility or transferred to criminal court. Thus, nonwhite youth, who were more likely than white youth to be detained, were sentenced more harshly both because of their race (a direct effect) and because of their custody status (an indirect effect).

Frazier and Bishop also conducted interviews with criminal justice officials. During the interview, the respondent was asked whether the findings of harsher treatment of nonwhites "were consistent with their experiences in Florida's juvenile justice system between 1985 and 1987."[109] Most of the intake supervisors and public defenders stated that they believed juvenile justice dispositions were influenced by the race of the youth. In contrast, only 25 percent of the prosecutors and 33 percent of the judges believed that nonwhites were treated more harshly than similarly situated whites.

Although some of the racial differentials in treatment were attributed to racial bias—that is, to prejudiced individuals or a biased system of juvenile justice—a number of respondents suggested that the race effects actually reflected differences in economic circumstances or family situations. As one prosecutor observed, "The biggest problem is the lack of money and resources. Blacks don't have the resources. Whites are more likely to have insurance to pay for treatment. The poor I saw were always poor, but the black poor were poorer yet." Other respondents cited the fact that white parents were more likely than black parents to be able to hire a private attorney and, as a result, got more favorable plea bargains. Other officials mentioned the role played by family considerations, noting that youth from single-parent families or families perceived to be incapable of providing adequate supervision were treated more harshly than those from intact families. Although they acknowledged that this practice had a disparate effect on minority youth, most officials defended it as "fair and appropriate." As one judge stated, "Inadequate family and bad neighborhood correlate with race and ethnicity. It makes sense to put kids from these circumstances in residential facilities."[110]

Frazier and Bishop concluded that the results of their study "leave little doubt that juvenile justice officials believe race is a factor in juvenile justice processing."[111] They noted that the fact that some officials believed that race directly affected juvenile justice outcomes, whereas others thought that the effect of race was subtle and indirect, meant that "policies aimed at eradicating discrimination must focus both on individual racism and on racism in its most subtle institutional forms."[112] They offered the following recommendations:[113]

- States should establish procedures for all the agencies comprising the juvenile justice system to require reporting, investigating, and responding to professionals whose decisions appear to have been influenced by racial or ethnic bias.

- State legislatures should mandate the development of a race, ethnic, and cultural diversity curriculum that personnel at every level of the juvenile justice system should be required to complete.

- Intake policies and practices should be altered so that youths referred for screening are not rendered ineligible for diversion and other front-end programs if their parents or guardians (a) cannot be contacted, (b) are contacted but are unable to be present for an intake interview, or (c) are unable to participate in family-centered programs.

- In any situation in which persons with economic resources (e.g., income or insurance benefits) are allowed to arrange for private care as a means of diversion from the juvenile justice system or less harsh formal dispositions, precisely the same treatment services should be made available at state expense to serve the poor—whether minority or majority race youths.

Frazier and Bishop acknowledged that these "fairly modest proposals" were unlikely to eliminate racial discrimination that had "survived for generations in a legal environment that expressly forbids it." Nonetheless, they were "cautiously optimistic" that their recommendations would have some effect. As they stated, "if implemented with a genuine interest in their success, such policies will both help reduce discriminatory actions and promote equal justice."[114]

Processing Juveniles in Pennsylvania   Kimberly Kempf Leonard and Henry Sontheimer[115] explored the effect of race and ethnicity on juvenile justice case outcomes in Pennsylvania. Although African Americans and Hispanics accounted for only 19 percent and 4 percent, respectively, of the general youth population in the 14 counties included in the study, they comprised 46 percent (African Americans) and 7 percent (Hispanics) of all referrals to juvenile court.[116]

Like the two studies discussed earlier, this study used a multivariate model to examine the effect of race / ethnicity on a series of juvenile justice outcomes. Leonard and Sontheimer found that both African American and Hispanic youth "were more likely than whites with similar offenses, prior records, and school problems to have their cases formally processed, especially in nonrural court settings."[117] They also found that minority youth were significantly more likely than whites to be detained prior to adjudication, and that detention was a strong predictor of subsequent outcomes. African American and Hispanic youth, in other words, were detained more frequently than whites and, as a result, were more likely than whites to be adjudicated delinquent and placed in a residential facility following adjudication.

Leonard and Sontheimer suggest that their findings have important policy implications. In particular, they recommend that

> [The] criteria used by individual intake officers should be evaluated to determine whether factors that may more often negatively affect minorities are accorded importance. Racially neutral criteria in detention decisions should be established … Cultural bias, including value judgments not based on fact (such as notions that minority parents may not provide adequate supervision for their children or that certain neighborhoods are not conducive to growing up well, must not influence detention.[118]

Intake and Disposition Decisions in Pennsylvania   A second study of juvenile justice decision making in Pennsylvania focused on two stages in the process: the decision to formally refer a youth to the juvenile court rather than handle the case informally and the decision to place the youth in a secure detention facility following adjudication.[119] As shown in Table 10.9, which displays the bivariate relationships between the two outcomes and the legal and extralegal variables that may affect those outcomes, Christina DeJong and Kenneth C. Jackson found that African American and Hispanic youth were more likely than white youth to be referred to juvenile court; they also were more likely to be committed to a detention facility. The likelihood of a formal referral also was greater for youth with the following characteristics: male, aged 15 and older, living in a single-parent (mother only) family, not in school, charged with a drug offense, charged with a felony, and with two or more prior arrests. A similar pattern of results was found for the decision to place the youth in a secure facility.

Further analysis of the data using multivariate techniques led DeJong and Jackson to conclude that race / ethnicity did not have a significant effect on either outcome once the other variables were taken into consideration. Although Hispanics were significantly more likely than whites and African Americans to be formally referred to juvenile court, the referral rates for African American and white youth did not differ. And neither Hispanics nor African Americans faced greater odds than whites of commitment to a secure facility. The race of the youth, however, did affect these outcomes indirectly. In particular, white youth who lived with both parents were less likely than those who lived in single-parent families to be formally referred to juvenile court or placed in secure confinement following disposition. Among African American youth, on the other hand, living with both parents rather than in a single-parent household did not have these positive effects. As DeJong and Jackson pointed out, "Black youths are treated the same whether they are living with parents or with their mothers only; for these youths, family status does not protect against [formal referral or] incarceration."[120] In addition, African American youth, but not white youth, were treated more harshly in rural counties than in urban or suburban counties.

DeJong and Jackson speculated that the fact that family status did not affect outcomes for African American youth might be due to juvenile justice officials' stereotyped beliefs about African American families. That is, officials "may view all black fathers as absentee" or "may view the black family structure as weak."[121] If this is the case, African American youth who live in two-parent families would not be regarded as better candidates for diversion or for treatment within the community than those who live in single-parent families. This type of subtle discrimination may be more common than the overt discrimination that characterized the system in earlier eras.[122]

Adjudication and Disposition Decisions in Georgia   A study of juvenile court outcomes in Georgia focused on the interaction between the race of the juvenile and admitting or denying the crime.[123] R. Barry Ruback and Paula J. Vardaman posited two opposing effects for admitting/denying guilt, one based on the youth's potential for rehabilitation and the other based on due process

**T A B L E   10.9   The Characteristics of Youth Formally Referred
to Juvenile Court and Placed in Secure Confinement
Following Disposition**

	Formally Referred (%)	Placed in Secure Facility (%)
Race / Ethnicity		
White	49.5	14.9
Black	61.4	17.8
Hispanic	59.4	22.9
Gender		
Male	57.5	17.1
Female	38.4	12.9
Age		
12 and below	43.7	11.8
13	50.0	14.3
14	51.9	17.5
15	56.9	12.7
16	58.6	21.0
17 and above	54.7	17.1
Living with mother only	65.9	17.8
Living with both parents	55.1	10.7
In school	61.0	15.8
Not in school	68.2	22.6
Charge Type		
Property	66.2	16.1
Violent	61.2	15.9
Drug	71.6	23.7
Other	29.6	15.6
Charge Seriousness		
Felony	78.5	19.5
Misdemeanor	35.8	12.5
Number of Prior Arrests		
None	48.7	10.5
One	64.7	22.9
Two	70.1	32.2
Three or more	76.4	35.8

SOURCE: Adapted from Christina DeJong and Kenneth C. Jackson, "Putting Race Into Context: Race, Juvenile Justice
Processing, and Urbanization," *Justice Quarterly* 15 (1998), pp. 487–504, Table 2. Reprinted by permission of the
publisher (Taylor & Francis Ltd, http://www.tandf.co.uk/journals).

considerations. They asserted that if the primary goal of the juvenile justice system was rehabilitation, then indicators of amenability to rehabilitation should be important predictors of case disposition. Since admitting guilt signals that the youth accepts responsibility for his actions and feels remorse and also indicates that the youth may be a good candidate for treatment rather than punishment, an admission of guilt should—again, if rehabilitation is the goal—lead to more lenient treatment. On the other hand, if the goal of the court is to punish the guilty, *denial* of guilt might lead to more lenient treatment. This might be particularly true, according to Ruback and Vardaman, in large urban jurisdictions with heavy caseloads. If the youth denies that he is guilty, the court must hold an evidentiary hearing and prove the charges. Prosecutors might prefer to dismiss the case rather than use their limited resources to secure a conviction.

Ruback and Vardaman found that whereas African Americans were overrepresented in juvenile court populations in the 16 Georgia counties they examined, white youth were treated more harshly than African American youth.[124] White juveniles (43 percent) were more likely than African American juveniles (39 percent) to be adjudicated delinquent, and African American juveniles (29 percent) were more likely than white juveniles (23 percent) to have their cases dismissed. The authors also found that white youth were substantially more likely to admit the crimes they were accused of committing: 66 percent of the whites, compared to only 51 percent of the African Americans, admitted their guilt.

When Ruback and Vardaman compared adjudication outcomes for African American and white youth, controlling for crime seriousness, prior record, whether the case was heard in an urban or rural county, whether the youth admitted guilt, and the youth's age and gender, they found that race had no effect. Admitting guilt, on the other hand, had a strong effect on the likelihood of being adjudicated delinquent. Youth who admitted their guilt were more likely to be adjudicated delinquent. The odds of being adjudicated delinquent also were higher in rural than in urban counties.

The authors of the study concluded that the harsher treatment of white youth could be attributed to two factors. First, whites were more likely than African Americans to admit guilt, and admitting guilt led to a higher likelihood of being adjudicated delinquent. Second, cases involving whites were more likely than those involving African Americans to be processed in rural courts, where the odds of being adjudicated delinquent were higher.[125] They also suggested that their results might reflect judges' beliefs that white youths would be more likely to benefit from the interventions and services available to the court. Thus,

> an intervention by the court may be deemed more likely to affect the future behavior of white juveniles (who generally have shorter legal histories), while the same intervention with Black juveniles (who generally have longer legal histories) may be perceived as wasted effort. It may be … that only white juveniles are believed to be worth investing resources in so as to reduce the chances of their committing future crimes.[126]

Ruback and Vardaman maintained that this also might explain why white youth admitted their guilt at a higher rate than African American youth. That is, juvenile justice officials might have urged whites to admit the crime so that they could receive an informal adjustment and court intervention.

Race / Ethnicity, Gender, and Age: Juvenile Justice in Nebraska

The studies discussed thus far all tested for the direct effects of race / ethnicity; that is, these studies examined whether African American and Hispanic youth were treated more harshly than white youth. Dae-Hoon Kwak used Nebraska data to examine the interactions among age, gender, race / ethnicity, and four juvenile court outcomes: detention, petition, adjudication, and disposition.[127] He controlled for the seriousness of the offense, the youth's prior delinquency referrals, whether the case was handled by a separate juvenile court or a regular county court, and the year of the referral. He found that each of the offender characteristics affected some or all of the outcomes: youth of color generally were treated more harshly than white youth, younger offenders were treated more leniently than offenders who were between the ages of 13 and 17, and males were more likely than females to be petitioned and transferred to legal custody.[128]

Kwak then compared outcomes for African American males who were 16 or 17 years old with outcomes for other categories of offenders. Although he found differences for each of the four outcomes, the most consistent outcomes were found for the disposition decision, which was measured by a dichotomous variable that differentiated between decisions that transferred the legal custody of the youth (that is, transferred the youth to a secure facility or into the custody of a public agency) and those that did not (that is, probation, dismissal of charges with a warning from the judge, or a fine). As shown in Table 10.10, African American males, aged 16 and 17, received substantially harsher dispositions than all of the other groups, except for Hispanic females aged 10 through 12, black males aged 13 through 15, Hispanic males aged 13 through 15, and Native American males aged 16 and 17. Of particular interest is the fact that white males, regardless of age, were substantially less likely than 16- and 17-year-old African American males to have their legal custody transferred to a secure facility or a state agency. The probability differences were 21.0 percent for white males aged 10 through 12, 13.9 percent for white males aged 13 through 15, and 17.7 percent for white males aged 16 and 17. Overall, then, male teenagers of color, and especially African American male teenagers, were treated more harshly than other offenders.

In summary, the results of the studies reviewed here suggest that the effect of race / ethnicity on juvenile court outcomes is complex. Some researchers conclude that race and ethnicity have direct or overt effects on case outcomes. Research conducted in Florida and Pennsylvania, for example, found that racial minorities were treated more harshly than whites at several stages in the juvenile justice process, including detention, and that detention had significant "spillover effects" on subsequent adjudication and disposition decisions. Other researchers conclude that the effect of race / ethnicity is indirect rather than direct. Research conducted in Pennsylvania, for instance, found that living in a two-parent family benefitted whites but

T A B L E 10.10   Differences in the Probabilities of Placement in a Secure Facility or Transfer to a State Agency

Probability Differences Between African American Males, Ages 16 and 17, and...

White Female	
Age 10–12	–18.7%
Age 13–15	–17.2%
Age 16–17	–18.8%
Black Female	
Age 10–12	–26.1%
Age 13–15	–6.8%
Age 16–17	–19.6%
Hispanic Female	
Age 10–12	Not significant
Age 13–15	–12.2%
Age 16–17	–22.6%
Native American Female	
Age 10–12	–28.0%
Age 13–15	–12.0%
Age 16–17	–16.8%
White Male	
Age 10–12	–21.0%
Age 13–15	–13.9%
Age 16–17	–17.7%
African American Male	
Age 10–12	–12.8%
Age 13–15	Not significant
Hispanic Male	
Age 10–12	–26.3%
Age 13–15	Not significant
Age 16–17	Not significant
Native American Male	
Age 10–12	–24.0%
Age 13–15	–6.6%
Age 16–17	Not significant

SOURCE: Dae-Hoon Kwak, "The Interaction of Age, Gender, and Race / Ethnicity on Juvenile Justice Decision Making in Nebraska." Unpublished master's thesis, University of Nebraska at Omaha, 2004.

not African Americans, while research in Georgia found that the *harsher* treatment of white youth reflected their higher rates of admitting guilt and a greater likelihood of being prosecuted in rural rather than urban jurisdictions. And a study conducted in Nebraska revealed that teenage boys were singled out for harsher treatment if they were racial minorities, especially if they were African Americans.

These studies also suggest that the effect of race on juvenile justice outcomes may vary from one jurisdiction to another and highlight the importance of conceptualizing decision making in the juvenile justice system as a process. According to Philip E. Secret and James B. Johnson,[129] "in examining for racial bias in juvenile justice system decisions, we must scrutinize each step of the process to see whether previous decisions create a racial effect by changing the pool of offenders at subsequent steps." The importance of differentiating among racial and ethnic groups is also clear. As one author noted, "Circumstances surrounding the case processing of minority youths not only may be different from those for whites, but also may vary among minority groups."[130]

Transfer of Juveniles to Criminal Court

In 2009 juveniles accounted for 9.6 percent of all arrests for murder/manslaughter, 14.5 percent of all arrests for forcible rape, 25.2 percent of all arrests for robbery, and 11.9 percent of all arrests for aggravated assault.[131] The number of juveniles arrested increased 100 percent between 1985 and 1994[132] but declined by 18 percent from 1994 to 2003.[133] Juvenile arrests for *violent* crimes increased from 66,976 in 1985 to 117,200 in 1994 (an increase of 75 percent), but declined to 92,300 (a decrease of 32 percent) in 2003 and to 68,074 (a further decline of 26 percent).

The increase in juvenile crime during the 1980s and early 1990s, coupled with highly publicized cases of very young children accused of murder and other violent crimes, prompted a number of states to alter procedures for handling certain types of juvenile offenders. In 1995, for example, Illinois lowered the age of admission to prison from 13 to 10. This change was enacted after two boys, ages 10 and 11, dropped a 5-year-old boy out of a 14th-floor window of a Chicago public housing development. In 1996 a juvenile court judge ordered that both boys, who were then 12 and 13, be sent to a high-security juvenile penitentiary; her decision made the 12-year-old the nation's youngest inmate at a high-security prison.[134]

Other states responded to the increase in serious juvenile crime by either lowering the age when children can be transferred from juvenile court to criminal court and/or expanding the list of offenses for which juveniles can be waived to criminal court. A report by the United States General Accounting Office indicated that between 1978 and 1995, 44 states passed new laws regarding the waiver of juveniles to criminal court; in 24 of these states the new laws increased the population of juveniles that potentially could be sent to criminal court.[135] California, for example, changed the age at which juveniles could be waived to criminal court from 16 to 14 (for specified offenses); Missouri reduced the age at which children could be certified to stand trial as adults from 14 to 12. By 2004 there were 15 states with mandatory waiver in cases that met certain age, offense, or other criteria and 15 states with a rebuttable presumption in favor of waiver in

---

B o x 10.3   *Kent* v. *United States* [383 U.S. 541 (1966)]: Criteria Concerning Waiver of Jurisdiction from Juvenile Court to Adult Court

---

In 1996 the United States Supreme Court ruled in *Kent* v. *United States* that waiver hearings must measure up to "the essentials of due process and fair treatment." The court held that juveniles facing waiver are entitled to representation by counsel, access to social services records, and a written statement of the reasons for the waiver. In an appendix to its opinion, the court also laid out the "criteria and principles concerning waiver of jurisdiction." The criteria that courts are to use in making the decision are:

- The seriousness of the alleged offense and whether protection of the community requires waiver.

- Whether the alleged offense was committed in an aggressive, violent, premeditated, or willful manner.

- Whether the alleged offense was against persons or against property.

- Whether there is evidence upon which a Grand Jury may be expected to return an indictment.

- The desirability of trial and disposition of the entire offense in one court when the juvenile's associates are adults who will be charged with a crime in criminal court.

- The sophistication and maturity of the juvenile as determined by consideration of his home, environmental situation, emotional attitude, and pattern of living.

- The record and previous history of the juvenile.

- The prospects for adequate protection of the public and the likelihood of reasonable rehabilitation of the juvenile by the use of procedures, services, and facilities currently available to the Juvenile Court.

---

certain kinds of cases. Currently, all but four states give juvenile court judges the power to waive jurisdiction over juvenile cases that meet certain criteria—generally, a minimum age, a specified type or level of offense, and/or a sufficiently serious record of prior delinquency.[136] And 15 states have direct file waiver provisions, which allow the prosecutor to file certain types of juvenile cases directly in criminal court. (See Box 10.3 for the criteria that courts can use in making the waiver decision.)

A 2008 report by the National Center for Juvenile Justice noted that the number of delinquency cases waived to criminal court increased by 80 percent from 1985 to 1994 but declined by 51 percent between 1994 and 2001.[137] (The report attributed the decline in the number of cases waived to criminal court in part to statutory changes that excluded certain cases from juvenile court or allowed prosecutors to file serious cases directly in criminal court.) During most of this time period, the waiver rate was highest for person offenses; from 1989 to 1992, the rate was higher for drug offenses than for person offenses. Not surprisingly, cases involving older youth were more likely than those involving youths 15 and younger to be waived, and cases involving males were substantially more likely than those involving females to be waived.[138]

There also is evidence that cases involving racial minorities are more likely than those involving whites to be transferred to criminal court. For example,

- In 2005 the percentage of delinquency cases waived to criminal court nationwide was 0.7 percent for white youth, 0.8 percent for African American youth, 1.3 percent for Native American youth, and 0.4 percent for Asian youth. Among youth charged with drug offenses, the rate was 0.7 for whites, 1.0 percent for African Americans, 1.4 percent for Native Americans, and 0.3 percent for Asians.[139]

- In 1996 youth of color accounted for 75 percent of Los Angeles County's population between the ages of 10 and 17 but 95 percent of the youths whose cases were waived to adult court; Asian Americans were 3 times more likely than white youth, Hispanics were 6 times more likely than white youth, and African Americans were 12 times more likely than white youth to be waived to adult court.[140]

- African American youth comprised 60 percent and Hispanics made up 10 percent of juveniles waived to adult court in Pennsylvania in 1994; white youth made up only 28 percent of these cases.[141]

- African Americans made up 80 percent of all waiver request cases in South Carolina from 1985 through 1994. Eighty-one percent of the cases involving African American youth were approved for waiver to adult court, compared to only 74 percent of the cases involving white youth.[142]

Decisions to transfer juveniles to adult criminal courts are important because of the sentencing consequences of being convicted in criminal rather than juvenile court. Although there is some evidence that transferred youth are treated more leniently in criminal court than they would have been in juvenile court[143]—in large part because they appear in criminal court at a younger age and with shorter criminal histories than other offenders—most studies reveal just the opposite. Jeffrey Fagan, for example, compared juvenile and criminal court outcomes for 15- and 16-year-old felony offenders in New York (where they were excluded from juvenile court) and New Jersey (where they were not).[144] He found that youth processed in criminal courts were twice as likely as those processed in juvenile courts to be incarcerated.

A more recent study compared sentencing outcomes of juveniles (those under age 18) and young adults (those ages 18 to 24) processed in Pennsylvania's adult criminal courts from 1997 to 1999.[145] When they examined the raw data, Megan C. Kurlycheck and Brian D. Johnson found that the mean sentence imposed on juvenile offenders was 18 months, compared to only 6 months for young adult offenders. These differences did not disappear when the authors controlled for the seriousness of the offense, the offender's criminal history, the offense type, whether the case was settled by plea or trial, and the offender's gender. Once these factors were taken into consideration, juveniles still received sentences that were 83 percent harsher than those imposed on young adults.[146] Further analysis revealed that "'being juvenile' resulted in a 10-percent greater likelihood of incarceration and a 29-percent increase in sentence length."[147]

These findings led Kurlychek and Johnson to suggest that "the transfer decision itself is used as an indicator of incorrigibility, threat to the community, and/or lack of potential for rehabilitation, resulting in a considerable 'juvenile penalty.'"[148] Evidence that African American and Hispanic youth face higher odds of being transferred to adult court than do white youth suggests that this "juvenile penalty" is not applied in a racially neutral manner.

Explaining Disparate Treatment of Juvenile Offenders

The studies discussed above provide compelling evidence that African American and Hispanic juveniles are treated more harshly than similarly situated white juveniles. The question, of course, is why this occurs. Secret and Johnson[149] suggest that juvenile court judges may attribute positive or negative characteristics to offenders based on their race / ethnicity. Judges, in other words, may use extralegal characteristics like race to create "a mental map of the accused person's underlying character" and to predict his/her future behavior.[150] As Coramae Richey Mann notes, officials' attitudes "mirror the stereotype of minorities as typically violent, dangerous, or threatening."[151] Alternatively, according to Secret and Johnson, the harsher treatment of African American and Hispanic juveniles might reflect both class and race biases on the part of juvenile court judges. As conflict theory posits, "the individual's economic and social class and the color of his skin … determine his relationship to the legal system."[152]

These speculations regarding court officials' perceptions of minority and white youth have not been systematically tested. Researchers assume that findings of differential treatment of racial minorities signal the presence of race-linked stereotypes or racially prejudiced attitudes, but there have been few attempts to empirically verify either the existence of differing perceptions of white and minority youth or the degree to which these perceptions can account for racial disparities in the juvenile justice system.

A recent study by George S. Bridges and Sara Steen[153] addressed this issue by examining 233 narrative reports written by juvenile probation officers in three counties in the state of Washington during 1990–1991. The narratives, which were used by the court in determining the appropriate disposition of the case, were based on interviews with the youth and his/her family and on written documents such as school records and juvenile court files. Each narrative included the probation officer's description of the youth's crime and assessment of the factors that motivated the crime, as well as an evaluation of the youth's background and assessment of his/her likelihood of recidivism. The information gleaned from these narratives was used "to explore the relationship between race: officials' characterizations of youths, their crimes, and the causes of their crimes; officials' assessments of the threat of future crime by youths; and officials' sentence recommendations."[154]

Bridges and Steen's review of the narratives revealed that probation officers described black and white youth and their crimes differently. They tended to attribute crimes committed by whites to negative environmental factors (poor school performance, delinquent peers, dysfunctional family, use of drugs or alcohol), but to attribute crimes committed by African Americans to negative personality traits and "bad attitudes" (refusal to admit guilt, lack of remorse, failure to take offense seriously, lack of cooperation with court officials). They also found that probation officers judged African American youth to have a significantly higher risk of re-offending than white youth.

Further analysis, which controlled for the juvenile's age, gender, prior criminal history, and for the seriousness of the current offense, confirmed these findings. As the authors note, "Being black significantly reduces the likelihood of negative *external* attributions by probation officers and significantly increases the likelihood of negative *internal* attributions, even after adjusting for severity of the presenting offense and the youth's prior involvement in criminal behavior."[155] To illustrate these differences, the authors discuss the narratives written for two very similar cases of armed robbery, one involving a black youth and one involving a white youth. The black youth's crime was described as "very dangerous" and as "premeditated and willful," and his criminal behavior was attributed to an amoral character, lack of remorse, and no desire to change. In contrast, the white youth was portrayed as an "emaciated little boy" whose crime was attributed to a broken home, association with delinquent peers, and substance abuse.

Bridges and Steen's examination of the factors related to probation officers' assessments of the risk of re-offending revealed that youth who committed more serious crimes or had more serious criminal histories were judged to be at higher risk of future offending. Although none of the offender's demographic characteristics, including race, was significantly related to assessments of risk, probation officers' attributions of delinquency did affect these predictions. Youth whose delinquency was attributed to negative internal causes were judged to be at higher risk of future delinquency than youth whose crimes were attributed to negative external factors. According to Bridges and Steen, "This suggests that youths whose crimes are attributed to internal causes are more likely to be viewed as 'responsible' for their crimes, engulfed in a delinquent personality and lifestyle, and prone to committing crimes in the future."[156]

The authors of this study concluded that race influenced juvenile court outcomes indirectly. Probation officers were substantially more likely to attribute negative internal characteristics and attitudes to African American youth than to white youth; these attributions, in turn, shaped their assessments of dangerousness and their predictions of future offending. As Bridges and Steen state, "Insofar as officials judge black youths to be more dangerous than white youths, they do so because they attribute crime by blacks to negative personalities or their attitudinal traits and because black offenders are more likely than white offenders to have committed serious offenses and have histories of prior involvement in crime."[157]

The results of this study illustrate the "mechanisms by which officials' perceptions of the offender as threatening develop or influence the process of legal decision-making."[158] They suggest that perceptions of threat and, consequently, predictions about future delinquency are influenced by criminal justice officials' assessments of the causes of criminal behavior. Thus, "officials may perceive blacks as more culpable and dangerous than whites in part because they believe the etiology of their crimes is linked to personal traits" that are "not as amenable to the correctional treatments the courts typically administer."[159]

JUVENILES UNDER CORRECTIONAL SUPERVISION

As the previous section illustrates, the racial makeup of juveniles at key stages of the juvenile justice system varies by decision type. Generally, nonwhite youth (the majority of whom are African American) are overrepresented at every stage of decision making. Nonwhite youth also are at greater risk of receiving harsher sanctions than white youth. For example, nonwhite youth are detained in secure custody prior to their juvenile court hearing at rates that exceed those for white youth, regardless of the seriousness of the delinquency offense. Recently, there has been a decline in the proportion of white youth detained but an increase in the proportion of African American youth in custody.[160]

Table 10.11 presents data on the racial and ethnic makeup of juvenile offenders who were placed in a secure public or private residential facility in 2006 after being adjudicated delinquent.[161] White and Asian youth are underrepresented among youth in residential placement, while African American, Hispanic, and Native American / Alaskan Native youth generally are overrepresented. For all of the criminal offense types (violent, property, drug, public order), youth of color made up about two-thirds of all youth in secure residential facilities. For status offenses (running away from home and truancy), on the other hand, whites comprised the largest proportion of offenders placed in secure confinement. Among youth in residential facilities in 1999, racial minorities were overrepresented in every state in the United States, and in some states there were more

T A B L E   10.11   Racial and Ethnic Profile of Juvenile Offenders in Residential Placement, 2006

| Most Serious Offense | Percentage of Youth in Residential Placement in Each Racial/Ethnic Group | | | | |
	White	African American	Hispanic	American Indian	Asian
Total	35	40	20	2	1
Delinquency Cases	34	41	21	2	1
Violent Offenses	32	44	20	2	1
Property Offenses	37	37	21	2	1
Drug Offenses	32	44	22	1	1
Public-Order Offenses	34	40	22	2	1
Status Offenses	50	33	8	5	1

SOURCE: Bureau of Justice Statistics, *Sourcebook of Criminal Justice Statistics 2006*, online edition, www.albany.edu/sourcebook, Table 6.10.

than twice as many racial minorities in secure facilities as there were in the juvenile population. For instance, racial minorities made up 37 percent of the juvenile population but 84 percent of those in residential placement in New Jersey. The figures were 15 percent (population) and 59 percent (residential placement) for Wisconsin, 18 percent (population) and 55 percent (residential placement) for Rhode Island, and 25 percent (population) and 77 percent (residential placement) for Connecticut.[162]

There also is evidence that African American males are incarcerated in state prisons at disproportionately high rates. In 1999 youth under the age of 18 accounted for only 2 percent of all new court commitments to adult prisons; in the 37 states that provided data to the National Corrections Reporting Program, there were 5,600 new court commitments involving youth younger than 18 at the time of admission.[163] Almost all of these youth (96 percent) were male and more than half of them (57 percent) were African American males. African American males made up 57 percent of new admissions for homicide, 75 percent of new admissions for robbery, and 84 percent of new admissions for drug offenses.[164]

CONCLUSION

The victimization and offending patterns for juveniles mirror those for adults. Juveniles of color, and particularly African American males, face a higher risk of victimization than white juveniles. This pattern is found for property crime, violent crime, and homicide. In fact, the homicide victimization rate for young African American females is higher than the rate for young white males.

Although the common perception of the juvenile offender is that he/she is a person of color,[165] the data discussed above indicate that whites constitute the majority of juvenile offenders for most crimes. The notable exceptions (among the more serious index offenses) are robbery, where over half of those arrested are African American, and murder and non-negligent manslaughter, where African American youth comprise nearly half of all arrestees. The overrepresentation of African American juveniles in arrest statistics is not a constant, however. The most pronounced disparities are found for violent crimes, where from one-third to one-half of all arrestees are African American. There is less racial disparity for property offenses; for these crimes, between one-fourth and one-third of those arrested are African American. Further, whites are overrepresented among arrestees for many of the drug and alcohol offenses.

Recent methodologically sophisticated research reveals that racial and ethnic differences in juvenile victimization and offending rates can be attributed in large part to family and community characteristics. African American and Hispanic youth are more likely than white youth to be the victims of violent crime because they spend more time away from home and are more likely to live in single-parent households and disadvantaged communities. Similarly, the higher rates of violent offending found among minority youth, as compared to white youth, reflect the fact that minority youth are more likely to live in disadvantaged neighborhoods, to be members of gangs, and to have weak bonds to social institutions such as schools. The sources of risk of victimization and offending are similar for all teenagers, but the likelihood of experiencing these risk factors is higher for youth of color than for white youth.

The results of studies examining the effect of race / ethnicity on juvenile justice processing decisions suggest that the juvenile justice system, like the criminal justice system for adults, is not free of racial bias. There is compelling evidence that racial minorities are treated more harshly than whites at various points in the juvenile justice process. Most importantly, minority youth are substantially more likely than white youth to be detained pending disposition, adjudicated delinquent, and waived to adult court. They also are sentenced more harshly than their white counterparts, at least in part because of the tendency of criminal justice officials to attribute their crimes to internal (personality) rather than external (environmental) causes.

DISCUSSION QUESTIONS

1. Describe the characteristics of juvenile victims of crime. Are they similar to or different from the characteristics of adult victims of crime?

2. There is a common perception that the typical juvenile offender is a person of color. Is this an accurate perception?

3. The mayor of St. Louis has appointed you to a commission whose task it is to develop policy recommendations to ameliorate the high rate of violence against young girls in that city's disadvantaged neighborhoods/schools. What would you propose?

4. Why is there greater potential for racial discrimination in the juvenile justice system than in the adult justice system?

5. What are the dangers inherent in allowing police to use gang databases in investigating crimes?

6. Studies of the juvenile justice system reveal that racial minorities are subject to "cumulative disadvantage" or "compound risk." Explain what this means and why it is a cause for concern.

7. We suggest that preliminary evidence indicating that African American juveniles are more likely than white juveniles to be waived to adult court should be confirmed by additional research that incorporates legally relevant criteria other than the seriousness of the offense. What other variables should be taken into consideration?

8. Although studies reveal that African American, Hispanic, and Native American youth are treated more harshly than white youth at several stages of the juvenile justice process (even after the seriousness of the offense and the offender's prior juvenile record are taken into consideration), they do not tell us why these disparities occur. How would *you* explain these differences? How do Bridges and Steen account for them?

NOTES

1. Linda S. Beres and Thomas D. Griffith, "Demonizing Youth," *Loyola of Los Angeles Law Review* 34 (2001), pp. 747–767, p. 747.

2. Kate Randall, "Another Florida teenager receives harsh adult prison sentence." Available at: http://www.wsws.org/articles/2001/aug2001.

3. "Juvenile Justice Experts Decry Severity of Life in Adult Prison for Nathaniel Brazill." Available at: http://www.cjcj.org.

4. Ibid.

5. Susan Spencer-Wendel, "Nathaniel Brazill Would Have Graduated From High School This Week," *Palm Beach Post*, May 22, 2005.

6. "Lionel Tate Released," CNN.com, January 27, 2004. Available at: http://www.cnn.com/2004/LAW/01/26/wrestling.death/.

7. Andrew Ryan, "Lionel Tate Accused of Firing Mother's Handgun Randomly on Street," Sun-Sentinel.com. Available at: http://www.sun-sentinel.com/news/local/broward.

8. Office of Juvenile Justice and Delinquency Prevention, "Juvenile Victims of Property Crimes" (Washington, DC: U.S. Department of Justice, 2000).

9. Ibid.

10. Ibid.

11. Ibid., p. 5.

12. Ibid.

13. Ibid.

14. Bureau of Justice Statistics, *Criminal Victimization in the United States, 2009* (Washington, DC: U.S. Department of Justice, 2010), Table 5.

15. Bureau of Justice Statistics, *Criminal Victimization in the United States, 2007— Statistical Tables*, Table 7. Available at: http://bjs.ojp.usdoj.gov/index.cfm?ty=pbdetail&iid=1743.

16. Ibid., Table 10.

17. Bureau of Justice Statistics, *Weapon Use and Violent Crime*. (Washington, DC: U.S. Department of Justice, 2003), Figures 1 and 2.

18. Janet L. Lauritsen, "How Families and Communities Influence Youth Victimization," OJJDP Juvenile Justice Bulletin, (Washington, DC: U.S. Department of Justice, 2003).

19. Ibid., pp. 5–6.

20. Ibid., p. 7.

21. Ibid., pp. 8–9.

22. Ibid., p. 9.

23. Ibid.

24. Jody Miller, *Getting Played: African American Girls, Urban Inequality, and Gendered Violence* (New York: New York University Press, 2008), p. 9.

25. Ibid., p. 66.

26. Ibid., p. 73.

27. Ibid., p. 111.

28. Ibid., p. 149.

29. Ibid., p. 197.

30. Ibid., p. 197.

31. James Allen Fox and Marianne W. Zawitz, *Homicide Trends in the United States*, (Washington, DC: U.S. Department of Justice, 2010). Available at: http://bjs.ojp .usdoj.gov/content/homicide/homtrnd.cfm.

32. Ibid.

33. Thomas McNulty and Paul E. Bellair, "Explaining Racial and Ethnic Differences in Serious Adolescent Violent Behavior," *Criminology* 41 (2003), pp. 709–748.

34. Ibid., Appendix 1.

35. Ibid., p. 719.

36. Dana Peterson, Finn-Aage Esbenson, and Terrance J. Taylor, "Youth Violence in Context: The Roles of Sex, Race, and Community in Offending," *Youth Violence and Juvenile Justice* 5 (2007), pp. 385–410.

37. Ibid., pp. 397–398.

38. Ibid., p. 404.

39. Ibid.

40. James Allen Fox and Marianne W. Zawitz, "Homicide Trends in the United States," (Washington, DC: U.S. Department of Justice, 2010). Available at: http://bjs.ojp.usdoj.gov/content/homicide/homtrnd.cfm.

41. Ibid.

42. Ibid.

43. See, for example, Robert J. Sampson and William Julius Wilson, "Toward a Theory of Race, Crime, and Urban Inequality," in *Crime and Inequality*, John Hagan and Ruth D. Peterson, eds. (Stanford, CA: Stanford University Press, 1995); and Clifford R. Shaw and Henry D. McKay, *Juvenile Delinquency and Urban Areas* (Chicago, IL: University of Chicago Press, 1942).

44. Michael R. Gottfredson and Travis Hirschi, *A General Theory of Crime* (Stanford, CA: Stanford University Press, 1985); Douglas S. Massey and Nancy A. Denton, *American Apartheid: Segregation and the Making of the Underclass* (Cambridge, MA: Harvard University Press, 1993); and William Julius Wilson, *When Work Disappears: The World of the New Urban Poor* (New York: Knopf, 1996).

45. Stephen A. Cernkovich and Peggy C. Giordano, "School Bonding, Race, and Delinquency," *Criminology* 30 (1992), pp. 261–291; Travis Hirschi, *Causes of Delinquency* (Berkeley, CA: University of California Press, 1969).

46. Ronald L. Akers, *Social Learning and Social Structure: A General Theory of Crime and Deviance* (Boston, MA: Northeastern University Press, 1994); Malcom Klein, *The American Street Gang* (New York: Oxford University Press, 1995).

47. McNulty and Bellair, "Explaining Racial and Ethnic Differences in Serious Adolescent Violent Behavior."

48. Ibid., p. 709.

49. Ibid., p. 736.

50. Paula J. Fite, Porche Wynn, and Dustin A. Pardini, "Explaining Discrepancies in Arrest Rates Between Black and White Male Juveniles," *Journal of Counseling and Clinical Psychology* 77 (2009), pp. 916–927.

51. Ibid., p. 919.

52. Ibid., p. 922.

53. Ibid., p. 924

54. Lori Dorfman and Vincent Schiraldi, "Off Balance: Youth, Race, and Crime in the News," Executive Summary, Berkeley Media Studies Group, 2001. Available at: http://www.buildingblocksforyouth.org/media/.

55. Ibid., p. 3

56. Ibid., p. 4.

57. Ibid.

58. Ibid.

59. Ibid., p. 8.

60. Carl Werthman and Irving Piliavin, "Gang Members and the Police," in *The Police: Six Sociological Essays*, David J. Bordua, ed. (New York: Wiley, 1967), p. 58.

61. Gallup Poll data, reported in Bureau of Justice Statistics, *Sourcebook of Criminal Justice Statistics 2000*, online edition, http://www.albany.edu/sourcebook, Table 2.16.

62. Donald Black, "The Social Organization of Arrest," in *The Manners and Customs of the Police* (New York: Academic Press, 1980).

63. Carl E. Pope and Howard N. Snyder, *Race as a Factor in Juvenile Arrests* (Washington, DC: Office of Juvenile Justice and Delinquency Prevention, 2003.)

64. Ibid., p. 6.

65. Ryan Pintado-Vertner, "How is Juvenile Justice Served? Racially Biased System Just Sweeps Troubled Youths Under the Rug," *San Francisco Chronicle*, February 27, 2000.

66. Stacey Leyton, "The New Blacklists: The Threat to Civil Liberties Posed by Gang Databases," in *Crime Control and Social Justice: The Delicate Balance*, Darnell F. Hawkins, Samuel L. Meyers, Jr., and Randolph N. Stone, eds. (Westport, CT: Greenwood, 2003).

67. Texas Art. 61-02. Available at: http://www.iir.com/nygc/gang-legis/gang_data-bases.htm.

68. Leyton. "The New Blacklists," p. 115.

69. Reverand Oscar Tillman, senior official of the Denver NAACP, quoted in Dirk Johnson, "2 Out of 3 Young Black Men in Denver Are on Gang Suspect List," *New York Times*, December 11, 1993, at A8.

70. Leyton, "The New Blacklists," p. 120 and n. 114.

71. John Moreno Gonzales, "Response to Violence; Anti-Gang Bill Revived," *Newsday*, November 12, 2004, at A18.

72. Leyton, "The New Blacklists," p. 121.

73. Daniel C. Tsang, "Garden Grove's Asian Mug File Settlement." Available at: http://sun3.lib.uci.edu/~dtsang/ggamfs.htm.

74. Stella Richardson, "ACLU Wins Major Settlement for Union City Students," *ACLU News*, Summer 2005. Available at: http://www.alcunc.org/aclunews/news0508/unioncity.html.

75. Marjorie S. Zatz and Richard P. Krecker, Jr., "Anti-gang Initiatives as Racialized Policy," in *Crime Control and Social Justice: The Delicate Balance*, Darnell F. Hawkins, Samuel L. Meyers, Jr., and Randolph N. Stone, eds. (Westport, CT: Greenwood, 2003).

76. Zatz and Krecker, "Anti-Gang Initiatives as Racialized Policy," p. 192.

77. Philip W. Harris, Wayne N. Welsh, and Frank Butler, "A Century of Juvenile Justice," in Volume 1, *Criminal Justice 2000, The Nature of Crime: Continuity and Change* (Washington, DC: National Institute of Justice, 2000), p. 360.

78. Literally translated as "father of the country," this phrase refers to the government's right and obligation to act on behalf of a child (or a person who is mentally ill).

79. Anthony M. Platt, *The Child Saver: The Invention of Delinquency*, 2nd ed. (Chicago: University of Chicago Press, 1977).

80. Ibid., p. xvii.

81. Ibid.

82. Barry C. Feld, *Bad Kids: Race and the Transformation of the Juvenile Court* (New York: Oxford University Press, 1999).

83. Ibid., p. 6.

84. Ibid., pp. 3–4.

85. Ibid., p. 4.

86. National Center for Juvenile Justice, *Juvenile Court Statistics 2005* (Washington, DC: Office of Juvenile Justice and Delinquency Prevention, 2008), p. 19.

87. Ibid., p. 20.

88. Ibid., p. 53.

89. Judith A. Cox, "Addressing Disproportionate Minority Representation Within the Juvenile Justice System." Available at the website for Building Blocks for Youth (http://www.buildingblocksforyouth.org). The author of this report noted that steps taken by the Santa Cruz County Probation Office led to a decrease in the percentage of those held who were Hispanic; it declined from 64 percent in 1997/1998 to 46 percent in 2000.

90. Office of Juvenile Justice and Delinquency Prevention, *Disproportionate Minority Confinement, 2002 Update* (Washington, DC: U.S. Department of Justice, 2004), p. 3.

91. Building Blocks for Youth, *And Justice for Some* (Washington, DC: Building Blocks for Youth, 2000).

92. Ibid., p. 9.

93. Ibid., p. 15.

94. See, for example, Donna M. Bishop and Charles S. Frazier, "Race Effects in Juvenile Justice Decision-Making: Findings of a Statewide Analysis," *Journal of Criminal Law and Criminology* 86 (1996), pp. 392–413.

95. Barry C. Feld, *Bad Kids: Race and the Transformation of the Juvenile Court* (London and New York: Oxford University Press, 1999), p. 266.

96. Carl E. Pope and William H. Feyerherm, "Minority Status and Juvenile Justice Processing: An Assessment of the Research Literature (Part I)," *Criminal Justice Abstracts* 22 (1990), pp. 327–335.

97. Carl E. Pope, Rich Lovell, and Heidi M. Hsia, "Disproportionate Minority Confinement: A Review of the Research Literature from 1989 through 2001," (Washington, DC: U.S. Department of Justice, 2004).

98. Ibid., p. 6.

99. David Huizinga and Delbert S. Elliot, "Juvenile Offenders: Prevalence, Offender Incidence, and Arrest Rates by Race," *Crime and Delinquency* 33 (1987), pp. 206–223, p. 212.

100. Donna M. Bishop and Charles E. Frazier, "The Influence of Race in Juvenile Justice Processing," *Journal of Research in Crime and Delinquency* 25 (1988), pp. 242–263.

101. Panel on Juvenile Crime, *Juvenile Crime Juvenile Justice*, p. 254.

102. Pope and Feyerherm, "Minority Status and Juvenile Justice Processing," p. 334.

103. Ibid., pp. 254–258.

104. Ibid., p. 257.

105. Bishop and Frazier, "The Influence of Race in Juvenile Justice Processing."

106. Ibid., p. 258.

107. Charles E. Frazier and Donna M. Bishop, "Reflections on Race Effects in Juvenile Justice," in *Minorities in Juvenile Justice*, Kimberly Kempf Leonard, Carl E. Pope, and William H. Feyerherm, eds. (Thousand Oaks, CA: Sage, 1995).

108. Ibid., p. 25.

109. Ibid., p. 28.

110. Ibid., p. 35.

111. Ibid., p. 40.

112. Ibid., p. 41.

113. Ibid., pp. 41–45.

114. Ibid., p. 45.

115. Kimberly Kempf Leonard and Henry Sontheimer, "The Role of Race in Juvenile Justice in Pennsylvania," in *Minorities in Juvenile Justice*, Kimberly Kempf Leonard, Carl E. Pope, and William H. Feyerherm, eds. (Thousand Oaks, CA: Sage, 1995).

116. Ibid., p. 108.

117. Ibid., p. 119.

118. Ibid., pp. 122–123.

119. Christina DeJong and Kenneth C. Jackson, "Putting Race Into Context: Race, Juvenile Justice Processing, and Urbanization," *Justice Quarterly* 15 (1998), pp. 487–504.

120. Ibid., p. 501.

121. Ibid., p. 502.

122. A study of juvenile justice outcomes in Ohio also found evidence of indirect dis-crimination. This study revealed that African American youth whose families were receiving welfare benefits were more likely than African American youth whose families were not on welfare to be placed in secure confinement following adjudi-cation. The same pattern was not observed for whites. According to the authors, this suggests that "only minority families on welfare are regarded as unsuitable for supervising their delinquent children." Bohsiu Wu and Angel Ilarraza Fuentes, "The Entangled Effects of Race and Urban Poverty," *Juvenile and Family Court Journal* 49 (1998), pp. 41–53, p. 49.

123. R. Barry Ruback and Paula J. Vardaman, "Decision Making in Delinquency Cases: The Role of Race and Juveniles' Admission/Denial of the Crime," *Law and Human Behavior* 21 (1997), pp. 47–69.

124. Ibid., p. 52.

125. Ibid., p. 59.

126. Ibid., p. 67.

127. Dae-Hoon Kwak, The Interaction of Age, Gender, and Race / Ethnicity on Juvenile Justice Decision Making in Nebraska, unpublished master's thesis, University of Nebraska at Omaha, 2004.

128. Ibid., Table 5.

129. Philip E. Secret and James B. Johnson, "The Effect of Race on Juvenile Justice Decision Making in Nebraska: Detention, Adjudication, and Disposition, 1988–1993," *Justice Quarterly* 14 (1997), pp. 445–478.

130. Ibid., p. 274.

131. U.S. Department of Justice, Federal Bureau of Investigation, *Crime in the United States, 2009* (Washington, DC: U.S. Government Printing Office, 2010).

132. U.S. Department of Justice, Federal Bureau of Investigation, *Crime in the United States 1994* (Washington, DC: U.S. Government Printing Office, 1995), pp. 227–228.

133. Office of Juvenile Justice and Delinquency Prevention, *Juvenile Arrests 2003*, p. 3.

134. "Chicago Boy, 12, Will Be Youngest in U.S. Prison," *Omaha World Herald*, January 31, 1996.

135. United States General Accounting Office, *Juvenile Justice: Juveniles Processed in Criminal Court and Case Dispositions* (Washington, DC: GAO, 1995), p. 2.

136. National Center for Juvenile Justice, *Which States Waive Juveniles to Criminal Court?* (Pittsburgh, PA: National Center for Juvenile Justice, 2004).

137. National Center for Juvenile Justice, *Juvenile Court Statistics 2005*, p. 40.

138. Ibid., p. 43.

139. Ibid., p. 43.

140. Mike Males and Dan Macallair, *The Color of Justice: An Analysis of Juvenile Justice Adult Court Transfers in California* (Washington, DC: Justice Policy Institute, 2000).

141. Office of Juvenile Justice and Delinquency Prevention, *Juvenile Transfers to Criminal Court in the 1990s: Lessons Learned from Four Studies* (Washington, DC: Office of Juvenile Justice and Delinquency Prevention, 2000).

142. Ibid., p. 13.

143. See, for example, Office of Juvenile Justice and Delinquency Prevention, *Major Issues in Juvenile Justice Information and Training Youth in Adult Courts—Between Two Worlds* (Washington, DC: Office of Juvenile Justice and Delinquency Prevention, 1982).

144. Jeffrey Fagan, *The Comparative Impacts of Juvenile and Criminal Court Sanctions on Adolescent Offenders* (Washington, DC: Office of Justice Programs, National Institute of Justice, 1991).

145. Megan C. Kurlychek and Brian D. Johnson, "The Juvenile Penalty: A Comparison of Juvenile and Young Adult Sentencing Outcomes in Criminal Court," *Criminology* 42 (2004), pp. 485–515.

146. Ibid., p. 500.

147. Ibid., p. 502.

148. Ibid., p. 505.

149. Secret and Johnson, "The Effect of Race on Juvenile Justice Decision Making in Nebraska."

150. Ibid., p. 450.

151. Coramae Richey Mann, *Unequal Justice: A Question of Color* (Bloomington, IN: Indiana University Press, 1993), p. 255.

152. R. Lefcourt, "The Administration of Criminal Law," in *Criminal Justice in America*, Richard Quinney, ed. (Boston: Little Brown, 1974).

153. George S. Bridges and Sara Steen, "Racial Disparities in Official Assessments of Juvenile Offenders: Attributional Stereotypes as Mediating Mechanisms," *American Sociological Review* 63, pp. 554–570.

154. Ibid., p. 558.

155. Ibid., pp. 563–564.

156. Ibid., p. 564.

157. Ibid., p. 567.

158. Ibid., p. 567.

159. Ibid., p. 567.

160. Office of Juvenile Justice and Delinquency Preventions, *Juvenile Court Statistics 2000*.

161. Bureau of Justice Statistics, *Sourcebook of Criminal Justice Statistics 2006*, online edition, http://www.albany.edu/sourcebook, Table 6.10.

162. Office of Juvenile Justice and Delinquency Prevention, *Juveniles in Corrections* (Washington, DC: Office of Juvenile Justice and Delinquency Prevention, 2004), p. 10.

163. Ibid., p. 19.

164. Ibid., p. 21.

165. Jeffrey Reiman, *The Rich Get Richer and the Poor Get Prison* (Boston: Allyn & Bacon, 1995).

11

✳

The Color of Justice

R ace, ethnicity, and crime are bound together in American society. It is impossible to discuss policing, sentencing, the death penalty, or employment in the criminal justice system without confronting issues of race and ethnicity and the disparities that exist throughout the system. And as we explained in Chapter 3, it is impossible to discuss crime without considering the social and economic inequalities that exist in American society, which contribute directly and indirectly to criminal behavior.

One major contribution of this book is our effort to disentangle the misunderstandings that exist with regard to race, ethnicity, and the justice system and to gain a clearer understanding of the complex reality of American society. One problem involves the terms "race" and "minorities." As we have explained, it is important to distinguish between race and ethnicity. First, these are different parts of the social reality of America. They are also reflected in official data on crime and justice. Second, different racial and ethnic groups have very different experiences with the justice system. African Americans and Native Americans experience the highest crime rates and also the highest rates of victimization. Asian Americans have the lowest rates of crime and victimization. Hispanic Americans fall somewhere between non-Hispanic whites and African Americans, with lower rates of both criminal behavior and victimization.

Another contribution of this book is to highlight the great complexity of crime and justice in this country. We have done this for a reason. Debates over criminal justice are so often cast in oversimplified terms that distort reality. You hear sweeping statements such as "crime just keeps going up and up," or "dangerous criminals all get off easy," or "immigrants are responsible for the crime increase." Not one of these statements is true. If we know anything about criminal justice, it is that each and every topic—criminal behavior, policing, sentencing—is extremely complex. There are no simple answers.[1]

EXPLAINING PERSISTENT RACIAL
AND ETHNIC DISPARITIES

In the end, what can we say about race, ethnicity, and crime in America? Given all the complexities, can we make any generalizations? We believe that a fair assessment of the evidence indicates that the criminal justice system is characterized by disparities based on race and ethnicity. It is impossible to ignore the disproportionate number of minorities arrested, imprisoned, and on death row. Some of the decisions that produce these results involve discrimination. Michael Tonry, one of the leading experts on race, ethnicity, and criminal justice, concluded that in the end, after all the evidence is considered, "race matters."

Not everyone agrees with our conclusion. As we discussed in Chapter 1, some people argue that the over-involvement of people of color in criminal activity, along with some other factors, explains the disparities in arrests, sentencing, and imprisonment. We cited Heather Macdonald as one proponent of this view.[2]

Our conclusion is a modulated one. We do not claim that race and ethnicity explain all of the disparities that exist, but they are important factors that cannot be ignored. The best research indicates persistent patterns of racial and ethnic disparities in the critical decision points of arrest and sentencing. This view is reinforced by the technique of meta-analysis, which systematically reviews all the research on a particular topic. Our conclusion is supported by others. A recent review of all the studies of police arrest decisions concluded that race is a factor: "We report with confidence that the results are not mixed. Race matters." The evidence clearly indicates that "race does affect the likelihood of an arrest." The chances of a person of color being arrested are 30 percent higher than for a white non-Hispanic person. A similar review of all the studies of sentencing, meanwhile, also found that race matters, although the effect was not as strong as in arrests.[3]

Patterns of crime and justice are continually changing (another important complexity). One of the most important developments of the past 20 years has been the great American crime drop, which began in the early 1990s and continued for nearly a decade. African Americans have been the primary beneficiaries of the great crime drop. The dramatic decline in homicides, particularly gun crimes among young men, has meant fewer deaths among primarily young African American men. Nonetheless, the racial disparity in both offenders and victims continues.[4]

EXPLAINING THE DISPARITIES:
SYSTEMATIC DISCRIMINATION?

Do the racial and ethnic disparities that researchers have identified constitute discrimination? We believe the answer is yes, but (another complexity) it depends on how you understand the scope of discrimination.

As we explained in Chapter 1, there are different kinds of discrimination: systematic, individual, and contextual. (No one seriously argues that we have ever had a situation of pure justice.) Based on the evidence, we conclude that the system is characterized by *contextual discrimination*. Racial minorities are treated more harshly than whites at some stages of the criminal justice process (for example, the decision to seek or impose the death penalty) but no differently than whites at other stages (for example, the selection of the jury pool). The treatment accorded racial minorities is more punitive than that accorded whites in some regions or jurisdictions, but it is no different than that accorded whites in other regions or jurisdictions. For example, some police departments tolerate excessive force directed at racial minorities or the use of racial profiling, whereas others do not. Racial minorities who commit certain types of crimes (for example, drug offenses or violent crimes against whites) or who have certain types of characteristics (for example, they are young, male, and unemployed) are treated more harshly than whites who commit these crimes or have these characteristics.

Precisely because the discrimination that exists is buried deep within the justice system, and is often confounded by other factors (for example, different patterns of involvement in crime), it is often difficult to identify with precision. This also makes it easy for critics of our position to argue that no discrimination exists.

PAST AND PRESENT

We are not arguing that the U.S. criminal justice system never has been characterized by systematic racial discrimination. In fact, the evidence discussed in earlier chapters suggests just the opposite. The years preceding the civil rights movement (pre-1960s) were characterized by blatant discrimination directed against African Americans and other racial minorities at all stages of the criminal justice process. This pattern of widespread discrimination was not limited to the South; it was found throughout the United States. Crimes among African Americans were completely ignored by police. Among persons shot and killed by the police, the ratio in the 1960s was eight African Americans for every one white person. The overwhelming number of people given the death penalty for rape were African Americans. (The Supreme Court has declared capital punishment for rape to be unconstitutional.) Clearly, we have made some progress since the days of the segregation era. But that should not be our standard. The proper standard is found in the words engraved above the Supreme Court building: Equal Justice Under Law.

Many of the worst forms of discrimination have been substantially reduced through new laws, court decisions, and political pressure. For example:

- Police and other criminal justice agencies no longer refuse to employ people of color.
- Policy reforms and a major Supreme Court decision have placed controls over police use of deadly force, thereby reducing disparities in persons shot and killed.

- Police no longer completely ignore crimes against African Americans, as was often the case in the segregation era.

- The bail reform movement of the 1960s eliminated the worst discrimination against poor people, which disproportionately affected people of color.

- African Americans can no longer be excluded from juries, as was the case in southern states in the segregation era.

- Sentencing reforms since the 1970s have attempted to insure that sentences are based on acceptable legal factors (the seriousness of the offense and the offender's prior record), thereby curbing the worst forms of sentencing discrimination.

- Racial segregation in prisons has been declared unconstitutional and thereby eliminated.

- Supreme Court decisions on the death penalty have eliminated the uncontrolled discretion in death sentences that produced the mast blatant forms of racial discrimination.

THE STUBBORN PERSISTENCE OF RACIAL AND ETHNIC DISPARITIES

Despite the progress made in many areas, racial and ethnic disparities persist in the criminal justice system. Tonry puts it bluntly, pointing out that the unjust effects of race and ethnicity "are well known, have been well known, [but] have changed little in recent decades." We think he understates the change and progress that has occurred, but he is absolutely correct about the stubborn persistence of the inequities. He explains this in terms of public indifference. Much of the public and most policy makers do not "much notice or care."[5]

Public indifference to racial and ethnic discrimination is also affected by the increased racial polarization of American politics in recent years. A 2010 poll, for example, found that almost half (48 percent) of all white Americans think "discrimination against whites has become as big a problem as discrimination against blacks and other minorities."[6] Many non-Hispanic Americans feel that immigration, and unauthorized immigration in particular, is a major problem in this country. These feelings often lead to stereotyping of all immigrants and/or all Hispanic people. In this book, we have tried to provide objective evidence regarding immigration and crime (it is not a significant contributor to crime rates).

Tonry and his co-author Matthew Melewski suggest several strategies for reducing racial and ethnic disparities. First, they argue for "radical decarceration," dramatically reducing the number of people the United States sends to prison. For the same reason our current incarceration policies disproportionately affect people of color, so a radical reduction in imprisonment would reduce that impact. Second, they recommend the abolition of other "disparity-causing policies," including capital punishment, mandatory minimum sentencing laws, sentences of life without parole, and truth-in-sentencing laws. They should be replaced with what they describe as "principled" sentencing guidelines designed to implement shorter sentences proportionate to the harm done by the crime. Finally, they recommend "race and ethnicity impact statements." These would be similar to fiscal impact statements for new legislation. Such statements, based on good research evidence, would highlight likely disparate racial and ethnic effects and therefore provide a warning against flawed proposed laws.[7]

To Tonry and Melewski's list we would add reorienting the war on drugs. The long-standing American focus on criminalizing drugs, and indiscriminately treating all drugs the same in terms of their harm, lies at the root of many criminal justice policies that adversely affect people of color, in policing, prosecution, and sentencing. The drug war is solidly supported by public opinion, however, and so ending it would require a major public education effort, the likes of which we have never seen.

In the end, race and ethnicity are a major factor in crime and criminal justice in America. We hope that this book has clarified the issues, provided readers with the best current evidence on all the important topics, and sorted fact from fiction. This country has a long and tragic history with regard to race and ethnicity. Much progress has been made in recent decades, but as the evidence in this book indicates, unacceptable disparities continue to exist, and much remains to be done if we are to achieve the ideal of Equal Justice Under Law.

NOTES

1. For a discussion of popular myths about crime and justice, see Samuel Walker, *Sense and Nonsense About Crime, Drugs, and Community*, 7th ed. (Belmont: Cengage, 2011).

2. Heather MacDonald, "Is the Criminal-Justice System Racist?" *City Journal* 18 (Spring 2008). Available at http://wwwcity-journal.org/printable.php?id=2563.

3. Tammy Rinehart Kochel, David B. Wilson, and Stephen D. Mastrofski, "Effects of Suspect Race on Officers' Arrest Decisions," *Criminology* (Forthcoming, May 2011); Ojmarrh Mitchell, "A Meta-Analysis of Race and Sentencing Research: Explaining the Inconsistencies," *Journal of Quantitative Criminology* 21 (December 2005), pp. 439–466.

4. Alfred Blumstein and Joel Wallman, *The Crime Drop in America* (New York: Cambridge University Press, 2006).

5. Michael Tonry and Matthew Melewski, "The Malign Effects of Drug and Crime Control Policies on Black Americans," in *Crime and Justice: A Review of Research*, Tonry, ed., (Chicago: University of Chicago Press, 2008), pp. 1–44.

6. Chalres M. Blow, "Let's Rescue the Race Debate," *New York Times*, November 20, 2010.

7. Tonry and Melewski, "The Malign Effects of Drug and Crime Control Policies on Black Americans."

Selected Bibliography

Adler, Jeffery S. "The Dynamite, Wreck-age, and Scum in our Cities: The Social Construction of Deviance in Industrial America." *Justice Quarterly* 11 (1994): 33–49.

Akers, Ronald L. *Social Learning and Social Structure: A General Theory of Crime and Deviance.* Boston: Northeastern University Press, 1994.

Albonetti, Celesta A. "An Integration of Theories to Explain Judicial Discretion." *Social Problems* 38 (1991): 247–266.

Albonetti, Celesta A. "Criminality, Prosecutorial Screening, and Uncertainty: Toward a Theory of Discretionary Decision Making in Felony Case Processing." *Criminology* 24 (1986): 623–644.

Albonetti, Celesta A. "Sentencing Under the Federal Sentencing Guidelines: Effects of Defendant Characteristics, Guilty Pleas, and Departures on Sentencing Outcomes for Drug Offenses, 1991–1992." *Law & Society Review* 31 (1997): 789–822.

Albonetti, Celesta A., Robert M. Hauser, John Hagan, and Ilene H. Nagel. "Criminal Justice Decision Making as a Stratification Process: The Role of Race and Stratification Resources in

Pretrial Release." *Journal of Quantitative Criminology* 5 (1989): 57–82.

Alexander, Michelle. *The New Jim Crow: Mass Incarceration in the Age of Color-blindness.* New York: The New Press, 2010.

Allen, James Paul, and Eugene James Turner. *We The People: An Atlas of America's Ethnic Diversity.* New York: Macmillan, 1988.

Alschuler, Albert W. "Racial Quotas and the Jury." *Duke Law Journal* 44 (1995): 44.

Alvarez, Alexander, and Ronet D. Bachman. "American Indians and Sentencing Disparity: An Arizona Test." *Journal of Criminal Justice* 24 (1996): 549–561.

American Bar Association. *Race and the Law: Special Report.* Chicago: American Bar Association, February 1999.

American Bar Association. "Whatever You Think About the Death Penalty, A System That Will Take Life Must First Give Justice: A Report from the IR&R Death Penalty Committee." 24 W.T.R. *Hum. Rts.* 22 (1997).

American Bar Association Commission on Racial and Ethnic Diversity in the Profession. *Miles to Go 2000: Progress of Minorities in the Legal Profession.* Chicago: American Bar Association, 2000.

American Civil Liberties Union. *Driving While Black.* New York: ACLU, 1999.

American Civil Liberties Union. *Federal Death Row: Is It Really Color-Blind? Analysis of June 6 Department of Justice Report on the Death Penalty.* Available at http://www.aclu.org/Congress/10614la.htm.

American Correctional Association. *1993 Directory of Juvenile and Adult Correctional Departments, Institutions, Agencies and Paroling Authorities.* Laurel, MD: American Correctional Associations, 1993.

American Friends Service Committee. *Struggle for Justice: A Report on Crime and Punishment in America.* Boston: Little, Brown, 1971.

Amsterdam, Anthony. "Race and the Death Penalty." *Criminal Justice Ethics* 7 (1988): 84–86.

Anderson, Philip S. "Striving for a Just Society." *ABA Journal* (February 1999): 66.

Arab American Anti-Discrimination Committee. *2003–2007 Report on Hate Crimes and Discrimination Against Arab Americans.* Washington, DC: ADC, 2008. Available at http://www.adc.org.

Arthur, John A. "Correctional Ideology of Black Correctional Officers." *Federal Probation* 58 (1994): 57–65.

Auerhahn, Kathleen. "Just Another Crime? Examining Disparity in Homicide Sentencing." *Sociological Quarterly* 48 (2007): 277–313.

Austin, J., B. Krisberg, and P. Litsky. "The Effectiveness of Supervised Pretrial Release." *Crime and Delinquency* 31 (1985): 519–537.

Bachman, Ronet D., Alexander Alvarez, and C. Perkins. "The Discriminatory Imposition of the Law: Does It Affect Sentence Outcomes for American Indians?" In *Native Americans, Crime and Justice,* Marianne O. Nielsen and Robert A. Silverman, eds. Boulder, CO: Westview Press, 1996.

Bachman, Ronet, Heather Zaykowski, Rachel Kallmyer, Margarita Poteyeva, and Christina Lanier. *Violence Against American Indian and Alaska Native Women and the Criminal Justice Response: What is Known.* Washington, DC: Department of Justice, 2008. NCJ 223691.

Baldus, David C., Charles Pulaski, and George Woodworth. "Comparative Review of Death Sentences: An Empirical Study of the Georgia Experience." *The Journal of Criminal Law & Criminology* 74 (1983): 661–673.

Baldus, David C., George Woodworth, and Charles A. Pulaski. *Equal Justice and the Death Penalty: A Legal and Empirical Analysis.* Boston: Northeastern University Press, 1990.

Baldus, David C., George Woodworth, and Charles A. Pulaski. "Monitoring and Evaluating Contemporary Death Penalty Systems: Lessons from Georgia." *University of California at Davis Law Review* 18 (1985): 1,375–1,407.

Barak, Gregg. "Between the Waves: Mass-Mediated Themes of Crime and Justice." *Social Justice* 21 (1994).

Barak, Gregg, Jeanne M. Flavin, and Paul S. Leighton. *Class, Race, Gender, and Crime: Social Realities of Justice in America.* Los Angeles: Roxbury, 2001.

Barkan, Steven E., and Steven F. Cohn. "Contemporary Regional Differences in Support by Whites for the Death Penalty: A Research Note." *Justice Quarterly* 27 (2010): 458–471.

Barkan, Steven E., and Steven F. Cohn. "Racial Prejudice and Support for the Death Penalty by Whites." *Journal of Research in Crime and Delinquency* 31 (1994): 202–209.

Baumer, Eric P., Steven F. Messner, and Richard Rosenfeld. "Explaining Structural Variation in Support for Capital Punishment: A Multilevel Analysis." *American Journal of Sociology* 108 (2003).

Bayley, David H., and Harold Mendelsohn. *Minorities and the Police: Confrontation in America*. New York: The Free Press, 1969.

Bedau, Hugo A., and Michael L. Radelet. "Miscarriages of Justice in Potentially Capital Cases." *Stanford Law Review* 40 (1987): 21–179.

Beres, Linda S., and Thomas D. Griffith. "Demonizing Youth." *Loyola of Los Angeles Law Review* 34 (2001): 747–768.

Berk, Richard, and Alec Campbell. "Preliminary Data on Race and Crack Charging Practices in Los Angeles." *Federal Sentencing Reporter* 6 (1993).

Bernstein Nagel, Ilene, William R. Kelly, and Patricia A. Doyle. "Societal Reaction to Deviants: The Case of Criminal Defendants." *American Sociological Review* 42 (1977): 743–755.

Bernstein Nagel, Ilene, Edward Kick, Jan T. Leung, and Barbara Schultz. "Charge Reduction: An Intermediary State in the Process of Labeling Criminal Defendants." *Social Forces* 56 (1977).

Bing, Robert. "Politicizing Black-on-Black Crime: A Critique of Terminological Preference." In *Black-on-Black Crime*, P. Ray Kedia, ed. Bristol, IN: Wyndham Hall Press, 1994.

Bishop, Donna M., and Charles E. Frazier. "The Influence of Race in Juvenile Justice Processing." *Journal of Research in Crime and Delinquency* 25 (1988): 242–263.

Bishop, Donna M., and Charles E. Frazier. "Race Effects in Juvenile Justice Decision-Making: Findings of a Statewide Analysis." *Journal of Criminal Law and Criminology* 86 (1996): 392–414.

Black, Donald. *The Manners and Customs of the Police*. New York: Academic Press, 1980.

Black, Donald. "The Social Organization of Arrest." In *The Manners and Customs of the Police*, Donald Black, ed. New York: Academic Press, 1980.

Blumberg, Abraham S. "The Practice of Law as a Confidence Game: Organizational Cooptation of a Profession." *Law & Society Review* 1 (1967): 15–39.

Blumstein, Alfred. "On the Disproportionality of United States' Prison Populations." *The Journal of Criminal Law and Criminology* 73 (1982): 1,259–1,281.

Blumstein, Alfred, Jacqueline Cohen, Susan E. Martin, and Michael Tonry. *Research on Sentencing: The Search for Reform*, vol. I. Washington, DC: National Academy Press, 1983.

Bohm, Robert M. "American Death Penalty Opinion, 1936–1986: A Critical Examination of the Gallup Polls." In *The Death Penalty in America: Current Research*, Robert M. Bohm, ed. Cincinnati: Anderson, 1991.

Boland, Barbara. *The Prosecution of Felony Arrests*. Washington DC: Bureau of Justice Statistics, 1983.

Bowers, William. "Capital Punishment and Contemporary Values: People's Misgivings and the Court's Misperceptions." *Law & Society Review* 27 (1993): 157–176.

Bowers, William. "The Pervasiveness of Arbitrariness and Discrimination Under Post-Furman Capital Statutes." *The Journal of Criminal Law & Criminology* 74 (1983): 1,067–1,100.

Bowers, William, and Glenn L. Pierce. "Arbitrariness and Discrimination Under Post-*Furman* Capital Statutes." *Crime and Delinquency* 74 (1980): 1,067–1,100.

Box, Steven, and Chris Hale. "Unemployment, Imprisonment, and Prison Overcrowding." *Contemporary Crises* 9 (1985): 209–228.

Brennan, Pauline K., and Cassia Spohn, "The Joint Effects of Offender Race/Ethnicity and Sex on Sentence Length Decisions in Federal Courts." *Race and Social Problems* 1 (2009): 200–217.

Bridges, George S. *A Study on Racial and Ethnic Disparities in Superior Court Bail and Pre-Trial Detention Practices in Washington.* Olympia, WA: Washington State Minority and Justice Commission, 1997.

Bridges, George S., and Robert D. Crutchfield. "Law, Social Standing and Racial Disparities in Imprisonment." *Social Forces* 66 (1988): 699–724.

Bridges, George S., and Sara Steen. "Racial Disparities in Official Assessments of Juvenile Offending: Attributional Stereotypes as Mediating Mechanisms." *American Sociological Review* 65 (1998): 554–570.

Bright, Stephen B. "Discrimination, Death and Denial: The Tolerance of Racial Discrimination in the Infliction of the Death Penalty." *Santa Clara Law Review* 35 (1995): 901–950.

Bright, Stephen B., and Patrick J. Keenan. "Judges and the Politics of Death: Deciding Between the Bill of Rights and the Next Election in Capital Cases." *Boston University Law Review* 75 (1995): 759–835.

Brosi, Kathleen B. *A Cross-City Comparison of Felony Case Procession.* Washington DC: Institute for Law and Social Research, 1979.

Browning, Sandra Lee, Francis T. Cullen, Liqun Cao, Renee Kopache, and Thomas J. Stevenson. "Race and Getting Hassled by the Police: A Research Note." *Police Studies* 17, no. 1 (1994): 1–11.

Brownmiller, Susan. *Against Our Will: Men, Women and Rape.* New York: Bantam Books, 1975.

Building Blocks for Youth. *And Justice For Some.* Washington, DC: Building Blocks for Youth, 2000.

Bureau of the Census. *Income, Poverty, and Health Insurance Coverage in the United States: 2009.* Washington, DC: Bureau of the Census, September 2010.

Bureau of Justice Statistics. *American Indians and Crime.* Washington, DC: Department of Justice, 1999. NCJ 173386.

Bureau of Justice Statistics. *Asian, Native Hawaiian, and Pacific Islander Victims of Crime.* Washington, DC: Department of Justice, 2009. NCJ 225037.

Bureau of Justice Statistics. *Black Victims of Violent Crime.* Washington, DC: Department of Justice, 2007.

Bureau of Justice Statistics. *Capital Punishment, 2009—Statistical Tables.* Washington, DC: U.S. Department of Justice, 2010.

Bureau of Justice Statistics. *Comparing Federal and State Inmates, 1991.* Washington, DC: U.S. Government Printing Office, 1993.

Bureau of Justice Statistics. *Contacts Between Police and the Public, 2005.* Washington, DC: Department of Justice, 2007. NCJ 215243.

Bureau of Justice Statistics. *Correctional Populations in the United States, 2009.* Washington, DC: Department of Justice, 2010.

Bureau of Justice Statistics. *Criminal Victimization in the United States, 2009.* Washington, DC: U.S. Department of Justice, 2010.

Bureau of Justice Statistics. *Criminal Victimization in the United States, 2007—Statistical Tables.* Washington, DC: Department of Justice, 2010.

Bureau of Justice Statistics. *Felony Defendants in Large Urban Counties, 2006.* Washington DC: U.S. Department of Justice, 2010.

Bureau of Justice Statistics. *Hispanic Victims.* Washington, DC: Government Printing Office, 1990.

Bureau of Justice Statistics. *Police Use of Force: Collection of National Data.* Washington, DC: Government Printing Office, 1997.

Bureau of Justice Statistics. *Policing and Homicide, 1976–98: Justifiable Homicide by Police, Police Officers Murdered by Felons.* Washington, DC: U.S. Government Printing Office, 2001.

Bureau of Justice Statistics. *Pretrial Release of Felony Defendancy in State Courts.* Washington, DC: U.S. Department of Justice, 2007.

Bureau of Justice Statistics. *Pretrial Release of Felony Defendants, 1990–2004.* Washington, DC: U.S. Department of Justice, 2007.

Bureau of Justice Statistics. *Prison and Jail Inmates at Midyear 2009.* Washington, DC: U.S. Department of Justice, 2010.

Bureau of Justice Statistics. *Prison Inmates at Midyear 2009—Statistical Tables.* Washington, DC: Department of Justice, 2010. Table 18. NCJ 230113.

Bureau of Justice Statistics. *Reducing Gun Violence: The Boston Gun Project's Operation Ceasefire.* Washington, DC: Department of Justice, 2001. Available at http://www.ncjrs.org. NCJ 188741.

Bureau of Justice Statistics. *Sourcebook of Criminal Justice Statistics, 2010,* online edition. Available at http://www.albany.edu/sourcebook.

Bureau of Justice Statistics. *Weapon Use and Violent Crime.* Washington, DC: U.S. Department of Justice, 2003.

Burns, Haywood. "Black People and the Tyranny of American Law." *The Annals of the American Academy of Political and Social Sciences* 407 (1973): 156–166.

Butler, Paul. "Racially Based Jury Nullification: Black Power in the Criminal Justice System." *Yale Law Journal* 105 (1995): 677–725.

Bynum, Timothy S., and Raymond Paternoster. "Discrimination Revisited: An Exploration of Frontstage and Backstage Criminal Justice Decision Making." *Sociology and Social Research* 69 (1984): 90–108.

Cahalan, Margaret Werner. *Historical Corrections Statistics in the United States, 1850–1984.* Washington, DC: Government Printing Office, 1986.

Campbell, Anne. *The Girls in the Gang,* 2nd ed. Cambridge, MA: Basil Blackwell, 1991.

Campbell, Howard. *Drug War Zone: Frontline Dispatches from the Streets of El Paso and Juarez.* Austin: University of Texas Press, 2009.

Carter, Dan T. *Scottsboro: A Tragedy of the American South.* Baton Rouge: Louisiana State University Press, 1969.

Carter, David L. "Hispanic Interaction with the Criminal Justice System in Texas: Experiences, Attitudes, and Perceptions." *Journal of Criminal Justice* 11 (1983): 213–227.

Carter, Terry. "Divided Justice." *ABA Journal* (February 1999): 42–45.

Casper, Jonathan D. *Criminal Courts: The Defendant's Perspective.* Englewood Cliffs, NJ: Prentice Hall, 1978.

Casper, Jonathan D. "'Did You Have a Lawyer When You Went to Court?' No, I Had a Public Defender." *Yale Review of Law & Social Action* 1 (1971): 4–9.

Cernkovich, Stephen A., and Peggy C. Giordano. "School Bonding, Race, and Delinquency." *Criminology* 30 (1992).

Chambers, David L., Timothy T. Clydesdale, William C. Kidder, and Richard O. Lempert. "The Real Impact of Eliminating Affirmative Action in American Law Schools: An Empirical Critique of Richard Sander's Study." *Stanford Law Review* 57 (2005): 1,855–1,898.

Chambliss, William J. "Crime Control and Ethnic Minorities: Legitimizing Racial Oppression by Creating Moral Panics." In *Ethnicity, Race, and Crime: Perspectives Across Time and Place*. Darnell F. Hawkins, ed. Albany, NY: State University of New York Press, 1995.

Chin, Ko-Lin, Jeffrey Fagan, and Robert J. Kelly. "Patterns of Chinese Gang Extortion" *Justice Quarterly* 9 (1992): 625–646.

Chiricos, Theodore G. "The Moral Panic of the Drug War." In *Race and Criminal Justice*, Michael J. Lynch and E. Britt Patterson, eds. New York: Harrow & Heston, 1995.

Chiricos, Theodore G., and William D. Bales. "Unemployment and Punishment: An Empirical Assessment." *Criminology* 29 (1991): 701–724.

Chiricos, Theodore G., and Charles Crawford. "Race and Imprisonment: A Contextual Assessment of the Evidence." In *Ethnicity, Race and Crime*, Darnell F. Hawkins ed. Albany: State University of New York Press, 1995.

Chiricos, Theodore G., and Miriam A. DeLone. "Labor Surplus and Punishment: A Review and Assessment of Theory and Evidence." *Social Problems* 39 (1992): 421–446.

Clarke, S. H., and G. G. Koch. "The Influence of Income and Other Factors on Whether Criminal Defendants Go To Prison." *Law & Society Review* 11 (1976): 57–92.

Cole, David. *No Equal Justice: Race and Class in the American Criminal Justice System*. New York: New Press, 1999.

Covey, Herbert C., Scott Menard, and Robert J. Franzese. *Juvenile Gangs*. Springfield, IL: Charles C. Thomas, 1992.

Cox, Judith A. "Addressing Disproportionate Minority Representation Within the Juvenile Justice System." Available at http://www.building-blocksforyouth.org.

Crockett, George. "The Role of the Black Judge." In *The Criminal Justice System and Blacks*, D. Georges-Abeyie, ed. New York: Clark Boardman, 1984.

Crutchfield, Robert D., Joseph G. Weis, Rodney L. Engen, and Randy R. Gainey. *Racial and Ethnic Disparities in the Prosecution of Felony Cases in King County*. Olympia Washington: Washington State Minority and Justice Commission, 1995.

Curriden, Mark, and Leroy Phillips, Jr. *Contempt of Court: The Turn-of-the-Century Lynching that Launched a Hundred Years of Federalism*. New York: Faber and Faber, 1999.

Curry, Theodore R., and Guadalupe Corral-Camacho. "Sentencing Young Minority Males for Drug Offenses: Testing for Conditional Effects Between Race/Ethnicity, Gender, and Age During the U.S. War on Drugs." *Punishment & Society* 10 (2008): 253–276.

D'Alessio, Stewart J., and Lisa Stolzenberg. "Race and the Probability of Arrest." *Social Forces* 81 (2003): 1,381–1,397.

Davis, Kenneth Culp. *Discretionary Justice: A Preliminary Inquiry*. Baton Rouge: Louisiana State University Press, 1969.

Death Penalty Information Center. *The Death Penalty in 2010: Year-End Report*. Washington, DC: Death Penalty Information Center, 2010.

Decker, David L., David Shichor, and Robert M. O'Brien. *Urban Structure and Victimization.* Lexington, MA: D.C. Heath, 1982.

DeJong, Christina, and Kenneth C. Jackson. "Putting Race Into Context: Race, Juvenile Justice Processing, and Urbanization." *Justice Quarterly* 15 (1998): 487–504.

Demuth, Stephen, and Darrell Steffensmeier. "The Impact of Gender and Race-Ethnicity in the Pretrial Release Process." *Social Problems* 51 (2004): 222–242.

Department of Health and Human Services. *Monitoring the Future* (2009).

Dixon, Jo. "The Organizational Context of Criminal Sentencing." *American Journal of Sociology* 100 (1995): 1,157–1,198.

Doerner, Jill K., and Stephen Demuth. "The Independent and Joint Effects of Race/Ethnicity, Gender, and Age on Sentencing Outcomes in U.S. Federal Courts." *Justice Quarterly* 27 (2010): 1–27.

Dorfman, Lori, and Vincent Schiraldi. "Off Balance: Youth, Race and Crime in the News" Executive Summary. Berkeley Media Studies Group, 2001. Available at http://www.building-blocksforyouth.org/media/.

Du Bois, W. E. B. "The Spawn of Slavery: The Convict-Lease System in the South." *The Missionary Review of the World* 14 (1901): 373–745.

Dulaney, W. Marvin. *Black Police in America.* Bloomington: Indiana University Press, 1996.

Elliot, Delbert, David Huizinga, Brian Knowles, and Rachel Canter. *The Prevalence and Incidence of Delinquent Behavior: 1976–1980: National Estimates of Delinquent Behavior by Sex, Race, Social Class and Other Selected Variables.* Boulder, CO: Behavioral Research Institute, 1983.

Equal Justice Initiative. *Illegal Racial Discrimination in Jury Selection: A Continuing Legacy.* Montgomery, AL: Equal Justice Institute, 2010.

Esbensen, Finn-Aage, and David Huizinga. "Gangs, Drugs and Delinquency." *Criminology* 31 (1993): 565–590.

Espiritu, Nicholas. "(E)racing Youth: The Racialized Construction of California's Proposition 21 and the Development of Alternate Contestations." *Cleveland State Law Review* 52 (2005).

Everett, Ronald S., and Barbara C. Nienstedt. "Race, Remorse, and Sentence Reduction: Is Saying You're Sorry Enough?" *Justice Quarterly* 16 (1999): 99–122.

Everett, Ronald S., and Roger A. Wojtkiewicz. "Difference, Disparity, and Race/Ethnic Bias in Federal Sentencing." *Journal of Quantitative Criminology* 18 (2002).

Fagan, Jeffrey. *The Comparative Impacts of Juvenile and Criminal Court Sanctions on Adolescent Offenders.* Washington, DC: Office of Justice Programs, National Institute of Justice, 1991.

Fagan, Jeffrey. "The Social Organization of Drug Use and Drug Dealing Among Urban Gangs." *Criminology* 27 (1989): 633–666.

Farnworth, Margaret, and Patrick Horan. "Separate Justice: An Analysis of Race Differences in Court Processes." *Social Science Research* 9 (1980): 381–399.

Farrell, Amy, Geoff Ward, and Danielle Rousseau. "Race Effects of Representation among Federal Court Workers: Does Black Workforce Representation Reduce Sentencing Disparities." *Annals of the American Academy of Political and Social Science* 623 (2009): 121–133.

Farrell, Ronald A., and Victoria L. Swigert. "Prior Offense Record as a Self-Fulfilling Prophecy." *Law & Society Review* 12 (1978): 437–453.

Federal Bureau of Investigation. *Crime in the United States, 2009.* Washington, DC: Department of Justice, 2010.

Feeley, Malcolm M. *The Process Is the Punishment: Handling Cases in a Lower Criminal Court.* New York: Russell Sage Foundation, 1979.

Feimer, Steve, Frank Pommersheim, and Steve Wise. "Marking Time: Does Race Make a Difference? A Study of Disparate Sentencing in South Dakota." *Journal of Crime and Justice* 13 (1990): 86–102.

Feld, Barry C. *Bad Kids: Race and the Transformation of the Juvenile Court.* New York: Oxford University Press, 1999.

Feldmeyer, Ben. "The Effects of Racial/ Ethnic Segregation on Latino and Black Homicide." *Sociological Quarterly* 51, no. 4 (2010): 600–623.

Fite, Paula J., Porche Wynn, and Dustin A. Pardini, "Explaining Discrepancies in Arrest Rates Between Black and White Male Juveniles." *Journal of Counseling and Clinical Psychology* 77 (2009): 916–927.

Fong, Robert, Ronald Vogel, and Salvador Buentello. "Prison Gang Dynamics: A Look Inside the Texas Department of Corrections." In *Corrections: Dilemmas and Directions,* Peter J. Benekos and Alida V. Merlo, eds. Highland Heights, KY: Anderson Publishing Co. and Academy of Criminal Justice Sciences, 1992.

Foote, Caleb. "Compelling Appearance in Court: Administration of Bail in Philadelphia." *University of Pennsylvania Law Review* 102 (1954): 1,031–1,079.

Fox, James Allen, Michael L. Radelet, and Julie L. Bonsteel. "Death Penalty Opinion in the Post-*Furman* Years." *New York University Review of Law and Social Change* 18 (1990–91): 499–528.

Fox James Allen, and Marianne W. Zawitz. *Homicide Trends in the United States.* Washington DC: U.S. Department of Justice, 2004. Available at http://www.ojp.usdoj.gov/bjs.

Frankel, Marvin. *Criminal Sentences: Law Without Order.* New York: Hill and Wang, 1972.

Franklin, Travis W. "The Intersection of Defendants' Race, Gender, and Age in Prosecutorial Decision Making." *Journal of Criminal Justice* 38 (2010).

Frazier, Charles E., and Donna M. Bishop. "Reflections on Race Effects in Juvenile Justice." In *Minorities in Juvenile Justice,* Kimberly Kempf Leonard, Carl E. Pope, and William H. Feyerherm, eds. Thousand Oaks, CA: Sage, 1995.

Freiburger, Tina L., and Carly M. Hilinski. "An Examination of the Interactions of Race and Gender on Sentencing Decisions Using a Trichotomous Dependent Variable." *Crime & Delinquency,* Online First, published on February 24, 2009.

Fridell, Lorie A. *By the Numbers: A Guide for Analyzing Race Data from Traffic Stops.* Washington, DC: Police Executive Research Forum, 2004.

Fyfe, James J. "Administrative Interventions on Police Shooting Discretion." *Journal of Criminal Justice* 7 (Winter 1979): 309–323.

Fyfe, James J. "Blind Justice: Police Shootings in Memphis." *Journal of Criminal Law and Criminology* 73 (1982): 707–722.

Fyfe, James J. "Who Shoots? A Look at Officer Race and Police Shooting." *Journal of Police Science and Administration* 9 (1981): 367–382.

Garfinkel, Harold. "Research Notes on Inter- and Intra-Racial Homicides." *Social Forces* 27 (1949): 369–381.

Geller, William A., and Michael S. Scott. *Deadly Force: What We Know.* Washington, DC: Police Executive Research Forum, 1992.

Geller, William A., and Hans Toch, eds. *And Justice For All.* Washington, DC: Police Executive Research Forum, 1995.

Gilliard, Darrell K., and Allen Beck. *Prisoners, 1993.* Washington, DC: U.S. Department of Justice, 1994.

Glaze, Lauren E., and Thomas Bonczar. *Probation and Parole in the United States, 2008.* Bureau of Justice Statistics, 2010.

Goldkamp, John S. "Danger and Detention: A Second Generation of Bail Reform." *The Journal of Criminal Law and Criminology* 76 (1985): 1–74.

Goodstein, Lynne, and Doris Layton MacKenzie. "Racial Differences in Adjustment Patterns of Prison Inmates—Prisonization, Conflict, Stress and Control." In *The Criminal Justice System and Blacks,* Daniel Georges-Abeyie, ed. New York: Clark Boardman Company, Ltd., 1984.

Gottfredson, Michael R., and Travis Hirschi. *A General Theory of Crime.* Stanford, CA: Stanford University Press, 1985.

Gottschall, Jon. "Carter's Judicial Appointments: The Influence of Affirmative Action and Merit Selection on Voting on the U.S. Courts of Appeals." *Judicature* 67 (1983): 167–173.

Greenberg, David F. "'Justice' and Criminal Justice." In *Crime Control and Criminal Justice: The Delicate Balance,* Darnell F. Hawkins, Samuel L. Meyers, Jr., and Randolph N. Stone, eds. Westport, CT: Greenwood, 2002.

Greenfeld, Lawrence, and Steven K. Smith. *American Indians and Crime.* Washington, DC: Bureau of Justice Statistics, 1999.

Grobsmith, Elizabeth S. *Indians in Prison.* Lincoln: University of Nebraska Press, 1994.

Gross, Samuel R., Kristen Jacoby, Daniel J. Matheson, Nicholas Montgomery, and Sujata Patil. "Exonerations in the United States 1989 through 2003." *Journal of Criminal Law & Criminology* 95 (2005).

Gross, Samuel R., and Robert Mauro. *Death & Discrimination: Racial Disparities in Capital Sentencing.* Boston: Northeastern University Press, 1989.

Hacker, Andrew. *Two Nations: Black and White, Separate, Hostile, Unequal.* New York: Scribners, 1992.

Hagan, John. "Extra-Legal Attributes and Criminal Sentencing: An Assessment of a Sociological Viewpoint." *Law & Society Review* 8 (1974): 357–383.

Hagan, John. "Parameters of Criminal Prosecution: An Application of Path Analysis to a Problem of Criminal Justice." *Journal of Criminal Law and Criminology* 65 (1975).

Hagan, John, and Kristin Bumiller. "Making Sense of Sentencing: A Review and Critique of Sentencing Research." In *Research on Sentencing: The Search for Reform,* Alfred Blumstein, Jacqueline Cohen, Susan Martin, and Michael Tonry, eds. Washington, DC: National Academy Press, 1983.

Hagedorn, John M. *People and Folks.* Chicago: Lake View Press, 1989.

Hall, Edwin L., and Albert A. Simkins. "Inequality in the Types of Sentences Received by Native Americans and Whites." *Criminology* 13 (1975): 199–222.

Hamm, Mark S. *American Skinheads.* Westport, CT: Praeger, 1994.

Hanson, Roger A., and Brian J. Ostrom. "Indigent Defenders Get the Job Done and Done Well." In *Criminal Justice: Law and Politics,* 6th ed., George Cole, ed. Belmont, CA: Wadsworth, 1993.

Harlow, Caroline Wolf. *Hate Crime Reported by Victims and Police.* Washington, DC: U.S. Department of Justice, 2005.

Harris, David. *Profiles in Injustice: Why Racial Profiling Doesn't Work*. New York: New Press, 2002.

Harris, Mary G. *Cholas: Latino Girls in Gangs*. New York: AMS Press, 1988.

Harris, Philip W. "Over-Simplification and Error in Public Opinion Surveys on Capital Punishment." *Justice Quarterly* 3 (1986): 429–455.

Harris, Philip W., Wayne N. Welsh, and Frank Butler. "A Century of Juvenile Justice." In *Criminal Justice 2000, The Nature of Crime: Continuity and Change*, vol. I. Washington, DC: National Institute of Justice, 2000.

Hartley, Richard D., Sean Maddan, and Cassia Spohn. "Prosecutorial Discretion: An Examination of Substantial Assistance Departures in Federal Crack-Cocaine and Powder-Cocaine Cases." *Justice Quarterly* 24 (2007): 382–407.

Hawkins, Darnell F. "Beyond Anomalies: Rethinking the Conflict Perspective on Race and Criminal Justice." *Social Forces* 65 (1987): 719–745.

Hawkins, Darnell F. "Ethnicity: The Forgotten Dimension of American Social Control." In *Inequality, Crime, and Social Control*, George S. Bridges and Martha A. Myers, eds. Boulder, CO: Westview Press, 1994.

Hawkins, Darnell F., ed. *Ethnicity, Race, and Crime*. Albany, NY: State University of New York Press, 1995.

Hawkins, Darnell F., and Kenneth A. Hardy. "Black-White Imprisonment Rates: A State-by-State Analysis." *Social Justice* 16 (1989): 75–94.

Hayden, George, Joseph Senna, and Larry Siegel. "Prosecutorial Discretion in Peremptory Challenges: An Empirical Investigation of Information Use in the Massachusetts Jury Selection Process." *New England Law Review* 13 (1978): 768–790.

Herbst, Leigh, and Samuel Walker. "Language Barriers in the Delivery of Police Services: A Study of Police and Hispanic Interactions in a Midwestern City." *Journal of Criminal Justice* 29, no. 4 (2001): 329–340.

Higgins, Michael. "Few Are Chosen." *ABA Journal* (February 1999): 253.

Hindelang, Michael J. "Race and Involvement in Common Law Personal Crimes." *American Sociological Review* 43 (1978): 93–109.

Hirschi, Travis. *Causes of Delinquency*. Berkeley, CA: University of California Press, 1969.

Hoffman, Morris B. "Peremptory Challenges: Lawyers Are From Mars, Judges Are From Venus." 3 Green Bag 2d 135 (Winter 2000). Available at http://www.lexis-nexis.com/universe.

Holmes, Malcolm D., Howard C. Daudistel, and Ronald A. Farrell. "Determinants of Charge Reductions and Final Dispositions in Cases of Burglary and Robbery." *Journal of Research in Crime and Delinquency* 24 (1987).

Holmes, Malcolm D., Harmon M. Hosch, Howard C. Daudistel, Dolores A. Perez, and Joseph B. Graves. "Ethnicity, Legal Resources, and Felony Dispositions in Two Southwestern Jurisdictions." *Justice Quarterly* 13 (1996): 11–30.

Harmon M. Hosch, Howard C. Daudistel, Dolores A. Perez, and Joseph B. Graves. "Judges' Ethnicity and Minority Sentencing: Evidence Concerning Hispanics." *Social Science Quarterly* 74 (1993): 496–506.

Howe, Scott W. "The Futile Quest for Racial Neutrality in Capital Selection and the Eighth Amendment Argument for Abolition Based on Unconscious Racial Discrimination." *William & Mary Law Review* 45 (2004): 2,083.

Huebner, Beth M., and Timothy S. Bynum. "The Role of Race and

Ethnicity in Parole Decisions." *Criminology* 46 (2008): 907–937.

Huff, C. Ronald, ed. *Gangs in America.* Newbury Park, CA: Sage, 1990.

Huizinga, David, and Delbert S. Elliot. "Juvenile Offenders: Prevalence, Offender Incidence, and Arrest Rates by Race." *Crime and Delinquency* 33 (1987): 206–223.

Human Rights Watch. *Punishment and Prejudice: Racial Disparities in the War on Drugs* 12, no. 2 (G), May 2000. Available at http://www.hrw.org/ reports/2000/usa/.

Human Rights Watch. *Shielded From Justice: Police Brutality and Accountability in the United States.* New York: Human Rights Watch, 1998.

Humphries, Drew, John Dawson, Valerie Cronin, Phyllis Keating, Chris Wisniewski, and Jennine Eichfeld. "Mothers and Children, Drugs and Crack: Reactions to Maternal Drug Dependency." In *The Criminal Justice System and Women*, 2nd ed., Barbara Raffel Price and Natalie J. Sokoloff, eds. New York: McGraw-Hill, 1995.

The Innocence Project, *250 Exonerated: Too Many Wrongfully Convicted.* New York: The Innocence Project, 2010. Available at http://www.innocence-project.org.

Jacobs, David, Jason T. Carmichael, Zhenchao Qian, and Stephanie L. Kent. "Who Survives on Death Row? An Individual and Contextual Analysis." *American Sociological Review* 72 (2007): 610–632.

Jacobs, James. *New Perspectives on Prison and Imprisonment.* Ithaca: Cornell University Press, 1983.

Jaynes, Gerald David, and Robin M. Williams, Jr., eds. *A Common Destiny: Blacks and American Society.* Washington, DC: National Academy Press, 1992.

Jenkins, Phillip. "'The Ice Age': The Social Construction of a Drug Panic." *Justice Quarterly* 11 (1994): 7–31.

Johnson, Brian D., and Sara Betsinger. "Punishing the 'Model Minority': Asian-American Criminal Sentencing Outcomes in Federal District Courts." *Criminology* 47 (2009): 1,045–1,090.

Johnson, Brian D., Jeffery T. Ulmer, and John H. Kramer. "The Social Context of Guidelines Circumvention: The Case of Federal District Courts." *Criminology* 46 (2008): 737–784.

Johnson, Elmer H. "Selective Factors in Capital Punishment." *Social Forces* 36 (1957): 165.

Johnson, Guy. "The Negro and Crime." In *Annals of the American Academy* 217 (1941): 93–104.

Johnson, Sheri Lynn. "Black Innocence and the White Jury." *University of Michigan Law Review* 83 (1985): 1,611–1,708.

Johnston, L. D., J. G. Bachman, and P. M. O'Malley. *Monitoring the Future: Questionnaire Responses from the Nation's High School Seniors, 2009.* Ann Arbor, MI: Institute for Social Research, 2009. Question C27.

Johnstone, J. W. C. "Youth Gangs and Black Suburbs." *Pacific Sociological Review* 24 (1981): 355–375.

Jost, Kenneth. "Rethinking the Death Penalty." *CQ Researcher* 11 (November 16, 2001).

Kalven, Harry, Jr., and Hans Zeisel. *The American Jury.* Boston: Little, Brown, 1966.

Katz, Charles M., and Cassia Spohn. "The Effect of Race and Gender on Bail Outcomes: A Test of an Interactive Model." *American Journal of Criminal Justice* 19 (1995): 161–184.

Kautt, Paula, and Cassia Spohn. "*Crack*-ing Down on Black Drug Offenders? Testing for Interactions Among Offenders' Race, Drug Type, and Sentencing Strategy in Federal Drug Sentences." *Justice Quarterly* 19 (2002): 2–35.

Keil, Thomas, and Gennaro Vito. "Race and the Death Penalty in Kentucky Murder Trials: An Analysis of Post–Gregg Outcomes." *Justice Quarterly* (1990): 189–207.

Kempf Leonard Kimberly, and Henry Sontheimer. "The Role of Race in Juvenile Justice in Pennsylvania." In *Minorities and Juvenile Justice*, Kimberly Kempf Leonard, Carl E. Pope, and William H. Feyerherm, eds. Thousand Oaks, CA: Sage, 1995.

Kennedy, Randall. "Changing Images of the State: Criminal Law and Racial Discrimination: A Comment." *Harvard Law Review* 107 (1994): 1,255–1,278.

Kennedy, Randall. *Race, Crime, and the Law*. New York: Vintage Books, 1997.

Kerner Commission. *Report of the National Advisory Commission on Civil Disorders*. New York: Bantam Books, 1968.

King, Ryan D., Kecia R. Johnson, and Kelly McGeever. "Demography of the Legal Profession and Racial Disparities in Sentencing." *Law & Society Review* 44 (2010): 1–33.

Kleck, Gary. "Racial Discrimination in Criminal Sentencing: A Critical Evaluation of the Evidence with Additional Evidence on the Death Penalty." *American Sociological Review* 46 (1981): 783–805.

Klein, Kitty, and Blanche Creech. "Race, Rape, and Bias: Distortion of Prior Odds and Meaning Changes." *Basic and Applied Social Psychology* 3 (1982): 21.

Klein, Malcolm W. *The American Street Gang*. New York: Oxford University Press, 1995.

Klein, Malcolm W., Cheryl Maxson, and Lea C. Cunningham. "'Crack,' Street Gangs, and Violence." *Criminology* 29 (1991): 623–650.

Klein, Stephen, Joan Petersilia, and Susan Turner. "Race and Imprisonment Decisions in California." *Science* 247 (1990): 812–816.

Klinger, David. "Demeanor or Crime? Why 'Hostile' Citizens Are More Likely to be Arrested." *Criminology* 32 (1994): 475–493.

Knepper, Paul. "Race, Racism, and Crime Statistics." *Southern Law Review* 24 (1996): 71–112.

Kramer, John H., and Darrell Steffensmeier. "Race and Imprisonment Decisions." *Sociological Quarterly* 34 (1993): 357–376.

Kramer, John H., and Jeffery T. Ulmer. "Court Communities Under Sentencing Guidelines: Dilemmas of Formal Rationality and Sentencing Disparity." *Criminology* 34 (1996).

Kramer, John H., and Jeffery T. Ulmer. "Sentencing Disparity and Departures From Guidelines." *Justice Quarterly* 13 (1996): 81–105.

Kurlychek, Megan C., and Brian D. Johnson. "The Juvenile Penalty: A Comparison of Juvenile Adult Sentencing Outcomes in Criminal Court." *Criminology* 42 (2004).

LaFree, Gary D. "The Effect of Sexual Stratification by Race on Official Reactions to Rape." *American Sociological Review* 45 (1980): 842–854.

LaFree, Gary D. *Rape and Criminal Justice: The Social Construction of Sexual Assault*. Belmont, CA: Wadsworth, 1989.

Lauritsen, Janet L. "How Families and Communities Influence Youth Victimization." *OJJDP Juvenile Justice Bulletin*. Washington DC: U.S. Department of Justice, 2003.

Lee, Harper. *To Kill a Mockingbird*. New York: Warner Books, 1960.

Lefcourt, R. "The Administration of Criminal Law." In *Criminal Justice in America*, Richard Quinney, ed. Boston: Little Brown, 1974.

Leiber, Michael J. "A Comparison of Juvenile Court Outcomes for Native

Americans, African Americans, and Whites." *Justice Quarterly* 11 (1994): 255–279.

Leiber, Michael J., and Anita N. Blowers. "Race and Misdemeanor Sentencing." *Criminal Justice Policy Review* 14 (2003): 464–485.

Levin, Martin Howard. "The Jury in a Criminal Case: Obstacles to Impartiality." *Criminal Law Bulletin* 24 (1988): 492–520.

Levine, James P. *Juries and Politics.* Pacific Grove, CA: Brooks Cole, 1992.

Lewis, Anthony. *Gideon's Trumpet.* New York: Vintage Books, 1964.

Leyton, Stacey. "The New Blacklists: The Threat to Civil Liberties Posed by Gang Databases." In *Crime Control and Social Justice: The Delicate Balance,* Darnell F. Hawkins, Samuel L. Meyers, Jr., and Randolph N. Stone, eds. Westport, CT: Greenwood, 2003.

Lujan, Carol Chiago. "Stereotyping by Politicians: Or 'The Only Real Indian Is the Stereotypical Indian.'" In *Images of Color, Images of Crime,* Coramae Richey Mann and Marjorie Zatz, eds. Los Angeles: Roxbury, 1998.

Lynch, Michael J., and E. Britt Patterson, eds. *Race and Criminal Justice.* New York: Harrow and Heston, 1991.

Lysakowski, Matthew, Albert Antony Pearsall, III, and Jill Pope. *Policing in New Immigrant Communities.* Washington: Department of Justice, 2009. Available at http://www.cops .usdoj.gov.

MacDonald, Heather. "Is the Criminal Justice System Racist?" *City Journal* 18 (Spring 2008).

Males, Mike, and Dan Macallair. *The Color of Justice: An Analysis of Juvenile Justice Adult Court Transfers in California.* Washington, DC: Justice Policy Institute, 2000.

Mangum, Jr., Charles S. *The Legal Status of the Negro.* Chapel Hill, NC: North Carolina Press, 1940.

Mann, Coramae Richey. *Unequal Justice: A Question of Color.* Bloomington, IN: University of Indiana Press, 1993.

Martinson, Robert. "What Works? Questions and Answers about Prison Reform." *Public Interest* 24 (1974): 22–54.

Mason, Alpheus Thomas, and William M. Beaney. *American Constitutional Law.* Englewood Cliffs, NJ: Prentice-Hall, 1972.

Massey, Douglas S., and Nancy A. Denton. *American Apartheid: Segregation and the Making of the Underclass.* Cambridge, MA: Harvard University Press, 1993.

Mather, Lynn. *Plea Bargaining or Trial?* Lexington, MA: Heath, 1979.

Mauer, Marc. *Americans Behind Bars: A Comparison of International Rates of Incarceration.* Washington, DC: The Sentencing Project, 1990.

Mauer, Marc. *Race To Incarcerate.* New York: New Press, 1999.

Mauer, Marc. "Racial Impact Statements as a Means of Reducing Unwarranted Sentencing Disparities." *Ohio State Journal of Criminal Law* 5 (2007–2008): 19–46.

Mauer, Marc. *Young Black Men and the Criminal Justice System: A Growing National Problem.* Washington, DC: The Sentencing Project, 1990.

Mauer, Marc, and Tracy Huling. *Young Black Americans and the Criminal Justice System: Five Years Later.* Washington, DC: The Sentencing Project, 1995.

Maxfield, Linda Drazga, and John H. Kramer. *Substantial Assistance: An Empirical Yardstick Gauging Equity in Current Federal Policy and Practices.* Washington, DC: United States Sentencing Commission, 1998.

McDonald, Douglas C., and Kenneth E. Carlson. *Sentencing in the Federal Courts: Does Race Matter?* Washington, DC: U.S. Department of Justice, 1993.

McIntyre, Lisa J. *The Public Defender: The Practice of Law in the Shadows of Repute.* Chicago: University of Chicago Press, 1987.

McNulty, Thomas, and Paul E. Bellair. "Explaining Racial and Ethnic Differences in Serious Adolescent Violent Behavior." *Criminology* 41 (2003): 701–730.

Meissner, Christian A., and John C. Brigham. "Thirty Years of Investigating the Own-Race Bias in Memory for Faces: A Meta-Analytic Review." *Psychology, Public Policy, and Law* 7 (2001): 3–35.

Melossi, Dario. "An Introduction: Fifty Years Later, Punishment and Social Structure in Comparative Analysis." *Contemporary Crises* 13 (1989): 311–326.

Melton, Ada Pecos. "Crime and Punishment: Traditional and Contemporary Tribal Justice." In *Images of Color, Images of Crime*, Coramae Richey Mann and Marjorie S. Zatz, eds. Los Angeles: Roxbury, 1998.

Michalowski, Raymond J., and Susan J. Carlson. "Unemployment, Imprisonment and Social Structures of Accumulation: Historical Contingency in the Rushe-Kirchheimer Hypothesis." *Criminology* 37 (1999): 217–250.

Michalowski, Raymond J., and Michael A. Pearson. "Punishment and Social Structure at the State Level: A Cross-Sectional Comparison of 1970 and 1980." *Journal of Research in Crime and Delinquency* 27 (1990): 52–78.

Miethe, Terance D., and Charles A. Moore. "Socioeconomic Disparities Under Determinate Sentencing Systems: A Comparison of Preguideline and Postguideline Practices in Minnesota." *Criminology* 23 (1985): 337–363.

Miller, Jerome. *Search and Destroy: African-American Males in the Criminal Justice System.* Cambridge: Cambridge University Press, 1996.

Moore, J. D., and Vigil R. Garcia. "Residence and Territoriality in Chicano Gangs." *Social Problems* 31 (1983): 182–194.

Mumola, Christopher J., and Margaret Noonan. *Suicide and Homicide in State Prisons and Local Jails, 2001–2007.* Washington, DC: U.S. Department of Justice, 2010.

Murphy, Clyde E. "Racial Discrimination in the Criminal Justice System." *North Carolina Central Law Journal* 17 (1988): 171–190.

Myers, Martha. *Race, Labor, and Punishment in the South.* Columbus: Ohio State University Press, 1999.

Myers, Martha. "Symbolic Policy and the Sentencing of Drug Offenders." *Law & Society Review* 23 (1989): 295–315.

Myrdal, Gunnar. *An American Dilemma: The Negro Problem and Modern Democracy.* New York: Harper and Brothers, 1944.

NAACP Legal Defense Fund, *Death Row, U.S.A, Winter 2010.* New York: NAACP LDF, 2010.

Nardulli, Peter F., James Eisenstein, and Roy B. Flemming. *The Tenor of Justice: Criminal Courts and the Guilty Plea Process.* Chicago: University of Chicago Press, 1988.

National Academy of Sciences. *Fairness and Effectiveness in Policing: The Evidence.* Washington, DC: National Academy Press, 2004.

National Center for Juvenile Justice. *Juvenile Court Statistics 2000.* Washington, DC: Office of Juvenile Justice and Delinquency Prevention, 2004.

National Center for Juvenile Justice. *Which States Waive Juveniles to Criminal*

Court? Pittsburgh, PA: National Center for Juvenile Justice, 2004.

National Opinion Research Center. *General Social Surveys, 1972–94, General Social Surveys, 1996.* Storrs, CT: The Roper Center for Public Opinion Research, University of Connecticut, 1997.

Neubauer, David W. *America's Courts and the Criminal Justice System,* 7th ed. Belmont, CA: Wadsworth, 2002.

Nobiling, Tracy, Cassia Spohn, and Miriam DeLone. "A Tale of Two Counties: Unemployment and Sentence Severity." *Justice Quarterly* 15 (1998): 459–485.

Note. *Batson v. Kentucky*: Challenging the Use of the Peremptory Challenge." *American Journal of Criminal Law* 15 (1988): 298.

O'Brien, Robert M. "The Interracial Nature of Violent Crimes: A Reexamination." *American Journal of Sociology* 92 (1987): 817–835.

Office of Juvenile Justice and Delinquency Prevention. *Disproportionate Minority Confinement 2002 Update.* Washington, DC: U.S. Department of Justice, 2004.

Office of Juvenile Justice and Delinquency Prevention. *Juvenile Court Statistics 2000.* Washington, DC: OJJDP, 2004.

Office of Juvenile Justice and Delinquency Prevention. *Juvenile Transfers to Criminal Court in the 1999s: Lessons Learned from Four Studies.* Washington, DC: Office of Juvenile Justice and Delinquency Prevention, 2000.

Office of Juvenile Justice and Delinquency Prevention. *Juvenile Victims of Property Crimes.* Washington, DC: U.S. Department of Justice, 2000.

Office of Juvenile Justice and Delinquency Prevention. *Juveniles in Corrections.* Washington, DC: Office of Juvenile Justice and Delinquency Prevention, 2004.

Office of Juvenile Justice and Delinquency Prevention. *Youth Gangs in Indian Country.* Washington, DC: Department of Justice, 2004.

Office of Management and Budget. "Revisions to the Standards for the Classification of Federal Data on Race and Ethnicity." October 30, 1997. Available at http://www.whitehouse.gov/omb/fedreg/ombdir15.html.

Olsen, Jack. *Last Man Standing: The Tragedy and Triumph of Geronimo Pratt.* New York: Doubleday, 2000.

Panel on Juvenile Crime. *Juvenile Crime Juvenile Justice.* Washington, DC: National Academy Press, 2001.

Passel, Jeffrey S., and D'Vera Coh. *A Portrait of Unauthorized Immigrants in the United States.* Los Angeles: Pew Hispanic Center, 2009.

Passel, Jeffrey, and Paul Taylor. *Who's Hispanic?* Washington, DC: Pew Research Center, 2009.

Pate, Anthony M., and Lorie Fridell. *Police Use of Force* (2 vols.). Washington, DC: The Police Foundation, 1993.

Paternoster, Raymond. *Capital Punishment in America.* New York: Lexington Books, 1991.

Paternoster, Raymond. "Discrimination Revisited: An Exploration of Frontstage and Backstage Criminal Justice Decision Making." *Sociology and Social Research* 69 (1984): 90–108.

Paternoster, Raymond. "Prosecutorial Discretion in Requesting the Death Penalty: A Case of Victim-Based Racial Discrimination." *Law & Society Review* 18 (1984): 437–478.

Paternoster, Raymond, and Robert Brame. "An Empirical Analysis of Maryland's Death Sentencing System with Respect to the Influence of Race and Legal Jurisdiction." Available at http://ncic.org/library/018518.

Paternoster, Raymond, and Robert Brame. "Reassessing Race Disparities in Maryland Capital Cases." *Criminology* 46 (2008): 971–1,007.

Peak, K., and J. Spencer. "Crime in Indian Country: Another Trail of Tears." *Journal of Criminal Justice* 15 (1987): 485–494.

Peffley, Mark, and Jon Hurwitz. "Persuasion and Resistance: Race and the Death Penalty in America." *American Journal of Political Science* 51 (2007): 996–1,012.

Petersilia, Joan. *Racial Disparities in the Criminal Justice System*. Santa Monica, CA: Rand, 1983.

Petersilia, Joan. *When Prisoners Come Home: Parole and Prisoner Reentry*. New York: Oxford University Press, 2003.

Peterson, Ruth D., and John Hagan. "Changing Conceptions of Race: Towards an Account of Anomalous Findings of Sentencing Research." *American Sociological Review* 49 (1984): 56–70.

Peterson, Ruth D., and Lauren J. Krivo. "Macrostructrual Analyses of Race, Ethnicity, and Violent Crime: Recent Lessons and New Directions for Research." *Annual Review of Sociology* 31 (2005): 331–356.

Pew Hispanic Center. *2002 National Survey of Latinos*. Los Angeles: Pew Hispanic Center, 2002.

Pew Hispanic Center. *Between Two Worlds: How Young Latinos Come of Age in America*. Los Angeles: Pew Hispanic Center, 2009. Available at http://pewhispanic.org/.

Pew Hispanic Center. *Hispanics: A People in Motion*. Washington, DC: Pew Hispanic Center, 2005.

Pew Hispanic Center. *Unauthorized Immigrants and Their U.S.-Born Children*. Los Angeles: Pew Hispanic Center, August 11, 2010.

Pew Research Center. *Muslim Americans: Middle Class and Mostly Mainstream*. Washington, DC: Pew Research Center, 2007. Available at http:pewresearch.org/.

Pierce, Glenn L., and Michael L. Radelet. "The Impact of Legally Inappropriate Factors on Death Sentencing for California Homicides, 1990–99." *Santa Clara Law Review* 46 (2005).

Platt, Anthony M. *The Child Saver: The Invention of Delinquency*, 2nd ed. Chicago: University of Chicago Press, 1977.

Police Executive Research Forum. *Police Chiefs and Sheriffs Speak Out on Local Immigration Enforcement*. Washington, DC: PERF, April 2008.

Police Executive Research Forum. *Racially Biased Policing: A Principled Response*. Washington, DC: PERF, 2001.

Police Foundation. *The Role of Local Police: Striking a Balance Between Immigration Enforcement and Civil Liberties*. Washington, DC: Police Foundation, 2009.

Pommersheim, Frank, and Steve Wise. "Going to the Penitentiary: A Study of Disparate Sentencing in South Dakota." *Criminal Justice and Behavior* 16 (1989): 155–165.

Pope, Carl E., and William H. Feyerherm. "Minority Status and Juvenile Justice Processing: An Assessment of the Research Literature (Part I)," *Criminal Justice Abstracts* 22 (1990): 327–335.

Pope, Carl E., Rich Lovell, and Heidi M. Hsia. *Disproportionate Minority Confinement: A Review of the Research Literature from 1989 Through 2001*. Washington, DC: U.S. Department of Justice, 2004.

Pope, Carl E., and Howard N. Snyder. *Race as a Factor in Juvenile Arrests*. Washington, DC: Office of Juvenile Justice and Delinquency Prevention, 2003.

Population Reference Bureau. *Large Wealth Gap Among U.S. Racial and*

Ethnic Groups. Washington, DC: PRB, September 2010.

Porter, Nicole D., *The State of Sentencing 2009: Developments in Policy and Practice.* Washington, DC: The Sentencing Project, 2010. Available at http://www.sentencingproject.org.

Portes, Alejandro, and Patricia Landolt. "The Downside of Social Capital." *The American Prospect* 26 (May–June 1996): 18–21, 94.

Quinney, Richard. *The Social Reality of Crime.* Boston: Little, Brown, 1970.

Rachlinski, Jeffrey J., Sheri Lynn Johnson, Andrew U. Wistrich, and Chris Guthrie. "Does Unconscious Racial Bias Affect Trial Judges?" *Notre Dame Law Review,* 84 (2008-2009): 1,195-1,246.

Radelet, Michael L. "Executions of Whites for Crimes Against Blacks: Exceptions to the Rule?" *The Sociological Quarterly* 30 (1989): 529–544.

Radelet, Michael L. "Racial Characteristics and the Imposition of the Death Penalty." *American Sociological Review* 46 (1981): 918–927.

Radelet, Michael L., and Glenn L. Pierce. "Race and Prosecutorial Discretion in Homicide Cases." *Law & Society Review* 19 (1985): 587–621.

Ralph, Paige H., Jonathan R. Sorensen, and James W. Marquart. "A Comparison of Death-Sentenced and Incarcerated Murderers in Pre-Furman Texas." *Justice Quarterly* 9 (1992): 185–209.

Ramirez, Deborah A. "Affirmative Jury Selection: A Proposal To Advance Both the Deliberative Ideal and Jury Diversity." *University of Chicago Legal Forum* (1998): 161.

Randall, Kate. "Another Florida Teenager Receives Harsh Adult Prison Sentence." Available at http://www.wsws.org/articles/2001/aug2001.

Reasons, Charles E., Darlene J. Conley, and Julius Debro. *Race, Class, Gender,* *and Justice in the United States.* Boston: Allyn and Bacon, 2002.

Reddy, Marlita A., ed. *Statistical Record of Black America.* Detroit: Gale Research, 1997.

Reddy, Marlita A., ed. *Statistical Record of Hispanic Americans.* Detroit: Gale Research, 1993.

Reiman, Jeffrey. *The Rich Get Richer and the Poor Get Prison.* Boston: Allyn & Bacon, 1995.

Reiss, Albert J. *The Police and the Public.* New Haven: Yale University Press, 1971.

Rise, Eric W. *The Martinsville Seven: Race, Rape, and Capital Punishment.* Charlottesville: University Press of Virginia, 1995.

Roberts. Dorothy. "Punishing Drug Addicts Who Have Babies: Women of Color, Equality, and the Right of Privacy." *Harvard Law Review* 104 (1991): 1,419-1,454.

Ruback, R. Barry, and Paula J. Vardaman. "Decision Making in Delinquency Cases: The Role of Race and Juveniles' Admission/Denial of the Crime." *Law and Human Behavior* 21 (1997): 47–69.

Rutledge, John R. "They All Look Alike: The Inaccuracy of Cross-Racial Identifications." *American Journal of Criminal Law* 28 (2001).

Sampson, Robert J. "Crime in the Cities: The Effects of Formal and Informal Social Control." *Crime and Justice* 8 (1986): 271–311.

Sampson, Robert J., Stephen W. Raudenbush, and Felton Earls. "Neighborhoods and Violent Crime: A Multilevel Study of Collective Efficacy." *Science* 277 (August 15, 1997): 918–924.

Sampson, Robert J., and William Julius Wilson. "Toward a Theory of Race, Crime, and Urban Inequality." In *Crime and Inequality,* John Hagan and

Ruth D. Peterson, eds. Stanford, CA: Stanford University Press, 1995.

Sander, Richard H. "A Systematic Analysis of Affirmative Action in American Law Schools." *Stanford Law Review* 57 (2004): 367–585.

Sarat, Austin. "Recapturing the Spirit of Furman: The American Bar Association and the New Abolitionist Politics." *Law and Contemporary Problems* 61 (1998): 5–28.

Sarat, Austin. *When the State Kills: Capital Punishment and the American Condition.* Princeton, NJ: Princeton University Press, 1998.

Sarat, Austin, and Neil Vidmar. "Public Opinion, the Death Penalty, and the Eighth Amendment: Testing the Marshall Hypothesis." In *Capital Punishment in the United States*, Hugo A. Bedau and Chester M. Pierce, eds. New York: AMS Publications, 1976.

Schermer, Laureen O'Neil, and Brian D. Johnson. "Criminal Prosecutions: Examining Prosecutorial Discretion and Charge Reductions in U.S. Federal District Courts," *Justice Quarterly* 27 (2010).

Schiraldi, Vincent, and Jason Ziedenberg. *Costs and Benefits? The Impact of Drug Imprisonment in New Jersey.* Washington, DC: Justice Policy Institute, 2003.

Secret, Philip E., and James B. Johnson. "The Effect of Race on Juvenile Justice Decision Making in Nebraska: Detention, Adjudication, and Disposition, 1988–1993." *Justice Quarterly* 14 (1997): 445–478.

Sellin, Thorsten. "Race Prejudice in the Administration of Justice." *American Journal of Sociology* 41 (1935): 312–317.

The Sentencing Project. *Facts about Prison and Prisoners.* Available at http://www.sentencingproject.org (April 2002).

Sentencing Project, The. *Felony Disenfranchisement Laws in the United State*

(2008). Available at http://www.sentencingproject.org/doc/publications/fd_bs_fdlawsinus.pdf.

Sentencing Project, The. *Schools and Prisons: Fifty Years after* Brown v. Board of Education. Available at http://www.sentencingproject.org/pdfs/brownvboard.pdf.

Serr, Brian J., and Mark Maney. "Racism, Peremptory Challenges, and the Democratic Jury: The Jurisprudence of a Delicate Balance." *Journal of Criminal Law and Criminology* 79 (1988): 1–65.

Shapiro, Thomas M. *The Hidden Cost of Being African American: How Wealth Perpetuates Inequality.* New York: Oxford University Press, 2004.

Shaw, Clifford R., and Henry D. McKay. *Juvenile Delinquency and Urban Areas.* Chicago: University of Chicago Press, 1942.

Silberman, Charles E. *Criminal Violence, Criminal Justice.* New York: Random House, 1978.

Sklansky, David Alan. "Not Your Father's Police Department: Making Sense of the New Demographics of Law Enforcement." *Journal of Criminal Law and Criminology* 96 (Spring 2006): 1,209–1,243.

Skogan, Wesley G., and Susan M. Hartnett. *Community Policing: Chicago Style.* New York: Oxford University Press, 1997.

Skolnick, Jerome. "Social Control in the Adversary System." *Journal of Conflict Resolution* 11 (1967): 67.

Smith, Brent L., and Kelly R. Damphouse. "Punishing Political Offenders: The Effect of Political Motive on Federal Sentencing Decisions." *Criminology* 34 (1996): 289–321.

Smith, Douglas A., Christy Visher, and Laura A. Davidson. "Equity and Discretionary Justice: The Influence of Race on Police Arrest Decisions." *Journal of Criminal Law and Criminology* 75 (1984): 234–249.

Smith, Michael David. *Race Versus Robe: The Dilemma of Black Judges*. Port Washington, NY: Associated Faculty Press, 1983.

Smith, Tom. "A Trend Analysis of Attitudes Toward Capital Punishment, 1936–1974." In *Studies of Social Change Since 1948*, Vol. 2, James E. Davis, ed. Chicago: National Opinion Research Center, 1975.

Song, John Huey-Long. "Attitudes of Chinese Immigrants and Vietnamese Refugees Toward Law Enforcement in the United States." *Justice Quarterly* 9 (1992) 703–719.

Sorensen, Jon, and Donald H. Wallace. "Prosecutorial Discretion in Seeking Death: An Analysis of Racial Disparity in the Pretrial Stages of Case Processing in a Midwestern County." *Justice Quarterly* 16 (1999): 559–578.

Spitzer, Steven. "Toward a Marxian Theory of Deviance." *Social Problems* 22 (1975): 638–651.

Spohn, Cassia. "Crime and the Social Control of Blacks: Offender/Victim Race and the Sentencing of Violent Offenders." In *Inequality, Crime & Social Control*, George S. Bridges and Martha A. Myers, eds. Boulder, CO: Westview Press, 1994.

Spohn, Cassia. "Decision Making in Sexual Assault Cases: Do Black and Female Judges Make a Difference?" *Women & Criminal Justice* 2 (1990).

Spohn, Cassia. *How Do Judges Decide? The Search for Fairness and Equity in Sentencing*. Thousand Oaks, CA: Sage, 2009.

Spohn, Cassia. "Race, Sex and Pretrial Detention in Federal Court: Indirect Effects and Cumulative Disadvantage." *University of Kansas Law Review* 57 (2009): 879–902.

Spohn, Cassia. "The Sentencing Decisions of Black and White Judges: Expected and Unexpected Similarities." *Law & Society Review* 24 (1990): 1,197–1,216.

Spohn, Cassia. "Thirty Years of Sentencing Reform: A Quest for a Racially Neutral Sentencing Process." In *Policies, Processes, and Decisions of the Criminal Justice System*, Vol. 3, *Criminal Justice 2000*. Washington, DC: U.S. Department of Justice, 2000.

Spohn, Cassia, and Jerry Cederblom. "Race and Disparities in Sentencing: A Test of the Liberation Hypothesis." *Justice Quarterly* 8 (1991): 305–327.

Spohn, Cassia, and Miriam DeLone. "When Does Race Matter? An Analysis of the Conditions Under Which Race Affects Sentence Severity." *Sociology of Crime, Law, and Deviance* 2 (2000): 3–37.

Spohn, Cassia, and Robert Fornango. "U.S. Attorneys and Substantial Assistance Departures: Testing for Inter-Prosecutor Disparity." *Criminology* 47 (2009): 813–842.

Spohn, Cassia, John Gruhl, and Susan Welch. "The Effect of Race on Sentencing: A Re-Examination on an Unsettled Question." *Law & Society Review* 16 (1981–82): 71–88.

Spohn, Cassia, John Gruhl, and Susan Welch. "The Impact of the Ethnicity and Gender of Defendants on the Decision to Reject or Dismiss Felony Charges." *Criminology* 25 (1987): 175–191.

Spohn, Cassia, and David Holleran. "The Imprisonment Penalty Paid by Young Unemployed Black and Hispanic Male Offenders." *Criminology* 38 (2000): 281–306.

Spohn, Cassia, and Lisa Sample. "The Dangerous Drug Offender in Federal Court: Intersections of Race, Ethnicity and Culpability." *Crime & Delinquency* (2009). Published in Online First on July 8, 2008, as doi:10.1177/00111287083928.

Spohn, Cassia, and Jeffrey Spears. "The Effect of Offender and Victim Characteristics on Sexual Assault Case

Processing Decisions." *Justice Quarterly* 13 (1996): 649–679.

Spohn, Cassia, and Jeffrey Spears. "Sentencing of Drug Offenders in Three Cities: Does Race/Ethnicity Make a Difference?" In *Crime Control and Criminal Justice: The Delicate Balance*, Darnell F. Hawkins, Samuel L. Meyers, Jr., and Randolph N. Stone, eds. Westport, CT: Greenwood, 2002.

Steen, Sara, Rodney L. Engen, and Randy R. Gainey. "Images of Danger and Culpability: Racial Stereotyping, Case Processing, and Criminal Sentencing." *Criminology* 45 (2005).

Steffensmeier, Darrell, and Stephen Demuth. "Ethnicity and Judges' Sentencing Decisions: Hispanic–Black–White Comparison." *Criminology* 39 (2001): 145–178.

Steffensmeier, Darrell, and Stephen Demuth. "Ethnicity and Sentencing Outcomes in U.S. Federal Courts: Who Is Punished More Harshly?" *American Sociological Review* 65 (2000): 705–729.

Steffensmeier, Darrell, John Kramer, and Cathy Streifel. "Gender and Imprisonment Decisions." *Criminology* 31 (1993): 411–443.

Steffensmeier, Darrell, John Kramer, and Jeffery Ulmer. "Age Differences in Criminal Sentencing." *Justice Quarterly* 12 (1995): 701–719.

Steffensmeier, Darrell, Jeffery Ulmer, and John Kramer. "The Interaction of Race, Gender, and Age in Criminal Sentencing: The Punishment Cost of Being Young, Black, and Male." *Criminology* 36 (1998): 363–397.

Stoudtland, Sara E. "The Multiple Dimensions of Trust in Resident/Police Relations in Boston." *Journal of Research in Crime and Delinquency* 38 (August 2001): 226–256.

Stryker, R., Ilene Nagel, and John Hagan. "Methodology Issues in Court Research: Pretrial Release Decisions for Federal Defendants." *Sociological Methods and Research* 11 (1983): 460–500.

Substance Abuse and Mental Health Services Administration [SAMSA]. *Results from the 2008 National Survey on Drug Use and Health: National Findings.* Washington, DC: Department of Health and Human Services, 2009. Available at http://www.oas.samhsa.gov/nsduh/2k8nsduh/2k8Results.pdf.

Sudnow, David. "Normal Crimes: Sociological Features of the Penal Code in the Public Defender's Office." *Social Problems* 12 (1965): 255–277.

Swift, B., and G. Bickel. *Comparative Parole Treatment of American Indians and Non-Indians at United States Federal Prisons.* Washington, DC: Bureau of Social Science Research, 1974.

Taylor, Ralph B., Jerry H. Ratcliffe, Lillian Dote, and Brian A. Lawton. "Roles of Neighborhood Race and Status in the Middle Stages of Juror Selection." *Journal of Criminal Justice* 35 (2007): 391–403.

Texas Civil Rights Project. *The Death Penalty in Texas: Due Process and Equal Justice … or Rush to Execution?* Austin, TX: Texas Civil Rights Project, 2000.

Thernstrom, Stephan, and Abigail Thernstrom. *America in Black and White: One Nation, Indivisible.* New York: Simon & Schuster, 1997.

Thomas, Jim. "Racial Codes in Prison Culture: Snapshots in Black and White." In *Race and Criminal Justice*, Michael Lynch and Britt Patterson, eds. New York: Harrow and Heston, 1991.

Thomas, Wayne. *Bail Reform in America.* Berkeley, CA: University of California Press, 1976.

Tonry, Michael. *Malign Neglect: Race, Crime and Punishment in America.*

New York: Oxford University Press, 1995.

Tonry, Michael. *Sentencing Matters*. New York: Oxford University Press, 1996.

Tonry, Michael, and Matthew Melewski. "The Malign Effects of Drug Control Policies on Black Americans." *Crime and Justice* 37 (2008): 1–44.

Toy, Calvin. "A Short History of Asian Gangs in San Francisco." *Justice Quarterly* 9 (1992): 645–665.

Travis, Jeremy, and Christy Visher. *Prisoner Reentry and Crime in America*. New York: Cambridge University Press, 2005.

Tuch, Steven A., and Ronald Weitzer. "Racial Differences in Attitudes toward the Police." *Public Opinion Quarterly* 61 (1997): 643–663.

Turk, Austin. *Criminality and Legal Order*. New York: Rand McNally, 1969.

Turner, Billy M., Rickie D. Lovell, John C. Young, and William F. Denny. "Race and Peremptory Challenges During Voir Dire: Do Prosecution and Defense Agree?" *Journal of Criminal Justice* 14 (1986): 61–69.

Uhlman, Thomas M. "Black Elite Decision Making: The Case of Trial Judges." *American Journal of Political Science* 22 (1978): 884–895.

Uhlman, Thomas M. *Racial Justice: Black Judges and Defendants in an Urban Trial Court*. Lexington, MA: Lexington Books, 1979.

Ulmer, Jeffery T., and John H. Kramer. "Court Communities Under Sentencing Guidelines: Dilemmas of Formal Rationality and Sentencing Disparity." *Criminology* 34 (1996): 383–407.

Ulmer, Jeffery T., Megan C. Kurlychek, and John H. Kramer. "Prosecutorial Discretion and the Imposition of Mandatory Minimum Sentences." *Journal of Research in Crime and Delinquency* 44 (2007): 427–458.

Unah, Isaac, and Jack Boger. "Race and the Death Penalty in North Carolina: An Empirical Analysis: 1993–1997." Available at http://www.deathpenaltyinfo.org.

Unnever, James D., and Francis T. Cullen. "The Racial Divide in Support for the Death Penalty: Does White Racism Matter?" *Social Forces* 85 (2007): 1,281–1,301.

Unnever, James D. "Direct and Organizational Discrimination in the Sentencing of Drug Offenders." *Social Problems* 30 (1982).

United States Sentencing Commission. *Report to the Congress: Cocaine and Federal Sentencing Policy*. Washington, DC: U.S. Sentencing Commission, 2002.

United States Sentencing Commission. *Sourcebook of Federal Sentencing Statistics*. 14th ed. Washington DC: United States Sentencing Commission, 2009.

United States Sentencing Commission. *Special Report to the Congress: Mandatory Minimum Penalties in the Federal Criminal Justice System*. Washington, DC: U.S. Sentencing Commission, 1991.

United States Sentencing Commission. *Substantial Assistance Departures in the United States Courts*. Washington, DC: U.S. Sentencing Commission, 1995.

U.S. Department of Health and Human Services, Substance Abuse and Mental Health Services Administration. *National Household Survey on Drug Abuse: Population Estimates 1994*. Rockville, MD: U.S. Department of Health and Human Services, 1995.

U.S. Department of Justice. *The Federal Death Penalty System: Supplementary Data Analysis and Revised Protocols for Capital Case Review*. Washington, DC: U.S. Department of Justice, 2001.

U.S. Department of Justice, Bureau of Justice Statistics. *Sourcebook of Criminal Justice Statistics, ONLINE EDITION*.

U.S. General Accounting Office. *Death Penalty Sentencing: Research Indicates Pattern of Racial Disparities.* Washington, DC: General Accounting Office, 1990.

U.S. General Accounting Office. *Juvenile Justice: Juveniles Processed in Criminal Court and Case Dispositions.* Washington, DC: General Accounting Office, 1995.

van den Haag, Ernest. *Punishing Criminals: Confronting a Very Old and Painful Question.* New York: Basic Books, 1975.

Vera Institute of Justice. *Felony Arrests: Their Prosecution and Disposition in New York City's Courts.* New York: Longman, 1981.

Vigil, James D. *Barrio Gangs.* Austin, TX: University of Texas Press, 1988.

von Hirsch, Andrew. *Doing Justice: The Choice of Punishments.* New York: Hill & Wang, 1976.

Wakeling, Stewart, Miriam Jorgensen, Susan Michaelson, and Manley Begay. *Policing on American Indian Reservations: A Report to the National Institute of Justice.* Washington, DC: U.S. Government Printing Office, 2001.

Walker, Samuel. "Complaints Against the Police: A Focus Group Study of Citizen Perceptions, Goals, and Expectations." *Criminal Justice Review* 22 (1997): 207–225.

Walker, Samuel. *The New World of Police Accountability.* Thousand Oaks: Sage, 2005.

Walker, Samuel. *Police Accountability: The Role of Citizen Oversight.* Belmont CA: Wadsworth, 2001.

Walker, Samuel. "Racial Minority and Female Employment in Policing: The Implications of 'Glacial' Change." *Crime and Delinquency* 31 (1985): 555–572.

Walker, Samuel. "Searching for the Denominator: Problems with Police

Traffic Stop Data and an Early Warning System Solution." *Justice Research and Policy* 3 (Spring 2001): 63–95.

Walker, Samuel. *Sense and Nonsense About Crime and Communities,* 7th ed. Belmont: Cengage, 2011.

Walker, Samuel. *Taming the System: The Control of Discretion in Criminal Justice, 1950–1990.* New York: Oxford University Press, 1993.

Walker, Samuel, and Molly Brown. "A Pale Reflection of Reality: The Neglect of Racial and Ethnic Minorities in Introductory Criminal Justice Textbooks." *Journal of Criminal Justice Education* 6, no. 1 (Spring 1995): 61–83.

Walker, Samuel, and Morgan Macdonald. "An Alternative Remedy for Police Misconduct: A Model State Pattern or Practice Statute." *George Mason University Civil Rights Law Review* 19 (Summer 2009): 479–552.

Walker, Thomas G., and Deborah J. Barrow. "The Diversification of the Federal Bench: Policy and Process Ramifications." *Journal of Politics* 47 (1985): 596–617.

Walsh, Anthony. "The Sexual Stratification Hypothesis in Light of Changing Conceptions of Race." *Criminology* 25 (1987): 153–173.

Washington, Linn. *Black Judges on Justice: Perspectives from the Bench.* New York: The New Press, 1994.

Way, H. Frank. *Criminal Justice and the American Constitution.* North Scituate, MA: Duxbury Press, 1994.

Weisburd, David, Rosann Greenspan, Edwin E. Hamilton, Kellie Bryant, and Hubert Williams. *The Abuse of Police Authority: A National Study of Police Officers' Attitudes.* Washington DC: The Police Foundation, 2001.

Weisenburger, Steven. *Modern Medea.* New York: Hill & Wang, 1998.

Weitzer, Ronald. "Racial Discrimination in the Criminal Justice System: Findings and Problems in the Literature." *Journal of Criminal Justice* 24 (1996): 313.

Weitzer, Ronald. "Racialized Policing: Residents' Perceptions in Three Neighborhoods." *Law & Society Review* 34, no. 1 (2000): 129–156.

Weitzer, Ronald, and Stephen Tuch. *Race and Policing in America: Conflict and Reform.* New York: Cambridge University Press, 2006.

Welch, Susan, Michael Combs, and John Gruhl. "Do Black Judges Make a Difference?" *American Journal of Political Science* 32 (1988): 126–136.

Werthman, Carl, and Irving Piliavin. "Gang Members and the Police." In *The Police: Six Sociological Essays,* David J. Bordua, ed. New York: Wiley, 1967.

Western, Bruce. *Punishment and Inequality in America.* New York: Russell Sage Foundation, 2006.

Wheeler, Gerald R., and Carol L. Wheeler. "Reflections on Legal Representation of the Economically Disadvantaged: Beyond Assembly Line Justice." *Crime and Delinquency* 26 (1980): 319–332.

Wice, Paul B. *Chaos in the Courthouse: The Inner Workings of the Urban Municipal Courts.* New York: Praeger, 1985.

Wilbanks, William. *The Myth of a Racist Criminal Justice System.* Monterey: Brooks/Cole, 1987.

Williams, Marian R., and Jefferson E. Holcomb. "The Interactive Effects of Victim Race and Gender on Death Sentence Disparity Findings." *Homicide Studies* 8 (2004).

Wilmot, Keith, and Miriam DeLone. "Sentencing of Native Americans: A Multistage Analysis Under the Minnesota Sentencing Guidelines." *Journal of Ethnicity in Criminal Justice* 8 (2010): 151–180, p. 152.

Wilson, James Q. *Thinking About Crime.* New York: Basic Books, 1975.

Wilson, William Julius. *The Truly Disadvantaged.* Chicago: University of Chicago Press, 1987.

Wilson, William Julius. *When Work Disappears: The World of the New Urban Poor.* New York: Knopf, 1996.

Wishman, Seymour. *Anatomy of a Jury: The System on Trial.* New York: Times Books, 1986.

Wolfgang, Marvin E., Arlene Kelly, and Hans C. Nolde. "Comparisons of the Executed and the Commuted Among Admissions to Death Penalty." *Journal of Criminal Law, Criminology, and Police Science* 53 (1962): 301–311.

Wolfgang, Marvin E., and Marc Reidel. "Race, Judicial Discretion, and the Death Penalty." *The Annals of the American Academy of Political and Social Science* 407 (1973): 119–133.

Wolfgang, Marvin E., and Marc Reidel. "Rape, Race, and the Death Penalty in Georgia." *American Journal of Orthopsychiatry* 45 (1975): 658–668.

Wood, Peter B., and David C. May. "Racial Differences in Perceptions of the Severity of Sanctions: A Comparison of Prison with Alternatives." *Justice Quarterly* 20 (2003).

Wriggins, Jennifer. "Rape, Racism, and the Law." *Harvard Women's Law Journal* 6 (1983): 103–141.

Wright, Bruce McM. "A Black Broods on Black Judges." *Judicature* 57 (1973): 22–23.

Wu, Bohsiu, and Angel Ilarraza Fuentes. "The Entangled Effects of Race and Urban Poverty." *Juvenile and Family Court Journal* 49 (1998): 41–53.

Young, Iris Marion. *Justice and the Politics of Difference.* Princeton, NJ: Princeton University Press, 1990.

Young, Robert L. "Race, Conceptions of Crime and Justice, and Support for the Death Penalty." *Social Psychological Quarterly* 54 (1991).

Zatz, Marjorie S. "The Changing Form of Racial/Ethnic Biases in Sentencing." *Journal of Research in Crime and Delinquency* 25 (1987): 69–92.

Zatz, Marjorie S. "The Convergence of Race, Ethnicity, Gender, and Class on Court Decision making: Looking Toward the 21st Century." In *Policies, Processes, and Decisions of the Criminal Justice System*, Vol. 3, *Criminal Justice 2000*. Washington, DC: U.S. Department of Justice, 2000.

Zatz, Marjorie S. "Pleas, Priors and Prison: Racial/Ethnic Differences in Sentencing." *Social Science Research* 14 (1985): 169–193.

Zatz, Marjorie S., Carol Chiago Lujan, and Zoann K. Snyder-Joy. "American Indians and Criminal Justice: Some Conceptual and Methodological Considerations." In *Race and Criminal Justice*, Michael J. Lynch and E. Britt Patterson, eds. New York: Harrow & Heston, 1995.

Zatz, Marjorie S., and Richard P. Krecker, Jr. "Anti-Gang Initiatives as Racialized Policy." In *Crime Control and Social Justice: The Delicate Balance*, Darnel F. Hawkins, Samuel L. Meyers, Jr., and Randolph N. Stone, eds. Westport, CT: Greenwood, 2003.

Zorn, Eric. "Dark Truths Buried in Nicarico Case May Yet See Light." *Chicago Tribune* (October 19, 1995), sec. 2, p. 1.

Index

"Not Your Father's Police Department"
(Sklansky), 173
NYPD. *See* New York Police Department
(NYPD)
NYS. *See* National Youth Survey

O

Obama, Barack, 331
O'Connor, Sandra Day, 434
Offenders
arrest data, 60–65
characteristics of, 69–70
community influence in rates of, 70–72
drug, 72–73
official arrest statistics, 58
perceptions by victims, 65
perceptions of, 66–68
picture of typical, 58–73
problems with NCVS data on, 65–66
problems with UCR data, 58–60
self-report surveys, 68–69
theoretical explanations for the racial
gap, 70
victims and, 39–95
Office of Community Oriented Policing
Services (COPS) report, 135, 140
Office of Federal Contract Compliance,
176
Office of Juvenile Justice and Delinquency
Prevention, 445
Office of Tribal Justice, 142
Oklahoma, race and death penalty in,
368
Olsen, Caroline, 242
Olsen, Kenneth, 242
Omnibus Crime Bill, 383
Orfield, Gary, 108, 122
Ousey, Graham C., 21
Oversight, of police, 172–173

P

Pacific Islander Americans, 46–48, 54, 55,
142, 451
Panel on Juvenile Crime, 464
Pardini, Dustin A., 456
Parole, 416–419
Patterson, Haywood, 197
PCR. *See* Police–community relations
Pearson, Michael A., 426
Peer officer comparisons, 159

Pennsylvania
intake and disposition decisions in, 470
processing juveniles in, 469
Peremptory challenges, 252–262
Perez, Dolores A., 204
Petersilia, Joan, 152, 224, 420, 428
Peterson, Laci, 41–42
Peterson, Paul E., 120
Physical force, 147–150
Pierce, Glenn L., 364
Piliavin, Irving, 138
Pitchford, Susan R., 425
Plea bargaining, 229–231
Police. *See also* Police employment
practices; Police–community
relations (PCR)
arrests, 150–154
attitudes and behavior, 165–166
brutality, 147–150
citizen complaints against, 170–172
citizen oversight of, 172–173
conflict between racial and ethnic
minorities, 134
corruption and people of color, 167
demographics of the United States and,
134–136
discrimination in arrests, 150–154
harassment and sentence enhancements,
459–460
perceptions of conduct, 138
policing racial and ethnic communities,
139–143
public attitudes about, 136–138
racial, ethnic minorities and, 129–194
shootings, 144–147, 153
stereotyping and routine police
work, 164
use of deadly force, 144–147
verbal abuse, 165
"Police and Immigration" (PERF), 143
Police employment practices, 173–181
affirmative action, 176–177
African Americans, 174–176, 179–180
discrimination, 173–174, 177–178
Hispanic Americans, 174–176
impact of diversity, 178
officers of color as supervisors and chief
executives, 178–181
Police Executive Research Forum
(PERF), 23, 131, 143, 159, 166